HOUSES OF THE GENTRY

HOUSES OF THE GENTRY
1480–1680

Nicholas Cooper

Published for
THE PAUL MELLON CENTRE
FOR STUDIES IN BRITISH ART
in association with
ENGLISH HERITAGE
by
YALE UNIVERSITY PRESS
NEW HAVEN & LONDON

Designed by Gillian Malpass

Printed in Italy

Library of Congress Cataloging-in-Publication Data

Cooper, Nicholas.
Houses of the gentry 1480–1680 / Nicholas Cooper.
p.   cm.
Includes bibliographical references and index.
ISBN 0-300-07390-9 (cloth: alk. paper)
1. Architecture, Domestic – England – History.
2. Gentry – Homes and haunts – England – History.
3. Architecture and society – English –History.   1. Title.
NA7328.C66   1999
728.8'0942'09031 – dc21   99-14919
CIP

A catalogue record for this book is available from
The British Library

Frontispiece   Chastleton House, Oxfordshire, *c.* 1612.

To Cecil Farthing,
Director of the National Monuments Record
1960–1976

Mapperton House, Dorset.
Mapperton was built in the mid-sixteenth century and was modernised
with a new, uniform front a century later.

Contents

Foreword

In 1954, when the great historical debate was still raging over the rise of the gentry in sixteenth- and seventeenth-century England, Eric Mercer of the staff of the Royal Commission on Historical Monuments wrote an article for *Past and Present* in which he drew attention to a distinctive group of country houses of middling size and novel plan.[1] These, he argued, were different from those of courtiers and the higher aristocracy, and he sought to explain their origin in the distinctive social and economic behaviour of an emerging class. Interest in the subject was not wholly abandoned within the Commission but lay dormant until 1990, when it was decided to undertake a more detailed study of the houses of the gentry during this period of radical social, economic and architectural change. The storm that prompted Mercer's original contribution has long since subsided, and in the intervening years a great deal of work has been done that now makes such a study incomparably easier.

Fundamental have been the books and articles of Mark Girouard, perhaps the initiator of a new kind of architectural history: concerned above all to understand houses as they were conceived and used and to see buildings as the scene of human action, Dr Girouard's work is central to this book. Malcolm Airs has illuminated the processes of building, while Lucy Gent, John Onians, Kristy Anderson, Vaughan Hart and others have greatly increased our understanding of contemporary perceptions of architecture. Simon Thurley has explored the exemplars of magnificence, the Tudor royal palaces, and Maurice Howard has discussed the contemporary houses of courtiers.

Besides the enormous amount of general work on the gentry and of their place in society, the study of their culture and social habits has been extensive. While Felicity Heal and Clive Holmes have offered hugely enlightening works on the gentry as a class and on their values, relationships and attitudes, there has also been something of a cottage industry, but a useful one, concerning what the early seventeenth-century country house poems have to say about changing social relations. The Stones' monumental analyses of the financial and social structures of the upper classes have included the use of their houses in order to illuminate statistically their economic circumstances, their social mobility and their aspirations. The works of Norbert Elias, Philippe Ariès and others have led to an increased understanding of the evolution of individual conduct and behaviour. Many other writers, as reflected in the bibliography, have taught how architectural historians need to understand something of contemporary developments in politics, economic history and literature if they want to advance beyond simply knowing what houses were like and to try to explain the reasons why.

Sources too have become vastly more accessible. Sir Howard Colvin's *Biographical Dictionary of British Architects, 1600–1840* (1954, rev. 3rd edn, 1995) has greatly facilitated the work of all architectural historians and comprises virtually a history of British architecture in itself. The monumental *History of the King's Works* (1963–82) has illuminated a much larger area than the works of the state. The publication of Roger North's writings and of John Thorpe's, Robert Smythson's and Inigo Jones's drawings has made the comparative study of Tudor and Stuart houses enormously more productive. The ever-growing volume of private records in local record offices means that more documentary source material is now available than any one person can comprehend, and there are still important discoveries to be made. The same is true of the houses themselves. More detailed analysis is casting new light on the development of houses that it was once assumed were well understood, besides drawing attention to others that were previously overlooked. The weekly issues of *Country Life* have for a century included descriptions of country houses, and if the writers were limited by the knowledge available when they wrote, at least this achieved the publication of a large body of material. Unpublished building records made by colleagues or by other recorders who have lodged them with the National Monuments Record have been invaluable in supplementing those made in the course of this study.

On the other hand, all of this work and the research that has been undertaken both on general issues and on specific problems, regions, dynasties and buildings have meant that any sort of overview of the subject has to take account of an enormous range of secondary material. In the present study much relevant work will inevitably have been overlooked, while much that has been published elsewhere cannot be omitted. Even with individual buildings one can seldom be sure that one has explored every source of information, or extracted as much information from the building as one might. In the past, the work of the Royal Commission has been based primarily on the detailed examination of buildings. This has been the case with the present study, which has sought both to throw fresh light on individual houses and to broaden the general picture. Many houses have long been recognised as key buildings but cannot be ignored if they contain some significant feature or illustrate some important development, and all need to be interpreted in the light of this great body of accumulated views and knowledge.

Yet in spite of this great volume of study there has been little by way of general overview of the subject since J. A. Gotch's *Architecture of the Renaissance in England* of 1894 and Thomas Garner's and Arthur Stratton's *Domestic Architecture of England during the Tudor Period,* published in 1911. The chief exceptions are James Lees-Milne's *Tudor Renaissance* and *Age of Inigo Jones,* both remarkable achievements for the early 1950s, and of course the relevant chapters of Sir John Summerson's *Architecture in Britain, 1530–1830,* first published in 1953 and frequently revised. These writers made a quantum leap in knowledge, and their books are still indispensable in that they illustrate or describe, in more or less detail, very many of the buildings that must be considered in any study of the sixteenth- and early seventeenth-century gentry house, and touch on many of the issues that any further work must address.

Of Gotch, who died in 1942, the *Dictionary of National Biography* says 'it is unlikely that his work will be rivalled or outdated by any other scholar'. However, the speed and the diversity of current research are now so great that no such claim could be made for any study of these houses today. The present work aims simply to sum up the present state of knowledge of how the houses of the gentry developed in the sixteenth century and the early seventeenth, to offer some possible explanations as to why this development took the course it did, to describe a number of individual houses as examples of that process, and to indicate lines for future research and investigation. With more time and space, other things should have been included. There is little discussion here of interior decoration or furnishing, except in so far as they throw light on the way in which houses were used, or of the dependencies, the outbuildings and the settings of houses, except in the context of the final chapter. To have included these topics would have prolonged the study and made the book unmanageable, but they are subjects on which, despite all that has been done, there is still a great deal to do.

Many of the houses included in this study are from that social region where the higher gentry merges with the aristocracy. Knights were generally regarded as upper gentry, and some men whose titles defined them as gentry enjoyed a thoroughly aristocratic life style. But the gentry embraced a wide range of income, overlapping with those both above and below them, and in any case social distinctions are blurred by Elizabeth's and James's capricious bestowal (or withholding) of titles. These builders were often performers on the national stage, but if a national survey is mainly concerned with the houses of the higher gentry this is because it was at this social level that architectural innovation took place and where its origins and motivation are most easily studied. But a national survey of this kind has to deal in generalisations which may fail to take account of local and regional circumstances and traditions, and of the needs of the full range of those who were recognised as gentlemen.

A national survey may show how certain models emerged, but it can do no more than suggest the ways in which they may have been diffused and the reasons why they were adopted. Much still needs to be tested by local studies. The finances and aspirations of the gentry and the variety of particular circumstances – economic and family, legal and tenurial – that prompted individuals to build what they did when they did also require further research. The uses of rooms in sixteenth- and seventeenth-century houses remain inadequately understood, partly because while something is known about entertainment, we know too little about people's private and everyday routines. More, too, needs to be done to synthesise the views of historians of architecture, painting, cartography and literature in order to explore how men and women viewed the world and their place in it.

It has been said that 'individual features do not define periods, if anything it is attitudes which do'.[2] Above all, this work seeks to be a study of a concept fashionable among historians: mentality. Its aim is to see the largely familiar story of the physical evolution of the gentry house in the light of the changing responsibilities and cultural attitudes of the upper classes, and in this objective, documents and buildings have been used together. At the beginning of the twentieth century Lord Curzon wrote of buildings that they were themselves 'documents just as valuable in reading the records of the past as any manuscript or parchment deed'[3] and he might have been repeating what Ruskin had said about Venice. Such an equation of documentary and artefact evidence is now a commonplace, but the inferences that can be drawn from buildings still need to be checked from other sources. Many of the interpretations advanced here may prove to be wrong or at best partial, but just as the initial, partial contributions to the great gentry debate of forty years ago were so fertile of later research, the present work will have been justified by whatever further studies it may stimulate. And if it in any way validates the correspondence between attitudes and houses, it will have succeeded in what it seeks to do.

Acknowledgements

This book arises from a study put in hand in 1990 by the former Royal Commission on the Historical Monuments of England (amalgamated with English Heritage in April 1999). In publishing this work, the Royal Commission was most fortunate to enlist the resources of Yale University Press, and is deeply grateful for the support, through the publishers, of the Paul Mellon Centre for Studies in British Art. In particular, I should like to thank Gillian Malpass of Yale for her skill, understanding and patience in handling all stages of negotiation, editing and design and for seeing this book through the press. Elizabeth McWilliams was constantly helpful, and Ruth Thackeray was an exemplary copy-editor.

On the Commission side, I am most grateful to former commissioners Malcolm Airs, Derek Keene, Gwyn Meirion-Jones and Anne Riches for their encouragement and for their very helpful reading of the manuscript, to the former Secretary, Tom Hassall, for his support and to Robin Taylor who patiently undertook the negotiations whereby the Commission was enabled to make a new departure in the publication of its work. Other colleagues provided not only essential help but also company that made the work very much more enjoyable. In the earlier stages Kate McGregor discovered existing owners and thus smoothed access to houses, discovered past owners and thus established these houses' historic status, and found printed inventories and other documentation relating to them. Dr John Gurney was able through his remarkable knowledge of primary source material for the period to explore the history of many of these houses and their builders in depth, and some important documentary discoveries are owing to him. George Wilson surveyed many of these houses and drew all the original plans that are reproduced here. Beyond those already available in the National Monuments Record or obtained from elsewhere, photographs were taken by Sid Barker, Steve Cole, James Davies, Derek Kendall, Pat Payne, Tony Perry and Peter Williams.

When it came to seeing houses and writing about them, an enormous number of people helped me and I visited very many more buildings than I have been able to discuss or include. If I acknowledge here only the people who allowed me to look at those houses that I have actually mentioned or described, or who otherwise facilitated access or shared information about them, this is not to say that I am not just as grateful to very many others. Any overview involves selection which may be made for quite arbitrary reasons: that there was already a good photograph of one house and not of another, that space could be saved by using one house to make several points (even though it may not be the best example of all of them), that illuminating research had already been carried out into the history of a particular building, or simply that when I saw a house I did not sufficiently understand what I was looking at. The omission of a house whose owner may have allowed me to see it is not to imply that it was in any way less interesting than those included.

I am thus deeply grateful to – among very many others – Joyce Abel-Green, Mr and Mrs D. M. Anderson, Tony Baggs, Richard Barker, Mrs Barr, Dr Sinan Bayraktaroglu, I. A. Bewlay-Cathie, Peter Bird, Mary Birkett, Mrs J. N. R. Bishop, Lord Boyd, Mrs Fiona Bridge, W. O. Brown, Mr and Mrs John Browne-Swinburne, Cherry Buckley, M. S. Bunn, M and Mme Georges Bureau, Viscount and Lady Camden, Catherine Chapman, Mr and Mrs Robert Charleston, John Chesshyre, Anthony Coghill, Edward Conant, Jo Cormier, John Culverhouse, Mr and Mrs Dale-Smith, Susan Denyer, Graham Derrick, Charles Dickens, Mr and Mrs Peter Dobree, Baron de Dosza, R. Douglas, H. A. Duffield, Mrs Dorothy Duffus, Mr and Mrs Ian Dyer, Mrs M. Falcon, Dr Jane Fenlon, George Ferguson, Sir Richard Fitzherbert, Mr and Mrs Robert Floyd, Dr Nancy Follett, Mr and Mrs John Ford, Mr and Mrs T. O. Frost, Julian Gibbs, Paul Girling, Peter Goide, Mrs Ahdaf Hamilton, Keith Hallett, Nim Haslam, Mr and Mrs Thomas Hatton, H. M. Henderson, John Hesketh,

Mr and Mrs Leonard Ingrams, Anthony Jaggard, T. R. Johns, B. M. Johnson, Sister Mary Julian, Lord Ralph Kerr, Nicholas Kingsley, Elfrida Knapp, The Landmark Trust, Peter Leach, Clifford Lee, Audrey Lefevre, Peter Lockhart-Smith, Anthony Loudon, Don Mackreth, Jonathan Marsden, Mrs M. P. Mills, Major and Mrs J. R. More-Molyneux, Alexander Moulton, A. H. Noon, Mr and Mrs Timothy Orbell, Anthea Palmer, Jeremy Pearson, Mr and Mrs J. Penoyre, J. P. M. Phillips, W. G. F. Plowden, Mr and Mrs Christopher Pole-Carew, Terry Power, Christopher Prideaux, Elizabeth Proudfoot, J. L. Puxley, Richard Roundell, Major and Mrs J. H. C. Sawrey-Cookson, John Schofield, Dr Constance B. Schultz, Mr and The Hon Mrs George Seymour, Chris Sharkey, Mrs S. N. Sinclair, Mr and Mrs Julian Spicer, Mr and Mrs Jack Stringer, Lady Stuart, The Marquess Townshend, Kit Turner, Anthony Vernon, Peter Vernon, W. G. Walker, Christopher Wall, R. M. L. Webb, Mr and Mrs John Weeks, Mr and Mrs Gordon West and Bill Wilson.

I cannot be absolutely certain that I have not left out anyone whose house is in the text and which I have seen, and I hope I shall be pardoned by them as well as by those owners whose houses I have not included. I have been struck throughout by the extraordinary generosity of the help I have received, by peoples' deep interest in their houses and by their willingness to allow a complete stranger to explore them (even though the name of the Royal Commission on Historical Monuments probably opened more doors than any other could). And I have included a few houses that I have not seen myself but that I have described from old records; I hope that the present owners of these important buildings will not mind their appearing here.

Finally, but to me most importantly of all, I should like to acknowledge what (in chronological order) I owe to three other colleagues, past and present. First, to Cecil Farthing, who many years ago gave me a job in the National Buildings Record and thus an incomparable opportunity to learn about the historic buildings of England. Second, to Eric Mercer, who taught me how to think about buildings historically and to analyse their building history constructively. And third, to John Bold for his companionship and his never-failing support – the last provided in ways that I suspect that I shall never know fully. But I do know how fortunate in all of this I have been.

Author's Note and Abbreviations

Except where another meaning is obvious, the word 'builder' is used throughout this book to denote the man or woman who caused a house to be built or altered rather than the artisan or architect who actually did the work or who was employed to supervise it.

Floors and storeys are denominated throughout in accordance with British usage, i.e. 'ground floor' corresponds to the American 'first floor', 'first floor' to the American 'second floor' and so forth.

Modern county names (i.e., post-1974) are given where a house was formerly in a different county. This is indicated in the index.

Nearly all the houses illustrated or mentioned in this book are private property. A few may be opened to the public by their owners; a few others are open by virtue of their belonging to the National Trust or to some other body, but in no case can their inclusion here imply any public right of access.

Abbreviations used on Drawings

Principal Rooms

H	Hall, Great Hall
B	Buttery
P	Parlour (often dining parlour after *c.* 1580)
LP	Low parlour, little parlour
GC	Great Chamber (often dining chamber after *c.* 1580)
W	Withdrawing room
C	Chamber
K	Kitchen
Ch	Chapel
St	Study

Secondary Rooms

Ic	Inner chamber
Cl	Closet
Pa	Pantry
Or	Oriel
Gr	Garderobe
Ps	Pastry, Bakehouse

Modern drawings are reproduced to the same scale of 1 : 300 (0.33 cm = 1 m.; 0.4 ins = 10 ft) unless otherwise indicated.

Abbreviations used in References

BL	London, British Library
CL	*Country Life*, 1898–
HKW	*History of the King's Works*, ed. H. Colvin, London, 1963–82 (see bibliography)
HMC	London, Historical Manuscripts Commission, Reports, 1870–
NMRC	Swindon, National Monuments Record Centre
PRO	London, Public Record Office
RCHM	London, Royal Commission on the Historical Monuments of England, Publications, 1910– (see bibliography)
RIBA, Smythson	London, Royal Institute of British Architects: drawings by Robert, John and Huntingdon Smythson (published as Girouard 1962)
RO	[County] Record Office
SM, Thorpe	London, Sir John Soane's Museum, MSS Vol. 101: drawings by John Thorpe (published as Summerson 1966)
SoL	London, The Survey of London, Publications, 1896–
VCH	London, Victoria Histories of the Counties of England, 1899–

Part I

BUILDERS

facing page   Brympton D'Evercy, Somerset.
Figures of sheep on the parapet of the house
announce the source of the builder's wealth and support shields with his coat of arms;
originally they probably held iron banners with his personal device.

I

The Image of the Gentry

Old Gentry and New: Wealth and Numbers

The houses of the gentry in the sixteenth and seventeenth centuries were more than just their homes. In a still largely rural nation, where authority and power were vested in the owners of land and where land constituted virtually the only permanent investment for capital, the houses of the gentry expressed the dominance of the landed class. Generally better educated than their forefathers, the leaders of society used their houses to express their knowledge and taste. More sophisticated than their poorer neighbours, their houses provided for a life of greater complexity in manners and in social relations. Aspirants and new arrivals expressed their ambitions in houses that proclaimed their gentility, while by rebuilding their old houses established members of the ruling class made sure that they were not out-shone by the newcomers. As the centres of largely self-contained communities, the houses of the gentry had to provide for a broad range of domestic functions. In an age where status still counted for much, they had to accommodate households where degrees of dignity were jealously observed, and when connections and affinities were still the cement of society, houses had to provide for the entertainment of friends and kindred, neighbours and dependants.

Over the two hundred years from the late fifteenth century to the end of the seventeenth, the duties, the education, the numbers and the life style of the gentry changed more radically than in any comparable period, and over the same time their homes evolved from buildings that were still medieval in appearance and in amenities into houses that are recognisably of the modern world. The expression of these changes was architectural, but in developing new plans and in adopting new styles of building, owners and builders were responding in ways that they felt appropriate to the changing demands of family and community, fashion and class. In building fine houses, the gentry

were fulfilling what they saw as their duty to society and to themselves. In the decoration of their houses they showed their taste, in the plans of their houses they provided for new standards of living, and both layout and appearance expressed the status and the evolving manners of the governing class.

No contrast could be stronger than that between two well-known pictures – Gillis van Tilborch's view of Tichborne in Hampshire, painted around 1670 to commemorate an ancient custom (pl. 1), and the anonymous painting of Wisbech Castle in Cambridgeshire, painted some ten years earlier to celebrate the building of a brand-new house (pl. 2). The picture of Sir Henry Tichborne and his children, handing out to all comers the annual dole of bread produced from a part of the Tichbornes' ancient estates as his ancestors had done since the thirteenth century, is one of the most evocative statements about traditional relations between the country gentry and the community. The family is accompanied by Sir Henry's two sisters and their husbands, indoor and outdoor servants, tenantry and a host of the neighbouring poor for whom the dole symbolised the importance of the house in local society. Family, household and the wider community are linked by reciprocal obligations of protection and service.[1]

As telling as the time-honoured activity of the picture are the details of the ancient house itself.[2] Though the house was pulled down in 1803, these are entirely convincing. Like a great many other gentry houses, it must have developed by a process of addition and subtraction, and its history and plan can easily be read. At the centre there is a great hall, still open to the roof, a medieval survival that was becoming unusual in the late seventeenth century but was not yet rare. The hall was superficially enhanced, perhaps around 1640, by the addition of an up-to-date classical porch. To the right of the hall window are those of the parlour and of the best chamber above it, perhaps added a little earlier than the porch but difficult to date closely in an

1 Gillis van Tilborch (active in England *c.* 1670): Sir Henry Tichborne and his family distributing the dole at Tichborne House, Hampshire. An ideal view of an old house, with an ancient family fulfilling ancient obligations to the local community. Like very many houses, the house itself shows work of many periods from the Middle Ages to the seventeenth century.

area with a strong tradition of timber building. In any case these windows give due prominence to the most important rooms of the house. To the right of this again a range returns forward with a tower gatehouse at its centre on which the family's coat of arms is prominently displayed. Such towers are commonly of the years around 1500. Left of the hall the accommodation is less clearly distinguished: here must be kitchen, pantry, buttery and the other normal service rooms of the manor house in which their owner did not need to make such a show.

The gatehouse suggests that there had once been an enclosed courtyard, with the house looking into it rather than out of it. Van Tilborch may have taken some artistic licence in ignoring it, or perhaps some predecessor of Sir Henry's may have pulled it down in order to transform the house from one that was inward-looking in the medieval tradition of such houses to one that looked outward, no longer presenting to the world the back walls of the house and courtyard with a domestic confusion

of chimneys and minor openings, but now by the size of its windows and the greater lavishness of its ornament announcing the wealth, the importance and the taste of the Tichborne family.

While the event that the painting records may have been unusual – few families were burdened with maintaining a charity quite so extensive as the Tichborne dole – the picture serves to make the point that at any given time few houses are modern, and most people make do with at best the piecemeal adaptation of the houses of their ancestors, and that even those individuals who do possess some architectural awareness may have no opportunity of demonstrating it. The rebuilding or even the substantial remodelling of a large house is an infrequent event, expensive and disruptive. Status, however, is displayed by the house's prominence and size and by evidence that the owner's way of life is suitable to his standing, and it does not follow that the house need be up to date. Tichborne is old and rambling, the product of generations of adaptation and accretion, but each part is distinguished appropriately to the internal hierarchy of the house's plan.

Wisbech was built in 1657 for Cromwell's Secretary of State, John Thurloe, and its architect was Peter Mills, a leading London builder who had already designed Thorpe Hall near Peterborough, some 20 miles away, for Thurloe's friend and colleague Oliver St John, Chief Justice under the Commonwealth.[3] Not only is the compact, finished composition of Wisbech Castle

2   Anon. (*c.* 1658): John Thurloe and his family at Wisbech Castle, Cambridgeshire. A new house and a new family. John Thurloe, Commonwealth law officer, bought the property in 1654, and immediately commissioned an up-to-date house from the mason Peter Mills of London. Both the building and its occupants contrast strikingly with the image of the Tichborne family.

a very long way from the rambling, accretive appearance of Tichborne, but the trim family of the Commonwealth statesman gathering on the balcony from what was probably their first-floor dining room presents an image as different as possible from the ancient hospitality being dispensed by Sir Henry. The scene of the Tichborne dole still seems medieval; Wisbech and its occupants are of the modern age. The Tichbornes claimed to have held their lands in Hampshire since two centuries before the Norman Conquest; the Thurloes of Wisbech had acquired the place in the 1650s. In wealth, lineage and sophistication the gentry were far from being a homogeneous group. Yet they shared a broadly based community of discourse and culture, and when these two pictures were painted both the Tichbornes and the Thurloes would have claimed membership of the same élite. Their radically different houses simply represent stages in the evolution of the gentry house and of the perceived responsibilities of the class.

The houses of the gentry are everywhere, ubiquitous evidence of a social system. It has been calculated that by the early seventeenth century one village out of every three in southern England (and in large areas elsewhere) had a resident squire,[4] equally concerned for his powers in the local community as for his right to be counted as a member of a national élite. Yet at the beginning of the sixteenth century perhaps only one village in ten had a member of the upper classes living in it, and the houses of the gentry are thus not only a demonstration of their standing, but an index of their rise.[5] From the fifteenth century to the seventeenth the gentry grew from a class broadly identifiable as minor nobility, overshadowed by a more powerful aristocracy, to a body that was numerous, vocal and self-confident.

There have been many attempts to estimate the numbers of the gentry and to produce figures that provide concrete evidence of a fact widely recognised by contemporaries as well as by later historians – the growth of the class in wealth and in numbers. The difficulties are formidable: the magnitude of the necessary analysis, the nature of the evidence and the prejudices and preconceptions of commentators.[6] There is a general consensus, however, that around 1500 the upper gentry numbered some four or five hundred knights and some eight hundred designated 'esquire', who together provided the great bulk of the members of parliament, the justices of the peace and the other office holders in the provinces. By the early seventeenth century numbers had grown to some 1500 esquires and some 1000 knights and baronets; by the end of the century, 3000 and 1400 respectively. The increase in numbers was far from steady, but in total it represented a large-scale transfer of land and power from the crown, the church and the higher nobility.[7]

The last figures derive largely from the late seventeenth-century hearth tax, a crude property tax introduced in 1662. The hearth tax was levied on the number of a house's chimneys and imposed not on the owner of the property but on its occupant, and it provides a rough guide to a house's size and its inhabitants' wealth. For many reasons the returns must be used with caution.[8] But although any one house may not be accurately described by the tax returns, taken together they provide a useful approximation of the range of sizes of the houses of the gentry at the end of the period with which this study is concerned. Furthermore, correlating these lists with lists of justices of the peace that are close in date confirms the economic position of members of the county élite. In a sample of seven counties there is a very clear difference in size between the houses of those lesser gentry described as 'gent'[9] and those called 'esquire', with the latter, on average, having houses some two or three times as large as the former.[10] While there is also a considerable difference in average size between the houses of knights and those of esquires, there is also a broad overlap between the two, and the magistracy was appointed from both classes.

Table 1   Average numbers of hearths in gentry houses in seven counties, 1662–75.[11]

County	'Gent'	'Esq.'	'Kt' and 'Bt'	JPs[12]
Derbyshire[13]	4.8	12.7	19.0	16.6
Dorset[14]	5.2	12.3	18.3	14.9
Norfolk[15]	7.1	13.8	23.6	20.9
Oxon[16]	8.1	14.5	22.6	18.5
Surrey[17]	8.0	14.9	18.8	19.8
Warwickshire[18]	5.7	10.6	16.3	
Westmorland[19]		9.0	14.4	12.1

As a class, the gentry included individuals with a broad range of wealth;[20] the range of house sizes reflects continuing regional variations in wealth and social structure (see table 1). In Surrey, the prosperity that London generated increased the wealth of the 'mere' gentry – those returned as 'mr' or 'gent', while the size of the houses of knights in Surrey is probably reduced by their including the suburban retreats of men who played little part in the life of the county, either London merchants or men whose principal country house was further off. At the same time, the high figure for the size of magistrates' houses indicates their selection from a genuine and wealthy county élite. In Westmorland, by contrast, poverty and absenteeism meant that houses were small and often ancient, even though the standing locally

of the county gentry was the equal of their richer peers elsewhere. In Warwickshire the 'gents' seem richer than those in Derbyshire and the higher gentry poorer, perhaps indicating a greater degree of gentrification in the latter county and a greater domination by great landowners in the former. However, despite enduring differences in local architectural resources and in the local economy, at least by the late seventeenth century the gentry shared norms of conduct and esteem that transcended localism.

Those who were called 'esquire' were, together with the knights of the shire, the leaders of county society in office, in wealth and generally in the culture through which they displayed their standing, and it is this county élite whose houses are for the most part the subject of this study. The title of 'esquire', properly limited to men of defined ancestry and to those who held certain offices (particularly Justice of the Peace) was already coming to be bestowed merely as a title of esteem on those whose wealth or evident standing impressed their neighbours. But the fact that the tax returns were a species of official document probably meant that the titles given were still used with care, and in any case the possession of substantial landed property was in general a necessary qualification for appointment to the magistracy.

The hearth tax returns come at the end of a hundred and fifty years of growth in gentry numbers, wealth and power. Although during this period the acreage owned by the knighthood and gentry probably doubled,[21] their numbers grew still more; this meant that though the size of the average, individual gentry estate might have fallen slightly (increasing their economic distance from the great aristocracy), their growth in prominence and in the pervasiveness of their control was even greater than is suggested by the bare increase in the area they owned. A land market of unparalleled freedom came into being for reasons which affected both sellers and purchasers. In the late Middle Ages, in response to the financial needs of the landed aristocracy as much as to demand from would-be purchasers, lawyers had devised means of selling feudal land holdings held from the crown.[22] Land came onto the market not only as a result of aristocratic extravagance but also through the exigencies of royal finance and the redistribution of church lands after the dissolution of the monasteries. Land was available and the mechanisms for selling it already existed when in the sixteenth century newcomers in unprecedented numbers were seeking to buy themselves a place among the landed élite.

Recruits to the gentry came partly from the landed class itself, from among the younger sons of existing landowners and from frugal yeomen making the most of a fast rising market for agricultural produce,[23] while existing landowners who were able to capitalise their rising rents or to add to their income by enclosures could invest the increase in the purchase of additional land. In the sixteenth century especially, before the rules of legal settlement and the customs of primogeniture were as strict as they would later become, many exisiting families were able to establish cadet branches on lands that had become available for purchase, providing new opportunities for house building.[24] Ownership of land was essential for membership of the governing élite, although the wealth that lay behind the building of almost all the greatest houses of the age came from other, more immediately remunerative activities. There was money to be made as the steward or as the confidential agent of greater men, in the service of the crown, by speculation in the land market itself, by trade at a time when the demand for luxury goods was rapidly growing, and notoriously and conspicuously at the law.[25] The increase in gentry numbers was probably most rapid between around 1570 and 1620, both when the greatest profits were to be made from land ownership and also the age of the greatest house building, but this increase in prominence was already foreshadowed by a growth in the class's powers.[26]

Status and Service: Public Duties and Private Culture

For three centuries the gentry were responsible for almost every detail of local administration. As county members of parliament they represented the landed interest to government and reported government back to their peers.[27] As magistrates they were responsible for the administration of local government as well as of justice in all except serious criminal offences. Their role in the community had long been established through the manor court, enforcing a combination of statute law and local custom, while as landowners their powers over the economic life of the community were as absolute as were their control of justice and local administration. By the seventeenth century their sense of class identity was well developed, confirmed by an education that fitted them for their role in society and in the state. Add to all this the wealth provided by land, by office holding and by provident marriages, as well as the dynastic security that was ensured by a gradually perfected system of entails to ensure the descent of their property, and there is a complete explanation for the prominence of their houses, recognisable at once as the homes of men whose standing required them to make an educated display of their position. In the long run the social prestige of the landed gentry outlasted their ultimate demise as a significant adminstrative and economic force, when by the end of the nineteenth century a system established three hundred years before would prove inadequate to administer a nation that was increasingly urbanised, increasingly mobile, increasingly democratic and whose population had grown some eight fold. But the strength of that prestige is evidence of the gentry's former power, and at the end of the period with which this book is concerned that power appeared unshakeable and as permanent as the homes that they built.

In the Middle Ages, society had rested on a series of reciprocal obligations. Tenure of a manor (whether directly from the king or indirectly from some great magnate as his overlord) was nominally conditional on a man's availability for military service; his own tenants held their lands in his fields by virtue of relatively insignificant and infrequent money payments but with dues of labour and beasts that could be onerous. That at least was the theory, and in such a view human organisations were essentially static. Society was held to be divinely ordained, the earthly reflection of an eternal order. Individuals might rise or fall on Fortune's wheel, but society itself was in a state of eternal equilibrium. Such a world was furthermore unalterably hierarchic, where everyone had his allotted place in an overall scheme of interdependence. There was no sense that to be dependent on some mighty nobleman for land and status was to demean oneself. Rather the reverse: the great man's honour reflected honour on the man who served him.[28]

In the classic, three-fold medieval classification of society – knight, priest and labourer ('I fight for all; I pray for all; I work for all') – the gentry were to be included in the first category. Contemporaries saw the great nobleman and the lesser, county gentry – the knight and the esquire – as members of the same noble class – nobilitas major and nobilitas minor.[29] The gentleman shared an identity of interest with the great magnate: both shared an ideology of military service, and while the lord of the manor might attach himself to a greater man in order to enjoy the fruits of his favour, the greater man relied on the lesser to keep him in touch with local sentiment and to maintain his regional power base.[30] The lesser man sent his children to be educated in the household of the great, to learn courtly behaviour and the gentlemanly (mainly warlike) arts and to form alliances that might in due course be useful for their advancement. It is not surprising that in 1500 the houses of the upper classes had changed little in a century or more, and that their appearance and layout were also fundamentally hierarchical. The house was built to accommodate a household in which everyone had his place in a mutually supportive and unchanging community.

However, there was potentially as much to divide the nobility from the gentry as there was to unite them.[31] Politically and economically the great nobleman was by far the more important of the two. Frequently committed to an extravagant display of his wealth and of the size of his following, summoned to parliament in his own right, attendant at court and involved in high politics (not infrequently at high risk) and lord of many manors, the great man led a peripatetic existence unless concentrating his attention on a few favourite houses. In either case most of his tenants would seldom see him, even though his house (or houses), built out of a sense of the honour due to his own exalted standing, would be a permanent reminder of his power and position. The mere knight or squire, on the other hand, holding only a few manors, would be a more familiar figure, already establishing a presence that would set a pattern for later developments.

The medieval status quo would be undermined by the harsh facts of demography and inflation, diminishing prospects of a military career and royal weakness, disruptions that would in due course propel the gentry into a new prominence in power and numbers. Demographic changes had been precipitated by the catastrophe of the Black Death, when the massive reduction of the working population had reduced income from land, had greatly increased the value of the labour of the survivors and caused the realities of supply and demand for land and labour to undermine the reassuring ideal of the interdependence of a community of the different sorts of men. The decline of opportunities for a military career – the established calling of the upper classes and the one which justified their position in the traditional scheme of things – arose from the progressive collapse of English power abroad and from the preference, in any case, for trained (and paid) soldiery to the personal service of an amateur knight and his following of part-time men-at-arms.[32] Royal weakness in the fifteenth century had provided opportunities for rival magnates to seek to expand their power and to build up their clientage, placing their own interests firmly before those of the state. But in so doing they created a situation where a revived, Tudor monarchy would feel the necessity of cutting the peerage down to size, so creating a species of administrative power vacuum which had to be filled from elsewhere.[33]

Fortunately, an alternative instrument for administering the regions already lay to hand: the county gentry. Members of the military classes – the *nobilitas* – were increasingly open to demands for services of alternative kinds: men with land and with time on their hands and who might once have gone to the wars were increasingly compelled to seek honourable avocations nearer home. The gentry were growing in numbers, were generally dispersed throughout the country, and were already experienced in local government as the class from which the magistracy was drawn, as the local clients of great men, through appointment to such crown offices as escheator and sheriff for the county, and through providing the bulk of the county members of parliament. The magistracy already existed as a relatively subordinate part of the existing establishment, protected by property qualifications from unsuitable candidates, and whose services could moreover be used for nothing. Nevertheless, it is doubtful whether the employment of the gentry in the running of the provinces was a coherent and planned policy of Tudor government; rather it was the *ad hoc* use of a tool that already lay to hand. Tudor monarchs, from Henry VIII onward, increasingly distanced themselves from day-to-day administration, leaving such routine to a council of ministers, themselves drawn from the landed classes. Such a system developed a community of interest between central government and its local agents and ensured continuing administrative stability for as long as such a community should endure.[34]

During the sixteenth century there was an ever-increasing weight of judicial and administrative tasks heaped upon the shoulders of local justices of the peace. Besides the enforcement of a growing number of criminal statutes, magistrates would find themselves administering poor relief, determining poor rates and dealing with vagrants; enforcing fair weights and measures and determining and imposing fair wage levels; enforcing laws that maintained public morality, the Protestant settlement and that penalised Catholics; overseeing measures for national security and fixing rates for the payment of the militia; supervising the maintenance and repair of roads and bridges, and enforcing a variety of laws for the encouragement of trade; and overseeing the appointment and conduct of a number of lesser, parochial officials – constables, guardians of the poor and the like. Although the leading magnates in each county were always included among the magistracy, these were always happy – until it became an established convention – to leave the actual work to the growing number of county gentry who saw in the office of Justice of the Peace an opportunity for service to the crown, a bulwark for the protection of the state, a means of personal advancement, an outlet for religious zeal and an instrument for moral and spiritual reformation, and a vehicle for their own self-importance – or probably, in most cases, an ill-defined mixture of several motives. Men of new families saw in the magistracy a means of identifying themselves with the county élite; men of old families saw in it the preservation of the status quo and the maintenance of their own dignity. Both saw the duty of the magistrate as the defence of property and of local interest, and while in the fifteenth century men had frequently been reluctant to serve, by the seventeenth those with the right credentials came to see appointment to the bench of magistrates as their rightful due. Through its increasing wealth, but still more through its members' increasing prominence in the government of the provinces, prestige accrued to the gentry class as a whole.[35]

The number of magistrates fluctuated, but tended to grow. Periodic reductions in the numbers on the bench (usually for political reasons, but sometimes in order to weed out the aged and the incompetent) might leave individuals with a sense of grievance, but generally the broad base of selection from among those qualified will have helped to consolidate a sense of class identity among the county élite. Only in the Civil War, when some existing justices tainted with royalism were replaced by men better disposed towards the regime, did the authorities find it necessary to go far outside the ranks of the county gentry in order to nominate men to the magistracy, and in most cases the Commonwealth appointees were removed at the Restoration. However, the precedent of such non-landed appointments had been established, and in the later seventeenth century increasing numbers of professional men were appointed – doctors, lawyers and the like – reflecting a community of interest, feeling and life styles between the landed gentry and the growing number of the genteel who lacked significant amounts of land.

The role of the upper classes as agents of central government, exercising control by authority rather than through powers that were founded in the community and in a theory of reciprocal duties, reinforced their sense of solidarity. At the same time the decline in their autonomous exercise of power can be paralleled by a deeper cultural shift towards a new concern for privacy and personal distinction.[36] This too has been seen as a product of the changing role of the state.[37] In the late Middle Ages government was weak and decentralised, and the individual was left by default to establish his own position and to maintain his own security by means of a personal affinity of retainers and a public display of strength. From the late fifteenth century onwards, however, not only in England but in much of Europe, states that were rapidly growing in authority were increasingly able to circumscribe the powers of the individual and at the same time better able to guarantee his freedom within strictly defined boundaries. No longer needing – or even permitted – to secure private power by his own efforts, the individual was left to make good his claims to status and authority through the exercise of powers bestowed on him by the state and by the cultivation of more personal distinctions.

The means of promoting such cultivation were at hand. Printing was bringing about a huge increase in the availability of books and in the number and range of titles, and at some stage in the sixteenth century it seems to have become normal to read silently to oneself and no longer to read out loud, reducing reading to the private reception of the ideas of one individual by another. Artists would progressively free themselves from conventions of representation that had been sanctioned by long usage, while growing concern with the individual would make possible the lifelike, painted portrait and the intimate, private contemplation of the face of the close friend or personal ideal.[38] In literature, the encapsulation of private feeling in the sonnet, the self-examination of Montaigne and the psychological insights of Shakespeare would have been impossible to express before the sixteenth century. In religion, monasticism – corporate devotion and obedience to a rule – was already declining in the previous century, to some extent superseded on the part of those who felt called to a holy life by a tendency to mysticism and a more private experience of God. With the Reformation the process was accelerated, and individualism reinforced: religous reformers stress the essential value of each person's own relations with the deity and the irrelevance of intermediaries. Protestants emphasise the importance of private prayer; Roman Catholics introduce the privacy of the confessional.

The emergence in the fifteenth and sixteenth centuries of so many parallel ways of establishing such private distinctions seems to indicate a changing mental climate that was perhaps no more than promoted and reinforced by evolving relations between the state and the ruling class. Such new attitudes found their intellectual strength in humanism, a new concern with the dignity of man and with his place in the universe. Humanists saw man as perfectable, and having a value in himself rather than simply in his relation to God or to the community. Such an attitude encouraged an exploration of the person's own feelings, opinions and experiences, and licensed their individual expression. It encouraged an appreciation of individual merit, and thus a new concern with the value of education for its own sake. While appealing to those who had the means to indulge in the refinements of civilised life, humanist teaching also appealed to those members of a rising class who were able to demonstrate a personal worth that was not dependent solely on the accidents of ancestry.

But while the cultivation of the individual led to an increased value being placed upon privacy, in their reading of the classics humanists sought examples of nobility and civic virtue. In Italy a view of civic responsibility was already developing by the first half of the fifteenth century, drawing upon Aristotle, Cicero and Plato, in which the performance of public duties was seen as a sign of virtue. 'Those whom Nature has endowed with the capacity for administering public affairs', wrote Cicero, 'should . . . take a hand in directing the government; for in no other way can a government be administered or greatness of spirit made manifest.'[39] Whereas in the Middle Ages goodness could be found in a withdrawal from the world, for humanists virtue comprised a wise engagement with it. While the purpose of education was to give the man of standing wisdom as a ruler, in conspicuous works he extolled the glory of the state that it was his duty to honour. But it was also the endeavour of humanist writers to assimilate the morality of classical writers to the teachings of the church.[40]

At the beginning of the sixteenth century, humanist ideals in England were confined to an élite of educators, statesmen and aristocrats: as the century progressed and such ideals became more widespread, beginning to inform the common culture of the upper classes, they inevitably became more diffuse and less rigorous. In due course the emphasis on individual virtue merged with Protestant reformers' concern with the signs of personal salvation and the importance of a private experience of God. But as the humanist message became less intellectually élitist, so it also became more practical, and in the sense that privilege brought duties with it, humanism and religion combined to promote in the gentry a sense both of the responsibilities of their position and of the underlying rightness of the distinction that they showed in their behaviour.

Members of the upper class were increasingly able to take advantage of new educational opportunities, and increasingly had a motive for doing so.[41] In the new century both Oxford and Cambridge universities saw a growing secularisation, with the foundation of new colleges and the reorganisation of older ones that made provision for the teaching of a classical curriculum to undergraduate laymen. Such teaching was encouraged by patrons who saw in it a means of educating men with the potential of becoming trained administrators, as well as the propagation of common values. In London – itself the unchallenged centre of civility – at the Inns of Court, young men in growing numbers would receive a training in the common law that would equip them as lawyers and magistrates. The universities and the Inns propagated a growing sense of the importance of active service to the public and of the righteousness of ordained power, together with belief in the superiority of the upper classes as the servants of the state. Even for those who attended neither, a growing number of grammar schools provided a basic education in the classics that underwrote the values of the rulers. The numbers of men educated at one or more of these institutions grew enormously in the course of the sixteenth century, broadening the culture of the gentry at the same time as the class was growing in size and expanding in influence.[42]

The first and most complete English exposition of an ideal of upper-class accomplishments that combined the courtly and the administrative, the martial and the academic in the service of the commonwealth was Sir Thomas Elyot's *Boke named The Governour* (1531), which had run to seven editions by 1580. Elyot was a platonist, believing with most of his contemporaries that the justification of civil government was the achievement and maintenance of order – a message that in any case appealed to contemporaries who remembered the disorders of the previous century and who were anxious about the continuing dynastic uncertainties of the present age. The ideal of the well-ordered, divinely ordained society had been the commonplace of the Middle Ages, and books about correct behaviour and the duties of good rulers were far from being a novelty, but what was new in Elyot was an explicit statement in the vernacular of the place of the upper classes in the service of crown and state, and the implicit rejection of older, feudal ideals of personal loyalty that transcended public duty.[43]

Plato's principles of a perfect society, perpetuated through Aristotle, Augustine and Aquinas and Christianised in the process, were applied once more by Elyot to secular ends: knowledge and virtue rather than divine dispensation justified authority and rank.[44] The model had been prefigured in Thomas More's *Utopia*, in which the rulers were to be a humanist aristocracy: the state itself was to be an incorruptible society in which order and responsibility were inseparable, backward-looking in the search for an ideal that was static and absolute but looking forward in its implicit rejection of divine sanction.[45] It can hardly be a coincidence that Elyot's *Governour* was written within three years of Niccolò Machiavelli's *Il principe* (*The Prince*) and within two of the publication of Baldassare Castiglione's *Il libro del cortegiano* (*The Book of the Courtier*), the two most influential books of instruction for the élite to be written in the sixteenth century.[46] All are fundamentally concerned with the organisation of the state and with the behaviour of the élite within it. Thomas Cromwell, Elyot's patron, certainly had a copy of Machiavelli, and probably a manuscript of Castiglione. Elyot was a thoroughly establishment figure, drawn by Holbein along with his wife and other leading figures of Henry VIII's court, and the ideals that he was promulgating were already current in ruling circles and met with the approval of his peers.[47] Erasmus, fêted in half the courts of Europe, described that of Henry VIII as 'a temple of the Muses rather than a court' and called More's household 'a gymnasium of Christian religion', deliberately using the epithet of a Greek academy.[48]

For Elyot, rule by a wise sovereign was the best guarantee of order. However, the ruler needed support:

it is expedient and also needful that under the capitall governor be sondry meane authorities, as it were aydyng hym in the distribution of justice in sundry parts of a huge multitude.[49]

In extolling the place of rank and order in society, he drew a parallel with the organisation of the house:

Where order lacketh, there all thynge is odious and uncomly. And that we have in daily experience; for the pannes and pottes garnisheth wel the ketchyn, and yet shulde they be to the chambre noe ornament. Also the beddes, testars and pillowes besemeth nat the halle, no more than the carpettes and kushyns becometh the stable. . . . Wherefor to conclude, it is onely a public weal, where . . . is also appoynted degrees and places accordynge to the excellencie therof; and therto also wold be substance convenient and necessarye for the ornament of the same, whiche also impresseth a reverence and due obedience to the vulgare people or communaltie; and with out that, it can be no more said that there is a publike weal, than it may be affirmed that a house, without the propre and necessarye ornamentes, is well and sufficiently furnisshed.[50]

It was the duty of Elyot's Governour not only to fill his place in society, but to be an ornament to it.[51] Erasmus had written: 'no man is born to himself, no man is born to idleness. Your children are born not to yourself alone, but to your country; not to your country alone, but to God.'[52] Lord Burghley may have been repeating Erasmus in a letter to his young protégé John Harington at Cambridge, when he wrote that the aim of his university studies was to make him 'a fytte servaunte for the Queene and your countrey for which you were born, and to which, next to God, you are moste bounde'.[53]

If service to the state was one way in which the functions and the image of the gentry was changing in the sixteenth and seventeenth centuries, a second aspect of change was in the relations of family and the larger household, and between both of these and the wider community of tenants, neighbours and connections. In the late Middle Ages the aristocratic household had been a close-knit community of carefully graduated ranks. With the status of its head depending to a great extent on the size and splendour of his establishment, households were often large, expensive and in functional terms overmanned: when the status of household members depended on their duties, the result was both inflexibility and a complex range of grades calling for careful definition if private honour was to be safeguarded. Rivalry and emulation between households in supporting the status of its head was normative in establishing a common culture, and the conventions of courtly behaviour described what was acceptable and unacceptable in one's behaviour towards one's peers. Such a household, in providing its own, self-contained structure of relationships and mutual obligations, had provided for all of its members both confirmation of status and a sense of personal identity.

The structured, extravagant, medieval household, inward-looking and self-sufficient in terms of personal relations, was gradually to be replaced by a household of a very different kind. As a writer of 1579 put it: 'honor and worship, resteth not either in your Country abroad, or in keeping of many servants, but rather in your own virtue'.[54] In the post-medieval household, grades of service would be slowly reduced in number, the higher servant level reduced in rank and the status of service itself diminished. As the distance increased between the lord and the upper servants who had once been his companions, so he would increasingly seek companionship among members of his close family at home, and among his peers beyond the confines of his household. For the lord and his family, the change in household relationships provided for a new source of identity by culture and affinity and for definitions that were familial and geographic. Within the county community, the growing numbers of gentry and their increasing responsibilities drew together neighbours of like position, with similar duties and with similar interests to maintain. Beyond it, the intermarriage of members of the same class created an extensive cousinage, connections that were cherished, consulted and visited, with a taste for the same company and a common concern for the maintenance of family standing. Friends and relations, women as well as men, corresponded with each other as well as visiting, enabled to do so by the growth of upper-class literacy. Godparents for the children of the gentry were chosen with a view not only to the future advantage of the child but to confirm the connections of the parents. These dense networks of peers and relatives reinforced the gentry's sense of its group identity and supported the self-esteem of every one of its members. The evolution of the inward-looking, self-defining household into the outward-looking yet exclusive family, defined by its social and kindred connections, parallels the development of the house itself.

In the Middle Ages, the important person's every action had been valueless unless performed in public, with suitable marks of status. But how a private man lived was ceasing to be public business. Once the individual had come to place a value on his own actions without regard to their public acclaim, it became not merely irrelevant that they should be done publicly but it might positively devalue them. Beyond his private beliefs he might be justified by his work for the public good and his standing displayed by proper ceremonial on public occasions, but the lines between public and private were increasingly tightly drawn. Whereas courtesy – courtly behaviour – had once been a sign that one was qualified to mingle with other courtiers, a cultivation of the self that went deeper than the acquisition of social skills was now leading to a recognition that manners are a sign of character as much as of social acceptability, and that in the practice of them one is showing consideration for others as much as one's own superiority.[55] In the cultivation of civility – a favourite word of sixteenth-century writers – a man displayed behaviour that set him apart from the lower orders, but the purpose of civility is no longer merely social distinction on

its own account so much as participation in a communion of like-minded, civilised individuals. Civility is a sign of inward morality, a message that was preached by Erasmus and in due course could easily be translated into religious terms by preachers who taught that a man's outward behaviour indicated the state of his soul.

But though the purpose of civility in forwarding human relationships was rather different from the purpose of courtesy in the Middle Ages, it tended to be no less exclusive in its application: the cultivated (or the saved) showed the fact in their daily lives, while those who were uncivilised remained beyond the pale. In the cultivation of friends a man excluded others whose claims to companionship were based solely on community or household, while the downgrading of service was itself an aspect of increasing privacy as the attendance in a servile role of those close in rank became less tolerable. Such a change led to a new importance of the family as an emotional centre and as a sanction for behaviour; the decline of the extended household of retainer-companions that had been brought about by the growing role of the state coincided with a decline in the felt need for such comradeship.

The gradual decline in the number and variety of servants and retainers and in the complexity of households takes place alongside an increase in consumption, in the physical complexity of houses themselves, in the specialisation of space within the house, in decoration that is increasingly specific to individuals or to particular usages, and – linking both the more specialised use of space and the growing separation of family from servants – the cultivation of exclusiveness and the increasing value placed upon privacy.[56] Personal identity would come to be provided not by servant companions but by objects and physical surroundings. The consequences of these changes for the architecture of the house were profound, as entertaining rooms became more specialised in their functions, more elaborate in their decoration and more exclusive in their use, and as family and servants moved in opposite directions, away from once-common household areas to regions of their own.[57] In 1624 Sir Henry Wotton saw the place of the house in the self-fulfilment of the individual as

> Every Man's proper Mansion House and Home, being the Theater of his Hospitality, the Seat of Selfe-fruition, the Comfortablest part of his own Life, the Noblest of his Sonnes Inheritance, a kinde of private Princedome.[58]

Such a domestic picture could not have been painted a century before.

Contemporary recognition of the new prominence of the gentry and an awareness of such changes in manners gave rise to a widespread concern with the qualities of gentility, prompting debate which itself contributed substantially to a sense of the class's coherence and to the establishment of its cultural identity.[59] The actual term 'gentleman', probably of French origin, began to acquire currency in England during the late fourteenth century.[60] The Statute of Additions in 1413 gave it legal force and its rapid adoption thereafter showed its usefulness in describing members of an increasingly identifiable class.[61] Courtesy books – books describing correct, courtly behaviour – had been current since the earlier Middle Ages, but by the sixteenth century they were evolving into works that combined rules of etiquette with discussion of who qualified as a gentleman.[62] At the centre of the debate was the question of whether gentility was bestowed by birth or by virtue – by nature or by nurture, so to speak.[63] Several factors might bestow gentility, and none of these was absolute. The claim to a coat of arms, either by grant from the heralds (having paid them their fee and satisfied them of one's birth and local standing) or better, by inheritance, was almost universal among the county gentry, and between the early sixteenth century and the late seventeenth the heralds conducted a number of regional visitations to confirm the rights of those who already bore a coat of arms and to satisfy the ambition of those who sought to acquire one. Yet a coat of arms was not a necessity, and the ease with which one could be acquired increasingly cast doubt on the value of what was on offer.[64] Office holding was not so much a qualification for gentility as a consequence of it, though the title 'esquire', normally only bestowed of right on the eldest sons of knights or of other esquires, was accorded by courtesy to justices of the peace. By the seventeenth century even the possession of land was not seen as a *sine qua non* of gentility, and leading lawyers and London merchants would be dignified with the title 'gentleman' though they owned no more than a few acres in the home counties. If there is no ready formula that can be applied retrospectively, there was a wide consensus that certain people qualified by a combination of wealth, birth, authority and behaviour, and general agreement about the manners appropriate to members of the class.

Rules of precedence in the sixteenth century often linked titles and income, but attempts to describe gentility constituted a search for a definition that involved more than mere economic and political power. For this power to be merited called for certain inherent virtues in those who exercised it.[65] The numerous books that discussed the qualifications of gentility in the sixteenth century and the early seventeenth clearly responded to a demand, from existing members of the upper class for reassurance about their status, and from aspirants for information and for asssurance of their capacity for joining the élite. Not unnaturally the writers of these books had to reconcile conflicting messages. The virtues of the ordered society had to be promoted, while daily recruitment to the ranks of its leaders seemed to threaten disorder. The solidarity of the class had to be supported, while facing the facts of social mobility. The claims of virtue to gentility had to be admitted without undermining the claims of lineage; above all, the claims of both virtue and lineage had to be maintained against the irresistible challenge of wealth.[66]

Yet wealth itself provided a framework of order, desirable in supporting the dignity of the governor and honourable in so far as it was the means whereby one achieved positions of honour

in the state. In granting coats of arms the heralds might favour the worthy *arriviste* 'who hath yet through virtue prevailed against the malignity of fate'[67] and Plato himself had urged that 'nothing is so dishonourable than [for a man] to be honoured, not for his own sake but on account of the reputation of his ancestors'.[68] In principle virtue might repose anywhere in society, but in practice the authority that virtue merited was only effectively exercised by those who were already in positions of prominence. The message of most observers was the same as Elyot's, that the ideal society was governed by men of birth who were themselves virtuous:

> Excepte excellent virtue and lernynge do inhabile a man of the base astate of the communaltie, to be thought of all men worthy to be so moche advanced: els suche governors wolde be chosen out of that astate of men whiche be called worshipfull, if amonge them may be founden a sufficient numbre, ornate with vertue and wisedome.[69]

Or, as it was put by the author of the *Institutions of a Gentleman* of 1555, it was the duty of gentlemen to show themselves 'worthy to possess such lands and inheritance as God hath prepared for them to the maintenance of their lives or estate'.[70] These were ideals, but they expressed what most people agreed: that by virtue of his wealth the gentleman did not work for his living, and that he ought to show by his behaviour that he merited his title.

In 1656 James Harrington published *The Commonwealth of Oceana* as a model for the government of Britain, describing an ideal social and economic balance between the classes of society. Harrington quoted Machiavelli's description of the gentry as 'such as live upon their revenues in plenty, without engagement either in the tilling of their lands or other work for their livelihood'.[71] But whereas Machiavelli saw such men as a threat to the power of the prince, for Harrington their independence made them an asset to the state:

> If his share [i.e. the gentleman's, in the wealth of the nation] be such as gives him leisure by his private advantage to reflect upon that of the public, what other name is there for this sort of man but . . . nobility? Especially when their families come to be such as are noted for their services done to the commonwealth and so take into their ancient riches ancient virtue.

By Harrington's time the idea of a secular balance of interests has wholly displaced the medieval notion of a divinely ordained society of three estates, and recognition of the importance of individual, public virtue has replaced the feudal notion of a society of mutual obligations and personal service. The idea of society as composed of a number of interdependent classes remains, but the ideal of service to the community has come to provide the gentry with a powerful moral justification for the exercise of power. Their status was confirmed by training that supported the ideology of an educated élite, but which was only open to those with the means and the time to acquire it. Education, leisure, status and service were intimately connected.

The Sanctions for Display

Concern for the definition of gentility embraced both qualifications and behaviour.[72] In the Middle Ages, great men had proclaimed their position by great buildings, by elaborate ceremonial and by the splendour of their retinue, but they had done so for the sake of their personal honour and as a symbol of lordship. In the sixteenth century an ideology was emerging that equally sanctioned display on the part of the leaders of society, but justified it as honouring the commonwealth of which they were members and as both the privilege and the duty of the servants of the state. The social and the household functions of sixteenth-century gentry still required a house of essentially conservative and hierarchical form, but architecture and decoration could be employed to advertise the culture of the owner as well as the common values of the leaders of a well-ordered society. There was too a didactic value in such expression. For humanists, virtue comprised both just principles and right action; for Cicero, perhaps the most revered of classical writers in the sixteenth century, rhetoric – essentially the province of the public man – had comprised the inculcation of such virtues and the means of connecting the real world with the ideal.[73] Such principles were clearly applicable to literature and were acknowledged by contemporary writers, could be expressed in painting in the idealisation of subject-matter, and could be realised in bricks and mortar in the erection of buildings that expressed the desired usages of society, that were appropriate to their function and to the distinction of their occupant and that embodied the ideal harmonies of the cosmos.

The idea of building suitably to the status of the builder was expressed in Vitruvius's notion of *decor* – characterised by Sir Henry Wotton in the early seventeenth century as 'the keeping of a due Respect between the Inhabitant and the Habitation'.[74] If such explicit statements of architectural ideology were not widely made, it is probably because such a notion was taken for granted. The connection between display and duty had long since been made by Aristotle.[75] Late medieval condemnation of governors (such as Henry VI) whose behaviour was inappropriate to their standing had been in direct conformity with the teachings of Aristotle, and in the sixteenth century Aristotelian thought remained powerful.[76] Visible distinction was an important element of the just society. But the word generally translated as 'magnificence' in Aristotle has now no direct English equivalent: in modern usage the term lacks the element of liberality in Aristotle's prescription for the magnificent man, and for Aristotle magnificence is a visible attribute of morality. Such a man

is by way of being a connoisseur; he has an eye for the suitable object and a talent for spending on it with taste . . . the

motive of the magnificent man in this expenditure will be fine, such a motive being an essential element in all the virtues.[77]

The vulgarian, by contrast, merely 'wants to make display of his opulence, since he imagines he is admired for that'. The essential point for Aristotle is that display by the man whose wealth and standing merit it shows the nobility of his mind, and as such is a virtue and even a public duty. The magnificent man's house ought also to be suitably furnished: 'it is also like him to furnish his house in a way suitable to his means, for that gives him a kind of distinction'.

Vitruvius had argued for fine building both in fulfilment of the duties of honour and on practical grounds. 'Men of rank', he wrote, 'from holding offices and magistracies, have social obligations to their fellow citizens', whence it followed that in their houses they needed imposing public rooms 'appropriate to their dignity. They need also libraries, picture galleries and basilicas . . . since public councils as well as law suits . . . are very often heard in the houses of such men'[78] – a good description of the contemporary ideal of the magistrate. Leon Battista Alberti struck a more rhetorical note in *De re aedificatoria* ('On Building'), which ran to seven editions (including two French) between 1485 and 1565:

When you erect a wall or a portico of great elegance and adorn it with a door, column or roof, good citizens approve and express joy for their own sake, as well as yours, because they realise that you have used your wealth to increase greatly not only your own honour and glory, but also that of your family, your descendants, and the whole city.[79]

Sebastiano Serlio, whose six-part *L'architettura*, written between 1537 and 1551, was to be the most widely read architectural manual of the Renaissance, would also praise 'the magnificent prince . . . to whom ignoble parsimony is an evil stranger'.

The point was repeated in Castiglione's *Il cortegiano* (1531), which had already, before its first English translation (as *The Courtyer* by Sir Thomas Hoby in 1561), established itself as the century's most successful and most penetrating prescription for civil conduct. Castiglione similarly recommended fine building as a species of duty. Describing the ideal ruler of the well-governed commonwealth, he repeated Alberti in recommending that he 'would seek to induce him to erect great buildings, both to win honour in his lifetime and to give a memorial of himself to posterity'.[80] In his *Compleat Gentleman* (1622), Henry Peacham quoted Machiavelli's praise of Cosimo de' Medici, whose 'buildings and every other of his actions were princely . . . yet so governed by wisdom as he never excelled the bounds of civil modesty'.[81] Magnates of the later Middle Ages such as Lord Cromwell at Tattershall and at South Wingfield, the Earls of Pembroke at Raglan, Lord Hastings at Ashby de la Zouche and Kirby Muxloe and the Duke of Buckingham at Thornbury had indulged in the most extravagant shows of building, and as a mode of conspicuous consumption building had probably been as great a drain on the resources of the late medieval nobility as the maintenance of great retinues of retainers – two long steps on the road to royal displeasure or bankruptcy. The humanist doctrine that fine building was an ornament to the commonwealth and an exemplar of the builder's virtue was acceptable because it provided an up-to-date justification for the parade of wealth and status.

On many houses (for example Barlborough in Derbyshire, Longleat in Wiltshire, Trevalyn in Clwyd and Ruperra in Mid Glamorgan) the coat of arms of a patron or overlord appears in addition to the owner's. This display in a conspicuous position was the equivalent of recognising and honouring an overlord in a medieval, feudal sense – an avowal that the man to whom the vassal owed such duty honoured the vassal in return by his acceptance of it. The concept of loyalty to a nation or class was only slowly emerging; in the late Middle Ages it had been through his personal affiliations that a man was placed, and by his position in a society where hierarchies of authority and dependency were taken for granted as the bonds that held the state together. The increasing display of the royal arms proclaimed the king himself as the fountainhead of honour and identified the splendour of the house and the honour of its owner with the glory of the state. Within the house too the royal arms over the fireplace of the hall or principal chamber would similarly announce to the visitor the owner's commitment to the legitimate order and imply his participation in its rule. In 1601 the nephew of Sir Thomas Smith, humanist, distinguished civil servant and builder of one of the most advanced classical houses of the age, declared that before he died in 1577 his uncle had planned 'a goodly and faire house of brick to be built annswerable [sic] to that honourable estate and calling wherein he served under the Queenes moste excellent majesty'.[82] The younger Smith neatly expressed how the standing that derived from service to the state coupled with the reciprocal duty due from the office holder to the crown as the source of honour, and how the house reflected both.

In the sixteenth century there was increasing demand for modes of behaviour and social control appropriate to the different levels of society.[83] Sumptuary legislation had originated in the fourteenth century, but during the sixteenth there was more active concern than ever before with the social distinctions of dress. Six sumptuary Acts were passed between 1483 and 1539, and for the rest of the century frequent royal proclamations reinforced the legislation. Laws regulating dress paralleled other attempts to police the ranks of society: to restrict the availability of higher education to the upper classes; to limit the amount of land that an 'inferior person' might buy; to restrict access to the English Bible to men of the rank of gentleman and above; to forbid the lower orders from playing games more suitable to their betters; and frequent measures to control wage rates. Some of this legislation, either enacted or proposed, sought to limit recruitment to the gentry by limiting the opportunities for

wealth, but much of it sought to preserve a hierarchy of rank in the interests of an ordered society. The sumptuary Act of 1533 complained of 'the great, manifest and notorious detriment of the commonweal, the subversion of good and politic order in knowledge and distinction of people according to their estates, pre-eminence, dignities and degrees'. Many people will have supported attempts at social control as no more than proper measures to keep the lower orders in their place.

Erasmus wrote that from a man's clothing one could deduce the attitude of his soul.[84] Elyot, more concerned with government than with the individual, phrased it more practically, recommending 'apparaile comely to every astate and degree'.[85] If there was no attempt to limit building by inferiors, it was probably simply because showy building was too expensive for anybody except a person whose wealth already made him socially acceptable, and it was only late in the following century that Roger North would write, in a phrase that almost seems a secular paraphrase of Erasmus: 'as the errors and prejudices of the mind proceed and are seen more or less in all the outward actions, nothing more exposeth than building. I can show you a man's caracter in his house.'[86]

Phillip Stubbes in 1583 approved fine clothes worn by 'the nobylity, gentylities, or magistracy . . . but not of every proud fixnet indifferentlie'; approved also was 'cloth of gold, Arase, tapestries, pendices and hangings in a house of estate [which] serves not onely to manuall uses and servyle occupations, but also to decorate, to bewtifye, & become the house'.[87] The most explicit sixteenth-century condemnation of extravagant building is by Thomas Starkey in his imaginary *Dialogue between Pole and Lupset* of 1529–32. The *Dialogue* concerns the place of the man of power and influence in the state, and Starkey pointed out with somewhat futile high-mindedness that true nobility did not rest in bricks and mortar. He condemns excessive ornament, 'the consumyng of gold apon postys & wallys . . . only a lytyl for the tyme hyt plesyth the ye, hyt ys a vayne pompe & of late days brought in to our cuntrey'.[88] On the other hand he followed Aristotle in accepting good building both as honourable and as a source of employment:

> So long as they byld but of tymbur & stone here got at home in our cuntrey wythout gyltyng & daubing the postys wyth gold me semyth hyt may be sufferyd ryght wel, for hyt ys a grete ornament to the cuntrey & many men are wel set aworke therby.[89]

The tendency of men to build like their superiors was, however, deplorable:

> mesemyth gentylmen & the nobylyte are in that degree over sumptuouse, they byld commynly above theyr degre, a mean man wyl have a house mete for a prynce . . . for now you schal see many men byld more then they themselfe theyr heyrys & successorys be convenyently abyl to maynteyn & repayre . . . because they were byldyd above theyr state condycyon & degre.

William Turner in 1555 similarly recognised the propriety of matching house and occupant:

> As for buyldyng of costlye houses and trimmynge of them wyth costly hangynges and fayre waynscot, manye merchauntes use to do these thynges, better the[n] many gentlemen do, and yet so, for all that, are no gentleme[n].[90]

Though contemporaries might more commonly complain about men of lowly birth swaggering like noblemen, it was more real a danger: a suit of clothes did not cost as much as a great house. But the many attempts to control other kinds of display indicate clearly the extent to which appearance was taken as the indication of the well-ordered society, and suggest the important place of the house in that society as an indicator of social worth.

Andrew Boorde, the first English writer to discuss the setting and layout of a house (albeit in the context of a book about bodily health) wrote in 1554 of the importance of the building's visual setting. Although his prime concern was with good air, avoiding damp and other common-sense prescriptions for the location of the house, there was a psychological value in ensuring

> that every thynge be desent and fayre to the eye, not onely within the precyncte of the place appoynted to buylde a mansyon or a howse, to se the commodyties aboute it, but also that it may be placable to the eyes of all men to se & to beholde when they be a good distaunce of from the place, that it do stande commodyously. For the commodyous buyldyng of a place doth not onely satysfye the mynde of the inhabitour, but also it doth comforte and reioyseth a mannes herte to se it, specyally the pulcrose prospect.[91]

The consequences of an ill-looking house were likely to be 'mortyfycacyon of the vytall, and anymall, and spirituall powers'. Leland, describing the buildings he saw in the years around 1540, used such phrases as 'a fair manor place of bryke'; a 'stately staire up to the haul . . . very magnificent'; 'a faire howse of sqwarid stone'. The limited vocabulary suggests no need to analyse the appearance of a house any further than this. It is enough to commend its appearance and to imply that others will be impressed with it too. What is remarkable about William Camden's opinion of Wollaton, built 'at great expense, in a foolish display of his wealth',[92] is how rare such condemnation is save when linked explicitly to a neglect of the social duties incumbent upon its owner. (By contrast, the Earl of Shrewsbury is above criticism: Worksop is 'superior to envy'.[93])

In the following century many more descriptions of houses interpret them as the expressions of their owners' quality. William Webb, among the most architecturally aware of seventeenth-century topographers, describing the approaches to Nantwich in Cheshire around 1622, wrote: 'into the same whichsoever way soever you come, your eye is entertained with a fair gentlemanly house'.[94] Church's House, one of the houses that Webb had in mind, is neither innovative nor otherwise remarkable and was

3   Church's House, Nantwich, Cheshire. Built in 1577, and described as 'a fair gentlemanly house' in 1622. Extravagant structural ornament announces the house of a man with money.

already forty years old, but by a lengthy inscription and an excess of ornamental braces to the frame it announces its owner's standing, and Webb's comment is an indication that for contemporaries conspicuous consumption was one of the characteristics of architectural gentility (pl. 3). The Hall at Bradford on Avon was equally old when John Aubrey approved of it as 'the best built house for the quality of a gentleman in Wilts' (pl. 4);[95] Celia Fiennes's comment on Shuckburgh is similar: 'not very rich, but in the general all things very well as any private Gentleman has whatever'.[96] Lord Wentworth advised his nephew Sir William Savile of Thornhill:

4 The Hall, Bradford on Avon, Wiltshire. Built around 1600 and described in 1660 as 'the best built house for the quality of a gentleman in Wiltshire'. The house combines the decorative exuberance of current London building with details of plan and ornament that are of more local origin.

Considering your houses in my judgement are not suitable for your quality, nor yet complete with furniture, I conceive your expenses ought to be reduced to two thirds of your estate, the rest saved to the accommodation of you in that kind.[97]

Wentworth's concern suggests that the inadequacy of Sir William's houses was not just a private matter, but that his public position demanded their improvement. Similarly, William Woolley in 1700 condemned Godfrey Clerk's house at Chilcot in Derbyshire as 'not equal to his estate and quality, being Knight of the County and married Catherine, daughter of Philip, Earl of Chesterfield'; by contrast, at Osmaston: 'Robert Wilmot Esq. has much improved the estate, especially the seat, by adding a noble pile of building of brick and stone and most curious gardens and other plantations . . . besides many other qualifications for a gentleman.'[98]

Sir Roger Pratt, the most knowledgeable of all writers on architecture in the seventeenth century and perhaps the first practising, erudite, gentleman architect (a characteristic product of the late seventeenth century, arising out of circumstances discussed further in the next chapter) concurred. 'As there are three sorts of persons for whom houses are built of any consideration,

viz. gentlemen, noblemen and princes, so there are so many kinds of building';[99] he continued by enumerating the difference in scale, decoration and ornament appropriate to each. The London Rebuilding Act of 1667, classifying the sizes of house suitable to each kind of street in the City, spoke of 'the fourth and largest sort, of mansion houses for citizens or other persons of extraordinary quality'.[100] There is some evidence, discussed further in chapter 6, that contemporaries may have recognised even within the ranks of the gentry forms or decoration appropriate to the builder. In practice money usually mattered more than degrees of gentility, and ambitious builders commonly built the grandest house they could afford. However, Pratt's comment confirms the basis of other contemporaries' remarks. All clearly recognised certain qualities as suited to the appearance of the gentry house, even though for those who lacked Pratt's architectural knowledge these qualities need not include an up-to-date style. Contemporaries knew gentlemanly architecture when they saw it, and felt no need to describe it further.

Nevertheless it is clear that architectural details were widely recognised as marks of status. It is at the lower range of gentry building that the distinction of their houses can be most easily shown. The lesser gentry of the countryside – the 'mere' gentry as they have been called, of whom by the seventeenth century many villages possessed two or three, living on the rents of a small estate – were little different in their living standards and in the layout of their houses from their yeoman neighbours; indeed the latter might very often be richer. Yet in a society where, in spite (or because) of an unprecedented degree of social fluidity, marks of status were jealously observed, a gentleman's house might be distinguished from that of his non-genteel neighbour in some small but telling way. It has been observed in a detailed study of part of Gloucestershire and Avon that the houses of these minor gentry more often had window mullions of stone, while those of rich farmers have wooden mullions.[101] In the Lancashire Pennines in the seventeenth century, distinctive gables marked the houses of those who were called gentlemen.[102] Widespread in areas of timber building are houses in which the rooms at the superior end of the house are distinguished by a jetty – the projection of the upper floors – or by more decorative exterior framing than are the service rooms at the opposite end.

Apart from such external distinctions, there were often no other differences between the houses of the village gentry and those of their inferior neighbours. In Yorkshire it has been observed that the plans of yeoman farmers' and village gentlemen's houses differ far less than do the latter from those of the county gentry.[103] The same has been found in Norfolk,[104] and the fact can be supported by contemporary comment. In 1613 Gervase Markham, a prolific writer on rural topics, published *The English Husbandman* in which he included a plan of a farmhouse (pl. 5). This (an old-fashioned house in many ways, with an open hall at the centre) has an H plan, a plan that was ubiquitous and long accepted, and as Markham says 'most plaine

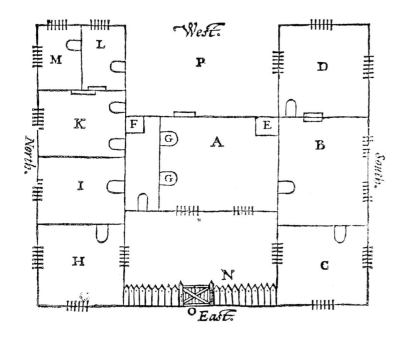

of all other, and most easie for convaiance [convenience]'. Markham's description of the plan commends its simplicity, but notes ways in which the exterior might be enhanced:

> Here you behold the modell of a plaine country mans house . . . yet if a man would bestow cost in this modell, the foure inward corners of the hall would be convenient for foure turrets, and the foure gavell [gable] ends being thrust out with bay windowes, might be formed in any curious manner: and where I place a gate and a plaine pale, might bee either a tarrisse, or a gatehouse, of any fashion whatsoever; besides all those windowes which I make plaine might be made bay windowes, either with battlements, or without; but the scope of my booke tendeth only to the use of the honest *husbandman*, and not to instruct men of dignitie.[105]

It is clear that, for Markham, what makes the gentleman's house superior to those of his inferiors is the way it looks as much as the way it works. There are numerous houses whose owners were probably keen to make such a show and whose ambitions went no further – or were no more intellectual – than that.

Even at the level of the village, concern about status showed itself in many and varied ways – in concern with titles, about precedence, and even in death with the kinds of church monument appropriate to the ranks of society. For the village gentry, the immediate point of such visual distinctions was no doubt to set themselves apart from their farming neighbours. For all the theoretical sanction for appropriate display, one must not discount the force of simple ambition and of rivalry between builders. At the highest level of society the example was set by the vast building programme of Henry VIII himself, a substantial number of whose forty-two houses and palaces he had bought, built or remodelled. Later stimulus came from another source:

the desire to entertain Queen Elizabeth. John Dodd, Sir John Thynne's agent at Longleat, described natural human responses when he wrote to his master that the house was 'the first house and hansomest . . . within the compasse of iiii shires round and about the same and so doyth all the countre report, some greved and some plesed'.[106] 'We see an emulation in the structure of our houses', wrote the Yorkshire squire Sir Henry Slingsby in 1640.[107] The inscription on the early sixteenth-century tomb of Sir Thomas Cockayn at Ashbourne recorded:

> Three goodly Houses he did build, to his great praise and fame
> With profits great and manifold belonging to the same.
> Three Parks he did impale, therein to chase the deere;
> The lofty Lodge within this Park he also builded here.[108]

It was with similar satisfaction that Ralph Sheldon's tomb at Beoley in Worcestershire (1613), Sir John Trevor's at Hope, Clwyd (1629), Sir George St Paul's at Snarford in Lincolnshire (1631) and most famously that of Elizabeth Hardwick, Countess of Shrewsbury (1607), also report their subjects' house building. The widespread practice of placing the builder's initials, date and sometimes longer inscriptions in a prominent place on the house itself expresses the same pride and it may be the identification of a house with a dynasty that is behind the belief that it was lucky to have a foundation stone laid by a child.[109]

But there is no regular pattern of innovation and imitation. Although the gentry from the highest to the lowest shared in a common culture that claimed distinction in its modes of behaviour, there was in practice a very wide variety in the degree of architectural sophistication and knowledge with which this distinction was displayed. Given the numbers of the gentry and their diversity, it was inevitable that individuals should differ in education, wealth and taste. This variety was partly too the practical result of the persistence of strong local building traditions. Though the village gentry might be at pains to announce their social distinction from their ungentle neighbours, there was a broader difference in wealth and in responsibilities between them and the county gentry. The lesser men might seek to emulate the fashions, architectural and otherwise, of the higher group, but they generally lacked the resources to build on a large scale, while their local roots, their education and their patronage of the same building craftsmen as their farming neighbours meant that they were unlikely to be innovators either in the decoration of their houses or in the amenities of their houses' plans. Such changes first occur among the houses of the higher gentry, and even these might take their cue from the class above them – courtiers, the nobility and others who were seriously rich.

But there is far less clear differentiation between the houses of the aristocracy and those of the gentry than there is between the latter and the houses of the classes beneath them. In the seventeenth century the hearth tax returns show how widely the sizes of gentlemen's houses overlapped with those of the classes above. Queen Elizabeth's notorious reluctance to grant titles meant that in the late sixteenth century some of the richest men in the land remained technically gentlemen (for instance John Thynne, the builder of Longleat, perhaps the most important house of the century, who rose no higher than a knighthood), and a clear distinction between the houses of the county gentry – the class of the magistracy – and those of the higher ranks of society is difficult to draw. Though in the middle of the sixteenth century the greatest architectural innovators were a small group of men connected with the court, others such as Sir Humphrey Stafford, builder of Kirby Hall in Northamptonshire, and Robert Corbet of Moreton Corbet in Shropshire were relatively obscure. Many of the most innovative houses of the early seventeenth century were built by men who had close financial or social connections with London or the court; but plan elements that these buildings incorporated, and the evolving life style for which they provided, were soon taken up by a broad spectrum of the upper classes and ultimately determined the form of the ubiquitous gentry house of the late seventeenth and eighteenth centuries.

Though some men eagerly – and with various motives – adopted the latest architectural fashions to build themselves houses that expressed their status, wealth and taste, others similarly failed to take advantage of the opportunities open to them. Such a variety of output can be explained only by the way in which building was organised, by a range of education and experience among the class of the builders, by diverse personal priorities, and above all by an aesthetic that recognised many dif-

ferent ways in which buildings might be used to make statements about qualities of class and culture that were essentially not visual qualities at all. In the way in which the house provided for its occupants there were similar tensions between innovation and tradition: between exclusivity and the demands of hospitality and community, and between the traditions of the self-sufficient, inward-looking household and the self-consciousness and self-confidence of a new and rapidly growing élite.

Many of these dialogues are implicit in a short, satirical description of an archetypal manor house in 1631. Wye Saltonstall's character book, *Picturae loquentes*, is one of a genre popular at the time, a small volume of light-hearted pen-portraits of contemporary types. Rather oddly among the individuals he describes – such as lawyers, maid-servants and Oxford students – comes 'a gentleman's house in the country'. This, he wrote, is

> the prime house of some village, and carryes gentility on the front of it. . . . At meales, you shall have a scattered troup of dishes, led in by some black puddings, and in the Reare some demolish'd pastyes, which are not yet fallen to the Servingmen. Between meales there be bread and Beere for all comers, and for a stranger a napkin and cold meate in the Buttery may be obtained. All the roomes smell of Dogges and Hawks, and the Hall beares armes, though it be but a muskitt and two Corsletts. . . . The Master of the house is ador'd as a Relique of gentility . . . his house is the seat of hospitality, the poore man's Court of Justice, the Curate's Sunday ordinary, and the only Exchequer of Charity.[110]

Satire must contain truth as well as appealing to its readers' prejudices, and the house of Saltonstall's country squire is as recognisable now as it must have been in the seventeenth century. This is not only the most important house in the village but has a respectable look to it as well; the old squire with his dogs and his guns is a model that has lasted to this day, but his role as the dispenser of charity and justice is one that goes back to the Middle Ages. The picture of the old manor house is both ideal and grotesque, reassuring in that the old place still preserved ancient values and patronising in its account of the rustic amusements of its occupants. Saltonstall's sophisticated readers (his grandfather had been Lord Mayor, and the writer must have known his readership) probably had an equally ambivalent attitude to the country and to countrymen. Houses were changing at the same time as the way in which contemporaries perceived them, and both houses and perceptions of them reflected changes in the gentry's view of themselves and of their place in the world.

2

Builders and Architects

Perceptions of Architecture

Well-informed men in the seventeenth century might not agree about what members of the gentry knew of architecture. While Sir Roger Pratt complained that men 'are apt to think nothing well but what is conformable to that old-fashioned house which they themselves dwell in, or some of their friends',[1] John Webb claimed that 'most gentry in England at this day have some knowledge in the Theory of Architecture'.[2] Their views were coloured by their own positions, but each could have quoted evidence to support his view. While the gentry owed it to their position in the world to make a decent show of their housing, there was a very wide variety in the nature of their involvement with the building process.

Evidence for the personal concern of members of the upper classes with the architectural detail of their houses is rare until the mid-sixteenth century, and even then confined to an élite.[3] None the less, the example of these men, for the most part highly prominent both socially and politically, almost certainly operated powerfully at a slightly lower level of society. Around the middle of the sixteenth century several highly educated individuals, sharing a common humanist background, had concerned themselves personally with building to an unprecedented degree. The links between them were close, by blood ties and by service. What appealed to these individuals was the opportunity through building to indulge their learning and their awareness of classical models, and a dawning comprehension that architecture as expounded by Vitruvius and by more recent continental writers involved principles that transcended detail. But while the correctness of the classical detail displayed in certain of these houses testified to a concern with the authenticity of sources, the incentive to adopt a classical vocabulary derived in large part from a perception of classicism as a language of status, culture and morality.

For some builders an interest in architecture may have arisen through their own experiences. Between 1568 and 1575 Sir Thomas Smith built Hill Hall in Essex, employing superimposed classical orders whose inspiration was probably French and which seems to be without English precedent in the treatment of a complete façade (pl. 6). He is known to have owned a set

6   Hill Hall, Essex, 1568–75. Sir Thomas Smith, its builder, may have acquired his known architectural interests through employment on foreign embassies. Hill Hall is essentially an inward-facing, English house with classical orders, almost certainly of French inspiration, applied to the courtyard façades.

of geometrical instruments[4] and his theoretical interest in architecture is shown by his possession of no fewer than six editions of Vitruvius.[5] Smith was Clerk of the Privy Council and Secretary of State, but his interest in building may have been prompted less by the enthusiasms of his colleagues in the 1550s and more by his experiences as ambassador to France from 1562 to 1566.

As notable as Hill Hall's external architectural decoration were the mural paintings inside the house – fragmentary but exceptionally rare survivals.[6] These comprise two sequences, one biblical and one classical, and the latter, a suite of the Cupid and Psyche myth, is derived from the same source as one at Ecouen, a house of Anne de Montmorency, Constable of France, who was Smith's host in 1563. Ecouen was a house of recent date, and of great size and sophistication. Smith's foreign travels had extended to Toulouse, Arles and Nimes – towns with abundant classical remains, and he had also been befriended by no less a person than Cardinal d'Este, patron of Serlio and the man to whom Daniele Barbaro dedicated his edition of Vitruvius. At Toulouse he could have met George d'Armagnac, Archbishop and friend of Philander (whose edition of Vitruvius Smith owned),[7] and he could have seen many French houses in which storeys are distinguished with entablatures and bays with columns or pilasters – effectively the system of Hill Hall, although it had already appeared on a smaller scale at Dingley in Northamptonshire (pl. 75) in 1560.[8] The details seem to derive from Hans Blume's *Quinque columnarum descriptio* of 1550, but Smith was described at his death as having had 'a very good genius in architecture, which that noble building at Hill Hall doth sufficiently demonstrate'[9] and his own involvement is unquestionable.

Yet while such experiences enabled Smith to put up a house in which classical elements are deployed as correctly as anywhere in England, this nevertheless amounted to little more than the application of a grid of classical orders to the walls of a building that is otherwise thoroughly conventional. Hill Hall remains essentially English, inward-looking and asymmetrical in its principal elevations. Even at Longleat, though it incorporates details that may have their origin at Somerset House of 1548–50, the frequent changes of design during his many years of work there suggest that Thynne was on a long, steep learning curve.[10]

Edward Hall in 1542 complained that when Englishmen returned home after foreign travels, they were 'all French in eating and drinking and apparel . . . and nothing by them was praised, but it was after the French form'.[11] But while foreign experiences may occasionally have prompted men to build when they returned home, the patterns they actually followed are almost always wholly English and the most that can be said is that their travels suggested some slight additional amenity modifying an otherwise conventional house. William Knight was employed before 1520 on embassies to Spain, Switzerland and the Low Countries, and in the later 1520s was sent to Italy on negotiations about the royal divorce. His house at Horton, northeast of Bristol, incorporates some of the earliest Renaissance

detail in England: it has a stone, classical doorcase and chimneypiece, an inscription with excellent roman lettering and a date of 1521 (which is not *in situ*), and a six-bay, open loggia with four crude classical portrait medallions on the interior back wall (pls 7, 8). These medallions (generally described merely as

8 (*above*) The loggia at Horton Court, Gloucestershire, *c.* 1520. Though wholly local in its details, such a free-standing loggia is unique at this date in England, but Horton Court's owner is likely to have seen such things on the continent.

7 (*facing page*) Classical medallions of heroes and anti-heroes built into the back wall of the loggia at Horton Court, and probably taken from northern European patterns. Representing good and evil Roman emperors and good and evil non-Romans, they make an appropriate reference to the diplomatic activities of the house's owner, William Knight, in the service of Henry VIII.

representing Roman emperors) are in fact a humanist iconographic programme of some sophistication, carefully chosen for their relevance to the career of a diplomat. These contrast heroes and anti-heroes, men from within the Roman world and men who would assault it: the emperors Augustus and Nero as types of virtuous and evil rulers and Hannibal and Attila the Hun as good and bad outsiders, identified in good humanist lettering which contrasts with the crudity of the carving. The source for these roundels is probably in northern European engravings, and the stone of which they are carved looks local.

The date of the loggia is not known. In 1521 Knight had not yet visited Italy, but loggias were already familiar in northern Europe – for example at the completely un-classical house of the humanist Jeronimus van Busleyden at Malines, and the Horton loggia could be the arcade of a Cotswold church.

An almost identical free-standing loggia is illustrated in a late fifteenth-century Burgundian Book of Hours.[12] There had been classical medallions in Cardinal d'Amboise's gallery at Meillant before 1511.[13] It is anyway not wholly without English precedent: open-fronted galleries already existed, giving on to gardens or forming links between separate parts of a building complex. Though he might not have employed classical details on his house or built his loggia had he not travelled abroad, these are best regarded as statements about his connections, his education and his experience rather than about his achitectural knowledge, and are to be seen in the same light as the antique ornament that occurs sporadically in other houses from the late 1520s: a generalised evocation of Antiquity intended to show its patrons' awareness of approved cultural models. In other respects the house seems wholly conventional.

A house whose form and details were said at the time to have been prompted by its builder's foreign travels is Moreton Corbet in Shropshire (pl. 9). Moreton Corbet was a medieval castle to which in 1579 Sir Andrew Corbet added a huge range of state rooms.[14] Responsible for it must have been Sir Andrew's son, Robert Corbet, courtier and diplomat, who on his return,

carried away with the affectionate delight of Architecture, began to build in a barraine place a most gorgeous and stately house, after the Italians model; but death prevented him so that he left the new work unfinished and the old castle defaced.

9 Moreton Corbet, Shropshire, *c.* 1579. Built by Sir Robert Corbet, 'carried away with the affectionate delight of Architecture'. Corbet had travelled abroad, but such 'affectionate delight' was in any case rapidly increasing among less-travelled members of the upper classes.

The building was damaged in the Civil War, repaired, but was again derelict by the end of the eighteenth century; as a result the original plan is not fully recoverable. The façade suggests that its builder regarded architecture as more than a sum of parts, and the composition is coherent and integrated, outward-looking and with a façade that is wholly symmetrical. But detail is less refined than at contemporary Longleat or Kirby and cluttered with emblematic ornament more typical of the contemporary delight in symbols and allusive devices.

Though foreign travel might have aroused an interest in architecture in the builders of Hill Hall, of Horton and of Moreton Corbet, a first-hand knowledge of foreign building was necessary to none of them. In their layout and in the overall composition to which classical elements are applied, there is nothing exceptional in any of these buildings when set against the houses of less travelled contemporaries. For the most part, those of the gentry who travelled abroad must have found their experiences too exotic to relate to their own needs. This must have been so, for example, for Sir John Leigh of Isel in Cumbria who rebuilt his house with an advanced, single-storey hall, probably some time in the 1540s.[15] In 1538 Leigh had been on official business to Rome and to Venice (where he seems to have taken a large house on the Rio di Santa Catarina)[16] and may even have brought some Italian pictures home with him, but his new house, innovative for so remote a region, reflects his knowledge of the fashionable English world and nothing at all of France or Italy.

Collacombe in Devonshire was owned in the 1570s by Edmund Tremayne who had been in Italy in the 1550s and subsequently entered royal service, working closely with William Cecil in the 1570s. To an accretive house which had been largely rebuilt by his father, Tremayne added a number of improvements. These combine traditional and classical motifs which suggest the work of a local mason who might have worked at such a house as Longleat, or whom Tremayne had supplied with a few prints of up-to-date detail (pl. 10). There are about the garden a number of loose Doric (or Tuscan) capitals and bases, of a size suitable to a single-storey loggia. But despite Tremayne's travels and connections there is nothing at Collacombe that could not be derived by English masons from sources available in England. Trevalyn in Denbighshire was the house of another well-travelled diplomatist, John Trevor, and has matching wings with pedimented windows and a Doric order to the gatehouse, but the most that one can suggest is that Trevor may have supplied his mason with engravings of classical detail.

The point is made still more forcibly by the Hobys, Philip and Thomas. Both had been extensively employed on diplomatic missions abroad, and the diary kept by Thomas (the translator of Castiglione) records his curiosity about much that he saw (though little relating to architecture).[17] He may have had his and his brother's joint tomb in Bisham in Berkshire made in a French workshop: both the workmanship and the attitudes of the effigies suggest it.[18] But although Bisham Abbey has little pedimented windows installed by Thomas (pl. 16), these could well have been imitated from those that the Lord Protector had employed at Somerset House (pl. 70); although the house has a loggia as well, this consists of one surviving range of a medieval cloister (pl. 323) (the Hobys pulled down the rest of it) and the alterations they made to their ancient house involved nothing either in plan or detail that could not be matched in England.

Nor was there any model for the house to be had from the ancient world. Indeed, architectural localism could be justified by reference to Vitruvius himself who with the entire Roman Empire as his field had explicitly recognised the necessary differences, founded on local conditions of culture and climate, between houses of different regions. Vredeman de Vries in 1572 concurred: that it was proper 'accomoder l'art a la situation et nécessité du pais plus que oncques a este besoing aux Ancoiens';[19] and Sir Charles Cavendish, recommending a plan of his own devising in 1603, wrote: 'There cannot be a sweeter house, keeping a form and the state of English building.'[20] Yet Aristotle and Vitruvius, in giving fine buildings a sanction derived from Antiquity, implicitly associated the architecture of the ancient world with moral excellence. In architecture, the earliest Renaissance ornament in England appears in small details, in furnishings, in heraldic devices and in tombs.[21] On the exterior of several houses whose architectural details are still wholly late Gothic, an armorial device is set in a Renaissance frame or is supported by putti that seem to derive from Italianate sources such as the royal tombs erected in Westminster Abbey after 1509: Hengrave (pl. 81), Cowdray, Glynde, a group of houses in Somerset, including Bingham's Melcombe (pl. 11), and several others. At Sherborne in Dorset Sir John Horsey gave his house an armorial frontispiece with a species of classical frame and would also be buried in a Renaissance tomb. Because of the association of classical ornament with ancient nobility, these devices made a statement about their subject that involved both education and morality: a man whose surroundings identified him with approved models of behaviour. But while the self-conscious use of classical ornament in these contexts was an explicit indication of cultural values, its incidental appearance on imported luxury goods probably made it also a mark of status.[22] Such distinctions will have been encouraged by a proclamation of 1523 which, with the ostensible purpose of encouraging native craftsmen, forbad the employment of foreigners by

10   Collacombe, Devon: the gatehouse, c. 1578 (photographed c. 1910). A blend of local and classical idioms, executed in the intractable local granite. Collacombe's owner was well travelled and no doubt demanded up-to-date elements in the improvement of his house, but classical detail was already entering the provincial craftsman's canon.

11 a and b Bingham's Melcombe, Dorset, c. 1555. Crude classical forms frame the coat of arms of the house's owner, on the oriel that lights the high end of the hall. Some of the earliest appearances of classical ornament in England are in association with a coat of arms or a tomb whereby it is directly associated with an individual about whom it makes an explicit, cultural statement.

anyone beneath the rank of members of parliament or men worth less than £100 a year.[23] Whatever its intention, the effect of the edict will have been to give to an élite privileged access to artists with a greater knowledge of fashionable continental styles.

From the mid-sixteenth century onwards the increasing availability of engraved patterns and examples placed in the hands of English craftsmen the means of satisfying their patrons' desire for classical ornament. The fact that as the century went on the sources of these inventions were increasingly northern European rather than Italian, and increasingly remote from any authentic ancient sources, was of less significance than their ingenuity and decorative richness. Its appeal was not only visual but cerebral as well.[24] Much sixteenth-century decoration is an art of symbols and allusions. Men had long been accustomed to reading signs: the emblems of the saints, merchants' marks, traders' signs and above all the displays of heraldry by which men proclaimed their lineage and affinities. To this was added a taste for more personal and private symbolism, *imprese*, signs and emblems of esoteric

meaning which were themselves felt to possess certain of the virtues which they represented. Symbols were didactic in that they reminded the beholder of virtues and truths, but exclusive in that their meaning was only apparent to the initiated.[25]

But heraldry, *imprese* and classical ornament are complementary, providing both factual statements about the individual and his connections and more general information about his culture, and there is no immediate falling-off of heraldic and genealogical display within the house when external classical detail becomes more widespread in the second half of the sixteenth century. Indeed, it is easy to gain the impression that heraldic ornament becomes more frequent since it is likely that earlier heraldic decoration was largely incorporated in textile hangings which have now vanished. Much of the earliest surviving heraldic display is in window glass, and the appearance of heraldry in chimneypieces, plasterwork and panelling probably corresponds to the spread of these fixtures in the last decades of the sixteenth century rather than to any new fashion for heraldry itself. But both heraldry and classical ornament made state-

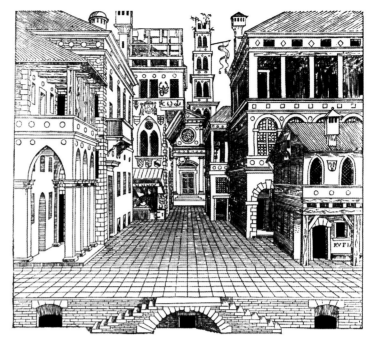

12 Classical palaces for princes, from Jean Martin's French edition of Vitruvius (1547), reprinted in 1575 and present in a number of recorded English libraries. The accompanying text makes an explicit connection between classical building and nobility.

13 'Houses of private citizens . . . built in the common way', from Martin's edition of Vitruvius.

ments about values, and there is a parallelism in the way in which they were perceived.

Classical ornament might also be associated more explicitly with status. Serlio (whose books are discussed further below) illustrated Vitruvius's discussion of theatrical scenery with plates of settings suitable for tragedy, comedy and satire; the tragic setting is a street of palaces (pl. 12), the comic a street of more traditional building (pl. 13). He explained the distinction by the fact that tragedies always concern the noble and great. But when Jean Martin used the same engravings to illustrate his French edition of Vitruvius in 1547 (reprinted in 1572 and recorded in several English collections) he explained that the palaces of tragedy 's'enrichissent de Colonnes, Frontispices, Statues, & autres appareilz sentans leur Royaulte ou Seigneurie', whereas 'ceulx [i.e. the buildings] de la Comique represent maisons d'hommes particulier & ont leurs fenestrages & ouvertures faicte a la mode commune'.[26] Serlio's and Jean Martin's palaces incorporate classical forms and ornament; their houses for private men do not. Henry VIII's palace at Nonsuch, built in the 1530s, was in two parts – the outer court for services and retinue, the inner for the king and queen. The outer court was still Gothic; the decoration of the inner court was rich, esoteric and classical.[27]

Use of the classical orders went beyond symbolising culture and class, linking both with virtue in a way that was wholly characteristic of the age. Italian writers of the early Renaissance had sought to imbue the orders themselves with a scale of moral values, a need that was the greater because of the historical identification of classical architecture with paganism. Such asso-

ciation was of course arbitrary, but the robust simplicity of the Tuscan order prompted its identification with civic virtue; the richness of the Corinthian, nobility and the responsibilities that accompanied status. Such analysis led to the development of a hierarchical theory of the orders that was as much moral as structural or decorative, and thus to a recognition of their fitness for purpose in a rhetorical sense that emphasised the appropriateness of classical references in the house of the governor.[28] How widely so sophisticated an interpretation of the orders was understood is debatable, but for half a century after about 1570 numerous English houses have porches with superimposed classical orders (pls 14, 97), including those of William Cecil and the Earl of Salisbury, chief ministers to Elizabeth and to James I.[29] The peculiar English popularity of the form – culminating at Oxford in the early seventeenth century, where Merton and Wadham Colleges have towers of four orders, the Bodleian has a tower of five – may often have been no more than a conventional device, but it may be seen as the expression of order in a civil sense: a rhetorical emblem of society.[30]

Although the ancients might provide cultural and rhetorical models for the ornament of the houses of the rulers, English architecture in the sixteenth century has often been described as still essentially Gothic, save for Renaissance detail increasingly appearing in the place of traditional ornament. There is much in this view: in the persistence of old-fashioned, hierarchical plan forms, of conservative building traditions that perpetuated gabled and pinacled silhouettes, of windows whose extravagant forms and whose quantities of glass can be seen as fulfilling medieval

15 (*above*) Barlborough Hall, Derbyshire, 1582. A number of castle-like houses of *c.* 1580–1610 looked for inspiration to chivalrous and national models.

14 (*left*) Cobham Hall, Kent, 1591–4. Renaissance commentators developed a hierarchical theory of the classical orders. Their use in sequence, superimposed from the lower to the upper floors of a house, not only expressed the relative status of the house's parts but can be seen as a rhetorical symbol of an ordered society in the houses of the ruling class.

ambitions, and in detail of late medieval origins used concurrently with more modern forms. Such survivals correspond to the strong persistence through the sixteenth century of many other aspects of medieval thought. But a reaction towards a home-grown historicism at the end of the century is, by contrast, evidence of increasing architectural self-consciousness. Between 1580 and 1610 the building of such romantic, castellated houses as Longford Castle, Barlborough Hall (pl. 15) and Lulworth Castle (pl. 121) corresponds to a heightening of national awareness in politics (at least twenty-nine books published between 1570 and 1601 deplored the neglect of military matters by contemporary gentry),[31] in literature and in historiography; their closest literary parallel is Spenser's *Faerie Queene*, in which Queen Elizabeth is seen as the heiress to an heroic national antiquity.[32] Late Elizabethan romanticism acknowledged humanist belief in ancient virtue while assimilating to it an idealisation of the culture of chivalry, providing both classicism and older, national forms with the sanction of morality. Samuel Daniel in 1603 used architecture as a significant metaphor: praising institutions that were of Old English origin, he continued 'look upon the wonderful architecture of this state of England

and see whether they were deformed times that could give it such a form'.[33]

In Italy the rediscovery of the values of the ancient world, at first through the critical analysis of manuscripts, found a second tool ready to hand in the physical remains of the civilisation that had produced them. The study of architecture and archaeology went hand in hand, and proceeded both by the reading of texts and by an increasingly careful examination of surviving buildings themselves in order to deduce the principles that underlay their design. In the plentiful remains of Roman buildings they were surrounded by material for exact record, analysis and emulation, and in Vitruvius contemporaries possessed a text on architecture that had come down from Antiquity. Vitruvius had claimed to write 'for all educated people' and not solely for professionals, and his treatise on architecture was central to the humanist view of mankind. His diagrammatic exposition of the human figure as embodying the geometry that underlay the natural world graphically expressed man's place in the cosmos and conformed to an existing, organic view of society as composed of a head and members.[34] For Vitruvius the architect should be philosopher, historian, musician and mathematician and should also have a knowledge of construction – an intellectual all-rounder, an appealing model for the universal man of the Renaissance. In Italy at least sixteen editions had been printed between 1486 and 1560, and he is by far the most frequently found architectural author in English libraries between 1560 and 1620.[35] Though employing terminology the meaning of which was not always clear, the text provided a starting point for the elucidation of the principles behind ancient architecture by purporting to provide a body of theory. In so doing, it made classical architecture a paradigm of order and imbued it with the respectability of an intellectual system. Amplified by Alberti and by Vitruvius's successive editors, a system of harmonic proportion that derived from Pythagoras and corresponded to the underlying laws that governed the Platonic cosmos purported to provide objective criteria of beauty.[36] Such an architectural system appealed to educated contemporaries: building makes real what until then exists as abstract ideas, images, systems of relationships and ideals of perfection.

Vitruvius's text enjoyed until the second half of the century a prestige that was disproportionate to its practical utility, though as with those works that gave a moral sanction to the classical orders it is questionable how widely such theory was understood. The first illustrated edition appeared in Italy in 1511 and was soon followed by others, all of which contained engravings of the classical orders with their entablatures and mouldings which were thereby made available for contemporary builders. Less theoretical and more fully illustrated were Serlio's first five books of architecture, published separately in Italy and in France between 1537 and 1547, by far the most widely used of all architectural source books before the mid-seventeenth century. Like the editors of Vitruvius, Serlio sought to illuminate Vitruvian principles by reference to ancient buildings themselves. But the absence in England of actual ancient buildings for examination, the difficulty of the Vitruvian rules and of the correct interpretation of his text meant inevitably that to aspire to an understanding of classical architecture that went beyond the imitation of detail was not for the uneducated craftsman, however practically skilled, but for the man of letters.

In sixteenth-century England the fullest endorsement of Vitruvius's claims to the architect's élite status was by John Dee in his preface to Henry Billingsley's edition of Euclid, published in 1570.[37] Dee owned both Latin and French editions of Vitruvius, Daniele Barbaro's modern commentary and Alberti's *De re aedificatoria* – the most influential of early Renaissance treatises – and his preface includes extensive passages from both Alberti and Vitruvius. Billingsley's Euclid was widely read, and for Dee the importance of Vitruvius is in his emphasis on mathematics as properly underlying all architecture. But Dee sees an important distinction between theory and practice, and a gulf between the educated man and the artisan:

> Plato affirmeth, the Architect to be Master over all, that make any works. Whereupon, he is neither Smith, nor Builder: nor, separately, any Artificer: but the Hed, the Provost, the Director, and Judge of all Artificiall workes, and all Artificers. For the true Architect, is hable to teach, Demonstrate, distribute, describe, and Judge all workes wrought. And he, onely, searches out the causes and reasons of all Artificiall thynges.[38]

For Dee, architecture's status was due to its inclusion among 'Artes Mathematicall derivative', which included music, astronomy and cosmography. Probably most English craftsmen felt themselves more in need of actual source material on architectural decoration. For those who could read Latin, Italian or French, successive editions of Vitruvius, Alberti, Serlio and of other continental writers sought to provide universal criteria of beauty and general principles of design. But in providing English builders and craftsmen with a decorative repertoire such works encouraged a species of bolt-on classicism: a view of classical architecture that divorced ornament from structure, encouraged its decorative or symbolic use and left both builders and craftsmen to follow the dictates of pragmatism or tradition in the overall form of their buildings. In any case such works were too expensive for most artisans, and classical ornament might also be derived as pure decoration from furnishings and through the employment (particularly but by no means exclusively by the king) of foreign artists.[39] As late as 1624 Sir Henry Wotton wrote that 'speculation [about Pythagorean proportional systems] may appear unto vulgar Artizans . . . too subtile, and too sublime'.[40]

While the education of the upper class might allow them to take an interest in the theoretical aspects of building, it also encouraged them to distance themselves from its practical side. In the Middle Ages the education of the ruling class had been predominantly military, ideally obtained by service in the household of some great man where the well-born youth might find models of courtly and chivalrous behaviour. Such an education was suited to a feudal society where honour, wealth and status ultimately lay in loyalty and service to the king or to some great lord. The new emphasis on learning and on the development of morality through the cultivation of the mind was, however, no less élitist than the old. Both tended strongly – though in different ways – to draw a line between the upper classes and the lower, and the sixteenth century's anxious debate about the qualities of gentility saw in the virtue that derived from education a bulwark against disorder and the breakdown of degree and rank. And the growing tendency in the sixteenth century for young men of the upper classes to acquire such education among their peers at schools, at the universities and at the Inns of Court, strengthened their sense of cohesion, class identity and exclusiveness.

Education was likely therefore to confirm most men in their sense of superiority to craftsmen and to do little to encourage them to acquire an understanding of what they saw as the craftsman's work. For most people there was a clear distinction between the academic learning proper to the gentleman and the practical skills necessary to the artisan. In 1581 Richard Mulcaster, master of Merchant Taylor's school and author of a manual of education, pleaded that those who practised 'laudable mechanicall Artes' might benefit from learning Latin, but he admitted that the response of most people would be to ask:

> What should marchauntes, carpenters, masons, shipmaisters, maryners, devisours, architectes, and a number such do with latin, and learning? do they not well enough without, to serve the turne in our countrie?[41]

Five years later Sir John Ferne numbered architecture among 'laudable' occupations that included agriculture, clothing manufacture, merchandising and 'the art and skill of plays' but though he admitted that such a man might aspire to the grant of a coat of arms, this could not be earned 'by the meere practize, of his mechanicall trade'.[42] While honour might be served by the erection of fine buildings, too close a personal involvement with bricks and mortar was not quite respectable. For Erasmus early in the sixteenth century, painting, architecture and sculpture had also been 'mechanical arts' which might perhaps be taken up by children who were slow at book learning.[43] Erasmus was less concerned with class distinctions than were most later writers and more with the cultivation of the individual, but such subordination of craft to scholarship inevitably lowered its esteem. For Castiglione, even drawing is 'now a dayes perhappes . . . called a handicraft and full little to become a gentleman'.[44]

Castiglione's *Courtier* is both more and less than a book of manners. Its writer assumed that his readers needed no instruction in mere etiquette, and the book is more a discussion (in the form of a Platonic symposium at the court of Urbino) of the graces and the virtues that ought to adorn the companions of the prince. Castiglione's perfect courtier differed from Elyot's governor, if chiefly because his functions as the paragon of the prince's court were rather different from those of the just magistrate that Elyot saw as the pinnacle of gentility. The courtier was a man of effortless accomplishments, complete self-assurance and disarming modesty; of perfect gallantry and perfect breeding, a knowledgeable patron of all the arts and a talented performer in those that were suitable to his high station. He should cultivate *sprezzatura*, the capacity of being surprised at nothing, the self-possession that comes of experience, noble thoughts and complete self-control. 'How low is his mynde', wrote George Whetstone in the person of a visitor to the idealised house of a great man, 'whose spirit hourely beholdeth not greater matter than eyther beautie, buylding or braverie.'[45]

But the very emphasis of humanists on the development of the all-round man might also promote a more active interest in the arts.[46] In spite of Castiglione's reservations about handicrafts, Sir Thomas Hoby, his translator, spent three years at Bisham Abbey between 1558 and 1560, evidently maintaining some kind of supervision of his brother's house while it was being modernised. Following the traditional calling of the gentleman, Elyot was prepared to admit the value of being able to draw out fortifications and the lie of the land during a military cam-

16 Bisham Abbey, Berkshire. A house of *c.* 1290, modernised 1557–60, with a new block with pedimented windows masking the medieval great hall. Beyond any cultural statement made by classical forms, the new works attempt to impose some regularity on the medieval building.

paign;[47] added to this, such skills enabled him to sketch the disposition of his own property. Furthermore:

> what pleasure and also utilitie it is to a man whiche intendeth to edifie [i.e. to build], hymselfe to expresse the figure of the warke that he purposethe, accordynge as he hath concevyd it in his owne fantasie. wherin, by often amendyng and correcting, he finally, shall perfecte the warke unto his purpose.[48]

Such experience was of value in developing connoisseurship, a proper ornament of gentility:

> The exquisite knowlege and understanding [that the gentleman] hath in these sciences [drawing and music] hath impressed in his eares and eies an exacte and perfect iugement, as well as desernyng the excellencie of them, whiche either in musike, or in statuary, or paynters crafte, professeth any counnynge, as also adapting their saide knowlege to the adminiculation of other serious studies and businesse.[49]

Whatever skill of drawing and painting the gentleman enjoyed should not, however, be exercised in public 'but as a secrete pastime, or recreation of the wittes, late occupied in serious studies'.[50] One would like to know more about the level of knowledge of Henry VIII himself, who had a set of drawing instruments, who involved himself closely in the royal works and who must have provided a powerful example to his courtiers.

In 1577 William Harrison published what was at that date the fullest account of contemporary building, with a new edition ten years later. In it he notes the improvement in chimneys and domestic comforts, in building materials and in window glass, and concludes: 'If ever curious building did florish in England, it is in these our yeares, wherein our workmen excell, and are in maner comparable in skill with old Vitruvius and Serlo.'[51] In the second edition he added 'Leo Baptista' to his two classic architects. 'Leo Baptista' is how John Dee had referred to Alberti, and one might guess that Harrison's knowledge of him was through Dee's preface to Billingsley's Euclid. For contemporaries something 'curious' (in Harrison's phrase) might be allusive, ingenious, symbolic or geometrical: each a quality to be enjoyed through the intellect. Harrison's claim for modern buildings thus goes beyond his catalogue of improved amenities, but suggests too what buildings themselves confirm: that contemporaries made no distinction between the pleasure of the eye and the pleasure of the mind and that neither was possible without the other. Appeal to Vitruvius justified the employment of geometrical principles of design; a sense of what was proper to the building and to its owner's status and education provided the rationale for ornament and composition; intellectual satisfaction was provided by the understanding of both. In claiming that English 'workmen' were comparable with these models, Harrison may have had in mind no more than the spread of a vocabulary of Renaissance detail (with its overtones of culture) among the class of the artisan – detail that for Harrison and other contemporaries sufficiently established the craftsman's architectural credentials.

In the dedication to Sir Thomas Bodley of his translation (1598) of Lomazzo's *Trattato della pittura* (1584), only the second book published in England to include details of the classical orders, Richard Haydocke wrote that 'many of [his] spare howers of recreation, have bin occupied in the sweete Contemplation, and delightfull Practice of the more curious kindes of Painting, Carving and Building'.[52] In a commendatory preface John Case, Aristotelian and writer on music, added that 'Geometricians heere-hence for Buylding may take their perfect Modelles.' Peacham in 1623 similarly extolled geometry 'who with her ingenious hand rears all curious roofs and Arches, stately Theaters, the columnes simple and compounded, pendant galleries, stately windows, turrets etc.'[53]

The same point plus the need for the gentleman's traditional military skills had been made by James Cleland, who included architecture in the chapter on mathematics in his manual of education, *Institutions of a Young Noble Man* (1607). Cleland wrote that the tutor should

cause [his] Scholler . . . to judge of the height of a Tower, the depth of a ditch. or of any such like thing appertaining to

military discipline, and principles of *Architecture*: which I thinke necessarie also for a Gentleman to knowe; not to worke as a Maister Mason.[54]

In 1623 Robert Burton included architecture among the recondite pastimes of the educated man:

To most kind of men it is an extraordinary delight to study. For what a world of books offers it self, in all subjects, arts and sciences, to the sweet content and capacity of the Reader? In Arithmetick, Geometry, Perspective, Optick, Astronomy, Architecture, Sculpture, Pictura . . . in Mechanicks and their mysteries.[55]

The emphasis on theory, on curiosity and on geometry preserves the distinction of the gentleman designer from the artisan.

Levels of Knowledge and Degrees of Involvement

On a chimneypiece at South Wraxall Manor in Wiltshire, probably put up around 1600, are the figures of Justice, Prudence, Arithmetic and Geometry (pl. 18). Arithmetic and Geometry had been elements of the *quadrivium*, the theoretical course studied in the medieval university, but at South Wraxall, besides her traditional attributes of a globe and a pair of dividers, Geometry is shown to have a practical value with a builder's level and square. It is as aspects of eternal order and eternal truth that all four are equally honourable in the house of the gentleman, but Arithmetic and Geometry are here placed on a level with the Justice and Prudence that the governor must make use of in his daily work.

'Our most handsome and artificiall buildings', wrote Fuller in 1662 with the benefit of seventy-five years' hindsight, 'bear their date from the defeating of the Spanish Fleet.'[56] William Harrison wrote of contemporary builders:

In the proceding also of their workes, how they set up, how they pull downe, how they inlarge, how they restraine, how they ad to, how they take from, whereby their heads are never idle, their purses never shut, nor their bookes of account never made perfecte.[57]

Harrison's is a vivid picture of the frenzy of house building in the years before the turn of the century, as recruits to the ranks of the gentry sought to announce their new-found status, while old families were determined not to be left behind in the expression of their standing and in the acquisition of comforts and luxury, and both took advantage of an economic situation when labour was cheap and landed incomes high.[58] A few years later Francis Bacon made the same point: 'as Augustus said that he had received the city of brick and left it of marble, so may [Queen Elizabeth] say she received a realm of cottages and hath made it a realm of palaces'.[59] At this date evidence of personal involvement in building on the part of individual owners is still rare, but it is impossible not to suppose that a great many builders took a keener interest in the design of their houses than is indicated by surviving documents.

Harrison suggested too the nature of this involvement – how

diverse men being bent on building, and having a dilectable veine in spending of their goods by that trade, doo daily imagine new devices of their owne, and to guide their workmen withall, and those more curious and excellent alwaies than the former.[60]

It is the gentleman's wish to maintain his distance from the craftsman as well as the contemporary fascination for cunning devices and conceits, in the understanding of which the man of culture could display his learning, that explains why some of the earliest buildings apparently to have been designed by gentlemen were above all expressions of ingenuity. The slight sketch and the casual note are almost as ephemeral as the suggestion by word of mouth, but there is evidence for the personal involvement of both men and women in the devising of such things.

The ingenious buildings of Sir Thomas Tresham are well known.[61] The inventory taken when he died in 1605 shows Tresham as having owned the largest known library of architectural books in sixteenth-century England, including modern French and Italian works as well as several editions of Vitruvius.[62] His most remarkable buildings are above all sophisticated plays with Catholic and Trinitarian symbolism; Tresham employed a variety of craftsmen in their erection, both local and from further afield. In the design of the Market Cross of 1578 at Rothwell in Northamptonshire he contracted with the mason William Grumbold on the basis of a drawing that Grumbold had made. The accomplished use of classical orders at Rothwell indicates either Tresham's own understanding or the possibility that the classicism already current in the county for thirty years had progressed further among an élite of local artisans than a rag-bag application of details. But though he may have lacked the skills to set down his requirements on paper with sufficient clarity to avoid misunderstandings over so sophisticated a building, there can be no doubt that the overall concept of the Trinitarian buildings was his own.

The scheme for the fishing pavilion that Sir Arthur Champernown designed for Richard Carew is often cited.[63] This was to have been a two-storey building standing on an island, with rounded turrets at the corners and intended as a miniature replica of Mount Edgcumbe, but it was also to be a geometrical conceit. The ground floor was to have comprised a round room inside a square block, with corner turrets containing kitchen, buttery, storeroom and a stair; the storey above was to have been round and tower-like, with a square room inside, and the odd spare space was to contain cupboards 'for keeping other necessarye utensiles, towards these fishing feasts'. Francis Bacon too devised a pavilion for an island in a lake as a place of retirement and entertainment: 'A howse for freshnes with an upper gallery open upon the water, a terace above that, and a supping roome

open under that; a dynyng roome, a bedd chamber, a cabanett, and a roome for musike'.[64]

Champernown's *jeu d'esprit* of squared circles very much resembles in spirit an anonymous design, preserved at Longleat, for a strange, square house with an octagonal, central tower (pl. 17).[65] The drawing appears English, but it seems to be derived from two plans for a house for a king in Serlio's unpublished sixth book of architecture.[66] More than one manuscript of this circulated in France, and though it is hard to imagine by what route such designs were known in England, French masons of considerable competence worked at Longleat.[67] If the Serlian derivation – however implausible – is accepted, it is significant that it was two of the most curious (by English standards) of Serlio's designs that appealed as the basis for this strange conceit. If the resemblance is purely coincidental, then the scheme can be seen as the work of someone like Champernown, playing with rulers and compasses and perhaps interested at some level in the fashionable cosmic and Platonic symbolism of perfect geometrical forms.[68]

Trinitarian or some more obscure symbolism may have motivated Sir Thomas Gorges, who built Longford Castle in Wiltshire in the 1580s as a triangular courtyard house and possibly

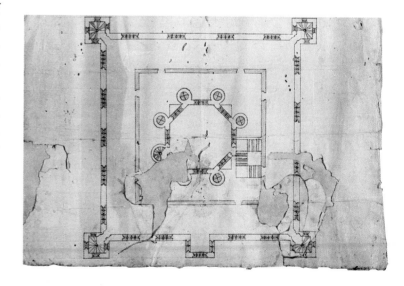

17 Anon. (*c.* 1570–80): A house with a centralised (upper-floor) plan. An unbuildable *jeu d'esprit* of *c.* 1570–80. Although possibly based on two designs in Sebastiano Serlio's unpublished sixth book of architecture. It is characteristic of the contemporary English fascination with ingenious forms.

18 (*facing page*) South Wraxall Manor, Gloucestershire: the great chamber chimneypiece, *c.* 1600. Decorated with figures of Justice, Prudence, Arithmetic and Geometry. All four are aspects, in a Platonic sense, of the way in which the real world connects with the ideal. Justice and Prudence are qualities demanded from the ruler in his everyday work; here they are associated with sciences whose practical application is implied by the attributes of the figures that personify them.

19 (*above*) Chilham (new) Castle, Kent, *c.* 1600. Battlemented, and polygonal in plan like the old castle, the house's meaning is made clear by the inscription 'The Lord is my House of Defense and my Castle' over the front door.

21 (*facing page*) Stapleford, Leicestershire, 1633. A wing of the house, remodelled by Lady Abigail Sherrard, with figures and coats of arms advertising her husband's ancestry.

20 (*left*) Chilham (old) Castle, Kent. The medieval castle at Chilham inspired the symbolism of its owner's new house nearby.

also Newhouse at Whiteparish in the same county, a house with three radiating wings.[69] Mark Girouard has suggested that the inspiration for the extraordinary form of Wollaton may have been in contemporary paper reconstructions of Solomon's Temple, an icon of Protestant ideology.[70] Chilham Castle in Kent is arranged around five sides of a hexagon, open on the sixth side (pl. 19): it has a battlemented parapet and its inspiration seems to have been antiquarian, in the polygonal keep of the Norman castle that stands on a motte a few hundred yards away (pl. 20). Lest anyone should miss the point its builder (the lawyer and diplomatist Sir Dudley Digges) wrote 'The Lord is my House of Defense and my Castle' over the the front door.[71] These inventions are similar in spirit to the seven-sided porch that Bishop Jewel added to the church at Sunningwell in Berkshire, with a column at each angle. The faceted plan is probably a play on Jewel's name, while the seven sides may symbolise the Sacraments. The ornament on the porch at Kirby (pl. 73) must have been placed there at the instigation of its builder and for

the learned to read. It makes a Biblical reference to the hospitality to be dispensed within the house.

Women too could involve themselves in such diversions.[72] At Callowden in Warwickshire around 1600 a banqueting house was built, 'the polite work of the Lady Elizabeth, wife of Sir Thomas Berkeley', which she occupied as 'the retired cell of her soul's soliloquies to God her creator'.[73] When the Countess of Arundel proposed a lodge at Gunborough (a place otherwise unidentified) she wrote to her husband: 'I hope you will let me be the architect.'[74] In the 1630s family zeal prompted Lady Abigail Sherrard to rebuild a range of late Gothic building at Stapleford in Leicestershire with ranks of medieval and fake-medieval statuettes as an extraordinary public display of her husband's ancestry (pl. 21).[75] There were few opportunities for the gentry to design fortifications, but Sir Francis Godolphin of Godolphin acted with the surveyor Robert Adams in 1593–4, building an artillery fort, Starr Castle, on the Scilly Isles of which he was governor.[76] An early Grand Tourist, Sir John Harington was

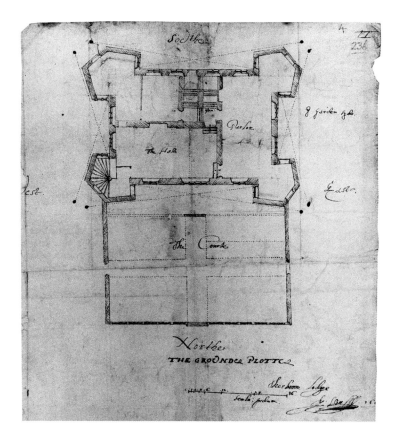

22 Simon Basil, *c.* 1600. Plan of Sherborne (new) Castle, Dorset, built *c.* 1593. Standing (like Chilham) close to an old castle, it was built as a house of retirement by Sir Walter Raleigh. The military inspiration is clear from the contemporary drawing: the angles of the polygonal turrets were determined by the fancied sight lines of an artillery fort. The derivation of the plan, however, may be French.

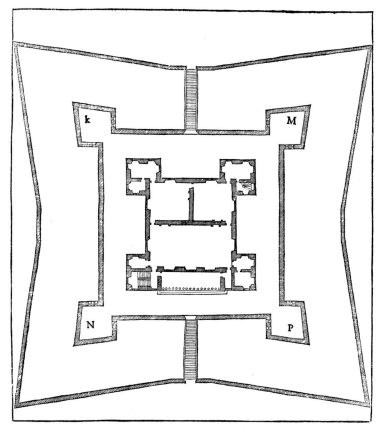

Les beaux ornements, belles façons, & enrichiſſements des logis, n'eſtre tant neceſſaires que la bonne ſituation d'iceux , & ouuerture bien accommodée aux vents.

23 A plan from Philibert de L'Orme, *Premier tome de l'architecture*, Paris, 1568. Possibly a source for the plan of Sherborne.

reported from Venice as sharing the same (unidentified) teacher of architecture and fortification as the English ambassador Sir Henry Wotton.[77] (Earlier, Harington's tutor had been James Cleland, whose recommendation of architecture and fortification as proper subjects of study is mentioned above.) Inigo Jones owned copies of Buonaiuto Lorini's *Le fortificatione* and Gabriello Busea's *L'architettura militare* and made extensive marginal notes in the former.

Alberti, Serlio, Vignola and the editors of Vitruvius had sought to rediscover and to set out the rules of ancient architecture. From the 1560s onwards an increasing range of French and Italian books was supplementing these analyses with illustrations of modern buildings, and it is clear from contemporary library lists and from correspondence that these works were finding their way into the hands of English builders who consulted them, derived inspiration from them and lent them to each other and to their architects. In his *Architecture in Britain, 1530–1830* Sir John Summerson pointed out the derivation of the plan of Hardwick from that of the villa Valmarana at Lisiera in Palladio's *Five Books of Architecture*.[78] The use of the Palladian plan when

the elevation is so wholly un-Palladian is itself a species of conceit: taking an exotic idea and adapting it for a house of a kind that Palladio could never have envisaged. The plan of Sherborne Castle in Dorset (pl. 22), as built by Sir Walter Raleigh, bears some similarity to one in Philibert de L'Orme's *Premier tome de l'architecture* of 1568 (pl. 23).[79]

Evidence from the late sixteenth century of the gentry's growing concern with the detail of building is afforded by the increasing esteem of architects themselves – a significant shift of emphasis from the exclusive, humanist identification of architecture with the liberal arts. Such growing respect for the educated craftsman suggests a number of things: awareness that erudition on its own was insufficient to achieve the erection of a creditable house, and recognition that leading craftsmen were themselves acquiring a measure of learning that enabled them to serve the needs of educated patrons. James Cleland had felt that even though it was not proper for a gentleman to practise the craftsman's skills, he should know enough of architecture to appraise it critically: 'that he may be able in looking upon any building . . . to tel what is *Frontispice, Tympane, Cornishes, pedestals, Frizes*, what is the *Tuscane, Dorik, Corinthian*, and *composed order*'.[80] Even if the builder himself knows little of architecture, the employment of a knowledgeable architect ensures that his credit is maintained with those of his peers who do.

The function of the architect and the evolution of the word have been studied in some depth.[81] In the late sixteenth century and the early seventeenth the title was sufficiently ill-defined as still to depend to a considerable extent on the claims of individuals. Very broadly, the architect was regarded as a general overseer of works: neither necessarily the contractor himself (though he might be) nor the principal craftsman involved (though he might be that as well) but having sufficient knowledge to ensure that the house was built according to such overall scheme as may have been agreed beforehand (a scheme which may have been his or another's). His background is likely to have been in the building crafts or in land surveying, and was often reflected in his evident versatility. Men of skill were highly regarded and increasingly sought after. John Thorpe, who certainly provided plans for building though perhaps not equipped to supervise it, was described by Henry Peacham in 1611 as an 'excellent geometrician and surveiour';[82] Robert Stickells was described in 1595 as 'the excellent architect of our time'[83] and recommended himself to William Cecil for the skills he claimed 'in the mathematical science, in the rules of architecture . . . of fortifying, house building, or any such ingenious causes' – a Baconian blend of the theoretical with the practical. When in 1610 Dorothy Wadham sought the services of the Somerset mason William Arnold on her projected new college at Oxford, Sir William Hext wrote to her: 'If I had not tyed him to this business we should hardly keep him; he is so wonderfully sought after being in deed the absolutest and honestest workman in England.'[84] In the previous year, when Arnold was remodelling Cranborne Lodge in Dorset for Robert Cecil, it was remarked that 'Arnold the workman . . . spends a whole hour in private with My Lord Treasurer about his buildings.'[85] He is designated 'Mr.' – the minimum title for a gentleman – in the Wadham College building accounts. Robert Smythson was buried in the chancel at Wollaton along with the village gentry, as were members of the Thorpe family at Kingscliffe. William Spicer, working at Longleat in the 1560s, rose through service to the Earl of Leicester and the crown to receive a grant of arms in 1591 and the lease of the Manor of Long Itchington.[86] Despite the strictures of Sir John Ferne, quoted above, by the early seventeenth century it was possible to rise through architectural skills from the ranks of the artisan to the lowest level of the gentry.

What was most often needed, in particular by the builder who took an active interest in the form and details of the house that he intended to build, was professional advice. When in 1605 proposals were made to build a new lodge for the king at Ampthill, John Thorpe worked up a design by an unknown amateur which Summerson described as 'remarkably classical': the work of a man familiar both with architectural texts and with the needs of royalty, but lacking the skill to produce a drawing sufficiently finished to serve as the basis for estimates or for the direction of workmen.[87] The example of Sir Edward Pytts of Kyre Park in Herefordshire has frequently been cited. Pytts was building – or at least intending to build – over many years. He opened his book of accounts – a large, handsomely bound volume with his monogram embossed on the cover – with a calligraphic flourish on the title page: 'A Viewe of the charges for the newe buildinge the House of Kyer Court nowe ruined.'[88] There followed a brief account of his distinguished predecessors as owners of the estate until its purchase by himself,

> who begynneth to provide Stone, Bricke, Tymber and other necessaries for the Reedefyeng therof, the yeare of our Lorde God one thousand five hundred and eightye eight . . . when God wonderfully vanquished the invincyble Fleet (as they cristened it) of the Spanyarde.

For Pytts, the building of his own house and the coeval defeat of the Spanish Armada were equal cause for celebration and their coincidence a happy omen. Among the earliest entries is 'To Ralph Symons of London for drawing my first platt for my house – 40s' which is immediately followed by a payment to him of £3 'for drawing my latter platt according to my newe purpose'. In 1611, on his way to Kyre from London, he persuaded John Bentley – who had come from Yorkshire to work on the Schools Quadrangle in Oxford – to accompany him to Kyre, 'to take instructions from me by veiyinge the place to draw me a newe platte for I altered my first intent'; presumably it was hard for Pytts to convey to Bentley the state of the incomplete house without Bentley's seeing it. He evidently consulted a Coventry mason 'one Sgianson'[89] as well, 'though he did nothing in that busines'. In 1613 Bentley was paid 10s 'for his paines in the platt', but he died in that year and Pytts resorted to Robert Stickells, who had earlier been employed by Tresham and had offered his services to Robert Cecil: 'Paid to Stickles of London for drawing the platt of my house anew.' It is clear that keen builders who lacked the technical, graphic or administrative skills with which to give direct instructions to workmen were anxious to find men of ability who would give their schemes practical effect.

Much of the design as well as of the direction of house building had always lain largely with craftsmen,[90] and the inventiveness of late sixteenth-century houses demonstrates the ability of leading practitioners to keep up with the demands of an increasingly educated clientele. In spite of Girouard's epoch-making study too little is known about the working practices of Robert Smythson, the greatest architect of the age, but his houses must have been substantially of his own devising, however instructed by his clients. Nicholas Stone in 1631 agreed with the Earl of Danby 'to desine a new House for him at Cornbury in Oxfordshire and to direct the workmen and to mak all their moldes' and visited the site thirty-three times over two years.[91] Gerbier too recommended that a good surveyor 'ought from time to time visite the work, to see whether the Building be performed according to his Direction and Moulds',[92] although it was also necessary, he said, to employ a good full-time clerk of works.

Further evidence that in spite of the geometrical amusements of the few, the detailed working-out of the house's design still generally remained in the hands of the working mason or brick-layer may be found in the proportional systems employed in the plans of executed buildings. Renaissance architects who sought objective beauty in harmonic proportions commonly employed simple ratios of real numbers, and those educated men who pursued their interest in architecture as far as the detailed drawing-out of their designs probably did the same. However, from the Middle Ages masons had very commonly employed irrational ratios in setting-out their buildings, such as root 2, root 3 and the Golden Section. The distinction between the architect and the artisan that was recognised by Dee corresponded to real differences of practice that have been characterised as two separate dialogues about design, the one 'Vitruvian' – theoretical, public and literary – and the other 'Euclidian' – composed of the inherited and reputedly arcane geometrical practices of the working mason and carpenter.[93] Analysis of the plans of a few of the most sophisticated houses of the early seventeenth century (including Holland House; Eagle House, Wimbledon; and Charlton House, all of which are considered in chapter 4) seems to show that the proportions most commonly occurring are the traditional ones of the working craftsman rather than those of the mathematician who has studied Vitruvius,[94] besides the continuing use of the standard, traditional builder's unit of length, the perch of $16\frac{1}{2}$ feet. They are different from the harmonic ratios widely used (with adjustment for their visual effect) by Inigo Jones.

But in the long term the decline of the craftsman-architect lay partly in the nature of the structures he was building. In the erection of Gothic buildings, the complex structures of arches, vaults and tracery called for a great deal of technical expertise on the part of the mason, who was thus out of necessity in large part the building's designer. With the abandonment of such intricate building and with its replacement by houses with plain walls and repetitious straight-headed windows, with roof structures that were concealed and purely functional and with details that were not in the traditional craftsman's canon, the craftsman was less able to insist on his own ultimate authority in design through the mastery of his craft.[95] It was thus not only new architectural and decorative styles and the education of patrons that brought about the change, but the Reformation: to make an obvious point, the decline of Gothic was partly brought about by the decline of church building.

Contemporary perceptions of the difference between the training of the architect and the education of the gentleman shows very clearly in the quarrel between Inigo Jones and Ben Jonson – a quarrel that involved many different issues but which could not have taken place but for the growing interest in the visual arts and changing attitudes towards artists that had made possible Jones's rise from humble beginnings to his acceptance as a man of culture in the very highest circles. Jones's architecture was based on a deep study of Palladio, Serlio, Vignola and the editors of Vitruvius, but was not dogmatic, recognising the need to temper prescriptive systems by the architect's informed use of his own eye (his conspicuous care in employing full-sized models to judge the effect of proposed new work at St Paul's must have been widely noticed).[96] Jones's influence as Surveyor General of the Royal Works,[97] as the architect of a few buildings for private clients, as adviser on others and as a professional member of the Commission for New Buildings (see p. 172 below) was out of proportion to the number of his own commissions. Backed up by his famed connoisseurship, his recognised professional skills must have enhanced the standing of architects and of architecture itself.

Jonson, writer of lyrics for royal masques for which Jones designed scenery, costumes and special effects, resented his own work being overshadowed by Jones's showmanship and arrogance, but his comments express more than mere pique.[98]

> Mr. Surveyor, you yt first begann
> From thirty pound in pipkins, to ye Man
> you are; from them leapt forth an Architect,
> Able to talk of Euclide, and correct
> Both him & Archimede; damne Architas
> The noblest Ingenyre that ever was!
> Controll Ctesibius: overbearing us
> With mistooke names out of Vitruvius![99]

The significance of 'thirty pound in pipkins' – earthenware jugs – is now lost,[100] but presumably referred to some then familiar and (to Jonson) disreputable tale of Jones's humble origins. Jonson's understanding of Vitruvius (he owned and annotated Barbaro's edition) was at least equal to that of Jones (who knew little Latin) and shows in the architectonic structure of many of his works.[101] Jones's architectural knowledge was less purely abstract, but among his affronts to Jonson were the claims that he made for himself as an architect. Jonson undoubtedly considered literature a nobler calling than architecture, and clearly considered Jones's aspirations grossly in excess of any to which an architect was entitled. He would have agreed with Dee that it was theory alone that justified architecture's inclusion among the liberal arts. He would have agreed with Vitruvius that even if the architect needed a broad knowledge of many things he could not claim omniscience or excellence in any other field than his own. Yet in denigrating the practitioner Jonson was swimming against the tide. His was the attitude condemned by Francis Bacon who complained that it was 'dishonoured among learned men to descend to inquiry or meditation of things mechanical'.[102] Jones, by applying practical competence and visual taste in adapting his models to English circumstances,

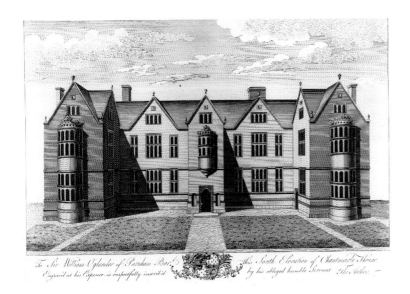

24 Anon. (late eighteenth century): Chantemarle House, Dorset, 1612. Chantemarle is a house of conventional form, but according to its builder its E plan was explicitly adopted for its religious symbolism, the E standing for 'Emmanuel: that is to say, God with us'.

was in a sense establishing the standing of practice in alliance with theory, and his social acceptability marks a changing attitude towards practical expertise.

Two cases illustrate particularly clearly how the concern of the builder and the practical skills of the craftsman-architect might interact. In one the builder's concern was with religious symbolism, in the other with architecture in a purer sense, but they have enough in common to suggest that they may represent a not infrequent level of involvement. At Chantemarle in Dorset Gabriell Moore oversaw the building of a new house for Sir John Strode between 1612 and 1619 (pl. 24). Moore was paid '20s. monethly wth his dyett, for his painis only to survey and direct the building in the form I conceived and plotted it', evidently recommending masons – the Rowes of Hamdon, 'preferred to me', wrote Strode, 'by Gabriell Moore my Surveyor'. The house incorporates an older range, projecting to the rear, and Strode recorded that the new building is 'fitly adjoyn'd to the old buildings by the care and discreccion of old Gabriell Moore (a skilful architect)'.[103] The main body of the house was on a familiar E plan, though Strode claimed not precedent but symbolism in its choice: 'Constructa est in forma, de littera E, p. Emmanuel, id est, Deus nobiscum in Eternum' and it differed from a conventional E-plan house in having its upper end wing mainly occupied by a two-storey chapel (of which there was no external evidence: symmetry dictated windows on both floors to match those in the opposite wing). Strode's explanation of its form is a typical contemporary conceit which he underlined by carving the word 'Emmanuel' over the front entrance, and only an educated man would have chosen a conventional layout for the sake of its symbolism and further proceeded to modify it in accordance with his private religious leanings. But presumably the overall scheme was no more than roughly described and sketched out by him; his architect was entrusted with ensuring that the conceit actually worked. If Moore was living on site, as is implied (and as was common practice), he must have main-

tained a close supervision of the works, and it is clear from Strode's subsequent account that he was happy with the result.

The other case is Raynham Hall, where between 1622 and his death in 1637 Sir Roger Townshend was putting up one of the outstanding country houses of the period (pl. 25).[104] The façades of Raynham are a medley of up-to-date elements, largely Jonesian and derived from London and probably also from the Prince's Lodging at Newmarket. Townshend had almost certainly been to see these for himself, and Pratt says that he 'bestowed his tyme to examine . . . ev'ry inch accor. to Mathematicks as he was able to do, witness his many Italian and French books of Architecture'.[105] For Pratt the Vitruvian link between architecture and mathematics was still a real one; and through the architectural library, which by implication only a man of Townshend's wealth and education was likely to possess, architectural knowledge remained – or indeed was anchored yet more exclusively – in the hands of an élite. At the same time William Edge, Townshend's mason, was provided with the means to travel and, presumably, to see for himself those features which Townshend wanted incorporated into his house. Whatever Edge's practical responsibilities, Townshend's responsibilty for the detailed planning of Raynham may be suggested by the harmonic, rather than the Euclidean, proportions that seem to determine its design. Townshend is a precursor of the gentleman architect who was to be characteristic of the second half of the seventeenth century and of whom Pratt himself was perhaps the most complete example.

A further, advanced feature of Townshend's work at Raynham was the making of a model. The making of architectural models seems to follow on from a growing interest in perspective drawing, which may itself be seen as the culmination of a long period of evolution in the graphic representation of buildings. In England, skilled craftsmen had been using isometric drawings in the late Middle Ages; schematic plans with dimensions written in were by the late sixteenth century being superseded by plans made to scale.[106] An interest in perspective seems to have been growing in the last decades of the century, at much the same time as English painters were tending to move from the flat, hieratic depiction of subject-matter to a greater use of chiaroscuro. In both, illustration feigns reality – a concept that is itself a species of conceit, but one which would lead naturally towards the appreciation of representation for its own sake.[107] Foreign works on perspective occur not infrequently in sixteenth-century libraries, and although their language as much as their mathematics will have limited their availability to the educated class – to those for whom their appeal was as much theoretical as practical – they suggest a changing attitude not

25 Raynham Hall, Norfolk, *c.* 1622–37. An assemblage of up-to-date architectural elements, many derived from Inigo Jones, and directly reflecting its builder's own architectural interests.

only to building but also to buildings: a wish not only to see the effect of a work before one committed oneself to it, but also a new recognition of the relationships between plan and appearance that must derive from an increasing degree of architectural awareness not only on the part of architects but also among builders. It can be seen too in the light of a huge expansion from the late sixteenth century in the production of estate plans and maps which similarly allowed the owner to visualise his possessions (see chapter 9 below).

The earliest English treatise on perspective is an unpublished translation by John Thorpe of Jacques Androuet Du Cerceau's *Leçons de perspective positive*, originally published in 1576.[108]

Among Thorpe's drawings at the Soane Museum is one drawn out according to Du Cerceau's rules,[109] and it is perhaps significant that of all late Elizabethan and Jacobean buildings and schemes Thorpe's are among the most fantastic, and those whose interrelated complexities of plan and elevation most clearly indicate the need for them to have been conceived as a whole. Thorpe's translation must predate by only a little the first work on perspective published in England which appeared in 1611, written by Salomon de Caus[110] – the same year as the first English translation of Serlio which also included a section on perspective. Henry Peacham proposed publication of 'a discourse of perspective' (possibly Thorpe's) in the same year. The coincidence of these works in the vernacular suggests that the science was emerging from a branch of mathematical theory to one with a perceived utility.

The use of the three-dimensional model as a means of working out a scheme and showing its intended appearance also suggests that the builder increasingly wished to see what his house was going to look like before work was begun, as well as the growing practice of working out its details in advance – itself an index of his growing sophistication.[111] References to a 'model' in the sixteenth century are likely to be to a drawing, but Sir Henry Wotton in 1624 – paraphrasing Alberti (of whose *De re aedificatoria* he owned what is now the earliest surviving manuscript)[112] – felt that even a perspective drawing was insufficient:

> Let no man that intendeth to build, setle his Fancie upon a draught of the Worke in paper, how exactly soever measured, or neatly set off in perspective; And much lesse upon a bare Plant thereof, as they call the Schiographia or Ground lines; without a Modell or Type of the whole Structure, and of every parcell and Partition in Pastboord or Wood.[113]

He continued that the model should be unpainted 'lest the pleasure of the Eye preoccupate the Iudgement'.

How a model could be used to enable the owner and his architect to sort out the design of his house is well shown in letters of 1651 from Lord Fairfax in Yorkshire to his cousin's husband James Challoner in London, about a house that Fairfax was proposing to build in York to designs by Edward Carter.[114] Carter's proposal was for a house larger than Fairfax intended, and Fairfax wrote to Challoner, as his intermediary, 'I shall shortly returne the platformes wth as full a description of the ground as I can.'

A week later he wrote again:

> I have returned the Models you sent downe but I doubt they are larger than I have space of ground for therfore I have sent a plaine draught of the ground with a calculation of yards as neere as I can gitt I have writt to Mr Carter though I have not skil enough to express my selfe so fully as I should like. . . . I desir you to put Mr Carter in mind to send me downe a perfait modle assoone as he can conveniently make it I will rather stay his time than that it should not be perfait.

Four months later Fairfax wrote once more, asking through Challoner that Carter 'will yitt perfait his designe & make that modle he sent me last in wood wch will be the best way to understand & surest way to worke after I shall satisfie him for it'.

Although the 'models' first referred to may have been designs on paper, Fairfax seems finally to have asked for one in three dimensions; though pretending to no architectural knowledge or skills, he was clearly keen to see what his house was going to be like before he started building. It is clear too that he intended Carter's model, in the necessary absence of Carter himself in London, to be the basis for the actual building work under the supervision of a local man.

The same process seems to have been followed by Lord Conway at Ragley in the 1670s.[115] Evidently Conway had a model made by William Hurlbert, a local carpenter and builder, which he then submitted to the scientist and architect Robert Hooke for his opinion. When in due course Hooke visited Ragley, the foundations had already been laid, but he 'viewd module, shewd many faults, made a great many alterations'. He followed this by sending to Ragley designs for extensive improvements, and later suggested that the model be sent up to him in London for alteration. Not all of Hooke's suggestions were followed, but both he and Conway clearly regarded the model as the means whereby they could communicate ideas to each other and to the workmen on the spot. On other occasions Hooke did not visit at all, and must have relied wholly on such drawings and models to make his designs understood.[116]

Sir Roger Pratt had summed up the uses of a model a few years earlier:

> It will not only prevent all future alteration in the building, a thing of a most vast expense, but will likewise avoid all complaint of the master, and abuse of the contriver, being that this will ever remain a justification of the invention of the one, and a most plain conviction of the consent of the other.[117]

Pratt also saw a model as better than trying to piece the overall effect together from a number of detailed drawings:

> Whereas all the other drafts . . . do only superficially and disjointedly represent unto us the several parts of a building, a model does it jointly, and according to all its dimensions. So that in one rightly framed all things both external and internal with all their divisions, connections, vanes, ornaments, etc. are there to be seen as exactly, and in their due proportions, as they can afterwards be in the work of which this is composed to be the Essay.

He added that if the model was made with sides that could be raised up, the internal layout could be seen. By the mid-seventeenth century no serious builder was likely to be satisfied with the somewhat haphazard way of proceeding that had been commonplace in the past.

But even in the seventeenth century the employment of a model or the use of a perspective drawing were always for a sophisticated minority, and for the most part the prospective builder proceeded by more traditional means: by the citing of an existing building as a pattern, by reference to a simple sketch plan, or else by less formal instructions still. In 1532 John Sydenham agreed with John Trevelyan of Nettlecombe in Somerset to build a new hall, 'as the olde halle made ys, and of the length of the same old hall or within 6 foote of the same length'.[118] Sydenham, however, had a lease of Nettlecombe from Trevelyan who may not have been greatly concerned for the details of a house he did not intend to occupy. At Little Moreton Hall in Cheshire (pl. 26), even though its extension around 1560 was in a vernacular style which had been little changed in the region over the previous seventy-five years, the work involved agreeing a drawing with the carpenter: when William Moreton died in

26　Little Moreton Hall, Cheshire, 1559: the hall and parlour windows. A prestigious display of glass and wood, facing into the courtyard and bearing the names of the house's builder and his carpenter.

1563 he requested that this be completed 'according to the devyse thereof devysed twixt me and Richard Dale the head wright and workman of the same frame'.[119] It is much more likely that Dale made the drawing than that Moreton did, and the most that can be said for Moreton is that he had presumably specified what he wanted and understood what he was shown. Against that is the contract between Sir Richard Edgcumbe and a local builder, Roger Palmer, for the building of Mount Edgcumbe in Cornwall in 1567.[120] No overall price or completion date is specified; all is to be done by piecework, so that at that stage a complete design need not have been decided. However, the contract does require Palmer's men to be 'followynge allwayes in their seyd worke the devyse advyse and platt of the seyd Sir Richard Eggecombe and his assignes'. The contract does not specifically name Sir Richard as the author of the design. Nevertheless the house is a sophisticated building on an unconventional plan which must have involved him in prior consultation about its form.

Widespread and time-honoured as a means of prescribing the builder's intentions was to cite an existing building as a pattern. Early in the sixteenth century the principal carpenter employed on Little Saxham in Suffolk was told to copy the new roof at Horham Hall in the next county, and also to go to London and look at a house in Tower Street.[121] In 1604 the roof of the Middle Temple Hall was taken as the pattern for that of the hall of Trinity College, Cambridge;[122] it had itself been modelled on that of Longleat some twenty-five years earlier. Together, the college bursar and a craftsman spent time in London examining possible patterns:

> Item for horshier to London for myself & John Symmes . . .xv.s.
> Item given at London to Carpenters and keepers of dyvers Halles to viewe and measure them . . . x.s.[123]

Henry Percy, 9th Earl of Northumberland, wrote to Robert Cecil: 'I must go and see Copthall, for now that I am a builder I must borrow of my knowledge somewhat out of Tibballs, somewhat out of every place of mark where curiosities are used.'[124] It is worth noting that Percy, the patron, planned to go and see these things for himself. It was no more than an extension of Percy's mix-and-match approach to sources for his intended building that prompted Sir Roger Townshend to send his mason sightseeing, probably as a result of his own realisation that in Jones's buildings there was something altogether new. In building two garden houses at Aston Hall outside Birmingham in 1637, Sir Thomas Holte specified initially that these were to be 'suitable unto the banquetting houses in the garden at Camden House in Gloucestershire', but later changed this so that they were to be built 'unto a plott which I have new made'.[125] Instead of following an existing pattern, the bricklayer was to be guided by his employer's own ideas.

Details as well as complete buildings might be taken from specified examples. In 1637 Richard Boyle, Earl of Cork, was enlarging his house at Stalbridge in Dorset to designs by Isaac de Caus ('the french architect, who belongs to my L. chamberleyn'[126]) and agreed with Walter Hyde of Sherborne to make '4 wrought [i.e. carved] chymneis, with ffigures answerable or better than the chymney in my own bed-chamber'.[127] The pattern cited supplied the general idea; the details were left to the craftsman or might be refined by discussion.[128] An entry in Boyle's diary a few days earlier suggests the informal way in which such models might be found:

> I dyninge this daie with thearle of Bristoll at Sherborn, did . . . agree with Gregory Brimsmead, his Lops. free mason, to pave the way from my owtmoste gate to my hall door at Stalbridg, and the Tarras before my howse . . . owt of the same vayne of hard ffree stoan [as] that [of] thearles Court going into his howse at Sherborn, and in the same manner that the same court is paved.[129]

Presumably Boyle was impressed by the quality of the new paving in his host's house, and lost no time in going to see the craftsman whom he had learnt was responsible for it.

There are numbers of houses so like each other that it can be assumed that one is modelled on the other even though one may have to speculate on how the imitation came about. Occasionally the connection is obvious: the idiosyncratic decoration of Moreton Corbet (pl. 9), built for Robert Corbet, is repeated exactly on a smaller house for a cousin a few miles away at Stanwardine (pl. 27); the cousin was clearly advertising his connec-tion with the builder of the grander house.[130] A well-known pair is Barlborough Hall (pl. 15) and Heath Old Hall (pl. 28), two tall, compact courtyard houses of the 1580s.[131] Barlborough in Derbyshire was built for Francis Rodes, a lawyer, Justice of the Common Pleas and at a slightly earlier stage in his career, steward to the Earl of Shrewsbury. Heath, pulled down in 1961, had a virtually identical façade, and though the plan is less sophisticated it is inconceivable that Barlborough was not its model.[132] The link may be Sir John Savile, whose arms occur in the much more modest Barlborough Old Hall.[133] John Savile was related to Sir Henry Savile, steward of the Honour of Wakefield;[134] Sir Henry's deputy (who probably did the day-to-day legal work of the office) was John Kay, builder of Heath Old Hall. John and Henry Savile were cousins, albeit not very close ones, but they lived near each other (Henry Savile's house was at Thornhill, south of Dewesbury; John's at that date was at Bradley, 6 miles away) and in an age which recognised and valued relationships

27 Stanwardine Hall, Shropshire. Built by a cousin of the builder of Moreton Corbet (pl. 9) and repeating the same ornamental motifs.

28 Heath Old Hall, West Yorkshire (demolished). The exterior almost certainly inspired by Barlborough Hall (pl. 15) though the plan is considerably less sophisticated.

and affinities, it may have been through these Savile connections that John Kay was inspired to emulate what was one of the most up-to-date houses of the north Midlands.

There is some further evidence of the Savile family's interest in architecture in that Sir John's brother, another Sir Henry, became Warden of Merton College, Oxford, in 1585 and in that capacity brought the Yorkshire mason John Akroyd to work at the college in 1608 and subsequently on the tower of the Schools Quadrangle.[135] Sir Henry founded chairs of geometry and astronomy, and on top of this theoretical knowledge Sir Thomas Bodley described him as possessing 'above all others . . . the judgement of a mason'.[136] Sir Henry's own statement that much of the detail of the Schools Tower was left to the workmen does not necessarily mean that the overall concept was not his, even though Akroyd will already have been familiar with frontispieces comprising superimposed orders in the north. It can anyway be assumed that in obtaining a Yorkshire mason he had the assistance of his brother Sir John: Akroyd's only other documented building is the (demolished) grammar school which was built at Heath while Sir John was chairman of the governors. Sir John himself bought Methley Hall, 5 miles from Heath, in the 1580s and rebuilt it in an up-to-date manner; Akroyd may have been his architect.

These are sophisticated buildings, easily compared and in which connections between prominent and educated builders can be traced without great difficulty. But it is often unnecessary to invoke such connections in order to explain why one building resembles another, and it is probably the widespread practice of taking an existing building as a pattern that partly underlies Pratt's criticism quoted at the beginning of the chapter:

that many of the gentry were content with a house like that of their neighbours. Probably for very many builders, resort to a standard plan or to an easily identified exemplar will have effectively saved them from making any more active decisions about the form of the house. Surviving estimates for building are scarce: the practice of financing building out of current income left less need to make preliminary, global costings, while the houses of the great – those which, for dynastic reasons, tend to be the better documented – were often built for reasons of prestige that damned expense.[137] Many such builders crippled themselves financially, but persisted. However, a rare set of estimates of 1558–61 survives for three separate schemes for a new house at Burton on Trent for William Paget, a member of Protector Somerset's circle but one skilled in the arts of political survival, who served successively King Henry, Queen Mary and Queen Elizabeth.[138] These estimates are attached to ground- and first-floor plans for each of the three schemes, and are effectively calculated on volume: on the making and laying of bricks for so many feet of wall of given thickness and height, of so many joists and rafters of given length and depth for floors and roofs, of so much lime to be burnt and the fuel for burning it, and so many windows of standard dimensions and forms. The calculations are detailed and exact, but they are essentially for the shell of the house and make no provision for anything that might be described as decorative work, inside or out. They suggest that it was impossible to cost such works at the outset because, as other evidence indicates, it was the practice to decide such details as the work proceeded – no doubt partly in the light of such additional money as might be found at that stage. Broad questions like the overall number of windows could be calculated from the plan; decisions about the precise placing of internal partitions, detailed finishes and ornament could come later, and the practice of making separate contracts for special items as they were required (for instance chimneypieces, doors or wainscot) made such piecemeal decision-making perfectly acceptable.[139] Once therefore the owner had decided to build, and decided more or less clearly the kind of house that he wanted, he might then take as much or as little interest in the detailed design of the building as his own inclinations prompted him.

It is in the light of such priorities that one can read a letter that the glass painter Bernhard Dinninghoff wrote to Sir Andrew Lumsden, offering a design for a house at Sheriff Hutton in Yorkshire in 1618.[140] The set of floor plans that Dinninghoff sent to Lumsden (pl. 29) are highly finished (apart from the eccentric spelling that reflects Dinninghoff's central European background), though his probable inexperience in building is suggested by the unsatisfactory character of the design. The general details of the scheme are clear enough from these plans. The house would have had towers projecting above the roof line, towers perhaps felt appropriate to the proximity of a large medieval castle of which substantial remains still existed, although such towers can be seen as a regional formula: they occurred in two houses just discussed – Barlborough and Heath

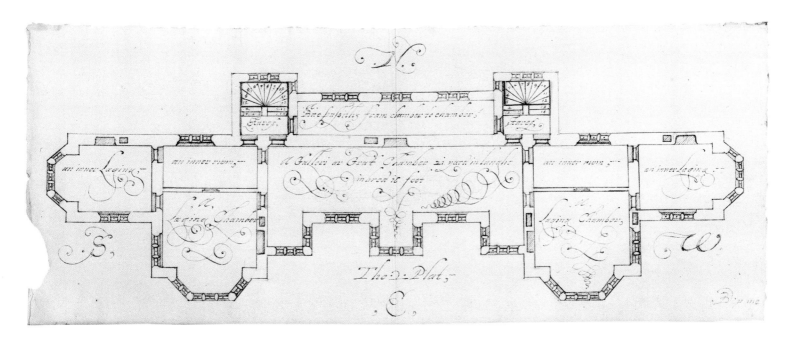

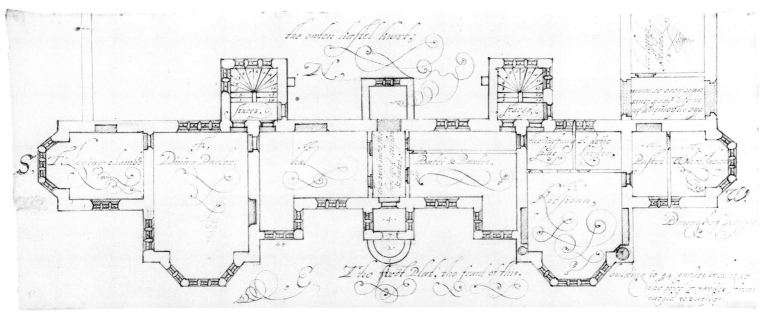

29   Bernhard Dinninghoff, *c.* 1620: ground- and first-floor plans for an unexecuted house. Dinninghoff was a central European glass painter working in Yorkshire. These finished drawings, with rooms named to demonstrate the attractions of the layout, were intended to advertise his architectural skills to a potential client. The turreted form may have been inspired by houses such as Fountains Hall and Hardwick, as well as by the proposed site, adjacent to a medieval castle at Sheriff Hutton.

Old Hall – and in a more sophisticated form at Hardwick and at Fountains Hall. Dinninghoff was then living outside Leeds, only a few miles from Heath, and he will have been familiar with all of these houses. Compared with them (and particularly

with Hardwick) Dinninghoff's house would have been ill-proportioned and gawky. But Dinninghoff sent Lumsden no elevation drawings, either because he did not feel competent to draw them or, which is more probable, because Lumsden was likely at this early stage to be concerned mainly with the layout and with the nature of the accommodation, and it would be time enough to settle the details of the façades once the plan had been agreed.

Dinninghoff's house was proportioned to the status of the builder: 'I have drawne 3 plattes with such adisson as is needful and convenient for a gentleman to dwell in.' But the details needed to be worked out in consultation with the client:

> if your worshipe bee amynded to build I will com to London and more exactly confare upon it and the business thereof you

bearing apart of my charges. . . . I would have you begin upon the south part towards the parke and so to build halfe the same a haule a dining parler a lodgeing chamber and for those roumes above and many other thinges I have to confare with you if I were with you my selfe.

Dinninghoff offered an estimate of £440 for 'all manner of workemanshipe and all laborrers and workemen towards the finnishing of the saide building' (Lumsden was to find the materials), but even if this suggests that he already had a good idea of the architectural detail of the house, it was clearly on the merits of the plan that he hoped to sell his scheme. The same can be seen in a letter from Sir Charles Cavendish written when the Earl of Salisbury was canvassing advice before embarking on Hatfield. Cavendish sent a plan of his own devising, writing 'there is some mislike in it, and something mistaken by the drawer in my absence; but if the general conveniency be liked the rest will easily be amended, as windows, chimneys, doors and such like'.[141] Beyond the stage of sketch design, the basic layout and overall form had necessarily to be determined before setting out foundations, but much else could be decided on the trot. At Blickling, surviving correspondence shows that there was a continuous development of the architectural vocabulary in the course of building.[142]

The plans in John Thorpe's book, heavily outnumbering the elevations, can be seen in the same light.[143] These represent the largest single body of architectural drawings preserved from the late sixteenth century and the early seventeenth and are a mixture of original designs (both executed and not), surveys of existing buildings, schemes for alteration and others that can only be described as essays, some of them based on continental models. Several plans which can be linked to known houses do not show them precisely as built but seem more in the nature of proposals for discussion or else schemes to be worked out in detail on site once there was general agreement to what was suggested. The preponderance of plans among Robert and John Smythson's surviving drawings suggests the same thing: that the prime need was to agree the general principles of the house's layout and that there would be opportunities for detailed adjustment at the stage of setting-out and more so in the details of elevations. As late as 1663 Balthazar Gerbier recommended that 'The readiest way to try a Surveyor, is to put him to draw a ground Plat in the Builder's presence.'[144]

Unquestionably one reason for gentlemen to acquire a knowledge of building was a purely practical one. A drawing or a model might be used to agree the form of the building with local craftsmen, and to show them the builder's intention in undertaking a house of perhaps unfamiliar form. But someone had to supervise the work, if not in a purely technical sense (in which one hoped in any case for the services of competent workmen) then in the resolution of architectural problems. For a great man the most natural person to do this was his steward, since his was the responsibility for looking after the funding of

the project.[145] In some cases this meant no more than making requisite payments and trying to keep the men on the job. 'I know you are in the Right that there might be more Care in the Supervising the Workmen', wrote Sir John Lowther to his agent William Atkinson, 'but Since tis from you alone that I can have anie Punctuall account off the Progress off my Work, so from you onlie tis that I hope ffor anie Life in my Businesse, tho I know tis not yr Proper Imployment.'[146]

Letters from Sir Arthur Ingram in London to his agent John Matteson, who in the early 1620s was in charge of his new building at Sherriff Hutton (a different house from Lumsden's, described above), show Matteson discussing with the carpenters the form of the principal stair, while the mere business of directing masons and carpenters in framing walls, in getting lead, window glass and stone suitable for fireplace openings, and in checking the quality of bricks and timber will have made serious demands on his knowledge in which he evidently satisfied the extremely demanding Sir Arthur.[147] The need for an educated man as steward necessitated the employment of at least minor gentry, and will have done something at least to propagate the knowledge of building among the class. Gentlemen who acted as their own men of business (or whose wives acted for him, as did Mary Coke of Hall Court; see chapter 6) might have to acquire such knowledge for themselves.

The first original, English book on architecture to be published since John Shute's in 1564, Sir Henry Wotton's *Elements of Architecture* of 1624, was written very much more for gentleman builders than for the artisan. It has no plates. 'Speculative Writers . . . are not bound, to comprise all particular Cases, within the Latitude of the Subject, which they handle; Generall Lights, and Directions, and pointings at some faults, is sufficient. The rest must be committed to the sagacitie of the Architect.'[148] Wotton's book is mainly aimed at enabling the gentleman who commissions a building to understand what is important about its layout and construction. 'As I passe along', he wrote, 'I will touch also the naturall Reasons of Art, that my discourse may be the lesse Mechanicall',[149] and he cites what Vitruvius, Palladio, Alberti and Philibert de L'Orme write about foundations, walls and roofs rather than discussing the actual practices of English workmen. The popularity of Wotton's book is shown by its later reprintings and by those cases where builders are known to have bought it. It evidently supplied a need. Nobody could have built a house with the information it contained, and its purchasers would not have expected to: that was the craftsman's job as was the knowledge necessary to do so. But Wotton's book would be of considerable use in helping the builder to form his own idea of how a house might be arranged, and with its aid he could take an informed interest in its planning and erection.

Webb's comment on the general level of architectural knowledge among the gentry by 1660 may be an overstatement, but a growing degree of personal architectural involvement on the part of their owners can be illustrated in a number of houses of the middle years of the seventeenth century. While the spread of stylistic innovation was in part due to the advancing knowledge of craftsmen, such increase was itself partly a response to the requirements of their employers and there is substantial evidence of increasing knowledge of architecture among the gentry themselves. The regionalism of English building was yielding to an increasingly nation-based culture, but although individual craftsmen might be widely employed, the mobility of most artisans and their opportunities for experiencing new building at first hand were still limited in comparison with those of the gentry who employed them. The increasing concern of members of the gentry class with the details of their houses must have arisen in part from their recognition of these limitations.

Particularly revealing are the notes made by Sir John Coke, who had risen from relatively humble origins to be a minister of the crown, when he came to alter and to modernise the house that he bought towards the end of his life: Melbourne in Derbyshire. Clarendon described Sir John as 'covetous'; he was certainly careful with his money, and while there is little to suggest that he had any particular interest in architecture, such carefulness allied to the temperament of a bureaucrat – he was by then Treasurer of the Navy – led him to describe in the minutest detail what he wanted the masons and carpenters to do during his absence on official business in London.[150] His instructions are exact, comprehensive and practical, and they evidently derive from his own very precise measurement of the existing house and his careful consideration of how economically to provide up-to-date amenities. His memoranda contain no instructions of an architectural character – indeed they seem positively to abjure architectural pretension: thus he writes of the hall screen 'I desire it may bee handsomly wrought without carving or curious charge' – and they stress where possible the desirability of re-using serviceable materials. Later alterations have made it impossible to judge the effect of Coke's building at Melbourne: only a fragment of his work at the back of the house is still visible. But his instructions insist throughout on the need for symmetry and regularity:

In the passage that goeth from the haule to the great chamber staires . . . a window must be made (to give light out of the cort) . . . in al els answerable to the buttrie window towards the cort. . . .

A third window must be made to give light into the haule over the table on the other side of the chimney which must bee in like manner answerable in all proportions to the other two windows. . . . The haule chimney must be placed in the midst betwixt the two windows 4 foot distant from either of them. . . .

A window must be placed 3 foote from the grownd, having 4 panes or lights with a double morion or peere in the midst: & in al things els suteable to the that [sic] window wch was taken out of the ould waule of the said parlour towards the east, & must again bee placed in the new waule in the same maner. . . .

The roof fro. end to end bee al of one height & proportion in every thing.

Sir John's office placed him in a position to consult the officers of the Royal Works. He headed a memorandum 'I disire to bee informed of the officers of his M'ies Woorks, men of knowledge & experience what is iust and usual in these points following', yet every one of these is about how to couch contracts with workmen, calculations of cost, whether day-work is preferable to piece-work, and similar wholly practical matters that came naturally to a man whose job was as an administrator. He adds only one purely architectural note, and this almost as an aside: 'The rule for height of chimneys and under the mantletrees is this. Divide the widenes into 4 parts . . . three of them is the height but they use now to make them higher.'

Coke's failure to take full advantage of the architectural knowledge of Inigo Jones and his colleagues may have been a lost opportunity. He could, too, have approached the fountainheads of architectural knowledge in other ways since his brother Thomas, though by now dead, had been in the service of the Earl of Arundel and had evidently acquired a considerable knowledge of pictures and of the arts, while Sir John had earlier served Fulke Greville, who may himself have been a patron of Jones. But this very failure and Sir John's evident lack of interest in architecture makes his constant emphasis on regularity and symmetry the more significant: these were the absolute requirements of a builder who otherwise had little interest in building beyond the economic and practical.

It was probably very much the same level of awareness that prompted Sir John Chamberlain to describe Jones's Banqueting House as 'too faire and nothing sutable to the rest of the house'.[151] In Richard Brome's play *The Weeding of Covent Garden*, written in 1632 or 1633, a gentleman (a Justice of the Peace) is made to admire the Duke of Bedford's new buildings. He exclaims:

This is something like! These appear like Buildings! Here is Architecture expressed indeed! It is a most sightly scituation, and fit for Gentry and Nobility! . . . You cannot think how I am taken with that Rowe! How even and straight they are! And so are all indeed. . . . How [the surveyor] has wedded strength to beauty; state to uniformity; commodiousness with perspicacity! All, all as't should be![152]

By putting garbled Vitruvianisms into the observer's mouth, the satirist suggests how far the taste for architectural restraint and regularity – the taste which Sir John Coke had shown in his notes for the rebuilding of Melbourne – has travelled.

Sir John Bramston probably expressed a comparable degree of architectural concern when he recorded the impending collapse of Skreens, his house in Essex, and the measures taken by his son to repair it. Until then, the house had been entirely of timber: 'besides the underpinnings, chymnies and walls about the gardens, there was not any brick in my house, and not any stone but the kitchen and hall flues'. But it was clearly in a bad way.

30 (*left*) Yotes Court, Mereworth, Kent. The back of Yotes (possibly intended originally as the front) has an old-fashioned, gabled elevation dated 1656, and seems to have been built before its owner consulted a London master craftsman.

31 (*below*) Yotes Court. The front of Yotes is an up-to-date design dated 1658 and built after its owner had sought professional advice (for the plan of Yotes, see pl. 286 below).

A rome which is called the Low Parlour was in dainger of fallinge, and would indainger the dyning rome [presumably on the first floor] which also seemed to have slipt from the maine posts . . . [therefore his son] resolved to take down all that end from the stairs, and rebuild a handsome parlour where the old one was, of brick; and because that would not shew well, being brick alone, he tooke downe the wall of all the rest of the house next the garden, and made it of brick also. But the new building being higher roof'd than the old (as indeed it ought to be) some eye-sores there are; but [anyone] who considers the difficultie of joyning new and old worke will pardon some blunders.[153]

Sir John's summary account includes most of the reasons for rebuilding: to remedy a deteriorating fabric, to improve the accommodation and if possible the house's appearance. These comments do not show a very advanced degree of architectural understanding, but they do express an aesthetic that is in the first place a visual one. It is the entire building (or, in the case of the new street in London, a whole row of buildings) that shows the taste of its occupants or builders. By the end of the century Roger North would write that 'uniformity . . . is what all expect to find, and blame if not observed. . . . I add that the most knowing enjoys no more.'[154]

But other owners might show a deeper level of involvement. Yotes Court, at Mereworth in Kent (pls 30, 31, 286), was built by James Master between 1655 and 1658, soon after he had acquired the estate from his stepfather Sir Thomas Walsingham.[155] Master's diary, kept from 1646, records a succession of visits to the country and suburban houses of family and friends. Although these travels were by no means the systematic inspection of contemporary architecture that Sir Roger Townshend's of Raynham seem to have been, they took in several houses that he may have found instructive, notably Audley End (the home of his half-brother's sister-in-law) and Aldermaston, an advanced house of 1636 (discussed further in chapter 5). Brief entries in his diary suggest a serious attempt to learn something of architecture and building, though at the same time essentially amateur and perhaps at first ill-directed. In 1654 he spent a shilling on 'Sir Henry Wotton's Book of Architecture'; in August 1656 he took a Mr Vezy and a carpenter to survey Yotes, so that evidently something of the house already stood; in November he paid 'Goodman Hubble' for looking for brick earth; in March 1657 he paid Vezy for 'a plot for a house'. This may be Richard Vesey, carpenter, who had been involved in the Duke of Bedford's Covent Garden development (1630s), additions to Holland House (1638–40) and work at Northumberland House (1640s) under Edward Carter, who had been Inigo Jones's deputy at St Paul's and succeeded him as Surveyor of the King's Works.[156] If so, Master will have had the advice of a man with first-hand experience of some of the most up-to-date London buildings. In September 1656 he had bought '2 little books about measuring timber and land' and a year later, perhaps

defeated by them, he paid another local man, Goodman Browne, 2s 6d for teaching him how to measure timber. Twice, in 1656 and 1658, he bought a rule and compasses, presumably in order to try his own hand at drawing – as Sir Roger Townshend had done in 1619 when first considering the plan of Raynham.

His house was greatly altered in the eighteenth century, but there is evidence of a change of mind in the course of building, perhaps as a result of Vesey's intervention. The centre of the house is two ranges deep; wings project a short distance forward and backward on either side of the central range. The main, entrance front to the south has a hipped roof and rainwater heads dated 1658, but the north front is gabled and dated 1656, and details of the plan suggest that it may originally have been intended as the principal front. The house now has a central hall in the south range, but the arrangement of walls and of brick vaulting in the cellar strongly suggests that, as built, this was arranged on an old-fashioned service-passage plan (a plan type discussed on p. 78 below) with the hall entered at one end. Even as completed the house is thus a combination of old and modern elements – in this case a conservative plan with an up-to-date exterior. Although the precise degree of Master's personal involvement and knowledge cannot be known, his wish to take an active part in determining the form of his new house is clear. While few builders will have had Roger Townshend's wholehearted commitment to the most advanced architecture, the more amateurish involvement of James Master was probably not rare.

Exactly contemporary with Yotes is Lower Slaughter Manor in Gloucestershire (pl. 32), built in the 1650s by a local mason, Valentine Strong, for Richard Whitmore, whose family had owned the estate since 1611.[157] Though altered internally in the

32 Anon. (nineteenth century): Lower Slaughter Manor, Gloucestershire, c. 1655. Built by the local mason Valentine Strong for Richard Whitmore, whose interest in the appearance of the house is suggested by his wishing to approve Strong's 'moulds' – i.e. probably the drawings for ornament. The house still stands, but has been enlarged.

33 Lyndon Hall, Leicestershire. Built by its owner Sir Abel Barker, 1672–7, to a design made by himself with professional advice.

eighteenth century and extended in the late nineteenth, its original external appearance is largely preserved. In plan, Lower Slaughter is a near-square double pile (two ranges deep), and it has a hipped roof: a form of house whose origins, discussed in chapter 4, seem metropolitan. The contract for its building provides for Strong to build 'according to one moddell or platt forme by him lately received from the said Mr Whitmore, and according to such mouldes as hee hath given to the said Mr Whitmore concerning the same'. Responsibility for the design is now impossible to apportion. Strong's father had worked on

some up-to-date building in Oxford and elsewhere, and Valentine Strong seems already to have built an extension to Sherborne Park in Gloucestershire in a style similar to that of the building now proposed.[158] Nevertheless, the form of Lower Slaughter was unusual for the age and region, and Whitmore's personal interest in the design of the house is clear from the contract. He need not have designed the house himself – indeed he probably did not – but in providing Strong with a drawing (from whatever source) he ensured that his new house reflected contemporary architectural fashion; his apparently concerning himself with stonework detail before building began suggests the possession of some architectural knowledge.

A better documented example of a builder's personal involvement is that of Sir Abel Barker at Lyndon Hall, Leicestershire (pl. 33).[159] Sir Abel had bought the property in 1661 and between 1672 and 1677 was building a new house to replace an old one. In form the house is fashionable without being revolutionary: a square triple pile with the hipped roof, deep eaves, balustraded roof platform and roof lantern that were becoming the norm for late seventeenth-century gentry houses. No drawing survives, but an extremely detailed description in Sir Abel's own meticulous hand makes it clear that he must have made one. The beginning of the note reads: 'A house may be built in this manner, all sydes alike', which seems to imply that he devised the plan himself. In its exact external symmetry there are echoes of earlier pleasure in 'curious devices', as there is in the exact regularity of the chimney arrangements – '16 chymneys to come up square in 4 pyles, 4 in each pyle; each pyle 4ft. square 16ft. from other & 8ft. from railes & ballisters: lanthorne in middle'.[160] A page of miscellaneous stylistic and structural notes is headed 'Observations concerning Architecture taken out of Palladio, Gerbier and the Act for rebuilding the City of London' – a strange mixture, but all three were recent publications (if the Palladio is the English edition of 1663)[161] and probably reflect what was readily available at a London bookseller. A further list headed 'Haec varianda de Modello nuper fact. per Joh'em Sturges' consists of detailed changes recommended by John Sturges, a surveyor-architect who seems to have had a fairly wide contemporary practice in the east Midlands.[162] But the actual building of the house was entrusted not to Sturges but to a Stamford man, John Sutton, for whose design abilities there is no evidence: presumably with his own plan, what he had learnt from his books and with what he had gained from Sturges's advice, Barker felt able to give Sutton detailed guidance himself.

It is as a particularly knowledgeable member of the growing class of gentlemanly amateurs that one can see Roger North, whose writings, for the most part unpublished until 1981, are among the key sources for an understanding of late seventeenth-century architecture. North's interest in building was ancillary to his scientific interests acquired as a student at Cambridge, to his responsibilities as a country landowner, and to his legal practice: as a Bencher of the Inner Temple, his first experience of design was with the refitting of his own chambers in 1679, and in 1683–4 he designed his only complete work, the gateway leading from the Strand into the Middle Temple. In addition he produced a scheme for the modernisation of his brother's early seventeenth-century house at Wroxton in Oxfordshire and for the house that he bought at Rougham in Norfolk where he supervised the work himself and described in detail what he had done. The importance of his manuscripts for historians has perhaps led to an overestimate of his contemporary significance, and the degree of his involvement reflected the unusual extent of his knowledge among men of his class. But in his enthusiasm for building he is at one with Freeman of Yotes, Barker of Lyndon and probably many contemporaries who have left no record but who alongside the satisfaction of improving their estates must have derived some, at least, from the building process

itself. In apologising for setting down on paper the details of what he undertook at Rougham, North wrote:

Here is an account, like many given to the world, that concernes more the author's, than any else; and however insipid it may be to my posterity, who onely are like to be troubled with it, it hath a goust to me, even in the remembrance, and recapitulation of all the various doubdts and considerations I had, and the several felicitys as well as infelicitys in the execution.[163]

The architectural innovations of the seventeenth century may have compelled the craftsman to make a choice: either to acquire the greater knowledge and skills necessary to become a surveyor or architect, or else to abandon any aspirations to design houses of any pretension. At the very least, it was necessary for him to learn the appearance and the layout of the fashionable house. At the end of the century North could describe the alternatives as though such polarisation was already an established fact. On the one hand, one could consult 'a capitall surveyor [of whom he cited Jones, Pratt, Webb and Wren], which by the way is not known in every age'.[164] The disadvantages of such an expert were expense, remoteness, and the likelihood that he would pay too little attention to the builder's views and prefer his own. If instead you were to go to 'a head workman', then 'you must be content with diminutive low invention, aggreable to the spirit and education of a mechanical workman, and it shall neither credit nor please you'. The answer, said North, was if possible to acquire sufficient knowledge of architecture and building to take on the job oneself.

Ranking in importance with North's notebooks are those of Roger Pratt, which reveal him as the most knowledgeable of all gentry builders in the third quarter of the seventeenth century. Pratt, who was responsible for the design of four or five houses of the first importance, felt that there were better sources of design in foreign countries than in England. The would-be builder should therefore

get some ingenious gentleman who has seen much of that kind abroad and been somewhat versed in the best authors of Architecture: viz. Palladio, Scamozzi, Serlio etc. to do it for you, and to give you a design of it on paper, though but roughly drawn.[165]

Once a satisfactory sketch had been obtained one should then entrust its supervision to a home-grown professional. Pratt himself had been abroad and profited from his travels, but it is tempting to wonder whether in suggesting that the would-be builder should obtain a preliminary design from someone of experience he had in mind some memory of Inigo Jones. There is evidence for Jones's participation in some advisory capacity in the designs of Goldsmiths' Hall,[166] of Wilton, of Stoke Bruern and of Coleshill, built for Roger Pratt's cousin Sir George Pratt and in which the relative responsibilities of Roger Pratt and of

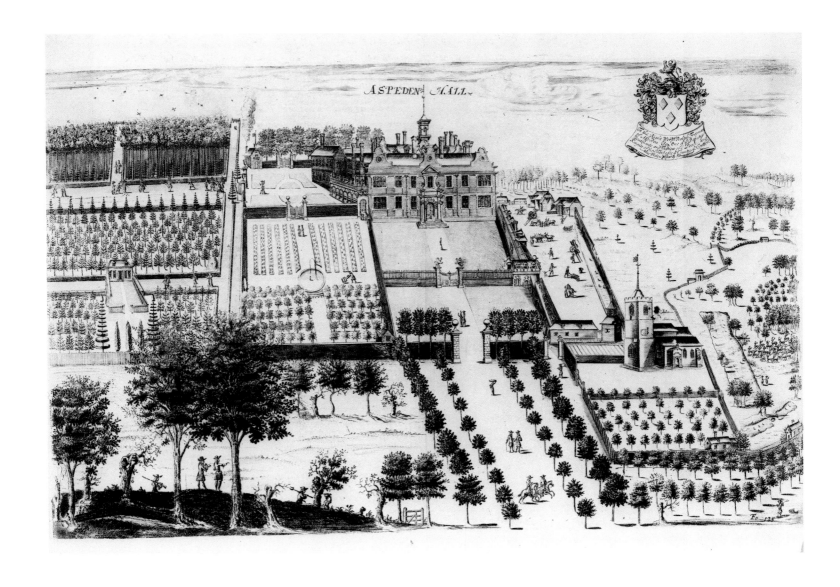

34 J. Drapentier: Aspeden House, Hertfordshire, c. 1650, engraved for Henry Chauncy, *Historical Antiquities of Hertfordshire* (1700). Built in the mid-seventeenth century by Ralph Freeman who according to Chauncy 'made his House neat, his Gardens pleasant, his Grove delicious, his Children cheerful, and his Servants easie . . . [and] had a general in sight in Architecture & Husbandrie'.

Jones have never been definitively established. In general Roger Pratt felt that the duties of an architect were not very different from those that Gabriel Moore seems to have performed at Chantemarle and Stone at Cornbury. He wrote:

> It is the part of a good architect not only to see his building truly laid out, and prosecuted by the Bricklayer, but also by the Carpenter, and daily to consider what trades are working there, what then in doing, and what worthy either of his observation or direction.[167]

It is clear that in combining the technical and professional knowledge shown in his notes with an ability in design, Pratt

possessed a combination of qualities that he did not expect to encounter widely elsewhere. Yet Wotton's concern in 1624, quoted above, to preserve his readers' distance from the artisan, contrasts strongly with Pratt's dismissal of Alberti as over-theoretical: 'rather contenting himself with showing the manner of things than giving himself the trouble of putting from antiquity any certain measures to them'.[168] If Jones had demonstrated the necessary connection of practice and theory, the pragmatic Pratt went a step further: against John Dee a century earlier, for whom theory took precedence over practice, Pratt effectively reversed the position. In stressing the importance of actual examples, of looking at buildings rather than theoretical constructs, Pratt rejected the fanciful 'curiosities' of two generations before.

Neither Pratt nor, later, North were objective observers of the status of the professional architect. Pratt's knowledge of architecture in the third quarter of the seventeenth century was without precedent among men of his social background, while North, though probably seeing himself as an amateur, evidently considered that he knew enough to be able to dispense with the services of a professional. However, both men represented no more than exceptional instances of the general advance in architectural awareness among their peers for which Master at Yotes and Barker at Lyndon are evidence. These men foreshadowed the emergence in the late seventeenth century of a significant group of architects – the most proficient of their day – who by virtue of their genteel background were similarly without any formal training in the building crafts but who had been drawn to architecture by their scientific curiosity or by their natural inclination and were able to indulge their aptitude through their connections. Besides Pratt and North, this group of gentleman architects included Robert Hooke, Hugh May, William Samwell and Christopher Wren. Wren and Hooke were scientists first (Wren an astronomer and Hooke a mathematician) and both were members of the gentry as the sons of clergymen. Samwell, like North, trained as a lawyer, May had been in royal service during the interregnum and both were sons of gentlemen. No generalisation about the class's knowledge of architecture is possible: individual awareness was too diverse. But the fact that gentlemen with education were engaged to provide finished schemes for the houses of their peers is the best indication that architecture had ceased to be merely a private 'exercise of the wits' to be indulged in when they had nothing better to do.

In 1700 Henry Chauncy published his *Historical Antiquities of Hertfordshire*, with rather crude engravings of the seats of many of the country gentry and with thumbnail biographies of leading men of the recent past. Ralph Freeman had built a house at Aspeden in the middle years of the century. From Chauncy's print it was evidently not particularly advanced: an outward-facing courtyard house (perhaps an old house remodelled) with shaped gables of the type of Swakeleys and Broome Park (see p. 180). But Freeman, a Justice of the Peace before the Civil War who retired from public life during and after it, was evidently a model of all that a gentleman should be. Chauncy wrote:

> He had a general knowledge of the Affairs of the Country. . . . He made his House neat, his Gardens pleasant, his Grove delicous, his Children cheerful, his Servants easie and kept excellent Order in his Family: He had a general in sight in Architecture & Husbandry, was very kind to his Relations, charitable to the Poor, and compassionate to the Afflicted.[169]

Freeman's architectural insight is bracketed with domestic virtue, estate management, charity and public service. While Aspeden's appearance suggests that this understanding was not particularly deep, the stigma of the artisan that once deterred such men from professing an acquaintance with building has vanished. The interest in architecture that had been shared by a coterie of humanists had now become part of the gentleman's approved sphere of knowledge and almost a commonplace.

Part II

BUILDINGS

facing page   Cold Overton Hall, Leicstershire.
Built around 1640 to an up-to-date, compact plan.
The pediment was altered in the nineteenth century;
the original form is shown in pl. 263.

3

Forms and Meanings, 1480–1600

Hierarchy

The plan and the appearance of the late medieval gentry house reflected its origins as well as expressing the social structure of the family and community that it was built to accommodate. In the early Middle Ages large houses had generally comprised groups of free-standing structures, with at their heart a hall open to the roof and a separate (but closely adjacent) building comprising a first-floor chamber raised over a basement which served both for security and for storage. Other accommodation – kitchen, chapel, additional lodgings – was in detached buildings nearby.[1] Such assemblages are known from archaeology and from their fragmentary survival, and the attainment of a satisfactory collective term to express the idea of a dwelling that united all its parts seems to have lagged behind its actual attainment. Fourteenth- and fifteenth-century descriptions of houses often refer not to a house as such but provide instead a list of its components. A Somerset knight, Sir Richard Cokke, in his will of 1483 referred to 'The hall parlur Chambers Chapell Kechin and other houses of my maner of Assheton';[2] for him a house was evidently a unit of accommodation rather than the totality that was by then required adequately to house a man of standing. The concept of the dwelling as the sum of its parts continued to be reflected in the use of other terms such as 'manor place' to describe the house of the great man.

However, long before the end of the Middle Ages the gradual coalescence of separate elements had produced buildings that were integrated complexes of hall, of living and sleeping chambers for the family and for guests, accommodation for services and servants, cellarage and perhaps a chapel.[3] The way in which these elements were gradually assembled had been determined by convenience and by a sense of what was proper, and by the fifteenth century the plan of the gentry house was already largely determined by precedent. The essential characteristic of the late medieval house, and one which it would retain throughout the

sixteenth century despite the elaborations of plans, the multiplication of rooms and increasing architectural uniformity, is that its layout is hierarchical. The house provided for a broad gradation of accommodation, from polite, entertaining rooms, through rooms for the family to those for servants and services, with at the centre a hall which was common both to the upper – the superior – and to the lower ends of the building. Though as a common room the hall mediated between the components of the household, it also formed a physical barrier between the ends of the house, preserving their separateness. But despite the central position of the hall, the plan itself was additive rather than strictly linear, echoing the house's accretive origins: rooms that were reached directly or indirectly radiated from the hall, and accommodation might extend into a wing or flank an inner or outer courtyard. The layout of the hall was itself hierarchical, in that its entrance was at one end and its upper and lower ends were clearly and publicly distinguished, inside and out.

At the same time as the almost universal high-end/low-end division of the house and household, there was another division that also combined status and location and which was equally persistent: that between upstairs and downstairs. From the late Middle Ages at least until the end of the seventeenth century all the most important rooms of the upper-class house apart from the hall were on the first floor. This arrangement, whose origins may have been in security and hygiene, continued as prestige. The essential principle of these divisions was universal. The upstairs/downstairs and the high-end/low-end divisions combined to form a layout in which the importance of each room was determined by its location in the house, and which ensured that everyone could be entertained or lodged appropriately to his or her rank.

A survey of the manor of Keevil in Wiltshire in 1387 includes a description of the manor house from which it is fairly easy to picture its general plan. This runs:

There is a hall, a capital chamber and a small chamber adjoining with a privy at the back of the high seat of the hall [i.e. at the superior end], roofed with tiles; a chamber under the said great chamber with a second chamber as a privy adjoining; a chapel and a cellar under it; a chamber called 'le Wardrobe', a large ['magna'] chamber at the end of the hall by the entry thereof [i.e. at the inferior end] with a privy and underneath the chamber a pantry and a buttery; a great kitchen newly repaired of late; a long building called 'Knighten chamber' [probably detached lodgings for superior retainers]; a bakehouse and a chamber for yeomen, a chamber above the gate with a privy entirely roofed with tiles; a long stable, a small stable and a barn to some extent new, roofed all over with straw.[4]

The house was arranged in a way that was already standard and would remain so for another two hundred years and more. The hall is at the centre, entered at one end next to the buttery and pantry and with the kitchen beyond; over these service rooms at the low end of the house is a good bedchamber. The best chamber and the chapel are at the high end of the hall, on the first floor, with rooms of lesser importance underneath. Two things stand out in this account of what seems to have been a very typical late medieval manor house. One is the polarisation of functions at opposite ends of the hall. The other is the small number of rooms and the simplicity of the accommodation. Save for the hall and the service rooms, there would have been beds in each chamber; bedchambers would have been shared with personal servants and beds with siblings. There is no parlour or other day-room named as such; the functions of chambers were essentially generalised, doubling as sitting rooms and as rooms for the entertainment of guests. There is a variety of outbuildings, some of which also provide servants' lodgings. How these outbuildings were arranged at Keevil is impossible to say, although the gatehouse (evidently a substantial structure with lodgings on the first floor) implies some sort of a forecourt around which these outbuildings may have been arranged.

While the accommodation at the heart of the house was essentially simple, the household requirements of a man of high rank called for a quantity of subordinate buildings. Shute House at Axminster in Devon is now a small fragment of a great house of medieval origin, but an unusually comprehensive survey taken in 1559 describes its layout in considerable detail and makes it possible to reconstruct its layout (pl. 35).[5] There was an outer courtyard around which were gatehouse, barn, stables and inferior servants' lodgings. An inner gatehouse, next to which were brewhouse, bakehouse and granary, led to an inner court flanked by lodgings for upper servants and by the hall, which had at one end the parlour and two wine cellars with good chambers above them, and at the other the buttery and pantry, together with a suite of rooms for the auditor who kept estate and household accounts. Beyond these lay the kitchen courtyard, which besides larders and a large kitchen with three fireplaces also included

three chambers for cooks and another for the clerk of the kitchen. Behind the hall was another little courtyard and an enclosed garden overlooked by rooms for family and guests and by a range of lodgings that had formerly been the nursery. Circulation was by walking through the hall, by crossing courtyards or by climbing stairs. The house can still be seen as a set of accommodation units, largely (but by no means wholly) assembled under common roofs.

Although the house was large, what emerges from the survey is an impression of simplicity: of rooms which though big (the hall was 54 by 25 feet; the wine cellars together 60 by 20 feet) and presumably intended to accommodate a sizeable establishment, are few in number and have a very direct, functional relationship to each other. The secondary buildings at Shute were largely of cob and timber, and virtually all surviving fifteenth- and sixteenth-century houses of any size have similarly lost most of the outbuildings that once were necessary to the functioning of the household. Even at such a house as Cotehele in Cornwall (pl. 36), which exceptionally retains an outer, an inner and a service courtyard, the original functions of many of these buildings are impossible to discover. The hierarchical layout even of the secondary buildings is clear at Shute, graded from outer courtyard to inner and with a private garden for the family's own use, but so too is its accretive character, with functions served by buildings that stood wherever it was both thought proper and found convenient to place them.

It would be misleading to say that principles of architectural composition did not exist in the Middle Ages, but of importance equal to an aesthetic of abstraction was a sense of fitness: from a perception of conformity between the object and its purpose. Over and above functional need, the design of secular buildings was largely determined by the proper display of dignity and status, and the form of the late medieval house distinguished externally between the relative importance of each of its elements. This might be done in a number of ways: by their relative size or prominence, their degree of decoration or by the visible extravagance of their construction. The result was a house whose layout could be read from the outside. Such external marks of distinction paralleled other forms of aristocratic display and a personal honour code that flourished in the relative absence in the late Middle Ages of strong central government.

Between 1500 and 1700 the outward appearance of the gentry house would change totally. The considerations that determined the design of the house evolved from hierarchical to architectural, from expressing an aesthetic of propriety to one of form, as the house evolved from one whose different parts announced their relative importance to one in which the entire building proclaimed the taste and standing of its owner. In the course of the sixteenth century this change affected the house's appearance in four closely connected ways: in the spread of innovative decorative styles; in the advance of symmetry, in a change in the house's aspect from inward-looking to outward-facing; and

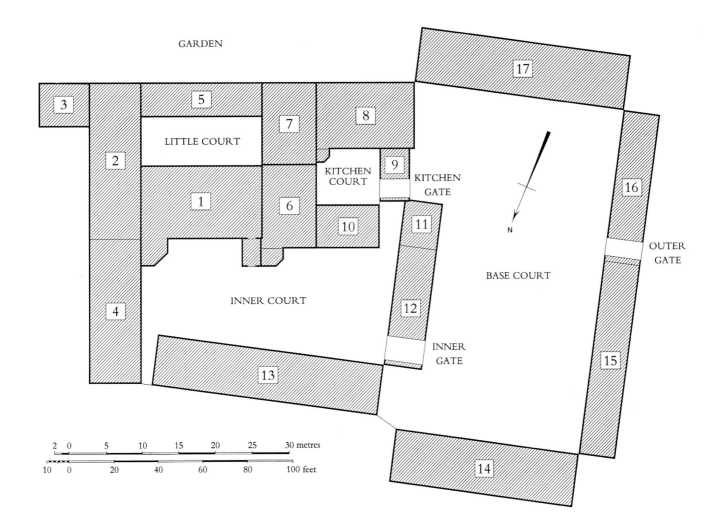

GARDEN

3

5

7

8

17

LITTLE COURT

2

KITCHEN
COURT

9

KITCHEN
GATE

16

1

6

11

10

N

BASE COURT

4

12

INNER COURT

OUTER
GATE

INNER
GATE

15

13

14

2 0   5   10   15   20   25   30 metres

10   0   20   40   60   80   100 feet

35   Shute House, Axminster, Devon. The house was built *c.* 1460 and enlarged *c.* 1510, and though most of the building has since been demolished, the information in a written survey of 1559 makes it possible to reconstruct in some detail a schematic layout of this representative aristocratic house at that date.

1   Hall, with a small chamber over the porch reached by a stair at the southern end of 6

2   Ground floor: wine cellar in two parts
    First floor: 'old' great chamber; small chamber for a 'gentleman'; door to churchyard (on the east)
    Stair at the junction of 2 and 4, and serving both

3   Tower, 48 feet high, on three floors, each with a 'fair' or 'handsome' chamber and garderobe

4   Ground floor: great parlour (*c.* 1510); garderobe at north end
    First floor: 'new' great chamber, bedchamber, two servants' rooms and a garderobe

5   'Garden lodgings'. Ground floor: three chambers, formerly the nursery
    First floor: three chambers; two garderobes

6   Ground floor: pantry and buttery
    First floor: 'auditor's chamber'

7   Ground floor: pastry (i.e. superior bakehouse); wet and dry larders
    First floor: inner bedchamber for auditor; servant's chamber; garderobe

8   Ground floor: kitchen
    First floor: three cooks' chambers (originally built *c.* 1450 as a single chamber)

9   Ground floor: kitchen gate
    First floor: clerk to the kitchen's chamber

10 Ground floor: bakehouse
    First floor: granary

11 Ground floor: brewhouse
    First floor: malthouse

12 Ground floor: gatehouse and porter's lodge
    First floor: four servants' chambers

13 Ground floor: two chambers 'for servants of the best sort'; 'wardrobe for beds etc.'
    First floor: two servants' chambers

14 Ground floor: two 'fair' stables; one 'lesser' stable
    First floor: three servants' chambers

15 Two 'extraordinary' (i.e. supplementary) stables

16 Ground floor: gatehouse and porter's lodge
    First floor: two servants' chambers

17 Great barn.

36 Cotehele, Cornwall. A late medieval house whose buildings typically face into a series of courtyards: forecourt or base court (top), inner court (centre, entered through a gatehouse), chapel court (a service court, right of the inner court). The hall is in the inner court, opposite the gatehouse; the tower was built *c*. 1620 to provide superior private accommodation for the house's owner.

in evolving from a building whose internal organisation was evident on the outside to one whose exterior provided no information about what happened within.

Most late medieval houses of any importance were originally approached by way of a gatehouse, a structure suggestive of authority even though by this time its defensive function was generally negligible and there might be other entrances for general use. Some of the greatest houses possessed two gatehouses, one into an outer forecourt or base court and a grander gatehouse that led into the inner courtyard in front of the main body of the house. The elaboration of the gatehouse reinforced the hierarchical layout by stressing the progressive nature of the approach to the house, with some people admitted to it and received according to rank while others progressed no further than the gates. The house made its principal display towards the courtyard, and though elements might be recognised at a greater distance – notably, in grander houses, a substantial block of superior lodgings, and sometimes the chapel which serviced the entire community – typically the exterior of the house comprised an irregular, uninformative display of chimneystacks and minor window openings. Equally uninformative was the range of buildings flanking the gatehouse in which any difference in function was suppressed (pl. 37). While the other outer faces of the house were largely functional, in many great houses the gatehouse range was wholly symmetrical, the only symmetrical element of the entire assembly.

Oxburgh, Norfolk. Typical of late medieval great houses, the gate-house proclaims the power of the house's owner, but the symmetrical range flanking it – the only symmetrical elements in the entire house – otherwise display nothing of the internal arrangements.

Along with other forms of hierarchical display, tower gate-houses increased in popularity and in prominence in the late fifteenth century and the early sixteenth. Such gatehouses evoked the dignity of castles and their occupants, without the need for the house itself to be strongly defensive with concomitant discomfort for those who lived in them. Many late gatehouses such as those at Tixall, Shute (built after 1559) (pl. 42),[6] Lanhydrock or Coughton Court, have great windows that transform them from defensive structures into statements about wealth and sophistication: far from protecting their owner's dwellings, any of these buildings would have been wrecked by

a handful of stones. Others, such as Layer Marney or Oxburgh (pl. 37), rise to a great height. At the same time, while the very vulnerability of these gatehouses emphasises their purely symbolic function, they continue to express the inwardness of the house: a building whose household was self-sufficient, interdependent and self-contained.

A courtyard was an extremely convenient way of organising the house's accommodation. Even when (by the fifteenth century, in most places save in the north) defence was no longer a major consideration, there were still advantages in securing an internal service court or an approach to the main body of the house from which those with no business could be excluded. A larger amount of accommodation could be included without stretching out a linear plan to inconvenient lengths, and a courtyard could act as a circulation area in which it was possible with relative ease to go from one part of the house to another without passing through intermediate rooms. Services could be segre-

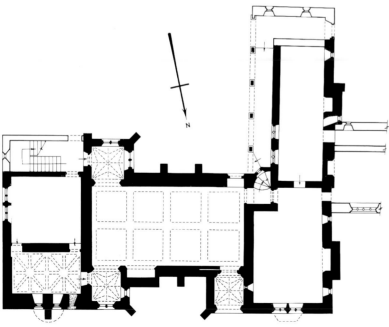

38 (*above*) Great Chalfield Manor, Wiltshire, *c.* 1480. Within a superficial, overall symmetry, external ornament as well as the form of the house differentiates between the functions and the importance of its various parts. However this display was made towards the forecourt into which the house formerly faced, with the church on the left and the gatehouse – through which the house was approached obliquely – on the right.

39 (*left*) Great Chalfield: ground-floor plan. The hall has two high-end oriels, one to light the dais and the other to give access to a parlour and to the stair (rebuilt in the twentieth century) leading to the chamber above it. There was formerly a service court to the rear (south), with an open-sided passage leading down the side of the rear wing from the screens passage to the (demolished) kitchen.

gated but still brought within an overall envelope, while for as long as architectural uniformity was not a desideratum any part of the sequence of structures around a courtyard could be replaced or rebuilt without disturbing the remainder.

Great Chalfield Manor in Wiltshire demonstrates clearly the way in which display towards the courtyard reflected internal hierarchies (pls 38, 39).[7] Great Chalfield was built around 1475 for Thomas Tropenell, a man of relatively obscure gentry origins but who made a great deal of money in the cloth industry: a clothier. The partial destruction of the front enclosure has opened up the main body of the house to view in a way in which it would not have been visible originally. Part of a moat survives, but the perimeter wall between moat and courtyard has been destroyed. A gatehouse remains, attached to a long range

40   East Barsham Manor, Norfolk, c. 1520–25: the façade. The importance of the house's different parts is displayed (towards a narrow courtyard) by their size and ornament, with its owner's lodging tower both the largest and the most highly decorated. The use of terracotta makes possible the mass-production of decorative detail to differentiate the various parts of the house. The roof was originally steeply pitched.

41 (following page)   East Barsham Manor: the gatehouse. An impressive display of the royal arms publicly announces its owner's commitment to the Tudor state. The closeness of the gatehouse to the façade is characteristic of a number of contemporary Norfolk houses.

42 (page 63)   Shute: the gatehouse, c. 1565. By the time gatehouses went out of fashion, they had wholly ceased to be defensive. The new gatehouse at Shute displays wealth, not strength. It was aligned symmetrically on the hall (note that it does not appear in pl. 35).

of building that flanks the forecourt on the west side and which probably originally contained stabling. There may have been a further range on the east side to provide lodgings for retainers, though the intimate association of house and church (which Tropenell largely rebuilt) and the probable need to pass through the house's forecourt in order to reach it neatly demonstrates the community of secular and religious authority. There was originally a second courtyard to the rear with service accommodation giving on to it and with a passage running down its side that served to bring food from the kitchen and bakehouse to the rear door of the hall.

The hall is at the centre of the house, entered through a porch which is a prominent invitation to those with claims on the owner's hospitality. This is lit by a tall window and by a second one in a small bay projection – an oriel – that provided a measure of privacy for those who were engaged at the room's superior end. The hall's height and its large window declares its continuing importance, but the finer windows of other rooms express the greater social importance of their occupants. On the ground floor are a parlour and cellar at the high end, beneath the best chamber (an arrangement similar to that of Shute but smaller in size); at the low end is a second parlour and a room that probably served as a buttery, with a second chamber of high status above it and another chamber beyond. The windows express the importance of both principal chambers, but that at the high end is the finer; this may have been Tropenell's own, but it will also have provided accommodation for distinguished guests (the question of where owners and guests may have slept is discussed in chapters 7 and 8). The fundamental, tripartite symmetry of Great Chalfield's façade, created by the centrality of the hall between the high-end and low-end wings, gives unity to a composition whose details clearly distinguish its elements. The hall porch does not match the oriel bay, and the difference between the bay windows to the high- and low-end chambers makes it clear which is the more important room.

East Barsham Manor in Norfolk shows the principle of hierarchic display particularly well (pl. 40).[8] The building was partly ruinous by the late eighteenth century and was heavily repaired in the twentieth, but although many details of its plan are lost the location of important rooms is clear. East Barsham was mainly built between 1525 and 1530 (though begun earlier) and already incorporates certain features that were to be more characteristic of later houses, but in the way in which the façade is composed it is a notable example of principles of composition that were already becoming old-fashioned. The house is fronted by a gatehouse (pl. 41), standing unusually close to the house itself but in its prominence typical of its period. Besides its size and the profusion of its terracotta decoration, the chief ornament of the gatehouse is a huge royal arms. This, rather than the arms of its owner Sir John Fermor (which appear on the front of the house itself), was probably not placed in any anticipation of a royal visit: Henry VIII seldom travelled so far afield, and increasingly preferred to stay in one of his own innumer-

able houses. The royal arms at East Barsham proclaimed the dignity of the house's owner. In the course of the sixteenth century such statements about identity and loyalties would increasingly be confined to the interior of the house, but at this date these coats of arms continue to make an explicit public statement about how he saw his relations with the world.

The most obvious things about East Barsham's principal front are its irregularity and the lavishness of its terracotta ornament. The terracotta ornament, which is applied solely to the gatehouse and to the main façade (it stops abruptly 6 feet along the side of the service block on the right-hand side), was a short-lived fashion of the 1520s, but one with the highest recommendations. Wolsey employed terracotta in his work at Hampton Court before he surrendered it to the king;[9] Charles Brandon, the king's brother-in-law, employed it at his houses in London and at Westhorpe in Suffolk;[10] Lord Marney, recipient of a number of lucrative grants from the king, employed it at Layer Marney; and Sir Richard Weston, who moved in the innermost court circles, used it at Sutton Place in Surrey. Terracotta occurs on a number of contemporary, gentry houses in Norfolk, for example at West Stow, Great Cressingham and Denver Hall. In these as at East Barsham there are few traces of the Renaissance detail that occurs in houses in the London region, but Fermor was making use of the most fashionable and showy of contemporary decorative materials and one which by the ease of its manufacture could be used with appropriate extravagance on each of the most important parts of the house.

The irregularity of the principal façade results from the need to distinguish each of these parts (pl. 43). The hall is precocious in being of a single storey only and its windows (save for the oriel bay) are therefore less prominent than those of a tall hall would be, but its location is made clear by that of the porch while the bays of the service rooms immediately to the right of the porch not only have smaller windows and less lavish decoration, but ceiling heights are lower. The upper end of the hall is marked by an oriel projection, beyond which is a parlour with a chamber above it – rooms of a status comparable with that of the hall. But the most prominent element of all is a three-storey tower which almost certainly provided lodging for Sir John Fermor himself. This is located at the lower end of the hall and close to the kitchens, but from its scale and external ornament there is no mistaking its importance. Internally, the house retains few original features, but the tower has elaborate brick-vaulted chambers on ground and first floors.

The tower at East Barsham is in a tradition that extends back to the early fifteenth century, of grand residential towers either for the house's owner or for the reception of guests.[11] Their origins lie partly in the residential gatehouses of English castles of the fourteenth century, and partly in the continental practice of placing the principal accommodation of the house in such a great residential block – a *corps-de-logis*. However introduced, they may have been popularised by Lord Cromwell in his great houses of Tattershall and South Wingfield in the 1450s.

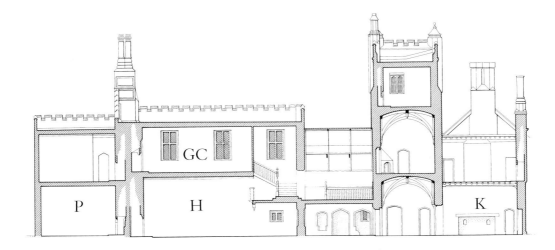

43 East Barsham Manor (section). East Barsham was built with a single-storey hall, with a great chamber (the principal entertaining room of the house) above it. There has been much alteration to the centre of the house, but the overall form remains clear.

They are sometimes at the high end of the house (as at Buckden and Gainsborough, sometimes at the low end (Tattershall and Farnham), are sometimes closely integrated with the body of the house (Faulkbourne and Broughton) and sometimes located more remotely (Minster Lovell and South Wingfield). The largest of all were effectively detached, as at Raglan, Ashby de la Zouche, Richmond and Warwick; in the last two cases the tower lodgings were built or begun for the monarch himself. The form persists through the sixteenth century – there are a number of examples in Northamptonshire: Canons Ashby (pl. 44), Deene, Dingley – and even into the early seventeenth at Cotehele in Cornwall (pl. 36). Sometimes, as at Compton Winyates in Warwickshire (pl. 45), the appearance of the tower apartments is that of a block of building of greater bulk rather than of a structure that actually evokes defence, but whether by its tower-like form or by its greater mass, attention is still drawn to the most important lodgings in the house.

Whether for the use of the house's owner or for his guests, these towers are the means of ensuring that their occupant is seen to be honourably housed. Although these great residential towers of the late fifteenth century sometimes have gun-loops, they would have been quite unable to withstand any serious attack. They were rather the architectural equivalent of these men's bands of liveried retainers: the semblance of castles as the retainers were the semblance of private armies, but in fact intended to overawe rather than to do battle. The system of retaining – of making legal agreements with men who in return for payment or land would thereafter attend at need upon the great – has been called bastard feudalism; fifteenth-century castle-like houses had a similar relationship to the genuine castles of earlier centuries. Interiors were decorated with appropriate

distinction: the chimneypieces in the three superimposed tower rooms of Tattershall are among the finest of the period; the brick vaulting in the tower of East Barsham is structurally unnecessary; and an inventory taken in 1506 of the goods of Sir Robert Brewton of Denston in Suffolk[12] values the contents of the 'Tower Chamber' as the best in the house, higher than those of parlour or great chamber which were in general the most lavishly furnished rooms in the houses of the upper classes. The tower chambers at Shute were also described as 'fair' and 'handsome' in 1559.

Athough Chalfield and East Barsham now face outwards and are easily comprehended, they were less so originally when their courtyard enclosures were intact. Furthermore, the gatehouse at Chalfield is at right angles to the façade; that at East Barsham is very close to it, and entering through either of them one would not take in the full extent of their façades at one glance. In both cases, hierarchy is displayed piecemeal towards the courtyard rather than immediately towards the world. Two other well-known houses, Ightham Moat in Kent (pls 46, 47) and Little Moreton in Cheshire (pl. 26), wholly surround courtyards and look entirely into them; except for their gatehouses they present little information externally. The earliest surviving evidence at Ightham Moat is for a house of the early fourteenth century, with a large open hall to which are attached at the high end, in an apparently haphazard way, two chamber blocks and a chapel.[13] Of services of that period nothing remains, though they must have been accommodated elsewhere on the tight, rectangular, moated site. Very little of the fourteenth-century exterior survives behind later additions and refacing, but there is nothing to indicate that the major apartments were originally distinguished by anything more than their greater size. Over the next two centuries the building evolved by additions and replacements, with more rooms and with rooms of more specialised function, until the entire moated area was surrounded by ranges of building that looked into the courtyard. But towards the courtyard the status of rooms came to be marked as it is elsewhere. The early chambers remained in use as the best in the house,

46 (*above*)   Ightham Moat, Kent. An accretive house of *c.* 1320–1600, the development of which was determined by its medieval, moated site.

44 (*facing page top*)   Canons Ashby, Northamptonshire. A house of conventional form, given a lodging tower *c.* 1550–70. There are a number of such sixteenth-century towers in Northamptonshire, though by this time they were going out of fashion in favour of houses that made a more general statement about their owner's standing and culture.

45 (*facing page bottom*)   Compton Winyates, Warwickshire, early sixteenth century. The house faces into a courtyard; externally, it presents an irregular series of windows and chimneys. The large window lights the chapel, but otherwise the importance of its various parts is shown by little more than their greater mass.

47 Ightham Moat: the courtyard. Hall to right (formerly entered through a porch), principal chambers to left. These, built in the late fourteenth century, had their external appearance enhanced in the sixteenth century with ornamental timber gables. Further to the left is the start of an open loggia leading to rooms in the gatehouse range, with a gallery of *c.* 1525 above it.

but in the sixteenth century the only one with a wall to the courtyard was enhanced with an ornamental, timber-framed gable (pl. 47).

Other changes in the course of the sixteenth century were typical of those required to meet the needs of fashionable living. A tall gatehouse was built above an entrance that had probably formerly been less ostentatious; a great chamber for the entertainment of guests was formed out of a flanking range that had probably earlier provided lodgings for retainers. A gallery (partly prefabricated from the remains of some temporary,

decorated pavilion) and an open loggia were built to link this front range with the body of the house on the other side of the courtyard; good chambers were added at the low end (the only space remaining) to supplement those at the high end; and the medieval chapel was converted into further bedchambers. At Ightham almost all accommodation of any distinction (save for the hall) is on the upper floors: except for two parlours the ground-floor rooms seem to have housed services and servants' lodgings, storage and perhaps in part little more than dead space in order to create sufficient floor area in the storey above. Save for the central position of the gatehouse, formal symmetry is precluded by the way in which the building developed, and the plan of Ightham Moat is dense and complex as a result of these successive additions. But its layout remains essentially sequential in its gradations from rooms of high status to those of low.

Despite its distance from Ightham Moat and the difference in its materials, Little Moreton illustrates many of the same principles of aspect and display (pls 26, 48, 49). The extravagant timber

48   Little Moreton Hall, Cheshire: the east side. Little Moreton is conservative, built in several stages from *c.* 1400 to *c.* 1560, but the later work perpetuates both the styles of its building and the way in which its parts are distinguished. The principal display (pl. 26) is into the courtyard, and apart from a towering gatehouse and the window of the chapel (left) the exterior is irregular and shows nothing of the status of its owner or of the parts of the house itself.

framing that embellishes every phase of the house except for the earliest is an advertisement of the wealth of the Moreton family. (The Moretons' jealousy for their reputation, characteristic of contemporary concern with status, was shown in a lawsuit they fought with a family of neighbouring gentry in 1513 about their precedence in seating and in processions in church.) The house stands within a moat, on a rectangular island of about an acre. It occupies only a small proportion of the site; the date of the

moat is not known, and the early history of the building may be of concentrating into one structure functions that were formerly more widely dispersed. At Great Chalfield there was both a forecourt and a service courtyard to the rear. At Little Moreton as at Ightham one enclosure serves both functions, and the body of the house faces into it (pl. 49).

The house is now of many periods from the early fifteenth century to the late sixteenth, though given superficial unity by its decorative framing. The oldest part of the house is the hall and a high-end cross wing; towards the end of the century a new low-end wing was built, providing services but including a new great chamber; in the early sixteenth the high-end wing was extended; in the middle of the century the hall was floored, the parlour remodelled and both provided with huge bay windows, while later still a new front range was built with a spectacular timber gatehouse surmounted by a long gallery and probably a suite of guest accommodation, and the north façade

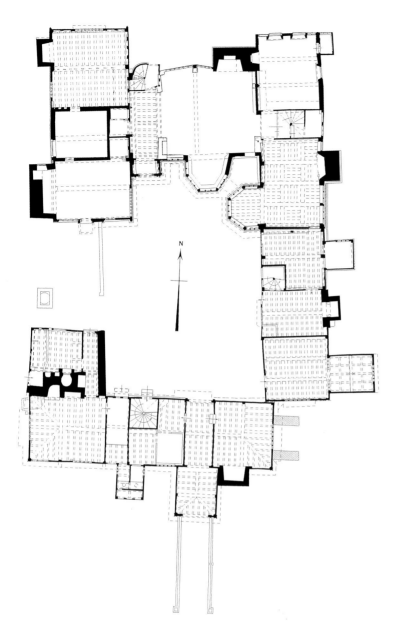

(pl. 312). The outer faces of the house consist mostly of an irregular succession of chimneybreasts, garderobe bays and unimpressive windows which except for the chapel provide no information about what happens within (pl. 48).

Great Chalfield and East Barsham demonstrate similar principles of display in houses with straight façades, but of different materials and from different parts of England. Ightham and Little Moreton similarly illustrate common principles in courtyard houses that otherwise contrast strongly with each other. All four show how the exterior of the late fifteenth- and early sixteenth-century house made a visual equation between house and household, and between status, function and order. These were public statements, probably more comprehensible to contemporaries than they are today. Yet despite the variety in the forms of these houses, it is unlikely that contemporaries would have been conscious of any fundamental difference between them that transcended that between their materials – stone, brick or timber – and this probable failure to recognise such formal distinctions may be a part of the reason for the diversity in the plans of the houses of the upper classes in the early sixteenth century.

To compare houses of the period on a purely formal basis is to present a picture of chaos: beyond the hierarchical principles of planning that have been described, and the general occurrence of courtyards in the larger house, there often seems no objective reason why the plan of a house should be arranged as it is. Within broad conventions and traditions, there was considerable licence for variation. The site itself, family circumstances and private whim, local practices, the emulation of preferred models and the adaptation of existing fabrics all played a part. Of at least equal importance, the uneven rise in standards of comfort and refinement among the gentry class created a demand for the improvement of amenities and for the incorporation of new facilities into the plan for which there was no existing precedent: any such departure required a degree of improvisation. Yet despite formal differences there is a general similarity between all of these houses in the overall principles of planning and display and in the scale and range of the accommodation they provide.

Two further houses may illustrate this functional similarity, their formal diversity the more striking in that they are functionally very similar, geographically very close to each other and similar in date and social class. These are Gurney Street Manor[14] and Blackmore Farm[15] at Cannington in Somerset. The plan of Blackmore Farm is roughly linear, with asymmetrical wings at either end that bring rooms into prominence or the reverse (pls 50, 51). At Gurney Street Manor there is a small internal court-

remodelled. In this complex evolution Little Moreton is typical, but the principles governing its growth are consistent: a steady multiplication of chambers (discussed further in chapter 8) with an evolving attitude to external display.

The mid-sixteenth-century modernisation of the main body of the house is easily dated by the inscriptions on the massive oriel that were added to hall and parlour, rising through two storeys and making an extraordinary display for which William Moreton explicitly claimed the credit: 'This windous Whire made by William Moreton.' Yet they look out on nothing save the courtyard: they neither command a view nor can they be seen from any distance; apart from providing the hall and parlour with convenient extra space, their principal function must have been to show off his wealth to immediate visitors. Their redundancy is particularly clear on the first floor, where that over the hall window lights nothing except a small chamber behind it

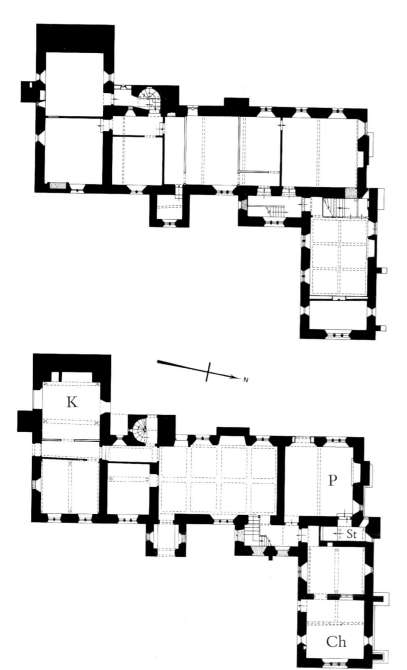

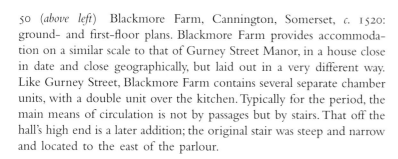

50 (*above left*) Blackmore Farm, Cannington, Somerset, *c.* 1520: ground- and first-floor plans. Blackmore Farm provides accommodation on a similar scale to that of Gurney Street Manor, in a house close in date and close geographically, but laid out in a very different way. Like Gurney Street, Blackmore Farm contains several separate chamber units, with a double unit over the kitchen. Typically for the period, the main means of circulation is not by passages but by stairs. That off the hall's high end is a later addition; the original stair was steep and narrow and located to the east of the parlour.

51 (*above right*) Blackmore Farm from the north-east. The house is built to give the greatest prominence to the wing that contained the chapel and probably the builder's own chamber.

yard behind the hall with some sort of a barn occupying part of one side, and the principal rooms are given a greater height (pls 52, 53). Gurney Street originally had an open hall; at Blackmore Farm the hall was always floored with a chamber over it. Both houses, except for the later flooring-in of the originally open hall at Gurney Street, probably reached substantially their present form around 1520. Each house has a chapel. That at Gurney Street is small, little more than an oratory, and incapable of holding more than two or three people besides the officiant. At Blackmore Farm (which is further from the parish church) it is rather larger, with an ante-chapel with its own external door.

There was formerly some kind of enclosed forecourt at Gurney Street and presumably one at Blackmore Farm, but few traces now remain of either. The surviving rear courtyard at Gurney Street forms a circulation area which can be reached not only by way of the screens passage at the low end of the hall but also by separate doors in its east and west sides and by

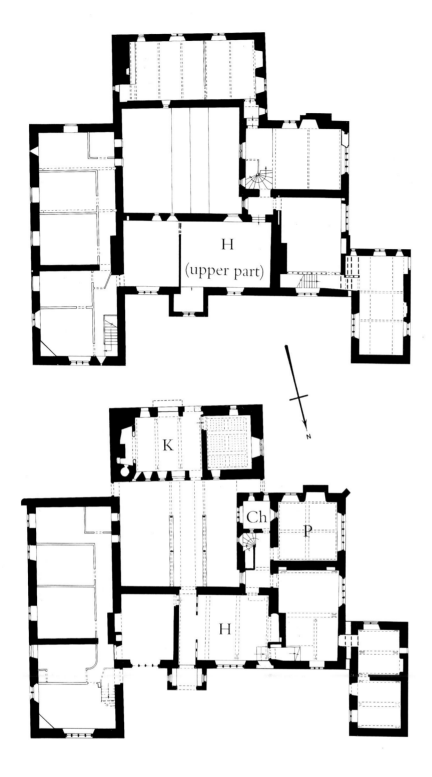

52 (*left*) Gurney Street Manor, Cannington, Somerset: ground- and first-floor plans. Gurney Street Manor reached its present form *c.* 1540, save for the much later flooring-in of the hall. There was probably originally some kind of a forecourt to the north with the hall facing towards it, as at Great Chalfield, but the house otherwise surrounds an inner courtyard (which at Chalfield has largely disappeared). The rooms at either end of the hall were probably built as cellars, with the principal accommodation on the floor above. This provided four separate units of accommodation: perhaps a set of two rooms off the hall's low end (with its own stair, since demolished), one off the high end, one beyond this flanking the courtyard, and another double set over the kitchens.

53 (*facing page top*) Gurney Street Manor from the west. The superior ('high') end of the house, with the two best chambers distinguished by their greater height, and the blank, rear wall of the kitchen.

54 a and b (*facing page bottom*) Gurney Street Manor: the pentice. A possibly unique survival of a covered passage built to shelter the bringing of food across the courtyard from the kitchen hatch to the low end of the hall.

way of the external door of the kitchen. This courtyard must have been semi-public; there was probably direct access from it to the chapel, and these doorways may have formed the normal approach for those who did not require direct access to the main body of the house. The courtyard serves for circulation in another important respect in that there was (and, exceptionally, remains) a single-storey pentice down the centre that leads from the rear door of the screens passage to the kitchen door and hatch (pl. 54). At Blackmore Farm the kitchen is incorporated into the body of the house so that eating rooms can be served by an internal passage, but there were similarly separate external doors to the chapel and kitchen. On the ground floor each house had a high-end parlour, reached indirectly from the hall, and a room off the hall's low end that probably served as a buttery: a low-ceilinged, cellar-like room at Gurney Street (later converted into a low parlour, given a fireplace and having its ceiling raised) and a room of normal ceiling height at Blackmore Farm.

Internal circulation is elementary in terms of an elaborate layout of passages and stairs, but in each house it is reasonably effective in securing independent access to the principal rooms. The hall itself constitutes the principal circulation space in these as in all late medieval houses. Beyond the hall, common space in each house consisted of no more than a lobby and modest flights of stairs at either end (the low-end stairs at Gurney Street are lost). The provision of high-end and low-end stairs, needed in any house with an open hall, was not strictly necessary in one like Blackmore Farm with a continuous first floor, but was a considerable convenience in order to save a long journey, to prevent intermediate first-floor rooms being used as passages, and to preserve a degree of social distinction between the house's opposite ends. The high-end stairs at Blackmore Farm were straight and steep and reached circuitously by a passage past the parlour; at Gurney Street the route to the stair is more direct, and space used more economically; parlour, chapel and a winder stair are all entered off a lobby.

Counting as one the two-room units situated over the kitchen in each house, the chambers are relatively few in number (five at Blackmore Farm, four at Gurney Street) and relatively large in size. Few need be used as passage rooms, nor do they appear from size or decoration to differ very greatly in status except that in each house one principal chamber overlooks the chapel. All those at Gurney Street have or had open roofs with well-finished, arch-braced trusses, while at Blackmore Farm there are two chambers with such open roofs (one with its own garderobe) and one room with a ceiling and with access to a further room beneath the roof above it. None of these rooms seems to be a subordinate room in the sense of a closet or servants' chamber. The broad similarity of the accommodation provided by these two houses, in amenities and quantity, contrasts strongly with the difference between their plans.

But though in general the functional arrangements of the late medieval house were formulaic, circumstances occasionally determined unusual layouts. The opposition of high end and low end was not always sacrosanct, and local traditions or the accidents of reconstruction sometimes compelled departure from the ideal or the perpetuation of arrangements that originated at an earlier stage of the house's development. At Little Moreton a new great chamber was built at the low end of the hall, around 1480, presumably because the high-end accommodation was still relatively new and the owner did not want the expense of demolishing and replacing it. At Plowden in Shropshire, to a medieval hall with a high-end chamber block there was added in the mid-sixteenth century a low-end wing comprising a kitchen with a great chamber above it (pl. 55).[16] In all of these examples the builder seems to have wished to retain the old rooms at the same time as enjoying the comforts and prestige of new ones.

Occasionally the ends of the house seem to have been completely reversed.[17] Ufton Court in Berkshire (whose large recusant household is described in chapter 7) is a much altered house of medieval origins (pls 297, 298). The earliest part of the building seems to be an open hall, with a range of good rooms at right angles to it at the east end. Around 1480 a new hall was built beyond these rooms, the old hall relegated to serve as a kitchen, what were formerly the best rooms in the house retained in an inferior position, and a new, best chamber and parlour built at the opposite end of the new hall. At Speke in Cheshire and at Knole in Kent equally substantial changes in their layout are implied in the late fifteenth century or the early sixteenth, since old halls were similarly retained when new ones were built in a new position. But such transformations were rare. When a house was renewed piecemeal, those parts that remained standing continued to determine the use of those that were rebuilt. Before the mid-sixteenth century most builders valued convenience and hierarchical appropriateness at least as much as architectural uniformity and were not troubled by owning a house of various dates and apparently discordant styles.

Symmetry and Regularity

The houses described above accommodated households that were assemblies of interdependent functions and communities of different status groups; within an overall architectural unity each house discriminates in an appropriate manner between the accommodation of the household's different parts. Nevertheless

55 Plowden Hall, Shropshire. The hierarchy of 'high' and 'low' ends of the house was seldom disturbed, but when at Plowden in the sixteenth century a new kitchen was built at the low end of the medieval hall, a new great chamber (right) was built above it, preserving the older high-end rooms (left) for the sake of economy.

the functional symmetry of the tripartite layout that had been developed by the late Middle Ages prefigured the gradual development of formal, visual symmetry that went beyond the balance of complementary parts. In thirteenth-century houses the solar – the owner's chamber and principal living room – was often located above service rooms at the low end of the hall, creating with the hall a house of two parts rather than of three.[18] The subsequent addition of a high-end chamber, the incorporation of the kitchen within the body of the house, and in due course the introduction of ground-floor parlours at one or at both ends, produced a three-part plan that would prove immensely fertile, both functionally and formally. With the hall placed between flanking blocks, the three-part layout was fundamental to the subsequent development of house plans in the sixteenth and seventeenth centuries, equally capable of refinement as an H, E or U and serving as the point of departure for the development of revolutionary new plan forms. The symmetry of the gabled wings at Great Chalfield must have satisfied a purely aesthetic sense, and the development of formal, external symmetry is a fundamental trend of the following century. At the great house of Cowdray, the central block is wholly asymmetrical, composed in a very similar manner to East Barsham; the wings that frame it, flanking the forecourt, are on the other hand mirror images of each other.

That the symmetrical model would supplant the more visibly hierarchical might seem surprising. It might seem more likely that the development of the house would have tended to distinguish the polite rooms more strongly rather than less so, and in some areas – particularly at the level of the lesser gentry – hierarchic forms continued to be followed well into the seventeenth century. Society itelf was evolving away from the medieval ideal of mutually supportive elements and towards a greater fragmentation and polarisation of interests, and towards households where the gentry proclaimed their sophistication while the servants were tucked away. Yet while in the sixteenth and seventeenth centuries the development of the house reflected that of society in the evolution of greater internal specialisation, of rooms for particular functions and of spaces for exclusive and private use, externally the house was evolving towards an ever greater uniformity. The late medieval house was a building of relatively few rooms with generalised uses whose plan can be clearly read from the outside; by contrast the Renaissance house has a greater number of rooms with more specialised functions, but its exterior provides no clue to the arrangements within. Externally, it is illegible. The development of this illegibility and the growth of symmetry are very closely linked.

The advance towards symmetry can be followed in a well-known group of houses in the south-west, in an area that was prosperous in the early sixteenth century from the wool trade. The demolished house at Kingston Seymour, south-west of Clevedon and only 25 miles from Chalfield, repeated the Chalfield formula very closely on a slightly smaller scale and achieved a precocious uniformity between the windows of its various parts.[19] Thirty miles to the south, Poundisford in Somerset, south of Taunton, survives, developing the Chalfield and Kingston Seymour formula with considerable ingenuity (pls 56, 57).[20] The date of the house is uncertain, but it was probably begun soon after the merchant William Hill took a lease on the property in 1546. The plan forms a symmetrical H, with the hall occupying the central stroke in the normal manner. Symmetry is not complete: the hall porch is balanced by the oriel as it is at Chalfield, while window levels in the high-end gable are slightly higher than those in the low end. However, this distinction may result from a difference in ceiling heights rather than being adopted deliberately to display the better rooms. The hall rises through two floors and is lit by a tall window, but being central to the house it does not interfere with its symmetry; indeed its axiality is emphasised by a gablet that lights a superior attic chamber above it. The interior has been partly remodelled, but seems always to have had a parlour at each end of the hall as well as having the kitchen integrated into the rear of the low-end wing. Above is a symmetrical disposition of chambers, disposed front and back in each wing and with stairs between them; the rear chambers are served by projecting garderobes. It is no longer entirely clear how closets – of which there are several – related to the chambers, but the plan is not only remarkably coherent and extremely efficient functionally, it also has considerable formal clarity – a clarity repeated from the treatment of the exterior of the house.

Poundisford approaches symmetry by playing down as far as possible the differences between its high and low ends. Barrington Court in the same county employs the same formula in a larger house (pls 58, 59). Barrington, once dated to 1514 and hailed as an example of precocious symmetry, is probably of a few years later than Poundisford, having being built in the late 1550s by a London merchant, William Clifton, who had been building up an estate in the county.[21] Barrington can be seen as an extended version of Poundisford. Whereas the hall at Poundisford occupies the whole of the central range, at Barrington it takes up only half the centre of the house. This made it possible to preserve the low-end entry to the hall while placing the porch at the centre of the façade, with the hall to one side and services – buttery and pantry – to the other. Symmetry is not complete: there is still a tall hall distinguished by taller windows, but in other respects the house achieves a uniformity comparable with that of Poundisford.

Two other up-to-date features of Barrington call for comment. The first is the way in which, although the wings of the house project so as to frame a forecourt, the approach to the house is centred on the façade. Before the second quarter of the sixteenth century it was exceptional for the gatehouse to be aligned with the hall porch – a dislocation probably inherent in the conflict between a symmetrical gatehouse range and an asymmetrical elevation to the main body of the house. Not infrequently, as at Chalfield, the gatehouse actually opens into

57 (*below*) Poundisford Park: ground-floor plan.

56 (*above*) Poundisford Park, Pitminster, Somerset, *c*. 1550. Poundisford develops the potential for complete symmetry provided by the Great Chalfield formula, with the hall oriel and hall porch matched in mass and fenestration.

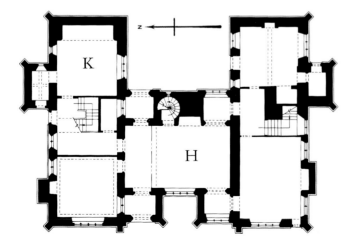

58 (*facing page top*) Barrington Court, Somerset, late 1550s. Barrington combines the Poundisford formula with an expanded façade. This is wholly symmetrical except for the taller window that is needed to light the tall hall which was still felt necessary in the house of a man of standing.

59 (*facing page bottom*) Barrington Court: ground-floor plan. At Barrington a service passage leads off the low end of the hall, past the buttery and against an order wall, to reach the kitchens and other offices. This systematisation of an earlier formula provided a layout that would be very widely followed up to the mid-seventeenth century and would continue to influence the evolution of plans beyond that date.

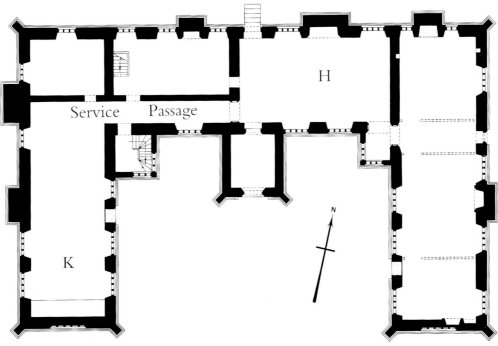

60 Kentwell Hall, Long Melford, Suffolk, *c.* 1563. Kentwell has a broadly extended, near-symmetrical façade, with (like Barrington) an axial approach entered by a small gatehouse that is placed well away from the front so that the totality of the house should make the fullest impact on the visitor.

the courtyard at one side, and still more indirect approaches are not uncommon: at Sandford Orcas in Dorset the gatehouse is attached to the low-end cross wing and the visitor has to double back to reach the front door (pl. 209). Although the surroundings of Barrington were greatly altered in the early twentieth century, the approach to the house seems to have been axial from the first. Similarly, while at East Barsham the gatehouse is close up to the front of the house, making it difficult to take in the full extent of the façade, increasingly the immediate approach to the house would be at a distance that made it possible to confront the entire elevation at a glance. At Shute before the building of the new gatehouse around 1565 the entrance was from one side of the courtyard; the new gatehouse seems to have been directly on the line of the hall porch. At Godolphin in the late sixteenth century there seems to have been a similar realignment.

The second modern feature of Barrington is its plan. Although severely damaged by fire in the early nineteenth century and largely remodelled internally in the twentieth, the layout of the central range remains clear: the hall occupies the left-hand side while to the right of the entry a pair of service rooms occupy the forward part and a passage runs behind them to reach the low-end wing. The Barrington formula may be described as a service-passage plan. Whether or (probably) not introduced here it is no more than the systematisation of the medieval arrangement of a passage leading past buttery and pantry to a kitchen, but its compatibility with a house of a certain size and an overall regularity of form would lead to its adoption in a huge number of houses over the next hundred years.

A house of very similar external form is Kentwell Hall in Suffolk (pl. 60) which the builder, John Clopton, described as new in his will in 1563.[22] There is evidence in the house that in its present form it is a remodelling of an earlier building, perhaps incorporating at the high end a residential tower of the East Barsham type, and there are certain inexplicable irregularities in the plan; none the less the date can be accepted stylistically, perhaps for a major overhaul. While the sixteenth-century plan is unclear, the principal elevation exactly parallels the Barrington formula: forward-projecting wings, a central entrance and to one side of it (originally) a tall window for the hall. The broad entrance courtyard is entered by a relatively small gatehouse set well away from the façade. The regularly composed and near-symmetrical courtyard elevations contrast with the utilitarian treatment of the back walls which are punctuated with windows, garderobes and chimneys at need, but the opening-out of the courtyard at such houses as Kentwell and Barrington, so that this uniform composition could be seen, is a matter of architectural display rather than the display of hierarchies.

The tension between symmetry and hierarchy, evident in the tall hall windows of these houses, is well displayed at Pitchford Hall in Shropshire (pl. 61). Here the overall layout is symmetrical, with a central porch between flanking wings, but the parlour wing has more elaborate framing to gable and first floor and a jetty – the first-floor projection which was almost universally employed in timber-framed houses of any status to distinguish the superior end from the lower. A group of houses of the 1560s and 1570s in the south-east – Baynards, Danny, Loseley (pl. 62) and Parham – are of a size and status similar to Pitchford, Barrington and Kentwell, but their façades are extended to the maximum extent.

Among the earliest gentry houses in the south of England to achieve complete symmetry is a small group of houses which seem stylistically related: Shaw House outside Newbury,[23] Corsham Court near Bath, which was enlarged and remodelled internally in the eighteenth century,[24] and Whittington in Gloucestershire (pl. 66), which seems never to have been complete in the form originally intended.[25] Shaw survives very more completely than either. Shaw is dated 1581, Corsham 1582; the date of Whittington is not known but was sufficiently complete by 1595 for Queen Elizabeth to be entertained there.[26] Shaw (pls 63–5) has a broad entrance front with wings that project a relatively short distance forward, giving the maximum exposure to the central façade; at Corsham as at Kentwell the entrance courtyard is very deep, similarly enhancing the approach. Although because the hall windows of Shaw were

61 Pitchford Hall, Shropshire, late sixteenth century. The Barrington formula expressed in a timber-framed house, with the high-end wing (on the right) still distinguished by a jetty from the inferior accommodation.

62 (*above*) Loseley House, Surrey, *c.* 1570. Built with no wings and with the maximum extension to the front. A number of contemporary houses in the region are built to the same formula.

63 (*facing page top*) Shaw House, Newbury, Berkshire, as originally built in 1579–82. Shaw is among the earliest houses to have a wholly symmetrical front, in which not even the location of the hall is displayed. The impression of privacy – of the disposition of the rooms of the house being no business of the outsider – is reinforced by the tone of Greek and Latin inscriptions (see p. 268).

64 (*facing page bottom*) Shaw House from the south. The present asymmetry of the façade is a result of hall windows' having been lowered in the eighteenth century at a time when internal regularity was more greatly valued than external symmetry.

deepened in the eighteenth century the façade is no longer symmetrical, it was so originally. All three houses have single-storey halls, and all have or seem to have had service-passage plans of the kind first described at Barrington. At Shaw chimneystacks project from outer walls but are regularly placed; the windows on the return sides of the house are largely uniform. In their façades Shaw, Corsham and Whittington, as probably intended, achieved the complete formal symmetry and external uniformity which earlier houses were moving towards, and in so doing they deny the internal layout any part in determining the house's outward appearance. Shaw and Corsham have been linked to the regional school of classicism engendered by John Thynne's long and extensive work at Longleat, and remarkably correct classical detail appears in all.[27] In all these houses (as at Longleat) classical entablatures run round the building at storey height, and windows with correctly detailed, pedimented heads appear at Whittington and Corsham; Shaw is of brick, but good classical detail appears on the porch and on a side door into the parlour wing.

It has been customary to explain the advance of symmetry as due to the increasing influence of classical architecture from the continent. For this there is no evidence before the 1570s, when the increasingly consistent use of classical detail informs a regularity and symmetry that is already on the point of attainment. When elements of classical architecture first appear in English buildings it provided superficial embellishment to the otherwise conventional houses of fashion-conscious patrons. A few tombs and chantry chapels of churchmen and of great territorial magnates from the 1520s onwards are evidence for aristocratic patronage of the new style, and antique detail appears in domestic interiors during the same decade. The decoration of

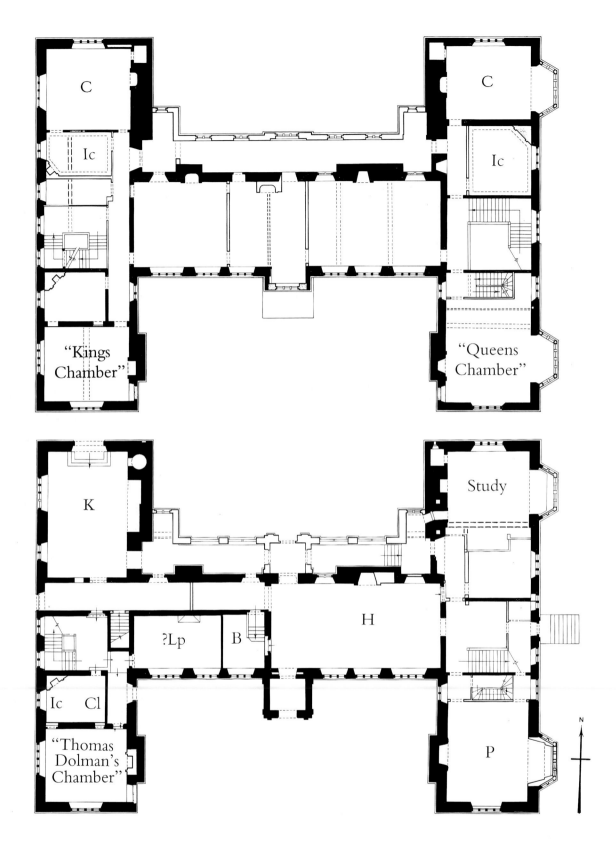

65 Shaw House: ground- and first-floor plans. Shaw may have been begun to a different plan: there are remains of a basement kitchen at the house's high end and other irregularities on the ground floor, but as built it is a classic example of the service-passage layout (cf. Barrington, pl. 59). The arrangements of the first floor, centre, have been substantially altered, and additions were made in the eighteenth and nineteenth centuries, but otherwise the house preserves its internal layout unusually intact. Rooms are identified from an inventory of 1620, and their functions are discussed on p. 296.

66 Whittington House, Gloucestershire, *c.* 1595. Incomplete and probably unfinished, but intended to have been similar to Shaw in layout and in its external symmetry. Classical ornament embellishes an otherwise plain façade.

the royal houses employed classical motifs widely; a very few ceilings remain at Hampton Court and at St James's Palace, while an exceptional survival in a gentry house is the fragment of painting in the great chamber at Acton Court (pl. 67), new built for Henry VIII's visit in 1535 and by its style and competence almost certainly painted by a craftsman of the Royal Works.[28] At Thame Abbey in Oxfordshire the last abbot incorporated classical motifs in the decoration of the ceiling of a room in his lodgings (pl. 69) – probably the kind of decoration that prompted Starkey's condemnation, quoted in chapter 1.[29] Documentary evidence for such taste is more widespread: 'antick' decoration and furnishings start to be mentioned in

inventories from around 1530, and from the late 1520s classical ornament appears as surface relief on terracotta window surrounds and conveys the impression of richly textured internal decoration in an antique style, as it were oozing through the windows to the outside of the building. But the first examples of classical architectural detail in the background of English portrait paintings probably denote cultural aspirations rather than actual domestic circumstances.[30]

Classical ornament features almost apologetically as subordinate decoration on a number of houses in the south-west from the late 1520s in combination with native, Gothic forms and in houses which are otherwise in a wholly native tradition, and its appearance is probably at first due to the employment of foreign stone carvers (pl. 68). Classical pediments to windows occur in the gentry houses of much of East Anglia from the mid-sixteenth century onwards, though difficult to date from their very persistence and uniformity (pls 217, 229, 246). Wainscot, frequently imported from across the North Sea and incorpo-

69 (*above*) The solar, Thame Abbey, Oxfordshire, *c.* 1525–30. The ceiling of this room is decorated in the most fashionable contemporary style, incorporating classical medallions and grotesques.

67 (*facing page top*) Wall painting at Acton Court, Iron Acton, Avon. Classical ornament, almost certainly by a painter employed at court, in a range built for the entertainment of Henry VIII. The internal use of classical decoration preceded its widespread application externally.

68 (*facing page bottom*) Forde Abbey, Dorset. Figures of classical derivation, probably by French masons, incorporated into otherwise Gothic work of *c.* 1525–30.

rating repetitious antique detail, provided a further means of introducing a superficial classicism into houses along the eastern seaboard, and such importations can be seen in the context of a long tradition of trade and of cultural links with northern Europe. At the level of the cultured humanist, classical ornament might indicate identification with ancient virtue; for most people, from the royal palaces to the parlours of North Sea merchants, it was more probably seen at best as an evocation of superior learning, more generally as fashionable decoration, but not indicating any deeper comprehension of classical architecture as a set of design principles. Nor could it do so in view of the period of a century (from Alberti to Vignola) during which such principles would evolve in Italy itself. Its most obvious effect was in gradually widening the decorative repertoire available to the craftsman, and in increasingly identifying such ornament with the broad cultural aspirations of the builder. The

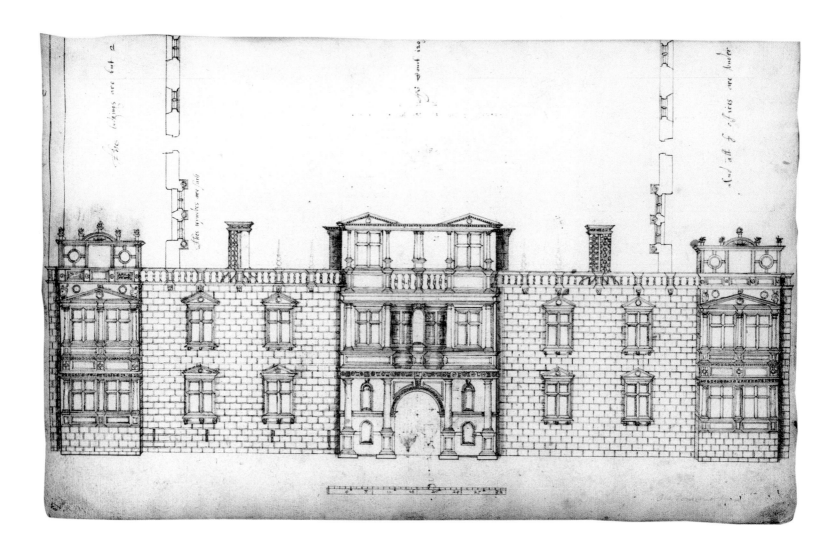

70 Somerset House, London: the gatehouse range. All ornament – doors and windows – is classical and comparable with contemporary work in France, but the symmetrical layout preserved the traditional English layout of a central gatehouse flanked by matching blocks (cf. Oxburgh, pl. 37).

most up-to-date building of the mid-century, the gatehouse front of Somerset House of 1547–9 (pl. 70), combined complete symmetry with sophisticated classical detail, but such gatehouse ranges had for long been the only part of the large house in which symmetry was normal and there was therefore no reason to associate the one with the other.

Before the 1570s, the building in which classical ornament was most fully and spectacularly displayed was Henry VIII's palace of Nonsuch (pl. 71). Nonsuch was built between 1538 and 1547 as a kind of glorified hunting lodge within easy reach of Hampton Court – Camden in 1586 called it 'a retiring place' – and it lacked, as did all of the king's later houses, a great hall. It was built of brick, stone and timber around two large courtyards, the outer (northern) one containing services and housing for attendants and officials (and a dining hall specifically for them),

and the inner containing the royal lodgings, arranged as was usual in two separate but communicating suites, for king and queen. The exterior appearance of the northern part of the palace, containing the outer courtyard, was conventional for an early Tudor great house: the entrance front was symmetrical, with ranges flanking a central gate tower, while the return elevations to east and west were less regular, their appearance determined by the variety of accommodation within. The inner courtyard was entered from the outer one by a taller and more elaborate gate tower, but its appearance was in other respects completely different. Both to the exterior and towards the courtyard it was decorated with a series of classical, mythological and heroic figures, executed in stucco in high relief and set within frames of carved and painted slate. Some at least of the carvers of these figures were foreign and had worked on similar figures at Fontainebleau for Francis I, and the number of these figures was evidently matched by their unprecedented quality. But equally significant for the overall appearance of the house was that it was thus not only within the courtyard that the onlooker was invited to admire the profusion and the splendour of this decoration, but outside as well: the extravagantly decorated outer walls were clearly meant to signal the royal lodgings to the

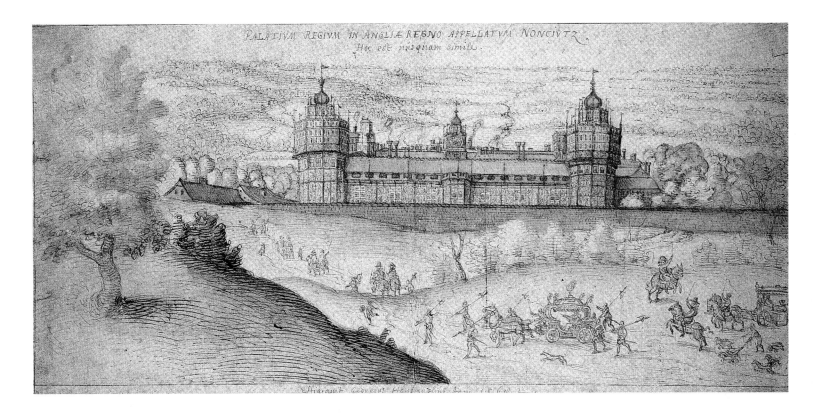

71 Joris Hofnaegel: Nonsuch Palace, 1568: the royal apartments from the south. The royal lodgings at Nonsuch (in contrast to the more architecturally conservative outer range) were highly decorated with classical figures whose dense and recondite iconography was calculated to accord with the magnificence of the house's owner. Divided into a king's suite and a queen's, the royal lodgings were almost symmetrical about a central stair turret.

distant viewer as well as to the visitor who had passed both gatehouses and reached the entrance to them.

The southern part contrasted strongly with the northern in expressing the magnificence of its occupants. Although symmetry was to an extent inherent in the balance between the king's suite and the queen's – itself a comparatively recent innovation (before the building of Greenwich Palace in the 1530s king's and queen's lodgings had generally been superimposed in the tradition of the lodging tower) – the greater size of the king's suite meant that symmetry was not axiomatic. The best surviving illustration of this south front (Joris Hofnaegel's often-reproduced drawing of 1588) places the southern stair projection at the centre of the façade. Excavation in 1959–62 showed that this projection was in fact a little off-centre towards the east, probably because the king's suite occupied more of the south range than did the queen's. Hofnaegel's mistake is understandable in view of the extent to which by the last quarter of the century asolute symmetry was becoming a norm, and though symmetry was not achieved in the south front of Nonsuch, it is not far distant. Internal arrangements on the

ground floor did not match, side for side, but the inner elevations of the inner courtyard do seem to have done so, with each side mirroring the other to express the suites of first-floor rooms for king and queen opposite each other. The house's aspect was equally ambiguous, with its royal lodgings overlooking the park but its gallery overlooking the courtyard.

Nonsuch was a castle of romance. Its outlandishness and the specialised nature of its accommodation ruled it out as a formal model for the more conventional house, even though the tentative nature of its symmetry and its partly outward aspect conformed to contemporary trends. As a celebration of the monarchy through the application of classical ornament to native forms, the building is the supreme representative of its age. But the fact that foreign craftsmen generally worked for English overseers in the decoration of buildings that provided for English needs considerably limited their ability to influence the building's overall form, and there is no evidence that they did so.

Kirby in Northamptonshire is the only house in which before the completion of Longleat around 1580 there seems to be a correspondence between the use of classical forms and the achievement of symmetry (pl. 72).[31] Kirby was begun in 1570 as a large courtyard house on an odd, trapezoidal plan; its builder was Sir Humphrey Stafford, of whom little is known, and its mason architect may have been Thomas Thorpe, whose son John laid the foundation stone at the age of seven.[32] The hall occupies one half of the inner façade towards the courtyard; the porch is at the centre, and a low-end range of the same length as the hall occupies the other half of the range. The two-storey, low-end range is made to match the tall hall range by linking

72　Kirby Hall, Northamptonshire, 1572. Although still facing inwards towards a courtyard, advanced architectural decoration was employed to make the appearance of the hall, to the right of the porch and rising through two floors, match the two-storey range to the left by running blind window mullions and giant pilasters through the level of the intermediate floor. The left-hand range has lost its roof.

the upper and lower windows by mullions and blind panels; an order of giant pilasters marches the full length of the façade, and the porch is ornamented with superimposed orders and with an extraordinary confection of seven pilasters and shell motifs in the gable (pl. 73). Across the courtyard, the inner side of the entrance front has an open loggia with a similar giant order to that on the hall front.

Kirby is architecturally highly self-conscious. The pilasters on the gable of the porch are a characteristic Elizabethan device, a clear reference to Proverbs 9,1: 'Wisdom hath builded a house: she hath hewn out her seven pillars'; Kirby is the House of Wisdom. The giant order, whose details derive in part from John Shute and from Serlio, was without precedent in England. It had appeared at Monceaux-en-Brie in the 1550s (almost as early

as its appearance at the Campidoglio in Rome) and at Ecouen but was as yet rare even in France. Kirby is by far the most foreign-looking house of its generation, and the exceptional nature of its design accords with the exceptional character, for 1572, of its symmetry. There are other houses in Northamptonshire (notably Deene Park, pl. 74, and Dingley Hall, pl. 75) which from the 1550s onwards show some acquaintance with French models, at least at second hand, and the relatively high survival rate of mid-sixteenth-century houses in the county probably gives a false idea of the distribution of such work originally. But even allowing for the loss of so much contemporary work elsewhere, the very scarcity of parallels may suggest how small the influence of continental classicism was in achieving symmetry. Even at Hill Hall (pl. 6), the house where the builder's own continental architectural education is the best documented,

73 (*facing page*)　Kirby: the hall porch. A typical Elizabethan device: the seven pillars refer to Proverbs, ch. 9: 'Wisdom hath builded a house, she hath hewn out her seven pillars. She hath killed her beasts, she hath mingled her wine, she hath furnished her table . . . Come, eat my bread and drink of the wine which I have mingled.' The porch invites the visitor to partake of the hospitality within.

but transformed by a humanist functionalism, and the symmetrical house may be taken as expressing more perfectly than the visual asymmetry of the medieval house, the perfect balance and integration of an harmonious commonwealth. The country house poems discussed in chapter 7 are good evidence that such an ideal existed.

But for many people the explanation was probably simpler, and lay in the new freedom that such a view allowed for the indulgence of a taste of visual symmetry which is probably innate. A growing visual taste for regularity seems to be shown in the way in which some houses have been altered. Bisham Abbey in Berkshire, remodelled by Sir Thomas Hoby in the late 1550s, had been a late thirteenth-century house of traditional form though of considerable size and grandeur, with an open hall between cross wings at high and low ends (pl. 16). The medieval house remains largely intact but Sir Thomas disguised the contrast between the huge hall and its two-storey, forward-projecting appendages by adding across its face a two-storey screen range with a regular line of gables to echo those of the wings at either end. This screen block is lit by a regular line of windows with classical pediments. Perhaps the grandest and most revolutionary of such alterations – though in the house of a style-setting nobleman rather than in a gentry house – was the classical loggia that the Duke of Northumberland built across the front of the hall at Dudley Castle around 1550.[33] This loggia – of which only the imposts to the arcade survive – linked the hall porch at one end of the hall to the state apartments at the other. Architecturally it screened the great hall rather as Hoby's new range at Bisham had done; though at Dudley (unlike at Bisham) the hall windows remained open and visible above the loggia, the loggia provided in visual terms a ground floor to the hall and unified it with the scale of the three-storey blocks at either end.

Longleat (pl. 76) is the first house in England to be completed with a uniform scheme of external decoration, symmetrical on all fronts (or as nearly so as was possible, given that the façades mask earlier and irregular internal courtyards) and wholly outward-looking. While much is unknown about its form before its final completion around 1580, it seems likely that a major incentive for this was the wish to disguise a domesticated jumble of monastic buildings behind a uniform façade. If so, then just as at Bisham and Dudley Castle, the employment of classical detail was perhaps at first incidental to the wish to resolve an aesthetic difficulty. There are innumerable lesser houses whose exteriors were brought up to date by the remodelling of their façades and made to conform with fashionable norms in the simplest and most economical way, without necessarily reordering the internal layout. At Stonor Park in Oxfordshire, a large, rambling house of medieval origins and many building periods was given a unified front around 1600 with a plain brick front rising to a line of fourteen matching gables.[34] Stibbington Hall in Cambridgeshire (pl. 77), apparently an E-plan house of about 1615, is accretive, partly at least timber-framed, and

75 (*above*) Dingley Hall, Northamptonshire, *c.* 1560. Superimposed classical orders on the loggia.

74 (*facing page*) Deene Park, Northamptonshire. Classical detail on a re-set window, *c.* 1560. The unusually large amount of mid-sixteenth-century classical work surviving in the county (much of it fairly crude) may gave a false idea of the original distribution of such ornament nationally.

the principal façades towards the courtyard were not fully symmetrical.

But if stylistic classicism is an inadequate explanation for the increasing regularity of houses in the later sixteenth century, another explanation is needed. While Vitruvius was well known to English humanists, 'symmetria' in the Vitruvian sense did not mean symmetry in the modern meaning of the word – of one half of a design being the mirror image of another. Rather was it the more general keeping of a due proportion between the parts of a building in accordance with their uses, a principle that conformed with existing notions of architectural decorum. As discussed in chapter 1, the medieval concept of the hierarchical society was not rejected in the course of the sixteenth century

76 Longleat, Wiltshire, completed by 1580. Longleat is symmetrical, outward facing on all façades and with very advanced classical detailing. The house incorporates medieval fragments, and its regularity may have been prompted at least in part by the wish to impose visual order on a very irregular internal layout.

77 Stibbington Hall, Cambridgeshire. Stibbington has a complex, accretive plan with work of varied dates, some of it originally timberframed. Around 1620 this irregularity was masked with a new, wholly symmetrical, stone front.

its complexity similarly cannot be deduced from its neat façade. At Little Moreton Hall, two contrasting gables on the north front were made more uniform late in the sixteenth century by the planting onto one of them of an ornamental frame with a decorative pattern similar to that of the other. At Speke in Cheshire – a highly irregular, timber-framed house of several periods – the hall oriel was matched at the end of the sixteenth century by another at the opposite end of the façade, although this new window lighted no room of any importance.

What these houses have in common is a repudiation of old-fashioned visual irregularity, and implicitly a rejection of hierarchical display – rejected because builders no longer wished to show externally the house's internal workings, and could thus satisfy a purely visual aesthetic. At the same time, changes inside the house were making external symmetry easier to achieve. While houses with tall halls continued to be built until the end of the century and beyond, a growing preference for single-storey halls (traced in chapter 8) was making uniformity easier: the single-storey hall made it possible to match the façade on one side of the entry with that on the other. While the desire to distinguish the ends of the house was declining, they were becoming more nearly equal in status as the owner's rooms were tending to move from the high end of the house to the low (also described in chapter 8), forming a kind of equilibrium with the best entertaining rooms at the high end. The importance attached to the appearance of the house is suggested too by the transformation in its aspect that was taking place at the same time. The late medieval gentry house had shown its front, often obliquely, to an enclosure which was its owner's private domain. By the late sixteenth century, it was increasingly making a display towards the outside world.

Aspect

One of the elements in the turn of the house from inward- to outward-looking, first completely achieved at Longleat, may be in the increasing tendency for the best rooms of great houses to expand towards a private garden or overlooking a park: on to an area that, as the preserve of the house's owner, was not public but which nevertheless lay beyond the strict confines of the courtyard.[35] This was itself in part the result of the multiplication of such rooms, the need to create space for them, and the lack of precedents for their location. At Thornbury Castle in 1520 suites of superimposed state rooms for the Duke and Duchess of Buckingham, with elaborate bay windows made by masons who had probably also worked at Windsor Castle, looked away from the inner courtyard and on to a private garden (pl. 78). At Hampton Court in the 1530s and 1540s, the queen's private rooms and her long recreational gallery extended to a great distance across the eastern face of the house, looking out over the park and including an open viewing gallery from which she could watch the deer hunting.[36] At Somerset House in the 1550s, ranges of grand lodgings spread out over the gardens to the south, between the great house and the Thames, and turn their backs on the more public courtyards to the north.[37] Such a private garden overlooked by the house's best rooms is described in the Shute survey (see p. 57 above). At Kirby Hall in the 1580s the need for a new range of state rooms was met by building them out from the body of the house with two broad window bays overlooking the gardens (pl. 79). In so far as they face towards private enclaves, these houses can be seen as a further regress into exclusivity, but in that they reject making their display towards the courtyard they are diminishing its importance in search of some other arrangement.

The evolution of the house's aspect can be followed most convincingly in houses that are built like Little Moreton and Ightham, with ranges that surround a courtyard. Although the courtyard was the most efficient way of organising the accommodation in a large house, several relatively small houses with internal courtyards, built in the fifteenth century, had also found a model for the form of the house in the tradition of the castle. Treago in Herefordshire, probably of around 1470–1500, is square in plan with round angle towers of differing sizes.[38] Faulkbourne in Essex was largely built during the half-century after 1439, and has an impressive four-storey lodging tower at one corner.[39] Wickham Court in Kent (pl. 80) is probably of around 1490, with a matching, octagonal turret at each angle which contained stairs or closets.[40] Both at Treago and Wickham Court the courtyard seems to have been a service area as much as a light well,[41] and all three houses must have been outward-looking from the first. (At each, the central area was small enough and sufficiently redundant as a source of lighting for it to be filled in subsequently to house a stair. At Faulkbourne this occurred around 1640; it is uncertain when it happened at the two other houses.) All three, however, have lost their original outer enclosures. The plans of all of these houses have been greatly altered and at Treago and Wickham Court the windows too have been very much changed so that it is not clear how much external differentiation of parts there may have been, but such distinction is very clear at Faulkbourne.

Hengrave Hall in Suffolk (pls 81–3), built between 1525 and 1538, marks a significant development from this evocation of the medieval castle towards something very much more domestic, even though built on a similar plan.[42] Though considerably altered in the eighteenth, nineteenth and early twentieth centuries, the house still embodies a number of significant aspects of this transitional period. Hengrave was built for Sir Thomas Kytson, originally from Lancashire but who as merchant and sheriff of London made enough money to establish himself in the county, to buy the place (which had formerly belonged to the Duke of Buckingham, the builder of Thornbury) from the crown, and to build the house. The base court has gone, though shown in a sketch plan of 1588. The house has a long façade corresponding to the inner gatehouse range at

78 (*above left*) Thornbury Castle, Gloucestershire, 1515–20. Large ornamental windows look out from the Duke of Buckingham's private apartments. A central development of the sixteenth century was a change in the aspect of the house, from inward-looking to outward-facing. One of the factors in this evolution may have been the multiplication of state rooms, with large windows overlooking a private garden.

79 (*above right*) Kirby Hall: windows of the best chambers, *c.* 1580. The descent of these windows from the Thornbury model is clear.

80 Wickham Court, Bromley, Kent, *c.* 1490. Much altered, but originally built around a small inner courtyard. Wickham Court has thin, brick walls, and its castle-like appearance owes more to the form of house felt appropriate to its builder than to practical defence. Fairly close to London, the house is likely to have been used by its owner (whose principal estates lay in Norfolk) at least partly for entertainment.

81 (*above*) Hengrave Hall, Suffolk, *c.* 1525–38. The way in which the projections of the front range diminish to pinnacles suggests that they may have been started as towers and were modified during building. Similarly, a gatehouse may have been intended originally, replaced by an ornamental bay window with classical putti – known to have been almost the last part of the house to have been built. The asymmetry of the front range is a result of nineteenth-century alteration.

82 (*right*) Hengrave Hall. The inner faces of the courtyard are surrounded by passages, which make possible a uniform arrangement of windows giving no indication of the internal layout.

Thornbury, originally more completely symmetrical than it is now, and with a gateway at its centre leading to a courtyard around which is built the principal accommodation. However, the entrance to the courtyard is very different from the massive, towered façade of Thornbury. In place of a tall gatehouse, fashionable Italian putti hold up the springing for three decorative, canted bay windows with little gables above them, and though there are massive projections flanking the gateway and at each end of the façade that look as though they were meant to have risen as towers, these are curiously and unsatisfactorily diminished at first-floor level and end as stubby pinnacles. Although some kind of a formal contract drawing was evidently made before work was started, there may well have been a change of plan and the canted windows over the entrance were not added until 1538 – almost the final piece of work in the house.[43] (A change in building material from brick to stone also suggests an interruption of work or a change of intention.) If there was indeed a scaling-down of the original intention then it was a significant change towards domesticity, and from the evocation of feudal power to the patronage of the most fashionable decorative style.

Once through the entrance, the courtyard is remarkably plain. It is not symmetrical, but except for the hall oriel the windows

83   Hengrave Hall. The outer faces of the house are still a traditional, irregular series of projections and openings.

are uniform. The reason for this is that the courtyard itself is not a circulation space and therefore not a space into which the house needs to be displayed: instead, circulation is by passages, on two floors, round three of the courtyard's inner sides. The arrangement was not entirely without precedent: at Herstmonceux Castle in East Sussex an inner courtyard, similarly fronting the hall range, had also been surrounded by an open gallery walk like a cloister, with corresponding passages on the floor above. Henry VII's royal lodgings – the donjon tower – at Richmond Palace may have been arranged similarly.[44] The base court at Knole is lined with suites of lodgings for retainers which are all entered off a continuous corridor that runs around the courtyard, but the novelty at Hengrave is that the passage fronts some of the principal rooms of the house. The courtyard passages mean that all of these rooms except the hall face outward rather than inward. Nevertheless the outer faces of the

house are irregular with projecting chimney bays, and apart from the entrance range, which has a tall bay lighting the chapel and formerly had another to balance it visually, no great prominence is given to the house's principal rooms.

Hengrave is a transitional building. The gatehouse is domesticated, and the courtyard façades are themselves almost wholly inexpressive of function or of status, but the other external elevations have not as yet acquired any elements of symmetry or of architectural display. It may be contrasted with Kirby of some thirty years later, whose internal faces play down still more strongly the functional and hierarchical differences between the high and low ends of the house. In addition to its symmetrical hall front, another innovative feature of Kirby was the regular line of windows to the garden front (pl. 84); by contrast, the opposite wing presented an irregular sequence of chimneys and windows towards the public road.

Contemporary with Kirby, and among the earliest surviving houses to face wholly outward and at the same time to achieve an exterior of almost total unformity, is Eastbury Manor in Essex (pls 85, 86).[45] Wings extend back from the façade (rather than

84 Kirby Hall. Uninformative but regular lines of windows towards the garden on the house's west side. The opposite side of the courtyard, facing towards the public road and containing services, is still irregular.

forward, in the usual manner of E- or H-plan houses) to present completely uniform, completely outward-facing elevations on three sides; on the fourth side is a service courtyard behind a high wall between the wings. Now engulfed in the eastern suburbs of London, the estate was acquired in 1557 by Richard Sysley of Sevenoaks in Kent who had already been buying up other land in Essex. The house was probably complete externally by 1573, and though altered slightly in the early seventeenth century and in the nineteenth, it preserves the essentials of its plan. The hall occupies the central range in the traditional manner (a later stair has been inserted in the position of the screens passage) with the entry still into one end of the hall and consequently off-centre to the façade. The winder stairs in the twin stair turrets seem still curiously old-fashioned. But in other

respects Eastbury is very progressive, as might be expected of a building that was close to the metropolis. The asymmetry of the façade is played down by the unassuming porch, and the single-storey hall does not need windows that are taller than any others. Almost all windows, regardless of the importance of the rooms they light, are identical, three-light mullions. At Poundisford and at Kentwell, stacks and garderobes projected on the flanks of the building; at Eastbury chimneystacks are either placed on the inner faces of the enclosed courtyard at the rear or else are incorporated within the internal plan, even at the cost of some irregularities at the high end of the hall. The exterior would be monotonous with its uniform ranks of windows, except that the stair turrets combine with the adjacent chimneys to give interest to the overall silhouette.

With the transformation of the house from inward-facing to outward-looking, the courtyard's value even as a light well would diminish, while its contraction made it increasingly unattractive as a circulation space. The equation of aspect and light was made by Sir Roger Wilbraham, writing of Wilton in 1603, thirty years before its remodelling by Inigo Jones and Isaac de Caus.

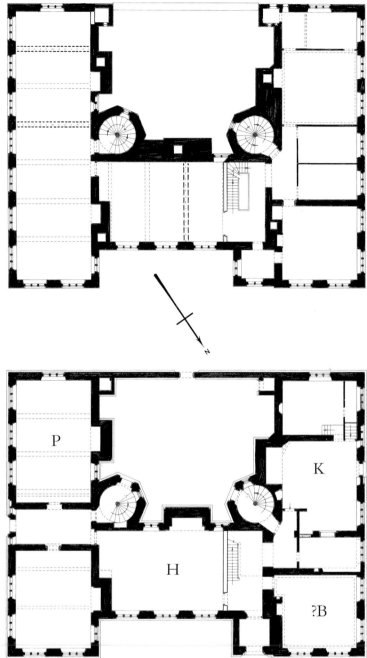

85 Eastbury Manor, Barking, Essex, *c.* 1570–75. One of the first entirely outward-facing houses. Its repetitive windows do not in any way distinguish the status or functions of its internal spaces.

Wilbraham wrote of 'a faire howse called Wilton . . . a large and high built square of hewen stone: the roames having ther lightes but one way into the square are melencholik and dark' (pl. 87).[46] Like Longleat, Wilton was a secularised abbey, and the outline of the cloister formed the courtyard of the house; Wilbraham's comment expresses an important change of attitude since the house's conversion sixty years before. Until late in the seventeenth century the house was further hemmed in with an outer courtyard: John Aubrey described the opening-up of Wilton to the country round after 1683:

> The Basecourt which was inclosed by a high wall, wch blinded the prospect of the house: as also the great Gate-house (wch. was a very good one) in the middle . . . were taken downe, as useless, by Tho: Earle of Pembroke, and the Court hath now an Enclosure with Piles, and Iron-barres, through wh. the passengers, and Travellers have a delightful visto of the area sett with Cypres-trees and [the] stately Palace.[47]

The eventual destruction of the forecourts at such great houses as Audley End, Hengrave and Wilton recognised their redundancy as the households of their owners had shrunk in size, as well as changing views of the relationship of house, grounds and countryside (discussed further in chapter 9).

86 Eastbury Manor, ground- and first-floor plans. The existing stair takes the place of the original screens passage; the original stairs are those in the polygonal turrets. Although partitions have been removed in the first floor, east range, there is evidence to reconstruct the original layout. There was a gallery on the second floor above these best first-floor chambers.

87 (*facing page*) Wilton House, Wiltshire. With the house increasingly turned from inward-looking to outward-facing, internal courtyards might become little more than large light wells. The courtyard at Wilton, formed from the cloister of a former nunnery, was condemned by Sir Roger Wilbraham in 1603 as 'melencholik and dark'.

Hanford in Dorset, of around 1610, is a rare example of an inward-facing Jacobean courtyard house:[48] the courtyard was small enough to have been ceiled over in the nineteenth century to house a staircase, but the porch of the house survives, facing into it. Although a small courtyard allowed a house to adopt a compact overall form, it meant that circulation had to remain linear, from room to room save in such an exceptional house as Barlborough, built with continuous passages around the inside of the courtyard, or as at Calke, where such passages seem to have been added, perhaps as part of the remodelling of a monastic grange around 1600. Only when a small courtyard was filled in would it become a satisfactory circulation area, and then there would be problems of lighting it. The small

courtyard, adopted largely as a means of achieving a compact silhouette, would ultimately be done away with, replaced by a house with a solid centre – a form whose origins are described below.

Sawston Hall in Cambridgeshire, Castle Bromwich Hall in the West Midlands and Chastleton in Oxfordshire usefully illustrate the development of the courtyard house in the late sixteenth century and the early seventeenth. Sawston was built in two phases round a square, internal court, probably shortly before 1557 and 1583, the dates inscribed on the house (pls 88–90).[49] The later phase comprises the greater part of the two ranges on either side of the courtyard, together with the front range with the hall at its centre. Porch and oriel are matched in

89 (*above*) Sawston Hall. The rear range (1557) contains a gallery on the first floor – an up-to-date amenity at that date – but only two of its windows look outward. The range is otherwise inward-looking in the traditional way.

88 (*facing page*) Sawston Hall, Cambridgeshire. The front range of Sawston (1583) faces outward from a courtyard. The porch balances the oriel: such a balance had by the late sixteenth century become a standard means of achieving a near-symmetrical front without abandoning the traditional layout, in which the entrance to the house is at the hall's low end.

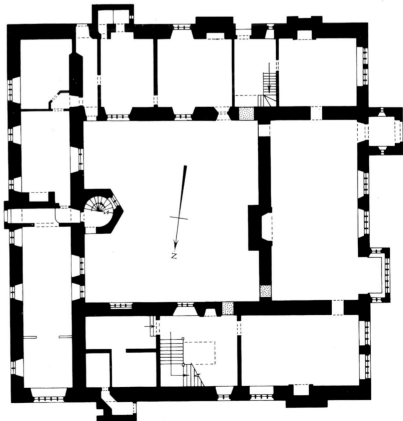

90 Sawston Hall, ground-floor plan. The courtyard still forms an essential part of the circulation of the house: the stair turret within it is a principal means of access to the gallery.

the conventional way, the hall stack juts back into the central courtyard, and the house looks outward across the site of the former, outer court. The earlier part of the house comprises the rear, south range, with a first-floor gallery. Although at each end the gallery has large windows in its outer walls, it has also a long stretch of blank wall punctuated only by the gallery stack. Other large windows overlook the courtyard. Similarly, save for the front range, all the other faces of the house present an old-fashioned, irregular alternation of chimneybreasts, windows and garderobes. Although the gallery was an up-to-date amenity in the 1550s, the open courtyard still performed an important function in reaching it: the only access to the gallery apart from passing through adjoining chambers at either end was by a stair turret at its centre with a door leading out of the courtyard. Sawston combines two courtyard traditions: that of the service courtyard at the rear of the hall range – the Great Chalfield model – and the formal courtyard surrounded by rooms of high status: the tradition of Compton Winyates and Hengrave. Sawston is architecturally considerably more regular than either. But it would be wrong to see Sawston simply as a fusion of such forms. The house is better regarded as an illustration of a continuing flexibility of planning in which, although the functional relationship of the principal parts of the house was established and formulaic, their realisation was not: of a flexibility that allowed for an evolution in architectural taste.

The date of Castle Bromwich Hall (pl. 91) is not known, but it was built for Edward Devereux who was High Sheriff of the County in 1593–4 and knighted in 1611; either of these honours might have provided the occasion for putting up a new house.[50] The basic formula is not unlike that of Sawston: an outward-facing hall range that fronts a rectangular courtyard of similar size. The difference, however, lies in the treatment of the other outer faces of the house and in the original form and subsequent history of the courtyard itself. No stacks project from the outer walls of the house; all face into the court so that virtually all lighting comes through the house's outer walls which are pierced by large, uniform windows, regularly spaced like those of Eastbury. As at Sawston there is a first-floor gallery, but this is placed on the front of the house with no window into the courtyard. Castle Bromwich was modernised, probably in two phases, following its purchase by a new owner in 1657. In the 1680s (the porch may have been given a new front a little earlier) it acquired new stairs and internal plasterwork, and the plan was in part remodelled. It seems likely that at the same time corridors were built on both floors against the internal, flank walls of the courtyard so as to improve the circulation.

The third of these late, outward-facing courtyard houses is Chastleton in Oxfordshire (pls 94, 95). Chastleton was built for Walter Jones, who bought the estate from Robert Catesby (of the Gunpowder Plot) in 1602[51] and whose descendants or close relatives continued to occupy it until 1990. Walter Jones came of a minor gentry family in Monmouthshire, and his father established himself as a clothier in Witney. Walter Jones himself was trained as a lawyer at Lincoln's Inn and for some years served as Town Clerk of Worcester and three times as Member of Parliament. It is not known when he began building the house, but an eighteenth-century rainwater head bears the date 1612, and either this date was there originally or else it represents a continuing family tradition for its completion. The form of the house is largely conventional, except for the matched, flanking stair turrets (a form discussed in the next chapter). There are three storeys above a full service basement, essentially outward-facing and symmetrical on each front. The house is built around a small service courtyard which descends to basement level and is deep and unpleasant, fully justifying Wilbraham's strictures on that at Wilton, but it makes possible a circulation that is, literally, circular – most rooms have two approaches, and the only dead ends are those first-floor chambers that abut against the upper part of the tall hall.

The front elevation is one of the most satisfying of all contemporary architectural designs. The hall is at the centre, rising through a storey and a half; flanking it are high-end and low-end ranges, and flanking these again are turrets that contain the stairs and which rise to low, battlemented towers above roof level. There are three essential elements to this composition. First, the advancing and receding planes of the towers, flanking bays, projecting bays and centre. Second is the counterpoint of differing window levels, created by the taller hall windows at the centre, the lower windows of the parlours and parlour chambers flanking the hall, and beyond these the windows of the stair towers which appear by perspective to break levels again.

91 Castle Bromwich Hall, West Midlands, c. 1600. The flank of a wholly outward-looking, symmetrical, courtyard house.

The effect is accentuated by the efforts made to preserve total symmetry: first, placing the hall door, which is in the traditional off-centre position, in the inner flank of the porch, and second, carrying the porch window up to match that of the hall oriel, even though this meant making the upper part blind where it cuts the floor level of a little room above the porch. The final element in the design is the way in which the ratio of glass to wall becomes greater at the centre of the house.

The problem of combining a hierarchically organised hall entered at one end with a symmetrical elevation was one that continued to exercise builders well into the seventeenth century. In a house with a long façade (as at Shaw) it was possible to balance the hall, on one side of a central front entrance, with other rooms on the other side. In a house where the hall occupied the whole of the centre of a more compact façade, other solutions were necessary. At Fountains Hall in West Yorkshire (pl. 93) a screen between forward-projecting wings contains a central doorway; once passed this, the visitor turns into a short, open passage leading to the hall doorway in one wing. A similar solution was adopted at the much smaller Hambledon in Leicestershire (pl. 204), where wings project a short distance on both the front and the back of the house. On both fronts there is a screen of this sort, arcaded to the front and colonnaded to the rear.[52]

A commoner but more drastic solution than to hide the doorway with a screen was to attempt to conceal the entrance by placing it so that it does not directly face the visitor but lies in the porch's flank wall. Chastleton is one of a group of houses built after 1600, including Burton Agnes in Humberside, Ludstone in Shropshire (pl. 92), Dorfold in Cheshire, Shipton

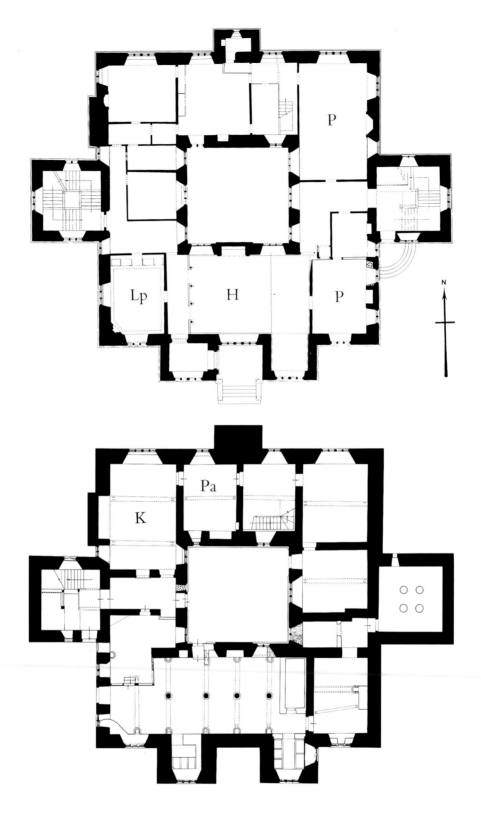

94 (*above and facing page top*) Chastleton House: basement, ground- and first-floor plans. The flanking stair turrets provide stairs of near-equal importance at each end of the house, for state and for family use, an arrangement (discussed in chapter 5) that may have originated in the London area. All services were in the basement. The first-floor rooms in the north range formed (from east to west) a sequence of great chamber, withdrawing room and bedchamber. There is a gallery above them on the second floor, running the length of the northern range and easily reached from these state rooms by the stairs at either end.

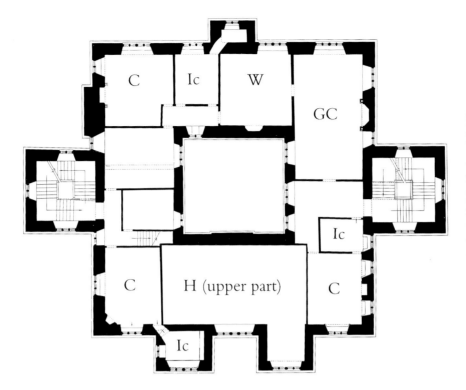

95 (*below*) Chastleton House, Oxfordshire, *c.* 1612. The façade is still composed in a traditional manner, with projecting porch and hall oriel matching each other, but the massing of projections, windows and flanking stair towers is precisely calculated and forms one of the most satisfying architectural compositions of the age. The front door is disguised in the flank of the porch for the sake of symmetry.

96 Littlecote, Wiltshire, *c.* 1590. Typical of a large group of late sixteenth- and early seventeenth-century houses with outward-facing, extended façades, with their halls still entered at the low end, and generally with service-passage plans.

Court in Oxfordshire and Quidenham in Norfolk (pls 174, 175), which make the final sacrifice of external hierarchy to symmetry, in that the very entrance is initially denied. Perhaps still more drastic a treatment of symmetry, and equally significant in terms of the changing hierarchies of the house, was to provide not one front entrance but two, leading into the central range of the house at either end. Two equal doors to the hall occur (or occurred) at Audley End, at Aldermaston in Berkshire (1636; pl. 191; see also p. 181 below), at the Priory at Mansfield Woodhouse in Nottinghamshire (*c.* 1630?),[53] at Norgrove in Worcestershire (1649; pl. 265; see also p. 228 below) and at Raynham as originally built (1622–38); Barton on the Heath in Warwickshire may have been similar[54] as well as Broadlands in Hampshire, where Celia Fiennes observed that 'the hall is in the middle with double doors',[55] and there are houses with this arrangement both among John Thorpe's and John Smythson's plans.[56] All save Barton and Mansfield Woodhouse were architecturally advanced houses; Audley End is the most palatial house of its day. Groombridge in Kent, a house of around 1660 whose details are architecturally up-to-date but whose plan is curiously old-fashioned, combines a double entry of this sort with a centrally entered screen (pl. 240).

It is far from clear how the entrances in these houses were actually intended to work. Faced with two identical doorways, the visitor cannot have known which one to approach; this might or might not have mattered, though the fact that at Norgrove and at Raynham the two doors were in due course replaced by a single one (central at Raynham, into one end of the house at Norgrove) suggests that the arrangement was not considered satisfactory. These houses are a compromise. The provision of doors at both ends of the hall was externally a denial of its hierarchical layout, even though builders clearly still felt it proper to enter the hall at one end and not at its centre. At the same time, these houses offered an alternative entrance by which one might bypass the hall and approach the polite rooms of the house more directly.

The preference for symmetry and regularity over the marking of the house's internal hierarchies, the change in the house's aspect from inward-looking to outward-facing and the taste for ornament that expressed the learning of the builder, have in common a parallel in evolving manners. By not expressing externally their internal arrangements, these houses seem to be making a statement about privacy: to deny that anyone outside the household has any right to know its internal workings or anything of the life of the house's owner beyond obtaining a favourable impression of his cultivation. Only when admitted

97 Gayhurst, Buckinghamshire, 1597. The house with recessed centre and projecting wings provided an image for the houses of the upper gentry that would persist in spite of changes in style and amenities for over a century.

into the house and beyond the hall is the visitor entitled to know such of the life style of his host as his host chooses to show, and the decreasing external prominence given even to the hall seems to indicate the reduced importance that its owner places on its traditional functions. Indeed, in these houses in which the principal entrance is suppressed, public functions seem actively denied. A taste for symmetry and uniformity is universal; a century before the first truly symmetrical façade, Great Chalfield showed how it was possible to approach visual symmetry while preserving marks of distinction. But such principles were fundamentally incompatible, and ultimately architectural changes were licensed by social ones. With the gradual abandonment of the expression of hierarchy as the guiding principle in the appearance of the house, more purely formal considerations might be invoked in its design.

The achievement of the 1570s was to have produced a model for a house that was outward-looking, whose principal elevations were symmetrical and whose appearance was unconstrained by any need to reflect its internal workings. By the end of the century, houses of the type of Shaw and Corsham – the typical, late Elizabethan and Jacobean E-plan house with long façade and short wings such as Burton Agnes (Humberside), Littlecote (Wiltshire) (pl. 96), Gayhurst (Buckinghamshire) (pl. 97), Montacute (Somerset) and Quenby (Leicestershire) – and outward-facing courtyard houses with their façades similarly arranged such as Barlborough, Chastleton, Chipchase (Northumberland) and Horton Kirby (Kent) – were ubiquitous, norms for the form of house suitable to the higher gentry. Central both to this modern house and to the older model, inward-looking and accretive, was an aesthetic in which the recognition of fitness for purpose was an essential aspect of visual appreciation. However, whereas the parts of the hierarchical house expressed the way in which it provided for household and community, in the developed, symmetrical house the entire building is appropriated to the standing of its owner and the house expresses to the world his place in the community of his peers. For as long as tension had remained between the demands of uniformity and those of hierarchy, the external form of the house was largely determined by attempts at its resolution. The attainment of such uniformity in houses of the generation of Shaw made regularity a new standard of architectural fashion, and opened the way for the overall design of the house's exterior to be determined by considerations that were purely architectural.

4

Alternatives and Experiments, 1550–1630

The Lodge

By the late sixteenth century, exteriors of the most advanced houses no longer expressed their internal hierarchies. It is not a coincidence that while designs for houses were becoming more purely formal than they had ever been, interest in architecture among builders was growing and esteem for architects was increasing. At the same time, changing domestic relations and demands for rooms for the disposition of which there were no precedents – the subjects of chapters 7 and 8 – meant that the needs of the household were becoming increasingly difficult to accommodate within the constraints of traditional plans. Taken together, these factors would engender a period of unprecedented inventiveness in the form of the house.

Many of the greatest houses of the age were built by members of a small number of families linked by marriage, by royal service, and by the early acquaintance of individuals. Even more than those of lesser men, their huge houses were vehicles of entertainment whose justification, over and above the display proper to members of an élite, was the reception of the monarch. They are the most spectacular expressions of the contemporary explosion of building, and they are houses of great sophistication. But although the lavishness of Burghley, Holdenby and Theobalds, of Hardwick, Worksop and Wollaton, of Audley End, Hatfield and Knole may have been beyond the reach of lesser builders, these houses could still provide an education for craftsmen and patterns of polite living in accommodation, amenities and display.

98 Wothorpe House, Northamptonshire. Built by Thomas Cecil as a lodge to Burghley House and described in 1662 as 'the least of Noble Houses, and best of Lodges'. The contemporary taste for architectural 'curiosity' found its readiest expression in the lodge, where hierarchical forms could largely be dispensed with and experiments indulged.

Although the sheer size of these houses prevented them from providing direct models for those of lesser men, there was another kind of building that might do so, often associated with these great houses and sometimes of equal sophistication. This was the lodge. The lodge had for a long time already provided the landowner with a more limited range of accommodation for occasional use only. But although lodges provided for less than the full range of functions of the gentry house, the varied needs of their builders meant that lodges ranged in size from buildings of no more than two or three rooms to houses which at first seem little different from the permanent dwellings of the aristocracy. Lodges varied in form as much as in size, with exteriors less bound by precedent than conventional houses and more flexible in their plan, and this freedom was to make the lodge a powerful model when in due course changes in the layout of the great house became inevitable as a result of changes in the household and communal functions that traditional arrangements had served. As models, lodges functioned by example, by a simplification and concentration of plan which tended to eliminate redundant spaces, and by their aptness for the employment of innovative forms. The lodge could be the vehicle for conceits and architectural experimentation.

More directly, lodges might influence the design of more conventional houses by becoming regular dwellings themselves when circumstances induced their owners to live in them permanently or to dispose of them to someone who would. The lodge had much in common with the secondary seat on an estate that a landowner would seldom visit but where it was expedient to maintain at least a symbolic presence, and a well-found lodge might readily be placed at the disposal of an heir before he inherited the family's principal house, of a younger son for whom lifetime provision should be made, or of a widow in need of a dower house. Sons and dowagers were people for whose duties and life styles a fully equipped house might be inappropriate, but who for honour's sake must be decently housed.

A lodge might come to be occupied for considerable stretches of time, but the accommodation it provided differed essentially from the house whose owner expected to exercise the full range of household and community functions. Life at the lodge did not normally call for a great hall for the entertainment of tenantry or to mediate relationships within a highly structured household, nor in general for a range of state apartments in which to receive distinguished visitors. It did, however, call for a building of visual distinction which would announce the standing of its owner in a manner comparable to his principal house, and for rooms in which he and his friends could be entertained for a period that might be short or long: where he could, so to speak, rough it in style.

There were lodges everywhere. Lodges of the kind that provided simple accommodation for occasional use in a building of some architectural distinction often lay a few miles from the owner's principal seat: an easy ride into the country and a distance that was neither too close to responsibilities for relaxation nor too remote from them for speedy return at need. In parks they were frequent, and in the sixteenth century parks were ubiquitous;[1] in some places, notably in the old royal forests and deer parks, lodges might be thick on the ground. In 1634 in addition to the chief lodge in the royal park at Woodstock there were 'many more old, handsom lodges, wherein many gentlemen of quality do reside';[2] in 1649 parliamentary commissioners recorded four of them, three with six rooms or more. In the 1670s John Wilmot, Earl of Rochester, succesfully sought the keepership of Woodstock Park for the sake of the privacy that its lodge gave him for writing and to entertain his intimates, at a convenient distance from his nephew's house at Ditchley and his own at Adderbury, some 14 miles to the north.[3] Celia Fiennes wrote that in the New Forest 'there are fifteen lodges, and these are disposed to gentlemen that have under keepers that have the care of it'.[4]

The sixteenth- and seventeenth-century lodge had a dual origin. Its functions had evolved centuries before, and were well summed up by the Earl of Dorset, writing in 1605 to justify the building of a new lodge for James I at Ampthill.[5] It was to be a house where the king might stay, 'not in state, yet sufficient for to serve for the enjoying of his pleasures of hunting and hawking, by the presence of necessary officers, and no more than are requisite for his royal person to have' and the house was to contain 'convenient rooms, such as are for necessity, not for pleasure'. Sir Philip Sidney must have conceived the star-shaped lodges to which Basilius and his queen retire for a year as something rather similar, situated in the depth of the forest, remote from court. The Ampthill scheme was for a building large enough to accommodate the great officers of state as well as the king, but what was needed on a large scale for the monarch was needed at an appropriate level for any landowner with an outlying estate that he might wish to visit but not to reside on.

Historically, hunting had probably been the most usual reason for needing a lodge, for resort within a deer park with no more than a group of intimates; when in the mid-sixteenth century the Earl of Leicester invited Lord Berkeley to Kenilworth Castle, hoping to persuade him to show the earl some documents that he possessed, he flattered Berkeley by 'lodginge him, as a brother and fellowe huntseman, in his owne bed-chamber'.[6] Lodges were also of value for occasional lodgings in the course of the peripatetic stag hunting of the sixteenth and seventeenth centuries. In 1559 the same Lord Berkeley,

His hounds being come Away goes hee and his wife a progres of buck hunting to the parks of Barkewell, Groby, Bradgate, Leicester forrest, Toley, and others on that side his house: And after a small repose, Then to the parks of Kenilworth, Ashby, Wedgenocke, and others, on the other side his house: And this was the course of this lord (more or lesse) for the thirty next somers at least: not omitting his own at Callowden and in the County of Gloucester.[7]

But as well as for hunting, lodges were built by great men as a place of occasional escape from a formal and a public life. Randle Holme in 1688 described lodges as 'Houses built in Forest Chases and Parks for preservation of the Deere; also for recreation, and to see the game hunted'; such lodges were clearly allied to 'Summer Houses, Bowers, Places to which the Gentry resort, and able there during the summer season, for their Recreation and pastime'.[8] At Claverdon in Warwickshire Thomas Spencer built 'a very fair tower' (pl. 99) which still stands, a most unconventional building but where 'for the great Hospitality which he kept thereat he was the mirrour of the County'.[9]

The lodge built as a place of private retirement has a long history. The elaborate complex of buildings in Woodstock Park must have had a purpose of this sort. Here in the twelfth century, in an architectural fantasy inspired by Sicily and by the legend of Tristram and Isolde, Henry II had kept his mistress, Fair Rosamond.[10] Francis Bacon's project for a pavilion on an island, described in chapter 2, was the prototype for a more elaborate lodge, Verulam House, close to the same site half a mile from his principal seat of Gorhambury.[11] This was square in plan with several heated rooms, the chimneys trunked together to form a central feature above and with an elaborate staircase in the middle of the house rising to a roof gallery surrounding, or flanked by, the chimneys. Kitchen and other service rooms were underground, and entertaining rooms were richly decorated. Bacon is said to have spent the summer at Verulam House and the winter at Gorhambury, and though this is probably an oversimplification, the nature of the lodge lent itself to such seasonal use. (It was at the Earl of Arundel's lodge at Highgate that Bacon himself died, having caught a chill in the winter of 1626 after experimenting with preserving a chicken by packing it in snow.)

This kind of lodge formed an ideal vehicle for architectural invention, and John Aubrey described Bacon's as 'the most inge-

lack of hierarchical organisation shows most immediately in the central entrance, although for convenience the parlour is still at the opposite end from the kitchens.

The situation is often the first clue to a house having been built as a lodge. It frequently stands on the brow of a hill, both to see and to be seen: the first, perhaps, to afford the best view of a distant prospect and the latter in order to advertise the owner's presence, his taste or simply to enhance a landscape where the lodge's builder was the principal landowner. A lodge at Risley in Derbyshire described around 1700 is typical of the genre: 'The main house is an ancient, large, convenient building . . . [with] a very fine park a little mile outside the town, in which stands a very handsome lodge on a considerable

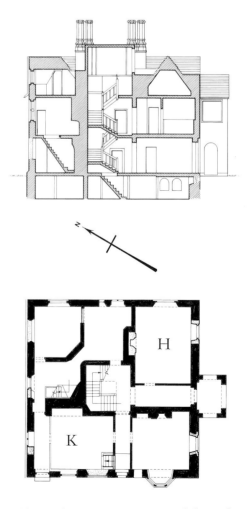

100   Little Walden Park, Essex, *c.* 1620: ground-floor plan and section (demolished *c.* 1955 and recorded in its final state). A park lodge for Audley End, with an unconventional plan and a central stair formerly rising to a viewing gallery.

niously contrived little pile, that ever I saw'. He was probably right in claiming that Bacon himself was 'the chiefest architect' though he had practical assistance – the frequent function of the contemporary architect, as has been seen – from a Mr Dobson, father of William Dobson the painter.[12] The house was demolished in the seventeenth century, but the same ingenuity with which a central staircase rose between chimneys to a viewing platform appeared at Little Walden Park, a lodge of Audley End, pulled down around 1960 but known from old photographs and from drawings made before its demolition (pl. 100).[13]

Better known is the ruin of Wothorpe House, outside Stamford (pl. 98). Wothorpe is a mile and a half from Burghley, and was built according to Fuller 'by Thomas Earl of Exeter, to retire to (as he pleasantly said) out of the dust, whilst his great House of Burleigh was a sweeping'.[14] The outer walls and floors have collapsed, leaving a central core containing the fireplaces and four gaunt towers, with windows derived directly from Serlio. A plan among the Thorpe drawings is so close to it that it may be of it.[15] The plan is geometric, unconventional, and above all completely unhierarchical, as suited a building whose function was simply to house its owner and his close family. The

101 Newark Park, Ozleworth, Gloucestershire, c. 1540. A small, symmetrical lodge with a central, classical door surround which is very advanced stylistically for its date. The battlements are for ornament, not defence, but evoke a parallel between hunting and war.

eminence, from which there is a noble prospect.'[16] Newark Park at Ozleworth in Gloucestershire (pl. 101) was built, probably in the 1540s, on an outlying estate of Sir Nicholas Poyntz, some 15 miles north of his principal seat at Iron Acton in Gloucestershire.[17] Poyntz had recently greatly enlarged his principal house in order to receive a visit from Henry VIII in appropriate splendour, and Newark is equally fashionable in terms of its precocious classicism. It stands castle-like on the edge of a high escarpment, and in the prominence of its site it is like many lodges; such settings would in due course be admired for important houses of any kind. Newark provides the limited

accommodation found in most lodges, but it offers this in a house of great sophistication. The front of the house is completely symmetrical – without precedent in the main body of any great house at the date of its building, though paralleled at another contemporary lodge, Beckley Park in Oxfordshire (pls 102, 103) – and the central entrance shows a remarkably correct, pedimented, Tuscan portico. Acton Court itself combines classical and late Gothic detail in an arbitrary manner; the porch of Newark is altogether more correct. Inside, the house provided two rooms on each of four floors, with a hall that is little more than a room of entry.

An anonymous painting (pl. 104) is an excellent illustration of a lodge in an appropriate setting. On the left is the lodge built by Henry Howard, Earl of Northampton, as Warden of Greenwich Royal Park – nominally a species of superior game keeper, but in fact an honorary post which gave one the right to hunt and to maintain the lodge as a retreat and as a place of

102 (*left*) and 103 (*above*) Beckley Park, Oxfordshire, *c.* 1540. A lodge for Rycote Park, 4 miles away. The rear view shows the tower-like projections that contain stairs and a garderobe.

104 Anon. (*c.* 1620): Greenwich Park, looking towards London. The Earl of Northampton's lodge (on the site of Sir Christopher Wren's Royal Observatory) was compact and architecturally sophisticated, and functioned both as a lodge and as a suburban house of retirement and pleasure. Deer and citizens disport themselves sedately in the park.

Cerea ſic torto capitur Ficedula reti,   Aurea frugiferos dum tollunt tempora vultus.

105 (*top*) Embroidered cushion cover from Hardwick Hall, Derbyshire. In being copied (perhaps by Bess of Hardwick – Elizabeth, Countess of Shrewsbury), the house in the background of the engraving in pl. 106 has been transformed into a castellated lodge of a kind with which the English were familiar, an appropriate setting for the subject of the picture.

106 (*above*) Phillips Galle, after Jan van der Straet, 1578: The Return from the Bird Hunt. The pattern for the cushion cover in pl. 105.

entertainment. The house is a little castle, an appropriately romantic image for a house at the top of a hill; it commands a tremendous view (Christopher Wren probably consciously imitated its general form when he built the Royal Observatory on the old foundations in 1675);[18] there are deer in the park and well-dressed citizens disport themselves sedately in a suitably pastoral setting. Another illustration is that on an embroidered cushion cover at Hardwick (pl. 105): a small, mixed party is out hawking; at the left foreground there seems to be some sort of a standing – a building that did no more than provide shelter (sometimes raised up) to watch the hunt; in the distance is another lodge, castellated like Howard's, and with smoke coming out of the chimneys – indicating, if not permanent occupation, at least entertainment of a fairly elaborate kind. The Flemish print that forms the basis for this cushion cover (pl. 106) shows a conventionalised Italian villa in the distance in the place where the lodge stands;[19] when the image was translated into needle-work by Elizabeth, Countess of Shrewsbury (Bess of Hardwick), or her companions, the alien form was rejected in favour of a building with turrets and battlements and of a kind with which they could identify.

Beckley Park, a lodge for Rycote, another vanished house, stands within the double moat that survives from a twelfth-century castle formerly on the site; the garderobe and stair turrets that project strongly from its back wall may be conscious echoes of the bastions of the demolished castle. Besides its setting, a castle style for the lodge was also popular because of the pleasing analogy between war and the pursuit of the stag. In 1567 Ludovic Greville decided to 'make a Castle about a quarter of a mile Southwards from the old Mansion House at Milcote and to call it Mount Grevill . . . on the top of a hill' and went so far as to obtain licence to crenellate it.[20] At Nonsuch the courtyard entrance to Henry VIII's suite was marked by a figure of Scipio, the Roman general, and Catherine Parr's by Penthesilea the Amazon queen: an iconography appropriate to the form and use of the house, even though its occupants will have engaged in nothing more warlike than hunting in the park at a pace adjusted to the king's great bulk, his ill-health and his ulcerous leg.[21]

Nonsuch is a link with a further source for the castle style in the fantastic banqueting houses built early in the sixteenth century at Hampton Court and the tower built to overlook the tilt-yard at Greenwich Palace.[22] For jousting, the symbolism of a castle is obvious. The banqueting house was a sort of summer house, generally in a garden but sometimes on the roof of a great house, and it was so called as a place of informal retirement for the taking of the banquet – the dessert – that followed a formal dinner. As with so much sixteenth-century building, the banqueting house was another aspect of the public display of exclusivity. The banquet itself was a species of elaborate picnic with fruits and sweetmeats, and the banqueting house provided an appropriately sophisticated setting for a rather precious entertainment. At Nonsuch there was an elaborate timber-framed building of two storeys with some sort of projecting balcony at each corner and a roof lantern, and surrounded by earthworks in the form of a miniature artillery fort.[23] There was a large room inside (44 by 20 feet) for feasting and entertainment. When as at Nonsuch the banqueting house was elaborated into a setting for large-scale picnics in the park and with rooms for retirement, it began to approach pretty closely to the functions of the lodge. It could serve, too, as the centrepiece for sophisticated play-acting and pageantry. The culture of Henry VIII's court had inherited much of the precious, artificial chivalry of the Court of Burgundy; under Elizabeth the ideals of knightly virtue might also seem appropriate to the courtiers of a queen. Such a self-conscious medievalism formed a counter-current to humanist classicism and engendered a great deal of make-believe in literature and in polite entertainment.[24] It was here that mock castles found their value as the scenes of allegory and fancy dress – for the courtier's mock assault on the castle of beauty, for pageants and jousting. The sixteenth century's delight in symbols and devices could easily be realised in the lodge: free from the practical constraints and precedents that controlled the plan and appearance of houses for regular living, the lodge provided a vehicle for architectural invention and experiment.

However, such artificial structures as these could not provide immediate models for the houses of ordinary gentlemen. Such a model was more readily provided by buildings of less precious and of more practical form. The lodge originated in the Middle Ages, and even the earliest are unconventional in terms of the standard forms of medieval housing. Lodge Farm at Pamphill in Dorset is compact, upright, with two heated rooms on each floor; the larger room on the ground floor is scarcely a conventional hall, nor the smaller a kitchen or parlour, and it is far from clear how the building was used in practice.[25] When the Royal Commission published the building in 1975, the house was thought to have dated to the seventeenth century, incorporating a re-used medieval window. The house is actually of the fifteenth century and the window (and medieval roof) are in place, but the misdating is significant, the result of the lodge as a type defying orthodox views of the development of house plans.

Equally unorthodox is Old Hall at Kneesall in Nottinghamshire (pl. 107), built probably around 1525 for Sir John Hussey.[26] This building too is anachronistic by conventional standards. The plan, with the principal entrance opening into a lobby against a centrally placed chimneystack, was to become a pattern for yeoman houses of the late sixteenth century and the seventeenth through a wide area of the Midlands and beyond, and its very early appearance at Kneesall as the secondary seat of a member of the aristocracy is anomalous both in date and in the social level for which it was built. The elaborate terracotta moulding to the front door establishes the house at once as the property of someone of a high social class, though the arrangement of rooms within seems little different from these farm houses of two generations later. Kneesall has been claimed

107 Old Hall, Kneesall, Nottinghamshire, *c.* 1525. A small house but with a highly decorated entrance, built as a hunting lodge for a great man but on a plan which would be widely adopted for the dwellings of lesser men.

108 House at Sutton Coldfield, Warwickshire. One of a group of farmhouses built *c.* 1490 on newly cleared woodland, and possibly taking the form of the lodge as their model. The house is not dissimilar to the Old Hall at Kneesall, but lacks Kneesall's prestigious entrance.

as the origin of the lobby-entrance plan (the layout in which the entrance leads into a lobby against a central chimneystack, with rooms off it on either side) but it is unlikely to have been unique: the group of small, sophisticated stone houses built by Bishop Vesey for his tenants at Sutton Coldfield around 1490 includes at least one which is very like it (pl. 108).[27] Bishop Vesey's houses were planted in cleared woodland, in a context not unlike that of lodges in a forest, and the form may already have been associated with such a setting. If so, then the subsequent adoption of the lobby-entrance plan by a large group of members of a somewhat lower, but newly prospering, social class – the class of the yeoman farmer – would be not unlike the way in which other characteristics of the lodge were ultimately to appear as elements in houses of the gentry.

The only constraint on the form of the lodge was its intended usage and the style of life to which its owner aspired. Many lodges – though the arangement was equally capable of a wide variety of forms – seem to have been relatively simple buildings, but with a resident caretaker to look after the place and perhaps to act also as park keeper (and presumably to attend on the owner and his party on their visits); one can only speculate from the amount and variety of lodging accommodation provided whether these visits were intended as brief or prolonged. A set of plans among the Smythson drawings (pl. 109) is for a building of this sort,[28] and the fact that these are inscribed in a later hand 'a good plan for small houses' shows how easily the distinctive conventions of the lodge could be forgotten once the planning needs of ordinary houses had come more closely to resemble the amenities of lodges.

In larger lodges the range of accommodation more nearly resembled that to be found in any conventional great house. This might be expected; the larger the house, whether for permanent or for temporary accommodation, the more complex the organisation required for its running and the more stratified the household. Sheriff Hutton in Humberside was a royal park on which Sir Arthur Ingram himself had a long lease, and around 1622, having pulled down an old lodge, he started to build a new one of considerable size and sophistication.[29] In plan it was U-shaped, with forward-projecting wings flanking a forecourt. Though a lodge, Sheriff Hutton had a great hall with a carved screen, great chamber, lodging chambers and gallery. The centre of the house was two ranges deep, still an innovative layout in 1622, and services were in a basement. The house still contains chimneypieces, plasterwork and woodwork of high quality, and the great chamber over the hall – presumably the principal entertaining room – was entered by a broad archway in line with the principal entrance from a stair that was particularly remarked on by parliamentary commissioners in 1650. Ingram's building clearly had most of the amenities of a conventional house, a fact remarked on at the time. Ingram's agent reported after a visit by a party of Irish peers in 1632 that 'the lords did much commend the house, and said it was a pity it was not continually inhabited'.[30] Its later reduction in size seems to have been due more to economics than to any basic irrationality in its plan. The royal lodge at Bagshot had a conventional hall with parlour at one end, pantry and buttery at the other, and when surveyed by parliamentary commissioners in 1650 it was described as 'large and usefull and fitt for any gent. of a large retinewe'.[31]

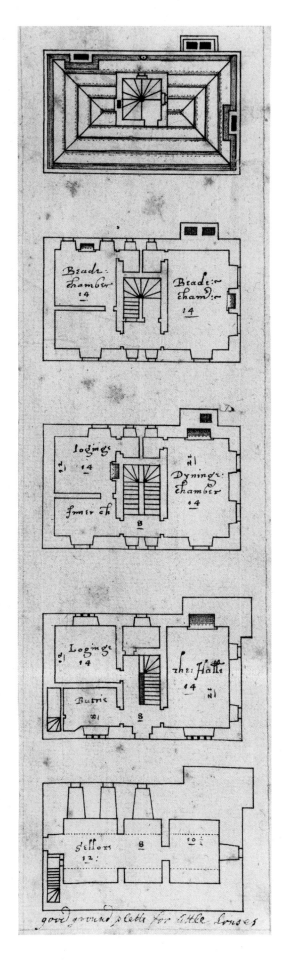

With such houses, temporary housing merges with buildings for permanent occupation. It is clear from many of these examples that in time the distinctive forms and functions of the lodge could easily be forgotten – and indeed, all of those whose history is known came in due course to be lived in as wholly normal houses. Fuller called Wothorpe (pl. 98) 'the least of Noble Houses, and best of Lodges'.[32] Wothorpe was for occasional use, but Fuller implicitly recognised – as explicitly did the parliamentary commissioners whose remarks on Bagshot Lodge have been quoted – that a suitably equipped lodge could perfectly well serve the needs of a conventional house. For the likely owner of a house the size of Ingram's, the presence of a traditional hall was still a valid amenity in a permanent residence.

Some lodges might become regular houses with virtually no changes whatsoever if their plans suited the way of life of their occupants. Rochford in Hertfordshire had been a royal park until the seventeenth century, when Charles I 'conveyed it to William earl of Salisbury, who (I suppose) granted it to Sir William Hartington, Knight, who converted the lodge into a good house, fit for his own habitation, where he lived sometimes'.[33] Such

110 (*above*)   Upper Swell Manor, Gloucestershire, *c*. 1630. Arranged for its owner's occasional use as a house of entertainment and to accommodate a resident caretaker. Immediately inside the front door a stair rises to a highly decorated dining chamber on the first floor.

109 (*left*)   Robert Smythson: plans for a lodge, endorsed in a later hand 'a good plan for small houses'. The form of the lodge would prove highly adaptable when a house was required without the full range of accommodation in the conventional country house.

conversion probably occurred most readily if their later inhabitants were lower in the social scale than their original builders, needing houses of less complexity, and such a change might take place naturally if outlying estates with lodges upon them were sold off. The so-called Royal Lodge at Huby in North Yorkshire (pl. 111) was another enterprise of Sir Arthur Ingram's, less grand than Sheriff Hutton and probably a little later in date, and built in another royal park on which Ingram held a lease.[34] Externally it looks like the farmhouse that it has long been, and only its early, deep plan and the sophistication of remaining internal decoration shows that it was originally anything else. The lodge at Little Walden (pl. 99) had long been a farmhouse when Richard Neville, 3rd Lord Braybroke, described it in 1836 and commended the view from the top;[35] he was evidently unaware of its original use. But such non-hierarchical houses could be permanently occupied by families of the class of their builders once a modification of traditional household relations had rendered obsolete traditional layouts. In the late seventeenth century Wothorpe was occupied for some time by the Duke of Buckingham and his family;[36] in the eighteenth it became a dower house for the Cecils of Burghley.

Other lodges required more or less of alteration to turn them into regular houses. An early example is Ightham Court in Kent (pls 112, 113), built for a branch of the Willoughby family whose principal seat was at Bore Place at Chiddingstone, some 7 miles off.[37] The detailed history of the building is obscure, but its earliest part seems to be a house of three storeys with a symmetrical front, central porch, and a tower at the rear in line with the front entrance, containing a staircase. Ightham had a

symmetrical front, with a central porch – the same layout as Beckley Park and Newark. Its date is as uncertain as its plan, but it may have been built in the 1550s. In 1575 it was enlarged and radically altered. The entrance was moved through 90 degrees and given a fashionable new porch with superimposed classical orders beneath a pediment, while a further range was built beyond the porch in order that the new entrance should still lie at the centre of a symmetrical façade. In 1596, having inherited Wollaton in Nottinghamshire, the family moved there and sold Ightham Court which seems to have been occupied permanently as a gentry house ever since. At Fawsley a building in the park which had originated as little more than a hunting tower or standing to watch the deer was enlarged in stages and in 1675 was the dower house of Anne Devereux, widow of Richard Knightley, who had the park as her jointure.[38]

Three lodges of the aristocracy are instructive in having a variety of origins as houses of temporary resort, and in their later transformation into permanent residences in an equal variety of ways. These are Cranborne and Sherborne in Dorset, and Bidston Hall in Cheshire, each built or acquired in rather different circumstances and each altered or enlarged in a rather different way. Bidston (pls 114, 115) stands on a bluff at the tip of the Wirral peninsula, where a park had been created by 1400; it was the property of the Earls of Derby, whose principal seats were at Knowsley and Lathom. Bidston seems to have been built in two phases, the first phase having been undertaken for Henry Stanley, 4th Earl, probably shortly before his death in 1593. Stewards' accounts mention frequent visits to the place by the earl for a few days at a time, the typical usage of a hunting lodge, and the date is suggested by the evident employment of the same masons as those working at Stoneyhurst between 1592 and 1597 for the earl's friend (and frequent visitor to Knowsley), Sir Richard Shireburn.[39]

Bidston Hall is a simple, two-storey building with a central hall and short cross wings extending to the rear, with a parlour and perhaps a study at one end and a second parlour and a kitchen at the other. Over the hall is a great chamber, with chambers of very similar size and status beyond. There is little in the layout to distinguish Bidston from the standard, hall-and-cross wings house plan that was widespread for the lesser gentry or higher yeomanry, represented by Gervase Markham's plan (pl. 5), save for a vital difference – the entry into the centre of the hall, which is virtually unprecedented at the date and which at once sets the house apart from conventional domestic parallels. The porch may be original or an addition, but window mullions in both house and porch are of an unusual, circular section and there is no indication that the central doorway into

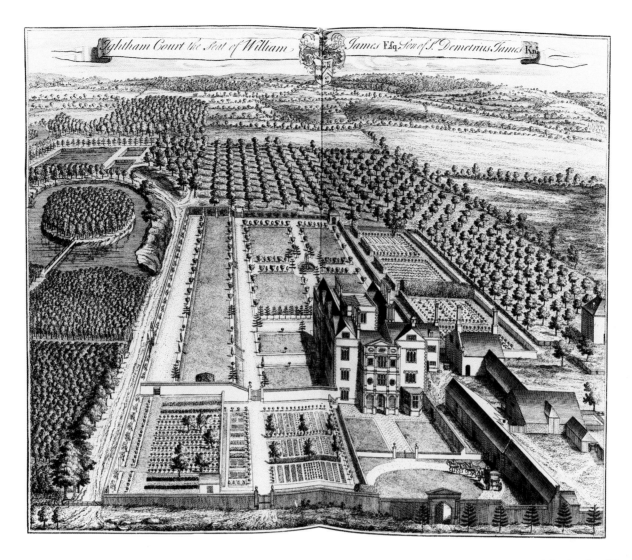

Ighltham Court the Seat of William James Esq. Son of S. Demetrius James K.t

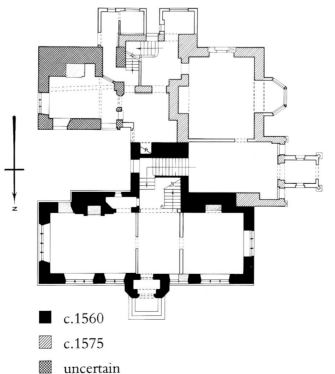

■ c.1560

▨ c.1575

▩ uncertain

112 (*above*) Jan Kip: Ightham Court, Kent, 1719 (engraving). A mid-sixteenth-century lodge, converted into a house for regular occupation in the 1570s. The conversion included the addition of an entrance porch with superimposed classical orders.

113 (*left*) Ightham Court: ground-floor plan. The sixteenth-century layout is not fully recoverable, but the northern range is the earlier building, with central entrance; the addition to the east comprised a more impressive entry, hall, and improved accommodation on the upper floors.

114 (*above*) Bidston Hall, Merseyside. Built as a hunting lodge for the 4th Earl of Derby, *c.* 1590–93, and modestly enlarged as a permanent house by the 6th Earl in the 1620s. The front was originally gabled.

115 (*right*) Bidston Hall: ground-floor plan. The centrally entered hall, from the first phase of building in the 1590s, was revolutionary at that date and was as yet unparalleled in a house for regular occupation and of otherwise conventional form. The hall of Bidston denies the hierarchical layout of the halls of conventional houses.

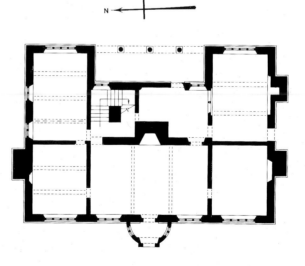

the house has itself been altered. Bidston does, however, show evidence of alteration within a fairly short time of its building. The park was leased out between 1596 and 1617, but thereafter the 6th Earl took it back in hand. William Webb in 1622 said of the building that

> though it be lesse than many other seats, which his Honour hath, wherein to make his residence, when he is so pleased; yet for the pleasant scituation of this . . . his Lordship seems much to affect the same, and enlargeth the conveniences therein for his pleasure and abode.[40]

After the death of his wife in 1627 the earl is said to have retired to Bidston and handed over the management of his estates to his son. The most easily distinguished of the 6th Earl's alterations was the deepening of the central range in order to provide a modest increase in the chamber accommodation on the first floor – presumably including dependent chambers which no longer exist – and to provide a south-facing, open loggia below. These are not great changes, and are dedicated more to the improvement of its amenities than to the radical restructuring or enlargement of the house. None the less, with these improvements it makes a house of considerable dignity, and one to which evidently even a nobleman need not be ashamed of retiring.

Sherborne in Dorset (pl. 22) was built for Sir Walter Raleigh, who acquired the estate in 1592;[41] John Aubrey described it as 'a delicate Lodge in the Park, of Brick, not big, but very convenient for its bignes, a place to retire from the Court in Summer time, and to contemplate etc.'.[42] Like Lumsden's project at Sheriff Hutton, the house lies only a little way from the ruins of the medieval castle, and it has polygonal corner turrets that may be an obeisance to the old building. The accommodation was limited: on the ground floor there were no more than a hall, a parlour of almost equal size, and two lesser rooms, one of which may have been a buttery. Entry into the house was into one of the angle turrets, an extreme (and early) example of the way in which an off-centre entrance might be disguised in the interests of achieving an apparently symmetrical elevation, and this same turret evidently contained a winder service stair up from a basement kitchen.[43] An oblong, well stair rises to the upper floors at the back part of the house – a plan that in the seventeenth century was gradually to become a norm, but again an arrangement of which Sherborne may be among the earliest surviving examples and which is discussed further below. In 1617 the house was acquired by Sir John Digby and transformed from a disgraced courtier's place of temporary retreat into a permanent seat of the aristocracy. As such, enlargement was necessary. This was done by throwing wings out beyond the towers, thus retaining the four original external elevations but doubling its accommodation. Probably only the contemporary fashion for curious planning would have accepted so bizarre a solution, although the same was done at another lodge, Westwood in Worcestershire, discussed below.

Cranborne, also in Dorset (pls 116, 117), is a lodge of different origins.[44] The original house was built as a royal hunting lodge in the thirteenth century, and it is not certain whether it was a self-contained building or whether the medieval structure that survives was built as a solar block attached to a great hall, since demolished without trace. In any case the medieval core of the present house still stood little altered in 1609 when Robert Cecil, Earl of Salisbury, who had acquired the estate in 1604, began work on its conversion and modernisation as a secondary seat – a seat that was to be the centre of his West Country estates but one which as James I's chief minister he would seldom find time to visit. Plans for the alteration and enlargement of the house, probably drawn up by William Arnold, allow the use of the house to be analysed in considerable detail, and these show both provision for the lodging and entertainment of distinguished visitors (the king made five visits to Cranborne) and at the same time that accommodation was arranged with considerable economy.

The centre of the house comprises the medieval building, and in William Arnold's plans this contains the conventional provision of hall, buttery and access from the kitchens. On the top floor of this block, over a tall hall, is a suite of great chamber, withdrawing room and 'king's chamber' – the royal bedchamber, with another room beyond it which is called 'lodging' on the plan but which could clearly be used as a closet or inner chamber at need. This central block is flanked by two lodging blocks. One of these, at the low end of the house, is probably for other guests and for important retainers (or possibly for a resident steward or caretaker): it has independent external access from beyond the house and none from within the building on ground-floor level. The other, at the high end, contains on the ground floor what is clearly a sort of two-room flat of parlour and chamber (neither of them large) for Cecil's own use. Above this is a dining room, on a level with the suite of state rooms. Also within this high-end wing is the great stair, providing the formal approach to these upper-floor entertaining rooms. On the top floor are further chambers and several rooms described on the plan as 'dead' – spaces, presumably, either inaccessible beneath the roof or at any rate not fitted up.

The interest of the Cranborne scheme (which was only partly carried out) lies less in how much was done but in how little. By comparison with Cecil's great house at Hatfield, Cranborne is tiny, and even though it has a formal, state suite these rooms are no more than what was provided for important guests in a great many permanent residences of the higher gentry who would never aspire to entertain the sovereign, while other lodgings are even more scanty. Cecil's own suite has besides his own chamber one small room for a personal servant or as a closet. The house has a study, but this is very small, difficult to get to (up a little newel stair that goes nowhere else) and of necessity private: there would scarcely be room for anyone else within it. In fact less seems to have been done to the house at the time even than the enlargements envisaged in these

116 Cranborne Lodge, Dorset. A medieval lodge, enlarged in 1608–12 for occasional visits on one of the outlying estates of Robert Cecil, 1st Earl of Salisbury, where he could entertain James I and indulge the king's passion for hunting.

drawings. Cranborne has many of the attributes of a conventional gentry house, but it is not the conventional house of a grandee. Though further work was done in 1647, in the later seventeenth century the house remained empty for long periods of time: it was only much later that the Earls of Salisbury were prepared to conform to what, if one was to live in the house, would have to be a less than aristocratic style of living.

What characterises nearly all these lodges is their unorthodox plan forms and often their equally unusual appearance. In both they show their builders' willingness to adopt elements that at the time when they were built were virtually unknown in houses for regular occupation: doubled-up ranges, centralised layouts, symmetrical elevations, low-end principal staircases and other features which when not positively bizarre were all in due course to be found in conventional houses. Two large lodges, Westwood

(pl. 120) and Lulworth Castle (pl. 121), illustrate these characteristics particularly clearly. Westwood in Worcestershire is of around 1600;[45] Lulworth Castle in Dorset is of 1608.[46] Externally they are very different: Lulworth is a mock-medieval castle with battlements and corner towers; Westwood, built for Sir John Packington in his capacity as Bow-bearer of Malvern Chase, is a riot of bay windows, shaped gables, emblematic cresting and high chimneystacks. But in layout they resemble each other very closely.[47] The plan of each comprises three parallel ranges of which the middle range provided for circulation, and in each the entrance is (or was) into the end of the central, passage range and leads directly towards the stairs. Lulworth was remodelled in the eighteenth century and gutted by fire in the twentieth; at an early date the entrance to Westwood was moved to the centre of the hall from its original position and the stair reconstructed, but the original arrangement is clear. (Another early alteration at Westwood was the addition of flying wings in order to increase its accommodation.) What may be preliminary plans for Westwood are among the Thorpe drawings (pl. 118):[48] if not, at least they represent a house of an identical kind. The entry lies similarly into the central cell, and the hall is located on one side,

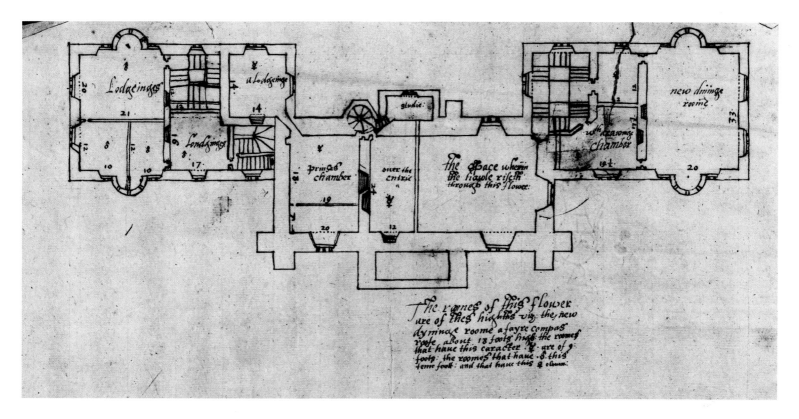

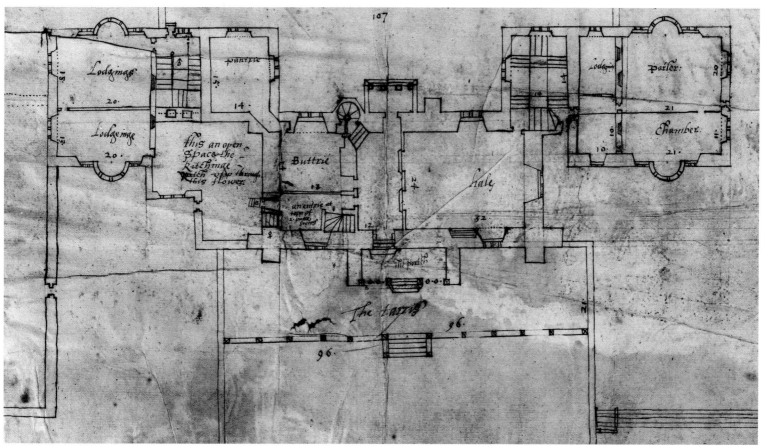

117   Cranborne Lodge: ground- and first-floor plans. Schemes (only partly carried out) prepared by the mason/architect William Arnold for the building's enlargement, *c.* 1609. Despite the standing of the builder and his intended guest and the richness of the external ornament, the accommodation is relatively modest; as built the house provided even less room than is shown in these plans.

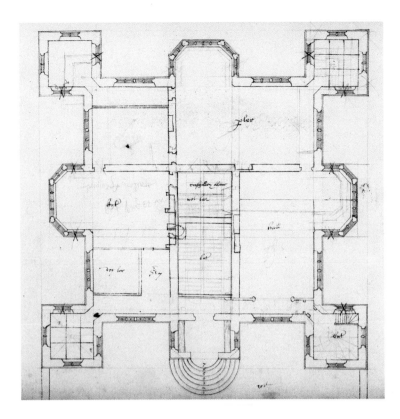

118 John Thorpe: plan for an unidentified lodge. Two large lodges have similar plans: Westwood, as originally built (pl. 120) and Lulworth (pl. 121). The drawing is for a rectangular house, three ranges deep, with the central range providing both circulation and the principal entrance so that the hall is bypassed and there is immediate access to a stair to the principal entertaining rooms. The deep, three-range plan seems first to appear in such large lodges as these.

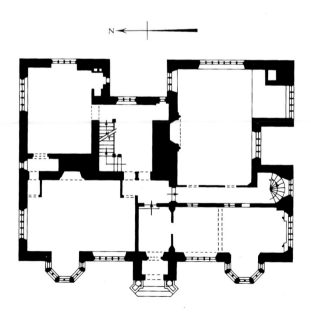

119 Gawthorpe Hall, Lancashire, 1599: ground-floor plan. The plan of Gawthorpe was altered in detail in the nineteenth century, but the essentials remain with the hall relegated to the rear and with almost direct access to a staircase at the centre of the house.

the services on the other. The place of the flying wings at Westwood is taken in the Thorpe drawing by square turrets, housing secondary stairs and closets. No scale is given on the Thorpe drawing and there are other significant differences between it and Westwood, but the possibility of a connection remains. Very much the same formula was employed at Shireoaks in Nottinghamshire, perhaps built around 1610;[49] Shireoaks, Lulworth, Westwood and the Thorpe drawing are the clearest evidence of a common formula for the type.

Three great houses in the north – Gawthorpe, Hardwick and Wollaton – seem to incorporate certain characteristics of the lodge in houses for permanent occupation. Gawthorpe, the latest of these in date, shows the application of these principles most clearly (pl. 119).[50] In its plan there are parallels with Westwood and Lulworth in the means of bringing the stair into prominence and subordinating the hall. The main entrance is in line not with the screens passage but with the great stair which rises in a belvedere-like tower to dominate the building. A species of screens passage remains, reached by a service stair from a basement kitchen; opposite the service stair were probably a buttery and pantry, placed there in the traditional way. But the whole hall/pantry/buttery unit is as it were relegated to one side of the house. The plan of Gawthorpe is closely paralleled at Bolsover.[51] There the layout is refined and regularised, the builder (Sir Charles Cavendish) was grander, and his architect is known to have been Robert Smythson. The setting and the purpose of Bolsover are altogether more lodge-like than Gawthorpe, but the similarities confirm the lodge as Gawthorpe's inspiration.

At Wollaton and Hardwick the lodge-like character is more subtle and lies as much in the meaning of the house as in its plan, although at both the placing of the hall is strikingly unorthodox. Neither is a gentry house in a strict sense, but both illustrate the power of the lodge as a model. At Wollaton the hall occupies the core of the house rather than being pushed to one side. But externally it is unrecognisable, rising as a glittering lantern with a prospect room on top, and internally the approach to it is not direct. Hardwick was equally revolutionary in its hall, whose long axis runs through the house from front to back, and its massive, flanking towers (pls 124, 331). The exactly contemporary Manor Lodge at Worksop is similarly a building of overwhelming height and incorporates the same revolutionary feature as Hardwick – a hall that runs straight through the house from front to back, entered at the narrow end. The Italian character of the great room at the Manor Lodge was remarked on in 1609,[52] and the plan of Hardwick seems to derive from Palladio's Villa Valmarana at Lisiera.[53] But the cross hall had already been used by Elizabeth Hardwick, Countess of Shrewsbury, in her recent reconstruction of Hardwick Old Hall (whose setting, next to the new hall, is equally lodge-like) and had previously appeared in a lodge of the 1580s at Holdenby (pl. 122).[54]

Hardwick may also be seen as a species of gigantic lodge, a fantasy castle standing at the highest point for many miles and

120 (*above*) Westwood, Worcestershire, *c*. 1600. One of the largest and most extravagant of all lodges, built with corner towers on a plan very like Thorpe's (pl. 118). The existing front entrance and the radiating wings were added soon after Westwood's first building so as to improve its amenities as a dwelling house.

121 (*left*) Lulworth Castle, Dorset, *c*. 1608. Built as a lodge, though later becoming a house for permanent occupation.

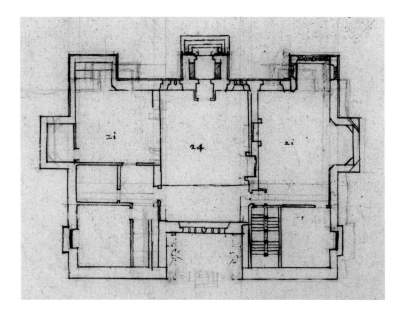

122 (*above*) John Thorpe: plan of a lodge at Holdenby, 1580–90. The Holdenby lodge is the first known building with a hall that runs through from front to back rather than side to side. Although less radical in denying the hall's conventional hierarchy than the hall at Bidston (pl. 115), by introducing an alternative axis the plan significantly weakens the traditional lateral separation of high and low ends.

123 Hardwick Hall: the frieze in the great chamber. Diana the huntress, symbolic of the virgin queen whom its builder probably hoped to entertain, sits with her attendants among the stags in the park. Stags are also the supporters of the Hardwick coat of arms.

124 (*facing page*) Hardwick Hall, Derbyshire, 1592. The apotheosis of the lodge, standing high above its surrounding park. Highly unconventional in plan (see pl. 331), with a through hall like that at the Holdenby lodge, in form Hardwick is a fantastic castle with windows for walls, monograms of Elizabeth Hardwick, Countess of Shrewsbury, for battlements, and prospect rooms (said to command a view of seven counties) for towers.

in which all conventions are fantastically inverted: not only does the hall run at right angles to the conventional direction but walls are replaced by glass, towers by belvederes and martial battlements by open balustrades and the cypher of its woman builder. Round the walls of the high great chamber runs a plaster frieze of deer in a forest together with Diana the virgin huntress and her attendants (pl. 123). Elizabeth Hardwick may have hoped that her namesake, the virgin queen, would visit the house and hunt her deer, and stags too are the supporters of her own coat of arms. But it is the craggy, forest-like setting of the house in its park that makes the allegory particularly apt.[55] In its relationship to the Old Hall, too, the New Hall is lodge-like (or perhaps harking back to the detached, private lodging blocks of fifteenth- and early sixteenth-century royal houses).[56] Its principal accommodation comprised suites of rooms for its owner and for a still greater guest, and with retainers largely accommodated elsewhere.

Wollaton and Hardwick were the supreme architectural achievements of the last years of the sixteenth century, and Smythson's own genius is unquestionable. Yet although

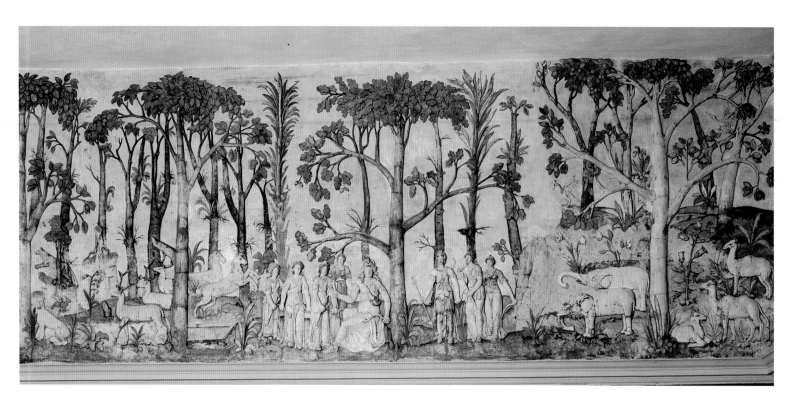

advancing a coherent and novel set of solutions to common problems – the creation of striking outlines, the enhancement of stairs and state rooms and alternative dispositions for the hall – in their high social standing and their geographical remoteness they did not immediately provide widely useful models for the housing of lesser men. They express the growing upper-class interest in architecture and the growing appeal of innovative plans and compact outlines, but when deep plans, novel relationships of rooms and compact silhouettes begin to appear among gentry houses, their immediate models were not these prodigy houses but the houses of the town and suburb: in particular, of London. These lodges and lodge-like houses would have a major role in introducing plans that broke down traditional hierarchies. But they would achieve that role indirectly: immediately, they would inform the plans not of the country houses of the gentry but of aristocratic houses of outer London, where from the end of the sixteenth century changing household relationships and a new social role of the capital city were creating a demand for a house of a rather similar kind.

The Villa

The single most important development in the layout and appearance of the upper-class house between the fifteenth century and the late eighteenth was in the introduction and spread of compact, non-hierarchical forms. Although these innovations had been prefigured in the lodge, it was in the suburbs and environs of London that the most powerful models, both architectural and social, were to appear. While in the country the lodge had from the Middle Ages offered the pattern of a different kind of house from the conventional homes of the landed classes, in the late sixteenth century a similar type of house was emerging in the neighbourhood of more than one English city, of which by far the most significant was London. These houses were, in effect, villas. Like lodges, their plans were not like those of contemporary country houses, nor did they serve the traditional role of the country house in the community. The households they accommodated were both more restricted and more strongly polarised between family and guests on the one side and essential servants on the other. Each makes a decisive break with hierarchical forms and each was to prove highly adaptable to the needs of a rapidly evolving society.

In 1700 the villa's function was described by Timothy Nourse as

> a litle House of Pleasure and Retreat, where Gentlemen and Citizens betake themselves in Summer for their private Diversion, there to pass an evening or two, or perhaps a Week, in the Conversation of a Freind or two, in some neat little House amidst a Vinyard or Garden, sequestred from the Noise of a City, and the Embarass or Distraction of Busines, or perhaps the anxious and servile Attendence of a Court.[57]

The similarity of the two types was remarked on by Roger North a few years earlier. 'A villa', he wrote, 'is quasy a lodge, for the sake of a garden, to retire to injoy and sleep, without pretence of enterteinement of many persons',[58] but the resemblances between them must have been apparent a very long time before that. In England, the compact, non-hierarchical house appeared at a time when both the social importance and the physical size of London were growing at an unprecedented rate.

The wish to enjoy rural amenities at the same time as urban pleasures was neither new nor confined to England. The moral appeal of the country goes back to the ancient world, as does expression of the physical pleasure of escape from noise, smells and smoke.[59] Sixteenth-century Italians had produced eloquent statements about the quality of rural life, though their writings would have been less familiar to educated Englishmen than those of their classical predecessors: Horace, Martial and above all Virgil and Pliny. For all of these the attraction of rural retirement had been its freedom from corruption, care and expense, and the opportunities for a cultivated and improving leisure. The lodge's resemblance to the Roman villa urbana will have struck everyone who read the classics, in particular the readers of the younger Pliny's description of his villa at Laurentum, just a few miles south of Rome. Few who visited Venice – the most accessible of Italian cities for the Protestant English – can have been unaware of the villa culture of the terra firma, and these houses had their parallels (albeit without their attached farms) round all the principal Tuscan cities as well as in the rural hinterlands of Rome and Naples. When Thomas Coryat visited the city (where he was taken about in the gondola belonging to Sir Henry Wotton, then English ambassador) he noted the villas along the Brenta,[60] but on his way there he had also remarked on the rich houses of French lawyers in the country-side about Paris.[61] The nearest parallel to the English experience was that of the Dutch. Both in England and in Holland a merchant aristocracy would build houses of great sophistication, aping the standard of living of the nobility but with no more land attached than was necessary for a garden and to secure a reasonable degree of seclusion from one's neighbours.

In the last decades of the century the attractions of London were increasingly felt, and would grow still further after 1603 as the residence of a less peripatetic court.[62] As the heart of government, where the best lawyers were to be found in a litigious age and where the finest merchandise was to be bought in a luxurious one, where the rich could best spend money and the extravagant best borrow it, where wives and husbands might be found for sons and daughters from among the host of other gentry resorting to the capital, where young men might learn law and urbanity at the Inns of Court and where there were better opportunities than anywhere else for attracting the favours of the great and the influential – there were ever more reasons for the gentry to visit the metropolis. In London there were 'Rich wines, spruce mistresses, pleasant houses, good dyet, rare wines, neat servants, fashionable furniture, pleasure and profits the best of all sorts',[63] to which one might add books, plays, poetry and politics, and opportunities for the exchange of ideas that could never occur in the country.

The culture of the late sixteenth century and the seventeenth was increasingly one of urban civility: through conspicuous consumption which was best served by the London markets, the gentleman displayed his wealth; through the emulation of manners and in the company of his peers he showed his taste and his breeding. London confirmed the gentleman in his sense of superiority. The urbanised gentleman was different from the rustic gentleman, the life of the town did not demand the same familiarity with inferiors as did the daily life of the country squire, and the amenities that he demanded in his town house were not all the same as those he needed in the country. But the life of the villa combined the culture of town with the virtues of the countryside.

The attractions of suburban life were well summarised in 1579 and their general acceptance seen as an established fact:

The manner of most Gentlemen, and Noble men also, is to house them selves (if possibly they may) in the Subburbes of the Cittie, because . . . the place is healthy, and through the distance from the bodye of the Towne, the noyse not much: Also for commoditie wee finde many lodginges, both spacious and roomethe [sic], with Gardaines and Orchardes very delectable. . . . When you lust to tarry alone, no man will presse you; if you wilbe accompanied, a small convitation will train freendes unto you, and those men of more civilitie, wisedome and worth than your rude Countrey Gentleman or rusticall Neighboures. If you delight in grave men & sober, you shal easily acquaint your selfe with such. If you pleasure in myrth and pleasant companions, they are at hand.[64]

Early in the following century, the suburban house was described as

erected by great persons or by provident gentillmen of the country, either to save Charge of hospitalitie or for some other their private use and pleasure, when they shall at any tyme have occasion to repayre unto the Cittie; or they are buylte by rytche Citizens in Gardens, and other conveniente places nere unto the Cittie, the better to recreate themselves in the Summer season.[65]

In the suburbs the city élite merged with a landed class, correspondingly displaced. And all these advantages were obtainable without having to maintain the household that went inescapably with a great house in the country, even though hardly seen as an advantage by servants for whom the reduced establishment offered no place:

Were it for the worship of a Gentleman, having good lande and revenues to keep no more servaunts then (as they do in Cities) those that for their necessary uses they must needes employ?[66]

Whether for a citizen moving out of town or for a countryman moving in, the suburban way of life involved the social duties of town rather than the territorial obligations of the country estate.[67]

In the early sixteenth century most upper-class houses in the London region did not differ substantially from such houses elsewhere. Nevertheless, the demands of a rich and cultivated clientele may at least have refined existing forms in the metropolitan area. It is the proximity of London that may in part explain the form of Wickham Court, near Croydon (pl. 80), an exceptional house of perhaps around 1480.[68] Wickham Court was probably built for Sir Christopher Heydon of Baconsthorpe in Norfolk, steward to the widowed Duchess of York, who also owned property in Berkshire and Gloucestershire and who by his wealth and his closeness to the Yorkist kings clearly moved in the highest circles. It can also be seen as a secondary seat (as in fact it was): not the owner's principal home, the centre of his principal estates, but a place of occasional residence in order to make himself known on an outlying property. None the less it is likely in view of his high standing that he would have made use of the house in connection with London visits, and the house's use as a place of entertainment for sophisticated guests may have influenced Heydon in choosing its form. Wickham Court is a compact, castle-like brick tower, three storeys high, with turrets that contained stairs and garderobes and with a small courtyard at the centre which has subsequently been filled in to provide a more spacious staircase. In spite of its military form and a few gun-loops at the foot of the turrets, the walls are thin and the house is clearly indefensible. In containing a hall and all the amenities of an up-to-date, aristocratic dwelling compressed within the envelope of a show castle, Wickham Court differs from late medieval tower lodgings (which it otherwise resembles) in an essential respect.

A later example of the same sort of sophistication – a house of a form that was essentially orthodox but which was enhanced on account of its proximity to London and its consequent social prominence – is Ham House.[69] When built in 1610 for Sir Thomas Vavasour, Ham had a wholly standard service-passage plan, with a long central range, one room deep, and cross wings at either end, but there were already certain features which set it apart from most houses of the kind: one, the basement kitchens which enabled the low-end wing to be used for dining parlours, and another, the size of the principal stair (which was further enlarged in the 1630s). The few sixteenth-century houses of the upper classes in the London area that survive or which are known in detail – Sutton House in Hackney, Beaufort House in Chelsea (known from a succession of contemporary plans),[70] Bruce Castle in Tottenham (pl. 125)[71] – are similarly conventional in their planning. However, from the end of the sixteenth century houses were built in the environs of London that were no longer merely adaptations of long established forms but adopted novel layouts to meet new social demands.

The villa plan had two separate origins. The largest and the

125   Anon. (*c.* 1685): Bruce Castle, Tottenham, London. A late sixteenth-century house of the outer London suburbs, built to a conventional plan with the turrets on the front of the house probably originally containing matched stairs. The clock tower was added after 1660. The early sixteenth-century brick tower to the left may have been a stand from which to watch the hunting in the park.

most spectacular embodied many of the most striking architectural refinements of the lodge and of the most innovative country houses of the last two decades of the sixteenth century, and they display a wide variety of forms, some of them unprecedented. However, others were built to compact plans which were equally revolutionary in terms of internal layout but were also simpler, more standardised, and derived from a very different source: from the town houses of the prosperous citizenry. Common to both groups was a deepening of their plans. The conventional country house had been linear, with a sequence of rooms from services at one end to entertaining rooms at the other, separated by a hall which mediated between them. Instead, all of these houses have plans which are two or more ranges deep. The simpler of these are rectangular, with four or six rooms to a floor. The more complex incorporate variations including halls that run from front to back rather than in line with the front of the house, as well as other layouts that were more revolutionary still. In both, this doubling-up of ranges created relationships of rooms that were unprecedented and which were largely destructive of traditional hierarchies.

126 E.M. Davison (1839) after John Vardy: Holland House, Kensington, London, *c.* 1606–7 (part destroyed). Holland House was among the most extravagant of all contemporary houses, and its location on the edge of London and the social prominence of its owner must have drawn widespread attention to its unconventional layout.

Of contemporary houses of the London environs that still stand or whose layouts are known, the most revolutionary were Camden House, Holland House and Nottingham House, all in Kensington; Eagle House in Wimbledon; Danvers House in Chelsea; and two larger buildings rather further out, Charlton House at Woolwich and Ashley Park at Walton on Thames. Probably the most prominent of these were Camden House and Holland House. Not only were they close to each other physically, their origins were also closely connected. Camden House was so called from Baptist Hicks, ennobled in 1627 as Viscount Camden of Chipping Camden in Gloucestershire, where around 1613 he built a large house with elaborately shaped gables of which nothing survives but a pair of detached pavilions.[72] Hicks was the son of a wealthy mercer, and hugely increased what was probably already a good fortune by supplying silks to the court and by continuing to maintain his business interests in the city after being knighted in 1607. Camden House may actually have been built not by him, however, but by Sir Walter Cope.[73] Cope's background was rather different: coming of an Oxfordshire gentry family of long standing, Cope was a gentleman of the Privy Chamber to James I, and in 1612 Master of the Court of Wards (a highly lucrative office if opportunities were well used) and a connoisseur whose visual taste may have been reflected in the elaboration of his house. He had a private museum in his house in the Strand,[74]

131

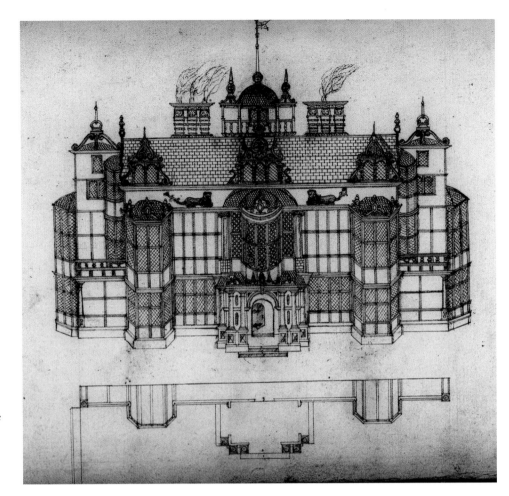

127 John Thorpe: Camden House, Kensington, London (demolished). John Thorpe's drawing for a timber-framed house has an extravagance equal to that of Holland House, nearby.

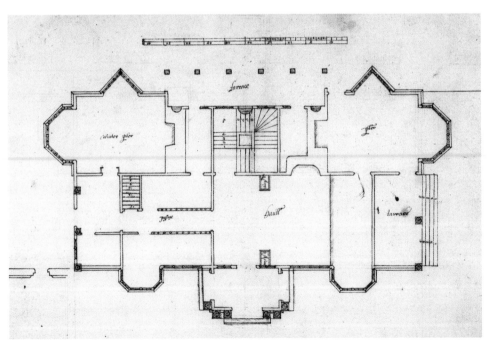

128 John Thorpe: Camden House, ground-floor plan, first scheme. Thorpe's drawings include two separate schemes identifiable as for Camden House. In the first, the hall is entered in the old-fashioned way at its low end, but the stair, leading to the principal entertaining rooms on the first floor, is set in line with the entrance rather than lying beyond the hall's high end. This relocation of the stair would have a profound effect on the hierarchical relationships of the plan.

was a member of the Elizabethan Society of Antiquaries, and died £27,000 in debt. He had been buying up property in Kensington from around 1590 and ultimately acquired manorial rights over most of the parish. Together, Cope and Hicks typified the two elements – the court and the plutocracy – that made up the Jacobean élite.

If indeed Cope built Camden House, he soon sold it to Hicks and followed it with Holland House (pl. 126), probably built in 1606–7 and further developing certain innovative elements of the earlier building.[75] Holland House derived its name from the title bestowed on Cope's son-in-law, Richard Rich; when first built it seems to have been generally known as Cope Castle, a name that reflected its upright silhouette, its upstanding position on the slope of the hill (a little lower down from Camden House), the elaboration of its external decoration and overall its lodge-like character. Neither house stands; Camden House was demolished, after successive alterations, in the nineteenth century, while Holland House was gutted in an air raid in 1940 and only fragments survive. However, the essential forms of both are known from drawings by John Thorpe, while Holland House was well recorded in later surveys, and the apparently innovative features of each are so significant for the later development of the gentry house as a type that it is worth examining them in some detail.

The Thorpe drawings include two sets that Summerson plausibly identified as successive schemes for Camden House,[76] one set consisting of a plan and elevation, the other of two plans (pls 127–9). Both sets seem to be for a house that was timber-framed, with an extraordinarily elaborate façade: continuously glazed on the ground floor, with projecting circular and polygonal window bays, fanciful scrollwork to dormers and stair turrets, and evidently some kind of loggia overlooking the garden at the rear (pl. 128). The whole appearance of the house would have been of an extravagance disproportionate to its relatively modest size, impressing the visitor with a sense of the luxury to be found within and creating above all the image of a house for entertainment. It is uncertain which if either scheme was followed in building: the earliest supposed view of Camden House, dating from around 1665, shows a generally similar house but built of brick,[77] and it may be (as Summerson suggested) that an original design for the timber-framed house was superseded and modified in execution. The overall effect of Thorpe's own elevation drawing is of a kind of architectural fantasy with such a degree of overwrought decoration that it is difficult to believe that it could ever actually have been built.

Inside, the earlier scheme provides for a hall entered in the conventional manner at the low end and with an old-fashioned dais at the high end, but the principal stair was also at the low end, beyond the screens passage. This stair was flanked by rear-projecting wings each containing a parlour which with the stair formed a plan that was a compact rectangle, one and a half ranges deep. No advantage of the second range was taken, at least on the ground floor, to improve circulation; passage from one end of the house to the other remained through the hall, and the purpose of the additional range seems partly aesthetic – to concentrate the visual mass of the house and thus to give the

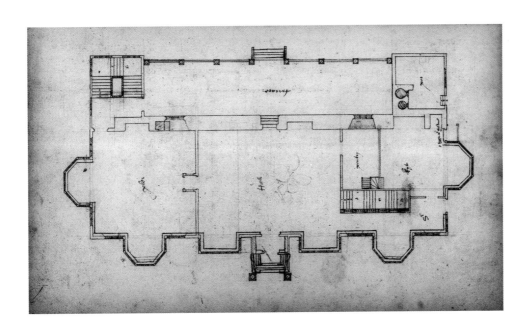

129   John Thorpe: Camden House, ground-floor plan, second scheme. In the second of Thorpe's schemes the entrance is placed at the centre of the hall. Although the hall retains a dais, the principal stair, to the great chamber over the hall, seems to be by a straight flight of stairs off the hall's low end. To the rear is an open loggia, with rooms above.

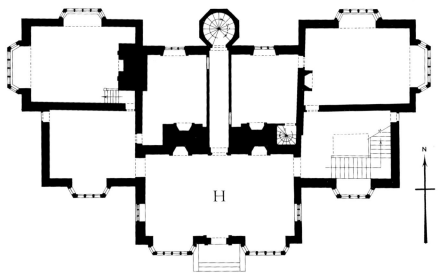

H

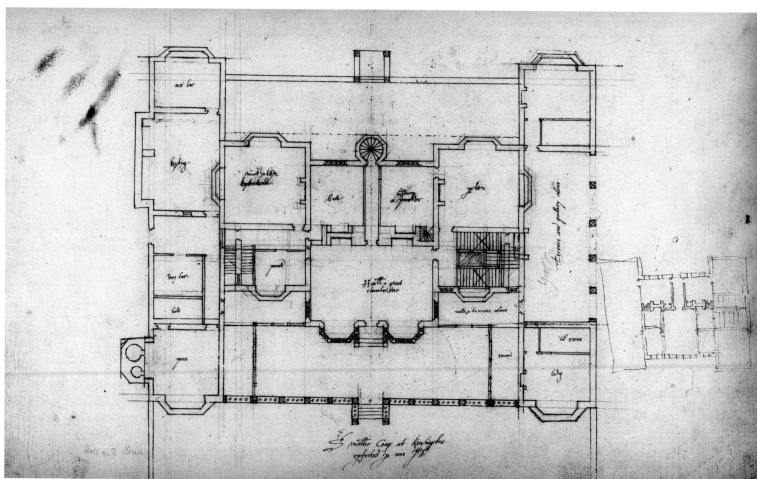

130 (*top*) Holland House: ground-floor plan, possibly as originally built. Even more than its flamboyant exterior and deep plan, Holland House was remarkable for its centralised, symmetrical hall, without any distinction of high and low ends. The similarities between Holland House and such lodges as Bidston (pls 114, 115) or Holdenby (pl. 122) appear more clearly in the original layout than after the house's enlargement.

131 (*above*) John Thorpe: Holland House, Thorpe's plan for alterations, *c.* 1612. Besides the addition of wings and possibly of tall stair towers, the scheme provided for the enlargement of the already large, principal stair.

elaborate frontispiece a more powerful impact. Flanking turrets, rising a little above the roof line and shown in the Thorpe drawing (though difficult to reconcile with the plan as drawn by him) further enhance the silhouette, and though no basement windows are shown in Thorpe's drawing the kitchens seem to have been below the ground floor perhaps in order to elevate the building as well as to relegate the services to a position out of sight.

For the second Camden House scheme there is no elevation drawing, but the plan differed from the first in having the hall entered at the centre of the long side. The central entrance into the hall was almost without precedent, although it seems to have occurred at Lord Derby's hunting lodge at Bidston. This entrance position made impossible anything like a traditional screens passage, but the hall retained a dais and a fireplace oddly placed, heating the room's lower rather than its upper end (though this may be a drafting error in the plan, copied from the first scheme even though the ends of the house have been reversed in scheme two). The kitchen in this second scheme is on the ground floor, and the service approach to the great chamber on the first floor (where Thorpe has outlined a large table at the centre of the room) is by way of a broad, dog-leg stair at the low end of the hall. It is far from clear whether this is intended as a formal approach for servants bearing food or for guests who were thereby enabled to reach the great chamber without having to pass through parlour and ante-room. The contradictions implicit in this arrangement were to be resolved in Holland House, but the entrance by which all visitors arrived at the centre of the hall anticipated the layout of an increasing number of houses from the second quarter of the seventeenth century until by the end of the century it was the norm.

At Holland House arrangements were perfected that at Camden House had been only partly worked out. The external decoration on the principal fronts was lavish, and the whole building was crowned by a line of shaped gables to each façade – thirty-four such gables in all (pl. 126). As originally built, Holland House consisted of three blocks, each two ranges deep with flues in the lateral walls in the urban manner (pl. 130). The hall occupied the middle block; the two flanking blocks were set slightly back from the line of the hall façade, and the forward projection of the hall was accentuated by a central entrance. The large, principal stair was in the conventional position at the hall's high end; there may have been subordinate stair turrets flanking the body of the house, though evidence from surveys of the building made before the house's destruction in 1941 (and of the basement made thereafter) suggests that these turrets were probably added as part of the house's subsequent enlargement (pl. 131). This, perhaps undertaken before Cope's death in 1614, comprised the addition of two forward-projecting wings with single-storey loggias to frame the principal entry. One wing contained services; the original kitchen was in a basement and rose into a half-storey. The other contained independent lodgings and a loggia on the ground floor, and a gallery on the first overlooking the park on the east side of the house.

The lack of distinction between the high and low ends of the hall is emphasised, not only by the central entry but by the room's completely symmetrical treatment with matching fireplaces and bay windows at both ends. As at Camden House it is doubtful whether the adoption of the deep plan did anything (at least on the ground floor) to facilitate communication between the ends of the house: the block to the rear of the hall (if Thorpe's drawing is to be relied on) probably comprised a buttery and a withdrawing room, with no passageway to bypass it but instead a passage to an octagonal stair turret at the centre of the north front – a curious conceit confirmed by a plan of the basement made before the house's destruction. The double-pile layout (i.e. of two ranges deep, discussed on pp. 141–52 below) otherwise brought rooms into convenient relationship to each other and reduced the distances between them, and (also like Camden House) made possible a more concentrated composition by centralising the mass of the building rather than by dispersing it into the wings. This was accentuated visually by the way in which the central range, comprising the hall and the great chamber above it, projected slightly forward of the blocks that flanked it on either side. This central emphasis was maintained after the addition of the wings, which were slightly lower than the original building.

The significance of Camden House is difficult to assess in view of the uncertainties about its completed form. If, as may have been the case, Camden House was among the first houses to have a principal stair at the low end of the hall, then its importance would be hard to overemphasise. For all its relatively compact size, the complexity of the Holland House plan and the elaboration of its façade made it a less obvious model. However, in no contemporary house does the layout of the hall so completely transform its function. The hall at Holland House, with its central entrance and undifferentiated ends, was clearly designed to be no more than a formal entrance and reception room, and it must have seemed revolutionary to those who were used to halls of more traditional form. The prominence of the building, an easy ride into the country from the most fashionable parts of town, and the home successively of two ambitious and well-connected men, must have ensured that Holland House was extremely widely known. At Camden House the placing of the principal stair identified the hall clearly with the superior rooms of the house, though the hall itself is still entered at one end and retains a dais. Holland House took the development a stage further, making no concessions whatever to traditional forms and making the hall into a room that was wholly adapted to contemporary social relations.

A further group of almost contemporary houses in the London suburbs shows an alternative development of double-pile elements in combination with a feature of quite different origin – a hall entered at the centre of its narrow end, running through the house from front to back and divided by load-bearing walls from blocks of accommodation on either side. Occurring at Hardwick, the arrangement had also been anticipated in a lodge of the late 1580s at Holdenby.[78] In three of these early houses, standing or known from other sources, the plan is simply that and no more: a rectangular block containing a hall flanked by rooms each side. Two others were larger, with flanking wings, but the central block is otherwise virtually the same as these smaller, rectangular houses. Nottingham House (pl. 132) was probably built by Sir William Coppin, Clerk of the Crown to James I, soon after 1605 when he acquired the site, some three quarters of a mile to the east of Holland House, from Walter Cope.[79] (Its name derived from the 1st Earl of Nottingham, a later owner; incorporated into Kensington Palace by William III, what remained was demolished during alterations to the palace in the eighteenth century.) It was simpler than either Camden or Holland Houses, its near neighbours, but it was like them in its compact, upright, symmetrical form with rounded and polygonal window bays. Despite the novelty of the through hall, the central entrance at its low end opened against a screen, and stairs were placed so that service stairs (from a basement kitchen) led into the screens passage while the principal stair gave off the high end of the hall. The overall arrangement is conservative by comparison with Holland House. At the high end of the hall, the end wall seems to have been entirely of glass: a great bay window that formed an oriel not beside the high table in the traditional manner but behind it. Facing north, it would have provided adequate light without the sun blinding onlookers.

Eagle House in Wimbledon (pls 133, 134) still exists relatively little altered.[80] Eagle House was probably built in 1613 for Robert Bell, one of the founders of the East India Company

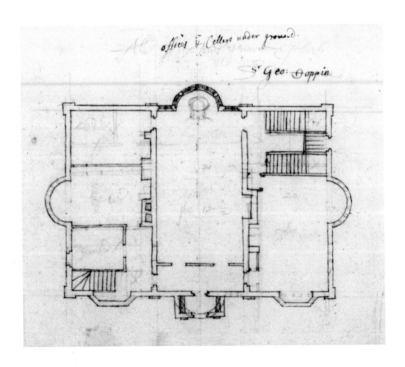

and 'an extraordinarie curious man . . . on gardens and walks'.[81] Eagle House resembled Nottingham House closely, but a minor point of difference is that the central block, containing the hall, lies slightly forward of the blocks that flank it – an unusual arrangement but one which occurs in precisely the same way at Holland House. Eagle House also has shaped gables very like those of Holland House, though by the second decade of the century such gables were widely used. Like Holland House, the kitchen is in the basement and rises into a half-storey. Like Nottingham House the service entry to the hall, by a stair from the kitchen, is still at the low end, and in the late nineteenth century the architect Sir Thomas Jackson, who lived there, believed that it had possessed a conventional screen.

Charlton House at Greenwich and the demolished Ashley Park at Walton on Thames show what might be made of the through hall model of Nottingham House and Eagle House in a larger building. Charlton House (pls 136, 137), of 1607–12, occupies a similar suburban location, and enjoyed a view over London like that of Henry Howard's lodge at Greenwich. The house's builder was Adam Newton, tutor to Prince Henry. Externally, it appears to be built on a conventional H plan, with a central hall and cross wings, and only the towers projecting from the outer face of either wing link it to Camden House, Holland House and other advanced London houses. The central range, however, is of Nottingham House form, with the hall flanked by double-pile ranges which also contain the principal and secondary stairs. Like Holland House as enlarged, the kitchen is on the ground floor in one wing, but as at Hardwick it is dropped into a semi-basement in order to provide greater ceiling height. Like Hardwick (but also like a number of other houses) the principal rooms are on the second floor, and also like Hardwick a passage across the top of the hall screen serves to connect the first-floor rooms on one side of the house with those on the other. In its scale, the house is more of a true country house than a suburban retreat, and Charlton can be seen as a fusion of suburban forms with others from further afield. Even if the hall arrangement derives immediately from London sources, it seems unlikely that Charlton can have been built without some knowledge of Hardwick, and in 1607 the Earl of Salisbury, beginning his great house at Hatfield, obtained a sketch of Hardwick from its then owner, the Earl of Shrewsbury,[82] who had recently inherited it. Curiously, the stair arrangement at Charlton more closely resembles that of a preliminary scheme for Hardwick, for which Smythson's plan survives (pl. 331), than the executed building.[83]

132 John Thorpe: plan of Nottingham House, Kensington, London (demolished). With Camden House and Holland House, the third of a trio of lodge-like houses in Kensington, and with a deep plan providing a through hall like the Holdenby lodge (pl. 122). The loss of all three of these houses has made it possible to overlook their significance, but their prominence must have made their novelties of planning widely noticed.

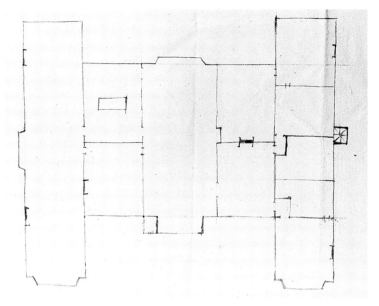

133 Eagle House, Wimbledon, London, *c.* 1613. A surviving, lodge-like, suburban house, the form of which resembles Nottingham House.

134 Eagle House: ground- and first-floor plans. The kitchen was in the basement, north-east, and partly rose through the ground floor. The hall now lacks a screen, but probably had one originally. The arrangements in the north-west corner have been altered (by the modern insertion of a lift) but the principal stair was always there.

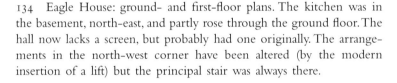

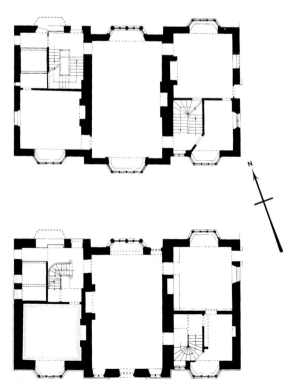

135 Anon.: Ashley Park, Walton on Thames, Surrey (demolished): first-floor plan, probably drawn *c.* 1615. Ashley Park, built 1602–5, may have been the first house in the London region to have a through hall. Social relations in the outer suburbs differed from those in the country, but it may also be significant that like Hardwick, the first great house to have a hall of this form, Ashley Park was built for a woman, who may possibly have found the hierarchical hall less appropriate to her mode of life.

Earlier, however, than Nottingham House, Eagle House or Charlton, but having like them a transverse hall, was Ashley Park at Walton on Thames.[84] While the other houses in this group were built for members of the court or the financial élite, the builder of Ashley Park was a female member of the landed aristocracy. The property was bought around 1600 by Sir Michael Stanhope for his sister, Lady Jane Berkeley, estranged second wife of Lord Henry Berkeley. Ashley Park was greatly remodelled at a later date; in the 1920s it was demolished, unrecorded, its importance unrecognised, but accounts for its building survive and the discovery by Dr John Gurney of an early seventeenth-century sketch plan, evidently of the first floor, has made it possible to appreciate its importance (pl. 135). If the (evidently single-storey) hall corresponded to the position of the great chamber, the house had a very similar layout to that of Charl-ton House, but its date of 1602–7 makes it earlier than any of the houses of this sophisticated suburban group. In the uncon-ventional placing of the hall, it may be more than a coincidence that both Ashley Park and Hardwick were built for women – owners for whom, possibly, the ceremonial use of the hall was less needed (or felt to be less fitting) than it was for a man, and whose requirements in this respect may therefore have been closer to those of the non-landowning, suburban magnate. Short of establishing a direct link between Ashley Park and Hardwick or Manor Lodge at Worksop, the two earlier great houses with

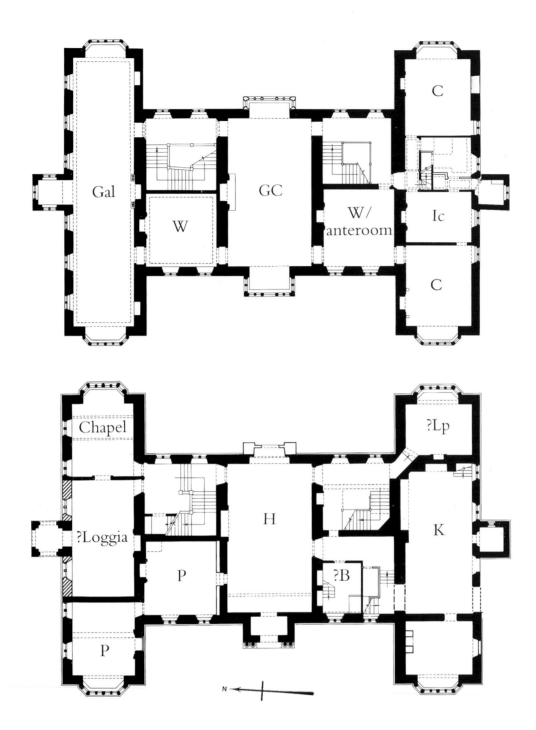

136   Charlton House: ground- and second-floor plans. Charlton displays the deep plan and hall of Nottingham House, expanded by the addition of wings. The arrangement of the kitchen in a semi-basement is identical with that of Hardwick, while the stair arrangement resembles that which may have been originally intended there (cf. pl. 331). Also like Hardwick, the principal entertaining rooms were on the top floor.

137 (*facing page*)   Charlton House, Greenwich, London, 1607–12. An aristocratic house of the outer suburbs, built for the tutor to Prince Henry, heir to the throne. Charlton House formerly commanded a view like that of the Earl of Northampton's Greenwich lodge (pl. 104).

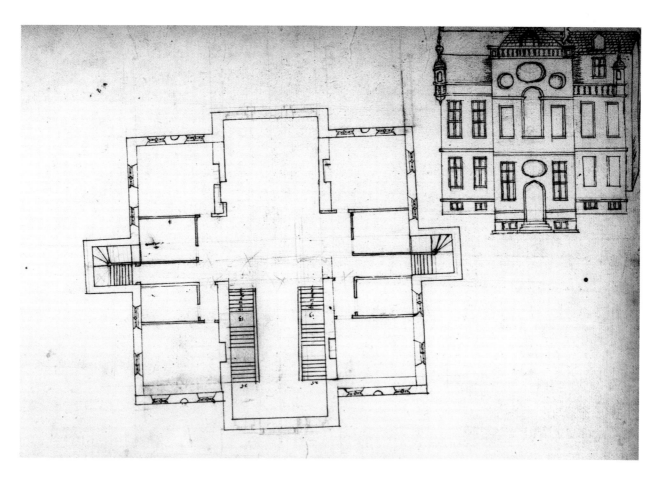

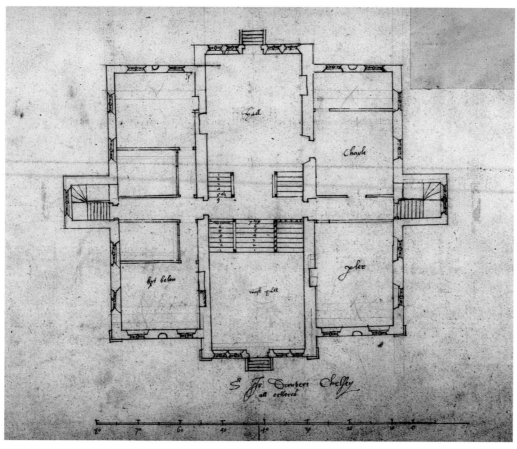

Sr Jo. Danvers Chelsey
all cellered

cross-hall plans, its antecedents – and thus perhaps those of these other cross-hall houses – are lost. But in any case it was probably through these houses of the outer suburbs that the innovations of the 1590s contributed to the mainstream of house design.

The last house of this group is Danvers House in Chelsea, similarly known from drawings by Thorpe (pl. 138) and in certain respects a further development of the Nottingham House/Eagle House plan.[85] The house was probably built by Sir John Danvers immediately after his acquisition of the property in 1622. Danvers came of good gentry stock in Wiltshire, where he acquired an estate by his second marriage; he was knighted by James I and later became a gentleman of the Privy Chamber to Charles I. He was a connoisseur and a patron of Rubens; John Aubrey reported that as a young man he travelled in France and Italy and that 'he had a very fine fancy, which lay chiefly for gardens and architecture'.[86] Nicholas Stone made garden statuary for him and built a house for his brother, the Earl of Danby, but the architect of Danvers house is not known. It has been attributed (without evidence) to Inigo Jones, but Aubrey remarked that 'the gardens . . . (as likewise the house there) do remain monuments of his [Danvers's] ingenuity' so that he may have had a large part in designing it himself.

The house was tall and compact, with services, as was becoming usual, in the basement. Again there was a hall running from front to back, but this was now of a still stranger form: there was no screen, and rather short of halfway down it there was a flight of seven steps which raised the rear, high end of the hall some 3 or 4 feet above the low end and made of it almost a separate room, thus given an extremely grand and formal approach. The stairs to the great chamber on the upper floor rose as two parallel flights either side of this upper hall, making the latter in effect a sort of prototype stair hall – a feature that would not become common until considerably later. The accommodation afforded was otherwise relatively conventional: principal chambers were paired with dependent rooms, and flanking stair turrets – reminiscent of Holland House and Camden House – rose through all floors. These stairs, on opposite sides of the house, provided an alternative, lateral circulation to supplement that of the principal staircase, and there may have been a gallery running from side to side of the house on the top floor, reached by these flanking secondary stairs.

The hall and great chamber were each lit by large windows at either end, again a development of the Nottingham House

scheme, though one that was inevitable given such a plan: no windows were possible on their internal, side walls, but John Aubrey commented on the pleasant views out onto the gardens of the house to the north – the high end – and over the river to the Surrey hills on the south. For Samuel Pepys, who visited Danvers House in 1661, it was 'the prettiest contrived house that I ever saw in my life'.[87] While the debt of the through hall to the Nottingham House/Eagle House model is clear, the layout may also owe something to Danvers's travels: if he had been to Venice, the setting of the house on the banks of the Thames could have reminded him of the Brenta, and the simplicity of the plan may be a conscious echo of Italy, with the hall and great chamber – effectively a *sala*, the great entertaining room of the Italian villa – dominating the subsidiary accommodation to an extent unprecedented in England.

The Suburban House and the Compact Plan

The aristocratic villa informed the development of plans that derived largely from other sources but which had in common a concentration of form that was only acceptable once traditional layouts could be rejected. In chapter 1, Wisbech Castle was taken as the epitome of the modern house, built by a leading London craftsman for a new man of the Commonwealth. By the middle of the seventeenth century, there were already quite substantial numbers of country houses of a form that had scarcely existed in the sixteenth: compact and rectangular, two or three ranges deep, typically without wings or other external projections, entered at the centre of the principal front and having internally a prominent, central stair and a hall that had ceased to function as anything more than a formal space by which to approach the entertaining rooms and the private accommodation of the family.

The house two ranges deep (or 'piles' in seventeenth-century parlance) has long been known to architectural historians as a double pile; by analogy, the house of three ranges may be called a triple pile.[88] The latter was generally larger, but their similarities were very much greater than their differences. Services are relegated to the rear, to a basement or sometimes even located outside the shell of the building. Such houses were the prototypes of the ubiquitous gentry house of the late seventeenth century and the eighteenth. Together with the achievement of external symmetry the compact plan constituted the most radical and far-reaching change in the layout of the upper-class house, not only within the two centuries with which this book is concerned but between the achievement of an integrated house plan in the thirteenth century and the advent of picturesque principles of design in the late eighteenth.

At the end of the seventeenth century, Roger North condemned the old-fashioned, H-plan house of a single range in depth, for its inconvenient circulation. It was, he said:

138 (*facing page*)   John Thorpe, Danvers House, Chelsea, London, 1622: ground- and first-floor plans. Built by Sir John Danvers, who may have designed the house himself. At Danvers House the through hall of Nottingham House became a stair hall as well. The windows of the great chamber, over the hall, commanded views of the Thames to the south and over Danvers's (extremely innovative) garden to the north. Samuel Pepys called it 'the prettiest contrived house that ever I saw in my life'.

Fit for a colledge or hospitall, to be devided into cells, and chambers independent of each other; but not for a dwelling house, that ought to have a connexion, and unity, without crossing to and fro one part to the other, thro the air, and abroad; and that cannot be avoided in such houses.[89]

In characterising the old-fashioned layout as cell-like – as a series of units – North put his finger on the essentially additive nature of the traditional, linear plan. By implication at least he recognised the greater possibilities for integrated circulation in the rectangular house. Francis Bacon recommended 'a double house, without through lights on the sides, that you may have rooms from the sun, both for fornoon and afternoon'.[90] Bacon's scheme was for a palace, but in 1660 Sir Roger Pratt wrote that 'the best form [of house] for a private man I conceive to be that which is an oblong square exactly'.[91] What he had in mind was a double-pile or triple-pile house of the Wisbech Castle type, and his recommendation is applicable to either:

We have there much room in a little compass, next that the chambers may be so laid out, as to be of use to each other . . . great convenience there for backstairs; item that it is warm, and affords variety of place to be made use of both according to the divers times of the day, and year also as shall be most requisite besides that herein a little ground is sufficient to build upon, and there may be great spare of walling, and of other materials for the roof.[92]

The practical advantages of the deep plan were clear too to the surveyor who in 1634 described a new house built by Sir Ralph Freeman at Betchworth in Surrey. Little of the building survives, though its appearance is known from an eighteenth-century painting. It was three ranges deep with the central range taken up by lobbies and stairs, and had

A hall and panterey in the front or north parte, a great Parler and Chapell in the reare and south parte, and in the middle ranke between theis, a lesser parler with a convenyent backe stayre Case severed apart, and a large lobby leading immediately and with great convenyency unto every one of the foresaid roomes and back stayres severally and a parte, and unto the great stayres; arising in the east side of the same lobby, which are spacious and fairely built and doe land into a like large lobby on the second story [i.e. the first floor] ministring like fitt opportunyty of passage from thence into the great dyning Chamber and unto the backe stayres and into all the other Chambers upon that flower. . . .

From this second lobby and flower doe arise likewise aswell the said great Stayres as also the backe stayres, into the theird half story [i.e. the attic floor] leading unto 7 other lodging roomes.[93]

But though the advantages claimed by Pratt and others for the compact house with a deep plan – warmth, convenience,

economy – recommended the form widely, they do not explain its origins.

Together with the lodge and with the villa of the London countryside these double- and triple-pile plans were evidence of a readiness to adopt layouts in which the hierarchical constraints of linear planning are superseded. Essentially, these compact forms can be seen as attempts to solve what would in the twentieth century be described as design problems. More significant than their typological variety is what they share in the treatment of the entrance, the hall and the staircase. The desire for symmetry made it increasingly desirable to place the front door of the house at the centre of the façade. For the hall, the problem was what to do with a room whose traditional, communal functions were obsolescent yet whose symbolism might still be valued, within a house whose other provisions were largely novel and whose exterior was symmetrical. In a large house the hall might be retained and transformed into a purely formal entry, but in the smaller houses that were built in increasing numbers for the ever growing numbers of the gentry even the symbolic reminiscence of the old-fashioned hall was becoming irrelevant. With the stair the difficulty was in finding space and the best location for a structure that was growing in importance, size and elaboration as the approach to the principal entertaining rooms, and which had generally been reached through the hall, a room whose associations were increasingly seen to be inappropriate on a route followed by polite visitors.

A solution to both problems – the problem of the hall and of the stair – was to place the stair directly in line with the house's front entrance. The arrangement shows perfectly in one of John Thorpe's small plans (pl. 139), where the parlour and hall lie to one side of the entry and stair, the buttery, pantry and a low parlour on the other, with the kitchen beneath the latter.[94] The origins of the compact plan are varied, but the facility that the deep plan provided for relocating the stair in this new position was a considerable recommendation of it, and the stair is so placed in some of the earliest houses of the new form. At the same time, this had an important effect on the hall. Since the new route to the superior rooms now lay in line with the front door – at the traditional low end of the hall, on the line of the screens passage – this had the effect of associating the body of the hall with the house's high end. By so doing, the hall ceased to be a space that mediated between the two parts of the household community and became increasingly associated with the polite accommodation. With the domestic community itself increasingly polarised, such a development was both acceptable and convenient.

The new position for the principal stair would have an equally revolutionary impact on first-floor circulation. In houses of any size, by the late sixteenth century the chamber used by the owner of the house was more often at the lower end, served by the low-end staircase – a move discussed in more detail in chapter 8. A stair at the centre of the house could be used by everyone; family chambers could be reached from it as readily

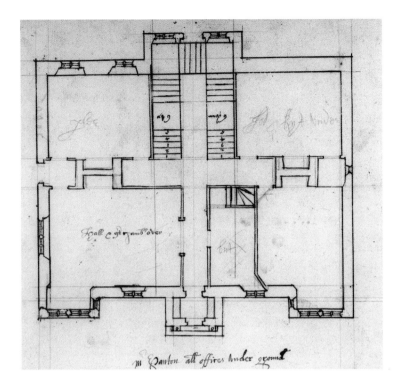

139 John Thorpe: plan for an unknown house. An archetypal, small, 'double-pile' plan – i.e. two ranges deep. The stair is immediately accessible from the front entrance, without having to pass the length of the hall to reach it.

140 (*below*) Whitehall, Shrewsbury, Shropshire, 1578. An extraordinarily early example of a house built to a deep rectangular plan.

as rooms for guests, and thus upstairs as well as on the ground floor the relocated stair would affect the disposition of family and guest rooms and allow for a greater flexibility in their use.

It was not, of course, essential to deepen the overall plan in order to relocate the stair. At a vernacular level houses are common from the sixteenth and seventeenth centuries that are a single range deep and have their stair in a rear turret projection, opposite the front entrance and often (in the lobby-entrance plan) at the back of a stack. In these the hierarchies that operated in the houses of the gentry scarcely existed, and as a common living room the hall is already a 'family' room. Camden House (pls 127–9) and The Hall at Bradford on Avon (pl. 4), which incorporates a number of features of the Camden House layout, showed how it was possible to align the stair with the main entrance without building a house that was two full ranges deep. Equally, in many large seventeenth-century houses with a deep plan, the stairs are still approached from the hall's upper end. A few early seventeenth-century double-pile houses have stairs at either end – a form discussed in chapter 6. Nevertheless by the mid-seventeenth century the central stair had become normal in compact, double-pile houses of gentry class, and there is a clear connection between the evolution of stair and hall.

The principle of the deep plan was capable of considerable variation, but four gentry houses may illustrate the basic forms around which development would take place. These are Whitehall on the edge of Shrewsbury in Shropshire, Thorpe Salvin in South Yorkshire, Hinton House at St Nicholas Hurst in Berkshire, and the Red House at Bourne in Lincolnshire. Two

141 Whitehall: ground-floor plan. The porch was originally central to the façade, leading into the low end of the hall and thence by a screens passage to the stair. The house has a full basement which may have contained a kitchen – again a very precocious innovation – and which has a lateral passage from side to side. Whitehall relates to the development of plans that are three ranges deep.

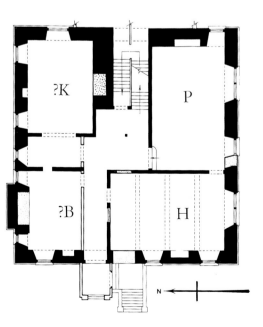

143

of these houses are of three ranges, and two of two. Whitehall (pls 140, 141) has long been recognised by architectural historians as a house of a novel form.[95] It was begun in 1578 and finished in 1582 by Richard Prince, a lawyer of local origins who after a successful career returned to his native town and built his house ('to hys greate chardge, wth fame to hym and hys posteritie for evr'[96]) on part of the property of a former abbey in what was then (and remains) a suburb. The porch has been moved sideways, creating a false impression of asymmetry, a cupola was added above the roof in the seventeenth century, and there have been internal changes that have obscured or altered the original circulation and the relationship of rooms. Nevertheless several novel characteristics can be distinguished. The plan is deep, compact, almost square and arranged around two axes, one running through the house from front to back in line with the former screens passage and the stair, and the other running laterally through the basement, providing access to front and rear rooms from the stair foot. The position of the stair is unprecedented, and the probable location of the kitchen, in the basement, was still very unusual.

The antecedents of Whitehall are not known, but its location is comparable with that of another early, compact, suburban house, Beckington Castle in Somerset (pl. 142).[97] These houses may be evidence of a tradition of compact suburban houses outside other towns. If so, it is unlikely that they did not occur at an earlier date on the edge of London as well.

The plan of Whitehall, though extremely logical, is of a complexity that does not often recur thereafter. A quite small house, Hinton House at St Nicholas Hurst in Berkshire (pls 143, 144) exemplifies the triple-pile layout at its simplest and clearest.[98] Neither its builder nor the date is known, though

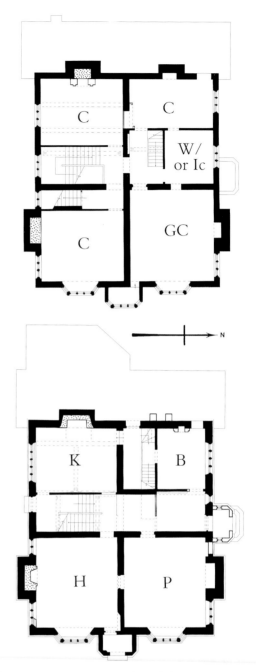

143 (*above*) Hinton House: ground- and first-floor plans. The central range contains circulation as at Westwood and Lulworth (pls 120, 121) but the house is entered conventionally through the hall. In the compact house, conventional hierarchies were sacrificed to formal innovations. When (as at Hinton) the front range comprises only hall and parlour, the central front door meant that a traditional, low-end entrance to the hall was impossible. A spine corridor on the top floor, essentially a means of providing separate access to each of the attic chambers, also served as a species of gallery.

142 (*left*) Beckington Castle, Somerset, *c.* 1570. The house is two ranges deep, with the stair in a forward projection, close to the principal entrance. It was probably built for a prosperous cloth merchant, on the edge of a small manufacturing town; such compact forms may have occurred at an early date in the outer suburbs of other towns besides London, where the principal evidence survives.

144 Hinton House, St Nicholas Hurst, Berkshire, *c.* 1615. Hinton is one of the earliest fully developed houses with a three-range ('triple-pile') plan.

puzzling origins.[99] Only its front wall now stands, but footings of circular turrets at four corners of the house show that as built the house was a substantial, rectangular block of building, two ranges deep. Early in the nineteenth century there was said to have been a large outer courtyard, a smaller inner courtyard fronting the house with its own gatehouse, and a third, probably a service court, to the rear.[100] The house rises through three floors, with the largest windows in the second storey, so that whatever courtyard enclosures there may have been, the principal rooms of the house showed well above them. Slight irregularities preclude complete symmetry: the high end of the hall breaks forward to form an oriel, but this is not apparent at first glance. The house deliberately evokes a castle by its full-height projecting porch, projecting chimneybreasts, end turrets and a battlemented parapet. The compact, double-depth plan (there was no internal courtyard or light well) was virtually unprecedented at that date, and Thorpe Salvin anticipates by its height and castle-like form (themselves almost certainly inspired by Chatsworth of the 1560s) an important group of later houses in the region culminating in Hardwick.[101]

Compact houses, two ranges deep with angle turrets, had been known in France since the fifteenth century, and plans of such houses had been published not long before by Du Cerceau.[102] There is evidence from the 1580s onwards of French and Italian plans adapted to the needs of English builders, but it is impossible to know whether Thorpe Salvin is an early example of this or if it is simply an adaptation of the native model of the compact courtyard house, contracted to the point at which the central courtyard had ceased to exist – and in either case, whether its plan was the initiative of its builder Henry Sandford or of his unknown mason. Nothing is known of Sandford that might have prompted him to adopt so unusual a form, although many of the same elements were soon repeated nearby in Barlborough Hall (pl. 15), the house of his son-in-law, Frances Rodes. Barlborough recalls the castle in a similar way, but had a small courtyard at the centre. This courtyard, however, was of no value in lighting the rooms of the house, which all look outward, but served instead to light a system of passages that run round the house on each floor and which somewhat resemble those of Hengrave. At both houses the compact plan seems to have been adopted primarily in order to concentrate the visual mass of the house and to provide, in a house of very different form, what was also achieved at Corsham Court and at Shaw: a house conceived and expressed as a totality and in which its internal arrangements were not displayed.

The fourth of these houses, offered here as types of double-pile and triple-pile plans, is the Red Hall at Bourne in Lincolnshire (pls 146, 147). This is a modest, brick house, built around 1620 for Gilbert Fisher, a local man of yeoman stock who may have chosen to celebrate his rise to the ranks of the gentry by building his house in a fashionable form and in a fashionable building material.[103] An inventory taken on Fisher's death in 1633 records hall, dining parlour, kitchen and pantry on

145 Thorpe Salvin, Nottinghamshire, c. 1570. Thorpe Salvin is possibly the earliest surviving country house to have been built to a double-pile plan. Its resemblance to Chatsworth of the 1560s (which was also outward-facing, with the best rooms on the top floor) may suggest one origin for the deep plan as a reduced courtyard house with the courtyard shrunk to nothing.

stylistically a date of around 1600–1620 seems most probable, and its builder a William Hide who died in 1624. The front of Hinton House is symmetrical, yet behind this symmetrical front the hall and parlour are also of equal size so that the entrance into the hall has to be arranged very oddly: the outer door to the porch lies at its centre, but the inner door from porch to hall is offset to one side. The central range is relatively narrow, occupied by the principal stair and probably formerly by a service stair as well. In the rear range are the kitchen and other services. The same arrangement, of two rooms to the front and two to the rear divided by a central range providing the main circulation, seems to have been repeated on the first floor, but on the top floor the main stair is repositioned so as to leave the central range free for a diminutive gallery, doubling also as a passage to serve the attic bedchambers on either side. These elements – the central entrance, the circulation arranged laterally in the middle range, and the upper gallery – could be elaborated beyond the basic, double-pile form, and would recur in a number of important buildings in the century following.

Thorpe Salvin (pl. 145) is probably slightly earlier than Whitehall and is a house of a very different class but of equally

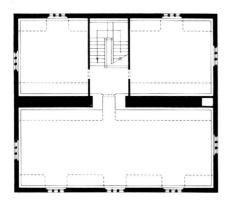

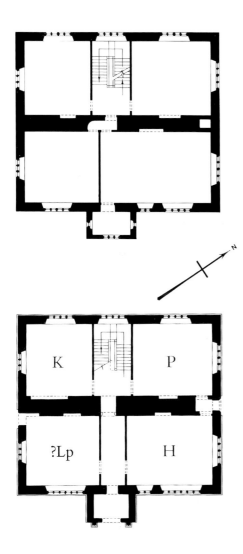

Red Hall: ground-, first- and second-floor plans. As in a very great many early double-pile houses, the original screen between hall and entry has been replaced by a partition. An inventory taken on the builder's death suggests that he slept over the kitchen, in the north-west. The top floor is partly occupied by what was described as a 'gallery' but its principal contents was a stock of cheeses.

for a grander neighbour, Sir William Rigdon, for which there is a preliminary plan (the same in its double-pile layout though very different in detail) among John Thorpe's drawings.[105]

Whitehall predated by almost two decades any close parallels, and without documentary proof one would have been very reluctant to give it so early a date. Thorpe Salvin is also without known English precedents. Nevertheless it is unlikely that any of the unusual features of either house made their first appearance there, nor that it was there that they first appeared together. Shrewsbury was a town of some administrative importance as the seat of the Council for Wales, but it was far from the centres of social or economic life; little is known of the builder of Thorpe Salvin, and the uncertainties surrounding the sources of both houses illustrate the difficulties in tracing the plan's ultimate origins. But elements of the compact plan had already appeared in town houses and in lodges. A few small medieval gentry houses[106] have their kitchen and parlour backing onto the hall, forming a plan which is near a square though far from symmetrical. An exceptionally grand house of 1431–42, Minster Lovell in Oxfordshire, has a two-storey range fronting onto a hall of great height which towers above it: the front range comprised a chapel on the first floor and some sort of parlour, accessible only from the dais end of the hall, on the floor below. Blocks of building that were more than a single range deep occur spasmodically in the sixteenth century as parts of larger houses. East Barsham may have had a precocious double-pile layout, if A. C. Pugin's nineteenth-century plan is to be accepted;[107] the evidence can no longer be checked, but the complex plan of Cowdray provides some parallels. They occur elsewhere in East Anglia. A range of minor rooms lies at the rear of the hall at Hengrave, possibly in order to diversify the circulation, though this is no longer clear. Rushbrook[108] and Seckford[109] in Suffolk, large E-plan houses of the late sixteenth century, had double-pile centres in which the second 'pile' seems to have been occupied solely by dependent rooms on the ground floor, though there may have been a lateral gallery on the first. Some large late medieval and early sixteenth-century houses such as Compton Winyates and Sutton Place incorporated substantial, deep blocks of lodgings for their owner.

The central range of Henry VIII's private palace at Nonsuch seems to have been two rooms deep, as was Princess Mary's lodgings at Whitehall, built in the 1530s with a front range 50 feet deep. These were self-contained units of accommodation and provided no precedent for the planning of a complete house, but their deep plans meant that even though one range of rooms

the ground floor, four chambers on the first floor (Fisher's plate was in the kitchen chamber, suggesting this as the room where he slept) and on the top floor a maid's chamber and the 'high gallery' which, though probably intended as a fashionable amenity, contained cheese and butter and spare beds.[104] Fisher was evidently not far removed from his yeoman origins, and may have built the Red Hall in emulation of Dowsby, a larger house

147 Red Hall, Bourne, Lincolnshire, *c.* 1620. A modest house with an up-to-date, double-pile plan, built for a man who was rising into the gentry class.

could face an internal courtyard, the other had to face outwards. But the house which more than any other building may have promoted both the double-pile principle and the outward aspect was Holdenby, the huge palace built for Sir Christopher Hatton betweeen around 1571 and 1583.[110] The plan of Holdenby, with double-pile wings flanking inner and outer courtyards, was unprecedented; almost as unprecedented was its appearance, with

the outward-facing rooms lit by a phalanx of identical bay windows looking over the gardens and park. Since rooms in a double-pile house can be lit from only one side, rather than both externally and from a courtyard, the double-pile plan was of necessity inseparable from the outward-looking aspect, and the symmetrical double pile was inconceivable until both symmetry and outward aspect had been accepted as principles of design.

But although these early experiments in deep planning must have been suggestive for later developments, the most influential model for the compact, double-pile house was probably the town house and subsequently that of the inner suburbs.[111] When space was not restricted, the rich man's town house occasionally approached the forms it would take in the country. But the impression one has from the plans of London property made by the surveyor Ralph Treswell early in the seventeenth century – the fullest contemporary record of the character of city-house plans – is largely of ill-lit dwellings composed of a chaotic jumble of rooms and divided by tiny alleys and narrow light wells.[112] Even some of the larger houses in his plans (identifiable as separate dwellings only by the name of the occupant written in each room) appear as haphazard accumulations of living space rather than organised on any coherent principle. Often there seems to have been no connection between the parts of such a house save through a small courtyard or across a common passage – a replica, though of different genesis, of the accretive medieval origins of the larger houses of the country. Pressure for room meant that ideal spatial relations could seldom be achieved. Significantly, inventories often show the halls of town houses as being very much better furnished than are those of the great men of the countryside: halls in town were more often used as living rooms, and in one of Treswell's plans he names a room as 'hall or parlour'; clearly he was himself uncertain about how to describe its use. Such density of building will have accustomed even the richer inhabitants to arrangements very different from those of the country: in particular, to rooms that were surrounded on three sides by other rooms, that were lit from one side only, and to living in houses where the conventional hierarchies of planning were unattainable.

Yet despite such impressions of chaos, house types had evolved, both in London and in other towns, that accepted these restrictions and were adapted to pressures on space. These served a mercantile class whose needs differed from those both of the gentleman in the country and of the medieval nobleman whose town house had served for no more than his periodic, ostentatious visits. The problem facing all but the wealthiest urban builders was how to make the best use of a site whose greatest value, whether for commerce or for making a public display of wealth and status, was the street frontage. Those rich enough to require a proper hall might place it as a wing at right angles to the front range, in which case it might lie close against a similar wing to the adjacent property. An alternative, not uncommon in town but exceptional in the country, was for a hall on an upper floor. However, the commonest solution to the commonest problem – that of fitting a house of the maximum size on a plot that was deep but narrow – was to build a house two rooms deep, with a transverse wall between the two which served for structural stability and as a fire break, could easily contain chimney flues and might support a staircase – in effect, a house to a double-pile plan (pl. 148).[113] Such an arrangement provided the maximum number of lit rooms, and also allowed for functional isolation of the dwelling house if, for instance, a front room was to be a shop or a warehouse.

Such a house could be extended to fill a plot of any given width. One of John Thorpe's plans shows the ground and first floors of a town house of just this kind (pl. 149).[114] This was

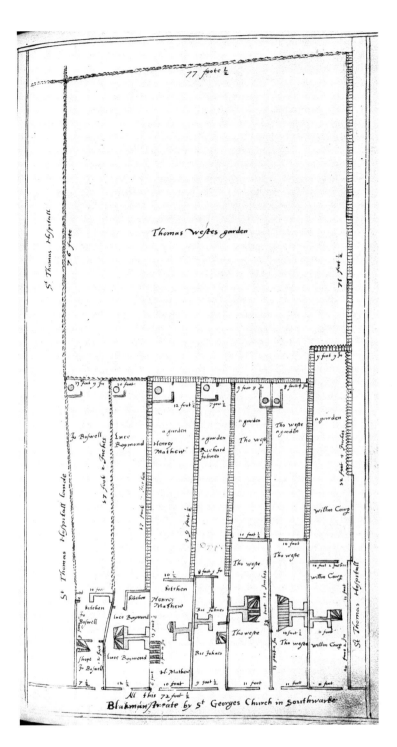

148   Ralph Treswell, *c.* 1610: houses in the inner suburbs. Deep plans were evolved in the Middle Ages to make the most use of space in the crowded conditions of town. Such conditions as these will have accustomed city dwellers to occupying houses in a different way from their use in the country.

fashionably situated in the Strand, had been occupied by a leading official of the Royal Works, Thomas Fowler, and was leased at the time of the survey by another royal official, Sir Thomas Lake. Party walls to either side and a spine wall down

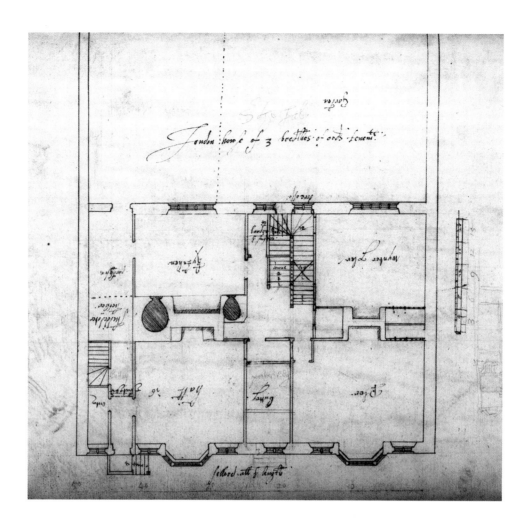

149 John Thorpe: house in the Strand, London, *c.* 1600. A town house in a prime location, probably surveyed (rather than designed) by Thorpe. The entry is still at one end of the hall, but it can be seen how by shifting it to the centre of the frontage one would create a house quite similar to that in pl. 139.

the centre confine windows to the front and back walls, but this is not a serious disadvantage. Entrance is via a side passage that leads to a yard at the rear and provides access to the hall as well as to the kitchen; a doorway at the high end of the hall leads in the normal way to a good staircase and to two parlours. The unusual width of the site makes it possible to preserve a hall which approximates at least to the traditional, hierarchical form with the entry leading in at one end and the best stairs and the best rooms leading out of the other. The side entry meets the practical limitations of a restricted site by providing access to the yard without the need to pass through the body of the house. But it is easy to see how, by simply placing the front door at the centre of the main front instead of tucked away down a side passage, the elevation would be made wholly symmetrical while the old-fashioned hall arrangement was destroyed.

Houses of this sort seem already to be by far the most widespread type shown in a bird's-eye view of the smartest part

of London engraved by Wenceslaus Hollar (pl. 150), probably made around 1660 and showing an area that had largely been built up in the previous seventy-five years in response to the burgeoning demand for fashionable accommodation. West of the City, in Holborn, St Giles and off the Strand that connected the City with Westminster (and where some of the greatest men of the land had long had their town houses), numbers of new houses were being built for those keen to enjoy the amenities of suburban life.[115] In the new century, a less peripatetic court provided a further incentive for the ambitious to resort to the neighbourhood of Whitehall. In 1598 John Stowe described the Strand as 'a continuall new building of divers faire houses'; Drury Lane as lined with 'diverse faire buildings, Hosteries, and houses for Gentlemen, and men of honor'; while green-field sites made room for gardens with 'many fayre summer houses . . . some of them like Midsommer Pageantes, with Towers, Turrets, and Chimney tops, not so much for use or profit, as for shewe

150 (*facing page*) Wenceslaus Hollar: engraving, *c.* 1660. A bird's-eye view of the most fashionable area of London, west of Holborn and north of the Strand. The area is filled with row houses and detached houses with deep plans.

S. Giles

huh Holborn

S. Giles Fields

Piazza in Covent Garden

Chapel

151 Pendell House, Bletchingley, Surrey, 1636. A villa-like house, built as a country retreat by a man who continued to maintain close political and commercial interests in the City of London. The plan closely resembles that in pl. 139, though there is no reason to suppose a direct connection.

and pleasure, bewraying the vanity of mens mindes'.[116] The new building boom encouraged the display of taste, wealth and architectural invention. In Hollar's view, substantial houses along the main streets back on to good gardens, while occasional freestanding ones occupy desirable open plots behind the principal street frontages. Whether isolated or part of a row, these houses are tall and compact in outline and deep and rectangular in plan, the systematisation of forms developed for the close densities of the city and for the styles of city living.

Those in the late sixteenth century and the early seventeenth who commended the amenities of the suburbs or remarked on their expansion were thinking primarily of areas relatively

close to the City such as that depicted by Hollar. But early in the new century free-standing, compact, upright houses, whose accommodation reflects urban rather than rural practices, begin to appear further afield. The versatility of the urban double-pile form was evidently recognised by Thorpe himself, who inscribed another drawing '3 howses for the cytty or for a country howse'.[117] The plan of these three houses could not have been adapted to the country without modification, yet Thorpe seems to see the country house simply as an extension of the double-pile layout in which the rich townsman would already have felt at home. The plan lent itself admirably to the specialised requirements of the suburban house, and when it first appears in the outer London area the resemblance of such houses to these models is so very close that there can be little doubt of their metropolitan origins.

Two houses close to each other at Bletchingley in Surrey illustrate particularly well the contrast between the novel, compact villa form and more traditional houses, since the careers and interests of their respective owners are precisely what one

152 Pendell Court, Bletchingley, Surrey, *c.* 1618–22. Within sight of Pendell House, but a house of traditional form, built by a man who had made his money as a City merchant but whose ambition (to judge fom the career of his son) was to establish himself as a country gentleman.

might predict from the differing forms of their homes. Pendell House (pl. 151) is a compact, four-square house of double-pile form with a symmetrical, hipped roof, built in 1636 by Richard Glyd, citizen of London.[118] Glyd had been a younger son of minor gentry in Sussex, apprenticed to a tallow chandler whose niece he had married. He had been buying landed property since 1617, but probably at first more as an investment than with any intention of building up an estate: his properties were scattered, included houses, and some he later sold at a profit. He bought the Pendell estate in 1633. London remained the centre of Glyd's financial and political activities as Governor and Treasurer of Christ's Hospital, Master of the Tallow-chandler's Company and

a member of the Common Council for the City during the Civil War. Pendell House, at 21 miles and a half-day's ride from the City, was a rural retreat rather than a county seat.

Pendell House is a compact, brick, double-pile building, essentially a square with a room in each quadrant. There is a full basement, probably containing the kitchen; the principal stair rises at the centre of the rear range. The plan is virtually the same as that of a house designed by Inigo Jones for Sir Peter Killigrew, probably at much the same date (pl. 178), and also closely resembles the Thorpe plan reproduced in pl. 139.[119] Pendell House was modernised in the eighteenth century and it is uncertain whether or not the front door opened (as now) into an entrance passage or directly into the hall that occupied one quadrant of the ground floor, though the latter seems more probable. In its plainness, its hipped roof and in the mannerist ornament of its brickwork the house is wholly typical of up-to-date building in the London region, and in view of Glyd's City connections it is safe to say that it must have been the work of London craftsmen.

By contrast, Pendell Court (pl. 152), less than half a mile away, is a house of wholly traditional form.[120] The house has been altered more than Pendell House, but essentially it has a linear plan, one range deep, with the best stair and parlour (with a short wing) at one end and the services at the other, and with the hall lying conventionally between. The elevations are gabled, the façade not quite symmetrical, and a tall, projecting porch similar to that at Pendell House leads into the low end of the hall. George Holman, the house's builder, purchased the manor of Pendell in 1617, and the house was probably complete by 1625, the year of his death. Robert Holman, his son, set himself up among the county community, increasing his local land holdings in the 1630s; a parliamentarian like Richard Glyd of Pendell House, he involved himself in the county rather than with London. During the Civil War he was named to a number of county committees, became a Justice of the Peace in 1646 and was elected one of six county members to the Protectorate parliament of 1654. He presented a pulpit to Bletchingley church, and as a Puritan was appointed to the Reigate Presbyterian classis in 1648. Of course, it is impossible to know whether George Holman, in buying Pendell in 1617, had aspirations to the county élite either on his own behalf or that of his son, but it seems probable: rather than buying a simple estate he had bought the manor with its rights and responsibilities, and the house he built was of precisely the form long associated with the manor house.

A few other compact, double-pile or triple-pile houses remain in the London area, and the Thorpe drawings provide – where their subjects are identifiable – evidence of several more of still earlier date. Thorpe's smaller double-pile plans are for the most part of two forms: one in which the principal stair is in line with the entry, and a second in which matched stairs project on either flank wall and which formed the model for a small group of surviving houses, away from London, discussed in chapter 5. The former is the more direct transfer from the town house. The house with flanking stair towers could not be built where other houses were to stand up against it, and in it the provision of both low-end and high-end stairs makes possible the preservation of hierarchy that is still appropriate in a rural context, even though the placing of the parlour to the rear of the hall already identifies the hall with the better rooms of the house rather than with the services. There is no surviving house of this latter form in the London area, but John Thorpe drew five such plans, one of which is inscribed 'Potters Bar 1596' (pl. 164).[121]

There are still five double-pile houses of the first type in the London suburbs, and all like Pendell House are the suburban seats of the mercantile élite. Boston Manor in Brentford is the earliest, dated 1622.[122] The builder was Lady Reade, widow of Sir Thomas Gresham's stepson who had died the year before, and was thus closely linked with the City aristocracy. The Dutch House (now Kew Palace) was built in 1632 by Samuel Fortry, a City merchant; Swakeleys in Ickenham by Edmund Wright, Lord Mayor; Forty Hall in Enfield (the earliest survivor to have a hipped roof) in 1629 by Nicholas Rainton, another Lord Mayor;[123] and Cromwell House in Highgate by Richard Sprignell who had City connections and married the daughter of the queen's apothecary. All have been altered more or less; each incorporates variations on the compact model. Common to them all is the placing of the main stair at the rear, in line with the front entrance. Forty Hall is a species of triple pile with some affinities to Hinton; Swakeleys is larger than the others, effectively a house with one traditional, service-passage range and another parallel to it containing the stair and additional rooms, and with cross wings at either end. Boston Manor has a passage and secondary stair running laterally through the service end of the house, creating a species of plan in which one half of the house is double pile, the other approaches three ranges deep. The plan of Cromwell House is oddly irregular, and may have been affected by a constricted site.

Architecturally they are equally varied. Boston Manor has straight gables, Kew Palace (pl. 183) has shaped gables, Swakeleys (pl. 188) gables of a still more elaborate form, Cromwell House a straight ridge behind a parapet, Forty Hall (pl. 176) a hipped roof. All are of brick, with deep windows, but the surface decoration of façades and of door and window surrounds is similarly varied, reflecting a wide variety of sources as well as the influence of the controls over London street architecture which were largely responsible for the development of the restless classicism of around 1620–60 that has been termed 'artisan mannerism' and which is discussed in the next chapter. But although the architecture of these houses is to an extent experimental in attempting to assimilate a variety of heterogeneous sources in the development of a native classicism, by the 1630s the compact form is well established as the appropriate mode for the suburban gentry house.

Early in the eighteenth century Daniel Defoe described the country south and west of London as

> so full of beautiful buildings, charming gardens and rich habitations of gentlemen of quality, that nothing in the world can imitate it . . . these houses and gardens are admirably beautiful in their kind, and in their separate, and distinct beauties, such as their scituation, decoration, architect, furniture, and the like . . . at a distance they are all nature, near hand all art; but both in the extremest beauty.[124]

Defoe ascribed the popularity of the outer suburbs to the example of King William and Queen Mary at Hampton Court. Certainly over the previous fifty years there had been a huge increase in the numbers of the upper classes who had houses in the London countryside, whether to live there permanently or simply to spend their holidays, but the movement to the suburbs went back a good deal further than that as did the development of the villa itself.

5

London and the Provinces, 1600–1650

London Plans

From the beginning of the seventeenth century London would assume a growing importance as the source of innovation both in the amenities of the upper-class house and in its architectural design. Away from London an increasing number of houses began to incorporate elements that can be directly paralleled in the visual extravagance or the inventiveness of planning of the most innovative houses of the suburbs. Holland House, with its riot of gables, its elaborately decorated frontispiece, its highly articulated elevations and its visual concentration had been the apogee of the style. At Blickling Hall in Norfolk (pl. 153) (the gables of which recall those of Holland House, even though they were already described as 'Dutch dormers' when they were built)[1] the house is approached on its short axis, creating a similar massing; so also is Bramshill in Hampshire. Aston Hall in Warwickshire presents a silhouette as elaborate as that of either Holland House or of Blickling, and was probably designed by John Thorpe; one of the Thorpe plans may possibly be a preliminary or variant design for Westwood. Whether this exuberance was engendered in London is debatable, but the wealth of Londoners certainly fostered it.

Somerhill, near Tunbridge in Kent and of which there is a plan among the Thorpe drawings,[2] closely resembles Ashley Park and Charlton House in layout in being a house of H plan with a double-pile centre and a hall running through the building from front to back. Like Nottingham House there was a dais in the hall, but unlike it there was no screen, probably because the service entry into the hall was not at the room's low end but close to the centre. Projecting from the centre of each wing was not a tower as at Charlton, but deeply projecting, semicircular bay windows like that which at Nottingham House had lit the end of the hall. Somerhill was built by Richard Bourke, Lord Clanricarde, an Irish peer who had acquired the

estate through marriage to Frances, daughter of Sir Francis Walsingham, who had already been married successively to Sir Philip Sidney and to the Earl of Essex. Through his wife, at least, Clanricarde's connections could not have been higher, and in his country house he made use of elements of planning that were appearing in the most fashionable houses of the London suburbs.

Clanricarde also built another house, Portumna Castle on his Irish estates (pl. 154), only the second house on a deep plan in that country.[3] Portumna has square, projecting angle turrets and

153 Blickling Hall, Norfolk, 1616–27. Blickling's compact silhouette and decorative gables (though described as 'dutch dormers' when built) suggests the influence of London buildings such as Holland House and Eagle House (pls 126 and 133).

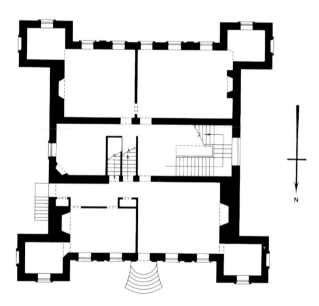

154 Portumna Castle, Co. Galway, Ireland. The house with a deep plan and rectangular corner towers derived from several models: from castellated houses such as Lulworth and Westwood, and from plans in French and Italian books. Portumna was built on the Irish estates of the Earl of Clanricarde, an Irish peer with close connections at the court of James I.

most notorious scandal of the age) came when he opposed Rochester's intended marriage to the divorced wife of the Earl of Essex – i.e. to the Countess of Clanricarde's former daughter-in-law. He was himself reported as paying court to the divorcée's half-sister, the Countess of Rutland, who was Lady Clanricarde's own daughter by her first marriage.

But while it is inconceivable that Overbury cannot have known the Earl and Countess of Clanricarde they need not have discussed architecture, and still less need Sir Thomas's father have shared an architect with the builder of Portumna. It is probably no more than coincidence that an English house which resembles Portumna in its combination of triple-pile plan and angle towers was put up by the father of a man whose connections with the Countess of Clanricarde's daughters was so close. At this exalted level of society everyone knew everyone, and to experiment with fashionable architectural forms was the vogue. But what this resemblance nevertheless illustrates (as much as does that between Somerhill, Charlton and Ashley Park) is how the primacy of London in the early seventeenth century as the fountainhead of architectural innovation was largely the result of the capital's social supremacy.

155 Bourton House, Bourton on the Hill, Gloucestershire, c. 1610: ground-floor plan. Bourton was much altered in the eighteenth century and some internal details are uncertain, but it preserves the essence of its three-range plan, combining it with the square turrets of Portumna and its models.

modest battlements. The defensible house still had a serious purpose in Ireland, and Portumna had a predecessor of a sort in Rathfarnham Castle, County Dublin, clearly based on current designs in fortification and with closer parallels in France than in the British Isles.[4] Rathfarnham combines a double-pile plan with sharply keeled angle turrets. There is no house in England with both of these features, but they occur in plans by de L'Orme (pl. 23) and Androuet Du Cerceau,[5] and the house thus combines interest in both fortification and architecture – the former sanctioned by tradition, the latter by fashion. But at Portumna the form is at least modified by English architectural practice, and only its small windows in any way distinguish it from contemporary houses of what may loosely be called the 'court school'.

Although there is now no house in the London area that combines such elements, there was a house at Bourton on the Hill in Gloucestershire with similar angle turrets and with which Clanricarde had an indirect but curious connection. The house was largely rebuilt early in the eighteenth century, but the original ground plan seems substantially intact (pl. 155).[6] It was probably built by a lawyer, Nicholas Overbury, who acquired the place in 1598 and died in 1643. One of Nicholas Overbury's sons was Sir Thomas, courtier, poet and wit (quoted on p. 271) and boon companion of Robert Carr, 1st Earl of Rochester. Sir Thomas Overbury's downfall (and his murder, the centre of the

156 Plas Teg, Hope, Clwyd, Wales, 1615. Built for John Trevor, a leading Jacobean civil servant, the house has angle turrets and a deep plan, with a through hall of the type already established in the London suburbs. The plan of Ashley Park (pl. 135) is among Trevor's papers, and it may be his own record of a house that had impressed him and whose form he wished to follow.

If there are links between the builders of these houses which might have played a part in their architectural similarity, the form of a Welsh house, Plas Teg in Clwyd (pl. 156), seems to depend directly on its builder's own knowledge of metropolitan building. The builder of Plas Teg, yet another house with a deep hall, was John Trevor, Surveyor to the Navy and son of the builder of another precocious, provincial house: Trevalyn, with matching wings and with pedimented windows.[7] Plas Teg has the angle turrets of Bourton and Rathfarnham, but the through hall of Ashley Park (pl. 135). While there is no demonstrable personal connection between Trevor and the builders of these other advanced houses, his service at court will have given him plenty of opportunity of visiting the London houses of his colleagues and peers. Most tellingly, it is among Trevor's papers, inherited by a Sussex family into which his descendants married, that a plan of Ashley Park has survived – looking by the draughts-manship as though made by an amateur, perhaps by Trevor

himself.[8] The houses are not identical: Ashley Park had projecting wings, Plas Teg angle turrets, but the correspondence of their hall layouts nevertheless makes it seem likely that the plan of Ashley Park was taken as a model for the building of Plas Teg: as good an indication of a London source for an advanced country house as one could hope to find.

The projecting turrets of Bourton, Plas Teg, Portumna and Rathfarnham are echoed at Ince Castle in Cornwall (pl. 157), built overlooking a branch of the Tamar estuary.[9] Ince was built in 1640 by Henry Killigrew, who had acquired the estate in 1638, although the Killigrews had owned property in the area since at least the previous century.[10] Killigrew was elected Member of Parliament for West Looe in 1639, and presumably intended the house as a species of local power base. He was well connected nationally; his father's first wife had been one of the five famously learned daughters of Sir Anthony Coke of Gidea Park, and thus through her he was related to the great patrons of architecture of the late sixteenth century, the Cecils and the Bacons. An uncle, Sir William Killigrew, had been groom of the chamber to James I; a cousin, Sir Peter was a protégé of the Earl of Pembroke and had a London house designed for him by Jones;[11] another cousin, Sir Robert, was Vice-Chamberlain to Queen Henrietta Maria.

Ince Castle is of brick, with square, projecting, corner towers and entrance into a species of *piano nobile*. An early eighteenth-

157 Ince Castle, Cornwall, c. 1640. Probably unfinished at the Civil War; a further storey may have been intended. A late example of the angle-towered house, but probably intended to have an up-to-date double-pile plan with the principal stair in an entrance hall like that of Chevening (pl. 177).

century view[12] shows battlements on the angle towers and the castellated appearance of the house may have been intended from the first, perhaps in conscious rivalry with Piers Edgcumbe's lodge at Mount Edgcumbe, overlooking the lower part of the estuary some 5 miles off. However, the overall, squat form of the house and the unusual entrance arrangements suggest that the political difficulties of the time prevented the completion of the house and that it may have been intended to have been at least one storey taller. If this was the intention, then perhaps Ince can best be seen as a very late version of the mock castles and the houses with corner towers of a generation and more earlier.

Much is obscure about the house's original form as a result of delapidation in the nineteenth century, drastic restoration in the early twentieth and subsequently a serious fire that gutted the interior, so that in reconstructing its original layout one must largely speculate. The plan provides six rooms of near-equal size on each floor, divided down its length by a spine wall. Detailed inspection following the fire showed that the principal internal divisions are substantially original to the house. The only evidence for original stairs is in two of the turrets, at opposite corners, but these could hardly have been sufficient for so pretentious a building. If the house was to have been taller, there would have to have been a stair rising in one of its six rooms

from the principal floor to the unbuilt storey above. At the centre of the front opposite the entrance are traces of a large window but with some kind of balcony projection (also overlooking the best view from the house) which may rule out a stair in that position; if so, then the most practical location for a principal stair must have been in the entrance hall. This would have provided a plan of a most up-to-date form – a house with the stair in the same position as that at Chevening (pl. 177).

The details of the execution to some extent belie its advanced form: there seems no earlier brickwork anywhere in Cornwall,[13] and the materials may have been shipped in, but stonework is not remarkable for its area and date and the one internal detail that remains – a plaster overmantel – has conventional strapwork of a kind that in the south-west might have been executed at any time in the previous forty years. But though there remain many unanswered questions about Ince Castle, enough survives to show that it was a house of unusual form whose building in so remote a place is inconceivable without the active involvement of a cultivated owner.

But the extravagant forms of some of these houses are of less importance in themselves than in suggesting the means by which architectural ideas were diffused. More significant in the long run than the adoption in a few large houses of the deep hall, running through the house from front to back, was the gradual spread of the hall arranged as it is at Bidston and at Holland House: running laterally, parallel with the façade of the house in the conventional manner, but entered at the centre. The deep hall of Eagle House and Charlton had practical drawbacks: suitable only to a house of a certain size or larger, and with an entrance end and a far end that still corresponded to the dis-

tinction between low end and high. The layout that appeared at Holland House was very much more potent for change in having no identifiable status gradation, although it seems to have taken a little longer to be adopted than the deep hall. It appears at Blickling, built between about 1618 and 1627 for a leading judge, Sir Henry Hobart. Aston Hall, built between 1618 and 1635, was designed with an end-entered hall and was either given its present, central entrance in the course of building or altered soon afterwards (conceivably as late as the 1650s following Civil War damage).[14] Among the first small houses to have a hall entered close to its centre is Newe House at Pakenham in Suffolk (pls 158, 159), dated 1622 and comprising essentially three rooms in line – parlour, hall and kitchen, with secondary services originally in a short wing to the rear. Despite the simplicity of its layout Newe House is a house of some sophistication, with shaped gables like those of Holland House. In the late 1620s and 1630s the centralised hall occurs in certain houses considered in more detail below: Chevening, St Clere and West Woodhay, houses which are very advanced stylistically and whose London affinities are unquestionable.

158 (*above*) Newe House, Pakenham, Suffolk, 1622. A small house with a sophisticated exterior, possibly built as a dower house.

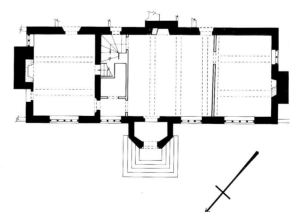

159 Newe House: ground-floor plan. Alterations have partly obscured the original layout, but Newe House has a hall which was entered at, or close to, its centre like that of Holland House (pl. 130) and Bidston (pl. 115).

160 Bidston Hall, Cheshire: the loggia added by the 6th Earl of Derby. There was a similar loggia at his London house.

The centrally entered hall cannot for obvious reasons be adopted in a double-pile house of the smallest sort, with four rooms to a floor – one to each quadrant. In a house like the Red Hall or Hinton, types of the small, compact house discussed in the previous chapter, the hall has necessarily to be entered at one end if the front entrance to the house itself is to be placed at the centre of the façade, and the awkwardness of the entrance arrangement at Hinton shows the initial difficulties in combining the four-square plan with the central entry. The fact that in some larger houses halls entered at one end still occur late in the seventeenth century suggests that the centrally entered hall was adopted at least partly for aesthetic reasons: because with hierarchy no longer significant, it was the most satisfactory way of achieving a symmetrical front in the house of middling size.

In a number of country houses of the early seventeenth century, plan elements that may be traced to London sources are combined with others that are more traditional or more local. A feature of Holland House as enlarged, probably of Charlton House as first built and of several other houses whose plans were drawn by John Thorpe, was the incorporation within the body of the building of a ground-floor loggia.[15] Both at Charlton and at Holland House this was located within the high-end cross wing, with a chapel in the extremity of the wing beyond it. At Bidston as enlarged by the 6th Earl of Derby around 1620 there is a similar loggia beneath first-floor rooms, in this case at the back of the hall (pl. 160). The same arrangement of loggia with a gallery over it occurs in a Thorpe plan of the earl's London house,[16] and it is easy to see how the novelties of London might be introduced into the provinces by such patrons as these. Dinninghoff's plan for Lumsden's house at Sheriff Hutton (pl. 29) also included a loggia between short wings, with a gallery above it which served also for communication between the two ends of the house – an arrangement commended by Francis Bacon.[17] There seems to have been a similar arrangement at Condover Hall in Shropshire (pl. 161), a large house probably finished before 1600 and built for the judge Thomas Owen to a scheme prepared by the architect-mason Lawrence Shipway.[18] Owen was a local man, typically returning to his roots after a successful career at a national level. With tall gables and a continuous frieze at storey height, Condover is reminiscent externally of Whittington (pl. 66), and in view of Shipway's wholly provincial career (so far as it is known) the house's innovations of plan may have been due to Owen. However, open loggias occur widely in contemporary books, notably in those of Androuet Du Cerceau, and like the deep hall, their ultimate derivation remains uncertain.

Chastleton House (pls 94, 95, 163), already described in some detail, shows the difficulty of separating elements of

London origin from those that may have evolved (or persisted) in the provinces. John Thorpe's possession of a plan of Wollaton and the likelihood that Hardwick provided a model for the group of London houses with cross halls, suggests the interaction of the two. At Chastleton the alternations of projection and recess, the visual syncopation of window levels and the increase in window area towards the centre of the house are highly accomplished. These have parallels with Dorfold in Cheshire, built around 1615 by Roger Wilbraham, lawyer at the Court of Wards and Liveries (pl. 162).[19] A plaster overmantel in the best bedchamber announces Wilbraham's service in the judiciary with a fine royal arms (unless it commemorates James I's visit to Nantwich in 1617 to see the salt works, when he was entertained at Wilbraham's house in the town).[20] Much altered internally, the plan of Dorfold was very advanced with a centre one-and-a-half ranges deep and with the principal stair origi-

161 Condover Hall, Shropshire, c. 1595. Condover has a loggia beneath a gallery. Such an arrangement may have been developed in London (cf. the slightly later example at Holland House, pl. 131) although it occurs widely elsewhere (cf. Bernhard Dinninghoff's plans, pl. 29). The exchange of ideas between London and the provinces was a two-way process.

162 Dorfold, Cheshire, c. 1615. An extremely accomplished design, with London parallels in its basement kitchen and its stair to the rear of the hall (since moved) and with a façade whose composition recalls that of Chastleton.

163 Chastleton House, Oxfordshire: the front elevation. The house is flanked by stair turrets that derive from current models in the outer suburbs of London (cf. pl. 164).

nally located behind the hall. What may also link it to metropolitan models is the placing of the kitchen in a tall, service basement as at Eagle House, with a much lower cellar beneath the hall. The floor of the hall is thus dropped so that the room can rise to a good height while allowing the first floor to maintain a continuous level throughout.

Mark Girouard has pointed out Chastleton's parallels with Burton Agnes in Yorkshire,[21] and hence the possibility of its having been designed by Robert Smythson, whose plan of Burton Agnes survives.[22] Burton Agnes has a similar, compact courtyard plan, a not dissimilar articulation of the front elevation, a concealed entrance in the flank of the porch (also found at Dorfold) and like Chastleton has a plaster, barrel vault to the long gallery. (Dorfold has a similar vault to the great chamber.) But while these three houses have common elements, they occur widely on their own and in combination elsewhere. Clearly

164   John Thorpe: ground-floor plan for a house at Potter's Bar, 1596. Paired, flanking stair towers appear in five of Thorpe's schemes for compact, rectangular houses. Although impractical in a house on an inner surbuban street, the number of Thorpe's designs that incorporate such stair towers suggests that the form originated in the London area and possibly originated with him.

some designer or designers of outstanding skill provided overall schemes for all three, but by the second decade of the seventeenth century such items had become the stock-in-trade of the well-informed builder or architect. When the qualities valued in a building were as much associative as architectural and while ingenuity, a striking silhouette and a show of wealth were among the most desirable qualities in the gentleman's house, builders were at liberty to pick and choose whatever fashionable elements they fancied. And when the person who made a draught for the house might not be the mason or carpenter who undertook or supervised its building, a combination of up-to-date and traditional features was to be expected.

At Chastleton this mixture of old and modern elements is particularly obvious in the flanking turrets. While incorporating old-fashioned, high- and low-end stairs of virtually equal size, their form here seems to have a suburban origin. Among the Thorpe drawings there are five plans in which an otherwise simple, double-pile house has the stairs similarly placed in flanking turrets rather than at the centre of the rear range. One of these (pl. 164) is inscribed 'potters bar 1596', an earlier date than any existing house with stairs of this kind.[23] The frequency of the layout among Thorpe's plans might suggest that it was a favourite design of his own, and such turrets were employed at

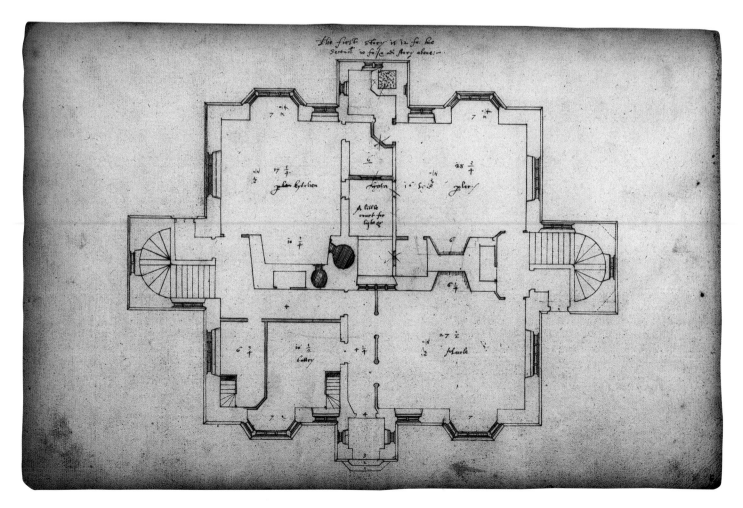

Camden House, later in Holland House as enlarged (and possibly as first built) and later still at Danvers House. The geographical spread of the few surviving houses to incorporate the motif also suggests London as the only likely common source: besides Chastleton, these are Gainford Hall in County Durham (pl. 165),[24] Gaythorne Hall in Cumbria (pl. 166)[25] and Kiplin in North Yorkshire (pl. 167).[26] At Grafton Hall in Cheshire of 1613, much restored in the nineteenth century and demolished in the 1950s, there were similar turrets which may also have contained stairs.[27] Although Gaythorne Hall replicates Gainford, the other examples are so widely separated in place, time or style that London is the only conceivable connection between them. The inspiration for such an arrangement may ultimately have been Worksop Manor or Hardwick, where stairs rise into towers at either end of the façade.

The advantage of the form was that by placing the high-end stair at one end of the house, its traditional position could be maintained in relation to the hall. A second advantage was aesthetic: the substantial, flanking towers provided visual mass to frame and support the façade and added to the interest of the skyline. However, the disadvantage of the layout was that in a larger house, placing the stairs at opposite ends might create circulation problems at the centre; in a small house this might be less serious, but in a small house two substantial stairs could be an unnecessary extravagance. Although the high-end stair might still be desirable in a house of traditional plan and in relation to a hall with traditional functions, it would become less so in due course, while changing household relations would make it increasingly unnecessary to provide a secondary, low-end stair of a grandeur almost equal to that at the high end.

Gainford Hall (pl. 165) was probably built in 1604 by John Cradock, vicar from around 1590 and third son of a middling gentry family, the Cradocks of Baldersdale. It is uncertain how he came by the money to build what was for a parson a large and sophisticated house and which was almost certainly the first compact, double-pile house in the north-west of England: it may have come through his wife (who on Cradock's death in 1627 was accused of having poisoned him) but he was a man of substance, Archdeacon of Northumberland and a magistrate. None the less, his status as a clergyman put him in a rather different position from that of most landowning gentry. The prosperity of Teesside and the southern parts of County Durham in the early seventeenth century meant that there were masons locally who would have been quite capable of executing such a house, given a plan to work to, but the form of the building cannot be of local origin.

Gainford Hall is two ranges deep, and the turret stairs are partly incorporated within the body of the house; there is virtually no difference in their size, and in ornament none. An odd feature of the building, partly a result of the sloping site but one that could easily have been avoided, is that the front and rear ranges are at different levels so that the social division of the house is between front and back rather than from side to side.

165 Gainford Hall, Co. Durham, 1604. Built for a parson, Gainford has the flanking stair turrets of Thorpe's drawings. Its remoteness and date make it inconceivable that the form could have been developed locally.

166 Gaythorne Hall, Asby, Cumbria. Built as a hunting lodge far up on the Cumbrian fells, either as a copy of Gainford (pl. 165) or erected by the same masons. Levens Hall, the main house of the Bellingham family who built it, is a house of conventional form.

The same arrangement occurs at a house that is virtually a twin of Gainford: Gaythorne Hall (pl. 166), standing in isolation in remote country between Kendal and Appleby in Cumbria. The resemblance between the two is so close – the double-pile,

split-level plan, the stairs contained in matching towers partly embedded in the house – that one must have provided the pattern for the other.

The third of these surviving double-pile houses with flanking stair turrets is Kiplin Hall in North Yorkshire (pl. 167), built for George Calvert, 1st Lord Baltimore. Calvert was effectively a career civil servant: clerk to the Privy Council in 1605, and thereafter holding a succession of appointments including Secretary of State (1619–25) and Lord of the Treasury (1620). He had been born at Kiplin, evidently in some property which his father had leased from Lord Wharton, and in buying the freehold of the estate in 1620 and in building Kiplin Hall shortly afterwards he was probably moved by a desire to proclaim his landed origins although as MP for the county in 1620–22 he may have had the same motives as Henry Killigrew at Ince: to provide a local power base. His principal interests were elsewhere: in London where his official duties lay, and in Ireland and in America where he was keenly promoting plantations. While Kiplin makes a bold outline with ogee caps to its turrets, it is basically an orthodox, four-square, double-pile building with rooms of large size and with the character rather of a villa than of a country seat.

The most unusual feature of Kiplin seems to have been the placing of the gallery, running through the middle of the house at right angles to its main axis and lit only at the ends – an arrangement that may have been paralleled at the more revolutionary Danvers House. Because of substantial later alterations many important questions about its original form cannot now be answered, but the kitchen seems to have been on the ground floor (or else detached) rather than in the shallow basement. There may in addition to the stairs in the flank turrets have been a principal stair at the centre of the rear range, the position

normal in the double-pile house and where there is now an eighteenth-century staircase. Kiplin is of brick with stone dressings, and in the quality of its details comparable with such great Jacobean houses as Hatfield and Blickling. Though not very far from Gainford, the status of its builder was very different, as is the house stylistically. It seems unlikely that Gainford was in any way a source for Kiplin, and much more probable that Calvert brought the plan directly from London.

London's position made it increasingly important in the national spread of novel forms, both as a centre of innovation and in developing and transmitting forms that may have been of provincial origin. In the creation of striking outlines, in the enhancement of stairs and state rooms and in plans that provided unprecedented locations for the hall, London houses advanced coherent and novel solutions to problems of form and layout that were felt increasingly widely. But when from the early seventeenth century novel, compact plans began to appear in numbers throughout England, they were at first generally executed within the context of existing regional building styles. In that they adopted the materials and the idiom of their locality, these houses must be the work of local craftsmen; in that they introduce novel layouts and sometimes novel outlines as well, it is tempting to attribute the spread of these forms not to craftsmen but to their clients who found in the metropolitan and suburban house a model that suited changing social relations and modes of living. On a visit to London in 1640 Sir Henry Slingsby of Scriven in Yorkshire was invited to supper at Holland House, where he was 'much taken wth ye curiosity of ye house; & from yt house I took a conceite of making a thorough house in part of Red-house wch now I build'.[28] Stylistically, Holland House was becoming old-fashioned, but it was the still innovative plan which appealed to Sir Henry. Builders like Sir Henry Slingsby and Sir John Trevor of Plas Teg were well travelled and had seen a broad range of the houses of their peers; only a handful of craftsmen whose reputation earned them wide employment could equal in their knowledge of a range of gentry houses, with their advantages and drawbacks, the experiences that were open to any reasonably observant member of the gentry class. In any case, these houses are also a reflection of the diversity of metropolitan culture itself. Even if the court was the centre of upper-class society, that society consisted of people who had a very wide range of contacts with it, from the intimate to the peripheral, and if many failed to comprehend the innovation in architectural styles of the 1620s, this did not mean that they were oblivious to other advances in civilised living. Many builders must have observed London innovations and returned home with them fresh in their minds. In the combi-

168 Garsington Manor, Oxfordshire, *c.* 1635. Outside Oxford, the house incorporates the highly characteristic motifs of contemporary college building in Oxford itself.

169 Garsington Manor: first-floor plan. The house has been altered, but is two ranges deep with a central, spine passage on the first floor providing access to chambers on both sides of the house.

nation of up-to-date plans and more conservative architectural detail, and in the preoccupation of most builders with the layout of their houses (rather than with architectural detail), there is a parallel with the reception of continental models by leading practitioners themselves. It has been suggested how the cross hall and perhaps the open loggia may have derived ultimately from continental sources, but even in the works of Robert Smythson and (in particular) of John Thorpe, where the inspiration of French or Italian patterns can sometimes be shown, this is very much more apparent in plans than in elevations.

A house of novel, compact plan whose stylistic affinities are extremely clear is Garsington Manor in Oxfordshire (pls 168, 169), built to a species of triple-pile plan in the mid- to late

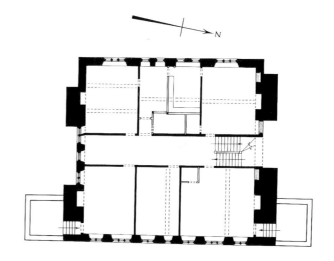

170 Anderson Manor, Dorset, 1622. Among the earliest double-pile houses in the county. Although brick was still a novel material locally, the use of different types echoed a regional taste for contrasting surfaces.

1630s.[29] Internal joinery is very close to contemporary work in Oxford. Equally close is the exterior, in which windows, string course and probably originally a battlemented parapet are identical with those of the new range of University College, begun in 1634. With certain distinctive variations, also recognisable at Garsington, University College follows an established local style, most notably in the perpetuation of late Gothic detail and windows with arched heads at a time when almost everywhere else in England these had been superseded by straight-headed windows. Yet the fact that there is an architect's model for the college, made of drawn elevations pasted on card – perhaps the first English model to survive – shows that the conservatism of these details was self-conscious rather than archaic[30] and there is nothing old-fashioned about Garsington's plan. Garsington resembles Hinton in that the central range is occupied by a stair and a lateral passage; like other houses of the same type, the difficulty of lighting this passage has led to later alteration.

A second example of local affinities is Anderson Manor in Dorset (pls 170, 171), built in 1622.[31] In its materials it is an innovation locally, being of brick with stone dressings. However, the use of brick may reflect not only the prestige of a fashionable material, but also a continuing local taste for striking or contrasting surfaces. A number of houses in the area and further north into Wiltshire deliberately use different types and textures of material in combination – notably flint with different stones – while the façade of Lake House at Wilsford,[32] with its similar, flat, gabled front and central porch also closely resembles Anderson in its proportions. Lake House was burnt out early in the twentieth century and rebuilt, but though the principal block is only one range deep (unlike the two of Anderson) its services were housed in a broad, rear-projecting wing which left the main front of the house to be wholly occupied by polite rooms. Thus, unlike Anderson, the hall occupied one half of the front, a parlour the other, while the stair was probably placed in line with the screens passage. Anderson can be seen as a mixture of influences: fashionable in its double-pile plan and its brickwork, regional in that the layout was to some extent prefigured by local tradition and in the decorative use of building materials.

A third, early, double-pile house which incorporates local idioms is Clegg Hall in Greater Manchester (pls 172, 173),[33] which stands forlornly on the edge of long-industrialised country near Rochdale, and is now only a shell. The property changed hands in the early seventeenth century and neither date nor builder is known, but a date around 1640 seems most plausible. In its architectural details it is wholly representative of local

171 (below) Anderson Manor: ground-floor plan. The plan of Anderson combines a distinctive regional tradition – a hall at one end of the house – with a second, parallel range to form a rectangular double-pile house. The small size of the original parlour, at the rear of the hall, and the prominent kitchen may reflect local usage; late in the seventeenth century the kitchen was rebuilt in the north-west wing, bringing its location into greater conformity with more general practice.

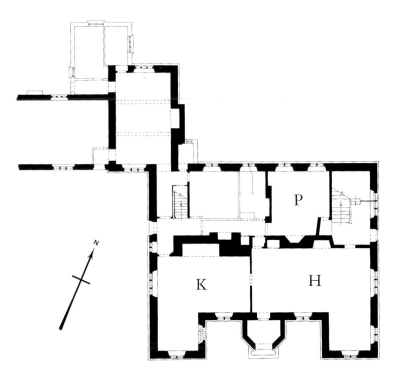

172 Clegg Hall, Greater Manchester, *c.* 1640. Photographed *c.* 1890 and now ruinous, Clegg Hall combined an up-to-date plan with local stylistic idioms.

173 (*below*)   Clegg Hall: ground-floor plan.

practices. But it shares with Gainford and Gaythorne Hall a split-level plan, front to back, and since a direct link between Clegg Hall and these seems unlikely, it may imply with them that some early, lost model for the form was similarly arranged. In the way in which there is a light well between stair landings and the windows in the back wall, the house resembles the arrangement of the secondary stair at Hardwick Old Hall.

A fourth double-pile house in a local manner is Quidenham Hall in Norfolk (pls 174, 175), much altered in the eighteenth century but known from an early model from which a plan can be taken.[34] The house was probably built around 1620 by Sir Thomas Holland, whose father John Holland (of old gentry

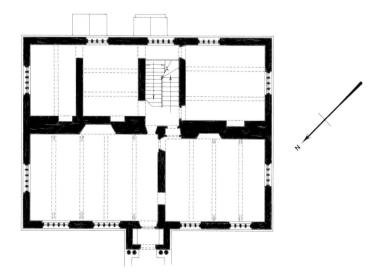

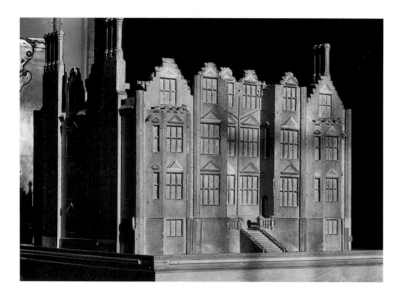

174 Quidenham Hall, Norfolk, c. 1620. Quidenham was altered in the eighteenth century, but its early form and arrangements are preserved in this model. A large, double-pile country house, it had the stepped gables and pedimented windows characteristic of contemporary East Anglian building, with the front door disguised in the flank of the porch.

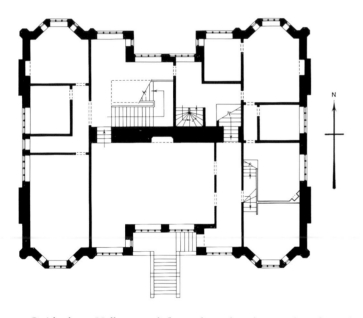

175 Quidenham Hall: ground-floor plan. The plan is taken from the evidence contained in the model and may not represent the internal layout precisely as built, but the general form is clear: overall, a double-pile plan adapted for a country house of quite large size which reflect the internal hierarchies but achieve regularity.

stock) was recorded in the eighteenth century as 'commended as an ingenious painter, in a book called the Excellent Art of Painting'.[35] This work has not been traced, but may indicate some family interest in the visual arts. In its externals Quidenham seems to have embodied many local idioms: of brick, with projecting window bays, pedimented surrounds and angle pinnacles and with a strong vertical emphasis, it closely resembled Heydon (pl. 217) and Barningham in the same county. Like many of these early, provincial double-pile houses, its plan is not otherwise formulaic; although in due course house plans would become increasingly standardised, as yet these houses often seem experimental, the adaptation by individual builders or masons of a layout which is understood as a principle but which requires interpretation in each case.

In the previous chapter, two houses at Bletchingly in Surrey – Pendell Court and Pendell House – were compared, the one built to a traditional plan and serving as the centre of a landed estate whose owner exercised the traditional responsibilities of his class, and the other, to a double-pile plan, the rural retreat of a Londoner. A number of these early, compact houses seem to have been built in circumstances where, as at the villa and the lodge, a traditional dwelling may not have been needed. Of those discussed, such were Gainford (a parsonage), Gaythorne Hall (a lodge), Kiplin and Ince (houses that did little more than establish their owners' territorial credentials), Anderson (a house of retirement, to be inherited by a younger son), and others not so far described including Quebec House at Westerham in Kent (for an unknown builder, but standing within the confines of a small market town),[36] Toseland in Cambridgeshire (probably a secondary seat for the Lake family of Cople in Bedfordshire),[37] Clanford Hall in Staffordshire (an unusual example of a timber-framed double-pile house, built as a dower house for Seighford Hall),[38] the Old Hall at Sandbach in Cheshire (also timber-framed, and on the edge of a town) and Wharton Court in Herefordshire[39] (a house for a man who was childless and cannot have aspired to found a landed dynasty in person). But though these examples might suggest that some builders regarded the form as exceptional, all were capable of functioning from the first as satisfactory dwelling houses. Though by 1650 such compact houses were not yet common, their wide geographical coverage probably gave them considerable influence as models and helped to make the form acceptable when in the mid- to late century such plans were associated with the spread nationally of architectural styles that were also of London origin.

London Styles

These compact houses demonstrate the importance of London as the source of innovative plan forms. However, at the same time as the emergence of new layouts, in the second and third decades of the seventeenth century new building styles were emerging in London and the suburbs. In terms of decoration these styles were diverse, ranging from the purism of Inigo Jones's Palladianism to the busy, cut brickwork of such a building as Cromwell House in Highgate, and from the simplicity of plain, hipped roofs to riots of shaped gables. One element in this diversity was an increasing availability of architectural pattern-books, and in this it is not surprising that London as the centre of trade, taste and building, led the way. The supply of native works was still very limited, although the first English edition of Serlio's first five books of architecture, translated by Robert Peake, was published in 1611. But the trickle of expensive, engraved Italian and French architectural books that during the sixteenth century had found their way into the libraries of a few connoisseurs was growing to a flood both of new works and of new editions of old ones, and now with works from Germany and the Low Countries. These illustrated books with immediate practical application were significantly outpacing the purely theoretical: fewer editions of Vitruvius and of Alberti (and these provided increasingly with illustrations), more works such as those of Palladio, Scamozzi, Serlio, Vignola, Bullant, de L'Orme and Du Cerceau. These too were supplemented by works more specifically on architectural decoration by writers such as Hans Blume and Jan Vredeman de Vries[40] and by a growing availability of single-sheet engravings. All of these had since the late sixteenth century placed in the hands of increasingly knowledgeable craftsmen a motley collection of motifs, some extravagant, some claiming classical authority but which – depending on their authorship and origin – were on any strict view not necessarily compatible with each other.

The diversity of London building in the new century was probably also encouraged by the capital's cultural diversity. Men of standing were increasingly concerned to express their personal distinction in their patronage of the arts, but the king's frequent absences weakened the court's monopoly of culture and fashion and left room for a number of different cultural groupings around the queen, Prince Henry and influential connoisseurs, collectors and the merely important such as the Earl of Arundel, the Duke of Buckingham and the Earl of Somerset. The embattled foreign policies of Elizabeth were giving place to a greater cosmopolitanism: easier relations with Spain, France, Flanders and the papacy brought men into contact with a wide variety of foreign cultural influences.

But mitigating the effect of the rag-bag of sources which certainly contributed to some of the decorative excesses of the beginning of the new century, was a more general tendency towards architectural restraint. In part this may have been a natural reaction from surfeit. Contemporary condemnation of architectural ostentation in the early seventeenth century is quoted in chapters 2 and 7, and it parallels changes in other kinds of behaviour: increasing concern for privacy and for public morals, a growing seriousness in religion, both sectarian and within the Church of England, and in personal conduct a greater sobriety in dress. A more serious moral climate exposed a fundamental dilemma in the nature of any class-based display which

was well expressed by John Weever, writing about church monuments in 1631:

Sepulchres should be made according to the quality and degree of the person deceased . . . for monuments answerable to men's worth, estates and places have always been allowed, and stately sepulchres for base fellows have always lain open to bitter jests. . . . [Yet] if one should seriously survey the tombs erected in our days, and examine the particulars of the personages wrought upon their tombs, he may easily discover the vanity of our minds, vested under our fantastic habits and attires.[41]

While it was right to express such distinctions, vanity was inherent in display itself. Sir Henry Slingsby, whose admiration for Holland House has already been quoted, nevertheless more than once expressed similar misgivings: 'A little thing sufficeth nature both for diet & habitation, & those buildings wch we aim at, serve more for magnificens yn [i.e. than] necessary use.'[42] There is a significant reaction from the Aristotelian precept that the magnificent man builds out of a sense of public duty. Once praiseworthy, magnificence is coming into question.

The principles of architectural restraint had been stated by Inigo Jones in a note of 1615:

all thes composed ornaments the wch Proceed out of ye aboundance of dessigners . . . do not well in sollid Architecture and ye fasciati of houses, but in gardens loggis stucco or ornaments of chimnies peeces or in the inner parts of houses. . . . For as outwardly every wyse man carrieth a graviti in Publicke Places, whear ther is nothing els looked for, yet inwardly hath his immaginacy set on fire, and sumtimes licenciously flying out . . . so in architecture ye outward ornaments oft [ought] to be sollid, proporsionable according to the rulles, masculine and unaffected.[43]

This contrast of the public with the private marked not so much a revolution in taste as a restatement of the direction in which architecture had been evolving over several decades. The growing demand for regularity, described in chapter 2, was already being realised in the growing taste for symmetry. Much late Elizabethan and Jacobean building was not highly decorated externally: while some houses boasted a riot of gables, turrets, advancing and receding planes, strapwork, pilasters, staggered window levels and glittering glass, very many others remained relatively sober as to their exteriors. One has only to compare Holland House with Charlton House of ten years later or with Shaw of twenty years before. Sophisticated men had for a generation indulged a growing interest in architecture by erecting a variety of fanciful and extravagant buildings, but in the long run the importance of these lay in their capacity for arousing and expressing a concern with the appearance of the house which would remain after the tide of opinion had turned away from such fancies.

Nevertheless as an explicit repudiation of decorative display, Jones's note is very significant. Sir Henry Wotton stressed the private nature of housing in 1624, in a passage quoted in chapter 1, and he continued by describing its proper adornment. Outwardly, good building did not depend on decoration:

A sound piece of good Art, where the Materials being but ordinarie stone, without any garnishment of sculpture, doe yet ravish the Beholder (and hee knowes not how) by a secret Harmony in the Proportions. And this indeede is that end, at which in some degree, we should ayme even in the privatest workes.[44]

He also repudiated the impractical curiosities that had been the architectural playthings of a generation earlier:

Sir Philip Sidney who well knowing that Basilius did rather want some extraordinary Formes to entertaine his Fancie, than roome for Courtiers; was contented to place him in a Star-like Lodge; which otherwise in severe Iudgement of Art had beene an incommodious Figure.[45]

Elsewhere he explained that 'designs of such nature doe more ayme at Rarity then Commoditie; so for my part I had rather admire them, than commend them'.[46] More particularly, he rejected the unthinking idolisation of the classical orders 'about which Architects make such a noyse in their Bookes, as if the very tearmes of Architraves, and Frizes, and Cornices and the like, were enough to graduate a Master of this Art'.[47] John Evelyn later in the century wanted not to reject but to purify them, believing that 'all the Mischiefs and Absurdities in the modern Structures proceed chiefly from our busie and Gothick Triflings in the Composition of the Five Orders'.[48] Meanwhile Pratt described the pleasure he had received from Raynham's unadorned simplicity:

Not long after it was first built [i.e. probably around 1640] . . . I was some while in it, when it had no ornament at all . . . there was somewhat in it divine in the symmetry of proportions of length, height and breadth which was harmonious to the rational soul.[49]

While architects and connoisseurs were able to analyse the elements of this greater architectural discipline, others like Sir John Coke (quoted in chapter 2) expressed the same, growing taste for restraint simply in terms of a preference for regularity.

Supporting this reaction from excess was an increasing number of foreign works which featured houses of greater simplicity. Serlio's seventh book of architecture was not translated by Peake, but appeared in a new Italian edition of 1619; this includes houses which have flat, pilastered fronts and hipped roofs. The same outline featured in the engravings in Rubens's *Palazzi di Genova* of 1622, though some of these had façades of riotous elaboration. Pierre le Muet's *Maniere de bien bastir* of 1623 included simple, rectangular houses with little ornament and

with swept, hipped roofs. In their size and amenities some of these houses closely resembled those demanded by the suburban builder; in their plainness they conformed to a growing taste.

The hipped roof would become increasingly common from the 1630s onwards, coinciding with the declining popularity of ranks of gables. It is uncertain whether Ham House, built in 1610, had a hipped roof originally. Its massing was not dissimilar to Charlton, but with turrets in the angles between the centre and the wings. The original turrets were lowered later in the seventeenth century, but are shown in combination with the hipped roof in a painting of around 1640.[50] Forty Hall at Enfield (pl. 176), Chevening (pl. 177) and St Clere (the last two close to each other in Kent) all seem to have had hipped roofs from their first building, and all were begun, at least, before 1630. Jones's design for a compact, hipped-roof house for Sir Peter Killigrew (pl. 178) may also be dated to before 1630.[51] Three demolished houses had deep plans and hipped roofs of unusual height with

176   Forty Hall, Enfield, London, 1629. An innovation in larger houses of *c.* 1620–30 was the hipped roof, possibly copying continental practice. Although much remodelled externally, Forty Hall had a hipped roof from the first.

177 (*facing page*)   Chevening, Kent, 1629 (from Colen Campbell, *Vitruvius britannicus*, II, 1717). Tall, compact, with a hipped roof. The stair was in the entrance hall, a revolutionary arrangement making impossible the traditional use of the hall but which may have been developed from Danvers House (pl. 138). The house has a double-pile plan, but like other London houses with deep plans the main structural divisions run from front to back, not from side to side.

30 Feet   Extends 88

The Elevation of Chevening house in Kent the Seat of the Rᵗ Honᵇˡᵉ the late Earl of Sussex. is most humbly Inscrib'd
to the Rᵗ Honᵇˡᵉ the Countess Dowager of Sussex .
Elevation de la Maison de Chevening dans la Comté de Kent .

50 Feet   Extends 88

Plan of the First Floor .   Plan of the Second Floor .
Plan du Premier Etage .   Plan du Second Etage .

Inigo Jones Inv: Ca: Campbell Delin: H. Hulsbergh Sculp.

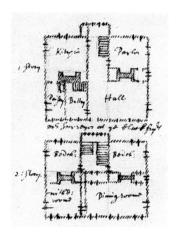

two ranks of dormers: Balmes House in Hackney of around 1634[52] and lodges at Bushey and Windsor (which may however have been put up after the Restoration).[53] Economising on the cost of gables may have been a factor, corresponding to the economic advantages claimed by Pratt for the double-pile plan. The appearance of hipped-roof houses in source books was another; yet another may have been the long acceptance of the hipped roof as a vernacular form among superior houses in the southeast of England. Despite the example of Ham, the hipped roof sits perhaps more happily on a rectangular building than on the wings of an old fashioned H- or E-plan house. In London the most up-to-date of uniform terraces of the 1630s have continuous cornices and dormers rather than gables, elements associated with the hipped roof which will have helped to spread it alongside other metropolitan forms.

A further ingredient of the characteristic London style was only indirectly the result of taste or knowledge. As the most crowded city in England, where pressure of population and the demands of developers were placing great strains on the physical and social fabric of the capital, the authorities were endeavouring to regulate both the form and quantity of new building.[54] Attempts to check overcrowding and to limit the danger of fire dated from the Middle Ages, but early in the seventeenth century to concerns with health and safety there began to be added a concern with visual amenity. In 1605 a royal proclamation had decreed that new building in main streets should be fronted in brick or stone and 'of that uniform order decreed by the magistrates for the street in which they were situated'.[55] The same ordinance recognised the economic value of superior building which would 'both adorne and beautifye his [James I's] sayde Citie . . . and can not fail to be inhabited but by persons of some ability'.

Repeated proclamations sought to check the spread of all sorts of building within varying distances of the city, but the common assumption was that it was slums and tenements that were in question: in 1616 suburban magistrates were reproved for doing nothing to check house builders 'of better quality and worth', while it was suspected that the unspoken objective in these

ostensible measures of control was principally to raise money by fining offenders or by selling exemptions – in which case, the bigger the house and the richer the builder, the better.[56] Already by 1615 the king was comparing himself with the Emperor Augustus:

> As it was said of the first emperor of Rome, that he had found the city of Rome of brick and left it marble, so Wee, whom God hath honoured to be the first of Britaine, might be able to say in some proportion, that we had found our Citie and suburbs of London of stickes, and left them of bricke, being a material farre more durable, safe from fire and beautiful and magnificent.[57]

On the face of it, it was a silly comparison, but it could not have been publicly made without there being some truth in the transformation that the king described. That it could be made at all suggests that a view of public improvements as a ruler's duty and a testimony of his taste was still accepted. The proclamation of 1615 announced that 'Wee doe exceedingly approve and commend all Edifices, Structures and works which tend to publique use and ornament'.[58] Individually, the buildings fostered by these regulations would be restrained; together, the new streets and buildings would be examples of Aristotelian magnificence. Under Charles I, keenly promoting the image of kingship through the allegorical power of spectacle and ceremonial, these improvements could be seen as tending towards the creation of the Platonic ideal of a capital city.[59]

While the king and the City authorities provided at least a passive encouragement of superior houses, in seeking by increasingly detailed regulation to control the form of building they would nurture an architectural style. Successive proclamations prohibited projecting window bays, prescribed arched brick heads for shop openings, regulated brick sizes, storey heights, wall thicknesses and the proportions of windows. In 1611 'cant windows' had been permitted provided they projected no more than 18 inches;[60] in 1620 they were specifically forbidden and the area subject to building controls extended to a radius of 5 miles.[61] The decree of 1619 had already attempted more thoroughly than any previous to impose uniformity on the appearance of the London house, demanding that walls should 'goe direct and streit upwards'.[62] Inigo Jones had been Surveyor-General of the Royal Works from 1615 and before 1620 had been appointed to the Buildings Commission, composed of members of the Privy Council and others, set up to control new building and to enforce standards.[63] He may thus have been the moving spirit in drafting the detailed terms of the proclamation of 1619, even though only from 1627 onwards is there direct record of his involvement with particular cases of contravention. It is difficult to assess the impact of the Commission from the small amount of building that still survives in London itself from the first half of the seventeenth century. Nor is there evidence for its directly interfering with a building's detailed design: the usual penalty for infringement seems to have been demolition. Nevertheless the controls that the authorities were beginning to place on the form and quantity of new building would promote the evolution of building styles that met their requirements.[64]

The style of the London bricklayer has been variously named 'artisan mannerist' from the way in which building craftsmen made wilful use of diverse and unrelated elements, and more recently 'subordinate' from its partial dependence on Jones's initiatives.[65] The earlier title (however reminiscent of Osbert Lancaster) still seems preferable, though the newer is capable of greater extension to cover the gradual refinement of the artisan style in the period before and immediately following the Restoration. Characteristic of the emerging style were shaped gables, quoining, architrave surrounds to windows, rustication, decorative window heads including the accentuation of alternate voussoirs, and a variety of classical elements which might include deep entablatures at storey height or at cornice level, giant or superimposed pilasters, sometimes with a label, and pedimented doorcases. The ordinary London builder is likely to have seen the style as essentially one of flat brick fronts and applied architectural decoration, and perhaps little more than refinements on the style of building he had been indulging already.

Scarcely any building in this style of street architecture now survives in London itself from the 1620s and 1630s, but there is a drawing by Jones (pl. 179) that may convey some idea of the character of the detached houses that he might have been asked to approve in his capacity as a member of the Buildings Commission.[66] This is his sketch for the scenery for a royal masque of 1638, glorifying the supposed political achievements of the 1630s.[67] This design is in a long and well-established Renaissance tradition of perspective stage scenery representing ideal locations, of which Serlio's engravings (pls 12, 13) are early and influential examples. But what is unusual in Jones's drawing is that what he idealises are the actual buildings and contemporary architectural styles of London. In the distance is a restored St Paul's Cathedral; the eye is led up to this through a broad street of detached, modern houses with flat fronts and gables of varying forms, quoins, strong cornices and platt bands (all but one of the houses are evidently of brick), tall windows together with smaller, round windows, and central front doors beneath bracketed balconies.[68]

The style reflects the diversity of its origins, drawing on Inigo Jones's own buildings and on the growing range of pattern-books. Much of the detail derives ultimately from Serlio, made even more accessible in the English edition of 1611. Above all the London style is an architecture of surface treatments, in which the façade provided the only opportunity for architectural display, and of street architecture in which regularity was emphasised by the repetition of detail along a complete frontage.

The royal proclamation of 1611 on new building in London said 'How much it would grace and beautifie the said Citie . . . if an Uniformity were kept in the sayd Buildings'.[69] A variety of unifying elements included lines of matching gables, long, horizontal cornices, and ranks of pilasters articulating each window bay. In the 1620s and 1630s a condition of architectural uniformity was already being written into building leases on the Bedford estate, presumably in accordance with the wishes of the ground landlord, the Earl of Bedford.[70] By the 1630s long rows of prestigious London houses were being built to a uniform design without gables, with a uniform parapet and sometimes with repetitive lines of pilasters, features that denied their separate expression as dwellings (pl. 180). This was the style of architecture that inspired the rhapsody on the architectural regularity of the Covent Garden area quoted in chapter 2.

The variety of this architecture makes difficult any simple characterisation of London building in the period around 1615–40. The potential for individual display of the narrow, terraced house had never been very great. But architectural idioms developed for the long, uniform terrace could easily be transferred to the façades of larger houses in the country. In being applied to the kind of rectangular, double-pile house which was already establishing its popularity in the London suburbs and would increasingly do so beyond, the artisan style of flat fronts and surface decoration would marry well with a form of house that was already more regular than the house that distinguished between centre and wings. So too would the hipped roof, while pedimented gables that probably derive from Jones's own work could be applied in a wide range of contexts. These distinctive building styles make it possible to trace over these twenty-five years the influence of London architecture and London building craftsmen through south-east England and beyond.

The pre-eminence of London as a centre of craftsmanship and in the provision of luxury goods was well established. In 1603 John Stowe remarked:

> not onely the Court, which is now a dayes much greater & more gallant then in former times . . . but also by occasion therof, the Gentlemen of the shires do flie and flock to this City . . . [and therefore] Artificers . . . do leave the Countrie townes, where there is no vent, and do flie to London, where they be sure to finde ready and quicke market.[71]

A measure of how widely London building craftsmanship was diffused at a fairly everyday level is the distribution of two easily recognisable types of carved, masonry fireplace surround which are almost certainly from metropolitan workshops. These chimneypieces occur quite widely in the home counties over a fairly long period from the last quarter of the sixteenth century. The first type (pl. 181) is basically a four-centred surround with the segmental curve at the haunch of jamb and lintel replaced by a straight cant.[72] The lintel is sometimes decorated with a repeated pattern of simple geometrical forms. Surrounds of this kind seem original at Eastbury Manor House, probably in the late 1570s;

179 Inigo Jones: sketch for scenery for the masque *Britannia triumphans*, 1638. In this masque, celebrating the peace and prosperity of the decade, a street of smart, new, detached (and hence suburban) houses leads up to a distant prospect of St Paul's Cathedral, in course of restoration. The houses may be taken as representative of those that Jones will have been asked to approve as the leading professional member of the king's Commission for New Buildings.

elsewhere they occur into the 1590s. The second type (pl. 182) has a straight head rather than a modified four-centred opening, an ovolo moulding to the arris which is frequently enriched, relief carving of birds, flowers or fruit to the lintel, and generally some kind of central device such as a shield of arms or a figure.[73] The haunch is occasionally filled with a small scroll. Strapwork, of French or Netherlandish origin and characteristic of much decoration from the 1580s, is notably absent from either type. The surviving numbers of these two types of chimneypiece, their distribution in time and the high quality of what are evidently stock items, suggests that they are the products of large and well-established workshops, and their geographical distribution in Essex, Kent, Middlesex, Surrey and Sussex (besides London itself) strongly suggests their London origin.[74] Their occurrence in houses of relatively modest status places them firmly within the ambit of builders of the gentry class, while their distribution suggests the area within which builders even at this level commonly looked to London as a source of architectural refinements.

At the end of the seventeenth century Roger North declared: 'it is scarce known that a person of quality hath built for himself in or neere London; but all is done by profest builders, and the gentry hire or buy of them'.[75] If true (and without documents it cannot be proved one way or the other) it implies that within the range of the metropolitan workman, responsibility for the spread of novel forms lay more with the architect and craftsman and less with the house's owner than it did in areas beyond. Such a difference was in any case inherent in the nature of suburban life: the man who buys or leases a house of retirement in the

PLAN THRO PILASTERS

SCALE OF 10   5   0   10   20 FEET

180 (*left*) James C. Cook (*c.* 1910): Houses in Great Queen Street, Holborn, London (destroyed). Originally part of a longer terrace, unified by a continuous cornice, straight ridge and repeated pilasters. Such repetitive elevations were easily applied to the façade of larger houses.

181 (*below left*) London chimneypieces: Eastbury Manor House, Barking, Essex. Surrounds of this type (and the pattern shown in pl. 182) occur widely in the home counties between *c.* 1575 and 1615 and indicate the geographical range within which builders resorted to London for stock items. Exceptional craftsmen ranged further afield.

182 (*below right*) London chimneypieces: Swan House, Wye, Kent. The second type of surround occurs in a similar area to those shown in pl. 181, but in the later part of the period. Very occasionally, elements of both types are combined.

183 The so-called Dutch House (Kew Palace), Richmond upon Thames, London, 1631. The styles of the seventeenth-century London building craftsmen were varied, and at Kew combined a busy texture of moulded brickwork with pedimented gables that occur in an early drawing by Inigo Jones.

184 Barnham Court, West Sussex, c. 1635. Almost certainly by the craftsmen who were responsible for the Dutch House at Kew. The plan is a double pile of the simplest kind – four-square, with a room in each quarter and a stair at the centre.

home counties for his own lifetime only has a different attitude to his house from the man who builds a seat for himself and his descendants, on a country estate that he has inherited or acquired for their continuing honour and support.

As early as 1593 John Norden had said of Middlesex:

This shire is plentifullie stored, and as it seemeth beautified, with manie faire and comely buildinges, especially of the Merchants of London, who have planted their houses of recreation not in the meanest places: which also they have cunningly contrived, curiously beautified, with diverse devises, neatly decked with rare invencions.[76]

Thomas Fuller in 1662 said much the same thing, describing the county as 'but the suburbs at large of London, replenished with the retiring houses of the gentry and citizens thereof'[77] and added that the Middlesex gentry 'seem sojourners rather than inhabitants'.[78] Of Berkshire, he wrote 'it is observed that the lands in Berkshire are very skittish, and often cast their Owners'[79] and in Hertfordshire the very much greater turnover of estates, by comparison with more distant counties, has been shown by Lawrence and Jeanne Fawltier Stone's calculations.[80] In these circumstances, it is not surprising if purchasers should have been satisfied with houses provided by architects who were themselves well versed in the taste and life styles of London and the suburbs. Beyond the region of the home counties sojourners and the range of the metropolitan craftsman, things were rather different. But in the area within reach of the London craftsman a high proportion of architects or contractors known to have been involved in the building of up-to-date country houses between 1620 and 1660 were also concerned with major developments in the fashionable areas of London itself, notably in the areas around Covent Garden, Lincoln's Inn Fields and Drury Lane.[81] Although many houses in the region from the 1620s and 1630s combine old-fashioned layouts and modern detail, there are fewer where the reverse is the case, and a growing number in which both plan and details show that craftsmen were aware of current metropolitan practices.

Some houses are so similar that they can be ascribed to the same craftsmen. The external similarity of Barnham Court in Sussex (pl. 184) to the Dutch House now known as Kew Palace (pl. 183) has been noticed before now, even though the two are 60 miles apart.[82] Both have shaped gables, deep entablatures and centre-pieces accentuated by rustication, though Barnham has two orders of superimposed pilasters (which Kew lacks) and is executed in English bond rather than in Flemish. Both also have double-pile plans, though Barnham's is simpler than that of Kew. Kew is dated 1631; neither the date nor the builder of Barnham is known and it was already tenanted before 1670 (when the rooms in the house were itemised in an inventory taken on the death of its late occupant). Though the largest house in the village, it seems not to have stood on the largest landed estate, a circumstance which suggests that it was some kind of retreat rather than a country seat. Still further from London than Barnham is the house now known as

185   The Old Rectory, Hamworthy, near Poole, Dorset. The front is a simplified version of Kew Palace and Barnham, and if not by crafts-men who had worked there it was certainly put up by men who knew the style well.

the Old Rectory (formerly the Manor House) at Hamworthy near Poole in Dorset (pl. 185), built for a branch of the Carew family probably in the late 1630s.[83] Hamworthy shows in a simplified form pilasters and gables characteristic of the style, and raises the possibility that both bricks and bricklayers (or if not bricks, then perhaps brickmakers) may have travelled to Poole from London by sea. The plan is similarly a more economical

variety of the double pile, only one and a half ranges deep, but the front range is three rooms broad with the hall occupying the centre and entered centrally.

Three large houses of the 1630s – Stratfield Saye in Hamp-shire, West Horsely Place and Slyfield in Surrey – form another group, in which lines of pilasters were employed to pull together façades of considerable length. West Horsely is a rambling house of several periods, unified in this way; Slyfield (pl. 186) has been in part destroyed, and the plan of Stratfield Saye has been so altered that its original form seems largely lost. Nowhere save at Lees Court in Kent are pilasters more clearly used in an attempt to treat the exterior of the entire building as a coherent whole, even if the monotonous repetition of pilasters in all of these

houses is architecturally naive, and the same craftsman must have been responsible for them all. In Kent, a few rather larger houses with essentially double-pile plans and pilastered fronts – Lees Court (pl. 187), Bay Hall at Pembury, Syndale at Ospringe and Bridge Place – also seem related to each other stylistically. They lack the gables of the Kew or Surrey groups, but have hipped roofs and deep eaves cornices.

A further group of houses in the Lewes area on the boundaries of East and West Sussex also have hipped roofs and pilastered elevations as well as prominent angle quoins – a combination that occurred also at Thanet House in Aldersgate Street in the City of London. All these seem to be double pile with the exception of the much-altered Folkington House, a larger house which was built round a small central courtyard. Some of these have superimposed orders of pilasters, some a giant order and there are other differences between them, but their proximity suggests strongly that in some way they are related. The

London affinities of Albourne, at least, are quite clear: the property was bought in 1639 by John Juxon, brother of William Juxon, Bishop of London, who was described variously as of St Gregory-by-Paul's and in 1655 when he died as being of St Benet's, Paul's Wharf.[84] The house is in part an extension and a recasing of a fourteenth- or fifteenth-century house, part of which remained to provide a service wing to the new building. Wotton Manor may be the last of this group in date, probably built between 1660 and 1665 and perhaps only indirectly imitating the London style: it appears cruder in details than the other houses in the group, and may have been modelled on Folkington nearby.

Other characteristic details of the London style appear at Swakeleys at Ickenham (pl. 188), built in 1638 for Edmund Wright, elected Lord Mayor (and knighted) in 1640–41 as a compromise candidate between parliamentary and royalist factions.[85] At Swakeleys, however, the roof is not hipped but each front is crowned by a riotous line of ornamental gables – eighteen in all – whose only concession to contemporary taste is the form of the gables themselves: these have swept slopes, scroll kneelers and pedimented heads. Inside, the plan is a combination of the double-pile with the service-passage plan that had been established for a century. Entrance is into the low end of the hall, and leads on through to the principal stair, lying at the centre of the rear range in what was by now the established double-pile mode. There is actually a screen forming a screens passage in the traditional position, placed there after the Civil War. The service passage leads north, leading past pantry, buttery and kitchen to a traditionally placed outside door at its end. A winter parlour is also reached off the service passage; other parlours lead off the high end of the hall. Effectively, Swakeleys is an old-fashioned, H-plan house with the central range doubled up and absorbing accommodation that would formerly have been placed in more substantial wings. However, the critical movement of the principal stair from the upper end to the centre of the house has polarised the plan between household and entertainment in the modern manner, effectively segregating the hall from the services.

Broome Park in Kent (pl. 189), of 1635–8, has detail comparable with that of Swakeleys, but of greater refinement; lines of pilasters which rise through an entablature into the attic provide a strong upward thrust to the façades, which are crowned by the most extravagant display of ornamental gables of any house in England.[86] Many of these gables are of the form that Inigo Jones may have introduced, in Fulke Greville's house in Holborn, with pediments and scrolled flanks, but others are still more inventive. At Broome a style that at Swakeleys tends towards a confused overloading of motifs combines them in a coherent and integrated manner. Broome remains (with Kew) the outstanding

187 Lees Court, Kent, c. 1640. A further variety of what has been called 'artisan mannerism', the style of the London bricklayer: giant pilasters beneath a continuous cornice and a hipped roof.

house of the London style. The plan was a conventional H, but the central range seems to have been two rooms deep: double pile. Alterations in the eighteenth and twentieth centuries have otherwise left little of the house's original interior, and even floor levels have been changed.

There is a further group of houses to which the term 'subordinate' may perhaps be more appropriately applied: less fantastic in their details than the houses with overblown gables and obsessive pilasters that have been considered so far as manifestations of the south-eastern style, but less restrained than a further group, considered below, where the influence of the staff of the Royal Works under Jones himself seems most easily recognisable. As noted above, Sir John Coke consulted the staff of the Royal

Works about the management of his building operations but not about the design of the house. Even those builders who moved in the innermost circles of politics or fashion did not necessarily build what with hindsight now seem the most advanced houses. Haines Hill, at St Nicholas Hurst between Reading and Windsor (pl. 190), was built by Sir Francis Windebank, Clerk to the Signet and Secretary of State from 1632 onwards.[87] The property had been acquired by his father, who through his earlier friendship with the Cecil family had also entered royal service. The house was built on a conservative E or H plan, with relatively long wings and a centre probably only a single room deep. Brickwork is plain, with ornament confined to rusticated quoins and window heads and a shallow cornice between first and second floors, but there are lines of shaped gables of the kind that had occurred at Holland House, and chimneys have octagonal shafts. Windebank, with his intimate connection with the court, could certainly have had access to personnel of the Royal Works if he had wanted to. But there is very little that is Jone-

188   Swakeleys, lckenham, Greater London, 1629–38. A flamboyant display of craftsmen's styles, built as a country seat for a Lord Mayor, within easy reach of the City of London.

189   Broome Park, Kent, 1635–8. A true country house rather than a house in the outer suburbs, and the most striking of all houses of the artisan mannerist style. Broome Park combines almost every stylistic element known to the building craftsmen of the home counties, but employs them with sophistication and flair.

sian about the rather conservative plan and its gabled elevations, and Haines Hill simply illustrates, as do many contemporary houses, the variety of stylistic options available at a time of rapid change in taste.

A house that no longer stands but which combined both innovative and more conservative details in a way that typifies the 1630s was Aldermaston Court in Berkshire (pl. 191).[88] Aldermaston was built in 1635 for Humphrey Forster, High Sheriff of Berkshire in 1619, Baronet in 1620 and a moderate Royalist during the Civil War, whose family had owned the place since the end of the fifteenth century. Neither the architect nor Forster's personal associations are known. Although a carved inscription on the stables is clearly by the same mason who carved inscriptions at West Woodhay, discussed below, other details of Aldermaston make it questionable whether it was built by an equally advanced architect – though in several contemporary houses there is a discrepancy between the advanced character of the overall design and conservative decoration and joinery. The house had a hipped roof and a double-pile centre with short wings projecting on both fronts, and the centre contained a two-storey hall with a gallery round it that provided chamber access.[89]

Although the overall appearance of Aldermaston seems to have been of the plainness that in the 1630s may be associated with the staff of the Royal Works, what is known of the detail does

191   Aldermaston Court, Berkshire, 1636 (demolished; from the *Illustrated London News*, 1842). Aldermaston combined a modern, hipped-roof outline with some old-fashioned features such as spiral chimneystacks. The house was one of a small group of early seventeenth-century houses with separate front entrances at either end of the hall.

not seem characteristic of their craftsmen. It was badly damaged by fire in 1843 and the remains pulled down, but the staircase was saved and re-used in a new house and indicates the original character of the interior (pl. 192). This has figures of soldiers standing on the newels, and there were evidently similar 'images' on the balustrade of the gallery that overlooked the hall. The source of the galleried hall may have been the Queen's House at Greenwich, newly finished, but nothing could be further from Greenwich than such decoration. Lees Court also had a galleried hall (pl. 193), though the decoration there was far more Jonesian. Aldermaston had two identical entrance doors, leading into screens passages at either end of the hall; these doorways had pedimented porches carried on Salomonic spiral columns. There were spiral chimney shafts of cut brick, described as linked by a cornice: another conservative feature, though possibly indicating that the house preserved some part of the fabric of its predecessor. As against this, twenty years later Evelyn described the house as 'à la moderne'. If it had survived, Aldermaston would have been a most instructive example of the uncertain taste of the 1630s, evidently combining up-to-date with conservative features both in plan and decoration.

190   Anon. (early eighteenth century; probably a sketch for an unexecuted engraving): Haines Hill, St Nicholas Hurst, Berkshire, *c.* 1630–35. Although built by Sir Francis Windebank, one of Charles I's Secretaries of State, Haines Hill is in the style of the London building craftsman rather than of Inigo Jones, Surveyor to the King. Political affiliations seem to have had relatively little to do with which architect or craftsman a builder would employ. The house still stands but has been much altered.

192 Joseph Nash (1846): Aldermaston Court: the stair re-erected in a new house when the old house was burnt in 1843. The figures standing on the newels are a long way from the architectural purism of Inigo Jones.

193 Lees Court, Kent: the hall. Not of the quality of Jones's work at Greenwich, but almost certainly influenced by interiors such as those of the Queen's House or Wilton. With the contemporary staircase from Aldermaston (pl. 192) it illustrates the variety of decorative styles in the interior of contemporary upper-class houses.

These south-eastern houses were the response of the metropolitan craftsman to the market for up-to-date houses in the country round. They are a very diverse group, some with hipped roofs and some with riotous gables, some with plain façades and some richly textured, influenced by the work of Inigo Jones and by the urban building styles for which Jones was partly responsible, by the work of other designers such as Nicholas Stone and Balthazar Gerbier, and by the mix-and-match possibilities afforded by the availability of printed exemplars. In none is there any real understanding of architecture as much more than a kit of parts, so to speak, with which to design the exterior of a house of a more or less modern plan and silhouette. There is, however, a further small group of houses with which there are reasons – tantalisingly inconclusive – to link figures associated with the Royal Works or else built by men known to have

moved in the most advanced artistic circles. It has been seen that connection with such circles was not in itself any guarantee that a builder would erect an up-to-date house. However, besides such associations these houses combine plans of striking modernity with exteriors that are plain and devoid of ornament to a revolutionary degree, and in their layout they incorporate features that were to be exceptionally fertile for the later development of house planning. Still within the orbit of the south-eastern, metropolitan craftsmen or architect, these houses are Chevening, West Woodhay, Ogbourne St George and Coleshill.

Chevening in Kent (pl. 177) was said to be by Inigo Jones when Colen Campbell published its elevation and principal floor plans (*Vitruvius britannicus*, II, 1717). *Vitruvius britannicus* is a manifesto for Palladianism and an advertisement for Campbell himself; by citing Jones as the first English Palladian, Campbell sought to place his own designs in good company. His plate and a crude perspective sketch of the 1680s provide the only documentary evidence for the external form of the house before its remodelling in the later eighteenth century, and his inscription the only authority for attributing the house to Jones. But though one need not necessarily believe Campbell, the house's upright silhouette with hipped roof, its rectangular outline and its plain exterior were all exceptional for 1629 when the house was apparently begun. The house's first builder was Richard Lennard, 13th Lord Dacre, who died in the following year; the house was finally fitted up by his son and heir in the 1650s,[90] but there is no real reason to suppose that its finished form did not substantially represent Dacre's original intention.

Still more remarkable than its elevations was Chevening's plan. This can be interpreted formally in a number of ways, but it is perhaps most easily seen as a development of the Nottingham House model with a through hall: in particular, it is perhaps Danvers House, the final development of the through hall, that is the point of departure for Chevening. Danvers House was eccentric in dividing the hall by a change of level and a stair: the space remained open, but effectively it performed the two quite different functions of hall and stair compartment. At Chevening the logical step has been taken of dividing the Danvers House hall into two, thus keeping the two functions of hall and staircase physically separate. The traditional relation of hall and stair have been reversed: while formerly the principal stair was reached through the hall, now the hall is accessible only past the stair foot. Chevening extends the Danvers House arrangement, with the immediacy of ascent that was already a feature of Lulworth, Westwood and Gawthorpe. The hall remains a passage room, but only for the family: it serves no function in relation to the service layout, and thus its only other plausible use is as a room for polite entertainment. Services, naturally, are in the basement.[91]

Equally revolutionary in both plan and the elevation is West Woodhay in Berkshire (pls 194, 195).[92] The house is of brick, ornamented by nothing more than discreet brick quoins and a chaste Ionic door surround to the front entrance, and has a hipped roof. The plan provides a double-pile central range, with shallow wings projecting on the front only; services are on the ground floor, and the principal stair is offset towards the opposite wing in the rear range. These features were not in themselves novel, but the hall is entered centrally and heated in the centre of the opposite wall.[93] The form of the hall at West Woodhay had been prefigured at Holland House (with two fireplaces symmetrically arranged, rather than one) and in a few houses of an unusual kind, such as Bidston Lodge, and partly at Newe House, Pakenham, but the only complete earlier example of the arrangement that has come to light in a country house for conventional, residential use is at St Clere, a house close to Chevening and contemporary with it. St Clere is double pile in plan, has a hipped roof and a centrally entered hall of the

Holland House kind, but has odd, polygonal angle turrets that recall the castellated lodges of the previous decade; the angle fireplace in the hall is unlikely to be in the original location.

Edward Carter has been suggested as the architect of West Woodhay.[94] Though not himself directly employed in the Royal Works, he served as Inigo Jones's deputy on the extensive repairs at St Paul's Cathedral between 1633 and 1641, worked on Jones's church in Covent Garden for the Earl of Bedford, and was thus in the closest contact with the fountainhead of innovation. However, the builder's own connections may go far to explain the house's innovative character. Sir Benjamin Rudyard, third son of a gentry family of Staffordshire origins, acquired the West Woodhay estate in 1634 and began his house immediately thereafter.[95] Rudyard was a friend of Sir Henry Wotton, Ben Jonson and William Herbert, 3rd Earl of Pembroke, whose poems were published jointly with Rudyard's own and whose brother and successor was to build Wilton in the 1630s. That Rudyard maintained a close connection with the Herbert family is suggested by the fact that he sat as MP for the town of Wilton in 1640. But his association with Inigo Jones was still more direct in that Rudyard was a member of the Privy Council's Commission for New Building, the body set up to regulate both the forms and the quantity of new building in London. Even if Rudyard did not discuss his own house with the commission's most expert member, it is likely that his tastes would have been influenced by the comments that Jones will have had to make on submissions to it.[96] The day-to-day business of the commission seems to have been conducted for the most part by its professional members, but such associations must have given Rudyard an education to decide for himself the kind of house he wanted. In considering a sophisticated house, it is often impossible to distinguish between the contributions of an advanced architect and a knowledgeable builder.

A house of equal sophistication but whose history is particularly tantalising is Ogbourne St George in Wiltshire (pls 196, 197).[97] The front of Ogbourne is immediately deceptive; it was transformed in the eighteenth century with new windows and in the twentieth with a new front door (itself a perfectly genuine Georgian one). But the original character of the house can be seen in the unaltered rear elevation: this has stone surrounds to tall, mullioned and transomed windows in a local vernacular manner. Until recently the house bore a date of 1619 on the chimney,[98] and this would be readily acceptable for these details as also for the principal staircase with turned balusters, the only substantial part of the original decoration to survive internally. However, the plan is a double pile of unusual form, with the front rooms heated in the spine wall, the rear rooms in the end gables. While in its plan the house is very advanced for such a date, in its silhouette it is unbelievably so. The rear range is gabled at either end, but the roof of the front range is hipped and swept in a manner occurring in Jones's house for Lord Maltravers, dated to the late 1630s.[99]

The dating of the house is made more problematical still in

194 West Woodhay, Berkshire, 1636. West Woodhay is among the plainest of all contemporary houses, and clearly prefigures post-1660 developments. It was built by Sir Benjamin Rudyard, who served with Inigo Jones on the Commission for New Building, established to monitor new building in London. Its architect is unknown but in view of Rudyard's connections some responsibility for its remarkable exterior must lie with him.

that its undoubted builder, Thomas Bond, did not acquire it (on a long lease from King's College, Cambridge) until 1621; his predecessor was described as 'yeoman' in his deeds. Most tantalising of all is the fact that according to John Aubrey (who as a Wiltshire man is likely to have known) Bond travelled abroad with Sir John Danvers, whose extremely advanced London house is described above (p. 141). Danvers's own country house, where he made a garden as renowned as the one he made in London, was at Lavington in the same county.[100] It is difficult to know how to interpret Ogbourne. The most obvious explanation is that it is an enlargement by Bond of a house built by his predecessor that had originally been only one room deep,

but there is no structural evidence for this in the house, nor do the details of the plan support it. Even if the date of 1619 has been misread and a date of some ten or even twenty years later has to be preferred on grounds of probability, Ogbourne is still an exceptional building and one that by its appearance and its plan one would have no difficulty in attributing to a member of the circle of the Royal Works. Through Danvers at least, Bond must have been in touch with the most advanced cultural circles.

The last of these houses is Coleshill (pls 198–200), built for Sir George Pratt, 2nd Baronet, who was married to the daughter of Sir Humphrey Forster of Aldermaston.[101] Work probably started around 1650; the shell at least was probably complete by the end of 1652 even though the fitting-up was not finished for another ten years. Like Sir Roger Townshend at Raynham, Sir George evidently made a false start, beginning on a different site and then, when the house was a little way up, starting afresh to a different plan in a different place. The authorship of Coleshill has been disputed as between Inigo Jones and Sir George's cousin Sir Roger Pratt, whose notebooks and whose fully documented buildings reveal him as the most competent gentleman-architect of the early years of the Restoration.

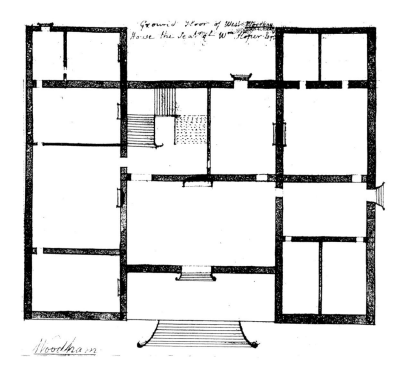

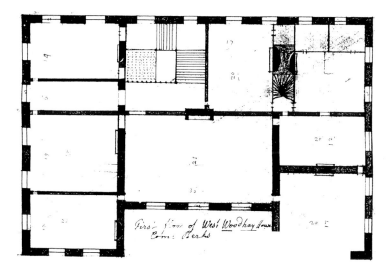

Although there is good reason for crediting Sir Roger with responsibility for completing the house (Jones died in 1652) there is also reason for giving Jones at least some share in the initial design, and unless and until fresh evidence comes to light the question will not be resolved.

Coleshill has attracted attention because of its attribution to Jones, because of the superb poise of its design, and through having been frequently cited as the classic example of the double-pile plan – a form whose recognition and whose name derives from Pratt's own remarks. In fact Coleshill is far from a typical double-pile house, but incorporates other significant aspects of advanced contemporary planning. Like Chevening, entrance was directly into the staircase hall, though the stair itself (pl. 200) was a double flight – an imperial, a form half anticipated at Danvers House but not otherwise known to have been executed in an English house before Coleshill. Although a few other houses may have had stairs of equal size, no contemporary staircase is so architecturally accomplished. Rising on either side of the entry, it provided a formal approach to the great dining room on the first floor as well as framing the approach on the ground floor to the saloon – called in 1652 a 'great hall' and in

195 Anon. (eighteenth century), West Woodhay: ground- and first-floor plans. West Woodhay is among the earliest true country houses wholly to abolish all traditional, high- and low-end distinctions in the hall: both entrance and fireplace are placed at the centre of the room.

196 (*above right*) Ogbourne House, Ogbourne St George, Wiltshire, formerly bearing a date stone said to read 1619. There is some internal detail compatible with such a date; Ogbourne's double-pile plan and hipped roof are extraordinarily precocious if the inscription can be credited. Its builder was a close friend of Sir John Danvers, builder of Danvers House (pl. 138). Door and windows have been altered, but the outline of the house is intact.

197 (*right*) Ogbourne House: ground-floor plan. Ogbourne is built to a double-pile plan of an odd form, with rear rooms heated at the end, front rooms in the spine wall.

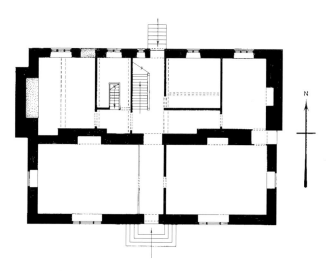

the 1670s the 'great parlour'. On the first floor the plan provides for a series of three-room apartments: chambers each with its dependent closet and dressing room or pallet chamber.

While numerous contemporary comments prove the general recognition of London as the centre of cultural activity, explicit recognition of the city as a source of architectural innovation is harder to find. Sir Henry Wotton deplored the lack of what he called 'artificiale tearmes' – language in which to describe architecture,[102] but though the lack of words in which to express and to compare architectural impressions may have limited the spread of architectural ideas, one may for the same reason underestimate people's knowledge and understanding of building. Contemporary comments do show that London buildings could provide a standard of comparison for buildings elsewhere. In an imaginary dialogue of 1618 between a townsman and a countryman, the former conmmended 'rich Apparell, precious Jewells . . . Princely Coaches, stately Horses, royall Buildings and rare Architecture'.[103] Writing around 1622, William Webb commended Crewe Hall in Cheshire (pl. 201), recently rebuilt by

198 Coleshill, Berkshire (demolished), *c.* 1649–62. The greatest architectural achievement of the mid-seventeenth century and the culmination of the stylistic and planning developments of the previous thirty years. Its authorship remains disputed.

199 (*facing page*) Coleshill: basement, ground- and first-floor plans from a late eighteenth-century survey. The kitchen is at one end of the basement, and in 1670 the first-floor chamber of Sir George Pratt, its builder, was at the same end of the house (an arrangement discussed in chapter 8), as was the common parlour, the family's everyday living room. The house has otherwise lost almost every distinction of high or low ends. As at Chevening, entry lies into a stair compartment providing immediate ascent to the grandest entertaining rooms on the first floor.

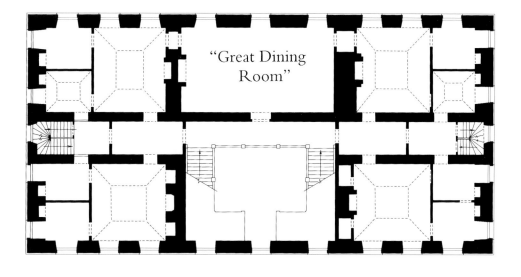

"Great Dining Room"

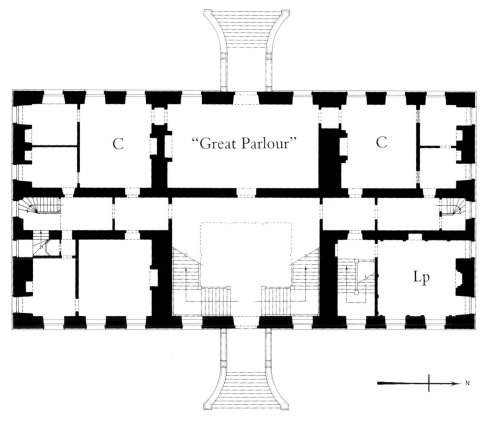

C   "Great Parlour"   C

Lp

N

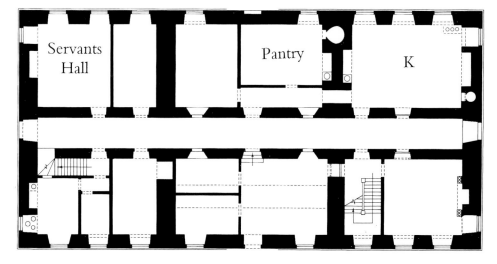

Servants Hall   Pantry   K

200 Coleshill: the stair. The stair was in the entrance hall, as at Chevening (pl. 177), but its imperial form (a double flight) was without English precedent.

the lawyer Sir Randolph Crew 'who hath brought into these remote parts a modell of that most excellent form of building which is now grown to a degree beyond the building of old times for loftiness, sightliness and pleasant habitation, as in and near London, we see many in this age of ours'.[104]

Richard Brome's *The Weeding of Covent Garden*, quoted above for what it has to say of attitudes towards architectural regularity, in satirising both the fashions and provincial ignorance equates town manners and town architecture and shows how both impressed the visitor. (It also enables him to indulge in some *double entendre* for the groundlings.) A scene opens: 'Enter

Dorcas above upon a Bellconie. . . . Dorcas is habited like a Curtezan of Venice.' After some exchanges in which the country bumpkin, Belt, asks who she is, the dialogue continues:

COCKBRAIN: O heresie! It is some lady or gentlewoman standing upon her Bellconie.
BELT: Her Bellconie? Where is it? I can spy from her foot to her face, yet I can see no Bellconie she has.
COCKBRAIN: What a knave's this! That's the Bellconie she stands on, that which juts out so in the fore part of the house; every house here has one of 'hem.
BELT: 'Tis very good; I like the jutting out of the forepart very well; it is a gallant fashion indeed.[105]

Short, narrow balconies above entrance doors were a London innovation of the late 1610s; they would be employed widely from the 1630s onwards. Capheaton in Northumberland was

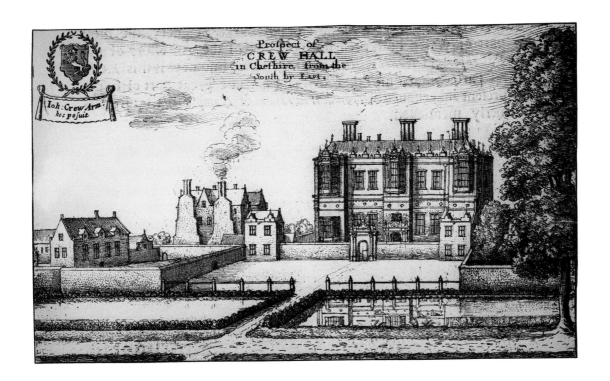

201 Wenceslaus Hollar, 1656: Crewe Hall, Cheshire. Built for Sir Randolph Crew, said by William Webb to have 'brought into these remote parts . . . that most excellent form of building . . . as in and near London, we see many in this age of ours'.

built with such a balcony in 1668. By the early eighteenth century they were outmoded, and Isabella Swinburne, the builder's widow, was again looking to London for up-to-date architecture. To her son in town she wrote: 'Sir Henry Lawson saith an Arch over the hall door . . . is fashionable and better than the balcony, if you se any howse so observe how you like it, and how it is made.'[106]

In 1632 a Lieutenant Hammond and two companions undertook a sightseeing tour in southern England, in the course of which they came upon the deer-coursing stand which John Dutton had just built at Sherborne in Gloucestershire: this they declared was 'not much unlike that goodly and magnificent building, the Banqueting House at Whitehall'.[107] The comparison is valid only when the building is compared with the vernacular of the Cotswolds. Lodge Park (pl. 202) is a curious pastiche of elements derived from Serlio and elsewhere and put together with little understanding: the kind of building that might have been put up by a provincial mason who had been working at Oxford or at Cornbury for Nicholas Stone (a leading mason-architect who worked for Inigo Jones and the purveyor of a mannered and over-detailed classicism of his own) and had misunderstood even Stone's eclectic style.[108] But Hammond's comments do indicate that the Banqueting House was itself seen as something exceptional, and perceptive builders must have

been led like Sir Henry Slingsby (whose comment on Holland House is quoted on p. 17 above) to build in conscious emulation of approved London models.

In 1622, for unknown reasons, Sir Roger Townshend abandoned the house at Raynham that he had started to build and made a fresh beginning (pl. 25). The house he built (which may have been finished externally in 1632, though it was probably still only part furnished when Sir Roger died in 1637) is on a complex double-pile plan; the outside is composed of a variety of up-to-date motifs including gables of a form that may first have been employed by Jones, in his London house for Fulke Greville, and a pilastered, pedimented centrepiece which probably derived from Jones's lodge for the Prince of Wales at Newmarket. While the detailed execution must have been left to Townshend's mason, William Edge, the wish to incorporate these metropolitan details must have come from Townshend, whose architectural interests and knowledge are recorded by Roger Pratt (see p. 37) and who provided Edge with the opportunity of travelling both in his company and on his own. In its mixture of motifs Raynham is perhaps the most complete example of the artisan mannerist style, and one that illustrates very clearly a builder's involvement in its spread.

If few architectural comments are recorded by members of the house-owning class, one can find still fewer made by the actual craftsmen who put them up. Nevertheless, the practice of resorting to London for high-quality architectural workmanship was established at least by the late sixteenth century, and in John Smythson, son of his greater father Robert, one has an example of a provincial architect visiting London and recording in his notebook some of the recent buildings that he saw there, includ-

ing a balcony of exactly the kind referred to by Richard Brome; Smythson called it a Pergola.[109] It is obvious that he recognised the metropolis as a rich source of architectural innovation. Among the buildings he drew are two houses in Holborn with pedimented gables and one with a rusticated façade; several features at Arundel House, including a chimneypiece, window shutters and a garden plan; and the rusticated basement storey – as far as work had proceeded – of the Banqueting House. Some of these details he described as 'Italyan', and it is remarkable how many of them can be associated, directly or with some probability, with Inigo Jones. (The hipped roof of Capheaton was also described as 'Italian' in the building contract of 1669 with the Newcastle mason Robert Trollope.[110]) One of the items that Smythson copied was a gateway by Jones – ultimately deriving from Michelangelo's Porta Pia – at Arundel House; another version of the same gateway was put up at Brasenose College in Oxford in the 1650s, perhaps by John Jackson, who had gone to Oxford from London some twenty years before. What evidently appealed to Smythson and doubtless to others were novelties of detail, and the crudity of his drawings made probable at best a mangled version of them when he got home. Smythson's appreciation of them seems little different from the comment of Sir John Chamberlain, who in 1617 described the Queen's House as 'some curious device of Inigo Jones'.[111] These architectural details were fashionable curiosities that the craftsman could use in his own buildings on his return to the country.

The direct employment of London architects and bricklayers and of craftsmen apprenticed in London must have been an important means of introducing metropolitan practices into the countryside. Grimblethorpe in Lincolnshire was probably built in the late 1630 for Sir Ralph Maddison, a writer on economics. Through the loss of its original gables and cornice it now looks more like some nineteenth-century factory than a

seventeenth-century house, and its façade always combined the up-to-date with the old-fashioned by virtue of its retaining an off-centre entry. But the similarity between its pilastered front and those of a number of houses in the home counties suggests very strongly that Maddison had it built by a London bricklayer. A late example of the style is Welford House in Berkshire (pl. 203), probably begun for Richard Jones, who died in 1664, and for which a contract exists mentioning the Oxford and London mason John Jackson. The house has a flat front with a line of pilasters and rear-projecting wings;[112] Jones's father was a lawyer at the Inner Temple, and his daughter (and heiress) married Sir John Archer, Judge of Common Pleas. The loggias on the front and back of Hambledon Hall in Leicestershire (pl. 204) so closely resemble those that Jones probably added onto the house of Mary, Countess of Pembroke, at Houghton Conquest in Bedfordshire (pl. 205) that they were probably copied from there: an instance of metropolitan fashions imitated at one remove. But the balustrade of Hambledon is identical with that formerly on the ruined Exton Hall nearby, built for the father of Sir John Harington, guest and fellow-student of Sir Henry Wotton in Venice[113] and intimate of Henry, Prince of Wales. Exton in turn had a very curious façade, with a tall parapet decorated with curious egg-shaped cartouches, both of which occurred on the front that had been placed on York House in the Strand in 1627–8, probably by Balthazar Gerbier.[114] The precise nature of the links between these three houses is obscure, but in all, by routes at present uncertain, advanced architectural forms were reaching the country.

London's dominance of the luxury crafts meant that it was already common for builders from far afield to resort to London workshops for particular architectural or decorative features. The best known of such work is probably that of the tomb carvers, since the Middle Ages supplying funeral monuments throughout England and by the late sixteenth century – though less well documented – carved chimneypieces as well.[115] In 1592 Sir Edward Pytts in Herefordshire engaged 'Garrett Hollyman a dutch carver' to make '2 chymny peices the carving therof being the storyes of Susanna & Mars & Venus'; the stone was to be local, but Hollyman came from London to do the work.[116] In 1622 Sir Arthur Ingram was ordering chimneypieces from London for his new houses in York and at Sheriff Hutton, 10 miles away. In due course he sent for London bricklayers, complaining of the incompetence of local ones.[117] In 1619 John Smythson obtained a design – copied from a chimneypiece in the Earl of Arundel's house – and a quotation for a chimneypiece for Welbeck or Bolsover from Thomas Ashby of London.[118] When in 1656 Richard Whitmore commissioned Valentine

203 (*above*) Welford House, Berkshire. Probably begun *c.* 1655–60 and intended to have a pilastered front rising to an eaves cornice, and completed *c.* 1680 with a by-then fashionable pediment. (Interruption of building is indicated by a clear break in the brickwork, from English bond to Flemish, at first-floor level.)

204 (*following page*) Hambledon Hall, Leicestershire, *c.* 1620. Hambledon is a house of a traditional form and in a regional style, save for the loggias which closely resemble those at Houghton Conquest (pl. 205). It is not clear what the connection is between the two, but copying and emulation was one of the principal processes by which new architectural forms reached the provinces.

205 (*page 193*) Houghton Conquest, Bedfordshire. The very pure, classical loggias at Houghton Conquest may have been provided by Inigo Jones, *c.* 1615, for the otherwise conventional house of Mary, Countess of Pembroke.

Strong of Taynton to build a new house at Lower Slaughter, the chimneypieces (save for the simple openings in the kitchen) were specifically excluded from the masonry contract. The implication is that Whitmore was going to obtain them from elsewhere, and their quality suggests strongly that London was their source. In 1655 John Webb wanted the hall chimneypiece at Lamport carved in London 'because of ye enrichments'.[119] In 1674 Sir John Swinburne of Capheaton sent for painters from London to decorate the inside of his newly finished house. Robert Crosby and Peter Hartshorne arrived by sea, with an extensive stock of paints, brushes and colours, and during their time in the north they decorated a number of other houses in the area as well.[120] After damage in the Civil War John Cartwright had rebuilt his house at Aynho in Northamptonshire to the designs of William Marshall, the London mason who had worked for Webb at Lamport, and subsequently commissioned further work from Thomas Turbet, a village plasterer; this was to be done 'all as well as the withdrawing room now is or as the best country workman can do'.[121] It was not to be expected that a local craftsman could match the workmanship of the metropolis.

Before the Civil War the houses in the home counties in which London mannerisms were employed constituted a regional rather than, as yet, a national style. But the importance of these regional developments, both of the exceptional, Jonesian houses and of the less sophisticated and more mannered productions of the home counties, was in developing a style of building that was new, conspicuous and acceptable. The style was born and consolidated during the first decades of the century: originating in London, already the national centre of fashion and taste, and consolidated through the building of houses in sufficient numbers for the style to cease to seem outlandish. In the same period there was an increasing spread of plan forms of London origin. Although the Civil War caused a very great falling-off in the volume of house building, the silhouette and the layout of the post-Restoration gentry house were already established in their essentials by 1640.

6

Conservatism, Innovation and Consolidation, 1620–1690

Conservatism: Differences

In tracing the development of the gentry house, this book has emphasised the houses, some of them for men of higher rank, that set the fashion. In their acceptance of innovations in layout, amenities and architectural style the gentry very generally followed the lead of the classes above them. However, in that many of these innovations were only slowly accepted, and that in very many houses conservative elements were perpetuated alongside the more modern, the gentry of the provinces might also in a sense – as Pratt implied – set local fashions themselves. This conservatism often distinguishes the houses of the lower gentry from those of the higher. It is partly a matter of simple economics, the greater wealth of the higher gentry providing them not only with more money to build but also with a broader educational and social background than lesser men. By contrast, the more limited circles in which the lesser gentry moved might be normative locally in providing acceptable architectural models.

The further from London, the more this provincialism is evident; on the other hand, the higher in society, the more people were likely to move beyond their immediate background.[1] Sir John Lowther's first wife had been a local girl, daughter of Richard Fletcher of Newbiggin, a few miles away, 'a lover of building contrivances, of houses, gardens and making of alterations rather for convenience than magnificence, she knew when to spend and when to spare'.[2] By contrast, he was anxious lest his second wife, out of Norfolk, should find northern barbarisms not to her taste: 'both shee and I were more tymorous, than in our former changes, by reason of the remoteness of friends to both distance of Cuntryes difference of the condicion of Cuntryes and manor of living betwixt north and south'.[3] In 1649 William Grey complained of Northumberland that 'since the union of both kingdomes, the gentry of this

countey have given themselves to idlenesse, luxury and covetousnesse, living not in their own houses, as their ancestours have done, profusely spending their revenues in other countries'.[4] At the other end of England, as early as 1602 Richard Carew had written of the Cornish gentry that 'little affecting so remote a corner [they] liked better to transplant their possessions nearer to the heart of the Realme'.[5]

The more limited experience of the lesser gentry made them more likely to employ craftsmen with no more knowledge of advanced architectural styles than their own. The roots of the craftsman's skills lay in the physical building materials of the different regions of England and in the particular techniques needed to work them. In separate areas, different structural and stylistic traditions had developed over long periods of time. There are very considerable visual differences between carpentry techniques in the south-east and those of the Midlands and the west, and a house from one or other area is instantly recognisable. Separating the two is the great swaithe of limestone hills – the Jurassic Belt, it has often been called, stretching from Somerset to Lincolnshire – where building stone is plentiful, generally of outstanding quality, and where high-quality external carpentry was in small demand. North again of the Midlands, a region for the most part of timber and brick, is the central mass of the Pennines, running north through Derbyshire into Yorkshire and beyond. Here, isolated from the stone building traditions of the south, houses were built with masonry details that were very different. In the south-west the fine limestone and the craft techniques that went with it peter out, and it tends to be replaced with sandstones, slate, cherts and granite – less tractable materials that imposed their own limitations on the quality of stonework and demanded different methods of working.

Within this broad range of regional materials and techniques, details and styles might be more localised still. Besides the geological bounds that restricted the craftsman's operations, there were economic ones: dependent on his trade for his living and on his connections and reputation for his employment, the building craftsman tended to be still further tied to an area within the broader region. His education and training also tended towards conservatism: essentially practical, acquired by apprenticeship to a master who instructed his pupil in traditional practices, each generation tended to follow the working style of its predecessor. Craft traditions might thus survive through geographical remoteness. But the strength of local building traditions that gave expression to the gentry's requirements related not only to geographical isolation, but also to the quality of the materials and to the level of economic prosperity that created a demand for the continued exercise of these skills. Where good materials existed there was scope for the exercise of traditional craftsmanship in their use, as well as the possibilities of experiment within an existing style; where there was demand for such skills they tended to be maintained.

The process was thus both centrifugal and centripetal. In spite of rapid change in the amenities that the gentry demanded in their houses, there was a strong and often conflicting tendency towards stylistic and technical inertia on the part of the craftsmen employed to put them up. Generalisations about either class or geography are dangerous. Pratt's comment on gentry conservatism is quoted at the beginning of chapter 2; in 1697 John Evelyn would write that 'especially in the Country . . . for the saving of a little Change, [builders] seldom consult an experienced Artist, besides the Neighbour Brick-layer and Carpenter'.[6] A craftsman's excursion beyond his usual sphere can occasionally be recognised by a house's alien style, as at Clay Hill, Ringmer, East Sussex, where a house in a characteristically Cheshire manner was built for a Cheshire lawyer, William Newton, who was steward to Thomas Sackville in the 1540s.[7] A tiny minority of craftsmen, like Robert Smythson and William Arnold, transcended local traditions and achieved skills and learning that led to their employment, sometimes far from their origins, by a fairly small group of sophisticated builders, and achieved a prominence and influence disproportionate to their numbers. Many builders, content to be comfortably housed in homes that would not disgrace them, were happy to leave their execution to craftsmen who satisfied local taste.

Regional architectural differences thus reflect economic circumstances, as well as tenurial differences which are frequently linked with economic ones. Over and above contrasts of building materials, there is for example a great difference between the architectural character of Devonshire, the Weald and the south Midlands: in Devonshire there were many small, old-enclosed manorial estates; in the Weald there were also small manors but few ancient gentry and something of a status vacuum filled in the seventeenth century by men who made money in the iron trades; and in the south Midlands in the sixteenth century there was much recent enclosure with foundations being laid of a pattern of large estates with rich and frequently

aristocratic owners – a pattern discernible in the high proportion of large houses in the region in which substantial sixteenth-century remains still exist. In Devonshire in 1674 there were ninety-one houses with between fifteen and thirty hearths but only one with more than that; in Warwickshire in 1663 there had been only forty-one in the first category, but fourteen in the second – Warwickshire was already a county of great houses and estates.[8] Builders who perpetuated traditional building practices did not ignore the importance of architectural display: what their houses show is how slowly up-to-date knowledge reached down to the middling gentry and their craftsmen or to the remoter parts of the country.[9]

Until the late seventeenth century houses in which regional mannerisms and traditions persisted were still being built. At the same time, innovation might be stimulated by local examples, fostering for the moment a style or a plan which was novel but which remained peculiar to a region. It is beyond the scope of a national survey to provide a full account of such regional diversity or to examine any group in depth, but five separate groups of houses may illustrate some of the factors involved: a distinctive type of house from Derbyshire, a south-western form and a group of related houses around Bristol, a characteristic East Anglian plan and an immediately recognisable type of house from West Yorkshire. The first of these shows the local influence of a single major building while the second and third may show a provincial city fusing local tradition with its own version of the compact plan of the London suburbs. The other two groups illustrate the persistence of regional building traditions and may reflect status differences among the gentry.

In Derbyshire there is a group of small, compact houses whose origins are difficult to guess at, though their compact character suggests the lodge. At least fifty parks are shown on Saxton's map of the county of 1570, and lodges must have been very familiar. The examples of such upstanding houses as Barlborough and Worksop may also have been a source of inspiration, or perhaps the prominent, three-storey block of lodgings added at the end of the sixteenth century to a medieval hall at North Lees.[10] Holme Hall at Bakewell and Bentley Hall at Hungry Bentley are both compact, rectangular houses probably of around 1620–40. Beyond their square footprint their plans are otherwise dissimilar, but a liking for such compact forms may explain the evident appeal of the cross hall of Hardwick, imitated in at least three houses in the area and which could only be incorporated into a house with a deep plan.

First of these houses is Tissington (pls 206, 207), built early in the seventeenth century for Francis Fitzherbert (d. 1619) or for his son (Sir) John.[11] Both served their turn as High Sheriff – one of the offices that fell naturally to members of the county élite. The hall is entered at the centre of its short side like that of Hardwick, and runs through the house from front to back. On one side lie two parlours with the principal stair between them; on the other, similarly divided by stairs, the kitchen and buttery. Low towers flank the house on either side, providing not

206 Tissington Hall, Derbyshire, *c.* 1625.

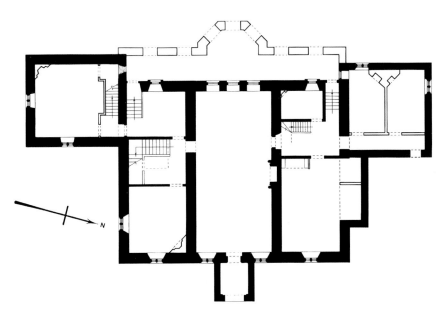

207 Tissington Hall: ground-floor plan (omitting nineteenth- and twentieth-century alterations). Tissington is one of three Derbyshire houses which have through halls, probably inspired by Hardwick in the same county.

stairs but additional rooms. Tissington was greatly altered in the eighteenth century[12] (when among other changes a loggia was built along the garden side and the upper floors of the house extended above it) but the essence of its highly unconventional layout is preserved. Away from London and except for houses whose links with London can be demonstrated, the only parallels at a comparable social level are also local: Park Hall at Barlborough[13] and Weston Hall at Weston on Trent (pl. 261).[14] Park Hall is a compact, rectangular house of three ranges, with the hall occupying the central range and running from front to back, as at Tissington. Weston (of which only a part stands; the Civil War and the impoverishment of the family prevented its completion) was to have been a large house on an H plan with a deep centre and projecting wings. The builders of these three houses are more likely to have emulated prestigious local models than the houses which adopted the deep hall plan in the London area.

These houses seem to show a local taste modified by a fashionable exemplar. By contrast, a group of houses in the west of England seems to be the end product of a long evolution. In Somerset, Dorset and part of adjoining counties there are a number of gentry houses of the late sixteenth century and the early seventeenth which have symmetrical fronts but whose halls extend to the end wall of the house. Although differing substantially in their details, the plans of Cold Ashton, probably of around 1630, Leigh of 1617 and Anderson of 1622 illustrate varieties of the form. Houses with end halls were the norm nationally before the general introduction of upper-end solars in the fourteenth century. Bisham Abbey, described in chapter 3, had been such a house when built in the 1280s; its high-end range was added early in the following century. Later examples in the region include the fourteenth-century manor house at Martock, Chantry Farm at Stoke sub Hamden and Woodlands

Manor at Mere. At Woodlands Manor, at the Court House at East Quantoxhead, perhaps originally at Athelhampton[15] and certainly at Sandford Orcas (pl. 209)[16] a small room seems to have stood back from the façade, almost detached from the hall and leaving its high end free. This probably provided, on the ground floor, no more than cellarage. Both East Quantoxhead and Athelhampton subsequently acquired high-end parlours (the latter probably built by the Sandford Orcas masons) but at Sandford Orcas itself there is still no high-end parlour.

It is almost certainly not from chance that houses with end halls occur in the area where the developed oriel is commonest. In the late medieval and early sixteenth-century house the oriel was a space that offered a measure of privacy, leading off the dais end of the hall. The oriel in a great house is often simply a deep bay, lit by a grand window; in a smaller house, it is sometimes almost a separate room, projecting on the front of the house and entered from the hall through an open doorway. It might be large enough to extend almost to the porch: at Dodington in Somerset there is only a small gap between them, while at Bradley Manor in Devonshire, of the late fifteenth century, the oriel merges with the porch to provide a complete passage along the front of the house to allow worshippers to a chapel at the house's high end without having to pass through the hall. In those cases where the oriel forms a virtually separate room off the hall, there is generally a small, distinct chamber above it, sometimes – as at Collacombe Barton in Devonshire – having a gallery from which to overlook the hall (pl. 211). Such a room at Penfound in Cornwall has its own newel stair, and is otherwise inaccessible. At Bingham's Melcombe (pl. 11)[17] a large, heated oriel bay on two storeys dwarfs what remains of the hall and provides the setting for a grandiose coat of arms of the family, while in the glass of the window itself are the arms of Queen Mary 1 and Philip of Spain along with those of numerous local gentry and family connections.

Leigh at Winsham in Somerset (pls 212, 213)[18] comes towards the end of this tradition, possessing a parlour but also retaining an oriel. Leigh was built in 1617 for Henry Henley, son of Robert Henley who described himself as a merchant of Taunton and who had been buying land in the neighbourhood since 1576.[19] The house is superficially a service-passage, E-plan house with forward-projecting wings (the service passage has been eliminated in later alterations). However, although the high-end wing contains the principal parlour, the hall extends to the end of the house and a small room that formed a projection to its rear (now partitioned off) was originally a heated oriel. When around 1695 Celia Fiennes visited the house, she remarked on the large dais and on the two hall fireplaces;[20] the oriel was

208 Manor Farm, Ashbury, Oxfordshire, c. 1480. Characteristic of a number of houses of lesser gentry in parts of the south-west is a plan in which the hall extends to the end of the house, with a small parlour off-set to the rear. The resemblance to Sandford Orcas (pl. 209) is clear.

evidently a feature she did not recognise. Fuller in 1655 had found it necessary to describe an oriel of this kind as 'that small excursion out of gentlemen's halls in Dorset';[21] he assumed that his readers might not be familiar with it.

A number of other houses in the region combine a symmetrical front with an end hall. Kingston Maurward in Dorset,[22] much altered internally, has an E façade with forward-projecting wings at either end; the high-end wing seems to have contained no more than an oriel off the hall. The original plan of Lake House at Wilsford[23] in south Wiltshire is not clear since the house was gutted by fire early in the twentieth century, but the main body of the house is five bays wide, probably with the hall and the entry occupying the larger part and the parlour the smaller. Services and the stair were in a broad, rear-projecting wing, thus placing the staircase in line with the front entrance and anticipating its location in the fully developed double-pile house. The plan of Anderson (pls 170, 171), the first double-pile house of the region, can be seen as the adaptation of the regional,

209 (*above*)   Sandford Orcas, Dorset, *c*. 1540. The hall is single storeyed, with a great chamber above it whose windows give it equal prominence. Sandford Orcas has a distinctive regional plan, with the hall extending to one end of the house and a small private room beyond it.

210 (*following page*)   Hazelbury Manor, Somerset, *c*. 1480. Hazelbury has two oriel bays off the high end of the hall, one forming a private alcove and the other leading to a parlour and a stair to the chamber above it. The arrangement of Great Chalfield (pls 39, 40) is similar.

211 (*page 201*)   Collacombe Barton, Devonshire, *c*. 1575. At Collacombe the hall oriel is developed into a small room (now partitioned off and entered by a door; early drawings show it open to the hall). There is a more private room on the first floor, with internal windows to overlook the hall. Like the off-set parlour, such developed oriels are characteristic of the south-west.

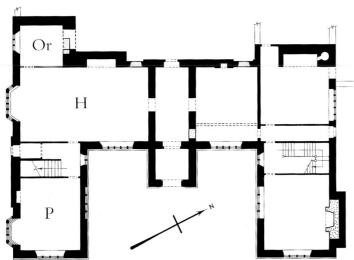

212 (*above*) Leigh, Winsham, Somerset, 1622. Leigh combines the E plan of innumerable contemporary gentry houses with the regional end hall.

213 Leigh: ground-floor plan. The left-hand wing contains a parlour, the right-hand the kitchen, which was probably originally in the front of the wing and subsequently moved to the rear. To the rear of the hall, and originally open to it and heated by its own fireplace, is an oriel which was remarked on as an unfamiliar feature by Celia Fiennes in the 1690s.

end-hall layout to new models. The regional tradition of the end hall meant that at Anderson all that was necessary was to add a rear range to the end-hall front range in order to create a double-pile plan of orthodox form. Here, as in some other areas, the novel, compact plan was able to assimilate and to build on existing traditions.

In the Bristol area the end hall provided an alternative compact model to the double pile. Cold Ashton (pls 214, 215) of about 1620 and later altered is odd and not wholly intelligible, but it has an end hall and a single staircase off the hall's low end. Comparable is Wick Court[24] (pl. 216) whose plan is no easier to understand but is similar in essentials with a stair

214 (*above*) Cold Ashton, Avon, *c.* 1620 and *c.* 1660: front elevation.

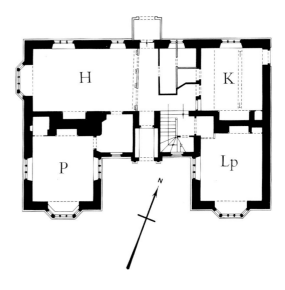

215 Cold Ashton: ground-floor plan. The development of Cold Ashton is not entirely clear, but an end hall is combined with a stair close to the front entrance: such a stair location parallels that of the compact double-pile house.

216 Wick Court, Avon: rear elevation. Wick and Cold Ashton are similar in overall form, though both have been much altered and at Wick the entrance is on the opposite side of the house.

217 Heydon Hall, Norfolk, c. 1625. Heydon employs the stylistic mannerisms of East Anglia, but the stair lies between rear-projecting wings in a way similar to the arrangement in the end-hall houses of the Bristol area. Both may have been influenced by metropolitan sources.

in the recess between the wings; the main difference between Cold Ashton and Wick is that at the former the entrance now lies between the wings, at Wick it is on the opposite, flat side of the house. Wick was remodelled by Thomas Haynes, grocer, who acquired it in 1665, probably substituting a small, modern entrance hall for an end hall (though the evidence is confusing). Naas House near Lydney on the opposite bank of the Avon is similar, as is Keevil, a few miles away, which seems to have been a radical remodelling around 1625 of an earlier building. All save Keevil were built for men with strong links to Bristol, and may be compared with the compact, double-pile villas of the London area. Such a plan is not a true double pile in that the wings are treated as separate projections rather than merging into a complete rear range, but otherwise the principal motive seems to be the same as that in the adoption of the double pile: the provision of an immediate approach to the upper floor and the by-passing of the hall.

Possibly the first house of the kind in the area is The Hall at Bradford on Avon in Wiltshire (pl. 4), built around 1600 by a rich clothier, John Hall, on the edge of a prosperous manufacturing town.[25] The house is not large, but it has an exterior of astonishing richness. It has been ascribed to William Arnold (whose father was probably a carpenter at Longleat) on the basis of details which occur elsewhere in work associated with him, and the semicircular window bays which are so prominent at Bradford on Avon occurred in a number of other houses in the south-west: at Montacute, Chantemarle and elsewhere. But

overall, the elaboration of the façade is more characteristic of London, and The Hall is in any case not a true country house. Like Wick, the house has a straight façade with short, rear-projecting wings, and the principal stair is in line with the front entrance. The form is not confined to the Bristol region. It occurred also at Marks Hall in Essex, perhaps built around 1610,[26] at Bletchingdon in Oxfordshire and probably at Heydon Hall in Norfolk (pl. 217), all three of them country houses with no known connection with Bristol. The type may represent a fusion of local traditions with ideas from further off, and although no house of the London suburbs now exists with such a layout it is almost precisely that shown in the first of John Thorpe's Camden House plans, described in chapter 4. In formal terms one may see the plan as a contraction of the Eastbury arrangement (pls 85, 86), merely substituting a single stair for Eastbury's two. However, the Bristol examples reinforce the suitability of the compact house in all its variety for the residence of the businessman who required fashionable amenities more than the full range of hierarchical accommodation to be found in the houses of an established landowner.

Very different from the layouts of these houses of the south-west, compact but with projecting wings, is an equally distinctive group of East Anglian houses of the lesser gentry which lack cross wings, even though houses of comparable size elsewhere (as well as in East Anglia itself) do have them. The sequence of rooms in these houses is identical with that in houses of similar rank elsewhere; what is often lacking is their

218 Flemings Hall, Bedingfield, Suffolk, *c.* 1550 and *c.* 1620. Flemings Hall belongs to a group of distinctive, East Anglian gentry houses which have long, rectangular plans without wings or other projections except for a porch and – in earlier examples – a stair turret.

external differentiation. An early and prominent example of the type, perhaps of around 1550 but very possibly earlier, is Flemings Hall at Bedingfield in Suffolk (pl. 218).[27] Flemings Hall is long, flat fronted (without a jetty) and timber framed save for the brick front to the centrally placed porch and (later) brick gables at either end.[28] Now exposed, the timber framing may originally have been covered in lime render, but it does not distinguish between the ends of the house. Flemings Hall has been

much altered and the arrangements of the lower end are now irrecoverable, but essentially the plan simply consisted of three or four rooms in line, with the stair (of around 1630 but probably a replacement of an earlier flight) in a compartment between the hall and the parlour.

Sharrington Hall in Norfolk (pl. 219), though of more than one building period in the sixteenth and seventeenth centuries, in its final form was also a long, plain-fronted house of brick and flint, its façade relieved only by a porch and by two projecting stair turrets of which the earlier rises at the junction between hall and parlour.[29] Like Flemings Hall its plan was extremely simple: parlour, hall, buttery and kitchen all in line, yet the size of the house indicates a substantial (though unknown) owner. Little Hautbois Hall (pls 220, 221) is a sophisticated

219   Sharrington Hall, Norfolk, of the sixteenth century, with a stair projection at each end of the façade.

house, possibly built as a secondary seat around 1580 (an earlier date on a Victorian doorway can be disregarded) and with its principal rooms in a taller block than the services (cf. Wilderhope, p. 310) and with the entrance at the junction of the two. Stairs rise in an ingenious manner round an open well, but it perpetuates the regional form with all rooms in line. A late example of these linear houses, Tharston Hall in Norfolk,[30] of around 1626, has decorative diaper brickwork and stepped gables, but its plan is a simple oblong whose proportions seem to be determined by simple geometry: the kitchen, the parlour and the hall within the line of the screen are square, the buttery and stair compartment are half-square, and the screens passage a quarter the width of the hall.

Thurston Hall in Suffolk (pls 222, 223) can be seen as a development of this long, narrow plan with the addition of a high-end cross wing.[31] The house is timber framed, with an extravagant display of closely set studs – an unnecessarily expensive mode of building, but one which at once announces the superior standing of its owner. The plan is wholly conventional, with a buttery beyond the hall and the kitchen beyond that at the end of the house; at the high end of the house is the parlour and a smaller, unheated room, with the principal staircase placed between them.

These long, plain-fronted houses may express a local predilection for extended fronts that appeared at East Barsham (pls 41–3), discussed above. The same taste can be found locally at Hunstanton Old Hall and Beaupre where the gatehouse, like that at East Barsham (pl. 41), stood remarkably close to the principal façade, reducing the forecourt between them to little more than

220   P. Gaymer, 1909: Little Hautbois Hall, Norfolk, *c.* 1580. At Little Hautbois there is a marked distinction between the tall, principal rooms and the lower rooms at the service end; the porch was placed at the junction between them. Little Hautbois may have been built as a species of secondary seat rather than as its builder's principal house.

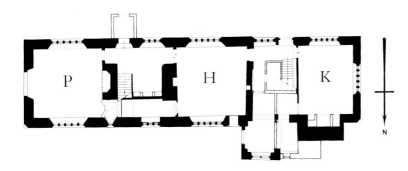

221   Little Hautbois: ground-floor plan. The long, rectangular plan of Little Hautbois is characteristic of the region.

a strip of land. At Hengrave (pl. 81) the courtyard around which stand the principal rooms of the house is narrower than the house's extended façade. The precise social level of the owners of these smaller linear houses has yet to be established, and their form may indicate recognition of a range of appropriate house types within the ranks of the gentry themselves. Their accommodation is limited, generally with a single parlour, yet in another of these linear hourses, Barnham Broome Hall, early in the seventeenth century its owner Leonard Chamberlain (cadet of an old East Anglian family) gave the house a new great chamber with some of the best plasterwork in the county.

Far from East Anglia, in Yorkshire the houses of the higher gentry were no less architecturally advanced than contemporary buildings and elsewhere. Great houses of the late sixteenth and early seventeenth century such as New Hall, Pontefract, Fountains Hall, Heath Old Hall, Howsham Hall, Burton Constable and Burton Agnes, while employing a decorative vocabulary appropriate to local materials, have elaborate, symmetrical fronts and sophisticated plans and are as innovative as houses of the higher gentry elsewhere. However, among the lesser gentry of the Pennine foothills the prevailing form from the mid-sixteenth century until the late seventeenth was one that incorporated highly distinctive external ornament, in which hierarchical

207

222   Thurston Hall, Suffolk. At Thurston a type of long, straight, regional house of the lesser gentry is modified by the addition of a high-end cross wing – a feature that occurs widely elsewhere. The house is further enhanced by the lavishness of its exposed timberwork in an area where at this date timber-framing was often light in weight for economy and concealed by plaster.

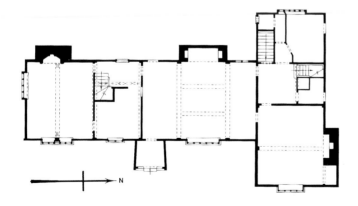

223   Thurston Hall: ground-floor plan.

functions remained very strongly marked and in which plans evolved of a kind that had few parallels elsewhere. Wood Lane Hall at Sowerby Bridge (1649) is a late example but typifies many of their characteristics (pls 224, 225).

Of the many ways in which these houses are unusual, one may note four in particular. Externally, their façades are often highly asymmetrical, with the porch and the upper end strongly accentuated. Internally, the passage at the lower end of the hall does not open directly into the hall through the openings in a screen, but is separated from it by the back of a fireplace that heats its lower end. Such a passage is generally termed a hearth passage, and though widespread in upland areas of the country in houses of a lower social class, it is only in the north that it occurs in houses that are unquestionably of gentry status. In many of these houses the kitchen lies not in a low-end wing but in a block directly to the rear of the hall, often forming an irregular projection. Finally (a point discussed further in chapter 8), they often have more ground-floor parlours than houses of similar size and status elsewhere. In all of these characteristics, they are distinct both from the great houses of the region and from houses of lesser gentry elsewhere.

These houses can be related to the houses of social classes both above and below them. Locally, the hearth passage is

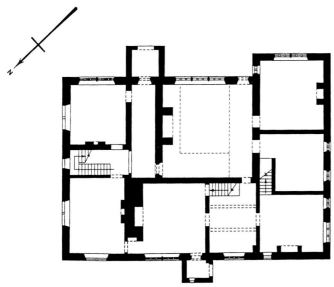

224 (*above*) Wood Lane Hall, Sowerby Bridge, West Yorkshire, 1649. In the clothing districts of West Yorkshire a highly distinctive type of gentry house emerged during the sixteenth century in which external differentiations remained very strong. These characteristic local forms were gradually superseded by more national forms only during the late seventeenth century.

225 Wood Lane Hall: ground-floor plan. The layout of these Yorkshire houses was also distinctive, with a multiplicity of ground-floor rooms and with the kitchen unusually placed in relation to the hall. The owners of these houses were largely involved in the production and sale of woollen cloth, and these arrangements suggest a community whose relations were rather different from those of gentry households elsewhere.

common in yeomen's houses, but absent in those of the higher gentry. In the Lancashire Pennines to the west, the hearth passage does not appear in surviving houses until the early seventeenth century, and its origins are not known.[32] However, in Cumbria hearth passages do occur in earlier houses of a higher social status: at Isel,[33] at Middleton Hall[34] and at Yanwath,[35] which date from the late fifteenth century and the early sixteenth; in the fifteenth century they may have been present in the houses of the higher gentry over a wider area of the north. It may be that in Yorkshire both the lesser gentry and, imitating them, the yeomen were perpetuating the practices of a higher social class. The persistence of hierarchical marks of distinction in the external appearance of these Yorkshire houses and also the perpetuation of open halls well into the seventeenth century suggests that the builders were very conscious of their position;

it seems unlikely that they would have adopted a plan that they associated with the houses of inferiors.

On the other hand, the location of the kitchen in some of these Yorkshire houses, directly to the rear of the hall, does suggest that the relations of these middling Yorkshire gentry with their household and community may not have been quite the same as those implied by house plans elsewhere. At East Riddlesden, where there are two parlours in a large, rectangular, low-end block, one of them can only be reached by passing through the kitchen.[36] These unusually sited kitchens, almost as large as the hall itself, may have evolved out of some former cooking function in the hall which made their owners accustomed to their continued proximity. They may have served also as servants' eating rooms, prefiguring the removal of servants from halls elsewhere; but the relatively small size of most of these houses (East Riddlesden is an exception) implies that their households would probably not have been very large nor probably very strongly stratified. Of equal importance, the direct entrance from the kitchen into the centre of the hall will have made difficult any lingering ceremony that may have been attached to the service of the meal. Whatever the ultimate social origins of the hearth passage plan and the rear kitchen, the social relations implied by the layouts of these gentry houses seem by 1600 to have more in common with those of the class beneath them than the class above. From these lesser houses they differed more in appearance and in specific amenities – in the number of parlours and chambers and in many cases in the quality of the plasterwork and wainscot with which they are decorated – than in their overall plan. In this they conform to the suggestion of Gervase Markham whose description of a farmhouse is quoted in chapter 1: that it was in the appearance of the house more than in its layout that the houses of the lesser gentry differed from those of prosperous yeomen.

These houses tend to conservatism in other ways. A number of them still incorporate open halls at a date when in most houses of men of a similar rank elsewhere a single-storey hall was already the norm (pl. 314). The exteriors of these houses are as striking as are their unusual plans. The high end is frequently strongly marked in contrast to the lower, by a forward-projecting gabled wing – even though the practice of placing the kitchen behind the hall means that it is not visible from the front of the house. In a number of houses the porch is accentuated by a species of rose window. It has been suggested that Robert Smythson may have been responsible for the introduction of the form: one of his drawings is for such a window, probably from as early a date as any of these windows that exists.[37]

Although studies of Robert Smythson have concentrated – rightly – on his work on major buildings, it is clear from his surviving drawings that he was also involved at least with the modernisation and alteration of houses of a much lower rank: more particularly, with houses in which regional idioms and more traditional, hierarchical forms were perpetuated. While it was suggested above that a reason for conservatism in the

houses of lesser men might be their resort to local masons, this possible involvement in the design of such houses by one of the greatest designers of the age may support what is also indicated by the contrast between the very different forms of the houses of greater and lesser gentry in East Anglia: that while any gentry house was distinguished as such, there was a recognisable formal distinction between the houses of the higher gentry and those of the lower that was dependent on more than mere size, the degree of architectural embellishment and the competence with which it was executed. On this, as on so many aspects of the subject, more work is needed.

The wish for visual distinction in the houses of the gentry was met in accordance with regional building traditions. Very often this is concentrated on the upper part of the house, corresponding to the wish that it should stand well when seen at a distance (as discussed in chapters 1 and 9). In Cornwall a group of early seventeenth-century houses have exteriors that are very plain, with long, unbroken façades, uniform windows, shallow pitched roofs, but battlemented parapets. These occur at Godolphin (pl. 262), Trelowarren, Penheale and Lanhydrock, while the battlements and roof occur on a conventional, E-plan house at Prideaux Place. On the borders of Gloucestershire and Worcestershire a number of houses both in stone and in timber rise to a massed line of small gablets: Preston Court (pl. 234), Middlebeam Hall and Mere Hall at Hanbury (pl. 258) among timber-built houses, Beckford Hall and Postlip Hall among those built in stone. In very many houses of Lancashire and Cheshire the use of decorative framing in gables often seems competitive, if not obsessive. Such local decorative idioms, not all as prominent as these, may in any particular instance be due either to the perpetuation of regional traditions or to the activity of a single craftsman. In either case their employment marks the houses of men of a certain rank and links them by a strong visual identity.

Innovation: Similarities

By contrast with these regional house types, there are by the late sixteenth century other houses for men of the same class which though still differing widely in details and materials are essentially similar in their overall forms. In this they parallel the early spread of houses building on compact plans, and their distribution suggests that even among the lesser gentry norms of layout and form may have evolved independently of the practices of local building craftsmen and that against the centrifugal and conservative tendencies of regional craft traditions, social behaviour and concern for the builder's image was having an opposite effect. Houses with a pair of gabled wings but with an off-centre entrance to the hall – the plan illustrated by Gervase Markham (pl. 5) – are ubiquitous and can be numbered in their hundreds. Simply to illustrate their range in time, place and building traditions one might cite Church's House (timber framed; pl. 3),

226 (*above*) Staley Hall, Greater Manchester (demolished; photographed *c.* 1895). The hall with cross wings is a form of house that occurs among all ranks of the gentry in the sixteenth and seventeenth centuries, and variations are largely confined to differences in materials and the evolution of internal amenities.

227 (*right*) Staley Hall: ground-floor plan. Staley Hall is a sixteenth-century, timber-framed house, cased in stone for fashion's sake a generation after it was built and without any major alteration to the traditional form of the plan.

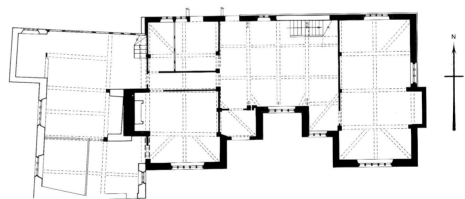

Staley Hall (timber, stone cased; pls 226, 227), Hambledon Hall (a conventional house embellished with up-to-date details; pl. 204), Shipton Hall in Shropshire (stone, with a tower porch characteristic of the region; pl. 228), Morley Old Hall in Norfolk (a brick house with pedimented windows ubiquitous in East Anglia; pls 229, 230), the dour Barlborough Old Hall in Derbyshire (pls 231, 232), or Old Hall Farm at Mayfield in Staffordshire (pl. 233), a stone house bearing a date as late as 1680. What is remarkable is the long persistence of the form,

with the last example – in the Staffordshire uplands – in an area that in the late seventeenth century was still very isolated. At Old Hall Farm one is at the social margin between the gentry and the yeoman farmer, and seeing the perpetuation of a form which had already been superseded in houses of the higher class.

Equally common are houses whose off-centre porches still betray their old-fashioned plan but which otherwise have a flat façade crowned with gables and with wings that project to the rear. Preston Court in Gloucestershire (pl. 234) has a tall front

228 (*left*) Shipton Hall, Shropshire, *c.* 1600. Shipton combines a local mannerism – a porch with a tower – with the ubiquitous plan of off-centre entry, central hall and matching wings. The porch was originally balanced with an oriel.

231 (*below*) Barlborough Old Hall, Derbyshire, *c.* 1600. A hall-and-cross-wings house of wholly representative form (cf. pl. 5).

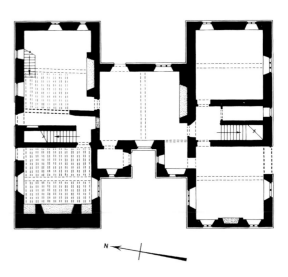

229 Morley Old Hall, Norfolk, *c.* 1610. Morley Old Hall has crow-stepped gables and pedimented windows typical of contemporary East Anglian gentry houses, but otherwise represents a common formula.

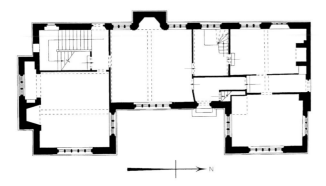

232 Barlborough Old Hall: ground-floor plan.

230 Morley Old Hall: ground-floor plan. Essentially, despite local variations, almost all hall and cross-wing houses functioned in the same way. Unusually, Morley Old Hall has an entrance lobby with the buttery behind it rather than having its front door opening directly into the hall's low end, but the overall relationship of spaces and entrance is the same as occurs elsewhere.

233 Old Hall Farm, Mayfield, Staffordshire, 1680. Old Hall Farm is the house of minor gentry (or even of a superior yeoman farmer) in a fairly remote part of England and is from the end of the hall-and-cross-wings tradition.

234 (*below*) Preston Court, Gloucestershire, *c.* 1600. Preston Court represents an alternative form to the house with cross wings: a house with a plain front and wings to the rear. There seems to have been a local taste for many-gabled façades (cf. Mere Hall, pl. 258) and many lesser gentry houses made their display with a distinctive roof line. The only external differentiation between high and low ends is in the closeness of the timber framing.

rising through three floors; the top floor is jettied, and there is also a little jettied upper chamber in the high-end wing that projects to the rear.[38] Although there is a structural break between the high and low ends of the house, the entire building was clearly conceived as a single architectural entity. The only external difference between the ends is in the character of the framing: close studded to the hall and parlour, box framed (or with wider studding) to the services. Of a similar character, though later in date, is Tunstall House in Kent (pl. 235; see also p. 301 below).[39] Tunstall seems to be a house of more than one period whose exterior was cased in brick around the middle of the seventeenth century (and which was possibly enlarged at the same time) so as to improve a building whose original form may have been less regular.[40] The house comprises essentially a hall with a large parlour at the high end, a smaller parlour at the other, and a kitchen beyond that. Far from either of these, and in a very different building tradition but of similar character and plan is Friars Head Hall at Winterburn in North Yorkshire (pl. 236), probably of around 1610.[41] Friars Head Hall has four, tall, matching bay windows along its front, rising to the peculiar gable windows which are characteristic of gentry houses in the area and which may first occur here. At the rear are shallow, irregular wings like those at Preston Court.

In these houses, as with those that frame their centre between matching gables, the slight hierarchical reminiscence preserved in the off-centre porch is simply a matter of conservatism. Wings exist, but they are placed at the rear (like those of The Hall at Bradford on Avon and its related buildings) and not used to express the differences in status between these houses' ends; they show how widely the taste for regularity has already travelled. Lacking any other articulation to their façades, they can be seen merely as lesser versions of such a house as Aston Bury in

235 (*top left*) Tunstall House, Kent. A straight front built in brick, *c.* 1660–70, to regularise the appearance of a house that had been built at a number of different periods.

236 (*above*) Friars Head Hall, Winterburn, North Yorkshire, *c.* 1600. Friars Head has a uniform, straight façade except for the off-centre front entrance determined by the traditional layout of the hall. Wings extend to the rear as at Preston Court.

237 (*top right*) Aston Bury, Hertfordshire. Probably *c.* 1610–30, the house has a flat front, with ground-floor windows of alternating size which reflect the internal hierarchies but achieve regularity.

239 (*right*) Red House, Eldersfield, Herefordshire, 1647. Red House has a plain front and rear wings, and up-to-date brickwork whose details are similar to London work of the previous twenty-five years.

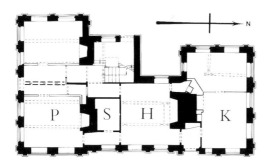

238 Red House: ground-floor plan. The plan is conservative. The combination of modern materials and old-fashioned plan is notably less common than the reverse and may suggest special circumstances: perhaps an owner prepared to make a display but not to adapt his way of life to a house of less familiar layout. There seems to have been a small parlour or study within the hall – a feature also provided at Tunstall (see p. 301).

Hertfordshire (pl. 237),[42] which has a façade of sufficient length for the porch to be placed at its centre. This is achieved by the simple means of creating a large buttery and pantry and a relatively small hall. While the fenestration of the first floor of Aston Bury is wholly uniform (awkwardly cutting across internal partitions) on the ground floor the windows corresponded to the importance of the rooms behind them. It has been suggested that this may be due to alteration during the course of building: to a changing view of what it was right for the outside of the house to express. However, these ground-floor windows still create a regular rhythm: uniformity is not achieved, but symmetry is. The date of the house is not known, but two large, square, stair turrets at the rear, almost equal in size, recall suburban houses of around 1600 to 1630.

The use of modern building materials did not necessarily mean the adoption of up-to-date plans, although the combination of new materials and old-fashioned plans is significantly rarer than the reverse. Comparable with these houses in its layout and external massing is in Worcestershire, Red House at Eldersfield (pls 238, 239).[43] Red House is said to be dated 1647, and its name reflects the use of brick – still unusual in an area that was traditionally one of building in either timber or (not very high-quality) stone. This exploitation of its decorative possibilities is comparable with the mannerism of the home counties and has contemporary parallels elsewhere, in particular in the east Midlands and in Shropshire although the actual detailing to window heads resembles work in London itself. The

240 Groombridge Place, Kent, *c.* 1660. Groombridge has up-to-date architectural detail, but its plan (with its centre one room deep and the hall entered at one end) is conservative. The combination of modern style and old-fashioned plan is very much less common than the reverse.

241 Hall Court, Much Marcle, Herefordshire, 1608–12. A simple, plain-fronted house, the circumstances of whose building can be followed in unusual detail from surviving documents. At the time of its building its owner was described as 'gentleman'; only later in a successful career would he be addressed as 'esquire'. The hipped roof is unusual at this date in the west of England, but occurs in two or three other contemporary houses in the area.

work may perhaps be that of a bricklayer apprenticed in London – as so many men were – and returning home to practice his craft. Walls are panelled and pilastered and windows are given ornamental heads in a display of the fashionable material, but the very crudeness of the craftsmanship corresponds to the conservative character of the plan. Though there are wings at either end of the building the high-end wing is very much longer to the rear than the other. The Red House may be compared with a house of a very different kind but comparable in uniting up-to-date architecture and a conservative layout: Groombridge Place in Kent (pl. 240).[44] Its hipped roof with eaves cornice, the well-proportioned brick quoins and the correct detail of doors and mouldings are comparable with some of the most up-to-date buildings in the south-east; the single-pile centre and a screen masking the two entrances to the hall (a feature described in chapter 3) are already anachronisms for its class and region.

The wide distribution of houses with similar layouts, still executed in the craft traditions of the region, may be illustrated by comparing two other gentry houses which were far apart geographically: Hall Court at Much Marcle in Herefordshire and Hacking Hall in Lancashire. Both were the houses of men who were educated and travelled, and the plans of each are functionally identical. However, each is in the local building style, and for Hall Court (pls 241, 242), built between 1608 and 1612, documents survive that identify the craftsmen and make it possible to follow the circumstances of its building in detail – unusual for so small a house.[45] It is also possible with unusual clarity to place the builder precisely in his social class, building a house that was appropriate to his wealth, station and prospects. Hall Court was built for Sir John Coke, who late in life bought Melbourne in Derbyshire (see above, p. 45). Coke was the second son of minor gentry, married to a girl from a similar family and making his way upwards, socially and economically, through the law, through patronage and through office holding until he was finally able towards the end of his life to buy a larger estate in his home county and to found a dynasty.

Architecturally Hall Court is unsophisticated, but marks a stage in Coke's career: sufficient for his status, income and needs when he built it, and conveniently close to the house of his wife's parents at Preston Court (pl. 234). He expressed their circumstances himself when he wrote to her of the options before them, evidently in response to her concern that while he was working in London, she was having to remain in the

242 (below) Hall Court: ground- and first-floor plans. The overall form, with rear wings, resembles that of Preston Court (pl. 234) where its builder's wife's family lived. The ground-floor plan is substantially unaltered, except that the porch has been moved and an entrance passage formed from the hall's high end. On the first floor the great chamber, at the centre, has had its fireplace cut off from the room by the later insertion of a passage.

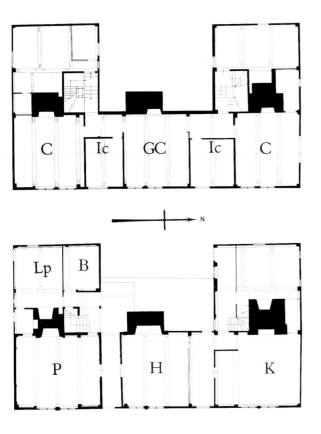

country. The choice, he wrote, was 'Either by this foreign attendance and striving with the world to such a better estate, or by a domestical frugality and united counsels and endeavours to improve that small condition which we have already.'[46] Although he was later able to leave Hall Court behind, he was already forty-five when he started building and though evidently still ambitious he probably had at the time no particular reason to anticipate his considerable further promotion. In so far as many men rose no further than Coke had done when he built Hall Court, the house typifies such men's requirements.

Even at this date Coke could have obtained up-to-date architectural advice if had wanted it. When Hall Court was built he was still in the service of Fulke Greville, courtier, statesman and literateur, friend of Sidney, Bacon and Dyer, and probably a little later to be a patron of Inigo Jones. Still nearer, his brother Thomas was already in the service of the Earl of Arundel. But the craftsmen who worked at Hall Court were all from the immediate neighbourhood and the house is entirely typical of the superior vernacular of the district. James Alcot, the principal carpenter, came from Bosbury, 6 miles away, masons came from Dymock, Berrow and Bromsberrow, other neighbouring villages, and ironwork came from the nearby town of Ledbury, as did casements and glass and the wainscot for the hall. Additionally, the craftsmen re-used stone and timber from an earlier building a little lower down the hillside on which Hall Court stands. Coke's papers make no reference to a preliminary drawing (though there probably was one of some kind, however sketchy); he seems to have contracted separately with each of the different craftsmen (though that again was normal) and while the overall scheme – which fairly closely resembles that of Preston Court – was probably determined by Coke and his wife, there was nothing in it that was new or which would have been unfamiliar to local craftsmen. While Coke was for most of the time away in London on business, his wife remained at her parents' house, frequently riding over to the building site to settle disputes, watching over the expenditure and writing to her husband about the progress of work.

Coke was probably unwilling to risk spending beyond his likely means or to embark on extravagant building when his own estate was one which he had himself entirely built up. He may also have felt that to make a sophisticated architectural display was not proper for someone who was still proving his own social position. During the period in which Hall Court was built, he was generally addressed only as 'Mr John Coke' – the designation to which he was properly entitled as a younger son. In 1623 he was described as 'esquire' – a signal of his advance: that year he sold Hall Court and moved back to London, prompted by pressure of work and increasing wealth. In 1624 he was knighted, and in 1628 he bought the Melbourne estate in his home county of Derbyshire, where at Melbourne Hall his descendants still live.

Hall Court is timber framed, and two storeys high. It makes little concession to display, though the superior end of the house is close studded on the ground floor, a more expensive form of construction than the square, box framing of the upper floor and of the whole of the service end. The roof is hipped, possibly as a result of alteration later in the century, though there is no obvious sign of this. There is a small group of other timber-framed, early seventeenth-century, hipped-roof houses in the neighbourhood. The house has a flat front facing east, with short wings projecting to the rear to form a U plan. The layout is conventional, with a central hall, kitchen and services at the north end and parlours at the south. Chimneystacks are in line, with the hall heated on its rear wall and other rooms heated by stacks between them. There are two staircases, each rising the full height of the house, and these are placed in the wings, at their inner angles. The construction appears modular, with a regular series of chamfered beams spanning the entire front range at ground- and first-floor levels and an arrangement of subordinate beams spanning the rear wings. These regularly spaced beams do not always align with the wall posts; though the majority are morticed into them, some are lapped or dovetailed over plates. Partitions generally coincide with ceiling beams and are tenoned into them; some, however, though evidently original, do not.

Many of the rooms can be identified through their being named in the building accounts, in glaziers' bills and in correspondence about the progress of work and from an inventory of 1680. The hall was at the centre of the house, entered originally from a porch at its northern end which gave into the usual screens passage between hall and kitchen. The parlour was at the southern end, with a little parlour behind it and also – unusually in this position – a buttery; the kitchen was north of the hall with what may be a bakehouse behind it: clearly a service room from its lack of any sort of decoration, the room has a fireplace opening into the back of the kitchen stack. (In 1680 a dairy house is mentioned which may be this room.) On the first floor the great chamber was over the hall, with the other best chambers over hall and kitchen. The high-end and low-end stairs each rose to a lobby which opened into the adjoining chambers and from which a short passage ran to either end of the hall chamber and provided access to smaller chambers between it and those at either end. The parlour was panelled, and payment is also recorded for a small amount of wainscot for the hall which may have been put up as some kind of a fireplace surround or as a reredos at the high end. The quantity mentioned (8 yards) is too small to panel the whole room, or even a dado. In both the east and west ends of the hall simple decorative framing was originally exposed.

Since Coke sold the house ten years after he had finished it, there are no contemporary inventories to show which rooms had beds in them, but the first-floor circulation achieved by this layout provided for maximum flexibility in use. The great chamber over the hall could be reached from the stairs at either end and could be used in conjunction with that over the parlour and the smaller room between them to provide a unit of great chamber, withdrawing chamber and bedchamber if this

243 Hacking Hall, Lancashire, 1607. Hacking, built of stone with forward wings, derives from a very different building tradition to Hall Court, but is functionally identical.

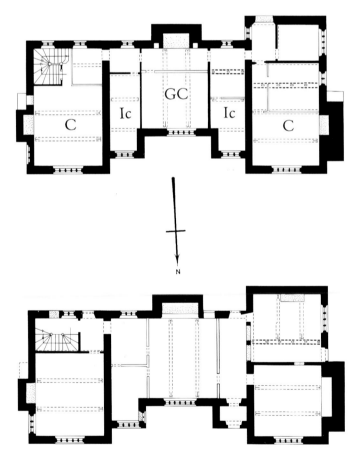

244 Hacking Hall: ground- and first-floor plans. The resemblance of Hacking to Hall Court is clearest on the first floor, where the great chamber was flanked by lesser rooms, east and west, and was reached in exactly the same way by short passages from high-end and low-end staircases. The low-end stair, now removed, was in the south-east angle of the west wing.

243 Hacking Hall, Lancashire, 1607. Hacking, built of stone with forward wings, derives from a very different building tradition to Hall Court, but is functionally identical.

was needed. The first-floor layout seems to resemble that of Arlescote in Warwickshire, a house probably of a similar date remodelled in the early eighteenth century. At the end of the seventeenth century (i.e. before its alteration) Arlescote's owner and his wife evidently slept in the central bedroom, over the hall, with their sons in one end chamber and their daughters in the other, and with male and female servants in smaller dependent rooms.[47] This might have been the original arrangement at Hall Court, but it is more likely that John and Mary Coke had slept in the chamber over the kitchen.

Alterations to make the house conform with later usage are themselves instructive. The principal change was to move the front door from the low end of the hall to the high end; this involved turning the original screens passage into a larder for the kitchen, and making a new entrance passage out of the opposite end of the hall, running through to the foot of the principal stair. There has been some remodelling in the area of these stairs, probably in order to provide a larger circulating space. The other change was to make a passage on the first floor, through the west side of the hall chamber. This separated the chamber from the fireplace that originally warmed it, but both of these alterations increased privacy as well as improving connections between the two ends of the house. One could now come directly into the house at the parlour end, rather than having to pass through the hall, while on the first floor servants could reach the best bedchambers at the south end of the house without having to pass through the hall chamber or to use the superior stairs.

The layout of Hall Court prompts comparison with Hacking Hall, north of Burnley in Lancashire (pls 243, 244), a house of almost the same date whose plan is also preserved unusually well. Hacking Hall is a dour, stone building, quite different from Hall Court externally but functionally identical, and their resemblance suggests that their builders had a common view of what they required in the amenities of their houses. The house's origins are a little uncertain. It is supposed to have been built, probably in 1607, for the son of a leading circuit judge, Sir Thomas Walmesley, who was close to the end of his career and who himself lived in a larger house, Dunkenhalgh, a few miles away. However, the initials that appear on the chimneystack are not those of any identifiable member of his family and it is possible that Walmesley acquired it immediately thereafter. The similarity to Hall Court is particularly striking on the first floor. Just as at Hall Court, stairs at either end of Hacking Hall rose to lobbies which provide separate access to each of the rooms in the wings. From these lobbies, short passages give access to small chambers at either end of the central range, and then open into a chamber at the centre of the house. Hacking has on

245 Wroxton Abbey, Oxfordshire, 1617. Symmetry was slow to become universal, and in a building of the complexity of many gentry houses was not easy to achieve; but asymmetry is unusual as late as this in a house of Wroxton's size, and the desire to achieve it was one of many factors in prompting a reduction in the height of the hall.

the second floor a gallery; there is none at Hall Court, but the possibility that its roof has been rebuilt leaves room for doubt about the original arrangement. What the similarities between these houses suggest (and the point could be made from a comparison of very many others) is that they are built to a local interpretation of a standard plan. The size of each house precludes a grand staircase in either, and though the low-end stair at Hacking has disappeared, it seems likely that at neither house was there a very great difference in size between the secondary stair and the principal one.

In spite of the survival of letters and accounts, the precise way in which these houses were conceived can only be surmised. There is no reason to suppose that the builders knew each other; though both were lawyers, they were separated by half of England and by half a generation in age. Nor probably was there one common source for the plans of these houses: in the details

of their arrangement they are not the same, even though the circulation and the relationships of rooms are identical. Many other contemporary houses resemble each other equally closely. What these houses demonstrate is that a common culture at the level of the gentry transcended the restraints of local craft traditions, that even where they were unconcerned with architectural detail owners probably specified the accommodation they required, and that for very many builders the model was in a sense Platonic rather than actual: the ideal house comprised the satisfaction of clearly perceived requirements of convenience and propriety while the details of its outward appearance as well as those of the plan could be left to the craftsman.

Among the higher gentry it is difficult after the second decade of the seventeenth century to find a house with asymmetrical elements to its façade. One of the last such is Wroxton Abbey in Oxfordshire (pl. 245), built in 1617 for Sir Thomas Pope. It has similarities to Chastleton in the advancing and receding planes of the façade and in having a tall hall lit by tall windows. With a longer frontage, it has a central porch (rather than the disguised entrance that Chastleton adopted in order to achieve symmetry) and a service-passage plan. But the hall windows which thus lie to one side of the porch are not matched by those which light the lower service room in the other half

of the central range. The same tensions between superficial symmetry and functional differentiation can be illustrated from widely different areas. Kirstead Hall in Norfolk,[48] Doughton Manor in Gloucestershire[49] and the Rectory at Guiseley in West Yorkshire,[50] though from regions with very different craft traditions, illustrate the spread of a common formula. The Rectory, dated 1601, is of the high-quality local limestone (pl. 247). Kirstead, built for a lawyer, William Roberts, and dated 1614, is of brick with a diamond pattern of burnt headers, and with the shallow pediments to its windows that characterise numerous contemporary East Anglian gentry houses (pl. 246). Doughton, built for a clothier of Tetbury probably of the 1620s, is of rubble covered with a lime render to disguise the poor quality of the masonry (pls 248, 249). Despite the differences of their materials, the layouts of Doughton and Kirstead are very similar, essentially half-H with service-passage plans and with two-storey central porches. The plan of Guiseley incorporates a number of local elements that set it apart from the other two houses, but all three combine a superficial symmetry with traces of hierarchical distinctions. At Guiseley and at Kirstead the high end of the house is marked by slightly larger windows. At Doughton parlour and parlour chamber are marked by a projecting bay window. Also at Doughton the mason seems to have had difficulties with chimneystacks in attempting to incorporate them within the body of the house, perhaps in order to avoid irregularities caused by their projection: the parlour stack is embodied in a gable on the principal elevation, the hall stack into a gablet on the back of the house, but in neither case does this achieve genuine symmetry.

The spread of innovative practices within the context of existing building traditions shows most clearly in the gradual adoption, in houses of relatively modest size, of the centrally entered hall. Its earliest occurrence has already been discussed, as has the fact that it was irreconcilable with the hall's traditional functions. The spread of the form after its first appearance in London and the home counties has yet to be traced, but by the 1660s it can be found adopted widely in smaller gentry houses, where any functional drawbacks were presumably outweighed by the architectural benefits of permitting a symmetrical façade. The plans of Stalham Old Hall in Norfolk (c. 1660; pls 250, 251) and of Forton in Staffordshire (1665; pls 252, 253) are of a form which in the next century would be ubiquitous (pls 254, 255), in which a house would have a central entry to the hall and a stair immediately to its rear. Their plans are neither true double piles nor have they the stair set between wings as with houses of the

247 The Rectory, Guiseley, West Yorkshire, 1601. In Yorkshire, symmetry (or even near-symmetry) is unusual at this date for a house of this size, but may be explained by the social difference between a rectory and the similar-sized houses of local clothiers which preserve hierarchical exteriors longer than elsewhere in the country (cf. pl. 224).

248 Doughton Manor, Gloucestershire, 1620s. A Cotswold clothier's house. Doughton's builder seems to have been at pains to promote regularity by the avoidance of chimney projections, but projecting window bays still distinguish the parlour and parlour chamber from the service end of the house.

250 Stalham Old Hall, Norfolk, c. 1660. The extravagant brickwork of London builders of the seventeenth century had regional parallels elsewhere, as builders seized upon its potential for decorative display.

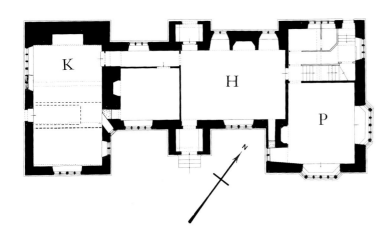

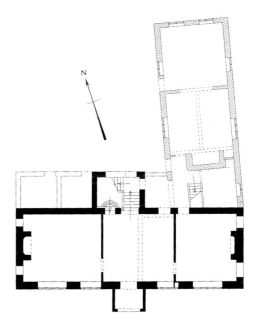

249 Doughton Manor: ground-floor plan. Doughton has a conventional, service-passage layout. That of Kirstead Hall (pl. 246) is similar.

251 Stalham Old Hall: ground-floor plan. The centrally entered hall was becoming widely adopted in houses of the lesser gentry in the second half of the seventeenth century.

252 Forton Hall, Staffordshire, 1665.

254 Crawford Manor, Lancashire, 1722.

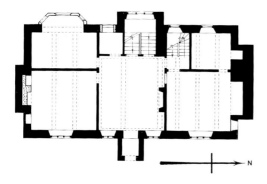

253 Forton Hall: ground-floor plan. At Forton the deep plan makes possible the provision of a shallow rear range: an element which could have been derived from the double-pile plan but which could equally have come about through the evolution of the house with rear-projecting wings, by the simple deepening of the centre. Such hybrid forms make tracing the sources and the evolution of the deep plan a matter of some complexity.

255 Crawford Manor: ground-floor plan. The plan is closely comparable with that of Stalham of sixty years before (pl. 251), and by the early eighteenth century was a form found throughout the country.

Bristol group, but the immediacy of access from front door to principal stair, achieved by centralising the stair at the back of the hall and close to the line of entry, is achieved here as in these other forms. At Eyam Hall in Derbyshire (1670–76; pls 256, 257) the stair is in a turret: a more traditional form than being incorporated in a half-pile but functionally identical, and the hall is entered at the centre in the modern manner.

In many existing houses, the entrance was moved to the centre from the traditional low-end location. Cote in Oxfordshire was partially remodelled late in the sixteenth century and again around 1700, when the present front door was created; however, the house retained a dais until the twentieth century.[51] Horton in Staffordshire, rebuilt in 1668, contains evidence of earlier work which includes traces of a low-end entry. So also does Braithwaite Hall in North Yorkshire (pls 259, 260), remodelled in 1667 as a modern, double-pile house with a gabled front in the regional style; Braithwaite still has its dais in place. Mere in Worcestershire (pl. 258) retains the porch of the original entrance, thus (one might have thought) negating the aesthetic advantage of moving it to the centre of the façade. Here, presumably, the internal advantage of the centrally entered hall was a more important consideration than the outward appearance

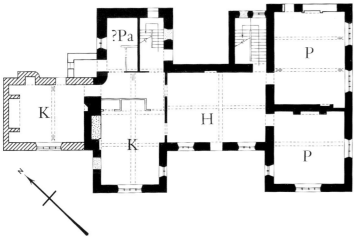

256   Eyam Hall, Derbyshire, 1670–76.

257   Eyam Hall: ground-floor plan. The centrally entered hall would spread rapidly after *c.* 1600, but Eyam is in a relatively remote part of the country, and despite having a hall of modern form the stair is a high-end turret in an old-fashioned manner.

259 (*left*)   Braithwaite Hall, East Witton, North Yorkshire. Braithwaite was reconstructed in 1667 as an up-to-date, double-pile house with central entry to the hall and regular, symmetrical façade.

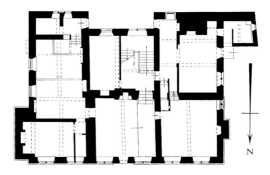

260   Braithwaite Hall: ground-floor plan. The irregularities of Braithwaite Hall's plan reflect the complex history of the house before its modernisation in the late seventeenth century. The hall dais survives, as does evidence of the original front door at the low end of the hall.

Mere Hall, Worcestershire. At Mere the hall entry was moved to the centre in the late seventeenth century, though the old porch was retained. Presumably the change was thought to be to the advantage of the plan rather than of the appearance of the house.

of the house. Among larger houses, Loseley acquired a central entrance early in the eighteenth century (pl. 296; subsequently moved back again), as did Raynham (though replacing the awkwardness of two identical entrances, discussed in chapter 3).

The houses of the gentry before the Civil War thus comprised a large number of houses of traditional forms, some of which had assimilated certain more up-to-date features, together with a smaller number of houses with advanced plans, widely scattered throughout the country. Some of these were two or more ranges deep, and in a number of them the location of the principal stair and the arrangement of the hall made for a radical departure from traditional circulation. In addition to these was an even smaller number of houses, still mainly confined to the home counties, which displayed significant innovations of architectural form and detail. The source of innovation both in the architecture and in the plans of these houses was in large part metropolitan, giving the compact model a national influence that local innovation could not achieve. But as such houses grew in numbers in the provinces, their power to influence provincial architectural developments steadily increased.

Consolidation and Diffusion

How the Civil War affected the development of the country house cannot be known.[52] Existing houses suffered more or less damage. Rarely, they were systematically demolished during or after a siege. They might be destroyed in pique, burnt by departing garrisons, ransacked by the enemy or ill treated by billeted troops. But besides the actual destruction caused by both sides during the fighting, properties were commonly harmed, more or less seriously, by high taxation, by fines, sequestration and loss of rents sometimes extending over years, by looting and by destruction of crops and woodland, and by arrears of maintenance. The war might leave a house's owner either unwilling or unable to arrest the processes of decay, as at Kimberley in Norfolk described in 1659:

> First fell Queen Elizabeth's brave lodging roome,
> Then the fayre statelye Hall to ruine came:
> Next falls ye vast great chamber archt on high
> With golden pendents fretted sumptuously;
> Yet of four parts, three still remayned ye seatt
> Unto that heyre who first was Baronett
> And to his son. Till ye Long Parliament
> Nobles and gentry sunk to discontent;
> In which sadd humour he lets all ye rest

> Of this fayre fabrique sink into its dust.
> Down falls ye Chappell: Last, ye goodly Towre,
> Though of materialls so firm and stowre
> Time scarce uncements ym.[53]

Probably many owners felt similarly demoralised.

While building never ceased altogether save during the actual years of fighting in the mid-1640s, financial losses and political uncertainties made for a climate in which most people felt disinclined to invest in an unpredictable future. There were exceptions: in the 1650s building in Hertfordshire seems actually to have increased,[54] but very generally the story is of unfinished schemes, houses neglected, damaged or worse, and of owners deferring the normal cycle of maintenance or rebuilding until times were more settled or fortunes restored. Hutton in the Forest has a grand, arcaded lodging range down one side of the forecourt, with Gothic piers that were probably adopted to conform to the existing work; the matching side was never executed and when eventually its owner came once again to build, he chose to replace the centre of the house (the former hall range) rather than completing the great project of a generation before (pl. 279). It has been seen how Ince (pl. 157) and Weston upon Trent (pl. 261) may have been left unfinished, the reason for their present strange appearance. Godolphin has a

261 Weston Hall, Weston on Trent, Derbyshire. Weston Hall was to have had a through hall like that of Hardwick. Only one wing survives, however, the Civil War having prevented its Catholic owners from completing it.

262 Godolphin, Cornwall. A double-sided loggia was added in the 1630s to the front wall of a Tudor house, supporting a new range of lodging chambers and intended as part of a larger programme of rebuilding which seems to have been abandoned at the outbreak of the Civil War.

grand entrance range with a double loggia built in the 1630s (pl. 262). Two piers of the loggia were erected (and still remain) within the late medieval house, anticipating its demolition to complete a larger scheme; twenty years later, when Sir Francis Godolphin might have had the opportunity to finish it, both his priorities and his taste may have changed. Coleshill was essentially complete by 1652, but the difficulties faced by Sir George Pratt – caused by gambling and by an accusation that his estate was crown land and thus liable for forfeiture – meant that he was unable to complete the house until after the Restoration (thus probably occasioning a dispute about the authorship of the house, as between Jones and Roger Pratt, which has bedevilled architectural historians ever since).

One effect of the war was to accelerate the breakdown of localisms in subjecting everyone to a national conflict over national issues; arguably, such a breakdown might not have occurred so soon or so violently had not London for a generation already provided a national forum for the formulation of national attitudes. Much of the architectural character of the last decades of the century was similarly prefigured before the war, and while some houses of 1640–65 perpetuate elements that are strongly conservative, others deploy with growing conviction the innovations of plan and style that in the previous decades had been largely confined to the London region. The period can be seen both as one of stagnation and of consolidation, in which a national architecture was emerging even though the Civil War may have slowed its appearance.

Few of the late king's supporters were in a position to build in the 1650s; some were in exile and many more had lost substantial amounts of money through fines, through supporting the losing side or simply through the turmoil that had left rents uncollected and estates neglected. But although the most advanced architecture of the 1630s can be associated with Inigo Jones or with builders or architects connected in one way or another with the Royal Works, there is no simple correlation between taste and politics, between architectural connoisseurship and war-time loyalties. Even the victors – those who had done well out of the war – built little.[55] Some of those who did built in the style of the London craftsman: Oliver St John at Thorpe; Edmund Prideaux, Attorney-General, at Forde Abbey; Sir Walter Erle, general of the parliamentary forces, at Charborough; John Thurloe, Secretary of State, at Wisbech; Sir Arthur Haselrig at Bishop Auckland. But John Lisle, builder of Moyles Court in Hampshire, a house of striking plainness that recalled the style of the Royal Works, was one of those who had signed Charles I's death warrant. John Webb, Jones's nephew and pupil, built in the 1650s for Sir John Maynard, one of the Commonwealth law officers, and for Edmund Ludlow, one of Cromwell's Lieutenants General, while Edward Carter, Jones's deputy on the restoration of St Paul's in the 1630s, was appointed by parliament to succeed him as Surveyor-General.

263 (*above*) Anon. (*c.* 1780): Cold Overton Hall, Leicestershire, *c.* 1640. The original, unorthodox central pediment in this view was replaced in the nineteenth century by a more conventional one, but the shallow central projection foreshadowed the pedimented centrepiece characteristic of many post-Restoration houses (cf. Eltham Lodge, pl. 283).

264 Cold Overton: ground-floor plan. The hall is entered at its centre, and advantage is taken of deepening the central range to provide service passages on both floors in order to bypass it and the dining chamber above it.

Four houses may be taken as typifying the stylistic diversity of the houses of the period; doubts about the dates of two of these that cannot be established from external sources are the result of the uncertain assimilation of a variety of styles. What they have in common is the adoption of the new, compact silhouette and deep plan. They differ in the details of their plans and in their architecture, reinforcing the impression that the general principles of the modern house were more readily understood and adopted than innovative detail. These four are Cold Overton Hall in Leicestershire, Norgrove in Worcestershire, Cheney Court outside Box in Wiltshire, and Thorpe Hall outside Peterborough in Cambridgeshire. The date of Cold Overton Hall (pls 263, 264) is not known, though is probably around 1640. It has unusual fireplaces, of markedly continental character, with a corbelled-out shelf carried on Tuscan columns.[56] Externally it appears more up-to-date now than it did originally. The central bays of the façade are now crowned by a plain pediment; when built, this pediment was of a curious mannerist form perhaps closer to those of Broome Park than to any other surviving examples. Nevertheless, the deep, plain plattband and the shallow, astylar central projection are reminiscent of Jones's second design for the Prince's Lodging at Newmarket, and it is not impossible that Newmarket suggested the design of Cold Overton just as it had inspired Sir Roger Townshend at Raynham. Inside, the hall is placed centrally with a central entrance. The stair leads off the upper end of the hall in the traditional way, but although the plan is not a true double pile there is on both floors a passage to its rear which provides efficient communication between its ends while preserving the exclusivity of the hall on the ground floor and of the dining chamber on the first. Its unknown

227

265 Norgrove, near Redditch, Worcestershire, 1649. Fashionable architectural elements – hipped roof, eaves cornice and roof lantern – are carried out with a certain lack of assurance that suggests their execution by provincial craftsmen.

date and its stylistic individuality make Cold Overton difficult to assess, but in its combination of the modern with the traditional the house is typical of provincial developments of the mid-century.

Norgrove, near Redditch in Worcestershire (pls 265, 266), bears a date of 1649, the year of the king's execution and a rare date for building. Externally, the house incorporates a number of fashionable elements. It is of brick, with stone dressings, in an area traditionally of timber and stone. It has a hipped roof, a cupola, deep eaves carried on brackets and (originally) small balconies of urban origin projecting above the doors. Of these there were two – a curious compromise mentioned in chapter 3 whereby symmetry could be attained without loss of the end-entered hall. Internally the house had a double-pile plan with services at the rear; a part of the rear range is raised up over a basement. At the same time the whole building has a provincial

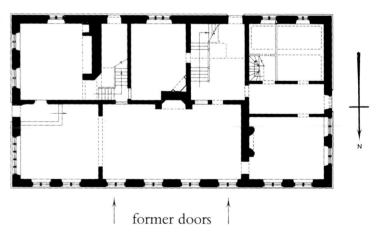

former doors

266 Norgrove: ground-floor plan. The house originally had matching front entrances, at either end of the hall (cf. Aldermaston, pl. 191). On the first floor, deep windows out of the great chamber opened on to balconies over these doors. The cupola was an up-to-date feature whose popularity would persist into the early eighteenth century.

267 Cheney Court, near Box, Wiltshire, c. 1650. Perhaps the work of a provincial builder experimenting in an unfamiliar manner. The extraordinary, staggered window levels correspond in part to stair arrangements within, but not wholly so: in some areas of the house they are purely for symmetry's sake. In their arrangement they recall the stair windows of Wick Court (pl. 216), a few miles away.

air, with odd solecisms in the design (such as the highly irregular placing of doors and windows in the rear elevation) and a number of awkwardnesses in the circulation. At Norgrove one feels the presence of a craftsman who had first-hand knowledge of metropolitan practices but was distinctly ill at ease in giving effect to them himself.

Cheney Court, a house of double-pile plan near Box in northern Wiltshire (pl. 267), is comparable with Norgrove in its combination of up-to-date elements and provincial execution. It is at the same time a house in which the underlying restlessness of the mid-century style is still more pronounced. Much is uncertain about it. Its builder was a member of the Speke family, established in the vicinity since at least the previous century. The decoration of its chimneypieces suggests that it may have

been built as late as 1660, although the principal stair – if this is original and has not been introduced from elsewhere – argues for a date no later than 1640. On the front elevation the high-end stair is lit by staggered windows which are certainly original to the house even if the staircase itself is not, and which necessitated a matching set of windows at the low end to maintain the symmetry of the façade. This play with window levels might be seen as some memory of the way in which windows were similarly joggled in some earlier houses like Chastleton or Dorfold, here applied wholly inappropriately to a façade of superficially more classical form. As if this window arrangement was not sufficiently bizarre, the low-end stair seems not to have taken advantage of the second set of joggled windows but to have risen elsewhere in the building: consequently, some of the rooms in this part of the house are lit by windows at levels which must always have been extremely inconvenient.

These stair windows seem very similar in detail to those of Wick Court (pl. 216), a few miles away, and one can assume the responsibility of a local craftsman. But even if local practice dictated the lighting of the stair by staggered windows, the extraordinary appearance of the front of Cheney Court could easily have been obviated by the placing of the stair at the rear of the

229

268 Thorpe Hall, near Peterborough, Cambridgeshire, 1654. Built for a Commonwealth statesman, Oliver St John, by the London mason Peter Mills.

hall in what was already the normal position in the double-pile house. If Norgrove is a local builder's *tour de force*, Cheney Court is almost more of a *jeu d'esprit*: incorporating local practices in a house of a form that was relatively strange to the area and in a way which can ultimately be explained only by individual tastes, knowledge and ignorance.

The largest Commonwealth house that still stands was Thorpe Hall, near Peterborough in Cambridgeshire (pls 268, 269), built for the Chief Justice Oliver St John by Peter Mills, a London bricklayer who had developed into a successful architect-contractor.[57] Externally, Thorpe is a refined, stone version of the style of the City of London: overall a house of simple form, but still with shaped gables, bay projections to windows and a restless alternation of window surrounds. In plan the house is a triple pile, three ranges deep with the stair the central range, a larger and more substantial version of the form encountered earlier and on a smaller scale at Hinton in Berkshire. The house still has a hall entered at its low end, and the principal stair still rises from its upper end. On the first floor, a suite of state apartments runs along the front of the building, while to the rear there is a bedchamber in each corner, entered – it would seem – rather unusually through a smaller room that doubled both as ante-room and closet. Compared with Coleshill, Thorpe is old-fashioned, but (as has often been pointed out) perhaps the supreme example of the taste of the City élite.

Thorpe would have an important influence regionally. Its immediate offspring was Wisbech Castle (pl. 2), also designed by Mills thanks to the friendship between its builder and Oliver St John. Lyndon (pl. 33), a four-square, compact house of 1672–7, almost certainly owes its overall form to the example of Thorpe, as does Thorney Abbey in Cambridgeshire, built by the local mason John Lovin on an outlying estate of the Dukes of Bedford which was then actively in course of improvement. In details, too, Thorpe illustrates how innovations might be spread. When John Webb was building Lamport Hall in the 1650s for Sir Justinian Isham and his contractor Sargenson raised a practical question as to how to deal with the water from the cupola on the roof, it was to Thorpe that Webb referred him.[58]

But the influence of Thorpe was also felt much further afield. In the breakdown of regionalism and in spreading innovations, both clients and craftsmen were involved, and the interaction of the two was critical. The process of innovation in the late seventeenth century can be illustrated from the north-west of England. In much of England the density of cultural and economic links generally makes the identification of individual influences at best speculative. However, the isolation of Cumbria (the former counties of Cumberland and Westmorland) from the rest of England makes the strands of influence a little easier to identify, though questions of attribution and responsibility that remain show how difficult it is to disentangle them even where buildings are few and where affinities between them seem demonstrable. The picture that emerges illustrates the themes that have already appeared: of the occasional patron whose orbit was at the highest social level and whose architectural ambitions transcended localism, of lesser builders and craftsmen with ideas

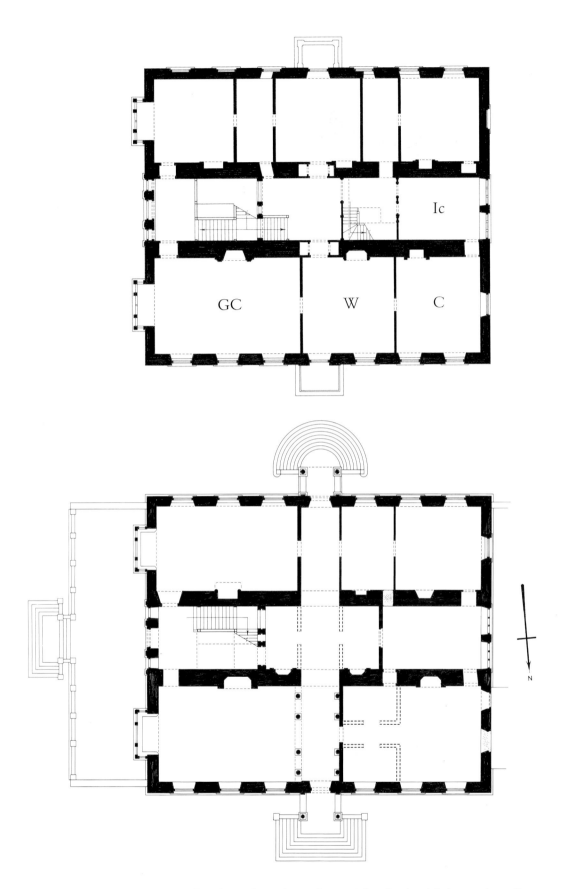

269 Thorpe Hall: ground- and first-floor plans. Thorpe has a triple-pile plan (cf. the much smaller Hinton House, pl. 143) with the central range largely used – as is normal in such houses – for circulation. The hall of Thorpe is still arranged in the old-fashioned way, with entry through a screen and with the principal stair reached off the hall's high end. On the first floor there is a standard, state-room sequence along the front of the house.

270 Halnaby Hall, North Yorkshire, *c.* 1660 (demolished 1958). The deep, rectangular plan of Halnaby may have been inspired by a house built by Sir Arthur Haselrig at Bishop Auckland, which was said to have been derived from Thorpe. The distinctive window pediments of Halnaby recur elsewhere in the north.

carried out by Rainbow's predecessor at Rose Castle in Cumberland. The economic prosperity of the Tyne and the Tees had in the previous half-century been reflected in a quantity of new building, and Rainbow's consulting Trollope may have been because of a lack of local craftsmen of comparable skill or repute, or because such as there were already implicated in the defective work. Over the next twenty-five years a number of moderately up-to-date houses were built in Cumberland and Westmorland whose origin may similarly have lain further east.

In 1649 Sir Arthur Haselrig, a radical both during the Civil War and under the Commonwealth, bought the castle of Bishop Auckland, a palace of the Bishops of Durham. According to a contemporary account,

> designing to make Auckland his principal seat, not liking the old fashioned buildings of the Castle, [Haselrig] resolved therefore on a new structure of a most noble and beautiful fashion, all of one pile, according to the most elegant mode of those times, taking for his pattern that curious and stately building at Thorpe, near Peterborough, which Oliver St John . . . newly erected.[61]

Haselrig's own origins were in the south-east Midlands: he was MP for Leicestershire, and his estates were within 30 miles of Thorpe, at Noseley. Appointed Governor of Newcastle on Tyne in 1649, he proceeded to build up property and influence in the north-east and his new house was no doubt intended as the seat of his territorial empire.

Restored to his see in 1660, Bishop Cosin had the new house pulled down and its form is not known; if Dugdale's description is to be taken literally (rather than simply meaning a rectangular block without wings) then it cannot have resembled Thorpe in plan since Thorpe is a deep triple pile. In the absence of more detailed information about Haselrig's house its impact is hard to assess, but it may have influenced a group of houses a short distance to the south. The largest of these was Halnaby Hall (pl. 270), demolished in 1958.[62] Halnaby was built on a double-pile plan, possibly before 1660, for a prominent alderman of Durham, Sir Mark Milbanke. Its original internal details were all destroyed in the eighteenth century save for a single fireplace surround. Halnaby was of brick with stone dressings, but these dressings together with the surviving fireplace included detail that was to be characteristic of a number of houses in the north and north-west between 1660 and 1690. Most notable are window heads with a pulvinated frieze and with curious pediments, straight and segmental, that are set in from the ends of the cornices from which they spring. The double-pile plan may

nevertheless obtained elsewhere, of other owners prepared to entrust their building to architects of more or less competence and knowledge, of the continuing strength of local styles, idioms and personal connections, and of craftsmen, far from the fountainheads of innovation, whose ability was fully equal to the demands of clients with no architectural knowledge but less than adequate to satisfy those with higher ambitions.

Cumberland, wrote Fuller in 1662, 'pretendeth not to the mode of Reformed Architecture'.[59] But there is evidence from around 1600 of competent craftsmen from Newcastle working in Westmorland,[60] and Gaythorne Hall (pl. 166), south-east of Penrith and the earliest house in the county of a sophisticated architectural form, has already been described as modelled on Gainford Hall (pl. 165) in County Durham. In turn, Gainford's plan had London origins, but Gaythorne stands far up on the moors and had no local influence. There is further evidence in 1671 that the hills dividing the north-east and north-west of England were not an insuperable obstacle to the movement of craftsmen, when Bishop Rainbow of Carlisle asked Robert Trollope of Newcastle to assess damages caused by failure of work

271 Moulton Hall, North Yorkshire, *c.* 1660. The distinctive gables and the overall rustication are unlike any other building in the region, and may derive from Haselrig's house.

272 Moulton Manor, North Yorkshire, *c.* 1660. Moulton Hall and Moulton Manor are close to each other and were built for two brothers. The manor is much cruder architecturally than the hall and more likely to be the work of local craftsmen, but incorporates the pedimented window heads that appeared at Halnaby.

derive from Bishop Auckland, but necessarily not so: there was an existing model equally near to hand at Kiplin of 1625 and in any case the form would by 1660 have been well known to the builder of such a house as Halnaby.

Two adjacent houses some 15 miles south may be further expressions of Bishop Auckland's influence. These are Moulton Manor and Moulton Hall, built for two brothers, George and Thomas Smithson,[63] probably in the 1650s or early 1660s. They are of similar size and status, but unlike in the quality of their detail. Moulton Hall has alternating, raised and recessed ashlar bands (pl. 271). Gables sweep upwards to be capped by pediments, a detail that ultimately derives from London but which is directly comparable with that of a garden house at Thorpe. Windows have pedimented heads of orthodox form. The plan is a double pile. There is no house like it in the region, and if Haselrig had recruited masons who were familiar with Thorpe, Moulton Hall is precisely what one might have expected from them.

Moulton Manor, however, is a different matter (pl. 272). Walls are of rubble, perhaps formerly rendered, and the illiterate classical detail includes windows with pedimented heads like those of Halnaby. The plan too is less sophisticated: a traditional hall with rear wings, though centrally entered and with a deepened central block to improve circulation. The two houses cannot be by the same masons, and Moulton Manor, the cruder of the two, is the more typical regionally. Thereafter these windows appear in a group of buildings in Cumbria with which the mason William Thackeray has been associated,[64] frequently in combination with unusual, deep and heavily incised voussoirs to door and window heads. These are Rose Castle, Drawdykes Castle and Ribton, to which one can add Moresby, the southern end of Acorn Bank and Branthwaite Hall at Dean. Although Trollope had been consulted in 1671 about the state of Rose Castle, William Thackeray was the master mason for the repairs, and Samuel Buck's print of 1736 which probably shows Thackeray's work shows the characteristic form of pedimented windows that occurred at Halnaby and at Moulton Manor.

Together with these curious window heads, another feature of some of these northern houses was a lavish use of rustication. Rustication had characterised much building of the court from Whitehall and the Queen's House onwards; John Webb's Lamport of 1655 (whence craftsmen had visited Thorpe to inspect the cupola) had a wholly rusticated façade, and it is clear from Bishop Cosin's instructions to his masons that Haselrig's house at Bishop Auckland was heavily rusticated. Their work was to include:

> Taking downe and laying safely and handsomely by the remaineing of all the rustick ashler worke, coyne stones, doors and windowes of Sir Arthur Haselrigg's building . . . [and] . . . sorting the same in convenient order.[65]

The overall rustication of Cosin's own rebuilding of the palace may be due to the re-use of much of this material (pl. 273).

273 The Chapel, Bishop Auckland, Co. Durham. At the Restoration, Sir Arthur Haselrig's house was demolished and the bishop's palace and chapel rebuilt, probably re-using rusticated masonry which is known to have characterised Haselrig's house. It may have initiated a local taste for such surface treatment which was carried by local craftsmen to the north-west.

His work at Bishop Auckland is a remarkable and self-conscious mixture of the Gothic and the modern – not unlike the similar architectural cocktails produced at Oxford, and perhaps for not dissimilar reasons[66] – and the rustication at Bishop Auckland is idiosyncratic and very prominent. Cosin clearly took a keen interest in what was to be done and sent drawings to his masons, citing 'this inclosed patterne which is taken from the best built plaine chappell in London. Let me hear from you how you like this.'[67]

What may also have recommended rustication to the bishop was Jones's employment of it in recasing Old St Paul's Cathedral. However, above plinth level that at Bishop Auckland is a

274 Moresby Hall, Whitehaven, Cumbria, *c.* 1670. By the local architect-craftsman William Thackeray, the house incorporates detail which may have had its origin among buildings influenced by Bishop Auckland and with craftsmen employed there after 1660.

peculiar chequer of raised and flush blocks. It seems unlikely that this was Cosin's invention and it has no resemblance to Jones's, but thereafter rustication (albeit generally less strange) was to recur on a number of houses in the north and north-west.

The most notable early classical house of the north-west is Moresby (pls 274, 275), built around 1670 for a leading local landowner, William Fletcher, overlooking a small harbour that he was trying to develop as a rival to the Lowthers' enterprise of Whitehaven 3 miles down the coast.[68] Fletcher's work comprised not a wholly new house but a new polite range: an entrance hall, staircase and flanking parlours with chambers above them, added on to an earlier house whose remains form three sides of

the service courtyard behind. Moresby can be attributed to William Thackeray through its extremely close resemblance to Ribton, where his involvement is attested by documents.[69] Ribton was demolished in 1929 and not all of its details are clear from old photographs,[70] but externally it seems to have been virtually identical. The rustication of Moresby differs from that of Bishop Auckland, but is almost as unconventional: alternating bands of short and long blocks are laid like headers and stretchers in the equivalent of English brick bond. Ribton, also rusticated, had the characteristic window pediments, set in from the ends of the cornice, of Branthwaite, Halnaby and Moulton Manor. Moresby's windows have true pediments to the first floor, but otherwise share another characteristic with these early classical houses of the region: bolection surrounds with pulvinated friezes to the windows of the upper floor, and architrave surrounds to the ground.

There seems also to be a link with the other side of the Pennines in the detail of Moresby's front-door surround. The source

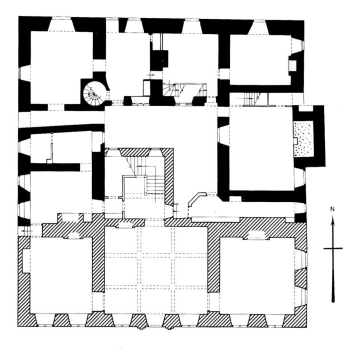

■ 16th century

▨ c.1670

275 Moresby Hall: ground-floor plan. Thackeray's work comprised the addition of a range of polite rooms fronting on to an older building which was retained in part to provide services.

of this is certainly Netherlandish, perhaps in Hendrik de Keyser's demolished Haarlem Gate of 1615–18 at Amsterdam[71] and plate XXVIII in his *Architectura moderna* of 1631 (pl. 276). Once again, Bishop Auckland may possibly be the link between them. The de Keyser family of master masons maintained close connections with England over three generations, beginning in 1607 when Hendrik visited London to inspect Sir Thomas Gresham's Royal Exchange and returned to Holland with Nicholas Stone.[72] In the 1660s his grandson, another Hendrik, was supervising work at Bishop Auckland for Bishop Cosin. Although it cannot be proved that he possessed his grandfather's designs nor that Thackeray worked with him, the coincidence might suggest it. Yet another link may be that in the west Thackeray's partner was a certain James Swingler; a Richard Swingler, joiner, worked at Bishop Auckland.[73] Moresby has other continental affinities: both the unusual double transoms to the windows (which also occurred at Ribton) and the deep, rusticated voussoirs which undoubtedly derive from continental sources such as Le Muet's *Maniere de bien bastir* of 1631.

These features also occur at Acorn Bank, a long, linear house of sixteenth-century origins to the south end of which new rooms were added probably in the 1670s (pl. 277). The gable end has yet another variety of rustication: continuous bands of ashlar with deeply grooved horizontal jointing, and the windows were originally double-transomed like those of Moresby and Ribton.

Thackeray is known to have undertaken work in 1677 at Newbiggin Hall, a mile away.[74] The Revd Thomas Machell wrote of Acorn Bank in the 1690s:

> That which is most to be noted here, is a curious and additional piece of building, of a parlour & drawing room, the outside of wch is of a red free stone, well wrought & polished ['smouthed' in margin] & plac'd (according to the Tuscan manner) wth excavations between every course.[75]

Thomas Machell, rector of Kirkby Thore, between Penrith and Appleby, himself claimed to have been instrumental in intro-

276 Hendrik de Keyser: *Architectura moderna*, 1631, pl. XXVIII. The front door surround of Moresby seems to derive from this Dutch example, and the windows of the house, with double transoms, are also of foreign origin. One of the de Keyser family worked at Bishop Auckland.

277 (*left*) Acorn Bank, Temple Sowerby, near Penrith, Cumbria. The gable end of a new parlour, added to Acorn Bank in the 1670s in Thackeray's characteristic style and almost certainly by him.

278 The Mansion House, Eamont Bridge, near Penrith, Cumbria, 1686. Probably by the local gentleman architect Thomas Machell. Machell, educated at Oxford (where he had seen new building by Wren), claimed responsibility for introducing 'regular architecture' into the region; his responsibility might have been disputed by Thackeray.

ducing a classical style into the north-west.[76] In his extensive manuscript collections for the history of Westmorland, he wrote of

> The most beautiful Art of Architecture wch (amongst many others) the present Rector [i.e. Machell himself] hath some knowledge of; He & one Addison (born in this towne & contemporary with him) being the first introducers of Regular building into these parts.[77]

Machell came of a gentry family that had been established at Crackenthorpe near Appleby since the fourteenth century, and when at The Queen's College in Oxford in the 1670s had watched the erection of Wren's new Williamson building and drawn both that and the Sheldonian. By then, as has been seen, there was already a handful of houses in the area which incorporated details and plans that were previously unknown in the region. Nevertheless his claim does have some substance for the area between Penrith and Kirkby Stephen, and as a gentleman

architect Machell is typical of his age. Returning to the north in 1679, he modernised his own rectory (into which he introduced a number of ingenuities of his own devising, such as a fireplace that needed cleaning out only once a year), rebuilt Howgill Castle for Sir Edward Stanford, Crackenthorpe Hall for his own brother and almost certainly designed a compact house of a very suburban form at Eamont Bridge near Penrith (pl. 278).[78] Crackenthorpe Hall had two matching cupolas on the roof, one to light the stair and the other disguising chimneys, but the house is otherwise very plain, very different not only from traditional building in the area but also from the mannerist façades of William Thackeray.

Three other houses need to be examined briefly in order to fill out the picture of local responses to what was still, in the north-west, a new architecture. Hutton in the Forest and Lowther Castle were both modernised in the 1680s in very similar ways. Both had formerly consisted of fortified towers at high and low ends, linked by a hall – a form typical of sixteenth-

279 Hutton in the Forest, Cumbria. The medieval hall between its flanking towers was rebuilt as a modern house around 1680. Probably the work of the mason William Addison, it incorporates some detail that is characteristic of Thackeray's work, notably the deeply splayed, rusticated voussoirs to the door head. These had become widespread regionally by the end of the century, and the exchange of details among craftsmen can make attributions difficult. The loggia to the right forms part of an earlier scheme of modernisation, abandoned at the Civil War.

century houses of the region and of which many remain. At both houses the hall range was fashionably rebuilt while the fortified towers were retained: their massive construction virtually forbade demolition, and at the basically similar Howgill Castle, which Machell had modernised, the walls of the tower ends are said to be upwards of 9 feet thick on the ground floor.[79] Lowther was burnt down and wholly replaced in the 1730s, and

Hutton in the Forest was greatly altered internally in the nineteenth century; the internal arrangements of neither is completely known, but in both cases the new central block, two rooms deep and three storeys tall, seems to have provided a centrally entered entrance hall with a good staircase and ranges of up-to-date accommodation above.

Responsibility for the two designs seems to reflect the relative standing of their owners. Sir George Fletcher of Hutton was related to William Fletcher of Moresby and to Christopher Dalston, heir to Acorn Bank. Hutton (pl. 279) is less mannered than Moresby and was apparently erected by Machell's protégé William Addison, but it has the characteristic window pediments and deep, rusticated voussoirs that Thackeray employed at Ribton: whoever was responsible for it, its affinities are essentially local. Sir John Lowther, however, was by that time among the greatest landowners of the region, his family long established, and in the course of the seventeenth century the Lowthers were

280 Stonegarthside Hall, Nicholforest, Cumbria, 1682. A mile from the Scottish border and built by Henry Forster, a man with strong Scottish connections, Stonegarthside is wholly Scottish in its architectural details. In the late seventeenth century regional influences were still important in the spread of new architectural styles.

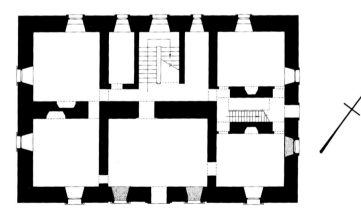

281 Stonegarthside Hall: ground-floor plan. Although of Scottish derivation, the general layout does not significantly differ from that of up-to-date contemporary houses in the south of England.

rapidly increasing their estates and their wealth by extensive purchases and sound management. Although executed by Addison, the design for Lowther Castle was probably supplied by William Talman, Comptroller of the Royal Works, who had a national country-house practice among the leading politicians of the day and regarded himself as a serious rival to Wren. But Sir John Lowther recorded that 'after I had directed Mr. Talman the King's Comptroller off his Works to draw me a design such as I thought convenient for me, I had the Correction and approbation off Sir Samuel Moreland'.[80] Moreland was a mathematician and experimental scientist with a particular interest in hydraulics, a man with much the same bent as the contemporary scientists-turned-architect, Wren and Hooke, and there is no other evidence for Moreland's interest in architecture apart from his possible authorship of a work on fortification (a traditional gentlemanly interest and the application of geometry). However, the association of architecture and mathematics, which had helped to make a knowledge of architecture acceptable in educated circles a century earlier, may still have operated in the mind of Lowther, who must have felt that Moreland's erudition made him a suitable man to advise about proposals advanced by professionals.

A third Cumbrian house, however, has a wholly different source. This is Stonegarthside Hall at Nicholforest (pls 280, 281), some 15 miles north-east of Carlisle and arguably the most remote country house in England.[81] It is only a mile from the Scottish border, and its affinities are with contemporary Scottish houses and not with any of those hitherto described. Despite its different genesis, Stonegarthside is no less a regional house than other houses of the region which can be related to each other. The house was built by Henry Forster, whose family had been prominent in the area at least since the previous century, and is dated 1682. Forster seems to have had a Scottish wife, and in that year was prosecuted for having his children baptised by 'a fannatical feild preacher in Scotland'.[82] Stonegarthside is built on a double-pile plan, but a number of features link it closely with Scottish houses: it has external details which include crow-stepped gables and decorated quoins like those to Heriot's Hospital in Edinburgh, the centre of the front range was originally flat roofed between flanking gables like Methven Castle of 1664 and Caroline Park, outside Edinburgh, of 1685, the stair position is identical with that of Methven, and the stair jambs have mouldings of a common Scottish form that occurs as late as 1697 at Melville House, Fife.[83] Although in England, Stonegarthside is thoroughly Scottish, confirming a continuing regionalism and the part played in the adoption of new architectural forms by the connections of the builders themselves.

Nevertheless, Stonegarthside incorporates elements of the most up-to-date building of a fashionable region, even if that region is Scottish rather than English. In four houses considered earlier – Cold Overton, Cheney Court, Norgrove and Thorpe – similarly fashionable features already occur, in a provincial context, that would be characteristic of houses of the late seventeenth century and of which some would determine the development of the country house through much of the eighteenth. These were partly matters of layout and partly matters affecting the house's overall appearance. In layout, they are the deep, rectangular plan of two or three 'piles', the centrally entered hall and in smaller houses, the central stair; externally, they are the eaves cornice, hipped roof and the central lantern. To these one can add in larger houses the increasing differentiation of staircases, the emergence of the vestibule as an alternative to the hall itself (developments traced in chapter 8), and

on the outside, the pedimented centre and the perpetuation of flanking wings.

The genesis of the hipped roof has been touched on above (pp. 170–72). The origin of the cupola is uncertain: it echoes the louvre of the medieval open hall (that at Gainsborough was reconstructed early in the seventeenth century) but a nearer antecedent is the roof turrets of Longleat, Burghley and other great houses of the previous century. Its appeal was both functional and aesthetic: providing a top light to a long, central attic corridor (as at Coleshill or Thorpe), access to the roof itself in order to admire the view (a taste coinciding with that for formal gardening, creating geometries best seen from above, and perhaps also to be associated with the taste for prospects that was most completely realised in the views of Kip and Knyff) as well as providing a satisfactory crown to the relative novelty of the hipped roof (as at Coleshill and Norgrove). On occasions it can be disproportionately large, as with that at Stedcombe in Devonshire, which is effectively a kind of glasshouse (from which there is a view of the distant sea), or at Oak Hall at West Bromwich – a grotesque provincial over-building of a fashion-

282 High Chimneys, Rowington, Warwickshire, *c.* 1680. An alternative to the roof lantern (cf. Coleshill, pls 197–9 and Norgrove, pls 265, 266): a roof platform. The four-square, centralised form of the house itself prompts comparison with larger, compact houses such as Lyndon (pl. 33).

able amenity. Where one was lacking originally it could be added, as at Oak Hall, Bruce Castle (pl. 127) and at Whitehall in Shrewsbury (pl. 142); or the effect of a cupola could be achieved by other means, as at the extraordinary High Chimneys at Rowington in Warwickshire, where chimneys (which frame the lantern at Stedcombe) simply flank a roof platform (pl. 282). Many houses that had cupolas originally have lost them: they were demanding on maintenance, and the changing taste of the eighteenth century diminished the appeal of the roof gallery as a place from which to admire the geometry of the planting around the house.

283   Eltham Lodge, Greenwich, London, 1665. Designed by Hugh May, one of a group of gentleman architects working in the late seventeenth century, the house is closely based on Dutch models. Eltham is among the earliest English houses in which a central frontispiece is surmounted by a true pediment – a form that would become extremely popular in gentry houses of every size. The plan is a triple pile similar to that of Thorpe, but with a centrally entered hall.

In its finished form the pedimented frontispiece is displayed at Hugh May's Eltham Lodge (pl. 283), a house whose Dutch origins have been widely recognised, the fruit of close architectural contacts between England and Holland since at least the 1620s. Relations were further strengthened by royalist expatriates living in the Netherlands during the Interregnum.[84] Evelyn was in Holland in 1641, Pratt in 1643–9, May in the 1650s, and between 1640 and 1649 there were 300 English students at the University of Leiden. For those who were aware of contemporary building in the town, it will have profoundly affected their view of architecture. Just as mannerist architecture in the Netherlands had been wilder than contemporary building in England (notwithstanding Holland House, an exceptional building in many ways) so the classical reaction in the 1620s and 1630s was also more radical and it will have appealed strongly to the growing English taste for restraint and regularity.[85] Houses with ranks of correctly detailed pilasters had been appearing in Holland from the 1620s, inspired by the same printed sources as such houses in England and probably also by Jones's Banqueting House. From the 1630s onward houses with hipped roofs

and pilastered fronts proliferated in The Hague, Leiden and Amsterdam, and the largest of these, together with public buildings, had central pediments as well. Eltham Lodge resembles Arent van 's Graavesende's Sebastiaansdoelen of 1635 at The Hague, which May would certainly have known, very closely indeed.

The pedimented façade was not without English precedents. As built, Wimpole (c. 1640) and Cold Overton (pl. 263) both had hipped roofs with central pediment-like devices of a fanciful kind; it has been seen that at Cold Overton this was combined with an astylar centre, breaking forward beyond the flanks of the façade. Princes Risborough Manor, probably of the 1630s, as built had a single, shaped gable placed against a hipped roof, a form that could easily be refined into a pediment. The form received a powerful boost with the temple front that Webb built in 1654–6 at The Vyne (pl. 284), and in his loggias to Amesbury and still more prominently at Gunnersbury on the edge of London. Webb's Palladian loggias were unnatural in the English climate – as unnatural as the great windows of Hardwick – and are without direct imitation. But the pilastered temple fronts of Eltham and of Welford (pl. 203) and the implied temple fronts of innumerable later seventeenth-century houses (Belton, Bourne Park, Clarendon House, Ramsbury and a host of others) are very much more 'natural' in that they observe architectural decorum and order, and conform to the requirements of the place.

It is similarly impossible to catalogue the variety of plan forms of the later seventeenth-century country house. The old-fashioned, linear plan left little room for varying the circulation of the house or the relationships of rooms, but one of the recommendations of the deep plan was the scope it provided for alternative layouts, individual preferences and individual ingenuity. But while the range of amenities required is discussed in chapter 8, some were common to every gentry house. Where a hall existed, it might still be used for polite entertainment, though in the largest house such a function would be performed by a saloon reached through an entrance hall or vestibule – an entrance passage – opposite. The other accommodation on the ground floor would comprise parlours – one as an absolute minimum (and a house with only one would scarcely be worthy of a gentry family), preferably two or more, of which one was for everyday use by the family and the other a more formal eating room, if possible with its own (with)drawing room. In a larger house there might also be a ground-floor apartment of bedchamber, dressing room (or closet) and servant's room, easily accessible from the parlour; in the largest houses there would be more than one such suite, as there would be a number of parlours. In such a house one such bedroom suite might be occupied by the house's owner, though more commonly he slept upstairs.

On the first floor there would be the principal dining room, perhaps still with a withdrawing room to it, and otherwise a range of chamber apartments. Children and servants would probably sleep in the garrets on the top floor, and if a new house was to be built with a gallery this was generally by now intended to serve as a spine corridor from which to reach these upper rooms. The principal stair would be placed prominently, at the rear of the entrance hall or else to one side of it, allowing easy and immediate access to the first-floor rooms. It was increasingly unusual for the principal stair to rise all the way to the top of the house; this would be reached only by service stairs, which were otherwise contrived to facilitate the servicing of bedrooms and also, as far as possible, to allow the principal stair to be used solely by the family and their guests.

Most large late seventeenth-century country houses combine the double-pile or triple-pile principle with the traditional model of central block and flanking wings, or else have long, plain façades. The house with a hall at the centre and wings at either end had an astonishingly long life. It had appeared in the fourteenth century, and endured long after the ends of the house had ceased to differentiate their internal functions. Such major late seventeenth-century houses as Clarendon House and Belton (both of them aristocratic houses, but the progenitors of numerous others for lesser men) combined modern, double-pile plans with wings at each end of their façades. Functionally these wings continue to perform as did those of E-plan houses of a century earlier: they provide additional accommodation without extending the façade to inordinate lengths. Aesthetically, wings articulate and terminate the elevation. Nor should one discount the likelihood of a view that was probably already an established convention: that the house with a central range and flanking wings constituted a normal and proper form of housing for members of the higher classes.

The house with wings and a double-pile central range first appeared in the 1630s – Swakeleys, if not the first, is a very early example; Yarnton in Oxfordshire (which has lost its wings) is another – and by the 1650s the form was well established. As noted in chapter 2, in the 1650s at Yotes the doubled central block consisted of no more than a block of additional rooms behind a traditional, service-passage range of hall and buttery (pl. 286), as at Swakeleys. Tyttenhanger in Hertfordshire (pl. 285) is close in size to Thorpe and almost exactly contemporary in date, but has a less sophisticated plan and short cross wings. The layout of Highnam in Gloucestershire was probably similar to that of Yotes. So, though larger, is Sudbury House in Derbyshire of 1665, and the same arrangement was created at Ham in 1673–5 by the building of a new range of rooms backing on to the old. The same service-passage arrangement appears in a slightly different form at Ollerton Hall in Nottinghamshire, probably of around 1675 (pls 287, 288). At Ollerton the hall is still entered

284 (*facing page*) The Vyne, Hampshire: the portico added in 1654–7 by John Webb, formerly deputy to Inigo Jones. Webb's porticos at The Vyne, Amesbury and Gunnersbury were the first pedimented, temple porches to appear on an English house, and the last – like Eltham, not far from London – must have given the form considerable prominence.

285 Tyttenhanger, Hertfordshire, c. 1655. The form of the house with a central range and cross wings was of medieval origin, but probably persisted partly because it had long formed part of the image of the ideal upper-class house. Furthermore, despite great changes in internal amenities, it remained a convenient means of separating out the functions of the house.

at the low end, and the principal stair is off its high end and at the rear. This part of the central block is only two rooms deep. A broad service passage, however, makes the lower end of the house more of a triple pile. These arrangements already appear in a plan among the Thorpe drawings,[86] in a contracted form at Boston Manor, and in a more sophisticated form in a sketch by Wren (pl. 317). The plan of Ollerton is unresolved, a provincial interpretation of fashionable forms. At the rear of the house there are two slightly projecting bays which it appears should contain stairs. Only one of them does so; the other does not and never did.

But at least equally representative of the houses of the gentry is the rectangular, hipped-roof house which by the end of the century is already ubiquitous. Out of about 250 drawings of

Yorkshire country houses made by Samuel Buck for the Yorkshire antiquary John Warburton in the 1720s, at least a third show buildings of this kind.[87] Pre-eminently a gentry form, the smaller of these rectangular houses were increasingly often built by members of a growing class whose claims to gentility rested on birth and on education but not necessarily on the possession of a substantial landed estate, the class that has been called the pseudo-gentry. The range of plan forms and size achieved in these compact, hipped-roof houses can be illustrated by four representative examples: Owletts at Cobham in Kent, the Rectory House at Stanton Harcourt in Oxfordshire, Melton Constable in Norfolk, and the demolished Tickencote Hall in Leicestershire. Owletts was built in 1684, to the simplest kind of double-pile plan, essentially with four rooms on each floor (pl. 289).[88] It was altered early in the eighteenth century by the building of closet projections at either end of the main front, but the plan remains substantially intact. Its layout is virtually identical with that of Pendell House, with that of one of Thorpe's simplest double-pile houses (pl. 139),[89] and with the plan drawn by John Webb of Inigo Jones's house for Sir Peter Killigrew (pl. 178). It is uncertain whether the existing entrance passage at Owletts was later partitioned off from a hall in one quadrant, or whether it

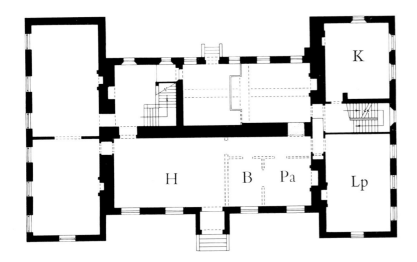

is original – in which case the two front rooms may always have served as parlours. The Rectory House at Stanton Harcourt is a little larger, with a deep, central entrance hall running through to a prominent stair and with two rooms on either side (pls 290, 291). None of the rooms on the first floor can be readily identified as a dining chamber; entertainment may have been confined to the ground floor. It was built in 1669 for Robert Huntingdon, who leased the estate of a little over 100 acres from All Souls' College in Oxford – probably an estate of a similar size to that of Bonham Hayes of Owletts.[91] The principal estate in the village was that of Sir Philip Harcourt, owner of the manor and of the large medieval manor house; Bonham Hayes's estate was also very much smaller than that of his aristocratic neighbour the Duke of Richmond and Lennox at Cobham Hall. The same kind of house suited both Hayes and Huntingdon, at a broadly similar social level in counties far apart.

Larger again than the Rectory House but embodying essentially the same elements was Tickencote Hall, built for the Wingfield family who had owned the manor since the late six-

teenth century (pls 292, 293). Tickencote has essentially six rooms to a floor, one of which was occupied by a staircase – a plan that goes back to Chevening of 1629 and before that to John Thorpe's plan of three London houses in line (discussed in chapter 4). Ince in Cornwall had embodied the form in 1640; Lower Slaughter in Gloucestershire (pl. 32) was built to a similar plan in the 1650s; Capheaton in Northumberland was clearly conceived in such a way in 1664.[91] Tickencote is a representative example of a plan type that by the time of its building was ubiquitous – the quintessential gentry house of the late seventeenth century and the early eighteenth.

By contrast, Melton Constable Hall, probably of 1665–70, shows the limitations of the deep plan, as well as being a further illustration of a builder's personal involvement (pls 294, 295). Melton is a large house, three ranges deep, in which the chapel and stairs are contained in the central range. Sir Jacob Astley, its builder, evidently devised the plan himself, having 'travelled with his bricklayer, whom he used also as surveyor, to most eminent houses in England, to take patterns, and observe the mode of

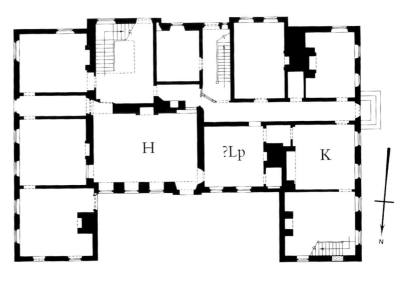

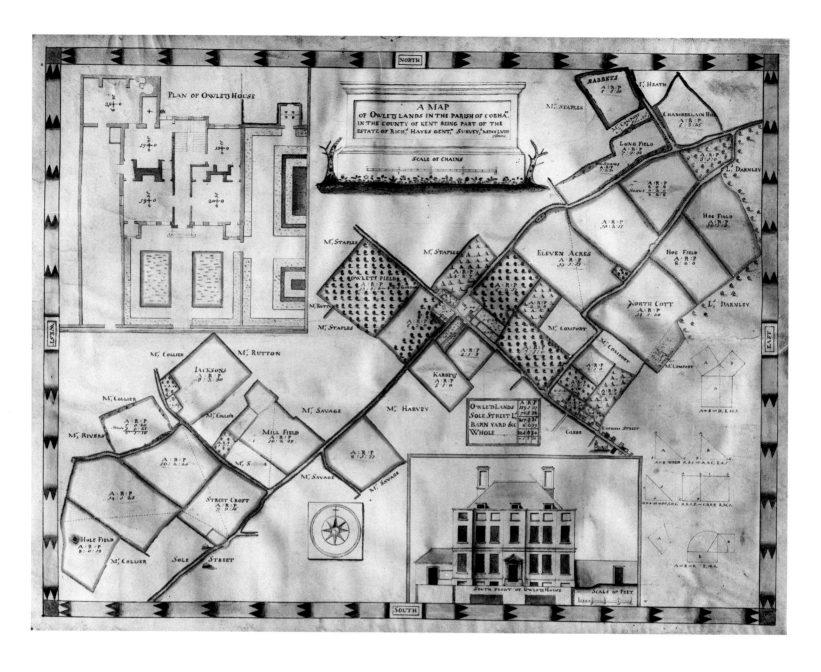

289 Anon. (eighteenth century), Owletts, Cobham, Kent, 1684: drawing of the house (plan at top left, elevation at bottom right) and map of its owner's lands. These were not extensive, but the form and size of the house were becoming ubiquitous for such modest gentry builders. The plan has a great similarity to plans by Thorpe (pl. 139) and after Jones (pl. 178) and it is from early seventeenth-century models such as these that such plans descended.

great houses'.[92] A model was made as a guide for the building of the house, and although some departures were made from it these were only slight. North condemned the result for its compact appearance, which he felt unsuited to a house which was to be the principal seat of a very large estate. He criticised too a number of details, some of which were particular to the house, some inherent in expanding the deep plan to such a size:

the low-ceilinged hall, the inconvenient arrangement of back stairs which partly impinged on the principal stair hall, the want of central light and the planning of the principal apartments on the first floor. The origin of the form is in earlier triple-pile houses such as Garsington and Hinton, developed through Wimpole and Thorpe. But if Melton is unsatisfactory in its overall form, it none the less shows what an informed amateur and his building craftsmen could do if left to themselves.

The relatively slow spread of the deep, rectangular plan form in the mid-seventeenth century can be put down both to the uncertainties of the times, to the slowing-down of the land market, to the saturation of the country with resident gentry, and to the fact that one result of the consequent building boom of 1580–1630 was that by then very many of these men's houses were still fairly new. But there were stronger reasons for its ultimate success. The form itself was coherent and neat, the

246

290 The Rectory House, Stanton Harcourt, Oxfordshire, 1669. Not in fact a rectory, but built for a minor landowner of similar status to the owner of Owletts and comparable with it in outline.

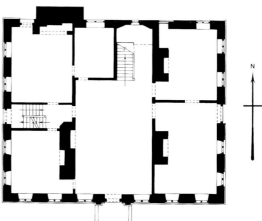

291 The Rectory House, Stanton Harcourt: ground-floor plan. The hall is quite large, but forms no more than an entry providing access to the stair and to the rooms on either side.

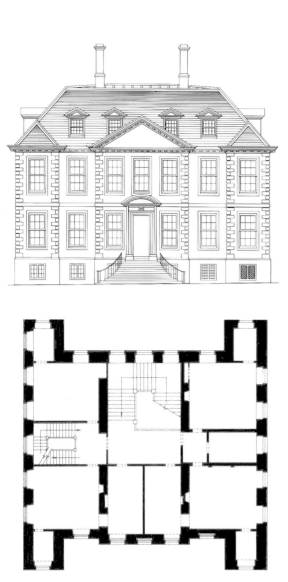

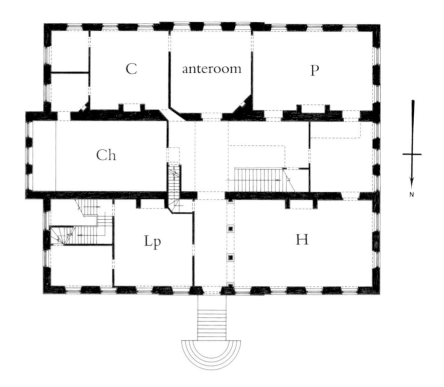

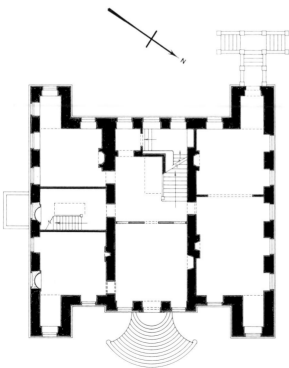

294 (*above right*)   Melton Constable Hall: ground-floor plan. The plan reproduced is taken from the builder's model and thus represents the original concept (though scaled to the dimensions of the executed house) in which there was to have been an old-fashioned hall and screen. It was slightly altered in execution, and there is now a solid partition forming a vestibule in place of the screen. The central room on the south side served both as a withdrawing room to the parlour and as an ante-room for the bedchamber to its east.

292 (*above left*)   Tickencote Hall, Leicestershire, 1702 (destroyed 1949). Tickencote was an enlargement of the type of Stanton Harcourt and Owletts, with a pedimented central bay.

293 (*left*)   Tickencote Hall: ground- and first-floor plans. The plan of Tickencote is a double pile, but like Chevening (pl. 177) it can equally be seen as being of three ranges side by side, an arrangement which illustrates another way in which the form can be conceived. It may similarly be compared with Forton (pl. 253). The kitchens were in the basement.

295 Melton Constable Hall, Norfolk, 1665–70: builder's model. By the end of the seventeenth century the use of a model was well established in building large or complex houses, as a means of visualising its final form and of helping all parties to the building process to agree on its layout. The model can be taken to pieces, floor by floor. Melton is the largest house of the compact, hipped-roof form, which was condemned by Roger North as 'suburbian' and unsuited for the main house of a major country estate.

apotheosis of 'regularity'. As Roger Pratt had recognised, it was economical to build and to live in. North acknowledged the origins of the form, condemning Melton Constable for being 'suburbian'. The metropolitan origins of the rectangular house, traced in previous chapters, were acknowledged at the time by other people besides North. John Evelyn called Hall Barn, built by the poet and politician Edmund Waller outside Beaconsfield,

'Mr Waller's City Box': it is a compact, square house, with pilasters of an artisan mannerist character.

But if the model was pushed to its limit at Melton, the smaller double-pile house was appropriate as the centre of a small or suburban estate, and the suburban landscape was itself appreciated. Even in the 1620s William Webb had commended the countryside around Wybunbury, 'on every side so garnished and adorned with the Seats and Habitations of Baronets, Knights, and Gentlemen, as scarce to be seen for the like in any Country Parish, so far remote from great and populous Cities'.[93] Workington Hall, a few miles from Moresby on the Cumbrian coast, was described in 1675 as 'A very fair Mansion House [with] woods and grass in the banks about: and brave corn fields and meadows below, as like as Chelsay fields'.[94] Such comments anticipate Defoe's (quoted at the end of chapter 4). At the end of the seventeenth century the ideal landscape was neat, productive and well peopled; for many people, their ideal house was something not unlike a villa.

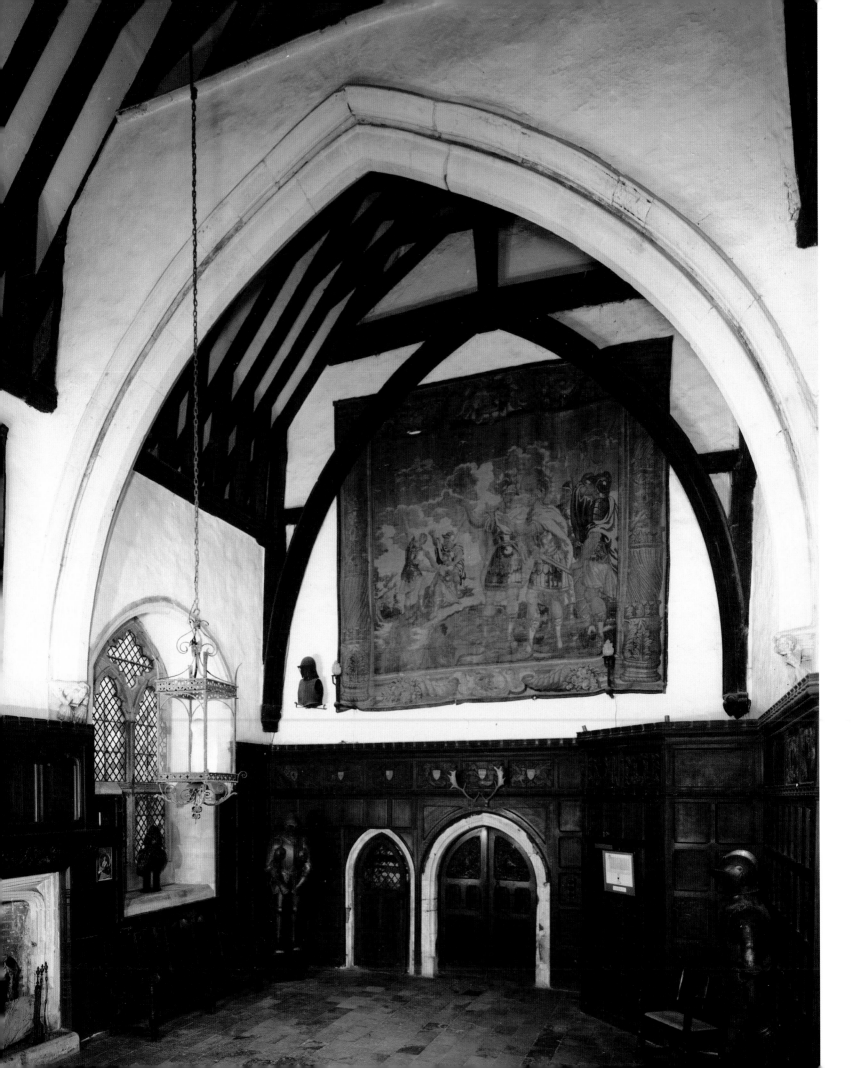

Part III

FUNCTIONS

7

Households and Hospitality

Households, Families and Relationships

For the gentry family the house was the focus of their lives in ways that were appropriate to each of its members. Relationships were central to the status of the gentry and to the fulfilment of their role in society, and it was with their maintenance that their houses were largely concerned. These relationships differed widely in their nature and over time. At home, the household contained blood relatives and servants, but the family might comprise no more than parents and children, or a more extended group of more than one generation and including siblings or cousins. The tendency over time was for the nuclear family to become more common, the extended family less so, but at no time was there a norm. Provision for members of an extended family might lead to structural alteration to the house or even to some substantial new building, but it need not do so; much depended on the individual family's style of living and on their personal relations. In time, an increasing polarisation of family and servants and a downgrading of personal service led to a reduction of communal areas which lies at the heart of the way in which the plan of the house was to develop, but once again the picture is not uniform: the conservatism of owners could lead to the persistence of familiar and symbolic arrangements that did not keep pace with the more general evolution of domestic relations, and some men kept up traditional housekeeping long after others had discarded old-fashioned modes of living.

Beyond the resident household, the relationships that the house had to accommodate were those with kindred and connections and with the local community of tenantry and poor. Kindred and connections required hospitality and housing, tenantry and poor called for entertainment or relief. In principle, all were received in a manner suitable to their position: relations and social equals treated or housed in chambers fitted for their reception, tenantry entertained in ways that observed proper social distinctions between the lord and his dependants, and the poor relieved at the gate or at the kitchen door. The accommodation within the house was largely devoted to the provision of hospitality at an appropriate level. But although individual families differed in the scale of their entertaining as much as in the composition of the resident household, it is remarkable how little houses themselves differed one from another in the type and extent of accommodation provided. In their own behaviour, individuals might deviate from the norm; in their houses, they sought to express their conformity to it.

When Robert Tatton of Wythenshawe in Cheshire died in 1579, he left a will that took account of a good many of the concerns of men of his time and class.[1] Primogeniture – inheritance of the ancestral estate by the eldest son – was normal among the gentry; it was also necessary to provide for widows, often desirable to provide too for other dependants and almost always a matter for concern to maintain the family's solidarity and to perpetuate the reputation for liberality and just dealing on which its standing depended. After providing endowments for his daughter and leaving all his real property to his son William, Robert Tatton went on to make an exception of

> my mansion howsse of Withinshaw &c. hereafter by me bequeathed to my seid wyeff for terme of her lieff onlye for asmoche as she hathe no convenient mansion house to kepe hospitalytie in but the manc'on manor housse of the Pele of Echells wch is not sufficientlye buyldid for her to dwell in and speciallye for asmoche as the same howsse is distant from her parishe churche two mylles she beinge not able to travell so farr in her olde yeres.

Having made provision for his tenants to remain in undisturbed possession of their holdings, he went on:

wheras Anne Mason my base sister hathe hitherto of my gifte a chamber wherin she now dwellethe at the psonage of Northerden wth a baye of housinge to laye her fuell and fyrewood in and also a lytle garden on the back syde of the same wthout rent painge therfore I desire my said sonn Willm to make to my seid sister the like graunt and my wyffe to fynde her as hetherto she and I have done duringe her leffe bothe wth meat drinke and clothe.

Northerden rectory (or parsonage), where his father's illegitimate daughter lived, was another of his houses; if his widow preferred to live there, he wrote, rather than at Withenshaw, his son William should let her. He concluded by leaving legacies to servants and by declaring what he had already done to set up his younger sons, and how for that reason he felt there was no need to do more for them. Acknowledgement of dependants and the provision of necessary accommodation for them, the temporary division of houses at need, recognition that a house should be fit for its occupant and for the exercise of his or her proper role in society – the considerations expressed in Robert Tatton's will, though more than usually wide-ranging and detailed, were wholly representative of the ways in which the social and family obligations of the gentry involved the proper use of their homes.

The commonest of all arrangements was probably that which made provision for the maintenance and lodging of a widow. Increasingly during the sixteenth and seventeenth centuries as family settlements became tighter, the wife's eventual position as a widow was anticipated on marriage, by her bringing with her a dowry which would be set off in part against the cost of providing her with a jointure – an annuity, and some further provision for income and residence if her husband should predecease her. On her own death, the jointure would revert to her husband's heirs. But the system of jointure was a specific legal contract between the parties to the marriage, and in its absence the widow enjoyed an entitlement under common law to a third of her husband's freehold. Thus – and especially before the general acceptance of strict settlement, which made formal provision at the time of marriage not only for a widow but for each child – many people were placed, as was Robert Tatton, with having to make formal arrangements for their widows by their wills; these arrangements frequently involved the setting aside of some part of the family house for her continuing occupation. At Squerries at Westerham in Kent in 1607 John Beresford left a substantial part of the house for his widow's use: the kitchen, five chambers, the little parlour, the buttery and the cellar beneath it and 'the new-built house for her poultry'.[2] The hall and great parlour were by implication excluded: the hall properly appertained to the owner of the house as a symbol of his position, and the principal parlour would be where he did much of his entertaining. On the other hand when John Reddish of Reddish in Lancashire died in 1569 and specified in detail how his house and its outbuildings were to be divided into three parts, he specified that his widow was to have two of

these three, including hall, parlours, chapel and most of the farm buildings.[3] His heir Alexander was to have the kitchen and other low-end rooms, the stable, hay-house and part of the turf-house. It is difficult to see how the house could have functioned with the main rooms in one occupation and the service rooms in another, but Alexander may already have been established elsewhere and this arrangement may simply have enabled him to keep an eye on his patrimony during his mother's lifetime. It is clear that in very many cases wills tell only a part of the story, and their terms need to be interpreted in the light of arrangements and relationships that are often speculative.

For a widow to occupy a house without trouble might necessitate further stipulations: thus Sir Richard Sackville of Buckhurst in 1556 required that 'she should have free goinge to the Chapell Closet throughe the Gallarie duringe her liffe'.[4] Such provision is more often left vague, as in Sir Francis Godolphin of Godolphin's will in 1665 that 'his wife should live and have her diett at Godolphin during her widowhood',[5] and Thomas Birch's in 1595, that his son George 'according to his promise doe quietly permit my wife to have twoe parlours or other conveniente places to her use if shee meane to continue heare'.[6] Such evident trust in the good intentions of the heir and the common sense of the widow implies that in very many cases it was felt unnecessary to specify any formal arrangements at all. Similar dispositions might be made during the lifetime of the owner if he felt inclined to give up responsibility for maintaining the house and the estate and to hand them over to his heir. At Grundisborough in 1647 William Bliss retained for his own and his wife's exclusive use no more than their own chamber over the kitchen and enough fuel to warm it;[7] presumably for the rest they shared in the general housekeeping of the family. Such arrangements need not call for any physical alteration in the house, save perhaps for the locking of a few doors. In the nature of things, they could not be permanent, and no tangible evidence for them is likely to remain.

A third, common form of house sharing, and one which would normally be equally temporary, was for young couples to spend the first years of their married lives in one or other parents' home before their growing family forced them to find housing on their own – and when they will have benefited by the experience they had acquired in the parental home. In 1622 Sir Hugh Cholmley of Roxby in Yorkshire married Elizabeth, the daughter of Sir William Twisden of Great Peckham in Kent; the couple lived with the Twisdens before moving north to a secondary seat of the Cholmley family at Whitby which Sir Hugh gradually restored while living in the gatehouse.[8] He clearly felt a deep and continuing affection for his wife's family, retiring to live with them in Kent after she had died.

In 1628 Sir John Coke, the second son of middling gentry, bought the estate and manor of Melbourne in Derbyshire.[9] As one of the king's principal Secretaries of State, Sir John himself could seldom be there, but his purpose in buying the Derbyshire property and in rebuilding the house had been to establish his descendants in the county of his birth (he was now aged seventy). Seven years later he wrote to the father of his eldest son's new wife, to persuade him to allow the young couple to move out of her parents' house and to set up at Melbourne on their own. A tactful man, he had to pretend that it was the reluctance of the younger John Coke to leave the comforts of his in-laws' home that prompted him to write; the real reason was that John wished to move to Melbourne but his wife and her parents would not let him. 'Brother Pudsey', wrote Sir John,

> [it is] my hope & ernest desire that you & my sister [i.e. Pudsey's wife] wil ioyne wth me to admonish & perswade both him & your daughter now at length to take upon them the charge of howskeeping at Melbourn when the howse is readie for them. They have had yr. good example to teach them how to govern a familie: Experience will make them capable if they applie themselves: wch if they put of longer they wil finde that new howse wil soone grow out of repaire & the ground wil also grow sadly out of heart. Tenants wil not be gotten & servants are in order but when they are under

the masters ey. It is also considerable that the place is not so far distant from their frends but they may visit and be visited as often as they please.[10]

Sir John's letter summarises many of the class's concerns with neighbours, duties and connections, which the house existed to serve. The process can be seen in successive generations. The younger John Coke had himself been born at his mother's parents' house of Preston Court outside Ledbury while his parents were building themselves a new house at Hall Court 5 miles away (described in chapter 6).[11] In Norfolk, John and Anne Townshend with two maid-servants and four other servants lived for two years with her parents at Stiffkey Hall in 1593–5 and at their expense.[12] When her father Nathaniel Bacon had been building Stiffkey (at his father's expense) he had lived in his father's house; in due course her son, Sir Roger Townshend, would himself live at Stiffkey when building his own new house in the 1620s and 1630s at Raynham.

Similar arrangements for heirs were made by the Mores of Loseley Park in Surrey, but here it is possible that they were anticipated or at least facilitated by an enlargement of the old house.[13] Loseley was rebuilt by Sir William More around 1570. His son Sir George More (1553–1632) rose in the service of the Earl of Leicester to become one of the leading men of the county, and in 1587 built himself a good new house at Baynards at Cranley, where he lived until inheriting his father's house at Loseley in 1600. On doing so, he promptly added to it a new wing which constituted virtually an independent dwelling (pl.

296 Anon. (late eighteenth century): Loseley Park, Guildford, Surrey. The house of *c.* 1570 is on the left (showing the front door in its eighteenth-century position at the centre of the hall; it has since been moved back). The wing on the right (destroyed in the nineteenth century) was added soon after 1600 and provided *inter alia* accommodation for the house's owner while his heir occupied the principal, older part of the house.

296). (The wing was destroyed in the nineteenth century, but it is shown in a plan by John Thorpe which may be a survey but is more probably a proposal for the new building.[14]) Sir George's intention to add to the old house still further by a matching wing on the opposite side, shown in Thorpe's plan, was probably frustrated by a subsequent decline in his political and financial fortunes which also led to the sale of Baynards, the obvious alternative seat for the family's heir. When in turn his son Robert married, a formal agreement between the two specified 'the allowance to Rob: More at Loseley so long as he shall kepe house there' and stated that he 'shall have the use of the old house for so many roomes as he shall have cause to use', presumably while his father occupied the new wing. Robert predeceased his father, dying at Loseley in 1626, and the house was thereafter divided between old Sir George and his grandson Poynings More. Four years later Poynings More was still living at Loseley when he had to flee abroad to escape his creditors; it was apparently some days before Sir George became aware of his absence – grandson and grandfather must have been occupying separate parts of the house.[15]

The evidence is far from rare for the accommodation of less immediate relatives, though it does not support the regular occurrence of extended families – two or more generations and groups of collaterals – living under the same roof. Wills might specify that unmarried daughters should continue to live in the family house; probably as often as not such arrangements were taken for granted. A great deal depended on circumstances that were particular to the family or to the individual. Sir John Bramston recorded family difficulties when his niece's husband lost his official job and the house that went with it, compelling the pair to move back into a house they had let to her widowed mother. Sir John's sister wrote to the old lady: 'If the worst come that my neice must have her house bringe your bed and come to me; you shall set it up in my dining roome and we shall be togeather.'[16]

In large households there might be permanent residents who were not family members at all. The painter Jan Siberechts seems to have lived for a considerable time in the 1680s at Cliveden, the house of the Duke of Buckingham.[17] At Berkeley in Gloucestershire there lived in 1574 and for many years 'Mr Francis Aylworth . . . then of Kington Magna in Warwickshire, a little old werish man, but an excellent well read practiced chirurgeon and physician'.[18] Kington Magna was a Berkeley property and leased by Aylworth, presumably to provide himself with an income, while his patron and landlord was evidently happy for him to live in his house as gentleman companion and family doctor. In providing a home for his former tutor, Thomas Hobbes, at Chatsworth and at Hardwick the Earl of Devonshire was presumably moved by old friendship, duty to an old servant and by the kudos of patronage. Architecturally the most famous such arrangement was that by which the 4th Earl of Pembroke granted a pension and lodgings at Wilton to Isaac de Caus, who had probably been responsible for designing the gardens and

garden buildings and involved (to a debatable extent) in the design of the house itself.[19] De Caus cannot be supposed to have lived there a great deal of the time, although a later reference to him as 'the french architect, who belongs to my L.chamberleyn' (see p. 41 above) suggests some sort of acknowledged client relationship perhaps like that of Aylworth and the Berkeleys.

The inducement to lodge members of an extended family may have been no more than the strength of kinship ties, but when there is evidence of large households of related members there may be particular circumstances to explain them. The Perkins family of Ufton Court in Berkshire (pls 297, 298) were staunch Catholics, and from the 1580s onwards the house was periodically raided in the search for priests and for evidence of the Mass. After the failure of one such search in 1586, a local informant reported that in addition to Francis Perkins and his immediate family, there regularly lodged in the house Mrs Tottersall (Perkins's mother), Mr Perkins (a cousin), Mr George Tottersall and his wife (presumably further relations), Mr Edward Tottersall (ditto), Mr Richard Perkins (another cousin), Mary Plowden (Francis Perkins's wife's sister) and Mr Richard Marvin (probably a relation of his stepfather's) besides others who are named as servants and others again whose status is unclear.[20] In 1599 one Thomas Perkins was described as 'keeper of the house' – presumably another relation, employed (as relations commonly were) as steward for its owner.[21] It is not clear whether all these people were present together in the house at any one time, or whether they were merely frequent visitors, drawn by kinship and possibly by the opportunity to practise their religion. Solidarity in the face of persecution undoubtedly led recusants to club together. However, although Ufton Court is not small and there is evidence of considerable extension and modernisation between around 1570 and 1620, it would be impossible from the house itself to deduce the presence (or otherwise) of such a household as is suggested.

Like the accommodation of widows and elderly parents, such arrangements would call for no structural alterations to the house beyond those that were so slight as to leave no unequivocal evidence of the way the building was occupied. Where there is

297 (*facing page top*) Ufton Court, Ufton Nervet, Berkshire. Ufton Court is a house of many different periods, but in the late sixteenth century it seems to have accommodated an extended Catholic family, the Perkinses, who may have come together out of solidarity.

298 (*facing page bottom*) Ufton Court: ground-floor plan. Ufton dates in part from the fourteenth century and has an extremely complex history, but the structure marked in black seems to have existed by around 1620. The near-detached wing on the left seems to have been added, *c.* 1600, for occupation by the owner's widowed mother, whose initials appear in the decoration of an oratory on the first floor. The kitchen was the hall of the medieval house, converted and replaced by the existing hall in the late fifteenth century.

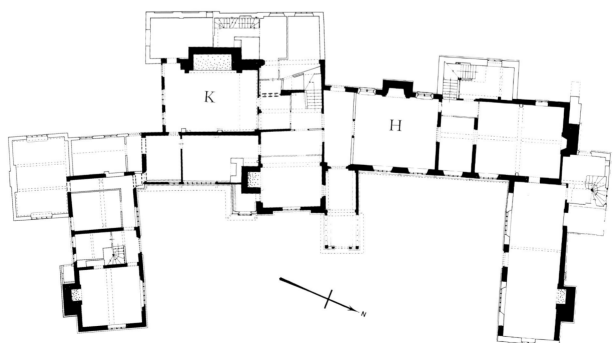

299 Brympton D'Evercy, Somerset. A house of several periods: the medieval hall was rebuilt as a two-storey block in the late sixteenth century (the porch is of *c.* 1850). Left of the hall (and at the low end of the house) is a block of *c.* 1530 which the owner reserved for his own use when he made over the rest of the house to his son. On the right-hand side of the forecourt is a range of building that seems to have been converted a little later as a dower house.

evidence for such separate provision, its form must depend on a combination of regional practice, individual family circumstances and in changing practices in marriage settlement and provision for children – both heirs and younger siblings. At some houses there is a subsidiary dwelling closely adjacent which evidence or tradition suggests were dower houses. At Ufton Court a self-contained house of two and a half storeys touches the main house at one corner, but probably without originally having any physical communication with it. This contains an oratory with painted decoration with the initials AP repeated in the frieze, probably for Francis Perkins's wife Anne, widowed in 1615 and living on until 1635. A formerly separate dwelling at Gurney Street Manor, at Cannington in Somerset (considered

in more detail in chapter 3) may also have been for a dependant.

At Brympton D'Evercy (pl. 299) there seem to be both a dower house of this sort and a lodging for the house's former owner.[22] The house traditionally known as the dower house is quite large (though very much smaller than the principal dwelling), and though probably of fourteenth-century origins was much enhanced in the late fifteenth. It may originally have been a range of lodgings for retainers or guests, subsequently adapted when the family's needs altered.[23] It provides two good rooms on the ground floor and three on the first, with a decorative fireplace and an open roof of high quality over them; in the early seventeenth century the principal upper room was given an ornamental plaster ceiling. The building has been seen as a priest's house, and it does stand on the edge of the churchyard between the main house and the parish church. On the other hand its identification as a dower house is of long standing; it turns its back on the church, clearly facing into the former forecourt of the main house, and its architectural quality and periodic decorative enhancement seem easier to explain in terms of its use by important members of the family.

300 Bisham Abbey, Berkshire (for the front of the house, see pl. 16). At Bisham the owner's brother, Sir Thomas Hoby, superintended alterations in the 1550s and may have added the two-and-a-half-storey block on the right, which is effectively detached from the main house, as a self-contained dwelling for his own use.

In 1534 John Sydenham of Brympton made over the main house to his son, reserving for himself and his wife only 'the nether parlour and two chambers over'. It seems probable that these rooms comprise the existing block of building at the low end of the hall, evidently built a short time before and probably replacing a service range that had earlier stood here, in the conventional low-end position. The block bears the royal arms and has a projecting bay window on two floors and a decorative stair turret, and its bulk and overall presence are enhanced by the extension of the upper wall as a screen, beyond the line of the pitched roof. It appears as a structure of similar character to the tower (described in chapter 3) that Sir John Fermor built for his own accommodation at East Barsham and stands in a similar relationship to the hall. Whether it was built specifically

in anticipation of the formal division of the house is uncertain.

Formal arrangements, requiring structural changes or additions, might be made in respect of other members of the family besides widows or eventual heirs. Bisham Abbey in Berkshire, a house of late thirteenth-century origins, was acquired by Sir Philip Hoby in 1552.[24] Sir Philip was as close as was possible in the sixteenth century to being a professional diplomat, and during his absence abroad in the 1550s the house was modernised and enlarged under the superintendence of his brother, Sir Thomas Hoby, the translator of Castiglione.[25] Besides the principal house at Bisham, centred around the medieval great hall, there is another, virtually separate dwelling, standing at a sharp angle to the larger house and in the sixteenth century touching it at one corner only (pls 300, 301). Architectural detail indicates that the smaller house is of the same date as the enlargement of the larger one. It rises through three storeys, with three rooms on each floor and with closets to the upper chambers in a narrower, rear range. It is possible that the block was built to provide additional lodgings for the older, larger house, but its aspect – looking away from the old house – and the fact that in all respects it could have functioned as a

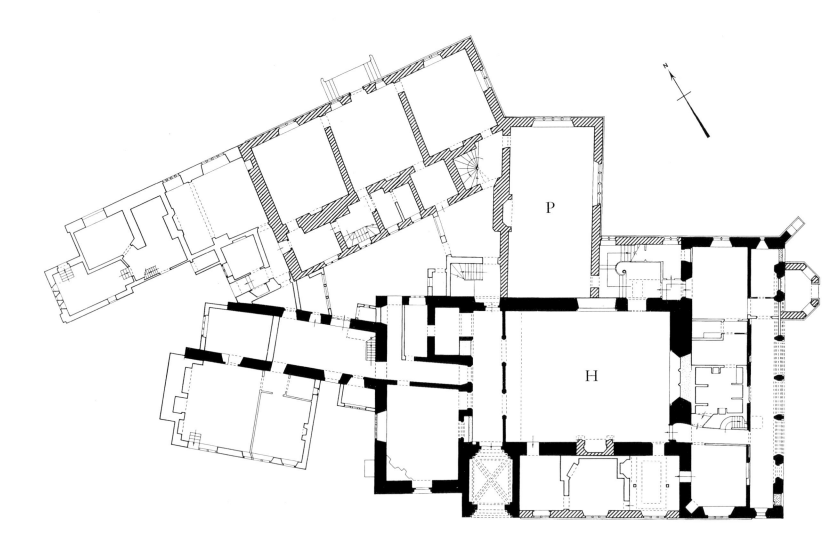

301 Bisham Abbey: ground-floor plan. Medieval work in black; the Hobys' work hatched. Sir Thomas Hoby's block is on the north-west, attached at one corner to a parlour built for Sir Philip, the house's owner.

separate dwelling, suggests strongly that it was built either by Sir Thomas for his own occupation or else as a dower house for eventual use by Sir Philip's widow. It seems only to lack a large hall, and a large hall was inappropriate in a house for a subordinate member of the family, immediately adjacent to the house of the principal landowner, lord of the manor and the family's head. In the event, Sir Philip and his wife both pre-deceased his brother, dying before the new work was finished. Sir Thomas himself (to whom the entire house had been bequeathed) died in the 1560s and his widow, though she remarried in 1574, was living at Bisham following the death of her second husband in 1586.[26] The purpose of this range remains unproven, but its physical relationship to the principal house seems most easily explained in terms of independent occupation by a close connection of Sir Philip's.

Sir Thomas's role in superintending the modernisation of Bisham Abbey on behalf of his brother parallels other instances of younger brothers acting as agents or stewards for their elders and evidently living in their house. Smithills in Lancashire is an accretive house of the fifteenth and sixteenth centuries with a conventional hall range at the centre, but low-end and high-end wings were virtually detached from it; they are of some archi-tectural pretension, and seem to have been capable of serving (save for the lack of a hall) as self-contained dwellings.[27] From the sixteenth to the eighteenth centuries the house belonged to the Bartons of Holme, near Newark, but in the late sixteenth century was occupied by Sir Richard Shuttleworth, Chief Justice of Chester who had married Anne Barton. The Shuttleworths' family seat was at Gawthorpe in Lancashire, at that date still occupied by Sir Richard's father. Either because Sir Richard (like Sir Philip Hoby) had a demanding and full-time job or else because he was childless, Smithills was also lived in successively by Sir Richard's two younger brothers who acted as his bailiff: first by Thomas, and after his death by the Revd Lawrence, absentee rector of Winderton in Warwickshire. On Sir Richard's death in 1599 Lawrence Shuttleworth moved away and built himself a new house at Gawthorpe, the Shuttleworth family's old home which Sir Richard had himself inherited in 1596. Work began so soon after Sir Richard's death that he may already have

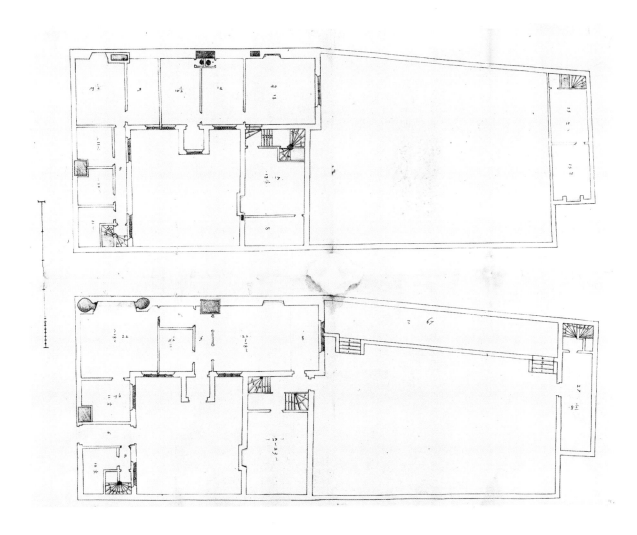

302 Anon. (late sixteenth century): unidentified plans, possibly connected with Redgrave in Suffolk. On the first floor the accommodation at the low end of the house (left) does not communicate with the better chambers of the house (top and right), but there is free communication on the ground floor. The low-end rooms may have accommodated a caretaker or steward; alternatively, the arrangement may simply perpetuate the division in earlier houses when the two ends were separated by a hall that was open to the roof.

prepared it, but in persisting with it Lawrence Shuttleworth must have been prompted by larger considerations of family and lineage since he too was childless and Gawthorpe was to be inherited by his nephew, the son of brother Thomas who had been his predecessor as bailiff at Smithills.

Smithills, Bisham, Ufton and perhaps Brympton are houses where a partially detached or independent block of lodgings may be accounted for by having been built or adapted for a widow or else for a younger brother who was superintending the family affairs, a post that released the senior brother for other occupations, provided the younger with a living and made good use of his commitment to the well-being of the family.

Elsewhere, a group of rooms set apart within the house itself may have been for a steward's use. At St Aylotts in Essex, a country house of around 1500 for the Abbot of Walden, there is no first-floor communication between the principal chambers and two at the low end, over the kitchen.[28] An undated plan of the second half of the century in the Suffolk Record Office (pl. 302) shows the same arrangement.[29] At Little Moreton Hall in the 1480s and at two nearly contemporary houses at Cannington in Somerset (discussed in chapter 3), there seem to have been self-contained lodgings over the kitchen which probably served a similar purpose. There is a similar arrangement at Wilderhope in Shropshire (pls 303, 304), of the 1580s (see p. 310),[30] and at Mackerye End in Hertfordshire,[31] though at both these houses it is more likely that the low-end rooms were for members of the family. These are discussed further in chapter 8 (pp. 309–10).

A number of other houses have been identified which seem to have comprised two separate dwellings, a principal building and a subordinate one in very close physical proximity to it.[32] Sometimes these can be simply explained as a result of modernisation. At Rufford Hall in Lancashire, the property of the Heskeths, an early sixteenth-century timber-framed house with

303 Wilderhope, Longville, Shropshire, *c.* 1590. The accommodation at the low end, left of the porch, is on three storeys; the main body of the house is on two.

an open hall survives in part; adjacent to it at the low end is a rectangular, self-contained, relatively modest red brick house probably of the 1660s (pl. 305).[33] In 1648 the widow of Thomas Hesketh, who held the estate for life as her jointure, leased it out together with part of the house to a Thomas Mawdsley. It seems from the hearth tax return of 1666 that Rufford was then occupied by a certain John Molyneux, who may have negotiated an extension or a transfer of the lease.[34] The house bears the Heskeths' initials; nevertheless it seems more likely that it was built by or for a tenant than for occupation by a leading county family, even one that had suffered heavily in the Civil War. Given a long lease – and leases for three lives, effectively

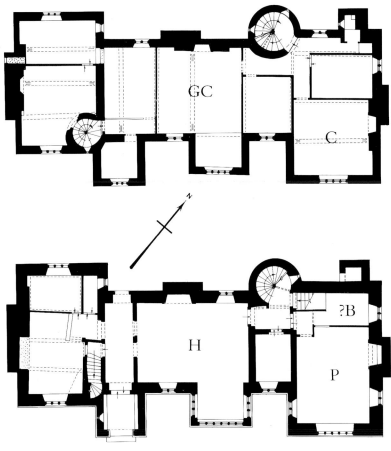

304 Wilderhope, ground- and first-floor plans. Originally there was no communication on the first floor between the rooms at the low end and the superior chambers over hall and parlour. There is evidence that Wilderhope was occupied by the brother of its owner, whose principal house was elsewhere but who may have used the better rooms at Wilderhope for periodic visits.

two generations, were common – substantial building by lessees was not unusual.

Nappa Hall at Askrigg in West Yorkshire was the medieval house of the Metcalfe family, once powerful but seriously impoverished by the seventeenth century. In 1637 a new wing was added, just touching the old house at one corner, and at least from 1655 to 1673 it and the old house were separately occupied by two brothers, one of whom – Thomas – was still a man of sufficient substance to be a Justice of the Peace.[35] Many families included hangers-on: 'younger brethren . . . who having Anuities for their maintenance, and noe houses wherein to settle themselves, must sojourn with friends or hire where they may for money'.[36] It has been suggested that in Lancashire and Cheshire, where such assemblages have been most noticed, they are the result of co-heirs living together in order to avoid the partition of estates. This seems improbable, granted the univer-

sal custom of primogeniture among the Lancashire gentry[37] and the fact that in some cases where two houses have been observed – as at Rufford[38] and at Astley Hall in Chorley[39] – property is known to have been held in tail male: i.e. its indivisible inheritance had been further guaranteed to a single, male heir by a series of specific deeds. At Livesey Old Hall, Blackburn, where the structure of the house and a series of initialled datestones seem to suggest similar enlargement to accommodate more than one generation, the property was similarly entailed so that whatever was done could not involve any ultimate diminution of the overall estate.[40] But men may have made temporary provision for younger sons and brothers in this way and these buildings may echo a practice that dates from before primogeniture had become the rule. Lancashire was an isolated community, relatively poor and inward-looking, with a strong following for the old religion and with powerful kinship ties.[41] There were few of the openings for the younger brothers of the gentry that were available in the prosperous Midlands and south, and a high proportion were commonly unemployed: their gentle birth deterred them from working, but there was in any case

305 Rufford Hall, Lancashire. At Rufford a new, self-contained house was built in the 1660s adjoining the medieval hall, possibly for a lessee.

little for them to work at. It was customary to provide them with life tenancies on some outlying part of the estate or with annuities that would die with them: to do what was necessary for the honour of the family, but not to dissipate the core of the family inheritance. In such circumstances, the provision of dwellings that could be used perhaps by an heir or a younger brother in one generation and by a widowed mother in another, might do something not so much to maintain the integrity of the family property (which was legally inviolable) as to mitigate some of the harsh effects of primogeniture and to honour the obligations of patriarchy and kinship.

Many of the richer gentry possessed more than one house on more than one estate, usable by other members of the family at need and sometimes leading to the permanent establishment there of a younger branch. Robert Burton, citing those Romans who had different houses for different times of year, wrote that 'an ordinary Gentleman of any fashion in our times hath the like . . . [and will] often shift places, and make choice of such as are wholesome, pleasant and convenient'.[42] In the Dorset hearth tax returns of 1662–4 several of the major landowners in the county are recorded as owning more than one house, such as Robert Coker, who was returned for a house of twelve hearths at Athelhampton and fourteen at Mapowder, or Thomas Freke with twenty-one at Bingham's Melcombe and twenty-five at Shroton. Other houses in the county were owned by gentry who mostly lived elsewhere: Colway Manor, with fourteen hearths, belonged to Henry Henley, whose principal seat was Leigh in the next county. At Dillington in Somerset:

> Sir John Speke next neighbour unto it, bought it, and being much taken with the pleasantness of the place and nearness of the mansion house there being only his parke between them hath built much at it, and made a fine convenient place of it where his eldest son now lives.[43]

If no suitable house existed, one might be built. Sir Christopher Lowther built Hackthorpe Hall, not far from his own house, as a dower house for his second wife; two generations later his grandson Sir John Lowther lived there after his marriage and before in due course inheriting Lowther Castle.[44] Newe House at Pakenham in Suffolk, built in 1622, has been variously described as a dower house for the Spring family of Lavenham and as a house for the heir; in due course it could have served as either. Poundisford in Somerset illustrates another way in which family seats might be multiplied.[45] Formerly a park belonging to the Bishops of Winchester, in 1533 the bishop leased it in two parts, the northern, with a house called The Lodge, to Roger Hill, and the southern part with no house to John Soper. When Roger Hill died his son William was abroad, and on his return in 1546 he found that The Lodge had been bequeathed to his mother. To maintain his connection with the place he was obliged to buy Soper's half of the park and to build a new house for himself on his new purchase, incidentally enabling The Lodge to be inherited by his younger brother.

In the same way that owners might hand over the use of much of the house to their heirs, retaining no more than a few rooms for themselves, they might on other occasions move out altogether. Sir William Pole of Shute, who died in 1635, had already made over the great house to his son and refurbished the ruins of Colcombe Castle, 3 miles off, for his own occupation.[46] John Tregonwell of Milton in Dorset – a large, monastic conversion – built a new house a few miles away at Winterbourne Anderson in 1622–4. When it was finished he handed over Milton to his heir (who married in the same year) and moved into the new, much smaller house; on his death he left Anderson to his second son Thomas and his descendants, thereby setting up a junior branch of the family in a house whose architecture was suitable to their standing and whose size was appropriate to their smaller estate.[47] In Henry Fielding's *Tom Jones* (1749) Squire Western similarly resigned his family seat to his daughter and son-in-law and retired to a lesser house, better suited for hunting, but as a regular visitor to his old home he kept the use of a parlour and ante-chamber where he could go and get drunk when he pleased.[48] Both Sir William Pole's and Squire Western's houses of retirement clearly possessed some of the character of a lodge. As discussed in chapter 4, lodges could easily be turned from places of temporary retreat into permanent residences.

Connections and Communities: Entertainment and Charity

Although in the sixteenth and seventeenth centuries there was no such thing as a standard gentry family, and provision within the household for heirs and parents, siblings and younger children seems not to have been undertaken on any systematic basis, their accommodation at need was generally regarded as a matter both of duty and of prudence, and was closely connected with broader obligations towards kin and community. Maintaining kinship links and esteem for one's family was a matter both of self-interest and of honour, and extended beyond the household to the wider circle of relatives, friends and connections. Concern for the standing of the house itself as the hub of such connections is frequently evident in the terms of people's wills. In 1556 Sir John Gage of Firle in Sussex left his house to his son Edward,

> upon full trust and confidens, that he the said Edward, will mayntayn, preserve and leave the same to John Gage his sonne and heire apparent in stock. And if the same John Gage dye before hym, then to suche myn heire male as shall fortune to have and to enyoie my mancion house of Firlez, as I have left it to hym, so as the said heire male may be able with the said stock and furnyture of his house and lande, to maynteyn and kepe hospitalitie and household upon that, the whiche I have left hym.[49]

Both house and contents were involved in supporting the duties and the honour of successive generations. Francis Fitton, who died in 1608, left to his nephew Edward, the owner of the ancestral house at Gawsworth,

> a summe of money . . . for and in respect of my love to him as heire to the Fittons of the house of Gawsworth, in which I and manie of my auncestors were borne, and for his better help to be the better able to stocke and store his demeasnes, and thereby also to be the better able to live in like countenance as his auncestors have donne there before him . . . he being my next heire in blood and the heire and lord of the house of Gawsworth, where my selfe and manie of my ancestors were borne, and continued many yeares and descentes.[50]

Heirs had their rights, but siblings should not feel excluded from the family home. Thomas Tremayne of Collacombe (see p. 23 above) in 1562 left his property to his eldest son, specifying that he should 'be left able to maintain the house with hospitalitie to the nourishing of love among the rest of my children', since 'no inheritance is to be compared to brotherly love and good agreement'.[51] Wills might specify particular objects bequeathed for such ends: Sir Cuthbert Clifton, who died in 1633, left six of his best beds with their hangings as heirlooms 'for the better enabling [his heir] to keepe . . . hospitalitie and to entertaine and entreate . . . kindredd and friends'.[52] How useful such a bequest could be to a recipient is suggested by the will of Sir Edmund Wright of Swakeleys in Middlesex, who in 1643 left the house to his daughter on condition that she allow other members of the family to come and stay for fourteen days every year.[53] Wright was a new man, recently Lord Mayor, and Swakeleys was newly built, but in making such a condition he presumably saw himself as having founded a dynasty which it was the duty of his heirs to support. In such a task houses played an essential part.

In the late sixteenth century and the early seventeenth bedchambers are often named for individuals. In many cases the rooms so identified in inventories are clearly those of upper servants: their furnishings are of relatively little value. Frequently, however, these named rooms are among the best rooms in the house. It is often impossible to know whether the people concerned were residents, regular guests or simply occasional visitors whose recognition in this way advertised the family's affinities and might flatter the room's occupant; nor can they always be identified, particularly when rooms appear to be named for friends rather than for family. Sir Edward Moore's inventory of 1670 included 'my Unkell Rob. Chamber' and 'my Brothers chamber' but it would be rash to assume that either lived permanently in the house.[54] The 'Mr. Wraye' whose chamber recurs in a series of inventories taken at Bassingthorpe in Lincolnshire, in the 1560s and 1570s, was Sir Christopher Wray, Chief Justice. Wray had been building himself a large house at Glentworth, some 30 miles to the north, and Bass-

ingthorpe may have been a convenient staging post on the way to London.[55] At Kimberley in Norfolk in 1588 Sir Roger Wodehouse's house contained 'My Lord of Surrey's chamber', well furnished but not so lavishly as the great chamber over the great parlour; Philip Howard, who as Earl of Surrey had been godfather to Sir Roger's son Philip, had by then been 1st Earl of Arundel for eight years, and his visits cannot have been frequent or the appraisers would not have used an incorrect title.[56] But in any event, names of individuals are evidence for the extent to which a family recognised and advertised its connections.

At Gawsworth in Cheshire, Edward Fitton's inventory in 1606 names bedchambers for Sir Percy Lee, Sir Ralph Egerton, Lady Holcroft, Francis Fitton and Richard Fitton.[57] Of these, Sir Percy Lee cannot be traced: he was certainly not any close relative.[58] Sir Ralph Egerton had been the husband of Anne Fitton, the youngest sister of Edward Fitton's father. Sir Ralph had died in 1596, and the name may recall some close attachment. Lady Holcroft was Edward Fitton's sister, married to Sir Thomas Holcroft of Holcroft (who would often be called on for financial assistance to the Fittons in the next generation) and though perhaps a frequent visitor did not live there. Francis Fitton, however, the childless brother of the deceased, was a resident; he had chosen to leave his own house a few years earlier and to spend his declining years at Gawsworth (his will is quoted above). His own house, Holleshotte, was occupied at the time of his death by his widowed sister. Richard Fitton may have been Edward's unmarried younger son, who had died a few years before.

At Lacock Abbey in 1575 the best rooms in Sir Henry Sharington's house included the duke's chamber, Lady Thynne's chamber, Mr Mildmay's chamber and Mr Talbot's chamber, and the names combine acclaim for a noble patron with acknowledgement of family alliances.[59] The duke was probably John Dudley, Duke of Northumberland, whom Sharington had served and who had also been a patron of advanced architecture at Dudley Castle before his death in 1553. Lady Thynne must be the wife of Sir John Thynne of Longleat, undergoing its final transformation in the 1570s and to be completed as the most up-to-date classical house in England. 'Mr Mildmay' is Anthony Mildmay of Apethorpe in Northamptonshire, husband of Sharington's daughter Grace. 'Mr Talbot' must be John Talbot of Salwarpe in Worcestershire, first husband of Olive, another daughter; she would inherit Lacock as co-heiress and eventually live there with her Talbot children. (Talbot's cousin, another John Talbot of Grafton Manor in Worcestershire, had rebuilt his own house a few years earlier, with very advanced detail whose roots go back to a group of buildings that include Somerset House, Dudley Castle, Longleat and Lacock itself.[60])

These bedchambers were the owner's provision for the entertainment of visitors of rank at least approaching his own. Visiting was frequent in the late sixteenth century and the seventeenth, and those who came from more than a few miles away would of necessity stay the night. In Cornwall, as described by Richard Carew late in the sixteenth century, it seems to have taken the form of a kind of spontaneous outbreak. The Cornish gentry, he wrote,

> keep liberal, but not costly builded or furnished houses; give like entertainment to strangers. . . . They converse familiarly together, and will often visit one another. A gentleman and his wife will ride to make merry with his next neighbour; and after a day or twain, the two couples go to a third; in which progress they increase like snowballs, till through their burdensome weight they break again.[61]

On more formal occasions, the accommodation of visitors and their entourage must have placed formidable demands on accommodation. Sir John Lowther left an account of the celebrations on the marriage of his daughter Barbara to John Beilby of Micklethwaite Grange near Wetherby, 'of an aunciente family', in 1661:

> Wee had most of the Gentry in the Country 3 or 4 dayes and about 20 horse with him [i.e. the bridegroom] out of Yorkshire a weeke, and then wee all sett them hombe; at Burowbrigge there mett us neare 80 horse and that night cost them above £25 and the next day wee went to the Grainge [the bridegroom's home] and stayed there 4 dayes were wee were intertayned with great freedom of Musicke and feasting 4 dayes. Then my Brother Will Lowther invited all the Companie to Swillington where wee had the like intertaynment. And from thence wee went to Skelton Castle to my son Trotters [i.e. Edward Trotter, husband of another daughter] and stayed there 4 dayes, And from thence were invited unto Sir James Penimans [father of the proposed husband of a third daughter] to Ormesby; and from thence to Marton [an outlying Lowther property], Soe to Egleston [ditto] and so hombe.[62]

Vivienne Larminie, charting the connections of the Newdigate family of Arbury in Warwickshire, has noted over seventy places visited between Preston in the north-west and Croydon in the south-east over the period 1610–21.[63] Friends and relations were under requisition when one travelled: thus Henry, Lord Berkeley (1534–1613), who lived at Callowden in Warwickshire but periodically visited his ancestral estates at Berkeley in Gloucestershire, travelled

> not commonly by one way, [but] lodging at the houses of gentlemen his friends and acquaintances, As at Claredon, Milcote, Clifford, Sainbury, Shirborne, Saperton, Lackhampton, Cassies Compton, Gloucester, Ellmore, Frocester, Lasseborrow, Downamny, and some others, by bending his journeys sometimes on the one hand and sometimes on the other.[64]

For fellow members of the gentry, visiting was the mirror image of hospitality: by visiting one established connections and confirmed alliances, sorted out family matters with relatives and local and national affairs with other members of the same county community, exchanged news and gossip and provided mutual entertainment in a society that without such a social life would have been introverted and reactionary, spiritually and intellectually impoverished.[65]

At Berkeley it was the duty of the gentleman usher

> to see all strangers of worth; and they shall be admitted into the great chamber, well entertained for the honour of the house; and that they want nothing necessary at their chambers; and when any gentleman of quality shall come, that he and the rest of the Gentlemen be ready to bring him into the great chamber; and when such a one goeth away, to bring him to his horse.[66]

At some houses people might arrive unannounced in the confident expectation of a suitable reception.[67] Late in life Edward Hyde, 1st Earl of Clarendon, recalled Lord Falkland's hospitality in the 1630s at Great Tew where like-minded friends from London and Oxford

> all found their lodgings there as ready as in the colleges; nor did the lord of the house know of their coming or going, nor who were in his house, till he came to dinner or supper, where all still met; otherwise there was no troublesome ceremony or restraint, to forbid men to come to the house, or to make them weary of staying there; so that many came there to study in a better air, finding all the books they could desire in his library, and all the persons together, whose company they could wish, and not find in any other society.[68]

Elsewhere it is unclear whether guests were invited or asked themselves, as in 1661 at Bridge Place, a new house built by the Flemish merchant Sir Arnold Braems who

> Since [he] is so amiable and hospitable and keeps a princely board, he has an extraordinary number of visits from knights and high born gentlemen and their ladies so that he is continually surrounded by his family and neighbouring friends at table.[69]

No less than the liberality of the entertainment, honour was involved in the quality of the accommodation. 'I pray finish your house as handsome as conveniently you may', wrote Edmund Sawyer to his father, who was rebuilding the family house in 1617.[70] Edmund was newly married and wished to invite some of his wife's family to stay, and his next letter anxiously repeats: 'I pray send me word howe forward you are wth yor house and I pray make it handsome though it cost the more money.'[71]

The entertainment of one's peers was enjoined by Cicero: 'it is most proper that the homes of distinguished men should be open to distinguished guests'.[72] But hospitality combined entertainment and practical advantage with duties that were regarded as the traditional cement of society: with Christian charity; with the display of largesse that in the Middle Ages was seen as an attribute of nobility and was readily transformed into the liberality that characterised the gentleman; and with functions that reinforced the links between lord and community. Hospitality was traditionally meted out in accordance with rank. At Wollaton, probably around 1572, the usher was required

> diligently to have good regard of every person that comes into the hall, to the end that if they be of the better sort, notice may be given to the master, or some head officer that they my be entertained accordingly. If of the meaner sort, then to know the cause of their coming . . . provided always that no stranger be suffered to pass without offering him to drink, and that no rascall or unseemly person be suffer'd to tarry there.[73]

On suitable occasions, hospitality towards inferiors was provided on a more formal basis. When Sir John Reresby of Thrybergh in South Yorkshire kept Christmas in 1682, he remarked that it was 'formerly the custom to observe [the festival] with great mirth and ceremony, but was much lessened, few keeping up the custom of it in thos parts but myselfe',[74] but what he did was formidable enough, differentiating carefully between his guests according to their social ranks. He entertained poorer tenants on Christmas eve and Christmas day (up to twenty-six of them at a time), farmers and better tenants on each of the next three days (up to fifty-four), on three following days neighbouring gentlemen and their wives (up to twenty of them), and finally on 4 and 6 January twelve local clergymen and 'seven gentlemen and tradesmen of Rotherham and other places'. On the only three out of the twelve days of Christmas when he did not himself entertain, he himself dined away from home. And above his normal family and household, he had fourteen people to stay in his house.[75] He concluded (as well he might) that 'The expense of liquor, both of wine and others, was considerable, as well as of other provisions, and my guests appeared well satisfyed.' One can assume, though Sir John does not say so, that the large numbers of tenants and poor would have been entertained in the hall, the smaller numbers of gentry and other select guests in the dining chamber – as the great chamber would by now have been called.

The great hall symbolised the place of the house and its owner in the community, and the periodic gathering there of household, tenantry and other dependants recognised this continuing relationship. The message conveyed by the ornament on the porch at Kirby has been interpreted above (pl. 73). On the hall chimneypiece at Deene (pl. 306), placed there in 1571, is a quotation from Ecclesiasticus 6, 14: it reads AMICUS FIDELIS PROTEXIO FORTIS ('A faithful friend is a strong protection'). In 1844 repairs were being undertaken at Newbiggin, a semi-fortified house of the mid-sixteenth century in the turbulent borderlands of Cumbria. In the course of the work, verses came to light dated 1569 and painted on what had probably been the hall's ceiling beams, and which ran in part:

306 Deene, Northamptonshire: the hall chimneypiece, 1571. Executed in an up-to-date style of French origin. The hall, as the entry to the house and the traditional place of entertainment, conveyed an important message to the visitor. The biblical inscription at Deene, 'A faithful friend is a strong protection', was clearly chosen for its appropriateness to the hall's long-standing communal and hospitable uses.

> If God have leade his hande upon the
> And mayde the lowe in all mens sight
> Contient the selfe wythe that degry
> And se thou walke there in upryghte. . . .
>   God save the quen
>
> [I] am ordaned in lande a knyghte
> To mantaine ye realme and ye church in ryghte
> To louke the pore be not over presced
> Nor that the ryche men be note sessed
>   In domino confido.[76]

The same note is struck at Grafton Manor near Bromsgrove, rebuilt in 1567 by John Talbot (cousin of the John Talbot who married a co-heiress of Lacock Abbey), who was described in

267

the next generation as having been 'in the lineall descent of the Talbots synce the Conquest . . . the fyrst man who was but an Esquyre yet in hospitality equallinge an Earle'.[77] On a pedimented window (ill. p. 252) are the lines:

Whyle everi man is plesed in his degre
There is both pease and uneti
Salaman saith there is non accorde
When everi man woulde be a lorde.[78]

Architecturally Grafton and Newbiggin are as different as possible, yet the message of the two inscriptions is the same: that in a properly ordered society every man has his duties and his place, and the great man's hall is both the proper expression of his responsibilities towards his household and his neighbours, and the place for the acknowledgement of their duties to him.

Beyond the entertainment of connections and retainers, the traditional duties of the householder extended to the relief of poverty. Robert Herrick in his *Panegirick to Sir Lewis Pemberton* extolled the hospitable use of the kitchen at Rushden in Northamptonshire in feeding both strangers and the labourers on the estate:

Where laden spits, wrapt with large Ribbs of Beef
Not represent, but give relief
To the lanke Stranger, and the soure Swain;
Where both may feed, and come again.[79]

The maintenance of a liberal table for one's servants characterised the gentleman no less than the relief of the poor, but in the seventeenth century such duties were to be justified as much by their being signs of salvation as because they were traditional attributes of gentility. On three fronts of West Woodhay House in Berkshire (pl. 194), built in 1636 for Sir Benjamin Rudyard (discussed further in chapter 6), are appropriate biblical inscriptions in Latin. That by the kitchen courtyard is based on Isaiah 58, 7, and reads *Exprome Famelico Animum Tuum* ('Show forth your soul to the hungry')[80] – and is less a message to the poor themselves (who would hardly have understood it) as an injunction to Sir Benjamin's peers (who would have recognised the biblical source); an announcement not only that he recognised traditional obligations but that his motives were correct in terms of contemporary theology.

In 1652 Sir George Sondes of Lees Court in Kent (pl. 187) – a new house built in a fashionable metropolitan style and described rather sourly at the time as 'a pile set out with all the cunning and pomp of magnificence'[81] – defended himself against varied accusations of ungodliness after his elder son had been murdered by his younger: their father, it was argued by his inquisitors, must have been singularly wicked to have incurred so dreadful a visitation from the Almighty. To the charge that he had neglected hospitality, he claimed that he

had three fair houses and at least 1.2000 per annum about them. . . . As to his house keeping, his house was open at all

times to rich and poor; twenty poor people at least were relieved in it weekly. The lowest proportion at his houses, whether he was there or not, was every week a bullock of about 50 stone, a quarter of wheat, and about a quarter of malt for drink, which made about a barrel a day for his household.[82]

Sir George's self-justification was couched traditionally, but Puritan reformers, critical both of worldly ostentation and of indiscriminate charity to the undeserving, readily translated the duties of hospitality into contemporary terms. In 1667 Bulstrode Whitelocke, using his own new building at Chilton in Wiltshire as a starting point for more general reflections on the sort of house that a Christian should inhabit, wrote:

Another braunch of charity is true hospitality, & if that be in the design of building it is a building with charity, & an evidence that the Lord doth build the house. I doe not call that hospitality, when the design is to build a large house to intertain & feast grandees, & to make high & sumpteous treatments. This is a building of luxury, not for true hospitality, which is to entertain strangers, and our poor neighbors, & those who are in want of bread.[83]

However, in being so translated, the essence of hospitality is changed. No longer a function of lordship and the cement of an integrated if hierarchical society, hospitality as charity becomes personalised, a sign of grace on the part of the charitable and of individual approval towards the recipient. Hospitality towards one's peers becomes a private function, and the place of the house in its exercise a private matter. The house ceases to have any place in the community beyond the statement it makes about its owner's status to which he can now add virtue, and if he cares to forgo the traditional duties of his station that is a matter for his own conscience.

In the strongest contrast to the inscriptions at Newbiggin and at Grafton is that at Shaw House outside Newbury – an architecturally very up-to-date house discussed in chapter 3. Its builder, Thomas Dolman, was the son of a successful clothier who inherited from his father in 1575, and promptly began to build. 'Lord have mercy upon us, miserable sinners; Thomas Dolman has built a new house and turned off all his spinners' ran a contemporary jingle. On the outside of the house are two inscriptions. That on the frieze above the porch reads EDENTU-LUS VESCENTIUM DENTIBUS INVIDET ET OCULOS CAPREREVM TALPA CONTEMNIT ('The toothless man envies the teeth of those who eat, and the mole hates the eyes of the goats'). On the porch itself, the inscription is in Greek: ΦΘΟΝΕΡΟΣ ΜΗΔΕΙΣ ΕΙΣΙΤΩ ('Let no envious man enter'). Far from offering traditional hospitality, Thomas Dolman seems to revel in the way in which his family's new money has raised him above the common herd. When in 1617 James Howell described Long Melford as 'so virtuous and regular a house as any I believe in all this Land, both for oeconomical Government and the choice Company', he commended the segregation of kitchen and 'other Offices of noise and drudgery' and 'a Back-gate for the Beggars and the meaner sort of swaines to come in at'.[84]

The continuous enhancement of the powers of the magistracy and of the modern, capitalist landlord since the early sixteenth century was creating a situation where it was difficult to pretend that relations between the gentry and the rural community corresponded any longer to nostalgic stereotypes. The whole structure of rural society was undergoing radical change. Enclosure and the transformation of customary tenures into rack rents were destroying the community of the manor court and the continuity of tenures. A powerful combination of capitalism and Puritanism was promoting an ethos that was increasingly individualistic. Drawn increasingly to the diversions of London, numbers of landowners were becoming absentees for at least a part of the year. At the end of the sixteenth century the numbers of the poor were rising, and traditional charity, less and less able to meet their demands, was being replaced by a coercive system of vagrancy laws and local rates. Falling wages and rising prices were creating economic tensions in which popular discontent was often voiced against the gentry as a class, whose growing numbers, powers and wealth at a time of increasing hardship seemed to suggest some causal connection. Phillip Stubbes in 1583 made a direct connection, attacking those who 'have so many houses that they visit them once in vii year; many Chimnies, but little smoke; faire houses, but small hospitalitie' and condemned together 'daintie Fare, gorgious Buildings, and sumptuous Apparel'.[85]

Between 1550 and 1650 traditional views of the place of the lord in the structured society were not so much abandoned as transformed. The Renaissance notion that public service was a necessary attribute of gentility and a manifestation of virtue tended to perpetuate the medieval idea that hospitality was among the duties of rank and a demonstration of the liberality proper to the nobleman. But it was also a crucial modification of the feudal ideal: whereas formerly the duties of the lord in the community arose as a consequence of his place in the hierachy, his liberality now proclaimed his virtues as an individual, and in practice such demonstration of virtue clashed with other modern ideals of polite behaviour. Indiscriminate charity was contrary to a growing sense that the poor had to show themselves deserving. The recruitment of so many new men to the class of the gentry in the sixteenth century inevitably meant a dilution of customary relations, and to the newcomers other ways of advertising their gentility might well be more congenial. In particular, it was difficult to reconcile open-handed housekeeping with the exclusivity that was becoming one of the attributes of the cultivated man. The man of culture showed his education and breeding among his intimates rather than by a public parade of his wealth and his retinue. He read and prayed alone; his taste was displayed in the rooms to which only his friends had access; his servants waited below stairs and his poorer tenants by the kitchen door. His cultivation was increasingly an urban one, taking its tone from the pleasures and company of the town, and the idealisation in contemporary literature of country life and rural values is similarly an urban view. It was a culture that rested on peer-group values: on emulation, education and consumerism rather than on community.

In the face of such changes, there is a group of early seventeenth-century poems in which established conventions of pastoral poetry are applied to real English settings, adapting the relationships of pastoral stereotypes in idealising those of actual lords and countrymen and the social functions of their houses.[86] These poems are a denial of contemporary social dysfunction. They are also political statements: a panegyric of the place of the landowning classes that was enunciated in royal proclamations which, beginning in 1595 and repeated with increasing urgency by James I and Charles I, endeavoured with only limited success to induce the gentry to quit the allurements of London where they spent their rural incomes and to reside on their estates where they might properly fulfil their moral and economic responsibilities and their part in the sound government of the kingdom.[87] The proclamation of 1615 complained that

> Noblemen, knights and Gentlemen of qualitie, doe rather fall to a more private and delicate course of life . . . by living in Cities and Townes, than continue the ancient and laudible custome of this Realme in housekeeping upon the principall Seates and Mansions in the Countrey . . . [and] the absence of Our Lieutenants, Deputie Lieutenants and Justices of the Realme out of the Shires where they have charge and Office, carrieth in itself a plaine neglect and contempt of that trust and charge which we have layd upon them.[88]

That of 1632 ordered that

> Baronets, Knights, Esquires and Gentlemen . . . that have Mansion-houses and places of Residence in other parts . . . [must immediately] resort to the severall Counties where they usually reside, and there keep their habitations and hospitalitie.[89]

The country house poems are not purely retrospective: their apparent nostalgia is a gloss upon contemporary change, while their explicit rejection of architectural ostentation anticipates the greater architectural restraint of the 1620s onwards.

But by commending traditional relationships, these poets implicitly recognise that reality was increasingly at variance with ideals. Pastoral poetry is highly artificial; its readership is sophisticated, its comments are often indirect, its rustic characters have little immediate correspondence to real life, and its landscapes are generally conventionalised. The longevity of the form, from its classical origins through its widespread popularity in the Renaissance, shows its extraordinary potential and versatility, but it is essentially a form that thrives on nostalgia, on escape and on being able to idealise the actual countryside. Late Elizabethan pastoral poetry had been allusive and symbolic, using the conventions of the rural idyll to comment allegorically on contemporary themes, on human nature, or else more generally to idealise the simple life. It is only gradually that real landscape begins to intrude on the conventional, and when it first does so, as in Edmund Spenser's *Shepheardes Calender* (1579) or Michael Drayton's *Poly-Olbion* (1612–22), it is itself treated mythologically. The country house poems celebrate real houses and real owners, but with an element of mythologising that sees them as heirs to an imagined past of good lordship and open-handed hospitality – a parallel to a growing interest in the origins, legendary and actual, of Britain itself.[90]

These poems are not many in number, and extend over forty years – from Ben Jonson's *Penshurst* of about 1612, to Andrew Marvell's *Appleton House* of 1652; between come Jonson's *To Sir Robert Wroth*, Herrick's *To Sir Lewis Pemberton*, Thomes Carew's *Saxham* and *To the King at his Entrance into Saxham*, probably of around 1620, and his *To my Friend G.N. from Wrest*, probably of 1639. All save the first owe a great deal to Jonson's prototype, and all contain numerous echoes of Martial, Horace, Virgil and Juvenal that would have been recognised with approval by their educated readers. Although the tone of Marvell's is very different from the rest, in almost all of these poems there are recurrent themes, both social and architectural: freedom from the corruptions of the city; the personal fulfilment afforded by a life of retirement; home-grown entertainment, moderation and friendship; the willing recognition of the obligations of lord and tenant; the free and open-handed hospitality afforded to every visitor according to his rank by lord and servant; the simplicity of the building itself, free from excessive and useless display and built without oppression of the poor; the notion that the generous owner and his satisfied guests are the building's greatest ornament; a Protestant satisfaction in resources being put to use rather than for display. Magnificence – and that only in the sense of liberality – lies in deeds, not in appearances. Underlying all these poems is a recognition of landed property as the basis for social stability and giving rise to reciprocal relations within and between the human and the natural worlds.

The tone is set by *Penshurst*. Penshurst was the medieval home of Sir Robert Sidney, whose elder brother, Sir Philip, had been the author of *Arcadia* in which his description of the house of Kalander prefigures Jonson's own description of Penshurst. When the shepherds and their companion arrive at Kalander's house,

Kalander knew that provision is the foundation of hospitalitie, and thrift the jewell of magnificence. The house it selfe was built of faire and strong stone, not affecting so much any extraordinarie kinde of finenes, as an honourable representing of a firme statelines. The lights, doores and staires, rather directed to the use of the guest, than to the eye of the Artificer: and yet as the one cheefly heeded, so the other not neglected; each place handsome without curiositie, and homely without lothsomenes: not so daintie as not to be trode on, nor yet slobbered up with good fellowshippe: all more lasting than beautifull, but that the consideration of the

exceding lastingnes made the eye believe it was exceeding beautifull. . . . The servants not so many in number, as cleanlie in apparell, and serviceable in behaviour.[91]

Penshurst in Jonson's poem is

> not . . . built to envious show
> Of Touch or marble, nor can boast a row
> Of Polish'd pillars or a roofe of gold . . .
> And though thy walls be of the countrey stone,
> They are raised with no man's ruin, no man's grone,
> There's none that dwell about them wish them down,
> But all come in, the farmer and the clowne,
> And no-one empty-handed, to salute
> Thy lord and lady, though they have no sute . . .
> Where comes no guest but is allowed to eate,
> Without his feare, and of thy lord's own meate:
> Where the same beere, and bread, and selfe-same wine
> That is his Lordship's, shall be also mine.[92]

Architectural extravagance and traditional hospitality are similarly contrasted in Carew's *Wrest*, which is also a model of good order in the traditional hierarchy of the hall:

> here the Architect
> Did not with curious skill a Pile erect
> Of carved Marble, Touch or Porpherie
> But built a house for hospitalitie . . .
> The Lord and Lady of this place delight
> Rather to be in act, than seeme in sight;
> Instead of Statues to adorne the wall
> They throng with living men, their merrie Hall
> Where at large Tables fill'd with wholsome meates
> The servant, Tennant, and kind neighbour eates.
> Some of that ranke, spun of a finer thred
> Are with the Women, Steward and Chaplaine fed
> With daintier cates; Others of better note
> Whom wealth, parts, office, or the Heralds coate
> Have sever'd from the common, freely sit
> At the Lord's Table, whose spread sides admit
> A large accesse of friends.[93]

All of these poems praise their central figure's hospitality, meted out appropriately to each rank and in willing conformity with the ancient duties of his high station, and meriting the ungrudging, reciprocal tributes of household and tenantry. That the relations they extolled were not wholly romantic seems confirmed by Sir Hugh Cholmley in his autobiography, writing of the Indian summer of the old regime before the Civil War:

In spring, 1636, I removed from the Gate-house into my house at Whitby, being now finished and fit to receive me; and my dear wife (who was excellent at dressing and making all handsome within doors) had put it into a fine posture, and furnished with many good things, so that, I believe, there were few gentlemen in the country, of my rank, exceeded it . . . and having mastered my debts, I did not only appear at all public meetings in a very gentlemanly equipage, but lived in as handsome and plentiful fashion at home as any gentleman in all the country, of my rank. I had between thirty and forty in my ordinary family, a chaplain who said prayers every morning at six, and again before dinner and supper, a porter who merely attended the gates, which were ever shut up before dinner, when the bell rang to prayers, and not opened till one o'clock, except for some strangers who came to dinner, which was ever three or four besides my family, without any trouble; and whatever their fare was, they were sure to have a hearty welcome. Twice a week, a certain number of old people, widows and indigent persons, were served at my gates with bread and good pottage of beef.[94]

Shutting the gates before dinner was not a denial of hospitality but rather for the maintenance of good order.[95] In his memoirs Sir Hugh contrasted his own ordered housekeeping with the behaviour of his grandfather, constantly accompanied by a riotous crowd of retainers who thought nothing of raiding the kitchen between meals until there was nothing left for Sir Richard's own dinner.

Nevertheless, Sir Hugh's traditional housekeeping was against the spirit of the age, and did not survive the disruption of his life with the death of his wife and the onset of the Civil War. 'I do not desire any more company in my house than my wife, children and servants', wrote Sir Henry Oxinden to his brother in 1636, adding 'I know you are none of them that when they are gotten into a friend's house continue there without shame or moderation longer than they are welcome'.[96] And in the circumstances of the country house poems there are a number of ironies. The message in all of these poems is that here, at least, the ancient virtues still hold sway – and their corresponding implication is that elsewhere they have vanished. One may see the architectural equivalent of these poems in the activity of Lady Anne Clifford, greatest of north country builders in the mid-seventeenth century, who restored the six northern castles that she owned and who progressed regularly from one to another, intensely tenacious of her ancestral rights and property and equally determined to perform the traditional duties of the great landowner. Her curiously and self-consciously old-fashioned triptych portrait includes Sir Henry Wotton's *Elements of Architecture*, conspicuously placed as a symbol of her passion for building.[97] But it was already eccentric to restore medieval castles, even in the north. In spite of their apparently real-life settings and their contemporary political subtext, the country house poems are equally nostalgic and their subjects hardly less unreal than is more traditional pastoral poetry. In the last of them (discussed again in chapter 9) there is a significant change of emphasis. Sir Thomas Fairfax, the retired Commonwealth general, has built a new house (rather than fulfilling traditional hospitality in an old one) in which he can enjoy a private retirement which is itself a sign of redemption, no longer communitarian but directly comparable with Sir Benjamin Rudyard's injunction that a man's public life displays the state of his soul.

The dream of a golden age of good lordship was nothing new, and housekeeping was certainly never so liberal as people liked to think it once had been.[98] Thomas Lever in a sermon preached before the king in 1550 had probably risked offending a distinguished congregation by stating that 'the chief cause why the commens doe not love, trust, nor obey the gentlemen and the officers, is because [they] buylde many fayre houses and keepe fewe good houses'.[99] Awareness of changing social relationships was prompted at least in part by contemporary enquiry for the sources of rising levels of poverty, unemployment and other social problems, and the decline of hospitality that is widely lamented is like its nostalgic celebration in the country house poems a single, readily identifiable aspect of a broader and deeper decay of relationships. Sir Thomas Overbury wrote early in the new century of the character of 'a Noble and Retired Housekeeper' that

> Nobility lightens in his eyes; and in his face and gesture is painted *The God of Hospitality*. His great houses beare in their front more durance than state; unlesse this adds the greater state to them, that they promise to out last much of our new phantasticall building.[100]

Nobility, hospitality and retirement go together: they do not go with the extravagant building that is characteristic of the modern world. In the light of the well-documented increase in the upper classes' resort to London, the royal proclamations that became ever more urgent – not to say frantic – in the 1620s and 1630s can be seen as objective confirmation of a widespread impression.

A lament by the author of *A Health to the Gentlemanly Profession of Serving Men* of 1598 shows another picture to that of the country house poems:

> The Haull boordes-end is taken up,
> No dogges do differ for the bones,
> Blacke-Jacke is left, now Glasse or Cuppe,
> It makes mee sigh with many groones
> To think what was, now these to be
>   By death of Liberalitie. . . .
>
> The Golden world is past and gone,
> The Iron age hath runne his race,
> The lumpe of Lead is left alone
> To presse the poore in every place;
> Nought els is left but miserie
>   Since death of Liberalitie.[101]

In the words of a modern editor, 'the ceremonial cameraderie of the feudal hall was giving place to below-stairs discipline'. By singling out a particular aspect of a broader change in manners, the writer was appealing to a more general concern about the breakdown of traditional social relations.

The function of the gentleman servant had been honorific as well as practical, an essential element in a socially graded household. The size of the aristocratic household had been falling in the sixteenth century, as the attendance of numbers of retainers was ceasing to be viewed as necessary to the nobleman's standing, and as a feeling grew among the gentry that service in the nobleman's household was not compatible with gentility. Such feelings spread downward through the households of the gentry themselves. The changes of the seventeenth century would tend to polarise relations between family and servants as the upper classes sought companionship among their peers and in their immediate family rather than in their wider household, as the distinction sought through behaviour and cultivation increased the gap between the educated classes and the rest, and as a Protestant ethic placed less value on service by mere attendance and more on labour. The decline in the size of the household and in its graded structure led to servants having more generalised duties and to the employment of more women – a sex generally less educated and invariably paid less for the same work.

Sir Roger Pratt, writing in 1660, strongly urged the segregation of servants, recommending basement kitchens 'that no dirty servant may be seen passing to and fro by those that are above, nor noises heard, nor ill scents smelt'.[102] Servants' garrets should not be placed over visitors' bedrooms, lest guests be disturbed by them going to bed. There should be sufficient back stairs and passages 'that the ordinary servants may never publicly appear in passing to and fro their occasions'. On the other hand, it would be misleading to suggest that this polarisation necessarily led to isolation. While the place for servants was no longer in the hall and still less as companions in the great chamber, practical commonsense meant that if an owner was to involve himself responsibly in the running of his household and his estate, he must be aware of what his servants are doing. Roger North, in his extensive description of the way in which he remodelled his own house at the end of the century, dwells constantly on the need to keep an eye on servants' activities. In his prescription for the arrangement of the back entrance, the same involvement is maintained. This should be

> as well for the comon servile part of the family, and buissness to make constant use of, as also for the master (whom I doe not suppose to be above economy) at ordinary times to pass at, whereby the dilligence and performances of his servants will fall under his eye, and also he can transact weith them, and other mean persons, without concerning his guest, or anoying the principall, and enterteining part of his house. Therefore this back entrance should be . . . somewhat cheerfull, and aiery, which the best of family at private times may make use of. . . . It is no unseemly object to an English gentleman to se his servants and buissness passing at ordinary times.[103]

By North's time the hall had for a generation ceased to be a servants' common room and it had been longer still since the gentlemanly retainers of great men had been on call to play at dice in the great chamber with their masters, but the very completeness of the change may have led North towards a more relaxed acceptance of the place of his servants than appears in the injunctions of Roger Pratt. Pratt writes to reinforce changes that he thought desirable; North advises on how best to accommodate a new status quo.

8

The Rooms of the House

Private and Public: Evolving Regions

The rooms of the house can be looked at in various ways. They can be seen as shared or exclusive, and as rooms for entertainment or for the private use of household members. They can be listed by status or by location: upstairs, downstairs or at the high or low ends of the house, locations that conform broadly to status but do not always do so completely. They can also be seen as old or new: rooms with origins in the Middle Ages, or rooms of new kinds, created to meet new requirements. Neither names nor functions remained the same in the course of the sixteenth and seventeenth centuries; new rooms came into being to meet new needs while some rooms dropped out of existence altogether, and all change to some extent in their functions and in the amenities they provide without always a corresponding change in terminology. But the fundamental change is an increase in their numbers as rooms changed from spaces that were shared to spaces that are private, and from rooms with more general functions to more specialised ones.

The simplicity of late medieval plans and the loss of furnishings – in particular of the hangings with which rooms of quality continued to be lined until the seventeenth century and which together with the beds formed by far the most valuable of their contents – now presents the impression of a very much greater uniformity within the house than would have appeared to contemporaries.[1] A letter of 1469 from Sir John Howard to his bailiff asks him to

> take the measure of the hall, . . . and likewise of the parlour, and of the chamber over the parlour, and the chamber where I lie in, and of the chamber over the pantry and buttery; of all these I pray you send me the measure in haste, and I trust before long ye shall see the chambers better hanged than ever ye saw them.[2]

Descriptions of rooms in inventories and the scale of values of their contents show in practice a very wide range of differences between them, intended to provide a setting appropriate to the functions of the room and to its occupant's dignity and honour as well as to advertise the owner's taste and wealth and to cater for his comfort.

But even when allowance has been made for such loss of distinguishing internal marks of status, the plan of the late medieval house appears very much simpler than it was to be by the seventeenth century. Not only did exclusive space scarcely exist but it was largely unwanted. Bedchambers doubled as sitting rooms, and the gradual separation of functions is the clearest evidence of increasing desire for privacy as rooms became more specialised both in their use and in their allocation to individuals. The common link betweeen the evolution of chambers, hall and parlours was in the increasing provision made in every part of the house for privacy and exclusivity and for activities that are the consequence of changes in education and manners.

While in providing rooms for entertainment owners broadly followed fashion, in their private quarters they were more likely to suit their own particular circumstances and the capacities of the house. Few people lived in new houses, and old inconveniences might have to be tolerated. Roger North made the distinction between formal and informal accommodation at the end of the seventeenth century, and it must have been valid long before. Having enumerated the principal rooms of the house and described the best contemporary practice for their disposition, he continued:

> All the rest of the house is family convenience, wherein an artist may help to contrive, by suggesting, and assisting to the invention and applycation of the master, but the judgement lys upon him, who knows his owne occasions, and therefore,

if not very dull, must be the best architect, as to what he is to use personally himself.[3]

The freedom of arrangements in such private rooms is suggested too by a letter from Sir John Lowther to his agent in 1694. Much work had just been carried out to bring his old house up to date, the family was on its way from London, and the steward was anxious to know who was to sleep where.

> My wife desires . . . that the Bedding may be made free from Mustinesse and that Beds may be sett up in those Rooms that are in the uppermost Storie on the south Side of the hous off the Old Building convenient ffor my Children &c. And that you may know as much as I can tell you My Son is to lie over the Room that is over the West End of the Dining Room, And My Cousin Temperence Kirkby in that beyond it, My 2 Eldest Daughters in that over the Room that Clarkson Wainscotted, My Wife's Maid in that little one Betwixt My Sons and my said Daughters Room, and my three youngest Daughters in the Great Room at the West End, and in the two little Rooms on each side the back stairs must the Maid Servants lie.[4]

Despite the modernisation of the house, there seems an air of the *ad hoc* about these arrangements. Not many even among the gentry lived on the scale of Sir John Lowther (who was ennobled two years later) but although the steady increase in the number of family rooms made such choices available to everyone who could afford a large, modern house, similar questions about the occupancy of rooms must always have arisen whether a house had many rooms or few. Sir John's teenage daughters were still expected to share bedrooms, and all were evidently housed on the second floor, above the more important chambers below. His having to decide who was to sleep where serves as a warning against making too facile assumptions about household arrangements from the scanty evidence that now survives, generations later and when almost all old houses have since had their layouts altered in one way or another.

Some of the fullest contemporary evidence about how rooms were used comes from inventories. Inventories are essentially catalogues of the contents of the rooms in a house. They have the advantage that one is not left to infer room uses from physical evidence that is often inadequate, and though not enough inventories of gentry households survive before the late seventeenth century to form the basis for accurate statistical analysis, enough remain to confirm an overall impression of increasing specialisation in the uses of rooms and a concomitant increase in the attainment of privacy. Certain caveats have to be borne in mind, some of which are purely practical. One is that most houses for which there are inventories have been pulled down, and even for those that do survive it is not always possible to match the rooms of an inventory – particularly bedchambers, often identified only by the name of an occupant or a scheme of decoration – with existing rooms. The appraisers who made

the inventory moved round the house in no predictable order: they might begin at the top or at the bottom, and after they had stopped for dinner they might start again somewhere quite different, so that indications of a layout derived from the room sequence in an inventory may not necessarily be valid. Another caveat is that when rooms are not listed, this does not mean that they did not exist. The inventory of Sir Richard Weston of Sutton Place in Surrey, taken on his death in 1542 and ostensibly complete,[5] can be shown to list only half (or less) of the rooms in the house: it seems possible, though it cannot be proved, that he may already have made over the bulk of his house and possessions to his teenage grandson and to his daughter-in-law, his grandson's widowed mother. Those who took inventories listed only the possessions of the person whose circumstances they were investigating, and ignored rooms that contained nothing. They differed too in what they might consider important and worth describing in detail, so that direct comparisons are not always possible.

A further reason for caution in interpreting inventories arises from the conditions in which they were made. Sometimes they were taken for some legal reason such as the confiscation of the goods of someone attainted for treason by the crown or of those of a recalcitrant Royalist by the Commonwealth. Sometimes they were made by the owner of a house who simply wanted to take stock of his possessions. Most commonly, however, inventories were taken on a person's death. The domestic arrangements depicted might thus be up-to-date when the inventory was taken, but often were not. In the case of an elderly individual, the inventory of his possessions may reflect arrangements created when he was in the prime of life, perhaps a generation earlier. Furthermore, furnishings could be moved about, and room uses altered with the furnishings. At Wollaton in 1541 there was 'other stuff gathered to gether and layed upp in the dyninge chambre' so that beyond its name one cannot tell how the room was usually used.[6] In 1624 the inventory of Sir Thomas Fairfax's possessions at Walton in South Yorkshire included 'other things not set in any particular place or belonging to it, but some in one and some in another';[7] the list included carpets, stools and chairs, though not beds, the presence or absence of which is perhaps the most fundamental distinction between the rooms in a house. Another reason why inventories cannot be used uncritically is that differences between the apparent uses of rooms may not be chronological but regional. Despite these provisos, inventories provide the fullest account of the evolving names, contents and functions of the rooms of the houses of the gentry. The overall consistency of the picture that emerges reinforces the impression of the houses themselves: that people of the gentry class shared certain habits and priorities, and that while an increasingly sophisticated way of life was provided for by a growing number of specialised rooms, usage and social convention prescribed the ways in which these rooms might be related and used, and created a broad, functional similarity between houses even of apparently very different form.

At the end of William More's inventory, at Loseley in 1556, is a list of 'things new bought' and presumably still waiting for allocation to particular rooms.[8] These include two chestnut chairs, a desk and three small cases, also of chestnut, a framed map of France, 'three pots of tynne to set flowers in', a great joined press and other items. Five years later More began to rebuild the house itself. Above all, in reading and comparing sixteenth- and seventeenth-century inventories, one is left with a sense of rapidly growing sophistication in taste, manners and comfort, and a sense that change is sometimes outpacing the power of terminology to keep up with it: that rooms have either several possible names or none, and that the appraisers did not always know what name they should be using.

The Hall

Until the early seventeenth century the most public room in the house was the hall, used by everyone who had access to the house and providing the central circulation space off which lay parlours or services and from which simple stairs rose directly to chambers at either end. The functions of the hall were both symbolic and practical, and its symbolic functions made for the perpetuation of the hierarchical, low-/high-end arrangement for some time after the exterior had ceased to display the building's internal layout. The hall expressed the organisation of the household in the same way that the outside of the house had done. In an age which jealously observed distinctions of rank, the decoration of the hall gave greatest honour to those areas that were used by the lord on formal occasions and represented his dignity when he was not there in person to preside over the community. But although its lord might seldom come there, its value in cementing relations and in expressing the unity of the household was recognised in aristocratic houses by levying penalties on servants whose rank qualified them to eat there but who preferred to eat on their own.[9] The importance of the hall in providing visitors with their first impression of the owner's wealth was recognised in its architectural decoration, traditionally the most lavish in the house and in strong contrast to the trestle tables and benches set out for the servants who ate there (illustration, p. 250). But it was above all its role in symbolising the ideal of the integrated but structured community that ensured the hall's long survival.

The principal entrance to the house lay at the low end of the hall. A porch would open into a cross passage with another external door on the hall's opposite side; this passage would generally be divided off from the body of the hall by a light screen through which two further openings gave into the hall itself. On the other side of this screens passage one or more doors led through to the service rooms beyond the hall's low end, from which food reached the hall from the kitchen. Besides serving to enhance the view into the body of the hall from the high table, a richly decorated screen served also to dignify the formal entry of food into the hall. The narrowness of the cross passage and its primarily functional purpose meant that on the passage side of the screen there was little scope for ornament. On the hall side, however, where it faced up the room and towards the high table, there was more reason and opportunity for decoration.

There were regional variations on this arrangement. Although a hall screen was found in almost all major houses (and most lesser gentry houses as well), in some northern houses the screen was replaced by the rear of a fireplace that opened into the hall itself. The screen might be formed partly out of the structure of the house: some medieval houses have an arrangement of posts on the line of the cross passage which rise to the roof, a structural device known as a spere truss. This arrangement itself provided scope for tectonic ornament, and a very few northern houses retain a free-standing structure, a spere, that stood between the posts of the spere truss and functioned as a screen. The decorative and honorific value of the screen was essential to the traditional hall, and it persisted into the seventeenth century as long as the hierarchical hall itself.

There were other means by which the upper and lower end of the hall were marked. In timber houses, decorative framing could be exploited internally to provide an extravagant display of constructive decoration at the high end, as a backdrop to the lord's own table on the dais. In a tall or open hall, the screen might carry some kind of gallery. Galleries are far from universal, and their function not wholly clear: traditional association with musicians should be treated with caution, though it is possible that they were occasionally so used; a physical resemblance to the west galleries of many post-Reformation churches may have prompted the belief that this was their common purpose. Some galleries such as those at Cothay and Poundisford are enclosed, and an enclosed gallery might be used in the same way as the small internal windows present in many houses that enable someone in a first-floor room at the high or low end of the hall to look down into it without themselves being observed. Such a window could have served a number of purposes: to monitor visitors first entering the house; to police the servants or others, sitting at meals; to enable non-participants to watch entertainment in progress in the hall. This squint might be no more than a narrow lancet, as at Chalfield; at Dudley Castle it comprises two arched windows with a pediment above them; at Collacombe in Devonshire it is elaborated into a small, arcaded gallery (pl. 210); at Horham in Essex around 1510 there is similarly a small room, placed on the side of the hall at the high end, with an internal window and reached from a passage beyond. In 1617 such squints were described as 'peeping windows for the ladies to view what doings there are in the hall'.[10]

At the high end of the hall a dais for the owner's table, and sometimes an ornamental canopy above it, formed a permanent reminder of his symbolic presence even though he may seldom have appeared there. (Although in many houses the dais has been subsequently removed in order to avoid an awkward step in the middle of the hall floor, evidence for it sometimes remains in a step up from the hall through the door that leads to the rooms beyond it.) Almost as universal as a dais was to mark the high end by an oriel window (pl. 307). The oriel (discussed further in chapter 6) could take many forms, and its persistence into the early seventeenth century in houses that were otherwise furnished with a full range of up-to-date accommodation is evidence both of the strength of regional traditions and also, perhaps, of its usefulness as a versatile and informal space. It was an intermediate stage in the provision for privacy, and in its prominence it seems to be an early manifestation of the desire which informs much of the development of the house in the sixteenth century: the apparently contradictory wishes both to attain privacy and to display it.

The layout of the hall thus emphasised the status of its high end. But as the centre of the house and a public demonstration of its owner's wealth and liberality, the hall's symbolic function called for its decorative enhancement over and above the hierarchic distinction of its ends. The commonest place for decoration was in the roof. In the houses of the gentry the hall that rose through two storeys was still all but universal in 1500. Structural carpentry may have been at its most inventive in the fourteenth century, but by the end of the fifteenth a variety of roof forms was available, to a considerable extent still regional in their

employment, each of which could provide the hall with a roof of appropriate grandeur. Evidence of painting seldom survives, but ornament took three other forms: the enrichment of the structural members with decorative mouldings; the addition of decorative or heraldic figures; and the use of redundant or gratuitous construction. Forms and examples of roof construction and ornament can be multiplied almost endlessly, and roofs have received more attention from scholars than any other aspect of medieval building construction.[11] But the reason for this elaboration beyond what was strictly required to keep the building weatherproof, must in every case have been the same: to impress the beholder with the wealth and standing of the man who owned so splendid a house.

The symbolic importance of the hall was reinforced by ritual as well by its architecture. The service of food in a great man's house was a highly formalised business, in which written household ordnances prescribed in detail the sequence of tasks, part practical, part ceremonial, of a large number of participants. Such tradition, inherited from the Middle Ages, continued in the houses of the great to the end of the sixteenth century and even beyond. The orders for the usher of the hall at Wollaton in 1572 are long and elaborate, and included much redundant ceremony:

> Upon intelligence given from the clerk or the cook that the meat is ready to be served, he is with a loud voice to command all gentlemen and yeomen [i.e. those who took their meals in the hall] to repair to the dresser. At the nether end of the hall he is to meet the service [i.e. the food and its bearers], saying with a loud voice 'Give place, my masters,' albeit no man be in the way.[12]

Having seen the food carried through the hall in solemn procession to the dining chamber, where the lord and his intimates ate by themselves, diners in the hall were to be seated according to rank, while the usher maintained order and commanded the waiters. The household regulations that are the evidence for such rituals in the houses of the great have no surviving equivalents for the households of the mere gentry, but Wye Saltonstall's satire quoted at the end of chapter 1 suggests that the gentry aped the nobility with comparable ceremonial.

An unsolved question concerns the heating of the hall. Anciently, it had been heated by an open fire on the floor, generally placed towards the lower end. Built-in fireplaces, common from the fourteenth century onwards in houses of the élite, are generally on the long wall away from the entrance so as to leave space for windows in the front wall, but other positions occur which raise questions as to the usage of the hall in particular cases. Halls are known where the fireplace heats the dais; these

307 Gainsborough Old Hall, Lincolnshire. Architectural detail emphasised the importance of the hall externally as well as internally, often calling attention by an oriel window to the location of its high end. Beyond is a lodging tower for the house's owner.

are generally found in fairly modest houses such as Gurney Street Manor, Mapperton and Poxwell in Dorset[13] and Rosewarne in Cornwall[14] but such fireplaces also occur at East Barsham and at Athelhampton,[15] houses of considerable grandeur. In the north, fireplaces are sometimes placed at the low end, replacing the screen and backing on to the through passage; once again, this position is commonest in smaller houses but in the north-west it can be found in larger ones such as Yanwath,[16] Isel[17] or Middleton Hall.[18] There may have been a difference between northern and southern practices in the use of the hall, but the distribution of dais fireplaces has not been adequately recorded.

Although tall halls would still be built in the seventeenth century (that at Rushton in Northamptonshire is as late as 1630, rebuilt by a new owner presumably to show what he regarded as the antiquity of his position[19]) the most important sixteenth-century innovation was the hall of a single storey, generally with a room of high status above it. There was no single factor that led to the tall hall being succeeded by a hall on one floor only, and in different houses where single-storey halls appear at an early date one can recognise a variety of different motives. Nevertheless, the reason why such a change could be entertained at all must be because in the long run, the prestige attached to the open hall was waning, its social functions were increasingly obsolete and its symbolic functions corresponded less and less to the image that its owner sought to present. The traditional recommendations of the open hall were increasingly outweighed by other and novel considerations.

An innovation that contributed to the flooring-in of the hall, although one that was not initially connected with any decline in the hall's prestige, was a matter of amenity: the introduction into the hall of a ceiling. Timber ceilings to upstairs chambers, hiding the roof and probably first introduced for the sake of warmth, appear during the second half of the fifteenth century, and from chambers it was a natural transition to insert a ceiling in the hall. There are several tall halls of the late fifteenth century with ceilings which are still lavishly decorated. The hall at Great Chalfield had from the first a slightly cambered, panelled ceiling beneath the timbers of the roof itself; substantial traces of painting survive along the cornice, and the whole ceiling may have been similarly painted.[20] Crosby Hall in the City of London, of 1467, has a cambered ceiling beneath an elaborate structural roof which is not intended to be seen, but the ceiling itself is treated as an opportunity for decorative experiment and in no way suggests any visual downgrading in the prestige of the hall.[21]

Having no rooms above their hall ceilings, both Chalfield and Crosby Hall suggest that their adoption may have been prompted by architectural fashion: the profile of the ceiling of Crosby Hall is precisely that of the four-centred arches of contemporary window and door openings and may have been preferred to the appearance of the steeply pitched structural roof, however decorated. None the less, once the practice of the ceiling-in of the hall was established, the possibility also arose of adding rooms above it. Great Chalfield anticipates this: two small stairs rise from first-floor closets into the roof space, and though the use of this space is entirely unknown (it lacks windows or floor boards, the cambered ceiling makes a level floor impossible, and at most it can have been used only as a passage or for storage) it is not a large step to the creation in other houses of a more useful roof space.

In the course of the sixteenth century the increasing complexity of chambers and galleries on the upper floors of the house, the result of growing concern for exclusivity and for the proper entertainment of guests, placed considerable demands on the ground floor of the house where room sizes and numbers were not increasing at a commensurate rate. Some increase in ground-floor area could be met by incorporating within it functions that in the Middle Ages had generally been housed outside the house, notably the kitchen – a movement that was already under way in the fifteenth century. More upper-floor accommodation could also be created by adding more storeys, a development that in any case suited contemporary ideas of what the ideal house should look like. However, a useful increase in upper-floor area could also be achieved by placing chambers over the hall, while the hall's decreasing status made acceptable the sacrifice of some of its architectural prominence. The extreme situation was reached at Worksop Manor in the 1580s where the house soared through three to six storeys and where apart from the hall the ground floor seems to have contained only services and storage.[22]

Single-storey halls seem to occur initially in houses of men of lower social standing, who had less need for display or to accommodate numbers of tenantry or retainers and were more likely to be moved by considerations of economy. However, there is some evidence of a temporary fashion around 1530 for single-storey halls in houses of men of the highest rank. East Barsham was described in chapter 3. Little is known of its owner, though he was clearly important enough to have been knighted and to have built an extremely fashionable house. The hall at East Barsham has windows no larger or more ornate than those of the great chamber, a room of equal size directly above it. East Barsham is contemporary with Sutton Place in Surrey, a house probably built between 1525 and 1532 and whose owner was still grander than Sir John Fermor.[23] Sir Richard Weston was an intimate of the king's, an intimacy which survived the execution of his son for a supposed liaison with Queen Anne Boleyn. The house has been greatly altered and its original form is recoverable only in part, but it is clear that the house had a single-storey hall when built. At Sutton Place the sources for the single-storey hall may have been both continental and, more immediately, in the example of the royal houses, where (unless they already existed) none of those altered or acquired for Henry VIII after 1530 has a hall at all.[24]

The reasons for this are partly in the development of machinery for ensuring royal privacy and in changes in the composition and daily routines of the royal household, but this temporary debasement of the hall may also be linked to the influence of French and Burgundian exemplars. The splendid court of the Dukes of Burgundy had influenced almost every aspect of English court culture under Henry VII, from clothing, through painting and music to the management of the royal library, and under Henry VIII Burgundy's place as a source for models of civility was to a great extent taken by that of Francis I of France. (A French poet even wrote an elegy on the death of Sir Richard Weston's son.[25]) Great halls do not occur in French or Burgundian great houses of the period, in which all rooms are of a single storey and in which a great block of superior accommodation – the *corps de logis* – assumes a prominence which was paralleled in several English houses of the period, notably at Compton Winyates (which does, however, have a tall hall) and probably also at Sutton Place.

A little lower in the social scale but nevertheless the home of a man of considerable standing is Rayne Hall in Essex, a timber-framed house of perhaps fourteenth-century origins which seems to have been very extensively remodelled in the sixteenth by Giles Capel (d. 1556).[26] Capel's father, younger son of a local gentry family, had risen from apprenticeship in the City of London to be knighted in 1482, Sheriff in 1491, three times MP for the City and Lord Mayor in 1501 and 1510; Giles Capel had been one of the Champions of England at the Field of the Cloth of Gold and with his son was among those deputed to receive Anne of Cleves on her arrival in England in 1540. The present house is fragmentary and its development is far from clear, but the hall (pl. 309) is of the same height as other ground-floor rooms and the moulded decoration of its ceiling and the form of its brick fireplace suggest a date before around 1550.

In these three houses the single-storey hall seems an anachronism: a premature departure from the hall's traditional prominence at a date when the economic, social and administrative changes that were to transform the gentry's relations with household and community were not yet complete. In these houses it seems difficult to explain the form of the hall other than in terms of fashion: the terracotta decoration of Barsham and Sutton Place is itself the clearest indication of architectural fashion-consciousness, and their internal arrangements may similarly reflect a temporary taste. If so, there was a reaction in great houses in the third quarter of the century from such low halls in favour of halls of a more traditional, tall form.

However, the examples of the royal houses and of such houses as these may have influenced those of lesser men at the same time that single-storey halls in still humbler houses may have been offering an example of economy and practical convenience. It is because their occupants have no need for the conventional hierarchical hall of the upper classes that single-storey halls tend first to appear in the houses of men of lower rank: lesser gentry, prosperous yeomen and priests. These were men – particularly the yeomen – who were rapidly growing in wealth as a result of the easy land market of the late fifteenth century and the

early sixteenth and whose living standards and desire for the comforts of life were increasing in proportion. They had no tenantry to entertain, no manor court over which to preside, no retainers to impress, and with their middling rank in society no grand neighbours to receive, yet they still needed a hall for the daily use and feeding of their own household of family and servants. It seems likely that numbers of the lesser gentry recognised in the houses of their rich farming neighbours amenities that were sufficient for their own relatively modest status. Distinctions could be perpetuated, however, within the single-storey hall: in many houses dais and screen continued to be provided into the early seventeenth century. Berry Hall at Solihull in the West Midlands is a fragmentary house, but retaining the hall and an upper-end cross wing. Although the hall is of a single storey and has lost its screen, the high and low ends are differentiated by progressive elaboration of the mouldings and ornament of the three cross-beams of its ceiling. While the hall no longer has an open roof, its decoration still respects the room's hierarchical use.

At Fulham Palace, the Thames-side country house of the Bishops of London, the hall (of around 1480) was of a single storey only and had its fireplace heating the dais. Though not a territorial magnate in the conventional sense, the Bishop of London was the third senior bishop in the Church of England, and elsewhere bishops' palaces had large, open halls. However, Fulham Palace was a relatively modest retreat, and there may have been no need for what would be normal elsewhere.[27] There are in Somerset and Dorset from the late fifteenth century a number of houses with single-storey halls that have chambers of high quality above them.[28] These upper chambers have sometimes been interpreted as first-floor halls, though there seems no reason why they should be so: the essence of the hall in any layman's house was that it should be immediately accessible from the outside, and the stair positions in these houses are conventional – they lead off the lower room at its superior end, furthest from the house's entrance. While certain of these are houses for churchmen who, like the Bishop of London at Fulham, had no need for a great hall, Blackmore Farm (described in chapter 3) is secular. The hall at Blackmore Farm is a relatively unassuming room, even allowing for the fact that it has lost its probable screen, and the first floor is at the same level throughout: the hall is no taller than any other ground-floor rooms. The fact that the upper rooms can be reached only by passing the length of the hall to the stair, in the normal manner, makes it impossible to interpret any of these chambers as a first-floor hall.

Sandford Orcas in Dorset (pl. 209) was probably built soon after 1533, and also has a ground-floor hall.[29] The house's probable builder, Edward Knoyle, was among the lesser of the county gentry: his grandfather had served as Lord Lieutenant in 1496, but though probably on the bench of magistrates he seems to have occupied no higher post. Sandford Orcas is smaller than East Barsham and much smaller than Sutton Place, and its architectural sophistication, like that of other houses in the

308 Rayne Hall, Essex: the hall. Probably built in the mid-sixteenth century by Giles Capel (chosen to be one of the Champions of England at the Field of the Cloth of Gold) or by his son: an early example of a single-storey hall in the house of a man of standing.

region, clearly has much to do with the availability of superb building stone that from the mid-fifteenth century to the late sixteenth gave much of Dorset, Somerset and Wiltshire a largely home-grown tradition of sophisticated house building. At Sandford Orcas, although the hall is taller than the great chamber above it, the fenestration is similar (as it was at East Barsham) and the external impression is of two storeys of almost equal importance, neither of which is dominant.

While the wide social and geographical spread of early sixteenth-century, single-storey halls in gentry houses is significant – those described are from Dorset, Essex, the West Midlands, Norfolk, Somerset and Surrey, to which one can add Doddershall in Buckinghamshire, Haslington in Cheshire and Isel in Cumbria – the low hall did not at once become the general practice in houses of the higher gentry, still less in those of the aristocracy; what is at present less clear is the social levels at which these distinctions operated. Sir Richard Weston of Sutton Place moved in the highest levels of society; Sir John Fermor at East Barsham and the Capels at Rayne were probably not very far behind. At the same time, other men of equal standing were still building houses with tall halls: Sir William Fitzwilliam, Treasurer of the Household by 1529 and a peer of

309 Longleat, Wiltshire: the hall ceiling. The tradition of architectural display in the hall persisted after the introduction of flat ceilings, which were partly the result of placing additional rooms above it on an upper floor. The hammer-beam roof of the hall at Longleat is not structural but perpetuates a medieval form.

Weston's, at Cowdray; Sir William Compton, Groom of the Stool, at Compton Winyates; Sir Thomas Kytson, Sheriff of London in 1533, at Hengrave (although the existing open hall is of the nineteenth century and little is known of its predecessor except that it may have been narrower).[30]

There is some evidence from the late sixteenth century of a reaction by the higher gentry in favour of tall halls, and the immediate influence of these ceiled, low halls was probably towards an intermediate form: a hall which still rose to a height

and which was enhanced by a ceiling whose decoration to some extent compensated visually for the loss of the open roof. Sutton Place demonstrates the change very clearly. It is known that there had been a serious fire at the house in 1561, and recent archaeological examination revealed that when the central part of the house was rebuilt some time later in the century, it was provided with a taller hall, rising through two floors and with a low attic storey above it. This reaction is clearest in houses where the hall ceiling has been enhanced in a way that seems a conscious evocation of roofs of the Middle Ages. At Longleat in the late 1570s (pl. 319) the hall has a further storey above it, yet its ceiling is carried on an elaborate false hammer-beam structure that is structurally redundant. At Wiston of the 1570s the hall has a true, structural hammer-beam roof, but on the façade the steep pitch is hidden by a blind parapet which reproduces the detail of the attic storey of the range on the low side of the porch. Kirby,

310 Poundisford, Somerset: the hall ceiling. The plaster ceiling at Poundisford is of the 1570s, some thirty years after the house was built. It is very similar to others of the same years which must be the work of a team of plasterers catering to a new fashion. The view is taken from the gallery over the screens.

too, has a tall hall, though (as already described) it is disguised externally by a uniform architectural treatment of the whole range (pl. 72). The increasing elaboration of decorative plaster-work from the 1570s onward provided a means of enhancing the ceilings of lesser halls with ribs and pendentives vaguely reminiscent of medieval vaults: existing halls at Collacombe, Poundisford (pl. 310) and Ufton all received such ceilings in the decade, and before the end of the century those of a very great many more gentry houses were similarly enhanced.

The extreme case is at Burghley, where – probably in the late 1570s – an enormous great hall of overwhelmingly medieval form was built on to a house which was otherwise being extensively modernised. This too has a hammer-beam roof, possibly by the same carpenters as those at Longleat and Wollaton and at the Middle Temple in London whose hall was rebuilt at much the same time. Originally the hall roof had a louvre as well – a purely formal echo, without practical use, of the chimney once necessary for the escape of smoke from a central hearth. The hall at Burghley is placed where it is not prominent externally; its intrusion into the symmetry of the house is as far as possible played down. The effect intended is internal, and at Longleat the hall is not detectable externally at all. Even at Wollaton, though the hall rises clear above the centre of the house, it appears less as a hall than as a gigantic lantern. The rebuilding of the hall of the Middle Temple, though scarcely comparable with the needs of a private citizen or his household, is perhaps similar in spirit in providing an appropriate image and setting for members of a community strongly conscious of their status, their antiquity and of the medieval foundations of their discipline. Inside the house, the great domestic hall presented an impression of the antiquity of its owner's family and of his continuing to perform the ancient functions of his class; on the other hand, the suppression from the 1580s onwards of external evidence for it (in strong contrast to its emphasis in the medieval house) seems to suggest an important change in the way in which its owner wished his duties to be perceived.

Those who owned a house with a traditional, open hall might retain it, alter it or replace it, and examples can be found of each approach. While a tall hall might survive in the houses of the great – for those whose wealth enabled them to retain a space whose importance was increasingly no more than an evocation of notional relationships – from the mid-sixteenth century it was already becoming the practice for owners of houses with old, open halls to insert a floor into them. The hall at Little Moreton, formerly open, was floored over in 1559 to make a new chamber above and a single-storey hall below (pl. 312); at the same time, the prominent windows on two storeys were created that overlook the courtyard. Nothing seems to have been done to remedy the unorthodox hierarchical arrangement in that access to the new chamber – which may or may not have supplanted the existing great chamber as the chief entertaining room of the house – remained by the low-end stair. At Ightham Moat there seems some evidence that flooring-over of the hall was contemplated, in that the hall chimney was rebuilt in the sixteenth century with an additional flue rising from first-floor level; in the event, nothing was done. At Little Moreton the evidence shows very clearly, as it does also at Northborough, where the medieval hall windows survive, floored across, with dormers

added above them to light the upper storey (pl. 311). A similar conversion of a medieval manor house took place at Howden on Humberside where a large aisled hall was floored in during the seventeenth century to create a complete (and quite substantial) house: externally, the origins of the house are almost as clear as they are at Northborough by virtue of its retaining its medieval porch and the outlines of the thirteenth-century windows. At Combermere Abbey after the dissolution the great chamber had been formed out of the hall of the abbot's lodging, identifiable by its retention of the oversailing canopy to the former dais (pl. 313). At Annesley in Nottinghamshire the medieval origins of the hall were discovered in 1988, when the inserted floor and fine seventeenth-century wainscot were stripped out, revealing a thirteenth-century aisle post in one end wall.[31] Such conversions were ubiquitous, and they can be found in houses of almost every level of society where there was a tall, open hall originally.

The perpetuation of the tall hall was facilitated by the continuing functional separation of the two ends of the house. In the medieval house, the open hall provided a physical barrier between the high and low ends on all but the ground floor, making necessary separate staircases and in particular limiting the means for servicing chambers. But although the ceiling-in of the hall and its reduction in some houses to a single storey might be expected to have a profound effect on internal circulation – making free passage possible from one end of the house to the other on the upper floors in addition to the ground floor – for some time no such advantage seems to have been taken of the new arrangement and until the advent of more radical changes in the layout of the house the traditional, essentially linear plan continued to determine the relations of its parts. In those houses where there was a great chamber over the hall, communication was probably incidental to the need to service such a chamber from both ends, and the inconvenience of using a room of high status as a thoroughfare probably discouraged it. Two exceptional northern houses, Wood Lane Hall at Sowerby in West Yorkshire[32] (pl. 314) and perhaps Westholme in County Durham,[33] combined an open hall with a first-floor link by providing a gallery around the hall at first-floor level, but neither have conventional plans with a central hall range between wings. Both are two ranges deep and the need in these houses to reach chambers that lay in the same central position as the hall itself called for

311 (left) Northborough Hall, Peterborough, Cambridgeshire. The windows of the medieval open hall were retained when a floor was inserted in the sixteenth century and dormer windows added to light the room that was created above it.

312 (facing page) Little Moreton Hall: the hall. Now open to the roof, as it was when built, the hall contains abundant evidence of having had a floor inserted in the 1550s in order to increase the chamber accommodation.

313 Combermere Abbey, Cheshire: the great chamber. Formed by the flooring-in of the hall but still preserving the original dais canopy at the hall's high end.

arrangements that were unconventional. When in the early seventeenth century galleries appear round the tall halls of a small number of architecturally sophisticated houses, their origin is very different.

There were other means of dealing with what might well be perceived as the problem of the hall. It might be entirely rebuilt, while retaining useful accommodation that adjoined it. Thus the hall range at Fyfield in Oxfordshire was rebuilt on three floors while keeping an early fifteenth-century range – possibly a parlour range originally – to house the services; the hall at Brympton D'Evercy was similarly rebuilt between earlier blocks at either end (pl. 299). Something similar was evidently done at Gorcott in Warwickshire, at Larden Hall in Shropshire and per-

haps (though the evidence is contained only in an eighteenth-century painting[34]) at Dixton in Gloucestershire. A hall might be retained but its use changed, as at Knole (albeit scarcely a gentry house) where a medieval hall seems to have become a kitchen with the building of a new hall in the sixteenth century. At Ufton Court the fourteenth-century hall seems similarly to have become the kitchen, though in this case probably as early as about 1480.

The decline of the social relations for which the hall had existed brought into question not only its size and architectural character but its function, its layout and ultimately its existence. Its function would change with the introduction of the servants' hall, a separate room specifically intended as an eating room and common day-room for them. Probably a traditional (though not a necessary) use of the hall was for the holding of the manor court. This was commemorated at Dunsland House, where in the eighteenth century the hall had become known as the Justice Room and the screen replaced by a pair of gates (pl. 315).[35] At

314 Wood Lane Hall, Sowerby, West Yorkshire. For reasons that are not clear, open halls persisted far longer in Yorkshire, in the houses of minor gentry, than they did elsewhere. The hall of Wood Lane is of 1649; a gallery provides first-floor circulation, connecting with rooms in a range to the rear.

Bishop's Cleeve in Worcestershire in the 1640s the tenant of the Manor House – the property of the Dean and Chapter of Worcester – was required 'to provide sufficient accommodation for the Dean Receivers and Steward their Servants and Horses for fore dayes and fore nights at their times of Keeping Court'.[36] However, at Owlpen in Gloucestershire there is a separate, detached court house which may have been built specifically to remove the court from the hall.

The low-end entry became not only irrelevant but also inconvenient when the hall's purpose was solely to enable the owner, his immediate family and his polite visitors to enter the house on their way to the rooms they habitually used. Halls entered at the centre of their narrow end occur from the end of the sixteenth century in exceptional houses (as described in chapters 4 and 5). Such halls remain hierarchical in their plan in that the entry both from services and from the outside of the house is still at the low end, and they may retain a high-end dais, but they already preclude the possibility of the screens passage being used as a common thoroughfare from the front of the house to a service court at the rear and even in the earliest examples the hall may not have been called on to provide the full range of traditional uses.

A more radical recasting of the hall took place when the hall remained lateral – in line with the length of the building – but when the entrance itself is moved to the hall's centre, at once making impossible any kind of low-/high-end differentiation in the hall itself. Equally radical is the effect (also described on pp. 142–3 above) which would become virtually a standard in the smaller gentry house, of the relocation of the stair on the way

315 Dunsland House, Devonshire (destroyed). The hall at Dunsland had by the eighteenth century come to be called the Justice Room, presumably because the holding of the manor court was the only one of its traditional functions that it still retained. The spiked, eighteenth-century gates at the screen end do not suggest hospitality.

the hall might be used. From the early seventeenth century there is an increasing tendency, particularly in houses with deep plans, for the principal stair to be sited no longer off the hall's high end, but at the low end of the hall in line with the entry. The traditional approach to the superior chambers of the house had been by entering through the hall screen, traversing the length of the hall from its low-end entrance, crossing the dais (if one existed), and then passing through an often modest doorway at the hall's high end before reaching and ascending an equally

modest high-end stair. Such an approach meant walking the length of a room that was still often used in the early seventeenth century as the servants' common eating room. Relocation of the stair in line with the front entrance made possible a direct approach to the house's most important rooms without the need to pass all down the hall.

The effect of this was to shift the approach to the best rooms, whether for family or for guests, to what was formerly the common entry: in these houses the polite functions of the household thus encroach on the domestic, and although the hall still exists, this change in circulation placed it firmly within the ambit of the superior rooms. With the absorption of the hall into the 'high' end of the house, its use as a common eating room was increasingly inappropriate; with a decline in the complexity of the household community such a use was in any case ceasing to be desirable or necessary. These arrangements first appear in lodges and in certain London houses in neither of which a traditional hall may have been needed. Their later proliferaton in houses for regular occupation is described in previous chapters.

With the decline in the hall's traditional functions, it could either be used for something else or done away with altogether. The 'great room or hall' at Tart Hall in London in 1641 was furnished with pictures, mirrors, and cupboards with plates and glasses, and though probably used for entertainment these are clearly provision for superior visitors.[37] When in the 1660s Roger Pratt saw the hall at Raynham (which he had earlier visited when it was bare) he found it 'furnished with pictures and other divertissements for the pleasure of knights and gentlemen that attend [the owner's] leisure to answer their suits and petitions [and is] not now fitt for the profane feet of vulgar serving men'.[38] At Ham, Roger North recorded that the 'noble room of entry' was used at the end of the century as a dining room,[39] and the same seems to have happened at Gayhurst and at Aston. At a different date the hall at Ham had been used for billiards,[40] as was that at Dyrham around 1700.[41] These were grand houses; in more modest gentry houses the evolving use of the hall is more difficult to trace, but the relocation of the stair and the occurrence of centrally entered halls from the mid-seventeenth century onwards can have been possible only with the hall's changing functions.

As an alternative to the entrance hall, the vestibule, a species of narrow entrance hall leading from front door to an inner hall, seems to have made its first appearance around 1660. Evelyn seems to have seen the vestibule as a species of internal porch: 'the Vestibule or Porch should precede the Hall; the Hall the Parlor'.[42] A plan by Wren of the 1660s for an unidentified country house (pl. 317) includes such a room as an approach to the great stair and to an ante-room that leads one way to the great parlour and the other way to the chapel; there is no other hall as such.[43] Two later plans from Wren's office (pl. 316) provide alternative layouts for a second house. In one there is a traditional arrangement with a low-end entry, lying between parlours, and in the other a vestibule between what are probably ground-floor chamber apartments.[44] Presumably according to current conventions either was acceptable and which one might be adopted was a matter of personal preference. At Tring, Wren's principal private house, built in the 1670s, Roger North noted a vestibule between the front door and 'the middle, or the hall'.[45] Tring was a large rectangular house, three ranges deep, with a tall, end-lit hall and the principal stair at its centre. The builder's model of Melton Constable (pls 294, 295) shows a traditional screens passage leading from the front door past one end of the hall to the centre of the house. As the house now stands, this is an enclosed passage (i.e. a vestibule), and it is not certain whether this arrangement represents the layout as actually built or whether it is an alteration. But in any case, at Melton the relationship between screens passage and vestibule is clear. While the origin of the vestibule may have been French, this resemblance

probably recommended it to English practice as a simple modification of traditional forms – merely turning the open screened passage into a wholly enclosed one.

In the sixteenth century and in traditional households of the early seventeenth, the hall had remained the formal eating room for the household servants, with the kitchen – the room in the house where activity, company and refreshment could probably be found at any hour – as the centre to which servants gravitated informally. The size and the furnishings of the kitchen suggest that in some small gentry households the servants may generally have eaten there rather than in the hall. There were inconveniences about both practices, which in the course of the seventeenth century were resolved by the creation in larger gentry houses of a servants' hall. Pratt in 1660 had recommended

316   Two plans from Sir Christopher Wren's office. In these two late seventeenth-century plans, alternative arrangements are suggested for the same house. One plan shows a hall entered at the low end; in the other, there is a vestibule leading through to a saloon which (in the absence of a hall) was presumably intended to perform the same social functions.

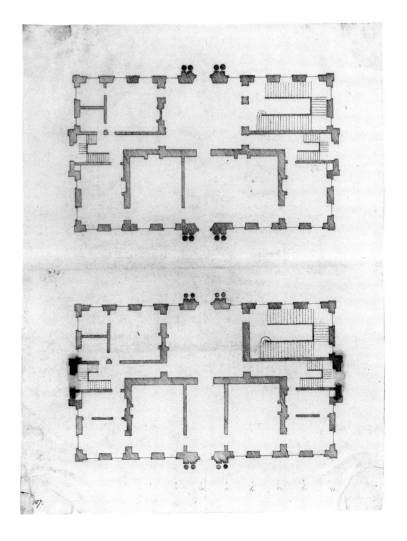

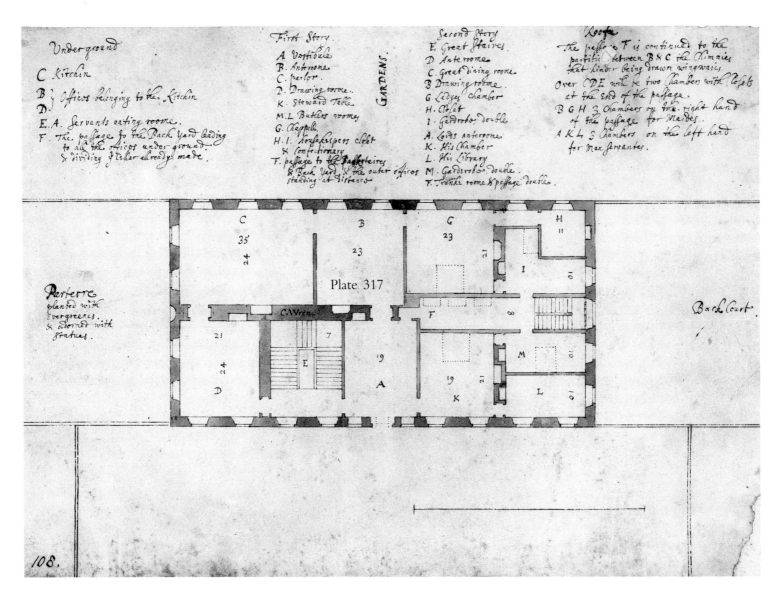

317 Christopher Wren: plan for an unidentified house, 1660s. Only the ground floor is shown, but the layout of the upper floors was to be similar. Every room in the house is clearly identified by Wren's annotations. These read:

UNDERGROUND
C   Kitchen
B,D Offices belonging to the kitchen
E,A Servants eating room
F   The passage to the Back Yard leading to all the offices under ground [i.e. in the basement] . . .

FIRST STORY [i.e. ground floor]
A   Vestibule
B   Anteroome
C   Parlor
D   Drawing roome [i.e. withdrawing room to the dining parlour]
K   Steward Table [probably an upper servants' hall]
M,L Butlers roomes
G   Chappell [placed to be accessible for servants]
H,I Housekeepers closet & Confectionary
F   Passage to the Backstairs & Back Yard, & the outer offices standing at Distance

SECOND STORY [i.e. first floor]
E   Great Staires
D   Anteroome
C   Great dining roome
B   Drawing roome
G   Ladyes chamber
H   Closet
I   Garderobe double [probably a dressing room]
A   Lords anteroome
K   His Chamber
L   His Library
M   Garderobe double [probably a dressing room]
F   Trunke roome & passage double

ROOFES [i.e. top floor]
The passage F is continued to the partition between B & C the Chimnies that hinder being drawn wingwaies
Over C D E will be two Chambers with Closets at the end of the passage.
B G H 3 Chambers on the right hand of the passage for Maides.
A K L 3 Chambers on the left hand for Man servantes.

a 'common eating hall' for servants, next to the kitchen,[46] though the phrase 'common parlour' in the late seventeenth century generally described a room for the family rather than for servants. At Coleshill both kitchen and servants' hall were in the basement, with a 'living parlour' on the ground floor at the kitchen end of the house. It was seen earlier how Pratt commended the changes at Raynham, and at the end of the century North remarked that it was only during his own lifetime that servants had left off eating in the hall at his father's house. 'As for servants', he wrote, 'I know it is usuall to clutter them all into a kitchen' but this was destructive of discipline and order – better a separate hall, 'the servants' dining room and place of attendance', not too close to the parlour because of the noise, nor too far 'that the servants may be in awe'.[47]

What may be an early servants' hall, and in a house where the most fashionable amenities are likely to have been found, was at Tart Hall in London, the house built in the late 1630s for Aletheia, Countess of Arundel. Here there was 'the first hall called the footmens hall', evidently in the basement, but possibly no more than a servants' waiting room and suggesting by the rather clumsy designation that it was a novelty. There was evidently a backstairs leading up from it to the ground floor – another modern contrivance whereby servants could go about their work unobserved by the Quality. Edward Carter's alterations to Northumberland House in London in the 1640s included dividing the hall with a floor and relegating the lower part to use as a servants' hall, 'the low hall'.[48] In some great houses later in the seventeenth century there were two servants' halls: at Hampstead Marshall, for the Earl of Craven, a contemporary plan includes both an eating room for servants and a grander one for gentlemen.[49] Though the grandeur of the earl's establishment was already old-fashioned, there seem also to have been two at Wroxton Abbey, the house of Roger North's noble brother, Lord Guildford: a servants' hall in a wing next to the chapel (equally a room which needed general access for all members of the household) and a 'gentlemen's parlour' off the hall, between high-end and low-end staircases.[50] In the houses of ordinary gentry such distinctions were superfluous and North was impatient with the niceties of servants' protocol, even though he recognised the demand for it: at his own house the servants' hall had a part divided off for the upper servants, 'for quality (forsooth) must be distinguish't'. Most gentry required but one, like the 'servants' parlour' at Barlborough in 1676 which contained three forms and a 'planke' for a trestle table.[51]

Parlours and Withdrawing Rooms

The most persistent of all rooms is the parlour. In the late Middle Ages this was on the ground floor at the high end of the house, though low-end parlours in addition were becoming increasingly common. The parlour was the family's everyday sitting and eating room, and where one entertained guests except when dining more publicly in the hall or more grandly in a great chamber – a function shown by the late medieval arrangement whereby the high-end stair generally rose not from the hall but from the parlour or from a lobby adjacent to it.[52] The inscriptions suggested by Thomas Tusser in 1555 for the decoration of the parlour indicate its hospitable function pretty clearly:

> The drunken friend is friendship very evil;
> The frantic friend is friendship for the devil.
> The quiet friend, all one in word and deed,
> Great comfort is, like ready gold at need . . .
> Woudst have a friend, woudst know what friend is best?
> Have God for friend, who passeth all the rest.[53]

Texts remain round the top of the walls in the parlour at Canons Ashby (pl. 318). Parlours had been a component of the late medieval house, but in the course of the sixteenth century several traditional functions that the parlour had served began to be distributed among different rooms. In the early sixteenth century, inventories frequently (though far from invariably) list a bed in the parlour although it is not clear who was intended to make use of it. However, given the tradition of chambers with combined functions as both day-rooms and sleeping rooms, the use of the parlour by the head of the household as an informal entertaining room did not rule out the possibility of his using it as his own bedchamber. Such usage will have freed the great chamber (discussed below) for the more ceremonious entertainment of guests while maintaining the location of the master's quarters at the high end of the house. At Steeton in South Yorkshire in 1558, the house of Sir William Fairfax, 'the parlour where he lay' was the most expensively furnished room in the house.[54] At Godinton in Kent in 1539 there had been a parlour, a new parlour, a chamber within the parlour and a great chamber, all of which contained beds, but by that time a bed in the principal parlour was already becoming unusual.[55] In 1585 at Michelgrove there was 'the chamber within the parlor called the inner chamber', in which despite its name there was no bed.[56] However, as late as 1660 Sir Roger Pratt recommended a ground-floor bedroom 'for those who are sick, old etc.'.[57]

In the course of the sixteenth century an increasing variety of furnishings occur in those rooms to which the term 'parlour' is applied, and more often than not the word is further qualified, either in recognition that it is inadequate on its own to describe a room's current function or else because of the need to distinguish between different parlours with different specialised uses. The use of the phrase 'dining parlour' seems to begin rather before the middle of the sixteenth century, at just about the time that beds were disappearing from the principal parlour, and it was probably the consciousness of this change that led contemporaries to use the new phrase to emphasise the exclusive usage of the room for eating and entertainment rather than for sleeping in. In Sir Thomas Lovell's house at Enfield (near London where one would expect the most fashionable arrangements)

318 Canons Ashby, Northamptonshire: the low parlour, *c.* 1600. A room for family use and for the casual, informal entertainment of close friends.

there was already a 'dining parlour' in 1524 with contents worth £16 17s and a 'great parlour' with contents worth £3 19s 8d, as well as a third room, also called a parlour but perhaps more of a common waiting room, apparently situated close to both the chapel and the porter's lodge, with contents valued at only 7s 4d.[58] None of these rooms contained beds. In 1571 Sir Thomas Pakyngton's house had a 'dining parlour' with a long table and twelve wainscot stools and a chair, and a draw-leaf table and a livery cupboard with carpets to put on both, all valued at

£3 17s 4d; he also had a smaller, 'new parlour', with green woollen hangings, a table, two leather chairs and seven velvet stools: fewer but finer furnishings and valued at £3 13s 8d.[59] The latter was clearly a more sumptuous room. The terms 'dining parlour' and 'parlour' (unqualified) very seldom occur together – further confirmation that this was increasingly the parlour's principal use.

From the middle years of the sixteenth century there is a steady growth in the number of houses with secondary parlours. Increasingly common is the 'little' parlour, generally so called in distinction from the 'great' parlour and sometimes adjacent to it. Beds tend to persist in little parlours after they have gone from the principal parlour (though at Kimberley in Norfolk in 1588 the position is reversed)[60] and the fact that there is sometimes a chamber next to or beyond the principal parlour – as the 'inner chamber next the parlour' at Leeds Castle in 1538,[61] with contents worth more than the parlour's – suggests that in such a position the terms parlour and chamber may have been interchangeable. Such a room may have been an informal guest chamber, called a parlour from its ground-floor location. At a much lower social level, Gervase Markham in his plan of a yeoman's house of 1629 (pl. 5) shows 'a stranger's lodging within the parlour'. Otherwise, the little parlour may have been a room for private relaxation and perhaps for the more intimate informal entertainment of close friends.

The little parlour can sometimes be a room that is more often called a 'low' parlour – a less pretentious room than a high-end parlour, and situated at the opposite end of the house where it probably served as a family eating and sitting room for everyday use. At Canons Ashby the panelling of the low-end parlour is painted with heraldic and other devices, a cheaper form of decoration than hangings, at least in the long run, but an indication that the room was intended to receive guests; there is also a built-in buffet for dishes (pl. 318). Those who listed the goods of Marmaduke Jennings of Curry Rivel in Somerset in 1558 recorded a high parlour and a little parlour (neither of them containing beds); on the first floor they noted a high parlour chamber and a low parlour chamber, with between them an up-to-date dining chamber, probably over the hall.[62] It is almost certain that his 'little parlour' must have been the room that they referred to as the low parlour when they had got upstairs. Around 1572 the City merchant Sir Thomas Cony seems to have retired from London to live permanently at his family home at Bassingthorpe in Lincolnshire. In anticipation of this move he built on to the old house a grand, new high-end block of building (which alone survives, altered; the rest of the house has been demolished). A remarkable series of inventories taken between 1564 and 1577 list the rooms in the house and their contents both before and after this work; both little and low parlours occur in such a way as to suggest that the former (listed in 1564, 1565 and 1569) has been superseded by the latter (1570, 1572 and 1577).[63] Both these rooms contained beds, and they may have been identical. There was still a 'faire bedstead well carved' in the low parlour at Bishop Auckland in 1628,[64] and although parlours no longer contained beds in the late seventeenth century, an inner parlour or little parlour might contain a day-bed or a couch.

The term 'winter parlour' occurs on several of John Thorpe's house plans made between around 1595 and 1620, where it is generally applied to a room off the low end of the hall: a family sitting and dining room close to the kitchen for warmth and convenience in the cold weather and probably equivalent to the low parlour. Francis Bacon used the term at much the same time in describing the accommodation in an ideal palace, but for a room at the same end of the house as a summer parlour; both were to be 'fair',[65] and Pratt gave the ability to provide rooms for summer and winter as one of the advantages of the deep plan. Balthazar Gerbier in 1663 says that an architect should be able to draw up a plan with proper accommodation for summer and winter.[66] The term is seldom found in inventories, though at Hengrave there were winter and summer parlours in 1605, and there was one at Wiston in Sussex in 1630.[67] In a contemporary plan of a large but compact London house by the architect Simon Basil, a winter parlour lies immediately beyond the hall and over the basement kitchen and is lit from a small internal courtyard; the summer parlour lies beyond it with a bay window overlooking a terraced garden.[68] The large windows of late Elizabethan great houses must have made it difficult to heat the grandest rooms and may have reinforced the need for a warmer, cosier parlour for winter use. (Wotton in 1624 complained that 'there is no part of the structure either more expencefull, then Windowes; or more ruinous (from the cold)'.)[69] Roger North described the parlour at Raynham as 'a warm winter room near . . . pantry and cellar'.[70] As late as 1668, when Sir Abel Barker drew up a specification for his new house at Lyndon in Rutland (now in Leicestershire), he provided for a 'winter parlour' off the low end of the hall.[71] When he died, however, in 1679, the appraisers of his goods called the room the 'Little Parlour'.[72] The near equivalence of 'low' and 'winter' parlour is suggested by the former term's increasing rarity around the time that winter parlours are first mentioned, but as a novel term the usage of the latter may not have been consistent. It seems anyway to be a phrase of transitory use, probably reflecting a fashionable amenity (as prescribed for Bacon's palace) which in practice had to be accommodated wherever it could, but it is a further aspect of the multiplication of specialist room functions and the difficulty of finding consistent locations for them.

At the end of the seventeenth century the function of the low parlour as the family's everyday living room is confirmed by Roger North. 'The comon dining parlor is usually at the other end of the house [from the great parlour and its withdrawing room], which is dedicated to the service of the family',[73] he wrote, and added:

For the comon parlor, this for economy sake must be layd neer the offices, and back entrance. . . . This room must not be great, but neat and pleasant, and posted so as to view the front and back avenew to the house; for, being the place of generall pastime, it is not amiss from it to see all the movements that happen neer the house. And if the walls can be brought to allow it, nothing is more usefull here than closets, cupboards, and presses, for the laying by books, swords, cloaks, and other things, which may be of quotidian use.[74]

At Broadlands in the 1690s the little parlour was next to the servants' hall.[75] As a room for informal entertainment at the low end of the hall the low parlour had much in common with the buttery where household members and respectable visitors might find refreshment between meals. The buttery originated in the Middle Ages. But in a number of late sixteenth- and seventeenth-century houses there is a room at the hall's low end which seems too large or too prominent just to serve the buttery's traditional functions, and it is likely that these tended to merge with those of a more private parlour as the traditions of open housekeeping gradually declined.

The number of parlours tended steadily to increase. In a series of inventories of Browsholme Hall only a low parlour and a high parlour appear in 1591 and in 1610, but in 1634 these are joined by a 'new parlour', with contents valued between the other two.[76] At Woodsome Hall in West Yorkshire in 1580 the former chapel was divided into two parlours 'for lakk of rowme'.[77] The growing number of numbers of parlours in the seventeenth century is general, and it is sometimes difficult to conceive their uses. At Gainsborough Old Hall – a large late fifteenth-century house, altered – there were in 1625 a Little Dining Parlour, a Little Side Parlour and a Garden Parlour as well as the Great Parlour.[78] At East Riddlesden in 1662 there was a dining parlour, the owner's 'own parlour', the 'old squire parlour' and 'old mistress parlour' as well as a 'servants' parlour' detached from the house.[79] At Gayhurst in 1673 there was a great parlour, little dining room, little parlour and parlour next to the buttery as well as a withdrawing room next to the hall and the great parlour, and a study.[80] This increase suggests that the process of differentiating between room uses was continuing: by the seventeenth century the parlour that was used as a family eating room or a formal dining room was normally described as such, while other parlours were becoming what would probably now be regarded as sitting rooms, serving the day-time functions that bedchambers had provided in the past.

In the late seventeenth century a specialised use for a parlour was for smoking: at Charborough Celia Fiennes noted parlour and drawing room, little parlour, servants' room and smoking parlour, 'all well wainscoted and painted'.[81] The low-end location was repeated at Tregothnan, where there was 'a large common parlour for constant eating in, from whence goes a little room for smoking that has a back way into the kitchen';[82] at Wolfeton 'Mr. Trenchard's smoking parlour' was a little panelled room behind the hall stack.[83]

The withdrawing room seems to originate in the sixteenth century in association with a great chamber, a usage discussed below, but from the early seventeenth century withdrawing rooms are increasingly found on the ground floor – an aspect of the multiplication of parlours and of the elaboration of ground-floor entertaining. The term occurs in a variety of contexts, generally seeming to indicate any space set slightly apart but dependent on some other designated room for its purpose. As early as 1600 at Salisbury House in the Strand there was a ground-floor suite of parlour, withdrawing room, bedchamber and pallet chamber; presumably the withdrawing room was either some kind of inner, more private parlour, or else a room with a similar function to its use in connection with the great chamber – a place into which people might withdraw between courses at dinner, or while the room was being prepared for another purpose.[84] There was a similar arrangement at Bayworth

in Berkshire in 1669.[85] At the Earl of Craven's huge new house of Hampstead Marshall of the 1660s, there was the usual 'litle parlor or Ordinary Roome to Eat in' but also a smaller room beyond it, the 'Withdrawing Roome or Roome for the Lord to Eat in'; there was also a 'Roome for the Lord's Records' and next to it a rather larger 'Withdrawing Roome to Repaire the Records' – probably in the sense of sorting them out and keeping them up to date: perhaps as it were an estate office. It is often unclear precisely what is the function of the withdrawing room, as at Gayhurst in 1673 where there were 'two new nether lodging rooms and withdrawing rooms and closets adjoyning to them' – possibly dressing rooms or ante-chambers (both discussed below).

But it is more common in the seventeenth century to find withdrawing rooms associated with parlours. Pratt in 1660 recommended a withdrawing room next to the great parlour, 'with its conveniences like a bedchamber', and evidently visualised a sequence of rooms with the principal parlour lying at the centre between a secondary parlour on one side and a withdrawing room on the other, 'all to lie in a row one into the other next the garden, though they have other doors to them besides, for thus the little parlour may be used as a Drawing Room, when the Drawing Room is used as a bedchamber'.[86] James Scarisbrick's inventory at Scarisbrick Hall in Lancashire in 1670 records a drawing room with a bed.[87] At Gayhurst in 1673 there was a 'withdrawing room next the hall and the great parlour', and Roger North proposed for Wroxton at the end of the century a 'parlour for ordinary use' and a 'withdrawing room' beyond it. There is an ideal sequence of this kind at Forde Abbey in Dorset, fashionably remodelled after 1649 for Edmund Prideaux, Cromwell's Attorney-General.[88] Beyond the hall's high end is a formal dining parlour, with a drawing room beyond that, both with fine plaster ceilings; off the lower end of the hall is a smaller room with comparable decoration and with a second withdrawing room off it.

In Sir Charles Raleigh's house at Downton in Wiltshire in 1698 there were two parlours, a great parlour with contents worth £28 1s and a little parlour with contents worth only £1 13s, but also a drawing room (so called) the contents of which were valued at £39 2s.[89] While the parlour presumably remains as a general eating room, the drawing room may be acquiring something of its modern functions as a ground-floor room for entertaining in comfort – indeed luxury – without the formal dispensing of food and drink, and representing too a stage in the movement of entertainment away from the first floor. In the late seventeenth century Raynham had a great parlour and a withdrawing room next to it, which also provided access to the garden as recommended by Pratt. Roger North uses the term solely with this meaning, as an adjunct to the best dining parlour.[90]

★   ★   ★

Great Chambers, Dining Chambers and Dining Rooms

Besides the parlour, the house's principal entertaining room in the sixteenth century was the great chamber. This too has medieval origins, and like the parlour its history is partly one of separating out different functions: those of eating and sleeping, and its use as the lord's family room and bedchamber from its use for the entertainment of his honoured guests. In the sixteenth century furniture included tables for dining and games as well as a superior bed. The bed was retained in some houses well into the following century, and changes in formal, state rooms may have taken place more slowly than in rooms for the family's more intimate daily use. In a house with an open hall, the great chamber lay at the high end, above the parlour; with the introduction of single-storey halls, it was frequently (though not invariably) placed above the hall. It was a room with multiple functions. When young John Coke was courting Elizabeth Willoughby in 1633, the great chamber featured prominently and had evidently ceased to be a bedchamber. He wrote to his father to describe how

> After Sir Henry had so freely the first night taken notice of the intention of my coming, I desired him next day to give me leave to have some speech with his daughter. He himselfe went in presently & sent her out to me into the great chamber where I had halfe an houres discourse with her. And bec[ause] I conceived it to be expected after supper I rose from the table when she did & toke her by the hand into a round window & tould her of the occasion of my coming. Next morning I had the opportunity to finde her in the great chamber by some favoor, & to speake with her againe. . . . At my departure [Sir Henry] called his Lady & Daughter himselfe into the greatt chamber that I might take my leave of them.[91]

(Francis Bacon remarked that 'Imbowed windows . . . be pretty retiring places for conference.'[92])

The principal development of the great chamber in the sixteenth century was its coming to be used exclusively as a room for formal eating and entertainment. The first known use of the term 'dining chamber' occurs around 1525, and seems to be applied to a grand first-floor room of entertainment which lacks a bed. In 1545 Vincent Munday of Markeaton Hall listed 'the Great Chamber where we dine' – an explicit statement of evolving terminology and use.[93] At Holcroft in Lancashire in 1559 there was 'the great chamber called the dynynge parler',[94] an unusual conflation of chamber and parlour which leaves the location of the room uncertain but leaves its principal function in no doubt. Houses that appear otherwise to resemble each other in size and in the evident quality of furnishings seem during the century or so during which the term is found, to have either a great chamber or a dining chamber but very seldom both – an indication of evolving use. Exceptionally at

Kimberley in Norfolk in 1588 there was a great parlour (£4), a little parlour (£3 1s), a great chamber (£19 12s 6d) and a dining chamber (£9 16s 8d) but Kimberley was a very large house and the fact that the dining chamber was described as 'ould' suggests that the arrangements were not coeval. Another exceptional case is that of Hatfield Priory in 1632, where the so-called 'dining chamber' contained no facilities for eating but did contain a new bed and a close stool.[95] The flooring-in of the hall facilitated the evolution of great chamber to dining chamber, since it became possible to place the dining chamber over the hall while still retaining the best bedchamber in its traditional location above the parlour.

Dining chambers first occur at much the same time as dining parlours. There was a dining parlour and a dining chamber at Middleton in Lancashire in 1675,[96] but by then both phrases have commonly been succeeded by a new, preferred term, 'dining room': at Chideock in 1633 there are both a great dining room and a little dining room, perhaps corresponding to great chamber and parlour which are not otherwise mentioned.[97] Both dining room and dining chamber are mentioned in the Berkeley household orders of 1601, made probably for Cranford in Middlesex by Lord Berkeley's wife, but it is clear that these are one and the same room and that the activities that take place in the room are those of a great chamber without a bed.[98] This was a formal room, though used by Lord and Lady Berkeley for dining and games even when there were no visitors. (As in many aristocratic households, the regime sounds old-fashioned. When the Berkeleys played there alone the gentlemen of the household might come and go as they wished, provided that they were properly dressed, but they were expected to be in attendance when there was distinguished company.)

When dining chambers, itemised as such, disappear from inventories to be replaced by dining rooms, it does not necessarily imply a change to formal eating on the ground floor. When remodelling Castle Bromwich Hall in 1688, William Wynde wrote to Lady Bridgeman that 'according to ye Rules of Building, ye upper Roomes (and specially ye Dining Roomes) are all wayes ye most ornamented'.[99] In 1681 Sir John Coryton was building a new downstairs dining room at Newton Ferrars in Cornwall,[100] but there was still one on the first floor at Branston in Leicestershire in 1684;[101] when used as a substitute for the great chamber, the new term 'dining room' may be primarily a mark of modernity as all associations with the old-fashioned great chamber with its bed are put out of mind. The last occurrence of a great chamber, so called, that has been noted in an inventory is from the 1660s, but the last in which the great chamber actually contains a bed is at Kew in 1643.[102] The 'french bed' there listed was more probably an elaborate couch; there is no mention of hangings for it. There had been a 'couch bed' in the great chamber at Lowther in 1637.[103] For a long time before that it had been normal practice for the distinguished visitor to be given a separate bedchamber rather than expecting him to sleep in the principal room of entertainment.

Chamber Sequences and Apartments

In the sixteenth century and the early seventeenth the great chamber in the grandest houses formed part of a suite of rooms, with a withdrawing chamber beyond it and an inner bedchamber beyond that, with perhaps a servant's bedchamber adjoining. Exceptionally, two great chamber sequences were described in the survey of Shute in Devonshire in 1559.[104] One of these was 'the olde great chamber of the howse . . . wtin wch chamber, ys a wthdrawing place and an house of offyce wtin that'. This old great chamber had no sleeping chamber beyond it: it was itself still evidently a sleeping room. (It also still kept its open timber roof, painted with coats of arms as a demonstration of affinities to the guests who used it.) The other was 'a ffayer great chamber . . . wthin wch is a vearye handsom bed chamber, And wthin that two lytle romes for srvantes and a howse of offyce' and conformed to modern practice. But in such a suite the great chamber might still retain its state bed as a symbol of a guest's presence, even though he or she was in fact sleeping in the more retired bedchamber beyond. There seem to have been two such sequences at The Vyne in Hampshire in 1540, one named for the king and the other for the queen: thus there was the queen's great chamber, the queen's lying chamber and the queen's pallet chamber (a servant's room), all of which contained beds, as well as a great chamber over the parlour, the 'portcullis chamber', the king's chamber 'within the portcullis', and a pallet chamber adjoining; both king's and queen's suites seem to have opened off the great dining chamber, which contained no bed and which will have served as a presence chamber during the royal visit.[105]

Such a suite of rooms, specially built for the visit of the king, survives at Iron Acton north of Bristol, where in 1535 Sir Nicholas Poyntz added – badly built and evidently in a great hurry – a suite of three rooms and a gallery on to a house of medieval origins, of relatively modest size and probably dwarfed by the new work. Fragmentary wall painting in the most fashionable antique taste of the court (pl. 67) still suggests the luxuriousness of the appointments. Something similar was probably intended at Heytesbury in 1540, where Sir Edward Hungerford had begun

> a fayre place, whiche if it had bene fynyshed, had bene able to have receyved the Kynges highnes: a fayre hall, with a goodly new wyndow made in the same; a new parlor, large and fayre; iiii fayre chambers, wherof one is gylted, very pleasant; a goodlie gallerie, well made, very long.

This terse and summary account almost certainly describes a comparable suite of formal rooms culminating in the king's bedchamber and a gallery for exercise and informal conversation.[106] The greatest houses would continue to have two great chamber sequences: Hardwick, Wollaton and Burleigh all have them, probably for the possible entertainment of the monarch (and if married, of his queen).

Plans for an unidentified house in Yorkshire, drawn up by Bernhard Dinninghoff around 1620, are rare in indicating on each floor the intended room uses (pl. 319). Although relatively modest in size, there is a proper sequence of state rooms, with the great chamber lying over the parlour and the dependent rooms over the hall. While not particularly skilful in the disposition of the rooms, the house incorporates a number of up-to-date features such as the concealed entrance in the flank of the hall porch and a passage to the rear of the central range, and Dinninghoff will have known the current requirements of members of the gentry class from his heraldic work for them. At Kirby, in the state-room block that had been built in the 1580s, withdrawing room and bedchamber were side by side, with deep, bay windows looking out over the garden (pl. 79).

State-room sequences can be recognised in houses where they are not otherwise documented. At Chastleton, the rooms recorded in an inventory of 1632 probably do not conform to what was originally intended.[107] Along the north side of the house on the principal floor (pl. 94), a sequence of rooms can clearly be identified as (from east to west) great chamber, withdrawing room, closet and bedchamber; the last was the most luxuriously furnished bedchamber in the house and was named 'Mr. Sheldon's Chamber' for a distinguished friend of Chastleton's owner, Walter Jones. The closet provides access to a garderobe. The withdrawing chamber is simply called 'the middle chamber' but from its location there can be no doubt of its intended function. At Godolphin in Cornwall a set of state rooms was added, probably around 1600, on the first floor beyond the high end of the (now demolished) medieval hall. The first room is clearly a great chamber, large enough for quite lavish entertainment. Beyond this is an inner room, a withdrawing room to be used either as a more intimate and exclusive place of retirement from the great chamber or as a private reception room for the distinguished guest; the door from the great chamber to the withdrawing room is placed in a species of lobby with its own small, oriel window and forming a place of slightly greater privacy within the great chamber itself. Beyond the withdrawing room is a bedchamber, later incorporated into a new range of rooms along the front of the house.

But not many houses were able to provide a complete, purpose-built suite of state rooms, and even houses visited by royalty need not have possessed the ideal sequence. At Kimberley in 1588 the queen's visit ten years before was commemorated in

319 (facing page) Bernhard Dinninghoff: ground- and first-floor plans for an unknown house, c. 1620. A compact, H-plan house with a number of fashionable amenities such as a concealed entrance in the flank of the porch (although the inclusion of a brewhouse within the body of the house would generally have been thought undesirable). Above the parlour and hall is a suite comprising great chamber, withdrawing room and lodging chamber whose location meant that the owner's own bedchamber (and its 'inner room') had to be at the service end of the house.

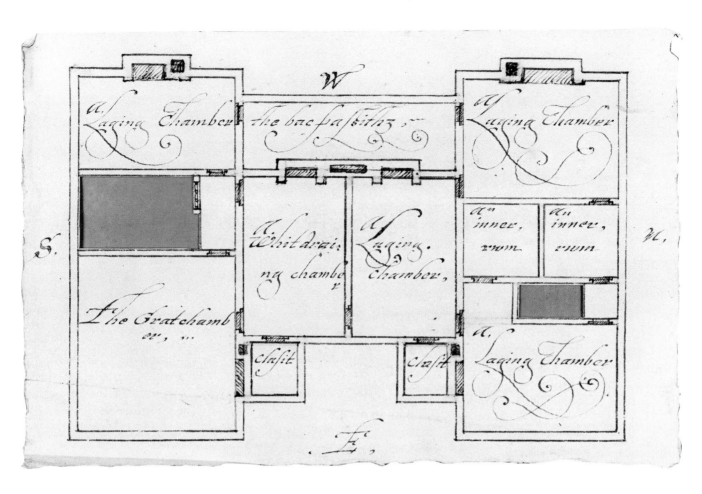
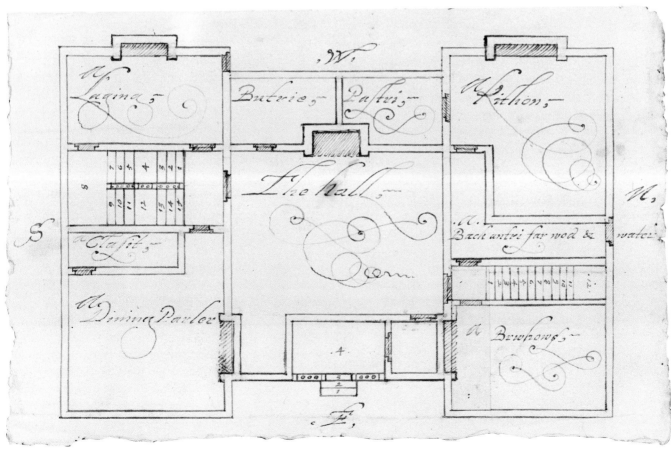

'the quenes chamber next ye great chamber' but there was no withdrawing room as such and it is likely that other rooms would have been pressed into service at need. At Ham in the early seventeenth century the withdrawing room doubled as a state bedchamber.[108] At Shaw, when James I and his queen spent a night in the house in their first Progress, the king was accommodated in what was probably the bedchamber of the house's owner, at the low end (pl. 65). This lay beyond what seems to have been a normal sequence of great chamber, withdrawing room and bedchamber which may have been insufficient for the usage of the monarch. The queen, by contrast, seems to have slept in the best high-end bedchamber: this was no doubt a luxurious room (with its own closet, as had the king's room) but it was less necessary that her chamber should be the climax of an increasing build-up of exclusivity.[109]

In a house large enough to possess a full great chamber suite, there would generally be at least one superior, guest bedchamber as well – at Shaw, the room occupied by the queen. At Chastleton, this is over the second of two high-end parlours and across a landing from the great chamber (so that anyone occupying it could easily retire to it from the entertainment offered in the great chamber). The Chastleton chamber has a chimneypiece bearing the arms of Jones, the family that owned it, impaling those of Fettiplace, for Anne Fettiplace who was married to Henry Jones, the heir. In 1617 the newly married Edmund Sawyer wrote to his father: 'I purpose to send a Bedsted & furniture for the same, I pray send me the height of yor plor Chamber now the flore is layd over it' (and added in a second letter 'if the Bedsted be too high you may cut it shorter').[110] In both cases the owner's heir seems to have lived elsewhere and been given the parlour bedchamber on his visits.

The fullest information about the relationships of rooms in the late sixteenth century and the early seventeenth comes neither from inventories (where the room sequence is not always explicit) nor from surviving houses (where alterations have generally obscured the original arrangement) but from the late sixteenth- and early seventeenth-century house plans left by John Thorpe and Robert Smythson. While there is a remarkable consistency between houses of diverse forms in the rooms they provide, it is clear too that flexibility was designed into many of these plans and that withdrawing rooms, servants' rooms or closets might be contrived so as to make possible different combinations according to circumstances. Dinninghoff's first-floor plan (pl. 319) shows this well: a doorway between the chamber at the end of the state-room sequence and the chamber over the brewhouse in the low-end wing enabled the best bedchamber to be serviced via the low-end stair, but it also made it possible to combine rooms in different ways.

The sequence of rooms commencing with the great chamber was for state: for the reception and entertainment of guests of exalted rank. For higher retainers and gentleman attendants the two-room lodging, beyond the main body of the house, had long been the norm. In 1585 Sir Amyas Paulet, reporting on the suit-ability of Dudley Castle as a prison for Mary Queen of Scots, remarked 'This Queenes gentleman servantes will not like wth their straight [i.e. restricted] lodgings, because they have no inner chambers',[111] but with the decline of such attendance, external lodgings fell into disuse. For the regular occupants of the gentry house the chamber provision was more modest. In the late Middle Ages, the principal chambers of the house generally had no secondary accommodation apart from a garderobe – a latrine – commonly opening off it. It is not unusual before the seventeenth century to find a pallet or trundle bed for a servant included among the furnishings of the bedchamber itself. In the course of the sixteenth century the ideal chamber unit within the house came to comprise two rooms, an arrangement that echoed that of the older, external lodging: a larger room which was initially used as both as a day-room and as a sleeping room by its principal occupant, and a smaller room, invariably more cheaply furnished, which could be used as a servant's bedchamber or as a closet for clothes, surplus furniture and for the safekeeping of linen and of hangings for the house and of other valuables. As such, it might evolve into a private study and in the seventeenth century into a dressing room.

Occasionally the function of the second room as an attendant's bedroom is made explicit, as in 1623 at Standon Lordship in Essex, where there were 'the chamber where my Master nowe lyeth' and 'the next chamber where his man useth to laye', as well as 'Mr. Wilson's chamber over the bowling alley' and 'the next chamber where his man useth to laye'.[112] The chamber suite (though not so called) – the bedchamber and smaller, dependent room variously described as a closet, an inner chamber or a pallet chamber (from the mat on which a servant might sleep) – was by the end of the sixteenth century the least that one could offer a guest or that the owner himself would generally require, though the poorer he was (or the more simply he aspired to live) the greater the proportion of chambers in his house with no secondary rooms.

The extent to which bedchambers were shared or occupied singly can only be inferred, since beds themselves might be shared. As late as 1679 at Lyndon 'Madam Eliz & Madam Thomasin Chamber' – the room occupied by the two younger daughters of Sir Abel Barker – had but one bed, though their maid had a separate room.[113] Growing numbers of bedchambers made it easier to allocate them to individuals or to allow access independent of servants, and both at Little Moreton and at Blackmore Farm, two-room units over the kitchen were altered in the mid-sixteenth century to create two separate chambers, each entered independently. A further indication of the sole occupation of bedchambers is the increasing use during the sixteenth century and the early seventeenth of individuals' names to designate them (a practice described in chapter 7). Although this often seems to have been a matter of commemorating a particular friend or honouring a frequent visitor rather than identifying a permanent member of the household, one must suppose that the individual named will have used the room named on

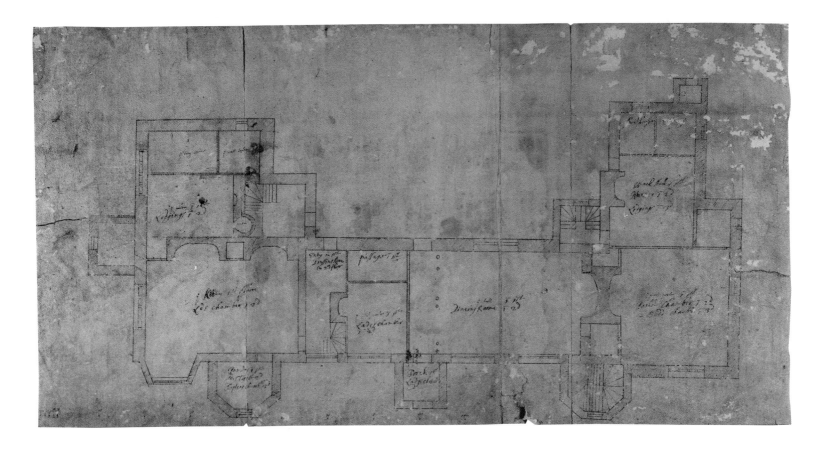

320 Bruce Castle, Tottenham, London: ground-floor plan, *c.* 1685, (cf. pl. 125). The inscriptions (which are partly defaced; spelling modernised) make room uses clear. Anti-clock-wise, from top left, these are:

Dry larder
Wet larder
Pastry [i.e. bakehouse] on ground floor, lodgings [i.e. a bedchamber, probably for visitors] on 1st floor
Kitchen on ground floor, 'Lord's chamber' on 1st.
Pantry on ground floor, lord's closet on first, chaplain's room on 2nd.
Entry on ground floor (a door to the garden), dressing room on 1st.
Passage on ground floor.
Little parlour on ground floor, 'Lady's chamber' on 1st.
Porch on ground floor, Lady's closet on 1st.
Hall on ground floor, dining room on 1st.
Great parlour on ground floor, parlour chamber on 1st, bedchamber on 2nd.
Back parlour [?] on ground floor, nursery [?] on 1st floor, bedchamber on 2nd.
[illegible]

his or her visits. In the course of the seventeenth century, however, there is a gradual shift away from bedchambers being named for individuals and towards their being given the name of a colour scheme – blue, green and so forth.[114] This change reflects, first, a constantly increasing level of comfort and the increasing sophistication of decoration (uniform schemes of decoration and upholstery were an innovation of the early seventeenth century); it also suggests a more private and less ceremonious attitude to the household and to entertaining. Whereas the naming of rooms recognised the family's links with a non-resident individual or else acknowledged the residence in the house of a member of the extended family or of a favoured retainer, the room that is identified only by its decoration is a room to be assigned more generally at need. The room named for a person has, at least symbolically, been abrogated to them and is to that extent a diminution of the self-sufficiency of the household. A room that is anonymous suggests that the family recognised no external commitments and may also indicate fewer non-family residents than in the past.

In the late Middle Ages garderobes were commonly attached to any chamber of consequence, as in the Keevil survey quoted in chapter 3. At Shute in 1554 there were six principal chambers or lodging units, each one of which had its own 'house of office' and the two best had a servant's room as well. (There were numerous other servants' chambers in addition, independent of the better chambers or lodgings, but none of these had garderobes.) Only one parlour is listed in what was evidently an extremely large house, and this too has its own house of office. The fact that garderobes contain no furniture means that they seldom feature in inventories, but there is ample evidence for them in late medieval houses themselves. Little Moreton (described in chapter 3) had one to each chamber.

From the mid-sixteenth century onwards the decline of such provision in new houses is extremely marked. One reason for this may have been purely architectural: the difficulty of incorporating a garderobe projection into an elevation that was increasingly regular and symmetrical. But there were alternative locations (commonly incorporated into a chimneybreast) and probably a more fundamental reason for this decline was a change in manners. The garderobe provided a measure of privacy for bodily functions: it was desirable when sharing a bedroom with other members of the family, but less necessary when the only other occupant of a bedchamber or of an adjoining room was a personal servant among whose duties was the provision at need of a close stool and before whom one had fewer inhibitions than one had in the presence of one's peers. A garderobe had also been desirable when bedchambers doubled as living rooms, and when they lacked closets or inner rooms where a close stool might be kept. However, once many of the functions of the bedchamber had become separated out into specialised day-rooms, there need be less restraint in using the bedchamber itself for private and personal needs. (There is little evidence of how bodily needs were catered for during the day. Presumably one used a close stool in a chamber, or else some provision outside the house: Andrew Boorde had recommended in 1544 'let the common house of easement be over some water, or else elongated from the house'.[115] There are still many houses with eighteenth-century privies in the garden which were obviously constructed not simply for the use of outdoor staff but for members of the family; one can assume that such provision had been made earlier, but hardly any evidence of it seems to survive.)

In the late seventeenth century, the chamber amenities of the best houses increasingly adopted a model of French derivation – the apartment. Sir Roger Pratt urged that 'the apartment for strangers . . . cannot well consist of less than four rooms',[116] which should be placed beyond the principal upstairs entertaining rooms, on the opposite side of the house from the rooms occupied by the family. Such a location was of course already usual for the best guest rooms. The four rooms that Pratt envisaged will probably have comprised an ante-room in which the distinguished visitor could himself receive visitors, a bedchamber beyond it, and beyond that a closet or dressing room and a room for a servant, preferably reached by a backstairs to avoid the servant's having to pass through the more important rooms – particularly when carrying slops. The system can be seen as providing an ante-room as an addition to the three-room apartment, or as a modification of the great chamber/bedchamber sequence but with the significant difference that the outer room was for the exclusive use of the person who occupied the entire

suite. The Wren plan (pl. 317) that shows the use of a vestibule in place of entry by a hall also indicates two chamber sets with ante-rooms on the first floor, each forming the approach to a suite of a different kind. One lies between the principal stair and the 'great dining room', beyond which there is still a (with)drawing room, while the other is part of a private sequence lying between the stair and the 'lord's chamber'; beyond this were his library and 'garderobe double', not in the medieval sense of a privy but probably rather a dressing room and a servant's room. The use of the term helps to confirm the French character of the arrangement.

When in the seventeenth century the apartment was employed in France, its usage was rather different from existing English practice in that its occupant will have received the most important of his (or her) visitors in the bedchamber. In England the entire trend of development over the previous century was against such a public display. The provision of an ante-room in the English seventeenth-century state-room sequence also conflicted to some extent with the increasing use of parlours as ordinary day-rooms, and at the end of the century the pragmatic Roger North described the room as 'fitt for many uses, and need not have a chimny, because it is for passage, short attendance, or diversion'.[117] Consequently in England such sequences are rare and confined to the grandest and most fashionable houses. Far more commonly, an apartment in an English gentry house of the seventeenth century consisted simply of a bedchamber and two inner rooms – an arrangement that can best be seen as a fashionable refinement of the chamber arrangements that had long been current. Pratt recommended that each bedchamber should have

> a closet to it, and a chamber for a servant, which has a door out of his master's chamber and another leading him upon some other passage near the backstairs, so that he need not foul the great ones and whatsoever is of use may be brought up and carried down the back way.[118]

North, while recognising that the ideal was to provide separate dressing rooms for man and woman as well as chambers for servants, admitted that these were 'too much for a private gentleman, who seldom entertaines guests of that nicety'.[119] He continued:

> of late, whether from the straitness of appartments at court, or of London houses I know not, the mode hath . . . delegated [the dressing room] to the use of the man . . . because of the roughness of his service and dressing, and the lady keeps the possession of the bedchamber . . . and doth not affect a different room for dressing, as formerly.[120]

The three-room arrangement already occurs at the Queen's House at Greenwich in the 1630s, in a mid-eighteenth-century plan of West Woodhay of 1636 (pl. 195)[121] (which may or may not reproduce the original arrangement) and at Tart Hall in 1641 there were just such three-room apartments as these.[122] 'My

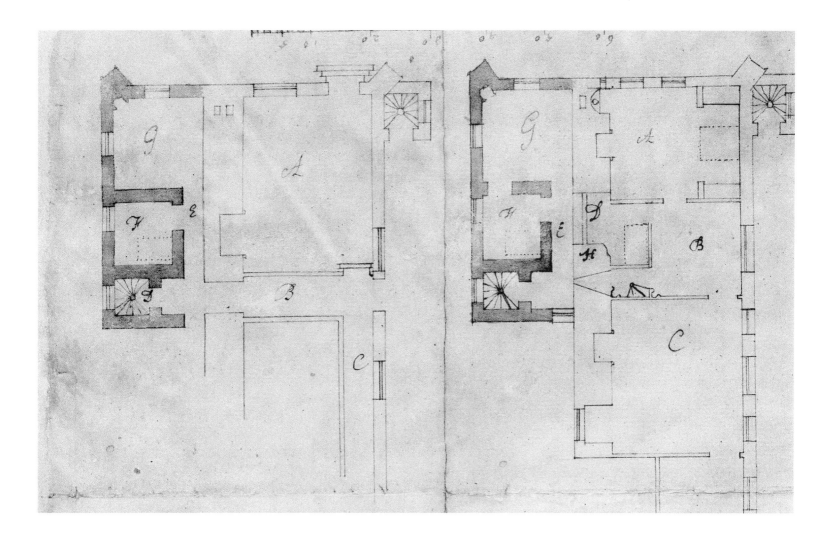

321 Towneley Hall, Lancashire: plan for alterations, c. 1700. Ground-floor (left) and first-floor (right) plans for alterations to one wing. What is proposed is the addition of a small block to provide a dressing room (G, right) and a room for a lady's maid (F, right), to serve a sequence of dining room, (with)drawing room and bedchamber (C, B, A, right). The ground floor contains a servants' hall.

Lord's room' and 'Mr. Thomas Howard's room' – the chambers of the Earl of Arundel and his grandson – were next to each other, with two smaller rooms to the rear of each. One of each of these dependent rooms was a closet, in one of which was a close stool while the other was evidently Thomas Howard's private sanctum. The other two were each described as a 'waiter's room', and though neither contained a bed, in one there was a porter's chair. Tart Hall was the Earl and Countess of Arundel's newly built London house – built for a couple who were rich, aristocratic and famous as connoisseurs, and it will have incorporated the most up-to-date amenities of fashionable living.

The ideal late seventeenth-century arrangement was well described at Coleshill in the 1690s (pl. 199) where there was 'a chamber on each side [of the dining room, on the first floor], with two closets to each, big enough for a little bed . . . and for dressing rooms, one of which has a door also out of it into [a] passage and so to the back stairs'.[123] A contemporary scheme of alterations at Towneley Hall in Lancashire (pl. 321) set out to provide this kind of fashionable apartment while allowing for flexibility in use. On the first floor, at the low end of the house, there was a family dining room (there was a formal dining room in the opposite, high-end range) with a small withdrawing room beyond it, off which was a servant's bedroom; beyond these again was a bedchamber for the lady of the house. It was proposed to enlarge the withdrawing room and to add a small block to contain a servant's stair and two small rooms reached by a short passage. One of these was to be Lady Towneley's dressing room. The other is described on the plan as being

A room with a bed for the ladys woman or a closet for the lady if she pleases with a door into her dressing room . . . if for a woman the door to the dressing room to be walled up and only that to the passage left open.[124]

Layouts need not be rigidly prescriptive and it was important to allow rooms to be used in different ways at need.

While hall, parlours and chambers evolved in the sixteenth and seventeenth centuries from medieval precursors, neither gallery nor study have true progenitors and their development is as clear an indication as any of the demands made by changing mental attitudes. When in 1523 Sir Thomas More erected his 'new building' for 'devotion, study or retirement' in his garden at Chelsea, at some distance from his dwelling house and where he evidently hoped to find peace and quiet from business and from his large household, it comprised a chapel, a library and a gallery.[125] Neither privacy nor the means of achieving it could be assured in the house of traditional form, and More's building may have been a conscious echo of the younger Pliny's *diaetia* at Tuscum: a separate building that comprised two or three rooms (including a bedchamber) set apart from his villa for still greater privacy and quiet, just as at his villa (like More in his own house) Pliny enjoyed retirement from town.

The study is a room for work and for contemplation, for reading and writing and for the safekeeping of books and documents and other private treasures. Roger North described it as 'a closet, for the person, who is supposed to be of quality, to retire to, for devotion, or study, whilst the chamber is cleaned, or company present'.[126] When Allan Bellingham of Levens in Cumbria died in 1579, he provided for his 'evidences [i.e. deeds, leases and settlements] to be safely kept under two locks and keys in my study at Helsington, and at the full age of my sons to be divided according to their rights'.[127] Studies are increasingly common from the mid-sixteenth century onwards, and their presence can be explained by growing literacy, by the Protestant practice of private devotions, by what seems to be a growing interest taken by the landowner in the detailed administration of his estates, by the increased business falling upon him by virtue of the public offices he assumed, by the growing connoisseurship of a sophisticated minority, and above all by a mental climate that was increasingly concerned with the cultivation of the individual and with the enjoyment of privacy as a good.

Studies are not always named as such, though the contents of a closet sometimes make it clear that its function was similar and the words might be used interchangeably. When in 1667 there was a fire at Godolphin in Cornwall, destroying most of Sir Francis Godolphin's papers a fortnight after his death, a letter from an associate described how 'it pleased God by an accident of fire to burn down the greatest part of his house: his closet wherein was most of his writings and to the great loss of his lady and children'.[128] At the same time, his widow writes to her sister-in-law of 'this aditionall losse and distraction amongst us by ye burning of yr deare brothers studdie & all yt was in it'.[129] Both studies and study-like closets are occasionally recorded in the early years of the sixteenth century, though they do not become frequent in inventories until the mid-century; it seems not to be before the 1570s that the word 'study' comes to be

generally prefered. When Edmund Dudley, statesman and notorious exploiter of the royal revenues, was attainted for treason in 1509 and an inventory taken of his possessions, some of his papers were in a closet within the great chamber, 'wherein is contained diverse evidence and other writings as well'.[130] Other papers were in the little wardrobe, probably beyond his own chamber, while the 'counting house' within the little parlour is most likely to have resembled a study in function. Cardinal Fisher in 1534 possessed three studies, so called, but one of these seems from its contents to have been more like a medicine cupboard or a stillroom.[131]

Studies are both their owner's place of business and his private sanctum. In his study within the great chamber in 1545 Vincent Mundy of Markeaton had a number of books, some of which were clearly chosen for pleasant reading – the poems of John Lydgate, John Gower's *Confessio amantis* and several chronicles. At Loseley in the 1550s – in an inventory taken during the lifetime of the house's owner, William More – the contents of 'my closet' included a table, a desk, maps, locked boxes, two other 'tables' (possibly pictures, possibly game boards), law books and a small but similarly eclectic collection of light reading: Chaucer, Gower, Froissart, and a 'boccas' – an edition of Boccaccio. Sir Thomas Elyot saw the study as a place for profitable, private recreation, where in books one might

> beholde those realmes, cities, sees, ryvers and mountaynes . . . [and] the diversities of people, beastis, fowles, fisshes, trees, frutes and herbes: to knowe the sundry maners and conditiones of people, and the varietie of their natures, and that in a warme studie or parler.[132]

Sir William More's wife had a closet of her own, also containing a desk and a table, but including drinking glasses, a case of knives, a case of combs, two pepper boxes and similar treasures.

Since studies and similar closets appear at an earlier date in inventories taken during an owner's lifetime than in those taken on death, the latter may often represent tastes and habits formed a generation before: the Loseley entries are thus not so exceptional as they seem in the immediate context of other contemporary lists. When in the sixteenth century either a study or a study-like closet is included in an inventory, often there are other items among the contents of the house to suggest the owner's cultivation and civility. Thus at Leeds Castle in 1534 the 'great closet' contained sixty-nine books 'emprunted on paper . . . of diverse storyes'. Besides the few in his closet, Sir William More's books in 1554 numbered 120, including history and literature in English and in Latin, Machiavelli, and works on husbandry, law and medicine that the educated head of a landowning family already found of value for the fulfilment of his duties in running his estate, administering his locality and caring for his household. William Glaser of Chester, who died in 1588, had 128 books and 'in the study within the gallery a frame of foure heights for a library',[133] Sir Henry Unton of Wadley in Berkshire in 1596 had two studies in his house (one of them a 'Mr

Payne's')[134] and 220 books; the theologian Richard Hooker of Bishopsbourne in Kent (though not quite of the same social class, but one of the greatest scholars of his age) had in his study and little parlour books valued at £300.[135] By the end of the century a study was familiar to contemporaries even if it contained few goods by which one might now identify it: when Sir Thomas Wodrington of Widrington in Northumberland died in 1593, the appraisers noted 'the study within the great chamber', even though they recorded nothing in it except a bed and bedding and fire irons; evidently it was a small, private room and heated.[136] In 1640 it was the term Sir Henry Slingsby used for the consulting room of Sir Theodore Mayerne, the royal physician,

> wch was a large roome furnish'd with books & Pictures; and as one of ye chiefest, he had ye picture of ye head of Hyppocrates yt great physitian; & upon his table he had ye proportion of a man in wax, to set forth ye ordure [sic] & composure of every part; before his table he had a frame wth shelves, wheron he set some books; & behind this he sat to receive those yt came for his advise.[137]

The location of the study, as a room that was not a component of the traditional layout, was more variable than that of the parlour, and it cannot always readily be identified on a plan. In Italy, where *studii* are recorded from the fifteenth century and from whence the name of the study probably derives, the *studio* (or *studiolo*) of the scholar or connoisseur was often within or beyond the owner's bedchamber, having developed from a writing desk or – as in England – from a closet.[138] This was the location of Edward Isaac's closet at Well Court in 1574 in which were a desk and books.[139] When Grafton Manor was rebuilt in 1567 after a fire, its amenities included 'My mr. new study the chamber adjoining the buttery chamber': a first-floor room, and from its location probably close to the owner's own bedchamber at the lower end of the house.[140] At Holcombe Rogus in Devonshire the study of perhaps around 1610 is situated in a tall tower over the porch, reached only by a private stair off a low parlour and ensuring both privacy and security. The study at Holcombe is lined with wainscot of high quality which incorporates built-in cupboards for title deeds, leases and other papers. Similar, built-in cupboards are shown in one of Robert Smythson's drawings (pl. 322).[141] Tower locations had occurred earlier; in the 1540s Leland noted that Henry Percy's private room in his castle Wressle on Humberside was called 'Paradise' from its location at the top of the house.[142] It could be a small room off the upper end of the hall (where it may have evolved from the oriel) and where it would be well placed as a business room, accessible for visitors arriving by the hall door. At Tunstall in Kent there is a small room beside the upper-end hall fireplace, which is clearly identifiable as 'the study in the hall' in an inventory of 1677. Although of modest size, Tunstall was the home of a rich man, John Grove (d. 1678), who had been steward to Sir Edward Hales (d. 1655), the richest commoner in Kent. Grove

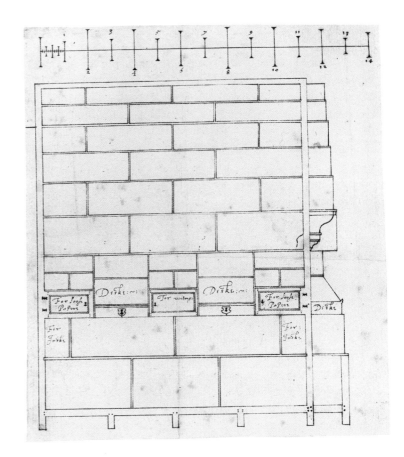

322 Robert Smythson (c. 1600): design for a fitted desk and shelves in a study.

himself, described as 'esquire', left an estate valued at £9400, including £5200 in cash. He will have needed an office for his work.

It is not before the third quarter of the sixteenth century that the gallery becomes at all general.[143] It originated as a species of covered or semi-enclosed passageway between the different parts of a complex of buildings; it was in due course exploited as an amenity in its own right for walking and for admiring the gardens or the park that it overlooked or enclosed, and although it is clear from their contents that references to galleries in the sixteenth and seventeenth centuries are generally to an enclosed space, open loggias are sometimes so described, particularly in the early years of this period. The most elaborate of early galleries were in the royal palaces at Richmond and Whitehall; at the Duke of Buckingham's great house of Thornbury in Gloucestershire the remains still exist of a two-tier gallery overlooking his privy garden. Three are listed in the inventory of the contents of Edmund Dudley's London house, one of which was rather a species of loggia, open to the garden with another, enclosed, probably lying over it – an arrangement like that at Thornbury.[144] A rare survival of such an arrangement is at Ightham Moat (pl. 47), where early in the sixteenth century a gallery above an open loggia was built down one side of

Kew.[146] There was a gallery on the second floor at Mendham Hall in Suffolk in 1548, which already contained a few pictures of various sorts (including needlework) anticipating a location and contents that were to become commoner as the century progressed.[147] Sir Richard Catesby had a gallery recorded in 1553, not in his principal house of Ashby St Ledger but in a secondary dwelling, perhaps in town.[148] Sir Thomas Pakyngton had one in 1571, with sparse and miscellaneous contents.[149] In 1574 Edward Isaac of Well Hall in Kent had two galleries, one over the hall which served also as an armoury, and a second which at the time of his death housed a good deal of furnishings including the hangings from the great chamber: it appears from other entries that extensive building work was going on at the time and one, if not both, of these galleries may have been newly made. But in general the gallery does not become an accepted feature of the houses of the upper gentry until late in the sixteenth century.

The location of the gallery varied as much as did that of the study, reflecting not only lack of precedent but the gallery's varied functions. Ideally it was accessible to the great chamber, and its usage complementary. In the great chamber the company found formal entertainment, while in the gallery the same people could engage less formally in talk, play, business or gentle exercise. Its length encouraged the formation of separate, intimate groups. On the other hand, it also reflected the great chamber's origins as a formal bedroom, and if possible the gallery therefore also lay adjacent to other guest chambers so that a visitor could use it as an amenity ancillary to his own suite of rooms. Although it needed to be close to the rooms used by upper guests, it was not always possible to place it in an ideal relationship with them.

In a house of a single range, of H or half-H plan, there were not many options available. It was most generally placed above the central, hall range of the house, where at Ufton Court in the 1570s a gallery was formed within the roof space of the fifteenth-century hall. Alternatively it might lie over the high-end wing, as it did at Eastbury of the same date, where there was a gallery within the roof on the second floor. There were more possibilities in a courtyard house, with four separate ranges available in which to accommodate it. At Sawston (which is compared with Castle Bromwich Hall in chapter 3) the gallery is on the first floor of the earlier (rear) range, overlooking a park. Within the house it is approached at each end but only through either of two bedchambers with garderobes; this limitation on its general accessibility was only partly circumvented by providing it with its own stair turret which had to be reached across the courtyard from the rear door of the screens passage. In contrast is the arrangement at Castle Bromwich where the

the courtyard to link the body of the house with rooms in the gatehouse range opposite. At Bisham Abbey, Sir Thomas Hoby preserved one range of a medieval cloister as a loggia (pl. 323). Bisham had humanist associations before the Hobys bought it, when it was the scene, real or imaginary, of Thomas Starkey's *Dialogue between Pole and Lupsett* (quoted in chapter 1): Cardinal Pole was the brother of the house's then owner, the Countess of Salisbury. The setting may recall the scene of the debates of the Stoic philosophers, a precedent for the garden gallery that provides the location for Erasmus's *Colloquies*.[145]

Galleries integral with the house (rather than as an external amenity) occur in the homes of great men early in the century. As early as 1523 Agnes Hungerford of Heytesbury possessed a gallery containing chests with documents and linen; this may have been simply a broad passage. The surviving gallery at The Vyne is probably of before 1527, and when he died in 1556 the Earl of Devon had a gallery in his far-away Cornish house at St

gallery occupies the forward part of the front range, opening immediately off the great chamber, though without direct access from what was probably the best bedchamber. In a third court-yard house of similar general form, Canons Ashby in Northamptonshire (a house whose entrance has been reversed – it now lies through a former service courtyard at the rear), the gallery originally overlooked the front of the house like that at Castle Bromwich. However, in the late seventeenth century it seems to have been altered so that it now looks on to the courtyard. The conversion is significant, suggesting that as the value of the gallery as an amenity declined so it was preferred that the bed-chambers that gave off it should have a pleasant outlook, while the gallery itself came to be primarily a passage for communication rather than a place of diversion.

Where galleries occur in relatively modest houses and in those of a linear plan, they generally run the length of the building. To describe such spaces as galleries may sometimes be anachronistic: the amenity value of such passages was often slight. When beds are noted in galleries, the space in question may simply have been a long, narrow passage room. Sir Henry Sutton in 1559 had both a long gallery and a little gallery; there was a trundle bed in the latter.[150] Where, as at Loseley and elsewhere, the hall rises through two floors, the gallery may be the sole link above ground-floor level between the ends of the house; in such cases its importance for the building's circulation must have been at least equal to its value as an amenity. Passage galleries cannot easily be equated with the recreational galleries of other houses, and it is likely that the term 'gallery' was often used in an inventory simply to denote an ordinary passage, as the increasing quantity of goods in the house made it necessary to describe the location of objects in circulating areas.

Small chambers frequently open off galleries, both those for recreation and for communication, and closets or chambers within galleries are often listed in inventories. This circulatory function in the linear house anticipates the use of the gallery as a developed upper-floor passage serving chambers off it in houses of more complex plan in the seventeenth century. That at Holcombe Rogus in Devonshire, clearly a recreational gallery from its plastered ceiling, has several rooms of small size occupying spaces beside roof trusses (pl. 324); internal door bolts seem to show that these were bedchambers rather than closets. In a number of seventeenth-century houses with deep, rectangular plans a top-floor gallery is primarily a central passage with servants' chambers off it. This is the arrangement envisaged in Wren's plan (pl. 317). At Coleshill Celia Fiennes recorded 'a gallery all through the house and on each side severall garrett roomes for servants furnished very neate and genteel'[151] and the same arrangement is described in Wren's notes to his plan. The arrangement survives on the top floor of Thorpe Hall.

In these houses the gallery is ceiled; at Stanwardine in Shropshire the long roof space over the main body of the house seems never to have been plastered, but nevertheless provides access to a chamber over the oriel bay of the hall and great chamber.[152] In a few inventories from the north-west, such as that of Sir William Norris of Speke in 1624,[153] there is reference to articles housed 'in the false roof', which may mean a roof space of this kind, above the ceilings of the rooms on the uppermost storey but not qualifying, by usage or by layout, to be described as a gallery. At Stanwardine and at Heskin Hall in Lancashire only one stair seems to have risen to the roof space so that it could never have served as a lateral passage. What the Stanwardine arrangement and these Cheshire inventory entries might imply is that where access existed (or could easily be contrived) to both ends of a long roof space – enabling it to be used as a passage – the owner might well choose to enhance it as some kind of gallery, regardless of how practical it was as an amenity: a ceiled gallery in so modest a gentry house is probably to be seen as a status symbol, a deference to fashion rather than as a true place of recreation.

Recreational galleries retained a limited popularity throughout the second half of the seventeenth century. 'I like a gallery in a house though it takes up lodging room', wrote Lord Fairfax in 1651 in respect of a new house he had thought to commission from Edward Carter,[154] and as late as 1683 Lord Weymouth consulted Wren about the building of a gallery at Longleat where previously there had been none.[155] But except in the grandest houses the precise function of the gallery remained slightly ambiguous, never wholly assimilated into the standard catalogue of accommodation. At the end of the century Roger North accepted its value 'for no other use but pastime and health',[156] though deploring galleries on the top floor of a house because no one could be bothered to go up there: a reluctance that would increase with the tendency that was emerging by the end of the century for dining and other entertainment to be removed from the first floor to the ground. North recognised two kinds of gallery, a grand one for the entertainment of guests and a more modest one for the use of the family, distinct both in their functions and in their location; the visitors' gallery should overlook the gardens, the owner's may be placed 'so that the master may in his promenade there see to the acting of his servants.' At Lower Slaughter in 1687 there was a 'long garret' with a shuffleboard[157] – probably a pastime for family and friends rather than an element in the formal entertainment of important guests (though there had also been a shuffleboard in the otherwise very impressively furnished gallery at Ingatestone Hall in 1600,[158] and there remains one at Littlecote in Wiltshire).

Roger North's own prescription was for a gallery

of a midle sort, not wholly dedicated to parade, nor to private use, but such as may serve reasonably to both purposes. . . . And therefore this should be placed with indifference so as to serve both the ordinary, and reserved apartments of the house. And a sort of moderation may be allow'd as to the decoration, and position of it, with respect to the offices of the family, being supposed for the use of the master and his family,

324 Holcombe Rogus: the gallery. This has small chambers off it, probably for servants (they have bolts on the inside of the doors). The distinction between galleries for recreation, corridors that give access to rooms off them and passages purely for communication was a flexible one, and the same term might be used for any of the three.

and his indulgent friends onely, and not for proud and ambitious enterteinements of grandure.[159]

It is clear that North regarded the gallery as an agreeable amenity but not as an essential part of the accommodation of the house. In discussing the fitting-up of his newly altered house in 1694, Sir John Lowther wrote to his agent:

I have been thinking that since there will need so much more Wainscott that it were best to take down the Wainscott in the Gallerie, and Putt it in those Rooms that want it in the Uppermost Storie, and so Wainscott the Gallerie anew more Fashionably which also may be done time enough when I come into the Countrie it not being a Room of Constant and Necessarie Use.[160]

More commonly, as at Tyttenhanger (pl. 325), it might be the gallery itself that would be lined with second-hand panelling. The high gallery was simply too far off, and when as in some lesser houses its attractions had not been great in the first place, it is hardly surprising that the contents of many galleries, listed in inventories, suggest that they might come to be used as repositories for junk. As such, together with their remoteness, they might make perfect children's playrooms: George Wither, describing the ideal palace for the senators of a reformed parliament in 1653, urged that there should be 'No little children in the garden sprawling/Or in the galleries or cham-

325 Tyttenhanger, Hertfordshire: the gallery. Re-used sixteenth-century wainscot in the passage gallery of a large mid-seventeenth-century house. Servants' bedchambers open off it. With the decline of the gallery as an amenity, fashionable decoration was no longer essential.

bers yawling'.[161] There was a 'garrett called the Scholehouse' at Loseley in 1633.[162] It may have been realisation that the top of the house was a good place for the children (it was evidently where Sir John Lowther placed his children, in the letter quoted on p. 274) that had prompted change at Shardeloes some time before 1698 – 'the new nursery formerly the gallery'.

★ ★ ★

Private Regions: Chambers, Nurseries and Service Rooms

As Roger North intimated, it is difficult to generalise about the disposition of the private areas of the house, but whereas at the beginning of the sixteenth century the house's owner generally slept at its high end, in the great chamber or in a second superior bedchamber, by the seventeenth century he seems more commonly to have slept at the low end. The great chamber had originated as the solar, the general-purpose, best room of the medieval house, where its lord customarily lived, slept and entertained; the solar towers and blocks of rooms of the feudal, fifteenth-century great house had been at the high end. The 'chief chamber' at Nettlecombe in 1525 was identified by the appraisers as 'my Master's chamber'.[163] But already before the mid-sixteenth century there is evidence for the owner's own chamber moving to the low end of the house. Sir John Fermor's lodging tower at East Barsham is mentioned above. At Melbury in 1559 Sir Giles Strangways's 'owne lyvinge chamber' and its inner chamber appear in the inventory between 'the lowe chamber next to the hall dore' and 'the chamber over the kechynge'. It has been seen how in 1534 the owner of Brympton D'Evercy retained for himself a low-end block of lodgings on handing over the rest of the house to his son. In 1616 Christopher Preston of Cricket St Thomas similarly handed over most of the manor house to his son John, retaining only (with other rooms) 'the chamber over the kitchen wherein the said Christopher Preston doth now and lately did usually lye'.[164] In Bernard Dinninghoff's plan (pl. 319) there would have been nowhere else for the owner to have slept since the space over the parlour and hall were occupied by the great chamber and its dependencies. At Chastleton in 1650 the owner's married heir, who lived in the house, was sleeping over the low parlour[165] while the house's owner probably slept above the kitchen. At the end of the seventeenth century Roger North placed his own room here, as did Lord Compton at his suburban house of Bruce Castle at Tottenham (pl. 320).[166] At Shardeloes in 1698 the appraisers noted 'the Roome over the Kitchen vizt Mrs Drake's Bedchamber' with the usual two rooms off it: 'Mrs Drake's closet' and 'Madam Oselles the Lady's Woman's room'.[167]

When the great chamber was at the centre of the house, over the hall, it could readily be reached by the owner from a low-end chamber. The low-end location allowed the bedchamber of most frequent occupation to benefit from some of the heat below, concentrated the everyday living rooms at one end of the house and made it easier for the occupant and his wife to oversee the daily running of the household. It may thus be linked to the increasingly active involvement of owners themselves in the management of their estates: it is the location of pairs of lodging rooms that existed early in the sixteenth century at Cannington, Little Moreton and St Aylotts and which it is suggested below were for the use of a bailiff or steward. But, more fundamentally, the factors which are apparent at Chastleton and in Dinninghoff's plan can be inferred more generally: that with the expansion of the best guest chambers at the high end of the house, its owner would have to move elsewhere. The move may have been a factor in the gradual abandonment of hierarchical distinction in the external form of the house. At East Barsham and at Brympton the owner's low-end lodgings are clearly marked: he has, so to speak, taken his rooms to the low end of the house with him.

There is evidence from the late sixteenth century and later of the owner's sleeping on the ground floor. This was certainly the case at West Auckland in 1633 when John Eden, esquire, was accused of adultery and witnesses testified that he slept in a chamber beyond his parlour.[168] When Thomas Dolman of Shaw died in 1620, he had been sleeping in the principal ground-floor room at the low end, though he was by then old and it is likely that he had had to move out of his own room for the king's visit in 1603 and he may never have moved back (pl. 65). But

in Gervase Markham's plan (pl. 5) the room beyond the parlour is identified as a chamber for visitors. Other ground-floor chambers beyond parlours have been mentioned already, and in the late seventeenth century these become more common in great houses. But whether for the owner or for guests, from the point of view of marking the location externally it had ceased to matter: with privacy increasingly valued, the location of rooms was no-one's business outside the household.

The rearrangement of first-floor hierarchies and the migration of the owner's rooms to the low end of the house was made more acceptable by the relocation of stairs, and as with so many of the ways in which the forms of houses developed it is impossible to know which of these interrelated developments has priority. One way of providing acceptable access to the low end was by providing matched stairs, as at Chastleton. The alternative was the central stair rising to a landing from which one could turn indifferently one way or the other: Coleshill of 1650–52 is the perfect example of the arrangement (pl. 200). At Coleshill, where all services were in the basement, the traditional notion that one end of the house was superior to the other has all but disappeared save for a few vestigial traces – arrangements which are of interest in showing how they lingered even in a house of revolutionary form. The kitchen is at one end of the house, and a service stair rises from opposite the kitchen to the 'living parlour' at the same end of the building on the ground floor: the equivalent of the old low parlour or winter parlour and now by its name admitted as the everyday eating room of the family. Immediately above this was Sir George Pratt's own chamber and its closets, perpetuating the now common practice of the head of the family sleeping at the low end.[169]

It is difficult to place children's rooms. Early in the sixteenth century children's chambers may sometimes have lain through their parents' rooms. John Aubrey recounted how Sir William Roper visited Sir Thomas More's house to choose one of More's daughters for a wife. He found them both asleep, according to Aubrey, 'in a truckle bed in their father's room'; a century later Aubrey was amused by what followed[170] but even in the early sixteenth century it seems surprising that grown-up daughters in one of the most cultivated families of the age should be sharing a bedroom with their father. The original tale may have been that they were sleeping not 'in' but 'within' their father's room – i.e. in an inner room beyond it. At Blackmore Farm there is a chamber under the roof, over and reached through the room that was probably occupied by the house's owner. In the sixteenth-century plan from Suffolk, mentioned above (pl. 302), one good chamber with a garderobe can be entered only through another, apparently identical in size and amenities: the lack of independent access suggests that at both places these may have been children's rooms.

Inventories frequently mention nurseries, and though from their contents they would seldom be identifiable as such their occurrence argues the perceived need for special provision for children. Occasionally there is evidence of children elsewhere, such as 'one folding table for children' in the parlour at Hanford in Dorset in 1611, and a child's chair in the queen's room at Kimberley in 1588. At Browsholme there was a children's chamber in 1591 and 1610, a school chamber in 1610 and 1634: room names may have changed as children grew older, though it seems unlikely that such rooms were in continuous occupation over forty-three years.[171] At Lady Dorchester's house at Gosfield in 1639 there was 'Mrs Elizabeth's chamber, or upper nursery'. This was evidently the bedroom of Elizabeth Bayning, an unmarried daughter, at least in her mid-teens (she married two years later), and the name of the room evidently changed as she grew up.[172] To judge by the other rooms that occur near them in the lists, nurseries were generally located at a little remove from the best rooms in the house, though (as now) sometimes a little less far from parents' own bedrooms.

Servants' bedchambers are sometimes identifiable by the name of the individual, by his function or by a group name such as the hinds' or menservants' chamber. The presence of personal servants can be inferred from secondary beds in or adjacent to their masters' and mistresses' rooms. A recurrent room name is the 'maids' chamber', whose location, to judge from the position of the room in the inventory, was usually close to the master's and mistress's own room. This was evidently a room for female, personal attendants when it was inappropriate for them to sleep in a secondary, dependent chamber. But while such chambers provided for personal attendants, in a high proportion of surviving houses there is now insufficient accommodation for all of the servants that must have staffed them, and the impression of inventories is that they lodged where they could with little system in the location of their rooms: the servants' chambers that are named are often interspersed among stables, brewhouses, bakehouses and other elements of the domestic complex, many of which were not structurally part of the main building. Hence, when – as has generally occurred – such ancillary buildings have been demolished, servants' chambers and garrets have been lost as well. Their furnishings are generally sparse, and beds may have been shared. There are sometimes two or three beds in a servants' room and occasionally more: at Markeaton, there was a 'great chamber where the servants lie' which contained three bedsteads, one of them 'larg of oke', and at Sir Richard Hutton's house in 1629 there were five bedsteads in the men's chamber, but in the sixteenth and seventeenth centuries such dormitories are not common.

Inventories, valuable in tracing the evolution of rooms of state as well as to some extent their disposition, are of much less help in following the history of service rooms which consists less in their progressive elaboration but rather the reverse. Their history is primarily of relocation, of a continuing tendency to reduce their impact upon the polite rooms of the house. The service rooms present in almost every house were kitchen, pantry, buttery, bakehouse, larders and brewhouse. The functions of the buttery and pantry, where beer and bread were dispensed to the household and to casual visitors, partook both of service and of entertainment, and their conventional position was off the low end of the hall, immediately adjacent to the screens passage, and the buttery was frequently sited above a cellar reached directly by its own stairs, for the convenient storage and retrieval of drink.

Its traditional associations with open housekeeping led Sir Henry Wotton to write that 'by the natural Hospitalitie of England, the Buttrie must be more visible'.[173] In the 1650s John Webb included a buttery next to the hall at Maiden Bradley, otherwise a house of very advanced plan.[174] But the buttery might occasionally be at the high end of the house, convenient for entertaining in the parlour, as at Bayworth in Berkshire in 1669.[175] Pantries, which had in the past been in a similar position, were tending during the sixteenth century to migrate to remoter regions, their functions partly assumed by the buttery. Larders – often both 'wet' and 'dry' – had to be adjacent to the kitchen, which by the early sixteenth century was normally within the body of the house. A bakehouse (often called the pastry) might be within the house or outside; dairies generally outside, though occasionally inside it; brewhouses almost invariably outside the body of the house because of the heat, wet and smells. (The inclusion of a brewhouse in Dinninghoff's plan is most unusual.)

The kitchen was of course the most important of service rooms. In inventories its equipment is often comparable in value with that of the better rooms in the house, both because of the demands of catering for a large household and because of the degree to which the household had to be as far as possible self-contained. In the classic plan of the late medieval house, a further passage ran at right angles to the screens passage, between buttery and pantry, to a kitchen which might be more or less detached from the main body of the house. This seems to have been the arrangement at Bisham Abbey, where the kitchen passage survives, even though the medieval kitchen itself has been demolished. There was evidently a similar layout at Haslington, where there is evidence for a passage running off the entry between rooms which probably functioned as pantry and butttery.

The concentration of service functions around a kitchen courtyard, though persisting in many large houses, was also an intermediate step towards the integration of services within the body of the house. The value of a kitchen courtyard was in bringing together related service functions – normally kitchen, bakehouse, dairy and brewery – while at the same time keeping them beyond the ambit of the polite rooms. A service passage was valuable in perpetuating this separation. At Woodsford Castle of around 1400 a line of corbels suggests that a service passage was contrived as a lean-to against the face of the building (pl. 326). At Great Chalfield such a passage is integrated as an open-sided corridor resembling a loggia, down the side of the low-end wing and beneath the upper storey (pl. 39); at Ockwells it wound round two sides of the service courtyard, providing access to successive service rooms on the way. At Hengrave, a small service court appears to have been created out of some earlier buildings, but this seems to have been connected directly with the hall and low parlour.[176] At Dorney Court in Buckinghamshire the services are grouped around a small internal courtyard and are reached by a passage within the body of the house. Similarly, at East Barsham a passage led past Sir John Fermor's lodging tower to a kitchen which overlooks a small courtyard behind the main front of the house.

Medieval kitchens in great houses had often been detached from the body of the house. A large household needed a kitchen of considerable size, often containing more than one fireplace, and open to the roof to lessen the great heat. By the sixteenth century, even when such huge kitchens persisted (as at Burghley, Cowdray and Hampton Court), they were incorporated within the house, and in lesser, conventional, U- or H-plan houses of the sixteenth and seventeenth centuries, the kitchen was integrated with the low-end wing. At Shapwick in Somerset there are fragments of an external kitchen of around 1500; the house was rebuilt with an internal kitchen a century later.[177] But the perennial problem with regard to the kitchen was its relation to the superior rooms: too near and the smells and the noise obtrude; too far and it is an inconvenience. In a small house there is little choice but to place it at the front of the wing, and this might be its preferred position in a larger building. Leigh has two rooms in the low-end wing which both have large fireplaces (pl. 213); an inventory of 1640 records both old and new kitchens, and may record the moving of the kitchen from the forward end of the wing to the rear.[178] However, with the introduction of more compact house plans around 1600 the kitchen might be brought into unwelcome proximity to the polite rooms of the house. Anderson in Dorset, an early and partial example of the form, when built may have had its kitchen in one half of the front range, the hall occupying the other (pl. 171). Such prominence for the kitchen, in a house which though small was the home of a man of standing, was clearly undesirable and before the end of the century it seems to have been relocated into a service wing at the rear. At Athelhampton, Bingham's Melcombe,[179] Haslington in Cheshire and Bowringsleigh in Devonshire services were similarly relocated in the seventeenth century in order to create an additional parlour. Boston Manor at Brentford is another compact house for an aristocratic owner and of the same date as Anderson; here too in 1670 the kitchen was moved from the body of the house to a wing.[180] At Thorpe Hall, a larger, rectangular house of 1654, the kitchen was located in a wing from the first. Eyam in Derbyshire (pl. 257) has an E plan of a more traditional overall form, although the hall is entered centrally in an up-to-date manner.[181] Here it is uncertain whether the kitchen was always in the inconspicuous wing that extends from the house's low end or whether it relocated there subsequently. At Winslow Hall, designed by Wren at the end of the century, the principal kitchen was in a low wing like that at Thorpe although there was a smaller internal kitchen as well.[182] It is not known how the work was divided between the two.

The problem of segregating the kitchen was one that was felt even before the emergence of compact houses in any number, and the solution increasingly resorted to was its placing in the basement. No definite English example has yet come to light earlier than Longleat, but the long building history of Longleat makes it uncertain when, before the house's final completion around 1580, a basement kitchen was first envisaged. The kitchen may have been in the basement at Whitehall in Shrewsbury (pls 140, 141), of 1578. The location of the kitchen at Longleat may have been of French inspiration, given the presence of basement kitchens in French houses at an earlier date and the involvement of French masons at Longleat; if so, it may be a rare example of foreign craftsmen having a direct impact on the overall form of an English house. After Longleat, basement kitchens seem to spread rapidly. Their occurrence has not been traced in detail, though they are much more commonly found in houses with compact plans than in those of more traditional layout.

The usual ground-floor ceiling height of an upper-class house in the seventeenth century – 12 or 14 feet – provided adequate height for a kitchen. In a basement, however, it was difficult to give it sufficient head room, even though there was a contrary advantage in that a basement raised the upper floor into greater prominence. In the early seventeenth century the solution sometimes arrived at – for example at Eagle House, Wimbledon, and initially at Holland House (both discussed in chapter 4) – was to raise it halfway into the ground floor, thus making necessary a species of low-ceilinged mezzanine immediately above it. At the end of the century North considered the arrangement unsuited to a country house, however acceptable it might be in the suburbs, and it certainly limited the usefulness of the room so treated. At Darsham Hall in Suffolk, the surviving low-end wing of a large house of around 1600, the kitchen lies forward, rising through two storeys; to the rear are two floors of other service rooms and family bedchambers. There is a continuous garret floor throughout.

There are other instances besides Darsham of low storey heights in service wings relative to those of the polite rooms of the house. Elsewhere in East Anglia they occur at Wood Dalling in Norfolk, perhaps around 1580 (pls 329, 330);[183] at Kirstead in the same county, probably after 1600 (pl. 246)[184] (where the overall symmetry of the flanking wings at first disguises their difference in floor levels); and at Little Hautbois[185] where, as at Wood Dalling, the services are in an asymmetrical wing (pls 220, 221). But the occurrence of the arrangement elsewhere suggests that it may have been widespread: for instance at Wilderhope in the 1580s (pls 302, 303); at Bradford on Avon around 1610; at the Old House in Mickleham in Surrey,[186] a house of the 1630s whose style connects it with contemporary building in London; and in the far north-west at Hayton Castle, perhaps in 1609.[187] The practice may sometimes have been adopted for the sake of economy where lower, service rooms are fronted by taller rooms in order to present a uniform façade; at Wilderhope and at Little Hautbois, on the other hand, it was probably still intended that the greater prestige of the polite rooms should be marked by their greater prominence.

Lodgings and Self-contained Accommodation

The rooms considered so far have been for resident members of the owner's immediate household, or for visitors whose status or close connection with him led them to be received as members of his family. Although inventories and contemporary plans reveal much about the amenities and arrangements of the house, there are features that occur in extant buildings that documents do not wholly explain. There is sometimes evidence of independent lodgings within the house; Little Moreton has two such. The high-end lodging now connects with the main body of the house, but originally did not: it comprises the chapel, a ground-floor room giving on to it, and overlooking it on the first floor a chamber of good size with its own garderobe. There seems to have been a similar arrangement at Smithills, 25 miles away, where (see p. 260) late in the sixteenth century two brothers successively managed the affairs of a third. It is possible that the physical separation of such accommodation means no more than that the use of the courtyard as a circulation area was preferred to the inconvenience of passage rooms – perhaps a survival from the still earlier origins of the house as an accretion of separate units (see p. 55). Until the late sixteenth century internal passages were rare except to provide access to services or when linking a series of lodgings for retainers. While it is not known who was intended to use this independent, high-end accommodation at Little Moreton, the fact that the upper room commanded a view over the chapel suggests that it was for a senior member of the Moreton family.

The front range of Little Moreton, probably built in the 1560s, was also independent when first built. This combines the gatehouse with what seems to be accommodation for guests: a gallery on the top floor and on the first floor a large room and two smaller chambers off it, one of which has its own garderobe, all approached by their own stair from the courtyard. There are somewhat similar arrangements of later date at Ightham Moat and at Godolphin: at Ightham a new great chamber was formed in the gatehouse range around 1600, reached both by a gallery from the main body of the house and by a grand staircase from the courtyard, while at Godolphin a new first-floor range containing two pairs of chambers with a large room between them was built across the front of the house in the 1630s (pl. 262). While from the Middle Ages it had been customary to provide lodging rooms for guests in ranges flanking the courtyard, at these three houses lodgings seem to be combined with a more formal room of entertainment. While all of these rooms may have been for visitors, it is not certain: they could have been used for permanent occupation by someone who lived an independent life but depended on the main house for eating – someone such as a widow or an heir.

In a few houses from the beginning of the period, where the evidence is displayed unusually well, it is possible to identify a pair of interconnecting and evidently self-contained rooms over the kitchen. These occur at Little Moreton, at both the Cannington houses discussed in chapter 3, and also at St Aylotts in Essex, an early sixteenth-century house of retirement for the Abbot of Walden.[188] In each, entry was into a heated, outer room from which a door led through to an unheated room with a garderobe. These paired chambers conform to the standard, late medieval form of self-contained lodging, frequently flanking the courtyard in front of the hall range, which was provided in many great houses for the use of retainers, upper servants and visitors whose distinction or whose degree of intimacy with the family did not warrant their accommodation within the main body of the house. An even earlier example is at Woodsford Castle in Dorset, of the late fourteenth century, where a surviving range of buildings provides both accommodation for the owner, a great man who was seldom there, and a self-contained suite of rooms beyond (pl. 326). These were timber floored, differing from the superior rooms which all lie above a stone-vaulted undercroft, and also have a lower roof; they seem to have had their own kitchen.

At Shute in 1559 the 'awditor's chamber' had been on the first floor close to the kitchen, and elsewhere this accommodation had probably been for a resident steward or bailiff who would probably act also as a caretaker in the owner's absence. At Gurney Street these rooms might be interpreted as the inner chambers of a great chamber sequence (pl. 52), but this can be discounted as an anachronism in a small gentry house of the early sixteenth century, and around 1600 the outer room was partitioned off

326 Woodsford Castle, Dorset, late fourteenth century. The lower range at the far right probably accommodated a resident steward, while the principal rooms were for the occasional occupation of the building's owner. The arrangement was perpetuated in a number of sixteenth-century houses.

from the stair head enabling it and the two lodging rooms to be used independently. Changes at Little Moreton and at Blackmore Farm are equally instructive. In both cases, alterations were made around the middle of the sixteenth century (at Little Moreton by a partition, at Blackmore Farm by a short bridge from the secondary stair (pl. 50) to allow each of the two lodging rooms to be used separately, thus destroying the original arrangement and increasing the number of the house's separate bedchambers. Some other provision may have been made for a steward, although it is tempting to link such changes to an increasing involvement of owners themselves in the running of their estates.

At St Aylott's the separateness of the low-end lodging is such that there is no physical connection between it and the principal rooms on the first floor. The Suffolk plans already cited (pl. 302) show the same arrangement: a normal relationship between low end and high end on the ground floor, but an unbroken division on the first between high-end chambers and those over the services.[189] Evidence for the same arrangement is preserved, exceptionally, at Wilderhope in Shropshire (pls 303, 304). The estate was bought in 1583 by Thomas Smalman, barrister of the Inner Temple and Justice of the Council of the Marches, whose principal seat was at Elton in Herefordshire; the house at Wilderhope seems to have been built for (or by) his brother Francis some ten years later. The almost complete loss of all internal decoration (long reduced to a farm, the house is now a youth hostel) has revealed its original layout with unusual clarity. The hall, of a single storey, lies in the conventional position between a great parlour to the south and kitchen and low parlour to the north. Above it lies a great chamber, retaining like the hall fragments of contemporary plasterwork to its ceiling, and communicating with further chambers and the principal stair in the parlour wing. Other chambers lie to the north, at the service end.

There was, however, no communication at all at first-floor level between these northern chambers (and the stair from the services) and the great chamber. Above the ground floor the only connection between one end of the house and the other is by way of a passage gallery within the roof; otherwise the two parts of the house are quite separate, and no advantage is taken of the fact that on the first floor the hall no longer divides them. These quite respectable low-end chambers may have been occupied by Francis Smalman as his brother's agent, and the grander high-end chambers used by Thomas on occasional visits. Since low-end accommodation on the ground floor is limited, presumably Francis as the regular occupant had the use of hall and parlour. At some stage a door was cut through what was originally the closed partition between the two ends of the house.

The arrangement may have been more widespread: it has been noted at Mackerye End in Hertfordshire (a house largely rebuilt in the 1670s, but old-fashioned in its plan and possibly in part the recasing of a building of earlier date).[190] It may have existed too at Little Hautbois in Suffolk, probably of around 1590, a house whose service end is smaller in scale than the block that contains the principal accommodation (like the arrangement at Wilderhope) and whose porch is very oddly placed at the junction between the two ranges (pls 220, 221). The early history of Little Hautbois is not known, and the two ranges now communicate with each other on the first floor, but this link is an awkward one and originally they may not have been connected. Both Little Hautbois and Wilderhope share something of the character of the lodge, with good rooms for the occasional use of its owner and with secondary accommodation for a caretaker. Though larger than most lodges and with secondary accommodation of unusual size, these may all be buildings of some similar kind.

The lack of first-floor communication may lead to some false conclusions. Until the introduction of the single-storey hall, it had been impossible to pass from one end of a house to the other above ground-floor level. The separation of the ends of the house may sometimes have been perpetuated out of conservatism, after the means had arrived of overcoming it, and the division may be due to no more than the wish not to use the central chambers – generally the best in the house – as passage rooms. But since such separation diminished the flexibility of room uses and made the servicing of these best chambers more difficult, it seems likely that where it has been noticed there was some conscious reason for it that outweighed its disadvantages.

Stairs

In the sixteenth century the growing sophistication of first-floor rooms for entertainment in all houses of the higher ranks made it increasingly important to dignify the ascent to them. Formal stairs at the entry to a castle keep (as at Castle Rising), to a monastic hall (as at Canterbury) or to a college hall (as at New College, Oxford) have a long medieval history. However, until the mid-sixteenth century most staircases in upper-class houses were quite modest. In the late Middle Ages there is occasional evidence for a stair of some grandeur: at Maxstoke Castle in Warwickshire a great window preserves the line of a stair that evidently provided a ceremonial link between the hall and the house's best apartments,[191] and there is a formal stair providing a processional approach to the great hall at South Wingfield in Derbyshire from Lord Cromwell's private apartments. But these are exceptional elements in exceptional houses, and in the more modest houses of the gentry it was normal for a stair to occupy as little space as possible, sometimes at the price of what often seems inconvenient narrowness and dangerous steepness.

Winder stairs are the general rule, making passage difficult and substantially limiting the capacity for furnishings to be carried upstairs (references to 'setting up' beds is evidence for the necessity of erecting them *in situ* out of parts taken upstairs separately). Where a straight flight was practicable, this was generally steep and narrow. Of the two stairs at Blackmore Farm, one was a winder, the other was straight; though at the high end, the latter was extremely cramped. The very scarcity of surviving staircases before the sixteenth century demonstrates how unsatisfactory later generations usually found them.

But until the late sixteenth century stairs rather than passages seem generally to form the primary means of communication – a feature now often disguised by the insertion of passages and the alteration of original stairs. The most frequent early use of passages seems to have been to provide access to sets of lodgings for retainers: hence (as at Speke) passages occur in the wings and in the courtyard ranges of houses more commonly than in the main body of the house, where the simple high-/low-end sequence provided little occasion for their use. The evolution of the stairs at Little Moreton is instructive. The high-end stair rose originally as a simple, straight flight directly into one of two equal-sized chambers; there is no sign of any original partition in this room, which thus served as a passage room for the second. In the 1560s, however, the stair was remodelled, broadened and enclosed in its own compartment formed out of the first chamber; doors at the head of the stair now gave separate access into each room.

Formal stairs, positively enhancing the approach to the upper floor, did not appear at all commonly until after the mid-sixteenth century, and it is possible that examples in the royal houses may have provided the inspiration for stairs of increasing grandeur in the houses of lesser men. The stair at Bridewell Palace, built for Henry VIII between 1515 and 1523, which rose directly and prominently from a courtyard to the royal apartments on the first floor, was reminiscent of medieval examples cited above. But it also resembled contemporary French practice in which the stair to the state rooms similarly rises immediately within the entrance to the house. At Dartford Palace, the conversion for the king of a dissolved Dominican nunnery, there was a winder stair 20 feet in diameter, making it similar in scale to those in such sixteenth-century French chateaux as Blois or Amboise.[192]

Among the earliest surviving formal stairs in a private house is that at Rayne Hall (pl. 327). Here the high-end accommodation was remodelled to provide a large parlour on the ground floor with a great chamber (now divided up) above it. A passage led to a side door from the high end of the hall, with on one side of it the parlour. On the other is a broad, ornamental doorway with heraldic carving to the spandrels which opens to a stair that rises in wide, straight flights round a solid, central core to a similar passage on the floor above. The planning is sophisticated, both isolating and enhancing the stair compartment. A small turret next to the existing staircase may have contained a more confined, earlier stair. The stairs at Beckley Park, of around 1540 (pl. 103), and at Broughton Castle, probably of 1558, are of very similar form. The rectangular well stair was to become the standard form in superior houses of the late sixteenth century and the early seventeenth, either with an enclosed core or, increasingly, round an open core which made it possible

to admire the structure and to decorate the staircase with balustrades.

The novelty of the formal stair is shown most clearly at Burghley House, where perhaps in the late 1560s William Cecil introduced a new stair in the course of his long programme of improvements (pl. 328). This rises to the second floor with straight, paired, return flights under a continuous coffered barrel vault. The form is unprecedented in England, and its model is clearly to be found in France where by the second decade of the century straight stairs occur at Josselin, Bonivet, Poncé sur Loir and Azay-le-Rideau and are thenceforward not uncommon.

327 Rayne Hall: the stair. Rayne, of the mid-sixteenth century, contains an exceptionally early example of a spacious stair providing a formal approach to the great chamber on the first floor. The spandrels of the doorways contain the arms of its builder.

At the date of Burghley's construction there was no published source available from which its form could be copied, and either it is the work of French masons (which is perfectly possible, given the evidence for their presence at Longleat and elsewhere) or else it was imported, ready-made, from the continent – something that Cecil is known to have done in respect of other work at Burghley. In either case the reason for the adoption of a French form is probably the lack of a suitable English model. The stair shows clear evidence of alteration to the steps (though not to the vault), which may be the result of its having been moved from elsewhere in the house or of its adaptation when the house was remodelled internally in the 1580s or 1690s, but also might be due to its having been originally cut to slightly different dimensions and requiring modification on site.

A straight stair of this sort was exceptional, and confined to the grandest houses. In 1579 Cecil wrote in praise of Sir Christopher Hatton's, at Holdenby, that he 'found no other thing of greater grace than your stately ascent from your hall to your great chamber'.[193] That at Hardwick of the early 1590s forms a similar grand ascent to the great chamber, rising in a modulated series of flights which enhance the approach more than a continuous staircase would do. There had been a slightly earlier attempt to provide something similar at the old hall at Hardwick, perhaps in the 1580s. At Wolfeton in Dorset a stone stair of the 1580s, with two straight return flights, survives in a fragment of a very large house that had been gradually enlarged in the sixteenth century. Perhaps with the fashion in the grandest houses for placing state rooms on the second floor, there was a greater need for stairs with room for resting places. Certainly at Hardwick neither the builder nor her intended guest were still young. Her son, Sir Charles Cavendish, may have been thinking of it when he sent his sister the Countess of Shrewsbury a sketch plan for a huge new house which he recommended as 'fair and easy, the great chamber at the first height and all the principal lodgings at the same height'.[194]

But until the 1590s such staircases do not represent those in the great bulk of upper-class houses where older arrangements tended to persist. At Eastbury of the 1570s (pls 85, 86), in many ways an up-to-date house, winder stairs are contained in two polygonal turrets in the angles between the central range and the rear-projecting wings. While conservative both in the spiral form of the stairs and in having a similar stair at either end of the house, the Eastbury arrangement evidently commended itself sufficiently for it to be employed in several other houses: at the lost Caron House in Lambeth of around 1580, at Wood Dalling Hall, perhaps of the 1580s, in Norfolk (pls 329, 330), at Plas

Mawr in Conway in Wales (where the high-end stair is markedly larger than the low-end one), at Plaish and at Moreville in Shropshire, at Syston in Gloucestershire and probably at Bruce Castle (pl. 125), while a number of houses in the Bristol area have (or had) single high stair turrets in a comparable position.

In these houses, stair turrets above roof level enhance the silhouette, though the stairs themselves are conservative in form and perpetuate the separation of high and low ends in providing independent access to the first floor of each. However, the lack of differentiation between the stairs corresponds to the practice, evident from the late fifteeenth century, of providing chamber accommodation of good quality at the low end of the house as well as at the high end, necessitating stairs commensurate with it. The provision of such paired stairs was not confined to such conservative forms as turrets. In a preliminary plan of Hardwick by Robert Smythson[195] (pl. 331) the hall is flanked by two well stairs of equal size, serving the two ends of the house – a scheme that may derive from Palladio or from Du Cerceau but whose acceptability must derive from English precedent. Smythson had already provided paired stairs of this kind at Wollaton. At Charlton of 1612, low- and high-end stairs flank the hall in a similar way (pl. 136); by the 1650s Lord Ducie's rooms at Charlton were on the low side of the hall, and the low-end stair must have been the one that he used every day. At Montacute of 1598 paired well stairs stand in the angles between the central range and the wings that project forward from it, and a similar arrangement was intended (or built) at Fawley Manor in Berkshire.[196] At Aston Bury in Hertfordshire, matching stairs are contained in a pair of turrets that project to the rear, while at Chastleton and in a group of houses of suburban origin (discussed in chapters 4 and 5), they are placed in flanking towers. Though the best stair at Chastleton is an open well, an architecturally more dramatic form than the closed well at the low end, the low-end stair would not have disgraced the owner in his daily use of it.

As discussed above (see also chapter 5), the formal, central stair was introduced in connection with the development of the deep plan. Paired high-end and low-end stairs long continued to be provided in H- or U-plan houses of traditional form; even in houses of service-passage plan, however, while each staircase may be similarly located within a wing, the high-end stair tends to be of steadily increasing grandeur. The original staircase at Shaw was replaced in the eighteenth century, but even when built it seems to have been substantially larger than that at the low end. The stair at Ham, shown in Smythson's plan of 1626 as already of considerable size, was remodelled in the 1630s to be larger still. Thorpe's preliminary plan for the addition of wings to Holland House, around 1620 (pl. 131), similarly envisaged the enlargement of the already large principal stair built fifteen years before. Whittington in Gloucestershire, a service-passage house probably conceived and begun in the 1580s and possibly intended to have a stair within the body of the high-end wing, was given an open well stair in a large external tower built in

328 (*facing page*) Burghley House, Cambridgeshire: the stair. The adoption of a continental form of stair at Burghley, probably in the 1560s, may have been because of the lack of any English precedent for a stair of the dignity required. William Cecil is known to have imported masonry from the continent.

329 (*above*)   Wood Dalling Hall, Norfolk, *c.* 1580 (from the rear). A large stair turret rises at the back of the rear of the hall.

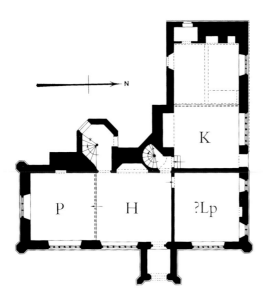

330   Wood Dalling Hall: ground-floor plan. The principal stair rises from the high end of the hall; a secondary stair is reached both from the end of the (former) screens passage and from the services in the rear wing.

331 (*facing page top*)   Robert Smythson, Hardwick Hall, Derbyshire: probably a preliminary plan, *c.* 1590. Two matching stairs rise at either side of the through hall. The right-hand stair provided access to the principal state-room sequence on the second floor, while the left-hand stair led to the rooms used daily by Elizabeth, Countess of Shrewsbury, and thus needed to be of nearly equal dignity. Near-matching stairs (variously arranged – cf. Chastleton, pl. 92, and Charlton, pl. 136, where they are arranged as they are here) are frequent in large houses of *c.* 1580–1630.

the angle between hall and wing after 1600. Thrumpton Hall in Nottinghamshire, a Jacobean, H-plan house which was probably built with a stair of some size, was given a still grander stair after 1660 (pl. 332), causing it to be described as 'very much improved and adorned . . . so that 't is now as pleasant and convenient both within and without, as can be wished'.[197] In the progressive enlargement of these stairs, builders were realising the precepts of Sir Henry Wotton, who recommended that 'to avoyd Encounters, and besides to gratifie the beholder, the whole Staire-case [should] have no nigard Latitude'.[198] In the seventeenth century the close resemblance of the stairs of many houses – for example,

332 (*facing page bottom*)   Thrumpton Hall, Nottinghamshire: the stair. Built in the early seventeenth century, Thrumpton was described in the 1660s as 'very much improved and adorned'; the stair, of *c.* 1660, must have been among the recent improvements that were commended.

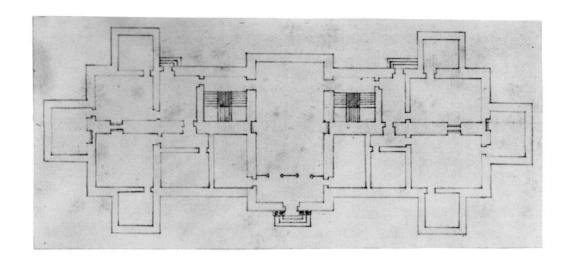

Benthall, Crewe and Aston; Thrumpton, Thorpe and Eltham – strongly suggests the establishment by then of teams of specialist craftsmen.

Alongside the increase in the size of the stair was an elaboration of its decoration. In most houses this consisted of the enrichment of balustrades and newels, so that by the 1620s balusters might be replaced by elaborate carved panels, while newels sometimes sprouted standing figures. The stairs of Cromwell House and that salvaged from Aldermaston (pl. 192), both of the 1630s, are of this kind. Francis Bacon recommended that staircases should be 'upon a fair open newel and finely railed in with images of wood cast into a brass colour; and [with] a very fair landing-place at the top',[199] and at Charlton House the main stair has a hierarchy of classical orders, more richly carved with each storey until it reaches the state rooms at the top of the house. Staircases occasionally grew into structures of some complexity. At Danvers House in Chelsea of around 1623 (pl. 138) duplicated flights filled much of the space of the hall, while further flanking stair turrets on either side of the building contained secondary stairs. Among the Thorpe drawings is an extraordinary variety of stair forms typical of the inventivess of the period, and the taste for 'curiosities' must have encouraged their development.

Of the more elaborate of the Thorpe forms none survives, but perhaps the most extravagant of all in an English house was that at Bletchingdon, illustrated in Robert Plott's *Natural History of Oxfordshire*: an extraordinary conceit, it comprised in effect four interlocking open well stairs.[200] (Interestingly, it must have been known to the young Christopher Wren who spent part of his youth with his mathematically inclined brother-in-law, William Holder, the rector of Bletchingdon.) The tiresomeness of it, which Plott remarked on in the 1670s, may have been an incentive for the rebuilding of the house in the next century.[201] Roger North complained similarly of the length of the stair recently built at Felbrigg, where

> a new apartment is layd to the old, so as the upper floor might range with that over the hall, which is 16 or 18 foot [high]. And this stair, however pompous and costly in the frame and finishing, doth not stupifie the sense, so as to make the pains of mounting 3 or 4 stretching flights insensible.[202]

The ideal stair should be 'as easy, delightfull, and inviting as is posible; or in short, as deceiving as may be, to perswade there is no such inconvenience as staires'.[203] By this time fanciful staircases were no longer the objects of admiration that they had been a century before, and they occasioned more general reservations about upstairs entertaining 'because it takes off mightily from the beauty, to endure the fatigue in the ascent'.[204]

★　★　★

Decoration and Ornament

The elaboration of staircases in the late sixteenth century can be seen as part of a developing taste for fixed decoration. This book is not intended to trace in detail the changes in the internal decoration of the house that took place in the sixteenth century and the early seventeenth, but it is important none the less to recognise the significance of the progressive introduction of increasingly elaborate fixed decoration – wall panelling, ornate chimneypieces and plasterwork. Early in the sixteenth century the character of a room had been mainly determined by its location in the house and by a decorative scheme whose elements were impermanent – the textile wall covering – and also non-specific – the plain fireplace opening, with or without an overmantel. At the same time that the external indication of internal hierarchies was breaking down and the creation of new kinds of room was upsetting traditional planning, the introduction of more permanent, architectural ornament that often included references appropriate to a particular context, such as the coat of arms of connections whom one hoped to entertain, created a need for careful planning in the layout and circulation of the house. Its increasing use is therefore a reflection of growing interest in architecture in two senses: not only in the immediate, obvious sense of a new appreciation of architectural ornament, but also in that its use suggests deeper consideration about how individual rooms were actually going to be used.

The famous wainscot in the gallery at The Vyne, probably the largest surviving display of early panelling, is probably of the 1520s, coeval with linenfold panelling at Hampton Court. That in the hall at Dorney Court is supposed to have been removed there from Faversham Abbey at the dissolution – around 1540. The wainscot in the parlour at Thame is illustrated above (pl. 68). The detailed survey taken in 1538 of Westhorpe, the great house of the king's brother-in-law Charles Brandon, describes many of the principal rooms as 'sealyd with englysshe oke' in a way which makes it clear that the panelling is on the walls, not on the ceilings.[205] (Some of this was presumably linenfold, described as 'waynsecotte drapery & drapery pannell'.) However, while grand rooms acquire wainscot of a quality and expense appropriate to their use, inventories confirm the impression of simple panelling increasingly introduced as a stock wall covering in rooms of many kinds from the mid-century onwards. The Mendham inventory of 1548 consists entirely of wall hangings, but mentions a 'seylyd chambre' and explains 'the seid chambre is seyled rownde'. There was a 'ceiled room' at Sutton Place in 1551, and by then wainscot is widespread throughout southern England. Besides the quantity that survives, from the late sixteenth century there is a perceptible decline in the listing of textile hangings in rooms of high status, implying the use of some other wall treatment. Sometimes wainscot is found concealing earlier wall painting – a clear mark of changing taste[206] – while in grand rooms there is a progressive elaboration of decorative panelling, often incorporating architectural detail and ornamental inlay.[207] By 1600 wainscot lined almost any room of quality, and one may exaggerate the impression of opulence that plain wainscot by then created for contemporaries. In discussing the fitting-up of the new gallery at Burghley in 1578, Sir Thomas Cecil urged that his father should 'ceil' it. Hangings, he wrote, are so expensive that they should not be used 'at all times that a man should have the use of a gallery'; the sunlight will make them fade; in any case, if there was to be a party, 'a great assembly', hangings could always be hung on top of the wainscot.[208]

Much early wainscot panelling was imported ready made, and the need to cut panels and lengths to make it fit rooms probably reinforced the sense of its being a decorative addition rather than a fixture. William Harrison in 1577, enumerating the amenities of modern houses, wrote of 'the wainscot that is brought hither out of the east countries, for our wainscot is not made in England' (though he also specifies 'oke of our owne' as an alternative 'sealing', and it is not clear what to him is the difference between this and wainscot).[209] In 1588 wainscot was among the stock-in-trade of the rich Newcastle merchant Robert Barber, together with 'Danske Chistes' imported from across the North Sea.[210] When the Revd Bernard Gilpin died in 1582, he left to his successor as parson not only the panelling but evidently some kind of an integral chimneypiece as well, specifying:

> all the wainscot, which I made in the east end of the great parlour, withe three lockes and keis over the fyre, if they be not lost. And I leave him all the wainscot which I made in the east end of the great chamber over the parloure, and in the studie joinynge to the same.[211]

Similarly, Edward Osbaldeston in 1590 left to his son 'all the wainscott within all and every part of the house',[212] while John Leigh of Ridge, presumably to avoid any possible debate about which things were movable and which were not, bequeathed 'all the glasse seelinge waynscotte hangeings tables formes leades brewinge vessels and ffurnaces at The Ridge in the hall kyttchen parlor chambers and howses off office there'.[213]

But whereas in Sir Cotton Gargrave's house at Nostell in 1588 the 'seeling' in the new great chamber was valued at £6, that in the gallery was said to be 'not praised' (i.e. appraised), possibly because it was felt to be an integral part of the room's structural decoration.[214] From the late sixteenth century, as wall panelling in gentry houses became ubiquitous, so the specific itemisation of wainscot became rapidly more rare, and although wainscot is occasionally thereafter included in inventories of fixtures, its exclusion from lists of chattels shows that it was by this time generally regarded as an inseparable part of the structure of the house.

The use of wainscot distinguished superior rooms from inferior, and in the late sixteenth century and the early seventeenth the grandest rooms might be further enhanced with chimneypieces of great elaboration. Decorative overmantels of brick or stone already occur in grand houses in the fifteenth century, and

their rarity is due not only to the early scarcity of fireplaces themselves but also to the wish to modernise old-fashioned decoration. However, with growing demands for comfort the number of fireplaces was growing, and the increasing architectural enhancement of the overmantel may partly have been because to place hangings immediately above the fireplace made them smokey and was a fire hazard. At Firle in 1556 there were special hangings for under the windows and over the chimney,[215] and at Hengrave there were in 1603 'two peeces of . . . arras which hangs over ye chimnees, whereof one hath Sir Thomas Kytson's and the Conwallis ther armes in ye border of it'.[216] (Hengrave was built in the 1520s, and the chimneypieces may have had no overmantels. A surviving overmantel in a ground-floor room is a painted allegorical scene of around 1630 set over an earlier fireplace surround.) The desire for appropriately decorated chimneypieces called increasingly for fixed ornament that was no less specific to its context than removable hangings, and relatively modest overmantels in wood, plaster or stone are increasingly general from the 1570s and seem to represent the more general adoption of fashions first established at a high social level.

Scarcely any surviving English overmantels of the first half of the sixteenth century rival those in contemporary French houses or those which were evidently made for the English royal palaces: in 1540 Sir John Wallop, reporting on Francis I's gallery at Fontainebleau, described the decoration as 'all antique of such stuff as . . . Modon [i.e. Nicholas of Modena] makith your Majestie's chimneys',[217] probably referring to work that was going forward at Nonsuch, while at an unknown date payments were made to 'certain ffrenche men workynge upon the frontes of chimneys for the privye chamber'.[218] A very few lavish chimneypieces survive from the mid-century to suggest those that may have inspired later emulation. At Reigate Priory the re-set wooden overmantel of a fireplace that is probably from a royal house at Bletchingley may give some idea of their quality. Its date has been debated, but it may be from the very end of Henry VIII's reign. At Broughton Castle in Oxfordshire, modernised in 1554–6, is a chimneypiece directly modelled on two prints of the Fontainebleau school; both the quality of its workmanship and the source make it reasonable to ascribe it to one of the craftsmen whom the king had been employing at Nonsuch.[219] The date of the chimneypiece in the parlour at Loseley has also been debated, but it seems most probable that it is contemporary with the house, rebuilt in the 1570s. Its remarkable decoration and the range of sources employed reflects the sophisticated taste which was already evident in the items listed in the family's inventories of 1556.[220]

Longleat has been seen as the centre from which a taste and a style spread throughout the south-western counties, and it is likely that other major houses had a similar impact regionally.[221] To some extent, Longleat provided models for direct imitation, as in the repetition of the aprons to the windows at The Hall at Bradford on Avon, probably around 1600. Otherwise, the

house nurtured a school of craftsmen keen for employment by builders who were equally keen to display their taste and their wealth. Longleat craftsmen must have been involved with the direct reproduction of Longleat motifs in the two extraordinarily lavish chimneypieces, looking far too grand for their setting, that were installed a few miles away at Woodlands Manor, Mere, probably in the 1570s; it may be seen too in a doorcase at Wolfeton, whose frieze precisely echoes that of the hall chimneypiece at Longleat.

Elsewhere features common to the chimneypieces of a number of houses in the region suggest the work of craftsmen who are likely at the least to have been apprenticed to Longleat masters or to have had access to the same sources. In 1959 Arthur Oswald identified a group that he associated with the work of William Arnold, whose father had probably been employed at Longleat as a carpenter.[222] These are characterised by a curious half-panel of strapwork on the lintel, and occur in Somerset and Dorset at Bradford on Avon, Charminster, Hanford, Herringston, Montacute, Stockton and Wayford. Anthony Wells-Cole's work of the 1990s has thrown much light on the engraved sources used by masons, plasterers and woodcarvers, and the recognition of common sources makes it possible to suggest that different works are the products of the same workshops and craftsmen. A second group that combines detail of Serlian origin with a characteristically flat relief and bold, leathery strapwork cartouches deriving from plates by the Italian engraver Benedetto Battini has been recognised further north at South Wraxall, Syston Court and in the church at Ampney Crucis;[223] to this list one can probably add chimneypieces at Chelvey Court (pl. 333), Doughton, Elmore, Seagry and Somerford Keynes. There are many other similar groups attesting to a demand that supported skilled local workshops, although similarities may also derive from the use – probably by different craftsmen – of common sources, for instance the engraving by Abraham de Bruyn that forms the pattern for plaster overmantels at Hardwick, Boston Manor House and Charlton. Over and above the information that such associations can provide about the organisation of crafts and trades, their importance is that they are evidence for a clear desire by builders for ornament that by its content and location was appropriate for the particular setting in which it appeared.

If discussion of the house's fittings and decoration cannot go beyond certain general principles, it is still less possible to do justice to its furnishings. But one aspect of these furnishings may be mentioned, in that the increasing display of pictures on the walls of the house, and changes in the subject-matter and in the places where pictures were hung seem to confirm some of the changes in taste that determined the way in which rooms were used and in which houses themselves were seen.[224] Again, there is space for only a few examples, but these show, first, a changing attitude to things visual: from the appreciation of artefacts for characteristics that are essentially moral and mental towards a greater connoisseurship; and second, a willingness to see the interior of the house as less the public expression of the owner's virtues than the personal indulgence of his taste. As such, the display of pictures parallels the multiplication of rooms and the inexpressiveness of the outside of the house. It is evidence too of the growing visual education that would lead knowledgeable individuals, by the mid-seventeenth century, to see buildings and works of art not so much in terms of meaning as of style.

Pictorial hangings had been an established part of the house's decoration before the sixteenth century. Elyot recommended appropriate subject-matter, making the essential humanist connection between ornament and virtue, didacticism and use:

> Semblable deckynge oughte to be in the house of a noble man or man of honour. I meane concernynge ornamentes of halle and chambres, in Arise, painted tables, and images containyng histories, wherein is represented some monument of virtue, most cunnyngly wroughte, with the circumstances of the mater briefely declared; wherby other men in beholdynge may be instructed, or at the lest wayes, to vertue persuaded.[225]

Although hangings might be purely decorative and admired for the quality and ingenuity of their workmanship, it is clear that they were often chosen for the appropriateness of their subject-matter. In this, they build on a taste for didactic inscriptions: Thomas Tusser's suggested text for a parlour is quoted above (p. 289), and at Acton Court there survive remains of the painted inscriptions in the gallery built in the 1540s (pl. 334). In Thomas Lord Seymour's bedchamber at Chesworth in Sussex in 1549 were tapestry hangings with 'the story of the magistrates' – evidently a moral tale suitable to the house of a high state official (he also had hangings with 'hawking and hunting' in his hall);[226] the Earl of Devon at his far-off house at St Kew in Cornwall had tapestry of 'wilde beasts byrds & flowers', and with 'pycturs of hawkyn and huntyng' which must have been among the principal entertainments at the place. Sir Thomas Smith's wall paintings at Hill Hall in Essex included a sequence narrating the story of Hezekiah, King of Judah, whose radical religious reforms had a particular resonance for himself as one of the architects of the Elizabethan church settlement. One may connect the tapestries in the high great chamber at Hardwick, telling the story of Odysseus, to Elizabeth Hardwick's own adventures before her final happy return to the place of her ancestors. Elsewhere, political and religious subjects made more general statements about the owner's support for the established order and the Protestant religion. Although hangings seem often to have been

333 (*facing page*)   Chelvey Court, Avon: a chimneypiece. The growing use of fixed architectural decoration such as chimneypieces of a quality appropriate to each room is partly the result of increasing demands for comfort, but it called for further thought in the planning and equipment of the house. It also promoted specialist craftsmanship. This is one of a number of chimneypieces in the region which must be from the same local workshop. It preserves original, painted decoration.

purely decorative, the relevance of their subject-matter was probably clearer to an audience reared on scripture and the classics than it is now.

The iconographic relevance of hangings to their settings or to the house's owner is paralleled by the use of heraldry as a means of connecting rooms with their users. Extravagant heraldic ornament tended to disappear from the exterior during the sixteenth century as the adoption of classical ornament, used alone, increased – a parallel to the way in which the hierarchic exterior, whose separate parts announce their function and status, gave place to exteriors that make no statement about the house's occupants beyond a general one about their class and culture. But inside the house the loss of early decoration may create a misleading impression of an increase in the use of heraldry. Of the two great chambers at Shute in 1554, the older one had a wooden roof painted with coats of arms. Some of the earliest surviving heraldic ornament is in windows, where glass tended to remain when decorative schemes in plaster, paint or wainscot have been superseded.

Heraldic references were statements about status and an acknowledgement of affinities, both self-advertisement and courtesy, and examples of such usage are ubiquitous. Windows at Coughton Court show the arms of the owner's sons-in-law. On the hall chimneypiece at Cadhay the owner, Robert Heydon, displayed the arms of his wife's family, of his great-uncle's wife, his wife's mother, his son's wife's mother and his daughter's husband along with his own. At Gilling Castle in the 1590s there had to be a book which visitors could refer to in order to identify the innumerable coats of arms they saw in glass and plaster.[227] When James I saw the all-embracing genealogical decoration at Lumley Castle, he is supposed to have said: 'I didna' ken that Adam's name was Lumley.' While chimneypieces, ceilings, windows and friezes were the most frequent places for heraldic decoration, it could be displayed elsewhere – for example on

staircases, as Sir Henry Slingsby did: 'upon every post a crest is set of my especial friends & of my brother-in-Laws' [sic].[228] Ultimately the profusion of heraldry would collapse under its own weight, with changing tastes and with growing cynicism about the credibility of a good deal of it and about the motives for its display. The use of heraldry within the house to advertise the owner's connections resembles the way in which chambers are named for them, and it declines alongside the change from named chambers to anonymous ones: just as rooms named for their decoration become more common from the mid-seventeenth century, so do chimneypieces and plasterwork that make no heraldic references.

In the seventeenth century the decline of heraldry coincides with a changing taste for pictures. Early in the sixteenth century the rare paintings in private houses were generally either religious pictures whose subjects had some particular relevance to their owner; these would gradually be supplemented or supplanted by portraits of friends, of the monarch or of other great men. These portraits might include figures from history as well as contemporary heroes, mythical figures as well as people from real life, but by displaying pictures of those with whom the owner recognised an affinity he realised a new way of endowing the decoration of the house with his own personality, extending and intensifying the functions of other kinds of decoration. Through the display of portraits, he was making a statement that was both public and private: to visitors his heroes announced his connections and loyalties, his values and his beliefs, while pictures of his intimates and those with whom he was connected reinforced his sense of their kinship to himself.[229] In the sixteenth century pictures, with heraldry and classical ornament, can be seen as complementary ways of making statements about the owner of the house.

Pictures listed in inventories were not hung indiscriminately. In the sixteenth century the division of pictures between parlours and galleries reflects essential differences between the two rooms. The parlour was for the private entertainment of friends; the gallery was among the rooms for grander and more formal entertainment, whether of an individual or of a party. Consequently one hung portraits of one's friends in the parlour where one could commune with them even in their absence; in the gallery one hung those pictures that made a more public statement. Most privately of all, one might keep miniature portraits in one's study or closet, to be contemplated alone or shown to privileged intimates to whom one opened one's heart.

The use of galleries for the display of works of art is of continental origin, but the social function of the gallery in England made it natural to accept the foreign fashion. The introduction of galleries and the taste for easel pictures grew together, and once associated many people probably regarded the association as a natural one. As a place of entertainment, it was in the gallery that one's visitors most readily had leisure and opportunity to appreciate them and through them to discern the personality and affiliations of their owner. To hang didactic pictures in the gallery was an extension of the practice of inscribing exhortatory texts – *sententiae* – on the walls.[230] Galleries seem to have been where one hung portraits of connections rather than of friends. As early as 1546 there were twenty-four portraits 'of diverse noble persons' in the Duke of Norfolk's gallery at Kenninghall.[231] When George Whetstone wrote in 1582 of an imaginary visit to the ideal house of 'Signior Philoxenus' (for culture's sake the setting is Italy, but the ideal is wholly English), in the gallery were

> the Pictures of all Christian Princes: and in an other place by themselves, the Pictures of certaine Heathen Rulers: and in an other rancke, the Pictures of so many learned men and grave Magistrates, as he could through freendship or rewarde obtaine.[232]

Like hangings, gallery pictures might also relate to the owner's particular circumstances: thus at Bishop Auckland in 1634 the Bishop of Durham had portraits of Protestant reformers.[233]

The great chamber was another place for didactic pictures. The scenes in the tapestry that hung in Signior Philoxenus's great chamber were (as Elyot had prescribed) specifically subjects for moral discourse. Mythological characters are not uncommon: the Nine Worthies (a favourite subject from the Middle Ages onwards) at Aston and in a passage at Harvington[234] and as figures on the exterior of the house at Montacute; painted Sybils at Chastleton and formerly at Hinton. In the high great chamber at Hardwick in 1601 (where the Countess of Shrewsbury had aspired to entertain the queen) the pictures were clearly chosen for their political correctness, juxtaposing prints of ancient philosophers and Roman emperors with portraits of Tudor sovereigns and statesmen. At Herringstone in Dorset there remains a group of high-relief figures in the panelling whose didactic qualities are clear, although it is difficult to see any particular programme in their selection: they include Hope, Sisera, Hercules, the Four Evangelists, Plenty and Geography as well as Adam and Eve before and after the Fall. They are paralleled by an indiscriminate group of modern worthies at Astley in Lancashire: Protestants such as Queen Elizabeth and William the Silent; Catholics including Philip II of Spain and Ambrogio Spinola; the explorers Christopher Columbus and Ferdinand Magellan; the Muhammadans Bajazet and Muhammad II.

But even in the late sixteenth century one cannot be dogmatic about the choice of pictures for particular settings. When pictures are mentioned in an inventory they may turn up almost anywhere in the house, and although portraits formed the bulk of them other subjects also occurred, in particular devotional pictures (though more often images) before the Reformation, tending to be replaced in Protestant houses by religious narrative, free from the taint of idolatry. And other subjects occur: in 1564 Richard Worsley of Appuldurcombe had a picture (probably an easel picture) of Cleopatra in his chamber,[235] while there was a 'table' of Henry VIII in the parlour. In 1565 there was already a mixed collection of monarchs and family members in the great chamber at Temple Newsam (the house of a great man – the Earl of Lennox), besides others unspecified of which 'some be verie smale & worth litle and some be bigger'.[236]

It would be wrong to suggest that there were many pictures in gentry houses even in the seventeenth century, but where they did occur collections were often quite eclectic, in their disposition round the house sometimes pervasive, and increasingly brought together from taste and connoisseurship rather than didacticism. At Ingatestone in 1600 seven miscellaneous portraits (Henry V, Henry VIII, Cleopatra, Diana, a Turkish couple and Sir William Petre, the house's owner) were listed in the gallery, evidently merely incidentals among the otherwise extensive furnishings of a very lavish room. In 1620 Lady Dorothy Shirley had fifteen 'English Pictures' as well as twenty-eight portraits of Romans and emperors in her gallery at Farringdon.[237] The mixture mainly of family and royalty in two galleries at Standon Lordship in 1623 was by then fairly typical, though the inclusion of Christ, Our Lady and Mary Magdalen was unusual and might indicate some precocious appreciation of contemporary Italian masters – the connoisseurship for which Charles I was widely condemned. One was more likely to find heroes of the Protestant Reformation, such as the portraits of Edward VI, Elizabeth I, Thomas Cromwell and Thomas Cranmer in Edward Isaac's parlour in 1574, and the portrait of Beza and 'two pictures of the Gunpowder Treason' at Hatfield Priory in 1626.[238] On the death in 1633 of Sir John Gage of Firle, there were in the house 109 pictures in sixteen different places,[239] while in 1643 Richard Bennett of Kew, though he had two galleries, had no fewer than fifty-nine unspecified pictures in his great chamber. The Countess of Dorchester in 1639 had an extremely catholic collection of landscapes, genre pieces, portraits, topographical views, mythological and religious subjects.[240] It is not stated where any were hanging, but so great is their variety that it would have been difficult to stick very rigidly to any prescribed programme of decoration.

Sir Henry Wotton in 1624 already felt bound to warn against an excess of pictures 'unlesse they bee Galleries, or some peculiar Repository for Rarities of Art'.[241] Although galleries might be the preferred place for the display of the collections of the connoisseur, and pictures an accepted mode of filling the walls of a long gallery (necessarily calling for a lot of them), for most people the placing of pictures in the gallery was probably no more than an aspect of furnishing: pictures were simply some of the things that made a gallery enjoyable, and they might be displayed anywhere else in the house. By Wotton's time the hanging of pictures had developed from a matter of acknowledging affinities to the expression of individual taste and the creation of mood, an approach to the furnishing of one's house that was less philosophical than the choice of heroes and the evocation of friendships but no less personal in its expression of the owner's preferences, and no less exclusive in its demonstration of his connoisseurship.

The appearance of easel pictures in the furnishing of the house has little direct connection with its layout or its architecture, but it is a pointer to its owner's greater personal involvement with the appointments of his house and to a growing tendency to see the whole house as an extension of private space. And during the seventeenth century landscape painting, a taste for which was growing rapidly from the 1620s onwards, would increasingly be used to idealise the actual appearance of real houses and their place and their owner's position in a real countryside.[242] Epitomised in the new taste for landscape was the shift that was taking place in the source of power itself: from lordship, in the medieval sense, to the physical possession of land.

9

The Image of the House

In 1618 Robert Reyce wrote of Suffolk that 'Our building at this day is chiefly to plan the houses where they may be furthest seen, have best prospect, sweetest air and greatest pleasure', noting a difference from the manner of former times, when men 'used in the scituation of their houses to regard profitt more than pleasure, and safety more than wholsomnes of the aire'.[1] In the following year James Howell wrote from the same county to his friend Daniel Caldwell that

> this house of Long Melford, tho' it be not so great, yet it [is] so well compacted and contriv'd with such dainty Conveniences every way, that if you saw the Landskip of it, you would be mightily taken with it, and it would serve for a choice Pattern to build and contrive a House by.[2]

The term 'landskip' was still new, and it is clear that Howell approved the overall appearance of the house as well as its plan.[3] By far the most usual approval for a house in the seventeenth century is that it stands well, and it is clear that the point of such commendation is not only that its prominence is suitable to the importance of its owner but also that the house in its surroundings makes an agreable spectacle. In 1633 Thomas Gerard described Leigh in Somerset (pl. 213) as 'a faire house finely seated, built by the now owner of it Mr. Henley';[4] Lieutenant Hammond similarly described the Royal Lodge at Woodstock in 1634 as 'neat and finely built . . . sweetly situated on a hill'.[5] John Evelyn in 1654 recorded his visit

> to Sir Ed. Baynton's at Spie Park, a place capable of being made a noble seat, but the humorous old knight has built a long single house of 2 low storeys on the precipice of an incomparable prospect. . . . The house is like a long barne, and hath not a Windo on the prospect side.[6]

From the mid-seventeenth century a growing number of painters depicted actual houses in their landscape settings. It would have been impossible to have done so had there not already been a willingness to idealise the landscape, not primarily in aesthetic terms but rather in ideological. In the work of continental painters English connoisseurs found a depiction of the natural world that appealed to them. Pliny (with whom more Englishmen would have been familiar than with these painters) had found the same satisfaction, commending the view from his Tuscan villa 'not as a real land but as an exquisite painting'.[7] Wotton associated the ideal landscape with the real, recommending 'chearefull Paintings in Feasting and Banquetting Roomes; Graver Stories in Galleries, Land-schips and Boscage, and such wilde workes in open Tarraces, or in Summer houses . . . and the like',[8] and recalling Vitruvius whose subjects for paintings in the *exedra* were also idealised nature: 'harbours, promontories, seashores, rivers . . . fanes, groves, mountains, flocks, shepherds'.[9] Not a great deal of landscape painting survives from early seventeenth-century English collections, but there is evidence of its growing popularity.

By implication such landscapes contrast the man-made artificialities of town and court (albeit where the taste for such a view was formed) with the eternal values of nature and with the imagined virtues of settled, rural society. Early seventeenth-century landscape is generally non-specific in its location and subject-matter, paralleling the conventions of pastoral poetry in the depiction of a golden age of the created world and of the beneficial enjoyment of the earth. It is formulaic, contrasting subjects, tones and moods: romantic crags with peaceful flocks, ruined towers with well-tilled fields and contented herdsmen; optimistic in expressing the divine providence by which the variety of the world is given for the benefit of man, and allegorical in that the hierarchies in the natural world reflect social order and degree.[10] The coherence of the ideal landscape, with the natural dependence of its parts, is a species of moral economy.

From the second decade of the seventeenth century landscape painting appears increasingly among pictures listed in inventories. The idealisation of the countryside in these early paintings can be paralleled by the idealisation of community and household relationships in the country house poems of the same period. In both poetry and painting a view of perfect worlds is substituted for a real one. This vision of a golden age is a product of the increasing cultivation of the house's occupants and is contemplated, developed and enjoyed in their private apartments. The growth of comfort and amenities, the increasing specialisation of room uses and the progressive segregation of servants are thus all part of a process in which in due course the painted landscape would come to express graphically how the owner saw himself within the countryside that he owned.

Against this ideological view of landscape and the growing popularity of the genre, from the mid-century there is a growing number of paintings that depict real houses in actual landscapes. Their owners had perhaps been prepared in another way as well, through the taste for maps that had already begun in the sixteenth century (John Dee had written in 1570 of how men were acquiring maps 'to beautifie their Halls, Parlers, Chambers,

Galeries, Studies or Libraries with'[11]) and with a great expansion of the work of surveyors who provided detailed (and often highly decorative) plans of a landowner's possessions. Such a growth coincided with the gradual emergence of a newer, capitalist view of property which – as argued in this book – influenced the development of the house itself. These surveyors not only provided accurate measurement of the landowner's estate; the maps and plans they made were often also decorative, worth hanging on the wall for the landowner to enjoy himself and to display to other people. Occasionally (though this was not their primary purpose) they were embellished with vignettes of the manor house itself, and among the earliest English representations of houses are views of this kind. By providing a means of visualising property, even if initially in two dimensions, they involved a growing number of landowners in a visual education.[12]

Painting reflected changes in how the owner saw himself relating to the wider world. The vogue for views of actual houses originated in France and Holland, but even before the Civil War there is evidence of a taste among connoisseurs for topographical painting in which idealisation of a real landscape could come to be associated with the idealisation of the country house within it, and both seen as realisations of an ideal, natural order. Here there is a new perception of the country, as in Hollar's engravings of Albury (1640s) – the rural retreat of his patron, the great virtuoso the Earl of Arundel. As prints

335 Wenceslaus Hollar: Albury, Surrey, c. 1640 (engraving). Hollar's views of the estate of his patron the Earl of Arundel are among the earliest examples of a taste for idealised views of real landscape.

· Alburgum in Comitatu Surria, vulgo Albury, olim mansio frequens Illustrissimi D.D. Thomæ Howardi Comitis Arrundeliæ et Surriæ, &c. Occidentem versus W Hollar fecit.

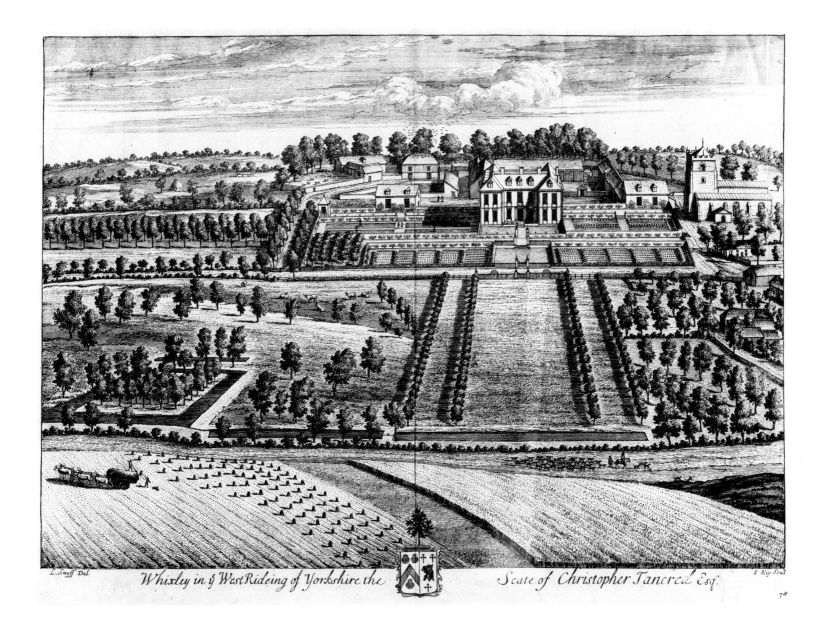

Whixley in ye West Rideing of Yorkshire the   *Seate of Christopher Tancred Esq.*

336   Jan Kip, after Leonard Knyff: Whixley, Yorkshire (engraving from *Britannia illustrata*, 1709). A new house surrounded by the property of its builder, a view that purports to be both factual and perfected. To the rear is the home farm; on the road his huntsman exercises his hounds, and in the foreground are his men making hay. The village church and the end houses of the village are to the right.

the Albury views are cabinet pictures – pictures for private contemplation and to satisfy a highly sophisticated taste – but they express an elegiac vision of enormous power (pl. 335). Arundel called Albury his 'darling cottage', preferring it increasingly to his suburban villa at Highgate, and though it was an escape from town he sought there the company of intimates, not the responsibilities of the country squire. Between the 1650s and the end of the century a growing number of painters – most of them from abroad, the chief of them probably Hendrik Danckerts and Jan Siberechts – practised in England to satisfy a rapidly growing demand.[13]

The most complete celebration of the country house is the great series of bird's-eye views engraved by Jan Kip at the beginning of the new century after drawings by Leonard Knyff (pl. 336).[14] These views idealise real houses: in them, houses and their grounds dominate the countryside which their proprietors own. Those of Kip's views that show the houses of the untitled squirearchy often include glimpses of the work of the estate. Roger North – whose notes are not primarily concerned with estate management – could write that 'care and management of husbandry is the only laudible means for a country family to live in plenty'.[15] The squire of the early eighteenth century took quite as keen a pleasure in his farming and in his sport and as much pride in his estates and in his seat on the bench of magistrates as his ancestors had done; the good landlord did not exploit his tenants, and he still dispensed charity to the poor. Useful and productive gardens immediately surround the house and further lines of avenues link these to the owner's broader estate. But at the same time these artificial gardens and frequently an extensive park seem to symbolise the cultural gulf between the occupants of the house and the cultivators of the farm land around. The overwhelming impression of these views taken together is of a land dominated by a class with common interests and a common culture, and in which the importance of landowning is the place it gives to the landowner in the community of his peers. These views express the change that had taken place during the previous two centuries in the nature of the gentry's authority: ownership rather than lordship had come to provide the basis for order, status and power.

These views were also the culmination of an interest in topography that over the previous century had helped the gentry to come to terms with their achievements and to confirm their own sense of their élite status. Effectively, topography – or, as contemporaries termed it, chorography, the description of place – begins with William Lambarde, whose *Perambulation of Kent* was published in 1576; this was followed by William Camden's *Britannia* (1586), Carew's *Cornwall* (1602) and a host of others in the next half century.[16] Typically such descriptions listed the places in each county, the rivers and other major topographical features, and increasingly they were concerned to provide the histories, genealogy and heraldry of county families. Some of these works were published, while others remained circulating in manuscript among the local gentry whose importance they celebrated. Detailed topographical description in these works varies from one to another and is generally slight, but flattering references to houses and their owners helped to confirm the gentry in the conviction of their permanent place in the government of the county and the nation. In the later part of the century local topographers became more concerned with natural phenomena, but their interest in family history persisted. Some works defy classification, such as Fuller's *Worthies of England* (1662), which combines topographical description with a catalogue of national heroes, listed by the counties of their birth and flattering provincial pride. More significantly, such works begin to include illustrations of country houses. These start with Hollar's views for King's *Vale Royall of England* (1656) and for Dugdale's *Warwickshire* (1658), while Lucas Vorsterman provided views of the principal houses of the Duke of Newcastle in the backgrounds to the plates in his great book on equitation that was published two years after Dugdale. With the Restoration, engravings multiplied: Robert Thacker and Gerard Winstanley produced suites of views of Longford Castle and Audley End; Robert Plott's *Staffordshire* (1682) includes a number of views of country houses engraved by Michael Burghers; Chauncy's *Hertfordshire* (1700) includes views by Jan Drapentier, as bad as Burghers's are good (pl. 34); and the demand for illustrations of the country houses of England reaches its full flood with Knyff's and Kip's great publication, their *Britannia illustrata* (1709), the climax of several years of preparatory work (pl. 336).

The significance of these publications is three fold. First of all, in their different ways they are statements about what is perceived as a settled order. Such depiction finds a parallel in contemporary political thought: in the acceptance by Bacon, Harrington, Locke and even Hobbes, from a variety of viewpoints and supported by a variety of arguments, of the landed proprietor as the natural governor, and of the duty of the state to incorporate the landed interest and its representatives. In their detailed family histories these works legitimise this order by looking backwards, but they express too a sense that this order is now both ideal and immutable – a perception that on one level is not unlike the medieval sense of an unchanging society, but which now has a basis in nature, legislation and reason rather than in divine dispensation and feudal law.

Such a perception was also implicit in the system of strict settlement of estates that was to be devised in the late seventeenth century and which effectively prevented the large-scale alienation of land by those families that in the previous century had been able to take advantage of a much freer land market to build up their position. By the late seventeenth century the land was, so to speak, saturated with the gentry. There was a limit, economically and socially, to the number of élite families that any one county could support, and by now it had been reached.[17] Indeed, thereafter it would tend inevitably to decline, as legal settlements prevented the sale or division of estates and when with the failure of male heirs, sought-after heiresses tended to carry their inheritance to other landed families.

These county-based topographies recognise the persistent regionalism of England: a regionalism that associated members of the county community with their own kind and kindred. When roads remained bad and travel slow, this local focus was partly from compulsion. But at the assizes, in the round of visiting and in the marriage market the members of the county community kept together, as much from liking and common concerns as from the restraints of geography. The result was a culture that was both centrifugal and centripetal. When business or pleasure took the gentry to London, there they were exposed to national fashions and there they would meet others of their sort who shared common assumptions about their place in the commonwealth and about their duties in society. But even in London they frequented the county dining clubs and remained conscious of their roots, and on returning home they took with them as much or as little of metropolitan sophistication as they chose.[18] Their houses reflect these contrary forces: in the increase of comforts and amenity inside the house, in the frequent persistence of regional mannerisms externally, and in the gradual spread of new architectural styles and plans whose occurrence is geographically haphazard, dependent on the particular interests and taste of individual builders and their craftsmen, and whose diffusion beyond the houses of individual innovators remained largely a regional, indeed a personal, function.

But besides the celebration of the county establishment and the recognition of an enduring regionalism, a further effect of these county histories and topographies is similar to that of the landscape painters, creating a view of the country in terms of the gentry established there and recording the economic and adminstrative prominence they had acquired over the previous century. The brief descriptions of the early chorographers, the illustrations of coats of arms that identified gentry families in graphic terms, culminating in the paintings and in the engraved views of country houses in the late seventeenth century – all of these place the gentry and their houses firmly at the centre of any picture of the country. Topographical artists of the late seventeenth century, by depicting the house surrounded by a broad sweep of the surrounding landscape, not only identified the house and its owner with all the country round but saw the whole countryside, as it were, in relation to its proprietors and their seats. By singling out the landowner's home for illustration, they shared his view of it as the proper expression of his importance. As lawyers found means to perpetuate landed interests irrespective of individual failures, and as the political theorists sought a rational defence of the established, propertied class, so contemporary writers and artists may be seen to provide emotional support for the landed order through a perception of the essential rightness of the house in the landscape, the owner on his estate.

The country house poems of the early seventeenth century had constituted a nostalgic evocation of a hierarchic community. The poem that is often taken as the last in the series, Marvell's *Upon Appleton House* of 1653, is rather different.[19] Nun Appleton in Yorkshire was the house to which Sir Thomas Fairfax retired after serving as the most distinguished of parliamentarian generals in the Civil War, and Marvell was tutor to his daughter. As a new house, built in 1637–8 on Fairfax's ancestral estate, perhaps it needed justification:

> Why should of all things Man unrul'd
> Such unproportion'd dwellings build? . . .
> What need of all this Marble Crust
> T'impark the wanton Mote of Dust
> That thinks by Breadth the World t'unite?

The house is partly justified by providing time-honoured entertainment:

> what needs there here Excuse
> Where Ev'ry Thing does answer Use. . . .
> A stately Frontispiece of Poor
> Adorns without the open Door:
> Nor less the Rooms within commends
> Daily new Furniture of Friends.

Wotton had said 'the place of every part is to be determined by use'. However:

> The House was built upon the Place
> Only as for a Mark of Grace;
> And for an Inn to entertain
> Its Lord a while, but not remain.[20]

What above all is celebrated in *Appleton House* is the contemplative as a complement to the active life, and the retirement that Fairfax had earned but which was equally, with his public successes, an outer sign of private virtue. The place of retirement is expressed in religious terms, and in being so translated, becomes a good in itself. The ability to fulfil the customary duties of Fairfax's station is chiefly valued as a further sign of divine grace. What is approved is moderation and Fairfax's own character:

> All things are composed here
> Like Nature, orderly and near:
> In which we the Dimensions find
> Of that more sober Age and Mind,
> When larger sized Men did stoop
> To enter at a narrow loop;
> As practising, in doors so strait,
> To strain themselves through Heavens Gate.

The past is evoked not as a golden age of good lordship, but simply as an architectural metaphor. The garden and further countryside are pressed into service as peaceful allegories of Fairfax's martial achievements, but mowers in the meadow and villagers chasing their cattle have no closer relationship to him than this.[21]

All of the country house poems contrast the virtues of retirement with the tumult of town or the corruption of business, but where *Appleton House* chiefly differs from the poems that descend from Jonson's *Penshurst* is that what is extolled in the earlier poems is the duties of good lordship and the life of the community with which their central figures have engaged; in *Appleton*, it is sufficient that in propitious circumstances Fairfax has separated himself from public life. His withdrawal to Nun Appleton can be paralleled on the Royalist side, in the enlargement of Cornbury in Oxfordshire by Edward Hyde, 1st Earl of Clarendon, who after the Restoration commissioned Hugh May (fellow exile with him during the Commonwealth) to add a wing on which is inscribed 'DEUS NOBIS HAEC OTIA FECIT'.[22] The façade of May's addition to Cornbury closely resembles the villa form of Eltham Lodge, and the quotation from Virgil recalls the rational pursuit of leisure in the classical villa with the addition that like Fairfax's, Clarendon's retirement was God-given.

Both Fairfax and Clarendon had been anticipated by those who withdrew from public life during the Civil War and by those who before it had sought the tranquillity of the countryside where with their friends they could enjoy the life of the mind: Lord Arundel in his devotion to his 'cottage' at Albury; Nicholas Ferrar at Little Gidding; the circle around Lord Falkland (including Hyde) at Great Tew; Pembroke at Wilton. Robert Dover's Cotswold games, celebrated in poems written for the occasion by many distinguished contemporaries, were an activist equivalent of the same quietism. In their level of discourse these communities were hardly typical of their class, but it is difficult to believe that the *otium* that was enjoyed in these places did not have an equivalent, at a less intellectual level, in many other contemporary households. Richard Fanshawe's *Ode* on the royal proclamation of 1630 ordering the gentry to live on their estates visualises a kind of moral hedonism:

> Who would pursue
> The smoaky glory of the Towne
> That may goe till his native earth
> And by the shining fire sit downe
> Of his owne hearth,
> Free from the griping Scrivener's bands
> And the more byting Mercer's books;
> Free from the bayt of oyled hands
> And painted looks?[23]

The peaceful, pastoral country that the *Ode* describes and extols is made pleasant with birds and flowers, but (contrary to the proclamation's intentions) actually involves the landowner in no communal responsibilities; Fanshawe may have felt that having to exercise such responsibilities would not have recommended the rural life to his urbane readers. He seems to anticipate the reactions to the troubles of the mid-century of many landowners who withdrew into the cultivation, sometimes in a literal sense, of their gardens: for instance rural improvers such as Sir Richard Weston of Sutton Place, John Evelyn with his planting, Isaac Walton with his fishing, and many others who in the country or abroad preferred to opt out of the political scene.

The movement embodies too the Protestant belief that wealth is given for use: while charity is one Christian use, because God has given man the providential diversity of nature for his benefit, a second right use of God's gifts is to enjoy and to improve them. Two later poems, John Pomfret's *The Choice* (published in 1702) and Matthew Green's *The Spleen* (written perhaps around 1720) extol in very similar terms moderation, the cultured life, agreeable rural surroundings and access to urban amenities. These are the virtues of a genteel retirement and a private use of benefits which is very different from the nostalgic, public charity and communitarianism of the early seventeenth-century country house poems. Pomfret's ideal is that

> Near some small Town I'd have a private Seat,
> Built uniform, not little, not too great:
> Better: if on a rising Ground it stood;
> On this Side Fields, on that a neighb'ring Wood.
> It should within no other Things contain,
> But what are useful, necessary, plain: . . .
> A little Garden, grateful to the Eye;
> And a cool Rivulet run murm'ring by: . . .

> At th'End of which a silent Study plac'd,
> Should be with all the noblest Authors grac'd . . .
> I'd have a clear and competent Estate,
> That I might live genteely, but not great:
> As much as I could moderately spend;
> A little more, sometimes t'oblige a Friend . . .
> And all that Object of true Pity were,
> Should be reliev'd with what my Wants could spare.[24]

Matthew Green's ideal house is smaller, but resembles this closely:

> A farm some twenty miles from town,
> Small, tight, salubrious and my own . . .
> May Heav'n (it's all I wish for) send
> One genial room to treat a friend,
> Whose decent cup-board, little plate,
> Display benevolence, not state,
> And may my humble dwelling stand
> Upon some chosen piece of land:
> A pond before full to the brim,
> Where cows may cool, and geese may swim;
> Behind, a green like velvet neat,
> Soft to the eye, and to the feet;
> Where od'rous plants in morning fair
> Breathe all around ambrosial air,
> With op'ning views of hill and dale,
> Which sense and fancy too regale.[25]

In Pomfret's poem, charity and hospitality – the proper use of status and resources – are still commended, but notable in these poems is how literally the houses and their settings are visualised: the landscape is seen as perfect in itself, wholly free of any metaphor such as Marvell's 'stately frontispiece of poor' at Appleton House. In this they express the further evolving view of the countryside and of the place of the landowner within it that is contained in the growing taste for landscape painting and in topographical literature.

When at the end of the seventeenth century Thomas Machell wrote about Crackenthorpe (see p. 237 above), the house he had rebuilt for his brother, he might have been describing a view by Kip. The Machells lived at Crackenthorpe from the thirteenth century to the twentieth, and in the words of an eighteenth-century writer 'above the degree of yeoman always; and seldom or never ascending to the degree of knight. Esquires or gentlemen constantly'.[26] The house still stands, though much enlarged. As described by Machell, it was

> a noble pile of building, exactly uniforme and of such a surpriseing symetrey, that it semeth greater by far than it Is. The N (as most of the Principal houses doe) haveing a pedament, & 2 Sp[h]eres or Cupiloes either side on the top of the house; the one being designed for pleasure only the other for a stack of chimneyes But so like you can scarce

desce[r]ne the one from the other. wch standing on either side of the pedament are very gracefull as you enter the house.

But nothing commendeth this mansion more, than Its scituation, on a plane at the foote of a hill, on the S of it from wch agayne you have a descent on the west side down a steep banke (all Coverd wth wood) to the River Eden and beyond that a great plane or meadow to Buly Castle wch stands in a wood. It has 2 Courtes before It, and a way wch flanketh them, from the Town to the Kitchen & other offices, so that none can com to the house upon any occasion but they will see the front & beauty of It.[27]

Machell fuses the long-standing view that the house should be seen to be a credit to its owner, with the view of regularity as a simple, easily comprehended constituent of architectural beauty. This is not a sophisticated critique, but (even allowing that Machell had designed Crackenthorpe himself) it is a complacent one, expressed in terms of architectural correctness, social prominence and of the house's place in the landscape. What Machell with his architectural knowledge was able to express, very many of his peers must have sensed.

Notes

FOREWORD

1 Eric Mercer, 'The Houses of the Gentry', *Past and Present*, v, May 1954, 11–32.
2 Eric Fernie, 'Archaeology and Iconography', *Architectural History*, XXXII, 1989, 20.
3 Quoted by David Cannadine, *Aspects of Aristocracy*, London, 1995, 80.

1 THE IMAGE OF THE GENTRY

1 P. MacNaghton, '800 Years of the Tichborne Dole', *CL*, CXIX, 1956, 565–6.
2 Harris 1979, 52.
3 Howard Colvin, 'The Architect of Thorpe Hall', *CL*, CXI, 1952, 1732–5; Mowl and Earnshaw 1995, 114. Thurloe had worked with or for St John through much of his legal and political career. Work at Thorpe was probably finished in 1656, the date on the stables; workmen may then have moved on to Wisbech, where work was in progress in the same year. In August of that year St John wrote to Thurloe 'we were all yesterday att yor howse att Wisbech & wth ye enlagments it will be a very fine seate', suggesting some change of plan; in September of the following year he wrote 'I have not adventured from home & therfore can give you noe informatio[n] of yor busines att Wisbich wch will be bettr done by Mr Mills' (BL, Add MS 4157, fol. 86). These references do not prove Mills's responsibility, but combined with circumstantial evidence make it extremely probable.
4 Stone and Stone 1984, 297–8.
5 Thompson 1983, 21. The figure is suggested for the West Midlands by early sixteenth-century poll tax returns; however, the likely overall numbers of the higher gentry class at the time suggest that such a distribution may be roughly true over a wider area.
6 Stone 1965b is a useful compendium of contributions to the long debate over gentry numbers and wealth among historians who were seeking economic causes of the English Civil War.
7 These figures derive from Cooper 1967, 422–3; Cornwall 1988, 279–80; Given Wilson 1987, 55–73; Guy 1988, 46–50; Habakkuk 1940; Mingay 1976, 2–11; Stone 1972, 72–6; Stone and Stone 1984, 256–66; Wrightson 1982, 24–37. They may be correlated with the estimate of '5000 or so country houses of all shapes and sizes scattered about England at any time after the mid-17th century' (Stone and Stone 1984, 297).
8 See the introduction to *Surrey Hearth Tax 1664*, ed. C. A. F. Meekings, Surrey Record Society, XVII, 1940, for a discussion of some of these problems.
9 Detailed discussion of the titles 'Gent' and 'Mr' is beyond the scope of this book. It is clear that they were often used interchangeably, though the former is very much more frequent than the latter. Men designated 'Mr' have been ignored in this analysis, since the title 'Mr' seems sometimes to be used to refer to an esquire whose principal dwelling has been identified elsewhere by his proper title, and is also often used to denote a parson; it is unlikely that this omission has greatly distorted the figures. Separate analysis of the use of 'Mr' and 'gent' in Derbyshire and in Surrey produces a slightly higher figure of 'Mr' returns for the former, slightly lower in the latter. In Norfolk parishes, with men being titled both 'Mr' and 'gent', average house sizes are 5.90 hearths for the former and 5.88 for the latter; this strongly suggests that in local usage, at least, there was no difference in wealth between them.
10 Gregory King, working for the heralds in the 1690s, evidently recognised the link between size of house and gentility in extracting all names appraised at five hearths and over with a view to identifying those who bore arms or who might be qualified to bear them (see Appendix A below). Philip Styles, 'The Heralds' Visitation of Warwickshire, 1682–3', *Studies in Seventeenth Century West Midlands History*, Kineton, 1978, 111–15.
11 Where one owner is given more than one house, the largest has been taken as his residence for the purposes of these calculations; however, some small secondary houses have certainly been included. In other cases a named individual's principal seat may have been in another county (for instance William Cartwright, Esq., JP, whose principal house was at Aynho in Northamptonshire, while he also owned the manor house, with twelve hearths, at Over Worton in Oxfordshire). It would require exhaustive research to eliminate these, but although including these smaller houses has probably reduced the mean figures, this is unlikely to have seriously distorted the relationships between them. A more serious source of error for individual returns is that when a proprietor owned two properties in the same parish, these were sometimes returned together: thus Lord Digby's sixty hearths at Sherborne in Dorset probably included both the old castle and the new, while the Earl of Devonshire's 114 at Hardwick certainly included both Old and New Halls and probably several ancillary buildings as well. The return may be compared with that for Chatsworth, a larger house than either, which was rated on seventy-nine.
12 All from PRO, C/193/12/3; esquires and knights (including baronets) but excluding peers, whose membership of the bench was nominal rather than active.
13 Derived from *Derbyshire Hearth Tax*

Assessments 1662–70, ed. David Edwards, Derbyshire Record Society, VII, 1982.

14 Derived from *Dorset Hearth Tax Assessments, 1662–64*, ed. C. A. F. Meekings, Dorset Archaeology and Natural History Society, 1951.

15 Derived from *Norfolk Hearth Tax Assessments Michaelmas 1664*, ed. M. S. Frankel, P. J. H. Seaman and P.T. R. Palgrave-Moore, Norfolk Genealogy, XV, 1983.

16 Derived from *Hearth Tax Returns, Oxfordshire, 1665*, ed. Maureen M. B. Weinstock, Oxfordshire Record Society, XXI, 1940.

17 Derived from *The Surrey Hearth Tax 1664*, ed. C. A. F. Meekings, Surrey Record Society, XVII, 1940.

18 Figures for 1662 from Styles (cited in n. 10), 152. For 1663 Styles gives 17.67 for knights, 10.6 for esquires, 5.18 for gents; also 2.44 for yeomen (1662) and 2.29 for 1663.

19 Derived from PRO, E179/193/73, E/179/259/14, and Carlisle, Cumbria RO, notebook of Daniel Fleming: all Westmorland houses of five hearths or more, 1674.

20 Brian Manning, *1649: The Crisis of the English Revolution*, London, 1992, 50–52.

21 Mingay 1976, 58–9.

22 Habakkuk 1940, 6–7; Bean 1968, 104–79.

23 Mildred Campbell, *The English Yeoman*, London, 1960, 20–63; Batho 1967, 276–305; Carpenter 1986, 49; Jones 1986, 42–4; Martin 1986, 129–40.

24 Thirsk 1969, 366; Cooper 1976, 215, 228–9.

25 Stone 1965a, 288–9; Stone 1966, 16; Everitt 1966, 56; Prest 1986, 127–83; Thompson 1983, 18–50.

26 For amount of house building, see Stone and Stone 1984, 361–94; for the profits of agriculture, see Heal and Holmes 1994, 101–16; Peter Bourdon, 'Agricultural Prices, Farm Profits, and Rents', in Finberg 1967, 593–609.

27 Carpenter 1992, 61.

28 Given Wilson 1987, 11–19.

29 Beckett 1986, 18–19; Cornwall 1988, 142; Wrightson 1991, 30–35.

30 James 1978, 78–82.

31 McFarlane 1973, 122.

32 Wrightson 1991, 37.

33 Carpenter 1992, 39–45, 95; Stone 1965a, 199–203.

34 Guy 1988, 154–77, 309–407; Martin 1986, 140–42; Fletcher 1986, 351–74.

35 Michael Broddick, 'The Early Modern English State and the Question of Differentiation, from 1550 to 1700', *Comparative Studies in Society and History*, XXXVIII/1, 1996, 92–111.

36 Chartier 1989, 21–48.

37 Elias 1978, xv–xvi.

38 Fumerton 1991, 104, 117–18.

39 Cicero, *De officiis*, Book I, chapter xxi; trans. Walter Miller, London and New York, 1913, 75.

40 Elton 1994, 209; Kelso 1924, 121; Simon 1965, 60–65, 104, 152.

41 Simon 1965, 246, 390; Stone 1965a, 16.

42 Charlton 1965, *passim*; Heal and Holmes 1994, 245–6; James 1978, 44; Barker 1948, 124–58; Stone and Stone 1984, 258; Caspari 1954, 132–42.

43 Barker 1948, *passim*.

44 Major 1964, 177–84.

45 H. Trevor-Roper, 'Sir Thomas More and Utopia', *Renaissance Essays*, London, 1986, 24–58; Major 1964, 89–139.

46 Starkey 1992, 157.

47 Simon 1965, 65, 80, 92–3, 152.

48 Charlton 1965, 68–70.

49 Elyot 1880, I, 25.

50 Elyot 1880, I, 7–8.

51 Stone 1965a, 674.

52 Quoted in Simon 1965, 104.

53 Sir John Harington, *Nugae Antiquae . . . newly arranged . . . by Thomas Park*, London 1804, 134. Cf. also the title page of 'The English Courtier . . . Cyvile and Uncyvile Life', 1579 (Anon. 1868): 'it beseemeth a Gentleman in all ages and times . . . to make him a person fit, for the publique service of his Prince and Country, and for the quiet, and comelinesse of his private estate and calling.'

54 Anon. 1868, 42.

55 Elias 1978, 53–83.

56 Fumerton 1991, 122; Stone and Stone 1984, 309.

57 Thurley 1993, 36.

58 Wotton 1624, 82.

59 Carpenter 1992, 73; Jones 1986, 1–20; Wrightson 1991, 38–40.

60 Mertes 1988, 27–8.

61 Jones 1986, 16; Carpenter 1992, 45.

62 There are useful summaries of contemporary literature in Thompson 1924, 127–72 and in Charlton 1965, 74–85.

63 Barker 1948, 147; Thompson 1924, 111; Mathew 1948, 39.

64 Styles (op. cit., n. 10), 110.

65 Mingay 1976, 2; Cornwall 1988, 11–12, 146, 154, 170.

66 Cressy 1976, 29.

67 Quoted in James 1978, 64.

68 Plato, *Menexenus*, XIX, quoted in Thompson 1924, 127.

69 Elyot 1880, I, 26.

70 Quoted in Simon 1965, 334.

71 James Harrington, *Oceana*, ed. S. B. Liljegren, Heidelberg, 1924, 119, quoting Machiavelli, *Discorsi*, I, 55. Machiavelli continued 'such men are a pest in any republic and any province' (Machiavelli, *Discourses*, ed. and trans. L. J. Walker, London, 1950, 335).

72 Heal and Holmes 1994, 245–6; Simon 1965, 334.

73 Simon 1965, 123; Baker-Smith 1989, 4–8; Kristeller 1979, 211–60.

74 Wotton 1624, 95.

75 See Carnes Lord, *Education and Culture in the Political Thought of Aristotle*, Ithaca, NY, 1982, 200–202; Lubbock 1995, 43–6; Thompson 1993, *passim*; the necessity for the symbolic

representation of magnificence is further discussed by Sydney Anglo, *Images of Tudor Kingship*, London, 1992, 6–10.

76 Kristeller 1979, 32–49.

77 Aristotle, *Nichomachean Ethics*, ed. and trans. J. A. K. Thomson, London, 1953, 99–100.

78 Vitruvius 1960, Book 6, chapter v, 182.

79 Alberti 1988, Prologue, 4.

80 Castiglione 1928, Book 4, 36.

81 Peacham 1962, 17.

82 Quoted in Paul Drury, 'A Fayre House, Buylt by Sir Thomas Smith: The Development of Hill Hall, Essex, 1557–81', *British Archaeological Association Journal*, CXXXVI, 1983, 116.

83 Harte 1976; Cornwall 1988, 10–14.

84 Elias 1978, 78.

85 Elyot 1880, II, 20.

86 North 1981, 7.

87 Stubbes 1879, I, 35.

88 Thomas Starkey, *A Dialogue between Pole and Lupsett* (written 1529–32); ed. T. F. Mayer, Royal Historical Society, Camden Society, ser. 4, XXXVII, 1989, 64–5. For the possible significance of the *Dialogue*'s setting, see below, chapter 8, p. 302.

89 Starkey, *Dialogue*, 64. Burghley's biographer reported him as having built Theobalds in part 'to sett [the] poore on worke' (F. Peck, *Desiderata curiosa*, 1779, 25; quoted in Mercer 1962, 13). The notion that to encourage building was to fulfil an economic duty to the Commonwealth was widespread: see Lubbock 1995, 61–9.

90 Quoted by Maurice Howard, 'Self Fashioning and the Classical Moment', in Gent and Llewellyn 1990, 213.

91 Boorde 1870, 234–5. Boorde's concern for health may be set against Erasmus's remarks on the unhygienic layout of English houses: 'their chambers built in such a way as to admit of no ventilation' (PRO, *Letters and Papers Foreign and Domestic*, Henry VIII, II, pt. 1, ccix). This is probably fair comment on many London houses, though probably equally true of town houses on the continent. It is difficult to see it as true of houses in the country.

92 William Camden, *Britannia* (published 1586); enlarged by Richard Gough, London, 1806, II, 395.

93 Loc. cit.

94 King 1656, 71.

95 John Aubrey, *Natural History of Wiltshire* (written *c.* 1690), ed. John Britton, Devizes, 1847, 19.

96 Fiennes 1947, 117.

97 Quoted in J. T. Cliffe, *The Yorkshire Gentry from the Reformation to the Civil War*, London, 1969, 103.

98 Woolley 1981, 116, 137.

99 Gunther 1928, 29.

100 Knowles and Pitt 1972, 31.

101 Linda Hall, 'Yeoman or Gentleman? Problems in Defining Social Status in Seventeenth- and Eighteenth-century Gloucestershire', *Vernacular Architecture*, XXII, 1991, 2–19.

102 RCHM Lancashire, 46–9.

103 RCHM West Yorkshire, 55–6.

104 Nigel Wright, *The Gentry and their Houses in Norfolk and Suffolk from c. 1550 to 1851*, unpublished PhD thesis, Norwich, University of East Anglia, 1990.

105 Gervase Markham, *The English Husbandman*, London, 1613, sig. A4–B.

106 Quoted in Girouard 1959, 202.

107 Slingsby 1836, 52.

108 Dugdale 1730, II, 1121.

109 E.g. Thomas Palmer, aged two and a half, did so in 1577 at Parham in Sussex for his grandfather, Sir Thomas Palmer. The best-known instance is the seven-year-old John Thorpe at Kirby, in that case the son of the master mason rather than of the builder. The term 'house' to mean a dynasty (e.g. the House of Lancaster) expresses the same identification of dwelling and family.

110 Wye Saltonstall, *Picturae loquentes* (written 1631), ed. Luttrell Society, 1946, 26.

2 BUILDERS AND ARCHITECTS

1 Gunther 1928, 61.

2 Bold 1989, 182. Compare also the remarks of North and Evelyn: 'All men pretend to judge, and thinck themselves masters [of building]' (North 1981, 6); 'most of our *Nobility* and *Gentry* . . . either imagine the Study of *Architecture* an absolute *Non-necessary*, or Forsooth a Diminution to the rest of their Education' (Evelyn 1723b, 6).

3 Mercer 1962, 60–66.

4 Paul Drury, 'A Fayre House, Buylt by Sir Thomas Smith: The Development of Hill Hall, Essex, 1557–81', *British Archaeological Association Journal*, CXXXVI, 1983, 98–123; Nancy Dewer, *Sir Thomas Smith: A Tudor Intellectual in Office*, London, 1964, 208.

5 Smith's architectural library is discussed in Drury, op. cit., 119–21.

6 Richard Simpson, 'Sir Thomas Smith and the Wall Paintings at Hill Hall, Essex: Scholarly Theory and Design in the Sixteenth Century', *British Archaeological Association Journal*, CXXX, 1977, 1–20.

7 N. Pevsner, 'Hill Hall', *Architectural Review*, CXVII, 1955, 307–9.

8 Superimposed columns as at Hill Hall are much rarer than pilasters, but they occur at Besançon of 1534–45. It is likely that the second storey at Hill Hall, within the roof, was lit by lucarnes completing the three-order sequence.

9 J. Strype, *Life of Sir Thomas Smith*, Oxford, 1820, 164.

10 For the development of Longleat, see Mark Girouard, 'The Development of Longleat House between 1546 and 1572', *Archaeological Journal*, CXVI, 1959, 200–222.

11 Edward Hall, *Chronicles*, ed. C. Whibley, London and Edinburgh, 1904, I, 175.

12 Reproduced in Strong 1979, pl. 12.

13 Babelon 1989, 66–8.

14 O. J. Weaver, 'Moreton Corbet Castle', *Archaeological Journal*, CXXXVII, 1981, 44–6, whence the following quotation from Camden.

15 For Isel, see NMRC, 87057; V. Rickerby, *Isel Hall*, guidebook, n.d.

16 BL, Cotton MS Vitellium B.14 283; PRO, *Letters and Papers Foreign and Domestic*, Henry VIII, XIII, pt 2, 353.

17 Hoby 1902, *passim*.

18 Whinney 1964, 4–11; Lees-Milne 1951, 27–36. It is tempting to link the possible French source of the Hobys' tomb with other near-contemporary monuments of continental origin or inspiration. See Lawrence Stone and Howard Colvin, 'The Howard Tombs at Framlingham, Suffolk', *Archaeological Journal*, CXXII, 1965, 159–71; Richard Marks, 'The Howard Tombs at Thetford and Framlingham: New Discoveries', *Archaeological Journal*, CXLI, 1984, 252–68.

19 Quoted in Mercer 1962, 77. For contemporary considerations of architectural nationalism, see Thompson 1993, 101–6.

20 HMC Salisbury, XIX, 1965, 121.

21 Nigel Llewellyn, '"Plinie is a weyghtye witnesse": Classical References in Post-Reformation Funeral Monuments', in Gent 1995, 147–62; Llewellyn, 'Claims to Status through Visual Codes: Heraldry in Post-Reformation Funeral Monuments', in *Chivalry in the Renaissance*, ed. Sydney Anglo, Woodbridge, 1990, 145–60.

22 Howard 1987, 120–35; Thurley 1993, 85–111; Maurice Howard, 'Self-Fashioning and the Classical Moment in Mid-Sixteenth Century English Architecture', in Gent and Llewellyn 1990, 198–217.

23 Quoted in Thurley 1993, 106.

24 Wells-Cole 1997, *passim*.

25 Anderson 1995, 259–64; Gent 1981, 29–31. For a discussion of *imprese* and the emblem books that popularised them, see Thompson 1924, 29–68.

26 Vitruvius, *Architecture ou Art de bien bastire . . . mis de latin en francoys par Ian Martin*, Paris, 1547, 77v, 78r.

27 For a discussion of the rich iconography of Nonsuch, see Geoffrey Quenby, 'The Image of Nonsuch Palace: Mythology and Meaning', in *The Image of the Building: Papers from the Annual Symposium of the Society of Architectural Historians of Great Britain*, ed. Maurice Howard, Milton Keynes, 1995, 17–36.

28 John Onians, 'The System of the Orders in Renaissance Architectural Thought', in Guillaume 1988, 169–78; Pierre Gros, 'Vitruve et les ordres' in Guillaume 1988, 49–59; James Ackerman, 'The Tuscan/Rustic Order: A Study in the Metaphorical Language of Architecture', in *Distance Points: Essays in Theory and Renaissance Art and Architecture*, ed. Jean Guillaume, Cambridge, Mass., and London, 1994, 495–546.

29 The earliest English appearance of superimposed orders was on the gatehouse of Somerset House of 1549–50. The antecedents of the Somerset House gatehouse have not been satisfactorily traced, but two or three near-contemporary French houses have entries that are not wholly dissimilar, e.g. Anet (the frontispiece to the inner court, no longer *in situ*), Fontainebleau (the Porte Dorée), and Fontaine Henri (applied to the face of the great lodging tower). The pedimented window heads of Somerset House are also characteristic of current French work. Perhaps Somerset House can be seen as a traditional English tower gatehouse modified by current French practice which included reminiscences of a Roman triumphal arch.

30 See Catherine Cole, 'The Tower of Five Orders in the Schools Quadrangle, Oxford', *Oxoniensia*, XXXIII, 1969, 92–101.

31 Kelso 1924, 44.

32 T. D. Kendrick, *British Antiquity*, London, 1950, 34–133; Girouard 1983, 210–31.

33 Quoted in Anderson 1995, 270.

34 Cf. the use by George Whetstone of the metaphor of the Vitruvian man in *The Mirror of Magistrates*, 1584, 7: 'Among the philosophers, MAN is called MICROCOSMOS, or a little worlde. . . . If he resemble the whole worlde, it were no absurditie to make him a Figure of a well-governed Common-wealth: a man consisteth of divers members, as head, body, Armes, legges &c. So doth a good Commonwealth of divers states.' The simile of the human body for the commonwealth is a medieval one. But Vitruvius and his commentators reintroduced a link between the proportions of the human body and the mathematics underlying the cosmos. Whetstone combines the old metaphor with the new.

35 Gent 1981, 85.

36 R. M. Smuts, 'Cultural Diversity and Change', in Peck 1991, 99–112.

37 *The Elements of Geometrie of . . . Euclide . . . Translated into the English Toung, by H. Billingsley . . . with a very Fruitfull Preface Made by M. I. Dee*, 1570. See F. Yates, *The Theatre of the World*, London, 1969, 20–42, 190–98; J. A. Bennett, 'Architecture and Mathematical Practice in England', in Bold and Chaney 1993, 23–30; Hart 1994, 136–54.

38 Dee, in Billingsley's Euclid (op. cit.), sig.d.iiii r–v.

39 Benno M. Forman, 'Continental Furniture Craftsmen in London: 1511–1625', *Furniture History*, VII, 1971, 94–120. For foreigners in royal service, see Thurley 1993, 102–11; *HKW*, IV, pt 1, 43–5; at Nonsuch *HKW*, IV, pt 2, 193–200. See also Howard 1987, 126–35.

40 Wotton 1624, 54.

41 Richard Mulcaster, *Positions*, London, 1581, repr. 1887, 242.

42 Sir John Ferne, *The Blazon of Gentrie*, London, 1586, 69–73.

43 Quoted in Major 1964, 64.

44 Hoby 1902, 64. For a discussion of the equivocal contemporary attitude towards graphic skills, see Gent 1981, 6–13.

45 George Whetstone, *An Heptameron of Civil Discourse*, London, sig. Biii.

46 John Buxton, *Elizabethan Taste*, London, 1963, 5–6.

47 For the practitioners of fortification, see *HKW*, IV, 409–14. It has been suggested that Sir William Sharington, whose mid-century work at Lacock is among the architecturally most advanced of the age, may have included fortification among his architectural knowledge; *HKW*, IV, pt 2, 591.

48 Elyot 1880, I, 45.

49 Elyot 1880, I, 48.

50 Elyot 1880, I, 48.

51 Harrison 1877, I, 238.

52 R. Haydocke, *A Tracte Containing the Artes of Curious Painting Carving and Building . . . Englishd by R.H.*, London, 1598 [unpaginated].

53 Peacham 1962, 85.

54 James Cleland, *Institution of a Young Noble Man*, London, 1607, 91.

55 Burton 1660, 279.

56 Fuller 1662, 84.

57 Harrison 1877, I, 338.

58 For the amount of house building in Dorset, Hampshire, Northamptonshire and Wiltshire (figures derived from the *Buildings of England* volumes), see Lubbock 1995, 56; for Hertfordshire, Northamptonshire and Northumberland, see Stone and Stone 1984, 384.

59 *The Letters and the Life of Francis Bacon . . . Newly Collected*, ed. James Spedding, I, London, 1861, 131–2.

60 Harrison 1877, I, 338.

61 G. Isham, *Sir Thomas Tresham and his Buildings*, Northamptonshire Antiquarian Society, 65, pt 2, 1965; J. A. Gotch, *A Complete Account of the Buildings Erected in Northamptonshire by Sir Thomas Tresham*, Northampton, 1883.

62 Tresham's library: BL, Add MS 39830, fos 155v–214r.

63 Carew 1602, 106–7; Champernown's scheme is mentioned in Girouard 1983, 9 and 23, and in Airs 1995a, 44.

64 J. C. Rogers, 'The Manor and Houses of Gorhambury', *St Albans and Hertfordshire Architectural and Archaeological Society Transactions*, new ser. 4, 1933, 35–132 (58).

65 Girouard 1983, 105.

66 Manuscripts in Munich (Bayerische Staatsbibliothek) and in New York (Columbia University, Avery Library) have both been published: *Sebastian Serlio: On Domestic Architecture*, ed. Myra Nan Rosenfeld, Cambridge, Mass., and London, 1978; *[Sebastiano Serlio] Sesto libro delle habitatione di tutti li gradi degli humani*, ed. Marco Rosci, Milan, 1966. These drawings are fos 36 and 43 in the New York codex, fos 35v and 41r in the Munich codex. The circulation of the text in France is discussed in Rosenfeld's introduction (p. 3) to the reprint of 1996.

67 Girouard 1983, 42–55. Chalcot House in Wiltshire (Girouard 1983, 63–4) has superimposed orders and windows in aedicules with alternating straight and segmental pediments and is by far the most purely Serlian house in England of the sixteenth century even though its rebuilding in the eighteenth century has left its original form irrecoverable.

68 Wittkower 1988, 15–40.

69 Christopher Hussey, 'Longford Castle, Wiltshire', *CL*, LXX, 1929, 648–55, 696–702, 724–30; Gotch 1894, 33, 70.

70 'Solomon's Temple in Nottinghamshire', in Girouard 1992, 187–96.

71 Christopher Hussey, 'Chilham Castle, Kent', *CL*, IV, 1924, 812–9, 858–65.

72 For additional examples of women involving themselves in building, see Anne Lawrence, *Women in England 1500–1900*, London, 1994, 152–7. As early as 1502 Robert Virtue, one of the King's master masons (previously involved at Bath Abbey and at Westminster) was building at Greenwich 'to a platt drawn by the Queen' (Thurley 1993, 34). Probably seldom recorded because taken for granted was the women's role in furnishing and maintaining the house. Elizabeth Cholmley, for example, 'contributed much to the beautifying of the house at Whitby, being a good contriver within doors, and having a most singular faculty to make and order furniture for houses, and dress it after the best mode . . . which gift she had from her mother, bred up in Queen Elizabeth's court' (Cholmley 1870, 51). Her domestic role may be contrasted with the wife of Francis Cholmley two generations earlier. Francis Cholmley 'resided most at Whitby, and built that house most from the hall downwards . . . and though the country affords plenty of stone, yet his wife would have the sides, even to the ground, all of wood, saying "that would serve well enough for their times", knowing she should not bear a child . . . She had got such a hand over her husband (though he was a very valiant man) that upon the porch, at the entrance to the hall door, she had set the first letter of her name before his' (Cholmley 1870, 13). Cf. also Sir John Lowther's characterisation of his first wife (p. 195 above).

There are many other cases of women involving themselves directly in the commissioning of building, though to an unknown extent in its design, most famously Elizabeth Hardwick. Other aristocratic woman builders in the seventeenth century included the Duchess of Rutland, at Belvoir in 1654 (Bold 1990, 75); Mary, Countess of Pembroke, at Houghton Conquest; Lady Anne Clifford, Marchioness of Ormond, at Moor Park; Lady Wilbraham at Weston, Staffordshire, and Lady Bridgeman at Castle Bromwich.

73 Smyth 1883, II, 362.

74 Howarth 1985, 65.

75 Christopher Hussey, 'Stapleford Park, Leicestershire', *CL*, LVI, 1924, 288–96.

76 *HKW*, IV, pt 2, 591–2. For Adams and his expertise in fortification, see Summerson 1958, 204–8.

77 John Stoye, *English Travellers Abroad, 1604–1667*, New Haven and London, 1989, 83.

78 Summerson 1993, 67.

79 Philibert de L'Orme, *Le premier tome de l'architecture*, Paris, 1568, 19.

80 See n. 54.

81 See especially Colvin 1995, 29–45; Airs 1995a, 31–56; Jenkins 1961, 1–40.

82 J. Summerson, 'John Thorpe and the Thorpes of Kingscliffe', *The Unromantic Castle*, London, 1990, 33.

83 Quoted in Jenkins 1961, 32.

84 Quoted in Nancy Briggs, 'The Foundation of Wadham College, Oxford', *Oxoniensia*, XXI, 1956, 67–8.

85 Quoted in Briggs, op. cit., 67. See also Oswald 1959, 25–30.

86 *HKW*, III, 97.

87 *HKW*, IV, 46.

88 BL, Add MS 62674. The form of the house is unclear; there is a sketch plan in the MS volume which suggests a double-pile house with square towers, a very up-to-date form discussed in chapter 5. But it is unlikely that such a house could have been contemplated as early as 1588, and the drawing, which is undated, may represent some later stage in what was clearly an evolving concept.

89 Thomas Sergianson supervised work at Lamport in 1654 under the direction of John Webb. Malcolm Airs tells me that Sergianson also built fortifications at Warwick and Coventry in 1641.

90 For the long-standing practice of masons making sketch plans for approval by clients, see P. D. A. Harvey, *The History of Topographical Maps*, London, 1980, 94.

91 *The Notebook of Nicholas Stone*, Walpole Society, VII, 1918–19, 70.

92 Gerbier 1663, 24.

93 See Joseph Rykwert, 'On the Oral Transmission of Architectural Theory', in Guillaume 1988, 169–78.

94 I am most grateful to Dr Peter Kidson for his analysis of these plans on my behalf.

95 Mercer 1962, 56–7.

96 John Newman, 'Inigo Jones's Architectural Education before 1614', *Architectural History*, XXXV, 1992, 18–50; Gordon Higgott, '"Varying with Reason": Inigo Jones's Theory of Design', *Architectural History*, XXXV, 1992, 51–77. Other works on Jones's design methods are listed in Higgott, op. cit., n. 1.

97 For Jones's work as Surveyor, see *HKW*, III, pt I, 129–53.

98 D. J. Gordon, 'Poet and Architect: The Intellectual Setting of the Quarrel between Ben Jonson and Inigo Jones', *Warburg Institute Journal*, XII, 1949, 152–78; Johnson 1994, *passim*.

99 Ben Jonson, *Works*, ed. C. H. Herford Percy and Evelyn Simpson, VIII, 1947, 402.

100 There is perhaps some reference to Jesus's betrayal for thirty pieces of silver which Judas Iscariot spent to buy the Potter's Field (Jonson would have been quite capable of comparing Jones to Judas).

101 Johnson 1994, 1–35.

102 Quoted in Mendyk 1989, 121.

103 Dorchester, Dorset RO, D/BUL/M4.

104 Christopher Hussey, 'Raynham Hall, Norfolk', *CL*, LVIII, 1925, 742–50, 782–90; H. L. Bradfer-Lawrence, 'The Building of Raynham Hall', *Norfolk Archaeology*, XXIII, 1927–9, 93–146; Linda Campbell, 'Documentary Evidence for the Building of Raynham Hall', *Architectural History*, XXXII, 1989, 52–67; John Harris, 'Raynham Hall, Norfolk', *Archaeological Journal*, CXVIII, 1961, 180–87; M. Airs, 'The Designing of Five East Anglian Houses', *Architectural History*, XXI, 1978, 58–67.

105 Gunther 1928, 133.

106 P. D. A. Harvey, *Maps in Tudor England*, London, 1993, 95–8.

107 Gent 1981, 22–8, 66–86.

108 K. J. Holtgen, 'An Unknown Manuscript Translation by John Thorpe of du Cerceau's *Perspective*', *England and the Continental Renaissance: Essays in Honour of J. B. Trapp*, ed. E. Chaney and A. Mack, Woodbridge, 1990.

109 SM, Thorpe 37, 38.

110 Salomon de Caus, *La perspective, avec la raison des ombres et mirroirs*, London, 1611.

111 The use of models is discussed more fully in Airs 1995a, 86–93.

112 Alberti 1988, 33–4 (Book II, chapter 1).

113 Wotton 1624, 64–5.

114 Sotheby's, London, sale 14 December 1993: Fairfax Library and Archive.

115 Peter Leach, 'Ragley Hall', *Archaeological Journal*, CXXVIII, 1971, 230–33.

116 Cherry 1988, 108–35.

117 Gunther 1928, 22–3.

118 Taunton, Somerset RO, DD31/2; VCH Somerset, V, 1985, 113–15; G. U. S. Corbett, 'Nettlecombe Court', *Field Studies*, III, 1961, 289–96.

119 The Little Moreton contract is printed in the current National Trust guidebook to the house.

120 Jope 1961, 221–2.

121 Airs 1975, 42.

122 T. D. Atkinson, *Local Style in English Architecture*, London, 1947, 77.

123 R. Willis and J. W. Clark, *Architectural History of the University of Cambridge*, Cambridge, 1886, II, 489–90.

124 HMC Salisbury, XV, 1930, 383.

125 Oliver Fairclough, 'John Thorpe and Aston Hall', *Architectural History*, XXXII, 1989, 30–51.

126 E. B. Grosart, *Lismore Papers*, London, 1886, V, 64.

127 Grosart, op. cit., 68.

128 It is interesting, too, that in spite of de Caus' eminence as the architect of Wilton (to a debatable extent; the extent of Jones's certain contribution is not universally agreed), designs for at least some of the chimneypieces at Stalbridge were left to others. The position at Wilton was similar.

129 Grosart, op. cit., 67.

130 H. E. Forrest, 'Stanwardine Hall', *Shropshire Archaeological Society Transactions*, XLI, 4th ser., 4, 1920–21, 85–7.

131 Girouard 1983, 120–25.

132 O. J. Weaver, 'Heath Old Hall', in *Ancient Monuments and their Interpretation*, ed. M. Apted, Chichester, 1977, 285–301; NMRC, 31963.

133 For Barlborough Old Hall, see NMRC, 87102: notes by J. Sinar.

134 T. D. Whittaker, *Lodis & Elmet*, Leeds and Wakefield, 1816, 314–15.

135 T. W. Hanson, 'Halifax Builders in Oxford', *Halifax Antiquarian Society Transactions*, XXV, 1928, 253–317.

136 'Akroyd, John', Colvin 1995; Lees-Milne 1951, 127–30.

137 For the financing of sixteenth- and early seventeenth-century country house building, see Airs 1995a, 94–104.

138 Stafford, Staffordshire RO, D1734/2/3/27,29.

139 At Hardwick Hall in Derbyshire masons' marks can be found everywhere on plain ashlar and on simple mullions and door surrounds; these were within the competence of the general team of banker masons whose employer will have contracted for the masonry of the carcass of the house and whose contractor kept a tally on his men's output in this way. There are no such marks on the more elaborate masonry, which will have been the subject of separate piece-work contracts. It must also be because of this way of working that there are original internal partitions built across window openings in sixteenth- and seventeenth-century houses.

140 Dinninghoff's letter is in the West Yorkshire District Archives, Leeds, TN/A/3/2; accompanying plans, TN/SH/A3/1–3. That Dinninghoff, a glass painter by trade, should provide plans for a house is not entirely surprising. At Hardwick John Balechouse, a painter, was in charge of building operations.

141 HMC Salisbury, XIX, 1965, 120–21. For Cavendish, see Girouard 1983, 183–5.

142 Caroline Stanley-Millson and John Newman, 'Blickling Hall: The Building of a Jacobean Mansion', *Architectural History*, XXIX, 1986, 1–43.

143 Published as Summerson 1966.

144 Gerbier 1663, 9.

145 Airs 1978, 59–62.

146 Carlisle, Cumbria RO, D/Lons/L1/3/4 (10 Feb 1692/3).

147 Leeds, West Yorkshire District Archives, Ingram letters TN/C *passim*.

148 Wotton 1624, 74.

149 Wotton 1624, 22.

150 Sir John Coke, MSS, BL and Melbourne Hall, Derbyshire.

151 *The Letters of Sir John Chamberlain*, ed. N. E. McLure, Philadelphia, 1939, I, 367.

152 Richard Brome, *Dramatic Works*, London, 1873, II, 1–2. The comment may be an echo of Ben Jonson, in whose *Poetaster* (Act III, scene 1) the bore of the play is made to say: 'By Phoebus, here's a most neat fine street, isn't it? I protest to thee I am enamoured of this street, more than of half the streets of Rome again; 'tis so polite and terse! There's a front of a building now! I study architecture too. If ever I build, I'd have a house just of that prospective.' See also pp. 40–41 for the practice of modelling new buildings on existing ones. Later in Jonson's play the same character (Crispinus) makes an oblique condemnation of architectural extravagance similar to Brome's when he likens ladies' head-dresses to 'high gable-ends, Tuscan-tops . . . arches . . . pyramids'.

153 Bramston 1845, 409.

154 North 1981, 149.

155 'The Expense Book of James Master Esq.', ed. Scott Holland, *Archaeologia cantiana*, XV–XVIII, 1883–9. John Cornforth, 'Yotes Court, Kent', *CL*, CXXXV, 1964, 1580–83, 1648–51; NMRC, 39704, where I offered a different interpretation of the house from that advanced here; the present one is to be preferred.

156 SoL 36, *The Parish of St Paul Covent Garden*, 1970, 6, 284, 287; Jeremy Wood, 'The Architectural Patronage of Algernon Percy, 10th Earl of Northumberland', in Bold and Chaney 1993, 55–80.

157 NMRC, 87132; Kingsley 1989, 126–8.

158 Reproduced in Kingsley 1989, 127.

159 Leicester, Leicestershire RO, D11/765 and DE 730/1 f178ff. Also John Cornforth, 'Lyndon Hall, Rutland', *CL*, CXL, 1966, 1212–15.

160 Cf. Chauncy's description of Ball's Park in 1700 as 'a very fair and stately fabric . . . consisting of a square pile with a court in the middle thereof, every side equally fronted, and exactly uniform' (Chauncy 1700, 260).

161 The reference must be to Godfrey Richards, *The First Book of Architecture by Andrea Palladio . . . with Diverse other Designers*, London, 1663, repr. 1668. See Rudolf Wittkower, *Palladio and English Palladianism*, London, 1983, 76–8, in which Richards's *Palladio* is described as 'a hodge-podge of Italian, French and English material'.

162 'Sturges, John', Colvin 1995.

163 North 1981, 87.

164 North 1981, 23.
165 Gunther 1928, 60.
166 For Goldsmiths' Hall, see John Newman, 'Nicholas Stone's Goldsmiths' Hall: Design and Practice in the 1630's', *Architectural History*, XIV, 1971, 30–39.
167 Gunther 1928, 83.
168 Gunther 1928, 285.
169 Chauncy 1700, 125.

3 FORMS AND MEANINGS, 1480–1600

1 John Blair, 'Hall and Chamber: English Domestic Planning 1000–1250', in *Manorial Domestic Buildings in England and Northern France*, ed. G. Meirion-Jones and Michael Jones, Society of Antiquaries Occasional Papers, XV, London, 1990, 1–21.
2 *Somerset Medieval Wills 1383–1558*, ed. F. W. Weaver, Somerset Record Society, XV, 1901–5.
3 The process is well summarised in Grenville 1997, 93–110.
4 PRO, Cal. Inq. Misc. 1392–9 137–8 281 (22 Oct 1387).
5 Exeter, Devon RO, 123M/E99. Christopher Hussey, 'Shute Barton, Devon', *CL*, CIV, 1951, 326–30, 398–401. Hussey had not seen this survey and he was therefore unable to interpret the building correctly. Nothing now remains of the house except the fifteenth-century kitchen and some other building around the kitchen courtyard, and a later Elizabethan gatehouse aligned with the entrance to the demolished hall.
6 The gatehouse at Shute is not mentioned in the survey of that year, and the heraldry suggests a date around 1565. It is aligned on the entry to the (now demolished) hall; in 1554 the entry was through a gate at right angles to the axis of the hall porch.
7 For Great Chalfield, see NMRC, 88324; H. Avray Tipping, 'Great Chalfield Manor, Wiltshire', *CL*, XXXVI, 1914, 230–37, 294–301.
8 For East Barsham, see NMRC, 88244; Garner and Stratton 1911, 51–4; Pugin 1840, III, 29–46; H. Avray Tipping, 'East Barsham Manor, Norfolk', *CL*, IV, 1924, 16–24.
9 R. K. Morris, 'Windows in Early Tudor Country Houses', in *Early Tudor England: Proceedings of the 1987 Harlaxton Symposium*, ed. D. Williams, Woodbridge, 1989, 125–38.
10 S. J. Gunn and P. G. Lindley, 'Charles Brandon's Westhorpe: An Early Tudor Courtyard House in Suffolk', *Archaeological Journal*, CXLV, 1988, 272–90.
11 These towers are discussed and a number of examples listed by Anthony Emery, 'Ralph Lord Cromwell's Manor at Wingfield', *Archaeological Journal*, CXLII, 1985, 276–339. See also W. Douglas Simpson, 'The Affinities of Lord Cromwell's Tower House at Tattershall', *Journal of the British Archaeological Asso-

ciation*, new ser., XL, 1935, 177–92; Thompson 1987, 87–102; Thurley 1993, 18–32.
12 PRO, Prob 2/180.
13 For Ightham Moat, see NMRC, 53012; *The Architectural Development of Ightham Moat*, National Trust, London [1992].
14 For Gurney Street Manor, see NMRC, 36479.
15 For Blackmore Farm, see NMRC, 94971.
16 Madge Moran, 'The Medieval Parts of Plowden Hall', *Shropshire Historical and Archaeological Society Transactions*, LIX, 1978, 264–71.
17 The principles of hierarchical planning are universal, though it has been suggested that in Cornwall the distinction between opposite ends of the house was not so rigidly observed as elsewhere: cf. Brian Anthony, 'Trerice', *Archaeological Journal*, CLXX, 1973, 247; Stuart Rigold, 'Cotehele', *Archaeological Journal*, CLXX, 1973, 258. However, at Godolphin the reversal seems linked to an alteration of the approach to the house (from west to north) which provided the occasion to build a new west range and to downgrade the former best rooms; see chapter 7 and NMRC, 88310.
18 Patrick Faulkner, 'Domestic Planning from the Twelfth to the Fourteenth Centuries', in *Studies in Medieval Domestic Architecture*, ed. M. J. Swanton, Royal Archaeological Institute Monograph, London, 1975, 84–117.
19 For Kingston Seymour, see Wood 1965, pl. ix.a, facing p. 52.
20 For Poundisford, see NMRC, 78322-3; Christopher Hussey, 'Poundisford Park, Somerset', *CL*, LXXVI, 1934, 116–20, 142–6; Garner and Stratton 1911, 61–2.
21 VCH Somerset, IV, 1978, 112–14.
22 For Kentwell, see NMRC, 94970.
23 For Shaw, see NMRC, 61583; L[aurence] W[eaver], 'Shaw House, Newbury', *CL*, XXVIII, 1910, 328–38.
24 Frederick J. Ladd, *Architects at Corsham Court*, Bradford on Avon, 1978, 7–22.
25 For Whittington, see NMRC, 87115. There are early twentieth-century plans of the house in the Gloucestershire RO.
26 The outside of Whittington has a profusion of masons' marks. One of these occurs also at Corsham. The two are only some 25 miles apart, but this is not sufficient to establish a link between them.
27 Girouard 1983, 65–8.
28 Kirsty Rodwell and Robert Bell, 'Acton Court, Avon, an Early Tudor Courtier House', in Airs 1994, 55–60.
29 For Thame Abbey, see NMRC, 5700.
30 Susan Foister, 'Sixteenth Century English Portraiture and the Idea of the Classical', in Gent 1995, 162–80.
31 For Kirby, see NMRC, 59962; RCHM Northamptonshire, 245–56.
32 John Summerson, 'John Thorpe and the Thorpes of Kingscliffe', *Architectural Review*, CVI, 1949, 291–300.

33 Harold Brakspear, 'Dudley Castle', *Archaeological Journal*, LXXI, 1914, 1–24; Douglas Simpson, 'Dudley Castle: The Renaissance Buildings', *Archaeological Journal*, CI, 1946, 119–25.
34 For Stonor, see VCH Oxfordshire, VIII, 1964, 142–7.
35 Thompson 1987, 57.
36 Thurley 1993, 79.
37 *Brittania illustrata*, London, 1709, pl. 4.
38 For Treago, see RCHM Herefordshire, I, 230–32.
39 For Faulkbourne, see RCHM Essex, II, 69–72. I am grateful to Anthony Emery for discussing his views of Faulkbourne with me.
40 For Wickham Court, see NMRC, 87150; SM, Thorpe 175.
41 At Treago there was a well in the courtyard; at Wickham Court it can be seen that there were very few windows looking into the central area and this area extended down to basement level, opening to cellars.
42 The fullest account of Hengrave is still that by John Gage, *The History and Antiquities of Hengrave in Suffolk*, London, 1822. The remarkable roof of the house, forming a series of ceilings with stepped coves to the first-floor rooms, was measured by Cecil Hewett whose drawings are reproduced in NMRC.
43 In 1530 there was a change in the way that building was organised; Airs 1995a, 67.
44 Thurley 1993, 28–32.
45 For Eastbury, see NMRC, 94949; English Heritage, London Division, report AR/HB/942 8019; *Eastbury Manor House, Barking*, 11th Monograph of the London Survey Committee, London, 1917.
46 *The Journal of Sir Roger Wilbraham*, ed. H. S. Scott, Royal Historical Society, Camden Miscellany, X, 1902, 65.
47 Bodleian Library, Oxford, MS Aubrey 2, fol. 30*v*.
48 For Hanford, see RCHM Dorset, III, pt 1, 102–4; Oswald 1959, 94–6. There is a plan for a similar house (perhaps a survey of an existing building) among the Thorpe drawings: SM, Thorpe 211.
49 For Sawston, see NMRC, 15957; VCH Cambridgeshire, VI, 1978, 251; Arthur Oswald, 'Sawston Hall, Cambridgeshire', *CL*, CV, 1954, 1902–5, 1998–2001, 2092–5; Michael Hodgetts, 'A House with Three Priest-holes', *CL*, CXXXI, 1962, 662–4; T. F. Teversham, *A History of the Village of Sawston*, Sawston, 1947.
50 For Castle Bromwich, see NMRC, 94972; VCH Warwickshire, IV, 1947, 43–4; Lawrence Weaver, 'Castle Bromwich Hall, Warwickshire', *CL*, XXXII, 1912, 228–35; Geoffrey Beard, 'Castle Bromwich Hall, Warwickshire', *CL*, CXI, 1952, 1408–11.
51 NMRC, 949971. Margaret Dickens, *A History of Chastleton*, Banbury, 1938, 17–21; *Chastleton*, National Trust guidebook, 1996
52 For Hambleton, see Gotch 1894, I, 11–12.

53 For Mansfield Woodhouse, see NMRC, 60137.

54 Barton has two matching porches. In their present form these are work of the 1890s; it is unclear to what extent they reproduce (or accommodate) an earlier arrangement.

55 Fiennes 1947, 55–7.

56 SM, Thorpe 31; RIBA, Smythson III/12(4). Smythson's arrangements somewhat resemble those of Fountains Hall with paired entrances behind a screen.

4 ALTERNATIVES AND EXPERIMENTS, 1550–1630

1 Some 700 are shown on Saxton's maps of 1575–80, and this is a diminution from the number earlier in the century. E. P. Shirley, *Some Account of English Deer Parks*, London, 1867, 22–3.

2 Hammond 1904, 119.

3 V. de Sola Pinto, *Enthusiast in Wit*, London, 1962, 147–8.

4 Fiennes 1947, 50.

5 Quoted by Mark Girouard, 'Designs for a Lodge at Ampthill', in *The County Seat*, ed. H. Colvin and J. Harris, London, 1970, 13.

6 Smyth 1883, II, 292.

7 Smyth 1883, II, 285.

8 Randle Holme, *Blazon of Armorie* (first published 1688), London, 1701, 453.

9 Dugdale 1730, II, 823. The tower is of three storeys, with one large and one small room to each floor. A well stair rises to the second floor, and a smaller vice rises from there to a flat roof. Tyack 1994, 237–8.

10 For Rosamund's Bower, see *HKW*, II, 1014–17.

11 For Gorhambury, see chapter 2, n. 64.

12 Aubrey 1947, 12–13.

13 For Little Walden, see RCHM Essex, I, 243.

14 Fuller 1662, 280.

15 SM, Thorpe 56.

16 Woolley 1981, 15.

17 For Newark, see NMRC, 94956; report by Kirsty Rodwell for the National Trust, Severn Region, 1988; Richard Haslam, 'Newark Park, Gloucestershire', *CL*, CLXXVIII, 1985, 943–7.

18 The cellars of the observatory seem to bear no relation to the structure above them; the most likely explanation for their layout seems to be that they date from the previous building.

19 The print is 'The Return from the Bird Hunt' from the set *Venationes Avium, Ferarum, Piscium* engraved by Philips Galle after Jan van der Straet. I am indebted to Anthony Wells-Cole for the reference.

20 Dugdale 1730, II, 710.

21 For the iconography of Nonsuch, see also chapter 2, n. 27.

22 Strong 1979, 23–43.

23 For the Nonsuch banqueting house, see John Dent, *The Quest for Nonsuch*, London, 1962, 125–30; *HKW*, IV, 201–2.

24 Girouard 1983, 217–30.

25 For Lodge Farm, see NMRC, 60096; RCHM Dorset, V, 48.

26 N. Summers, 'Old Hall Farm, Kneesall', *Transactions of the Thoroton Society*, LXXVI, 1972, 17–25; Anthony Quiney, 'The Lobby-entry House: Its Origins and Distribution', *Architectural History*, XXVII, 1984, 456–66.

27 For Bishop Vesey's houses, see P. B. Chatwin and E. G. Harcourt, *The Bishop Vesey Houses and other Old Buildings at Sutton Coldfield*, Oxford, 1947.

28 Girouard 1962, 44, 116.

29 NMRC, 94957; Christopher Gilbert, *A Short Historical Guide to Sheriff Hutton Park*, York, 1965 [unpaginated]; Gilbert, 'Sheriff Hutton Hall, Yorkshire', *CL*, CXL, 1966, 548, 628. The house was reduced in size around 1730 and drastically remodelled but the essentials of its original form and accommodation are known from a parliamentary survey of 1650 (PRO, E317/49/54), from a schematic sketch in an estate plan of 1624 (BL, MS Harl 6288) and from what remains of the house itself.

30 Quoted in Gilbert 1965 (op. cit., n. 29).

31 *HKW*, III, pt 2, 48–9; PRO, E317/49/54. There is an earlier seventeenth-century survey at PRO, SP14/53, with plan and sketch elevation. The house was not entirely conventional in its arrangement (it had an unusually large buttery, presumably for the refreshment of the huntsmen) but this evidently did not rule out its domestic use.

32 See n. 14, above.

33 Chauncy 1700, 272.

34 For New Parks, see NMRC, 94948; Christopher Gilbert, 'New Park Huby, an Early 17th Century Hunting Lodge', *Yorkshire Archaeological Journal*, XLV, 1973, 185–8.

35 Richard Neville, 3rd Lord Braybroke, *The History of Audley End*, London, 1836, 177.

36 W. Harrod, *Antiquities and Present State of Stamford and St Martin*, Stamford, 1785, 293.

37 NMRC, 94958; Mark Girouard, 'Ightham Court, Kent', *CL*, CXXIII, 1958, 1424–7.

38 For Fawsley, see NMRC, 61868; Garner and Stratton 1911, 67–8.

39 For Bidston, see NMRC, 94959; W. F. Irvine, 'Notes on the Ancient Parish of Bidston', *Transactions of the Lancashire and Cheshire Historical Society*, XLV, 1893, 33–80; John Brownbill, 'A History of the Old Parish of Bidston, Cheshire', *Transactions of the Lancashire and Cheshire Historical Society*, LXXXVII, 1935, 133–99.

40 King 1656, 124.

41 Oswald 1959, 130–35; RCHM Dorset, I, 66–9.

42 Aubrey 1947, 201.

43 A plan of 1600, drawn by the architect Simon Basil, is at Hatfield. This has some resemblance to a plan in Philibert de L'Orme, *Premier tome de l'architecture*, Paris, 1568, 19.

De L'Orme's plan differs from Basil's in having square towers rather than polygonal ones. Nevertheless a further French resemblance may be seen in the fact that Basil's plan, uniquely as far as is known among English house plans, is marked with sight lines as for an artillery fort. A number of French houses of the late sixteenth century have corner towers whose angles are canted in such a manner. The only other parallel in the British Isles is Rathfarnham in Ireland (see chapter 5, n. 4).

44 For Cranborne, see Oswald 1959, 123–7; RCHM Dorset, V, 7–12.

45 For Westwood, VCH Worcestershire, III, 234–7; Gotch 1894, 15–16; F. B. Andrews, 'Westwood', *Transactions of the Birmingham Archaeological Society*, XLIII, 1917, 63–72; Christopher Hussey, 'Westwood Park, Worcestershire', *CL*, L, 1928, 50–57, 94–100.

46 For Lulworth, see Oswald 1959, 140–42; RCHM Dorset, II, pt 2, 146–8.

47 I am indebted to Harry Gordon Slade for calling my attention to the original form of Westwood. Previous commentators have taken the present position of the front entrance as original.

48 SM, Thorpe 191–2.

49 Girouard 1983, 174–6.

50 John Martin Robinson, 'Gawthorpe Hall, Lancashire', *CL*, CLVIII, 1975, 158–61, 630–33.

51 For Bolsover, see Girouard 1983, 206–10, 234–44.

52 Howorth 1985, 16–19, quoting a letter from Thomas Coke to the Earl of Shrewsbury, in which he likened Worksop to the Medici villa at Pratolino; Girouard 1983, 131–3.

53 Summerson 1993, 67.

54 Girouard 1992, 205–6; there is a plan and sketch of the Holdenby lodge in SM, Thorpe 182.

55 A further lodge-like feature of Hardwick New Hall is the lack of accommodation for servants, almost all of whom must have been housed in the Old Hall or in a range of service buildings which survives, much altered, nearby. These are described and their original use discussed in Nicholas Cooper, report to the National Trust, East Midlands region, 1998.

56 Thurley 1993, 25–34. Perhaps the Queen's House at Greenwich, which was dependent (to a greater extent than Hardwick) for many amenities on the former royal palace, can be seen as a later parallel.

57 Timothy Nourse, *Campania Felix*, London, 1700, 297.

58 North 1981, 62.

59 Conveniently summarised in Ackerman 1990, 10–14, 35–42.

60 Thomas Coryat, *Coryat's Crudities* (written 1611), Glasgow, 1905, I, 300.

61 Coryat, op. cit., 168.

62 F. J. Fisher, 'London as a Centre of Conspicuous Consumption in the Sixteenth

63 Quoted in Stone 1965a, 388.

64 Anon. 1868, 78, 81.

65 Quoted in Laurence Gomme, *The Making of London*, Oxford, 1912, 211.

66 Anon. 1868, 35.

67 Cornwall 1988, 155.

68 For Wickham Court, see NMRC, 87150. Among John Thorpe's drawings is a plan (SM, Thorpe 175), probably for its modernisation, though later alterations have obliterated almost all traces not only of the original internal arrangements but also of the work done around 1600. It is only in the cellars that it can be confirmed that Thorpe's plan is of the existing building; even the location of the hall, though reasonably convincing archaeologically in the existing house, has been altered. The earliest known view of the house, in 1797 (BL, Add MS 32375, fol. 14) shows very different fenestration and candle-snuffer roofs to the towers.

69 The original plan of Ham House was recorded by Robert Smythson: RIBA, Smythson I/24.

70 The Beaufort House plans published in SoL (*Parish of Chelsea*, II, 1913, 20–25) are an extremely instructive series of drawings for the modernisation and subsequent rebuilding of this major suburban house, showing the successive enhancement of stairs, of passages for improved circulation and of other amenities. Beaufort House was conventional in its linear layout, though the continuous corridor proposed for the rear of the principal rooms in the final plan clearly acknowledged the disadvantages of the arrangement.

71 For Bruce Castle, see NMRC, 93513. Although the half-octagonal turrets that project from the façade of Bruce Castle are reminscent of a gatehouse range (cf. Hengrave), it is more likely that the house was originally something like Syston Court in Gloucestershire.

72 For the Camden House pavilions, see NMRC, 86401. The form of the gables of the demolished house seems to have inspired those of the (surviving) gatehouse at Stanway, a few miles away.

73 For Camden House, see SoL 37, pt. 2, *Northern Kensington*, 1973, 55–7.

74 *The Journals of Two Travellers in Elizabethan and Early Stuart England: Thomas Platter and Horatio Busino*, ed. Peter Razzell, London, 1995, 33–6.

75 For Holland House, see Earl of Ilchester, *House of the Hollands, 1605–1820*, London, 1937, 1–15; RCHM West London, 75–6; the plan on p. 134 is based partly on the RCHM plans and partly on those held by English Heritage, London Division.

76 SM, Thorpe 96–9; Summerson 1966, 72.

77 Harris 1979, 55.

78 SM, Thorpe 93, 182.

79 Patrick Faulkner, 'Nottingham House: John Thorpe and his Relation to Kensington Palace', *Archaeological Journal*, CVII, 1950, 66–77. Thorpe's plan is in SM, Thorpe 94.

80 For Eagle House, see NMRC, 94973; T. G. Jackson, 'Eagle House, Wimbledon', *Surrey Archaeological Collections*, X, 1891, 151–64. Also, English Heritage, London Division, MER 10.

81 PRO, SP14/103/89, Richard Harrison to Sir Dudley Carleton. The reference is to work going forward at Imber Court. Bell was also involved in planning the gardens at Hatfield for the Earl of Salisbury: Lawrence Stone, 'The Building of Hatfield House', *Archaeological Journal*, CXII, 1955, 100–180. It is tempting to guess that he may have had some involvement with the remarkable gardens less than a mile from Eagle House at Wimbledon Park, shown in Smythson's plan (RIBA, Smythson I/24) and executed for Salisbury's brother, Thomas Cecil, Earl of Exeter.

82 HMC Salisbury, XIX, 121.

83 RIBA, Smythson I/8.

84 For Ashley Park, M. E. Blackman, 'Ashley Park, Walton on Thames', *Surrey Archaeological Collections*, LXXI, 1977, 263–5; *Ashley Park Building Accounts 1602–7*, ed. Blackman, Surrey Record Society, XXIX, 1977.

85 For Danvers House, SoL, *Parish of Chelsea*, II, 1913, 11–14; Bodleian Library, Oxford, MS Aubrey 2, fol. 53 ff.; SM, Thorpe 21–2.

86 Aubrey 1947, 81.

87 Samuel Pepys, *Diary*, ed. R. C. Latham and W. Matthews, London, 1970, II, 187–8.

88 Maurice Barley's account of the double-pile house (in *Archaeological Journal*, CXXXVI, 1979, 253–64) is a useful discussion of the acceptance of double-pile planning at a relatively humble social level, but his definition of the form by roof structures cannot be sustained. A copy of Barley's unpublished index of such houses is in NMRC. The term is due ultimately to Pratt, but its adoption is unfortunate since it implies that the deep plan was generally conceived by contemporaries as a house of two parallel ranges. This was clearly not so, as is shown by the terms of other contemporary descriptions: cf. the contract for the building of Capheaton in Northumberland in the 1660s. This, a classic double pile of two ranges deep, was to have 'two main walls built through it' (Hodgson 1820–58, pt 2, I, 220) – i.e. at right angles to the axes of the front and rear ranges and an accurate description of the plan, e.g. of Chevening.

89 North 1981, 32.

90 Bacon 1858, 483.

91 Gunther 1928, 62.

92 Gunther 1928, 24.

93 Kingston, Surrey RO, survey book of the Manor of East Betchworth, 1633–4, 47v–48r. William Cotham, surveyor.

94 SM, Thorpe 176.

95 E. g. Mercer 1962, 127.

96 *Early Chronicles of Shrewsbury, 1372–1603*, ed. W. A. Leighton, Shropshire Archaeological and Natural History Society Transactions, II, 1880, 290.

97 For Beckington Castle, see NMRC, 51130 (where the suggested date is almost certainly too late). Garner and Stratton 1911, 189. The actual date of the house is hard to establish: much detail has been restored and much introduced, but it may be of around 1560–70. The very remarkable roof, with crossed purlins forming St Andrew's crosses, illustrates the sophistication of these small, suburban houses of rich men; it might be compared with the crossed rafters of the roof of the great hall of Kirby, 1572.

98 For Hinton House, see NMRC, 88232; VCH Berkshire, III, 1923, 249.

99 There is a modern plan of as much of the ground floor of Thorpe Salvin as survives above ground in NMRC, 94964. Girouard (1983, 119–20) suggests that it may have had a small internal courtyard; the evidence is against this.

100 J. Hunter, *South Yorkshire: The History and Topography of the Deanery of Doncaster*, London, 1828, I, 309–11.

101 For Smythson's role in refining and exploiting stylistic and formal elements that were already developing in the north Midlands, see Girouard 1983, 110–26. It seems fairly clear that Chatsworth exercised an influence in the region comparable with that of Longleat in the south-west, though its rebuilding at the end of the seventeenth century has made it easier to overlook its impact.

102 The relationship – if any – of these rectangular, compact houses to contemporary French examples such as Bailleul, Maulnes and Omesson (all descended from Chenonceaux) still needs to be explored. Girouard 1983, 103–4.

103 Joan Varley, 'New Light on the Red Hall at Bourne', *Lincolnshire Historian*, XII, 1965, 13–18.

104 Lincoln, Lincolnshire Archives Office, Ad. ac. 24/70, printed in Varley, op. cit., pp. 17–18.

105 SM, Thorpe 28. Thorpe's Lincolnshire connections are discussed in Summerson 1966, 7. For Dowsby, see D. L. Roberts, 'John Thorpe's Designs for Dowsby Hall and the Red Hall, Bourne', *Lincolnshire History and Archaeology*, VIII, 1973, 13–34. Thorpe's plan of Dowsby is a simple deep rectangle, like Red Hall; as built, the house was still two ranges deep but several bays longer.

106 E.g. Wanswell Court in Gloucestershire: Wood 1965, pl. 5; perhaps the Old Manor House at Lustleigh in Devonshire.

107 Pugin 1840, I, pl. 59.

108 There is a plan of Rushbrook in NMRC, Red Boxes, Suffolk.

109 For Seckford, see NMRC, 88251; Anon,

'Seckford Hall, Suffolk', *CL*, XXVII, 1910, 90–96; Gotch 1894, II, 43.

110 For Holdenby, Girouard 1992, 197–210; RCHM Northamptonshire, 235–8; Mark Girouard, 'Elizabethan Holdenby', *CL*, CLXVI, 1979, 1286–9, 1398–1401.

111 The idea that the deep plan may have originated in the town house was first made, as far as I am aware, by the late Arthur Oswald: 'Boston Manor, Middlesex', *CL*, CXXXVII, 1965, 603–7. However, this suggestion seems to have attracted no attention at the time.

112 *The London Surveys of Ralph Treswell*, ed. John Schofield, London Topographical Society, CXXXV, 1987.

113 Schofield (1994, 51–3) calls the form 'type 3' in his classification of London house plans. Examples, largely redrawn from Treswell's surveys, are in Schofield 1994, 52, 158, 163–4, 189, 192, 209, 263. Where like the last (Blackman Street, Southwark, taken from *Treswell*, fig. 53) these are in near-suburban locations, the houses are slightly more spacious and the layouts more completely worked out than those in more cramped, central areas. Other late sixteenth-century examples of houses with central stairs and stacks are provided by Roger Leach, 'The Prospect from Reyman's Row: The Row House in Late 16th and Early 17th Century London', *Archaeological Journal*, CLIII, 1996, 201–42.

114 SM, Thorpe 135, 136.

115 M. J. Power, 'The East and West in Early Modern London', in *Wealth and Power in Tudor England: Essays presented to S. E. Bindoff*, ed. E. W. Ives, London, 1978, 181–98.

116 *A Survey of London by John Stowe* (written 1598), ed. C. L. Kingsford, Oxford, 1908, II, 98, 78.

117 SM, Thorpe 18.

118 For Pendell House, see NMRC, 94966; VCH Surrey, II, 463.

119 The plan and elevation of Killigrew's house is reproduced in Harris and Higgott 1989, 312–14.

120 For Pendell Court, see NMRC, 94967; VCH Surrey, II, 479.

121 SM, Thorpe 225, 226.

122 RCHM Middlesex, 5–6; Arthur Oswald, 'Boston Manor, Middlesex', *CL*, CXXXVII, 1965, 603–6.

123 For Forty Hall, see RCHM Middlesex, 23–4; English Heritage, London Division, EN 53.

124 Daniel Defoe, *A Tour through England and Wales* (first published 1724–6), ed. G. D. H. Cole, London, 1928, 165–7.

5 LONDON AND THE PROVINCES, 1600–1650

1 Caroline Stanley-Millson and John Newman, 'Blickling Hall: The Building of a Jacobean Mansion', *Architectural History*, XXIX, 1986, 13.

2 SM, Thorpe 202. For Somerhill, H. Avray Tipping, 'Somerhill, Kent', *CL*, LII, 1922, 310–17.

3 Maurice Craig, 'Portumna Castle', in H. Colvin and J. Harris, *The County Seat*, London, 1970, 36; D. M. Waterman, 'Some Irish Seventeenth-century Houses and their Architectural Ancestry', in *Studies in Building History*, ed. E. M. Jope, London, 1961, 257–8.

4 Edward McParland, 'Rathfarnham Castle, Ireland', *CL*, CLXXII, 1982, 734–7. The plan of Rathfarnam is reminiscent of the Irish coast defence fort at Haulbowline, for which a contemporary drawing is reproduced in P. D. A. Harvey, *Maps in Tudor England*, London, 1993, 64. The form is little known in England, though a fort to this plan was begun in the Scillies in 1551 and abandoned (*HKW*, IV, 591) and its origin is continental. The house with angle towers is not uncommon in England before 1500 as well as in France. Thereafter it is virtually unknown in England until towards the end of the century (Thorpe Salvin, Barlborough, etc.) but in France the formula developed rapidly to provide one of the most universal forms for the larger house, whether a compact block or a range of buildings around a courtyard. The keeled turrets of Rathfarnham repeat those of the Château de Ferrals Aude; Babelon 1989, 564–6. A number of John Thorpe's plans repeat the general form.

5 De L'Orme, op. cit. (chapter 2, n. 79), 18.

6 For Bourton on the Hill, see NMRC, 87114; Benton Fletcher, 'Bourton House, Gloucestershire', *CL*, LXXXVII, 1940, 3012–15, 330–33; Kingsley 1989–92, I, 63. The house has generally been dated to 1570, the year inscribed on an adjoining barn. Stylistically, this is inconceivable.

7 For Plas Teg, see Smith 1975, 242; Mark Girouard, 'Plas Teg, Flintshire', *CL*, CXXXII, 1962, 134–7. For Trevalyn, see Mark Girouard, 'Trevalyn Hall, Denbighshire', *CL*, CXXXII, 1962, 78–81. For the Trevor famiy, *Archaeologia cambrensis*, 6th ser., V, 1905, 108, VI, 1906, 189. It is uncertain whether Trevalyn was to have had a wholly symmetrical façade, but it seems unlikely.

8 Lewes, East Sussex RO, Glynde 302.

9 For Ince, see NMRC, 94965; Christopher Hussey, 'Ince Castle, Cornwall', *CL*, CXLI, 1966, 592–5, 648–51.

10 The builder and date of Ince have been identified by Dr Stephen Roberts, working for Lord and Lady Boyd. I am indebted to Lord Boyd for permission to quote the historical information in this paragraph.

11 For Sir Peter Killigrew's house, see Harris and Higgott 1989, 312–14. For the Killigrew family, see H. M. Jeffrey, 'Two Historical Sketches of the Killigrew Family of Arwenack', *Royal Institution of Cornwall Journal*, IX, 1886–7, 178–216; *The Commons 1660–1690*, ed. B. D. Henning, London, 1983, 679–80.

12 *The Prideaux Collection of Topographical Drawings*, ed. J. Harris, Architectural History, VII, 1964, 51.

13 There was brick in Devon by the early sixteenth century: Pugsley 1992, 113.

14 Patricia Butler, 'Aston Hall', *Archaeological Journal*, CXVIII, 1971, 209–13; Adrian Oswald, 'Excavations at Aston Hall, Birmingham', *Transactions of the Birmingham Archaeological Society*, LXVIII, 1950, 107–10; Christopher Hussey, 'Aston Hall, Birmingham', *CL*, CXIV, 1953, 552–5, 620–23, 694–7.

15 Paula Henderson, 'The Loggia', in Gent 1995, 109–46.

16 SM, Thorpe 109.

17 Bacon 1858, 484.

18 Malcolm Airs, 'Lawrence Shipway, Mason', *Architectural History*, XXVII, 1984, 368–73.

19 NMRC, 88333; 'T', 'Dorfold Hall, Cheshire', *CL*, XXIV, 1908, 594–606; Figueiredo and Treuherz 1988, 77–80.

20 King 1656, 70.

21 Girouard 1983, 188–91.

22 The Burton Agnes plan is at RIBA, Smythson I/2.

23 SM, Thorpe 225, 226.

24 For Gainford, see NMRC, 87108; J. R. Walbron, *Antiquities of Gainford*, Ripon, 1846, 82–3.

25 For Gaythorne Hall, RCHM Westmorland, Asby, 6 (with plan).

26 For Kiplin, see NMRC, 35279; Richard Haslam, 'Kiplin Hall, North Yorkshire', *CL*, CLXXIV, 1983, 202–5, 278–81; Constance B. Schulz, *Kiplin Hall and its Families*, Kiplin, 1994. There are early nineteenth-century plans of the house in Northallerton, North Yorkshire RO, ZBL M 17–19. My account of the house (in NMRC and followed here) differs in its interpretations from that in *CL*.

27 For Grafton, see Figueiredo and Treuherz 1988, 235–6.

28 Slingsby 1836, 51. Holland House seems not to have provided a through vista when first built: there was originally a curious, polygonal service stair turret at the rear of the house in line with the front entrance. If this turret had been removed when flanking service stair turrets were added, this would have created the vista that Sir Henry approved, and his comment may be evidence that this is what in fact happened. The form of Red House is not known, but there is a service stair of the Holland House kind at Caverswall in Staffordshire, a grand, Smythson-like house of 1615 which is similarly two ranges deep though different otherwise.

29 NMRC, 88247. The stair balusters are identical with those at Pembroke College of around 1636.

30 The model is illustrated in Airs 1995a, 30.

31 For Anderson, see RCHM Dorset, III, i, 6–7; Oswald 1959, 102–4; J. Hutchins, *History of Dorset* (first published 1774), London, 1861, I, 160.

32 For Lake House, see NMRC, 50490; G. L. Morris, 'Lake House', *Architectural Review*, v, 1899, 171–9; 'T', 'Lake House, Wiltshire', *CL*, xxiii, 1908, 198–203.

33 For Clegg Hall, see NMRC, 32302.

34 It has been suggested that the model, now in the Union House Museum at Gressenhall, Norfolk, is an original architect's model for the house. This seems unlikely, although it remains a possibility.

35 According to Blomefield (1805, i, 344), the book was published in 1586, but the date seems improbable. It is possible that this is a confusion with Compton Holland, *A Book of Drawing, Limning . . . and the Art of Painting . . . Or, the Young Man's Time Well Spent*, first published (under a different title) in 1616–20; this title is that of the 1652 edition. It is not known what connection Compton Holland had with the Quidenham family. Sir Thomas Holland's son, born in 1607, was connected with advanced artistic circles as steward of the Earl of Arundel's park at Kenninghall.

36 The associations of Quebec House with General Wolfe seem to have overlain any earlier record of the house. From its fabric it appears to have acquired its present form by around 1630, but it incorporates work of more than one period.

37 For Toseland, see RCHM Huntingdonshire, 276–7.

38 For Clanford, see NMRC, 87070.

39 For Wharton Court, see RCHM Herefordshire, iii, 127–8. Wharton Court was built soon after 1600 by Richard Whitehall, 'a citizen of London, who had been High Sheriff of the County [and] built a handsom mansion house in the village, but had no issue' (J. Price, *Historical Account of Leominster and its Vicinity*, Ludlow, 1795, 164).

40 The most comprehensive and accessible list of manuscript and printed architectural writings before 1640 is by John Bury, 'Renaissance Architectural Treatises and Architectural Books: A Bibliography', in Guillaume 1988, 485–503. For the printed sources of architectural decoration, see Wells-Cole 1997, *passim*.

41 John Weever, *Antient Funeral Monuments* (first published 1631), ed. W. Tooke, London, 1767, xi.

42 Slingsby 1836, 45 (and cf. 52).

43 Quoted in Summerson 1993, 109.

44 Wotton 1624, 13.

45 Wotton 1624, 120.

46 Wotton 1624, 19.

47 Wotton 1624, 42–3.

48 Evelyn 1723a, sig. C(2).

49 Gunther 1928, 133.

50 In the background to a portrait of the Duchess of Lauderdale by Alexander Marshall, painted around 1660. However, important internal alterations had been made to the house in the 1630s; it is possible that the hipped roof was introduced then.

51 Harris and Higgott 1989, 312.

52 Priscilla Metcalfe, 'Balmes House', *Architectural Review*, cxxi, 1957, 445–6.

53 The Windsor and Bushey lodges are both known from eighteenth-century views. Their origins are obscure: more needs to be discovered about them, though Ernest Law (*History of Hampton Court Palace*, London, 1883, ii, 205–6) implies that the Bushey lodge is post-1660, granted to Edward Progers, Groom of the Bed Chamber.

54 Lubbock (1995, 165–7) sees these restrictions as a moral reformation of over-consumption, while Sharpe (1992, 407–12) sees them in terms both of aesthetics and of deliberate social engineering. In the present context the significance of these regulations is architectural, but they are rightly understood as part of a broader concern for social order.

55 Brett-James 1935, 81; Larkin and Hughes 1973, 112.

56 Brett-James 1935, 91–2.

57 Larkin and Hughes 1973, 346.

58 Larkin and Hughes 1973, 346.

59 Hart 1994, 155–87.

60 Larkin and Hughes 1973, 267–8.

61 Larkin and Hughes 1973, 485–8.

62 Brett-James 1935, 96; Knowles and Pitt 1972, 20. In commending bay windows, Bacon had made an exception in town: 'in cities, upright do better, in respect of uniformity towards the street' (Bacon 1858, 484). The Latin text expresses this slightly differently: 'ad planum aedificii, et minime protuberantes'.

63 Howarth 1985, 185–6; *HKW*, iii, pt 1, 140–47; SoL 36, *The Parish of St Paul Covent Garden*, 1970, 25–7; John Summerson, *Georgian London*, London, 1988, 15–19; Lubbock 1995, 25–36; Sharpe 1992, 406–12.

64 Brett-James 1935, 17–126; Lubbock 1995, 25–35.

65 The phrase 'artisan mannerism' was probably introduced by Summerson in 1953 (1st edn, p. 97, of Summerson 1993). Its characterisation by him there remains accurate and acute. In inventing this phrase, he was probably thinking of Jones's rejection of the 'composed elements . . . brought in by Michill Angell and his followers' (loc. cit.). The term 'subordinate' is used in Harris and Higgott 1989, 298.

66 Reproduced in Harris, Orgel and Strong 1973, fig. 329.

67 Harris, Orgel and Strong 1973, 178–9.

68 A preliminary version of this drawing shows houses of a very much more traditional kind, with timber overhangs and other old-fashioned features. The second version can therefore be seen as a conscious updating of the image that Jones wanted to convey.

69 Larkin and Hughes 1973, 270.

70 SoL 36 (op. cit., n. 63), 1–7.

71 Stow 1908, ii, 211–12.

72 This type has been recognised by Malcolm Airs (1995a, 56). To his examples at Eastbury, Little Belhus and Albyns one can add others at the Charterhouse in London, at Prittlewell and Stapleford Abbots in Essex, and in Kent at Bumpitts in Lynstead, at Harringe Court Farm at Sellinge, and at Skire Hall at Wilmington. The last was associated with wall paintings identical with those remaining at Bumpitts.

73 Examples occur at Brickwall at Northiam; at Wye College and at Swan's House in the High Street at Wye; in a house at Hampton Wick (RCHM Middlesex, pl. 36) and elsewhere. Both types occur at Knole. There was an example of the first type in the Palace of Westminster on which the decoration to the lintel resembled that of the second type: Colvin, 'Views of the Old Palace of Westminster', *Architectural History*, ix, 1966, 62.

74 A further indication of London workmanship may be that, although the overall forms are standard, the decoration of the second type of chimneypiece, the more ornamental of the two forms, is not repetitive. This may suggest the products of a workshop large enough to supply a good range of sources and/or a number of competent craftsmen.

75 North 1981, 25.

76 John Norden, *Speculum Britanniae: The First Part . . . Middlesex*, London, 1593, 12.

77 Fuller 1662, 176.

78 Fuller 1662, 187.

79 Fuller 1662, 112.

80 Stone and Stone 1984, 170–80; G. E. Mingay has calculated that in 1642 43 per cent of the gentry in Hertfordshire and 26 per cent of those in Essex had settled there since 1603, against 14 per cent in Norfolk and 12 per cent in Kent of whom most of the newcomers were in the west, closest to London (Mingay 1976, 9).

81 For example Richard Vesey (probably at Yotes), Peter Mills (Wisbech and Thorpe Hall), Edward Carter (perhaps West Woodhay), Isaac de Caus (Wilton) and Nicholas Stone (Cornbury and elsewhere). SoL 36 (op. cit., n. 63), 28.

82 For Barnham, see NMRC, 82745. Philip M. Johnstone, 'A Lesser Country House of the Seventeenth Century', *CL*, xl, 1916, suppl. 2★–6★. Chichester, West Sussex RO, STC 1/24, fols 132–3, will and inventory of Edward Boniface.

83 For Hamworthy, see RCHM Dorset, ii, pt 2, 238.

84 For Albourne, see NMRC, 88306; Christopher Hussey, 'Albourne Place Sussex', *CL*, lvi, 1924, 398–404.

85 For Swakeleys, see *Swakeleys, Ickenham*, London Survey Committee, Monograph xiii, n.d.

86 For Broome Park, see Arthur Oswald, 'Broome Park, Kent', *CL* lxxxvi, 1939, 494.

87 There is an early eighteenth-century bird's-eye drawing of the house in Hertford, Hertfordshire RO, D/EP/P18. The ownership of

88 For Aldermaston, see NMRC, 94950; Evelyn 1995, III, 100 (9 June 1654); *Gentleman's Magazine*, I, May 1843, 194; *Illustrated London News*, 7 and 14 January 1844, 28. Evelyn's comment ought, however, to be seen in the context of similar remarks about Burghley, Holdenby and Kirby Hall.

89 In 1841 the great drawing room was said to be over the dining room; when the house was built these rooms were probably a great parlour on the ground floor and dining chamber above, presumably either at the rear of the two-storey hall or else occupying the high-end wing. A damaged inventory of 1663 indicates dependent rooms beyond both parlour and dining room: 'the green cloth room' and 'garden chamber' beyond the parlour, and a withdrawing room probably beyond the dining room and another room by it.

90 Bold 1990, 154–5.

91 The plan of Chevening may have been determined in part by the presence of an earlier house: the spine wall between the front and back basement rooms may have been the front wall of the previous building. Chevening can be seen as an alternative to a house with a modified through hall, as a compact E-plan house with the space between the wings filled in. But this view does not affect the interpretation of the relationship of hall and stair.

92 Gervase Jackson-Stops, 'West Woodhay, Berkshire', *CL*, CLXXXI, 1987, 44–9.

93 West Woodhay was greatly altered in the nineteenth century, and subsequently reduced to its original size. That the layout described is substantially original, however, is suggested by an eighteenth-century plan (BL, K. Top. VII 516, c).

94 Gervase Jackson-Stops, op. cit. (n. 92). Carter's name is attached to the plan and elevation of an unbuilt lodge (reproduced in Mowl and Earnshaw 1995, 60) at Easthampstead in Berkshire, west of Windsor, designed for William Trumbull (d. 1635) or for his son, another William, shortly thereafter. The elder Trumbull was clerk to the Privy Council, and had been granted the royal park at Easthampstead in 1628; his son succeeded him. A connection with Rudyard of West Woodhay lies in that Rudyard was MP for Downton in 1628, Trumbull in 1625–6. The drawing for Easthampstead is the clearest indication of Carter's style: the house is spare and plain, with a hipped roof, little surface ornament, and an ingenious plan which may be founded on an Italian plan but substituting an open, square courtyard at the centre for the *sala*, and a conventional English hall for one of the two loggias. The other loggia remains open in Carter's plan, perhaps intended to function on two levels or to have had a gallery above it.

95 J. A. Manning, *Memoirs of Sir Benjamin Rudyard*, London, 1841.

96 A building licence dated 1634, signed by Jones, Thomas Fowler, John Hulse, Sir Henry Spiller, Laurence Whitaker and John Williams, names Rudyard among the commissioners. Those signing are likely to have done the commission's daily business, but though the first names on the list are largely honorific they nevertheless included men known for their architectural interest, notably the Earl of Arundel and his son Lord Maltravers for whom Jones designed a building scheme. Dorchester, Dorset RO, DD/WHL/2576.

97 NMRC, 94975; Christopher Hussey, 'The Manor House, Ogbourne St George, Wiltshire', *CL*, XCII, 1942, 1226–9.

98 Now removed, but preserved in the cellars.

99 Harris and Higgott 1989, 84.

100 John Aubrey, *Natural History of Wiltshire*, ed. John Britton, London, 1847, 93. See also Strong 1979, 179–81.

101 For Coleshill, see Lees-Milne 1953, 211–16; Gunther 1928, 4–8, 92–8; Bold 1990, 157–8; Mowl and Earnshaw 1995, 48–58; H. Avray Tipping, 'Coleshill House, Berkshire', *CL*, XLVI, 1919, 108–16, 138–44; 'Jones, Inigo' and 'Pratt, Roger', Colvin 1995; Nigel Silcox-Crowe, 'Sir Roger Pratt', in *The Architectural Outsiders*, ed. Roderick Brown, London, 1980. Even the date of Coleshill has been debated. In December 1652 parliamentary commissioners described Sir George Pratt's house at Coleshill as 'All that mantion house built of stone, and covered with tile, consisting of one great Hall, two Parlours, one Kitchen, one Larder, one Pantry, with severall other lowe roomes, with one greate seller, with one great Dyneing roome above stayers, wth aboute 18 chambers above stayers, with all the out Offices, and out houseing, Buildings, Brewhouse, Barnes and Stables wth the Courts, Gardens, and Fouldyards, to the same belonging' (PRO, E 317 Berks 4). An old house had been burnt down shortly before, and a house to replace it had already been abandoned at ground-floor level. The description, though fairly generalised, fits the house that Roger Pratt finished. John Webb designed capitals for Coleshill (Bold 1990, pl. 103) which were never installed. The most likely sequence of events seems to be that Jones provided some overall design for the house, perhaps not worked up in detail but with Webb suggesting some of what was required and Roger Pratt acting as an intermediary between Jones and Sir George; that building came to a halt around the end of 1652, with the house not yet completely fitted up; and that around 1659–63 Roger Pratt oversaw its completion, with remaining detail designed by himself or some unknown master-craftsmen.

102 Wotton 1624, Preface [unpaginated].

103 Brereton 1868, 178.

104 King 1656, 75.

105 Brome, op. cit. (chapter 2, n. 152), II, 8.

106 Morpeth, Northumberland RO, ZSW 510/9.

107 Hammond 1904, 115.

108 Stone's Botanic Garden buildings at Oxford survive: RCHM Oxford, 14–15. His work at Cornbury still exists in part.

109 RIBA, Smythson III/6(3).

110 Hodgson, 1820–58, pt 2, I, 218. For Capheaton, see A. A. Tait, 'Classicism in Eccentric Form: The Architecture of Robert Trollope', *CL*, CXXXVIII, 1965, 390–93; Anne Riches, 'Capheaton Hall', *Archaeological Journal*, CXXXIII, 1976, 169–73.

111 PRO, Cal. State Papers Domestic 1617, 70, Chamberlain to Sir Dudley Carlton.

112 There is evidence in the house itself for an interruption in building, perhaps consequent on Jones's death: the brickwork changes from English to Flemish bond at first-floor level, and the upper parts of the façade are more likely to date from the 1680s than 1650 or 1660. The space between the rear wings was filled in with a new dining room in the early nineteenth century. The original intention may have been to have built a façade similar to that of Milton Manor, nearer Oxford. This is probably of around 1655–65, has a hipped roof rather than a pediment, and (like Welford) a continuous line of pilasters to the front. These have labels, a London motif.

113 Exton was burnt in the early nineteenth century, and only fragments now remain. Late nineteenth-century photographs show the shell of a house of various periods, but evidently with a hall and porch of around 1620–30 incorporating a number of modern details. Little more appears from a superficial examination of the existing ruins except some evidence that the hall may have had a false hammer-beam roof, and that it was divided by the insertion of a floor in the early eighteenth century.

114 Drawn by Jacob Esselens and reproduced in *Drawings of England in the Seventeenth Century by Willem Schellinks, Jacob Esselens and Lambert Doormer*, ed. P. H. Hutton, Walpole Society, XXXV, 1959, II, 28. Colvin 1995, 397. For a discussion of the York House design, see Harris and Higgott 1989, 298.

115 Whinney 1964, 12–22.

116 BL, Add MS 62674.

117 Leeds, West Yorkshire R.O. TN/C.

118 Girouard 1983, 219.

119 Bold 1990, 85.

the house is given in VCH Berkshire, IV, 1911, 248–9, but it is ascribed to too early a building date. Both from its style and the history of Windebank's career, the house must be of 1630–40. It was enlarged in the eighteenth century. There is an inventory of 1670 in PRO, PROB 4/12738, Richard Bigg of Haineshill Esq.

120 Morpeth, Northumberland RO, ZSW 450/1–12.

121 N. H. Cooper, *Aynho: A Northamptonshire Village*, Banbury, 1984, 146.

6 CONSERVATISM, INNOVATION AND CONSOLIDATION, 1620–1690

1 Stone and Stone 1984, 36–40.

2 *Lowther Family Estate Books, 1617–75*, ed. C. B. Philips, Surtees Society, CXCI, 1976–7, 62.

3 Op. cit., 67–8.

4 William Grey, *Chorographia or a Survey of Newcastle upon Tyne*, Newcastle, 1649, 39–40. See also J. V. Beckett, 'Absentee Landownership in the Later Seventeenth and Early Eighteenth Centuries: The Case of Cumbria', *Northern History*, XI, 1983, 87–107.

5 Carew 1602, 63–4.

6 Evelyn 1723b, 57.

7 Hove, Rape of Hastings Survey, *Newsletter*, 1990.

8 Pugsley 1992, 96–118.

9 There is a telling anecdote (albeit of *c.* 1730, a later date than the period covered in this book) in Sir Thomas Robinson's letters: 'The overlooker or *Clerk of the Works*, often thinks himself wiser than the Architect. A remarkable instance happen'd att old Sir Wm. Strickland's [Boynton Hall] in Yorkshire; Ld. Burlington gave him a beautiful design, with a Palladian roof, & an Attic story, instead of garrets & the old wretched & ugly roof of our Gothick ancestors – when the house was completed Sir Wm. went down, pleasing himself that he had improv'd the bad taste of his County, & should be the object of the Envy of his neighbours, when alas he found the old fashion'd roof & many other material alterations from the plan . . . [the Clerk of Works' defence was] . . . that he took it for granted the Architect had made a *mistake* . . . a constant mortification [to Sir William] while he lived' (Margaret Lady Verney and Patrick Abercrombie, 'Letters of an Eminent Architect' [Sir Thomas Robinson], *Architectural Review*, LX, 1926, 51). The old house is illustrated in *Samuel Buck's Yorkshire Sketchbook*, Wakefield, 1979, 400. The plan of the eighteenth-century house, no more than a remodelling of the earlier one, is given in Arthur Oswald, 'Boynton Hall, Yorkshire', *CL*, CXVI, 1954, 280–83, 356–9.

10 The block was not a free-standing tower, as has sometimes been said, though it must have dominated the earlier structure to which it was attached. Girouard 1983, 125–6; NMRC, 88272.

11 'T', 'Tissington Hall, Derbyshire', *CL*, XXIX, 1911, 342–50, 378–84; Gervase Jackson-Stops, 'Tissington Hall, Derbyshire', *CL*, CLX, 1976, 158–61, 214–7, 286–9; NMRC, 88270.

12 The alterations of around 1755 were stylistically of some interest, including the creation of a Gothic revival chimneypiece and gate and the preservation and extension of Jacobean wainscot.

13 There is a modern plan of Park Hall in NMRC, 94963.

14 For Weston Hall, see NMRC, 78200.

15 For Athelhampton, RCHM Dorset, III, pt 1, 9–13; Garner and Stratton 1913, 121–7; Clive Aslet, 'Athelhampton, Dorset', *CL*, CLXXV, 1984, 1310–14, 1374–7, 1478–82; Oswald 1959, 65–9.

16 For Sandford Orcas, see Garner and Stratton 1913, 123–4; RCHM Dorset, I, 1952, 196; Oswald 1959, 75–8.

17 For Bingham's Melcombe, RCHM Dorset, III, pt 2, 163–8; 'Inventory . . . of Robert Bingham of Bingham's Melcombe', ed. C. W. Bingham, *Archaeological Journal*, XVII, 1860, 151–7.

18 For Leigh, see NMRC, 83983.

19 Taunton, Somerset RO, DD/TOR/154.

20 Fiennes 1947, 272.

21 Thomas Fuller, *Church History of Britain*, ed. J. S. Brewer, Oxford, 1845, III, 305.

22 For Kingston Maurward, see RCHM Dorset, III, pt 2, 254–6; Garner and Stratton 1911, 165–6; Oswald 1959, 91–223.

23 For Lake House, see chapter 5, n. 32.

24 For Wick Court, see NMRC, 33416. Kingsley 1989–92, I, 198–200.

25 Arthur Oswald, 'The Hall, Bradford on Avon', *CL*, CXXXII, 1962, 841–4, 900–902, 1020–23.

26 For Marks Hall, see RCHM Essex, III, 177–9; Christopher Hussey, 'Marks Hall, Essex', *CL*, LIV, 1923, 420–27.

27 For Flemings Hall, see NMRC, 78984.

28 These gables had their upper parts rebuilt in the early seventeenth century. The lower part of the front wall has also been rebuilt in brick.

29 For Sharrington Hall, see NMRC, 34414.

30 For Tharston Hall, see NMRC, 88280.

31 For Thurston Hall, see Garner and Stratton 1911, 182–3; NMRC, 88250. The date 1607 appears on the building; this is plausible, though it is carved on a member which is not integral with the structure. It was also carved on a chimneypiece, since removed. The suggestion that the house is of more than one building period is not the case.

32 RCHM Lancashire, 14–15.

33 For Isel, see NMRC, 87057; Taylor 1892, 327–31; see also chapter 2, n. 15.

34 For Middleton, see RCHM Westmorland, 170–72 (with plan); Taylor 1892, 232–8.

35 For Yanwath, see RCHM Westmorland, 250–52 (with plan); Taylor 1892, 52–64.

36 For East Riddlesden, see RCHM West Yorkshire, 206–7.

37 Girouard 1983, 168. The drawing is at RIBA, Smythson II/33/4.

38 For Preston Court, see NMRC, 61276.

39 For Tunstall House, see NMRC, 61297.

40 Edward Hasted, *History of Kent*, 2nd edn, Canterbury, 1797–1801, VI, 95, 572. His inventory is at Maidstone, Centre for Kentish Studies, PRC 27/27/247. It includes a quantity of building materials; it may be that when he died he was on the point of rebuilding his house, which is certainly small for so rich a man.

41 I am grateful to Dr Peter Leach for giving me his views on the date of Friars Head Hall.

42 For Aston Bury, see Garner and Stratton 1911, 77–8; NMRC, 77417; RCHM Hertfordshire, 1992, 72–4, 87–9.

43 For Red House, see NMRC, 38982.

44 Arthur Oswald, 'Groombridge Place, Kent', *CL*, CXVIII, 1955, 1376–9, 1480–83, 1524–7.

45 BL, Add MSS 69869, 69874–5, 69880. An inventory of the house taken in 1680 is in PRO, PROB 4/4610.

46 Quoted in Michael Young, *Servility and Service*, Woodbridge, 1986, 34.

47 Sarah Markham, *John Loveday of Caversham*, Wilton, 1984, 318–19.

48 For Kirstead Hall, see E. P. Willins, *Some of the Old Halls . . . in the County of Norfolk*, London, 1890, facing pl. XXIX.

49 For Doughton Manor, see NMRC, 87111; Garner and Stratton 1911, 162–3; Kingsley 1989–92, I, 84–6; Christopher Hussey, 'Doughton Manor House, Gloucestershire', *CL*, XCIV, 1943, 948–51.

50 For Guiseley, see RCHM West Yorkshire, 198; Ambler 1913, 58.

51 For Cote, see VCH Oxon, XIII, 1995, 65–8; NMRC, 88246.

52 There has been no systematic attempt to estimate the impact of the war on houses, or on house building, but see Thirsk 1985, 119–54, in which it is estimated that 150–200 houses 'of major local importance' (p. 134) were physically destroyed as a result of the war.

53 Quoted in L. G. Bolingbroke, 'Two Elizabethan Inventories', *Norfolk Archaeology*, XV, 1904, 94. A slightly different version is in Blomefield 1805, 544.

54 Stone and Stone 1984, fig. 11.8, p. 384.

55 Aylmer 1973, 280.

56 Such a fireplace is shown in an engraving of around 1640 reproduced in Peter Thornton, *Authentic Decor: The Domestic Interior 1620–1920*, London, 1984, fig. 33, p. 36. The engraving is English, so such forms were evidently not otherwise unknown at the time.

57 H. Avray Tipping, 'Thorpe Hall', *CL*, XLVI, 1919, 300–310, 330–38, 364–71; Lees-Milne 1953, 202–6.

58 Bold 1990, 87.

59 Fuller 1662, 216.

60 Wells-Cole 1997, 199–200.

61 Quoted from William Dugdale in Raine 1852, 107, n. 2.

62 Christopher Hussey, 'Halnaby Hall, Yorkshire', *CL*, LXXIII, 1933, 334–8, 362–7.

63 For Moulton Hall, see NMRC, 94946;

for Moulton Manor, see NMRC, 94947; Christopher Hussey, 'Moulton Manor [and] Moulton Hall', *CL*, LXXIX, 1936, 250–55; VCH Yorkshire North Riding, I, 1914, 191–5.

64 'Thackeray, William', Colvin 1995, 971–2; Blake Tyson, 'William Thackeray and his Work at Rose Castle, Cumbria, 1673–75', *Transactions of the Ancient Monuments Society* new ser., XXVII, 1983; Tyson, 'William Thackeray and James Swingler at Flatt Hall . . . and other Cumbrian Buildings', *Transactions of the Ancient Monuments Society*, new ser., XXVIII, 1984, 60–92.

65 Raine 1852, 104.

66 Eric Mercer suggested that the adoption of Gothic at Oxford was to avoid the declamatory classicism associated with the Counter-Reformation while at the same time staking the claim of the national church to legitimacy and continuity, 'treading a narrow path between Geneva on the one hand and Rome on the other' (Mercer 1962, 86). Neither style appears at the more overtly Protestant university of Cambridge.

67 Raine 1852, 85.

68 For Moresby, see NMRC, 8393.

69 For the attribution of Ribton and Moresby to William Thackeray, see Tyson 1984, op. cit. (n. 64). I am grateful to Mr Tyson for his comments on my own interpretation of Moresby.

70 For Ribton, see Taylor 1892, 334–6 (with photograph).

71 Illustrated in Kuyper 1980, pl. 66.

72 H. J. Louw, 'Anglo-Netherlandish Architectural Interchange c. 1600–c. 1660', *Architectural History*, XXIV, 1981, 1–23.

73 Raine 1852, 104.

74 Blake Tyson, note in *Transactions of the Cumberland and Westmorland Antiquarian and Archaeological Society*, new ser., LXXXI, 1981, 164.

75 Cumbria RO, Dean and Chapter of Carlisle, Machell MSS I, 540.

76 'Machell, Thomas', Colvin 1995, 631–2; Jane Ewbank, 'Antiquary on Horseback', *Cumberland and Westmorland Antiquarian and Archaeological Society*, extra ser., XIX, 1963.

77 Cumbria RO, Dean and Chapter of Carlisle, Machell MSS, I, 538.

78 Blake Tyson, 'The Mansion House, Eamont Bridge, Cumbria', *Transactions of the Ancient Monuments Society*, new ser., XXXI, 1987, 146–74. Tyson compares the house with Appleby Castle; the similarity to Crackenthorpe, definitely by Machell, seems as close or closer.

79 Taylor 1892, 146.

80 'Talman, William', Colvin 1995.

81 C. Roy Huddleston, 'The Foresters of Stonegarthside Hall', *Cumberland and Westmorland Architectural and Achitectural Society*, new ser., LXI, 1961, 169–201.

82 Quoted in Huddleston, op. cit., 176.

83 I am most grateful to Kitty Cruft for commenting on the Scottish affinities of Stonegarthside.

84 Kuyper 1980, 57–114. John Cornforth and Herbert Jan Hijmersma, 'Early Classicism in Leiden', *CL*, CLVIII, 1975, 438–41.

85 J. Rosenberg, S. Slive and E. H. Ter Kvile, *Dutch Art and Architecture, 1600–1800*, Harmondsworth, 1966, 229–40.

86 SM, Thorpe 62.

87 *Samuel Buck's Yorkshire Sketchbook*, Wakefield, 1979. The original is in BL, Lansdowne 914.

88 Christopher Hussey, 'Cobham, Kent, II: Owletts', *CL*, XCIV, 1943, 1168.

89 SM, Thorpe 176.

90 VCH Oxon, XII, 1990, 281.

91 See chapter 4, n. 87.

92 North 1981, 9.

93 King 1656, 67.

94 Edmund Sandford, *A Cursory Relation of all the Antiquities and Familyes in Cumberland . . . about the year 1675*, ed. R. S. Ferguson, Cumberland and Westmorland Antiquarian and Archaeological Society, Tract Series, IV, 1890, 20.

7 HOUSEHOLDS AND HOSPITALITY

1 *Lancashire and Cheshire Wills and Inventories*, III, ed. G. J. Piccope, Chetham Society Publications 54, 1861, 91–102.

2 Granville Leveson Gower, *Parochial History of Westerham*, London, 1883, 13. Squerries was rebuilt in the late seventeenth century.

3 *Lancashire and Cheshire Wills and Inventories*, ed. J. P. Earwaker, Chetham Society, new ser. III, 1884, 27–38.

4 W. D. Scull, 'Old Buckhurst', *Sussex Archaeological Collections*, LIV, 1913, 69.

5 PRO, PROB 11/345 fol. 128.

6 *Lancashire and Cheshire Wills and Inventories*, II, ed. G. J. Piccope, Chetham Society Publications 51, 1860, 129.

7 Lewes, East Sussex RO, HA/30/50/22/1.8 (10).

8 Cholmley 1870, *passim*.

9 For Sir John Coke, see Dorothea Coke, *The Last Elizabethan*, London, 1937; Michael Young, *Service and Servility*, Woodbridge, 1986.

10 BL, Add MSS 69873, fol. 49v.

11 BL, Add MSS 68969.

12 *Papers of Nathaniel Bacon of Stiffkey*, III, ed. A. Hassall Smith, Norfolk Record Society LIII, 1987–8, 252.

13 NMRC, 94952; Marcus Binney, 'Loseley Park, Guildford', *CL*, CLXV, 1969, 802–4, 894–7. Binney's suggestion that an old house at Loseley was retained to provide service accommodation after the building of the present house is not persuasive.

14 SM, Thorpe 39–40. The new wing is datable to 1602 by an agreement with John Saunders, mason of Guildford (Guild-

ford, Guildford Muniment Room, LM 826'15).

15 Reading, Berkshire RO, D/ELI/C1/ (5 July 1630).

16 Bramston 1845, 352.

17 Harris 1979, 46.

18 Smyth 1883, II, 385.

19 Bold and Reeves 1988, 42.

20 A. Mary Sharp, *The History of Ufton Court*, London, 1892, 95–6.

21 Sharp, op. cit., 100.

22 NMRC, 94954; Christopher Hussey, 'Brympton D'Evercy, Somerset', *CL*, LXI, 1927, 718–26, 762–9, 775–8 (furniture and pictures). J. D. Gray, 'Brympton D'Evercy', *Proceedings of the Somerset Archaeological and Natural History Society*, CIX, 1965, 40–46.

23 I am indebted to Anthony Emery for this very plausible suggestion.

24 NMRC, 94955; E. T. Long, 'Bisham Abbey, Berkshire', *CL*, LXXXIX, 1941, 3420–24, 342–6, 364–8.

25 See chapter 2, n. 17.

26 HMC Salisbury, III, 1889, 73; P. W. Hasler, *The House of Commons 1558–1603*, London, 1981, II, 320.

27 For Smithills, VCH Lancashire, V, 1911, 13–19 (with plan); H. Avray Tipping, 'Smithills Hall, Lancashire', *CL*, LXVI, 1929, 488–96; John Harbord, *The House and Farm Accounts of the Shuttleworths of Smithills and Gawthorpe*, Chetham Society, 35, 41, 43, 46, 1856–8.

28 For St Aylotts, see NMRC, 93446.

29 Ipswich, East Suffolk RO, HA 240/2508/1435. The plan is associated with others which are for Redgrave Hall, though it may not be for Redgrave itself.

30 NMRC, 94974; W. G. D. Fletcher, 'Sequestration Papers of Thomas Smalman of Wilderhope', *Shropshire Archaeological and Natural History Society*, 3rd ser., III, 1903, 1–36.

31 RCHM Hertfordshire, II, 70–71.

32 The so-called unit system, in which two self-contained houses of similar status stand close to each other on what is apparently the same property, has received a good deal of attention. See W. J. Hemp and C. A. Gresham, 'Park, Llanfrothen and the Unit System', *Archaeologia cambrensis*, XCVII, 1942–3, 98–112; J. T. Smith, 'Lancashire and Cheshire Houses: Some Problems of Architectural and Social History', *Archaeological Journal*, CXXVII, 1970, 156–81; R. Machin, 'The Unit System: Some Historical Explanations', *Archaeological Jorunal*, CXXXII, 1975, 187–94; K. Sandall, 'The Unit System in Essex', *Archaeological Journal*, CXXXII, 1975, 195–201.

33 H. Avray Tipping, 'Rufford Old Hall, Lancashire', *CL*, LXVI, 1929, 528–35, 570–76; VCH Lancashire, VI, 1911, 123–6.

34 Preston, Lancashire RO, DDHe/37/11,13B.

35 J. T. Cliffe, *The Yorkshire Gentry from the Reformation to the Civil War*, London, 1969, 137, 154; M. Hartley and I. Ingleby, *Yorkshire Village*, London, 1953, 77; Ambler 1913, 46, pl. 38.

36 Smyth 1883, II, 426. See also Thirsk 1969.

37 Mervyn James, *Family, Lineage and Civil Society*, Oxford, 1974, 25–6.

38 *Lancashire Inquisitions Stuart Period*, III, ed. J. P. Rylands, Lancashire and Cheshire Record Society XVII, 1888, 351–8.

39 *Royalist Composition Papers County of Lancaster*, II, ed. J. H. Stanning, Lancashire and Cheshire Record Society XXVI, 1892, 25.

40 *Lancashire Inquisitions Stuart Period*, II, ed. J. P. Rylands, Lancashire and Cheshire Record Society XVI, 1887, 277–83; J. T. Smith, op. cit. (n. 32), 172; VCH Lancashire, VI, 1911, 284.

41 J. E. Hollinshed, 'The Gentry of South-west Lancashire in the Later Sixteenth Century', *Northern History*, XXVI, 1990, 82–99; B. G. Blackwood, 'The Economic State of the Lancashire Gentry on the Eve of the Civil War', *Northern History*, XI, 1976, 53–8.

42 Burton 1660, 259.

43 Gerard 1990, 138.

44 *Lowther, Family Estate Books 1617–75*, ed. C. B. Philips, Surtees Society, CXCI, 1976-7, 233–4.

45 For Poundisford, see chapter 3, n 20.

46 Hussey, 'Shute Barton' (chapter 3, n. 5); T. Risden, *Chorographical Description or Survey of the County of Devon* (written c. 1620), London, 1811, 28–9.

47 Hutchins, 1861, I, 160; 'J', 'Anderson Manor, Dorset', *CL*, XXXVII, 1915, 446–51; Oswald 1959, 102–4. RCHM Dorset, III, pt 1, 6–7.

48 John Bold, 'Privacy and the Plan', in Bold and Chaney 1993, 109.

49 R. Garraway Rice, 'The Household Goods etc. of Sir John Gage of West Firle', *Sussex Archaeological Collections*, XLV, 1902, 51.

50 *Lancashire and Cheshire Wills*, II, ed. J. P. Earwaker, Chetham Society, new ser. XXVIII, 1893, 170–75.

51 Christopher Hussey, 'Collacombe Barton, Devon', CXXXI, 1962, 906.

52 Owen Ashmore, 'Household Inventories of the Lancashire Gentry', *Transactions of the Lancashire and Cheshire Historical Society*, CX, 1958, 65.

53 PRO, PCC 21 Crane.

54 Ashmore, op. cit., 61.

55 Lincoln, Lincolnshire Archives Office, MCD 864.

56 L. G. Bolingbroke, 'Two Elizabethan Inventories', *Norfolk Archaeology*, XV, 1904, 91–108.

57 Chester, Cheshire RO, WS 1607, Sir Edward Fitton of Gawsworth.

58 For Fitton genealogy, see George Ormerod, *History of Cheshire*, London, 1819, III, 59.

59 Thelma E. Vernon, 'The Inventory of Sir Henry Sharington', *Wiltshire Archaeological and Natural History Magazine*, LXIII, 1968, 72–82.

60 *The Elizabethan Estate Book of Grafton Manor*, ed. J. Humphreys, Birmingham Archaeological Society, XLIV, 1918, 1–124.

61 Carew 1602, 64v.

62 *Lowther*, op. cit. (n. 44), 169.

63 Vivienne Larminie, *Wealth, Kinship and Culture*, Woodbridge, 1995, App. 3.

64 Smyth 1883, II, 370.

65 Heal 1990, *passim*; Heal 1984, *passim*.

66 Smyth 1883, II, 365–6.

67 The practice was condemned by the author of 'The English Courtier . . . Cyvile and Uncyvile Life' (Anon. 1868, 31–3).

68 Quoted in Richard Ollard, *Clarendon and his Friends*, London, 1987, 31.

69 Willem Schellinks, quoted in *Apollo*, CVII, 1978, 9.

70 Norwich, Norfolk RO, MC 254/4/23.

71 Norwich, Norfolk RO, MC 254/4/24.

72 Cicero, *De Officiis*, Book II, chapter xviii; trans. Walter Miller, London and New York, 1913, p. 237.

73 HMC Middleton, 1911, 538–41.

74 Reresby 1991, 285.

75 Reresby 1991, 285–6.

76 Private information.

77 Habington 1895, 100.

78 Quoted in VCH Worcestershire, III, 1913, 124.

79 *Poetical Works of Robert Herrick*, ed. L. C. Martin, Oxford, 1956, 146–49.

80 M. H. McClintock, *Portrait of a House*, London, 1948, 126–7. This Latin version comes from no known text, and was evidently Rudyard's own.

81 Quoted in Christopher Hussey, 'Lees Court, Kent', *CL*, LII, 1922, 178–83, 210–16.

82 *Sir George Sondes his plaine Narrative to the World*, London, 1655, 49.

83 BL, Add MS 53728, fol. 29v.

84 Howell 1892, I, 106.

85 Stubbes 1879, 105.

86 There is an extensive literature on country house poems, among which are G. R. Hibberd, 'The Country House Poem of the Seventeenth Century', *Journal of the Warburg and Courtauld Institutes*, XIX, 1956, 159–74; Don E. Wagner, *Penshurst: The Semiotics of Place and the Poetics of History*, Wisconsin and London, 1984; Malcolm Kelsall, *The Great Good Place: The Country House and English Literature*, New York and London, 1993, 32–43; William A. McClung, *The Country House in English Renaissance Poetry*, Berkeley and London, 1977, 18–45, 104–46.

87 Lubbock 1995, 48–55, 149–55; Sharpe 1992, 414–17.

88 Larkin and Hughes 1973, pp. 356–8.

89 Larkin 1983, 352.

90 T. D. Kendrick, *British Antiquity*, London, 1950, 99–167.

91 Sir Philip Sidney, *The Countess of Pembroke's Arcadia*, ed. Albert Feuillerat, Cambridge, 1912, 15.

92 *Works of Ben Jonson*, ed. C. H. Herford Percy and Evelyn Simpson, Oxford, VIII, 1947, 93–6.

93 *The Poems of Thomas Carew*, ed. Rhodes Dunlap, Oxford, 1949, 86–9.

94 Cholmley 1870, 34.

95 Cf. the comparable injunction in the house-hold ordnances of 1566–92, reprinted in Harington, op. cit. (chapter 1, n. 53) 105–8.

96 *The Oxinden Letters 1607–1642*, ed. Dorothy Gardiner, London, 1933, 114.

97 Discussed and reproduced in Alice T. Friedman, 'Constructing and Identity in Prose, Plaster and Paint: Lady Anne Clifford as Writer and Patron of the Arts', in Gent 1995, 359–76.

98 See, for example, J. H. Hexter, 'The Myth of the Middle Class in Tudor England', *Reappraisals in History*, London, 1961, 82–3.

99 Quoted in Thompson 1993, 38.

100 Sir Thomas Overbury, *His Work with Additions*, 10th impression, London, 1618.

101 *A Health to the Gentlemanly Profession of Serving Men* (written 1598), ed. A. V. Judges, Shakespear Association Facsimile 3, 1931, fol. E2v–E3.

102 Gunther 1928, 27.

103 North 1981, 128.

8   THE ROOMS OF THE HOUSE

1 Thornton 1978, 105–6; Penelope Eames, 'Documentary Evidence concerning the Character of Domestic Furnishing in England in the Fourteenth and Fifteenth Centuries', *Furniture History*, VII, 1971, 41–60.

2 Turner and Parker 1859, 109.

3 North 1981, 135.

4 Carlisle, Cumbria RO, D/Lons/L1/3/4 (10 April 1694).

5 Considered complete when published by Frederick Harrison, *Annals of an Old Manor House*, London, 1893, 206–12. See N. Cooper, 'Sutton Place, East Barsham and some Related Houses', in Airs 1994, 33–54.

6 HMC Middleton, 1911, 474.

7 E. Rebecah, 'Inventories made for Sir William and Sir Thomas Fairfax', *Archaeologia*, XLVIII, 1885, 121–56.

8 Guildford, Guildford Muniment Room, LM 1109.

9 Turner and Parker 1859, 179; see also Michael Thompson, *The Medieval Hall: The Basis of Secular Domestic Life 600–1600 A. D.*, Aldershot, 1995, 110–17.

10 D. Lupton, *London and the Countrey Carbonadoed* (first published 1617), Aungerville Society, II, Edinburgh, 1884, 32.

11 A bibliography of roofs would be almost interminable. But see J. T. Smith, 'Medieval Roofs: A Classification', *Archaeological Journal*, CXII, 1955, 36–94; Eric Mercer, *English Vernacular Houses*, RCHM, London, 1975, 79–112.

12 HMC Middleton, 1911, 538–41.

13 For Mapperton, see RCHM Dorset, I, 154–6; Arthur Oswald, 'Mapperton House, Dorset', *CL*, CXXXI, 1962, 18–21, 66–9, 176–80. For Poxwell, see RCHM Dorset, III, pt 2, 260–62.

14 For Rosewarne, *Archaeological Journal*, CXXX, 1973, 260–62.

15 For Athelhampton, RCHM Dorset, III, 1970, 9–13; Oswald 1959, 65–9.

16 RCHM Westmorland, 250–52.

17 See chapter 2, n. 15.

18 RCHM Westmorland, 170–72.

19 RCHM Northamptonshire, 302–3.

20 The roof of Great Chalfield is illustrated in Pugin 1840, III, 31.

21 The roof of Crosby Hall is illustrated in *Crosby Place*, London Survey Committee, Monograph IX, 1908, pl. 30.

22 For Worksop Manor, see RIBA, Smythson I/8.

23 See n. 5 above.

24 Thurley 1993, 54–65.

25 Frederick Harrison, *Annals of an Old Manor House*, London, 1893, 84.

26 For Rayne, see NMRC, 83069; Baron de Cowson, 'The Capels of Rayne Hall', *Archaeological Journal*, XL, 1883, 64–79; VCH Essex, VI, 1913, 189. RCHM Essex, I, 219.

27 In 1500 the Bishop of London had ten houses in Essex, nine in Middlesex and three in Hertfordshire, though papal dispensation was sought for the surrender of some of the more remote, pleading lack of funds and the ruined state of many of them. J. A. Tremlow, *Calendar of Papal Registers*, London, 1906, 85–6, Papal Letter VII, quoted in London Borough of Hammersmith and Fulham, *Fulham Palace Management Plan*, London, 1987, 11.

28 Pantin 1957, *passim*.

29 For Sandford Orcas, see RCHM Dorset, I, 196–7.

30 The roof and the rear internal wall of Hengrave are nineteenth century; comparison with the plan in Gage 1822 suggests that the hall may formerly have been narrower.

31 For Annesley, see NMRC, 38654.

32 For Wood Lane Hall, see RCHM West Yorkshire, 57–62, 216.

33 The original form of Westholme is not quite clear. The hall has a gallery like that at Wood Lane; on the other hand this gallery also has a fireplace, suggesting that it could be the conversion of a former chamber over the hall.

34 Reproduced in Harris 1979, 270.

35 Arthur Oswald, 'Dunsland House, Devonshire', *CL*, CXXVIII, 1960, 18–21, 78–81.

36 Worcester, Worcestershire RO, BA 2602/91 b009:1.

37 Lionel Cust, 'Notes on the Collection formed by Thomas Howard, Earl of Arundel', *Burlington Magazine*, XIX, 1911, 278–86, XX, 1912, 97–100, 233–6, 341–3.

39 North 1981, 144.

40 Peter Thornton, 'The Furnishing and Decoration of Ham House', *Furniture History*, XVI, 1980, 39.

41 Karin-M. Walton, 'An Inventory of 1710 from Dyrham Park', *Furniture History*, XXII, 1986, 30.

42 Evelyn 1723b, 12–13.

43 Oxford, All Souls College, Wren drawings, II, 108; reproduced in *Wren Society*, XII, 1935, pl. II.

44 Oxford, All Souls College, Wren drawings, II, 107; reproduced in *Wren Society*, XII, 1935, pl. IV.

45 North 1981, 129.

46 Gunther 1928, 63.

47 North 1981, 138.

48 J. Wood, 'The Architectural Patronage of the 10th Earl of Northumberland', in Bold and Chaney 1993, 63–4.

49 Cornforth and Hill 1966, 142.

50 North 1981, 86.

51 S. O. Addy, 'Inventory of Robert Marples 1676', *Journal of the Derbyshire Archaeology and Natural History Society*, IX, 1887, 29.

52 Wood 1965, 133.

53 Thomas Tusser, *500 Points of Good Husbandry*, (published 1562), ed. W. Mavor, London, 1812, 287.

54 C. R. Markham, *Life of Robert Fairfax of Steeton*, London, 1885, 287–94.

55 PRO, PROB 2/503.

56 H. Michell Whitby, 'An Inventory of the Goods and Chattels of William Shirley of Michelgrove', *Sussex Archaeological Collections*, XL, 1912, 286–98.

57 Gunther 1928, 65.

58 PRO, PROB 2/199.

59 PRO, PROB 2/393.

60 L. G. Bolingbroke, 'Two Elizabethan Inventories', *Norfolk Archaeology*, XV, 1904, 91–108.

61 PRO, PROB 2/484.

62 PRO, PROB 2/721.

63 Lincoln, Lincolnshire Archives Office, MCD 864.

64 Raine 1852, 79.

65 Bacon 1858, 486.

66 See chapter 2, n. 144.

67 Maidstone, Centre for Kentish Studies, E272/1.

68 A. P. Baggs, 'Two Designs by Simon Basil', *Architectural History*, XXVII, 1984, 104–11, pl. 3.

69 Wotton 1624, 56.

70 North 1981, 133.

71 Leicester, Leicestershire RO, DE/730, fol. 178ff.

72 Loc. cit., fol. 81.

73 North 1981, 131.

74 North 1981, 137–8.

75 Fiennes 1947, 55–7.

76 Simon Jervis, 'Five Inventories of Browsholme Hall', *Furniture History*, XXII, 1986, 1–24.

77 RCHM West Yorkshire, 18. Early seventeenth-century houses in Yorkshire seem often to have had an unusual number of parlours, which may have been used as ground-floor bedchambers (loc. cit., 61–4).

78 Barley 1990, 15.

79 RCHM West Yorkshire, 206–7.

80 PRO, PROB 5/921.

81 Fiennes 1947, 14.

82 Fiennes 1947, 259. John Aubrey made what may be the earliest record of the impact of smoking on domestic arrangements: 'Sir Walter Raleigh standing in a Stand at Sir Robert Poyntz parke at Acton (which was built by Sir Robert's Grandfather to keepe his Whores in) tooke a pipe of Tobacco, which made the Ladies quitt it till he had donne' (Aubrey 1947, 256).

83 Arthur Oswald, 'Wolfeton House, Dorset', *CL*, CXIV, 1953, 414–17, 484–7; RCHM Dorset, III, pt 2, 63–7.

84 See n. 68 above.

85 Reading, Berkshire RO, D/AI/178/117D.

86 Gunther 1928, 65.

87 F. H. Cheetham, 'Two Inventories at Scarisbrick Hall', *Lancashire and Cheshire Historical Society*, LXXXIX, 1937, 123–38.

88 RCHM Dorset, I, 240–46.

89 Inventory of the Goods of Sir Charles Raleigh of Downton, 1698, *Wiltshire Archaeological Magazine*, XLII, 1922–4, 307–12.

90 North 1981, 72 (at Buckenham), 73 (Honington), 75 (Melton Constable), 76 (Raynham), 130–31 (general principles).

91 BL, Add MS 69870, fol. 39*v*.

92 Bacon 1885, 487.

93 W. C. Clark-Maxwell, 'An Inventory of the Contents of Markeaton Hall . . . 1545', *Derbyshire Archaeological and Natural History Society*, new ser., IV, 1931, 115–40.

94 *Lancashire and Cheshire Wills and Inventories*, I, ed. G. J. Piccope, Chetham Society Publications 37, 1857, 156.

95 Chelmsford, Essex RO, D/DBa E3.

96 Owen Ashmore, 'Household Inventories of the Lancashire Gentry', *Transactions of the Historical Society of Lancashire and Cheshire*, CX, 1958, 75.

97 Dorchester, Dorset RO, D16/F3.

98 Smyth 1883, II, 419–20.

99 Quoted in Geoffrey Beard, 'William Wynde and Interior Design', *Architectural History*, XXVII, 1984, 150–59.

100 PRO, PROB 4/3241.

101 PRO, PROB 4/3435.

102 PRO, PRO SP 46/103.

103 Carlisle, Cumbria R.O., D/Lons/wills 4.

104 Exeter, Devon RO, 123M/E98; see also p. 57 above.

105 Belvoir Castle, Rutland MSS.

106 'Inventory of the Goods of Dame Agnes Hungerford', *Archaeologia*, XXXVIII, 1860, 359.

107 M. Sturge Henderson, *Three Centuries in North Oxfordshire*, Oxford, 1902, 213–21.

108 Thornton, op. cit. (n. 40 above), 24.

109 The visit is recorded in James Nichols, *Progresses of James I*, London, 1828, I, 250. The location of the rooms used by the king and queen at Shaw is inferred from Thomas Dolman's inventory: Oxford, Bodleian Library, D/AI/62/54.

110 Norwich, Norfolk RO, MC 254/4/23–4.

111 Quoted in VCH Worcestershire, 1917, III, 93.

112 Ambrose Heal, 'A Great Country House in 1623', *Burlington Magazine*, LXXXII, 1943, 108–16.

113 Leicester, Leicestershire RO, DE 730/1/81.

114 Thornton 1984, 14–15, 22–4.

115 Boorde 1870, 236.

116 Gunther 1928, 64.

117 North 1981, 132.

118 Gunther 1928, 64.

119 North 1981, 134.

120 North 1981, 134.

121 See chapter 5, n. 93.

122 See n. 37, above.

123 Fiennes 1947, 24.

124 Preston, Lancs, Lancashire R.O., DDTO Acc 28 36/16.

125 William Roper and Thomas Harpsfield, *Lives of Saint Thomas More*, ed. E. E. Reynolds, London, 1963, 14. The building is shown in Bernard Lockey's miniature version of Holbein's group portrait of More's family (London, Victoria and Albert Museum), in which there is a hint – the size makes detail impossible – of a pedimented doorway: a classical allusion.

126 North 1981, 134.

127 *Wills and Inventories from the Archdeaconry of Richmond*, ed. James Raine, Surtees Society, XXVI, 1853, 284.

128 PRO, SP29/196/123.

129 BL, Add MS 28052, fol. 4.

130 C. L. Kingsford, 'On some London Houses of the English Tudor Period', *Archaeologia*, LXXI, 1921, 17–54.

131 'Two Inventories of the Goods of Cardinal Fisher, Bishop of Rochester', *Proceedings of the Society of Antiquaries*, 2nd ser., V, 1872, 294–9.

132 Elyot 1880, I, 77–8.

133 *Lancashire and Cheshire Wills and Inventories*, III, ed. G. J. Piccope, Chetham Society Publications 54, 1861, 132.

134 J. G. Nichols, *The Unton Inventories*, London, 1841, 1–9.

135 'Inventory of Richard Hooker', *Archaeologia Cantiana*, LXX, 1957, 231–6.

136 *Wills and Inventories from the Register at Durham*, Surtees Society 38, 1860, 228.

137 Slingsby 1836, 70.

138 Peter Thornton, *The Italian Renaissance Interior*, London, 1991, 296–8; Dora Thornton, *The Scholar in his Study: Ownership and Experience in Renaissance Italy*, New Haven and London, 1997.

139 PRO, PROB 2/402.

140 John Humphreys, 'The Elizabethan Estate Book of Grafton Manor', *Transactions of the Birmingham Archaeological Society*, XLIV, 1918, 1–124.

141 RIBA, Smythson II/13.

142 Leland 1904, I, 53. There is also a room traditionally called 'Paradise' at Newbiggin in Westmorland. At Hampton Court in 1597 there was 'a certain cabinet called *Paradise*, which besides that everything glitters so well with silver and gold, and jewels, as to dazzle the eyes, there is a marvellous instrument, made all of glass except the strings' (*A Journey into England in the years MDXCVIII by Paul Hentzner*, ed. Horace Walpole, Aungerville Society, I, Edinburgh, 1881, 47).

143 For the history of the gallery, see particularly Rosalys Coope, 'The Gallery in England: Names and Meanings', *Architectural History*, XXVII, 1984, 446–56; *HKW*, IV, pt 2, 20–21; Howard 1987, 88–93, 116–18.

144 See n. 130, above.

145 The Stoic tone of Starkey's *Dialogue* may be reinforced by a comparison of Starkey's condemnation of over-gilded decoration, quoted in chapter 1, with that in Seneca, Epistle LXXXVII.

146 'An Inventory of a Nobleman's Personal Property in the 16th Century', *Journal of the Royal Institute of Cornwall*, II, 1866–7, 226–33.

147 'Inventory of Furniture at Mendham Hall 1548', *Proceedings of the Suffolk Institute of Archaeology and Natural History*, II, 1859, 242–7.

148 PRO, PROB 2/254A.

149 PRO, PROB 2/393.

150 PRO, PROB 2/375.

151 Fiennes 1947, 24–5.

152 For Stanwardine, see H. A. Farrant, 'Old Shropshire Houses and their Owners', *Transactions of the Shropshire Archaeological and Natural History Society*, XLI (4th ser., VIII), 1920–21, 85–7.

153 E. B. Saxton, 'A Speke Inventory of 1624', *Lancashire and Cheshire Historical Society*, XCVII, 1945, 107.

154 See chapter 2, n. 114.

155 Colvin 1995, 1091.

156 North 1981, 135.

157 Gloucester, Gloucestershire RO, D 45 F 2.

158 *Ingatestone Hall in 1600*, Essex RO publication 22, 1954.

159 North 1981, 137.

160 Carlisle, Cumbria RO, D/Lons/L1/3/4.

161 I am grateful to Dr John Gurney for this quotation.

162 Guildford, Guildford Muniment Room, LM 1105.

163 *Trevelyan Papers*, ed. J. Payne Collier, Camden Society, 1857, 124; Exeter, Devon RO, DD/WO/49/2.

164 Taunton, Somerset RO, DD/HI/411.

165 Traditionally the room in the disguised closet of which he hid from Roundhead troops pursuing him after the battle of Worcester.

166 As shown in a late seventeenth-century plan preserved at the house.

167 *Buckinghamshire Probate Inventories 1661–1714*, Buckinghamshire Record Society, XXIV, 1988, 258–71.

168 *Acts of the High Commission Court within the Diocese of Durham*, Surtees Society, XXXIV, 1857, 44–8.

169 The rooms are identified in Gunther 1928, 93, following a lost manuscript discussed in H. Avray Tipping, 'Coleshill, Berkshire', *CL*, XLVI, 1919, 146.

170 'He [i.e. More] carries Sir William into the chamber and takes the Sheete by the corner and suddenly whippes it off. They lay on their Backs, and their smocks up as high as their arme pitts. This awakened them, and immediately they turned on their bellies. Quoth Roper, I have seen both sides, and so gave a patt on the buttock, he made choice of, saying, Thou art mine' (Aubrey 1947, 214).

171 Simon Jervis, 'Five Early Inventories of Browsholme Hall', *Furniture History*, XXII, 1986, 1–24.

172 'The Inventory of Anne Viscountess Dorchester', ed. Francis Steer, *Notes and Queries*, CXCVIII, 1953, 156.

173 Wotton 1624, 71.

174 Bold 1990, 54.

175 Reading, Berkshire RO, D/A1/178/117D.

176 The service range at Hengrave has gone, but is shown in plan and elevation in Gage 1822, pls I and II.

177 NMRC, 61274.

178 Taunton, Somerset RO, DD/TOR/27.

179 RCHM Dorset, III, pt 2, 163–8.

180 Arthur Oswald, 'Boston Manor, Middlesex', *CL*, CXXXVII, 1965, 603–6.

181 NMRC, 77896.

182 A. T. Bolton and H. D. Hendry, eds, 'Winslow Hall', *Wren Society*, XVII, 1940, 54–77.

183 NMRC, 44299.

184 NMRC, 88275.

185 NMRC, 88241.

186 NMRC, 87066.

187 This date is inscribed on the stair, when the house seems to have been substantially rebuilt in its present two-storey/three-storey form.

188 NMRC, 93446.

189 See chapter 7, n. 29.

190 See chapter 7, n. 30.

191 N. W. Alcock *et al.*, 'Maxstoke Castle, Warwickshire', *Archaeological Journal*, CXXXV, 1978, 195–234.

192 John Newman, 'The Development of the Staircase in Elizabethan and Jacobean England', in *L'escalier dans l'architecture de la Renaissance*, ed. A. Chastel and J. Guillaume, Proceedings of the Tours Colloquium, 1974, 175–77.

193 For Holdenby, see chapter 4, n. 110.

194 HMC Salisbury, XIX, 1965, 120.

195 RIBA, Smythson I/8.

196 NMRC, 87074. Only a part of the house survives; it may never have been finished, but it was clearly intended to have been of the type of Montacute and of Cannons shown by Thorpe (SM, Thorpe 44).

197 John Throsby, [Robert] *Thoroton's History of Nottinghamshire . . . with Large Additions*, Nottingham, 1790, I, 33; Christopher Hussey, 'Thrumpton Hall, Nottinghamshire', *CL*, CXX, 1959, 1138–41, 1194–7, 1254–7.

198 Wotton 1624, 5.

199 Bacon 1858, 486.

200 Robert Plott, *The Natural History of Oxford-shire*, Oxford, 2nd edn, 1705, 272–3, Tab. 13.

201 The plan of Bletchingdon as remodelled in 1782 perpetuated a huge stair hall between rear-projecting wings; the ghost of the original house is probably incorporated into the present building.

202 North 1981, 132. Christopher Hussey, 'Felbrigg Hall, Norfolk', *CL*, LXXVI, 1934, 666–71.

203 North 1981, 123.

204 North 1981, 131.

205 S. J. Gunn and P. G. Lindley, 'Charles Brandon's Westhorpe: An Early Tudor Courtyard House in Suffolk', *Archaeological Journal*, CXLV, 1988, 272–90.

206 Mercer 1962, 112.

207 Mercer 1962, 104–8.

208 HMC Salisbury, II, 1888, 200.

209 Harrison 1877, I, 233. But he also describes rooms as, alternatively, 'seeled with oke of our owne'; the difference between this oak 'sealing' and imported wainscot was not clear to him.

210 *Wills and Inventories from the Registry at Durham*, Surtees Society, XXXVIII, 1860, 176.

211 Op. cit., 88.

212 *Lancashire and Cheshire Wills and Inventories*, I, ed. G. J. Piccope, Chetham Society Publications 51, 1860, 75.

213 Op. cit., 93.

214 'Inventory of the Goods of Sir Cotton Gargrave of Nostell', *Yorkshire Archaeological Journal*, XI, 1891, 279.

215 R. G. Rice, 'The Household Goods of Sir John Gage . . . 1558', *Sussex Archaeological Collections*, XLV, 1902, 114–27.

216 Gage 1822, 22–37.

217 Quoted in Thurley 1993, 108.

218 Turner and Parker 1859, 117.

219 Martin Biddle, 'A Fontainebleau Chimney-piece at Broughton Castle, Oxfordshire', in Colvin and Harris 1970, 9–12; Wells-Cole 1997, 34–5.

220 Wells-Cole 1997, 25, 35–8.

221 Wells-Cole 1997, 135–53.

222 Oswald 1959, 24–5.

223 Wells-Cole 1997, 20–21, 142–6.

224 Susan Foster, 'Paintings and other Works of Art in Sixteenth-century English Inventories', *Burlington Magazine*, CXXIII, 1981, 273–82.

225 Elyot 1880, II, 22–4.

226 Henry Ellis, 'Inventories of Goods, etc. in the Manor of Chesworth . . . taken 1549', *Sussex Archaeological Collections*, XIII, 1861, 120.

227 Rebecah, op. cit. (n. 7 above).

228 Slingsby 1836, 6.

229 Compare the use of paintings in Italy, dis-cussed by Peter Thornton, *The Italian Renaissance Interior, 1400–1600*, London, 1991, 261–8.

230 Anderson 1995, 251–2.

231 Bolingbroke, op. cit. (n. 60 above).

232 George Whetstone, *An Heptameron of Civill Discourses*, 1582, sig. m.ii.*v*.

233 *Travels by Sir William Brereton*, ed. Edward Hawkins, Chetham Society, I, 1844, 80.

234 Elsie Matley Moore, 'Wall Paintings recently Discovered in Worcestershire', *Archaeologia*, LXXXVIII, 1938, 281–9; H. R. Hodgkinson, 'Recent Discoveries at Harvington Hall, Chaddesley Corbett', *Transactions of the Birmingham Archaeological Society*, LXII, 1943, 1–26.

235 J. L. Whitehead, 'An Inventory of the Goods and Chattels of Sir Richard Worsley . . . AD 1566', *Proceedings of the Hampshire Field Club*, V, 1904–6, 277–95.

236 E. W. Crossly, 'A Temple Newsam Inventory 1565', *Yorkshire Archaeological Journal*, XXV, 1920, 91.

237 J. G. Nichols, *The Unton Inventories*, London, 1841, 17–30.

238 Alan Lowndes, 'Inventory of the Household Goods of Sir Richard Barrington . . . in 1624', *Transactions of the Essex Archaeological Society*, new ser., III, 1889, 155–76.

239 Lewes, East Sussex RO, T266.

240 See n. 172 above.

241 Wotton 1624, 98.

242 For the growth of landscape painting in England, see Ogden and Ogden 1955, *passim*; Whinney and Millar 1957, 260–73; John Hayes, 'British Patrons and Landscape Painting: The Seventeenth Century', *Apollo*, LXXXII, 1965, 38–45.

9 THE IMAGE OF THE HOUSE

1 Robert Reyce, *Breviary of Suffolk*, ed. Francis, Lord Hervey, London, 1902, 50.

2 Howell 1892, I 107.

3 Edward Norgate in 1620 described landscape as 'an Art soe new in England, and soe lately come ashore, as all the Language within our Seas cannot find it a Name, but as a borrowed one, and that from the Dutch' (quoted in Whinney and Millar 1957, 260).

4 Gerard 1900, 71.

5 Hammond 1904, 119.

6 Evelyn 1955, III, 12 (19 July 1654).

7 Quoted in Simon Schama, *Landscape and Memory*, London, 1995, 530.

8 Wotton 1624, 99–100.

9 Vitruvius 1960, 211.

10 Ogden and Ogden 1955, 83.

11 John Dee, introduction to Billingsley's translation of Euclid (see chapter 2, n. 37 above), sig.a.IIII.

12 See Sarah Bendall, *Dictionary of Land Surveyors and Local Map-Makers of Great Britain and Ireland, 1530–1850*, 2nd edn, London, 1997, I, 4–42.

13 Harris 1974, 4–7, 40–48, 88–94.

14 Harris 1979, 91–4; Hugh Honour, 'Leonard Knyff', *Burlington Magazine*, XCVI, 1954, 337–8; for the place of these views in the history of architectural illustration, see Connor 1977, 14–30.

15 North 1981, 28.

16 Currie and Lewis 1994, 9–25; Mendyk 1989, *passim*.

17 Stone and Stone 1984, 360.

18 James M. Rosenheim, *The Emergence of a Ruling Order: English Landed Society 1650–1750*, London and New York, 1998, 89–129.

19 H. M. Margoliouth, *Poems and Letters of Andrew Marvell*, Oxford, 1963, I, 59–83. The complexities of *Upon Appleton House* are beyond the scope of this book, though see McClung, op. cit. (chapter 7, n. 86), 147–74, and Kelsall, op. cit. (chapter 7, n. 86), 49–58. What is known of Nun Appleton House (which still stands, greatly altered) is conveniently summarised in Bold 1990, 164–5.

20 The sentiment may be compared with those on houses in the north-west recorded in Taylor 1892. Early examples (e.g. Newbiggin 1533, Cliburn 1567, Askham 1574, Catterlen 1577, Huthwaite 1581) are in the vernacular and sometimes in rhyme, naming the builder. In the seventeenth century they tend towards religious epigram, in Latin (e.g. 'Non est haec requies' (Barton Kirk); 'Peregrinus hic nos reputamus' (Greenthwaite Hall) as well as more modest in giving the builder's initials, not his name. The change both of sentiment and language is significant, from direct statements in the sixteenth century to more exclusive and contemplative in the seventeenth.

21 Kelsall, op. cit. (chapter 7, n. 86), 49–58, sees the villagers as a potentially destructive, levelling force: such a reading actually heightens Fairfax's separation from the community.

22 John Newman, 'Hugh May, Clarendon and Cornbury', in Bold and Chaney 1993, 81–8.

23 *The Poems and Translations of Richard Fanshawe*, ed. Peter Davidson, Oxford, 1997, 58.

24 John Pomfret, *Poems upon Several Occasions*, London, 1736, 1–2.

25 Alexander Chalmers, *Works of the English Poets*, London, 1810, XV, 168.

26 J. Nicolson and R. Burn, *History and Antiquities of the Counties of Westmorland and Cumberland*, London, 1777, I, 345–6.

27 Carlisle, Cumbria RO: Dean and Chapter Archive, Machell MSS, III, 83.

Appendix

House and Household Sizes: The Hearth Tax

The hearth tax returns of the 1660 and 1670s provide an indication of the sizes of the houses of different social classes which
formed the basis for table 1 (p. 6 above). For several reasons –
architectural, social and adminstrative – these can form only a
rough basis for comparison. Older houses tended to have fewer
heated rooms for their size than newer ones; outhouses and
dependencies were usually returned with the principal dwelling.
Many gentry owned more than one house in a county, and it
is not always known which of these was his or her principal
residence, but if an owner used more than one house in a parish
they were sometimes lumped together. Returns were sometimes
made carelessly or even fraudulently. But although it is not wise
to take the return for any one house as an accurate count of its
fireplaces (and thus of its heated rooms), taken together the
returns show a wide difference between the amenities enjoyed
by different classes, as well as the range of house sizes that might
be occupied by different members of the same class.

But the averages in table 1 suggest too that ranks within the
upper classes broadly overlapped. Figs 1–6 below show how
broad was the range of house sizes occupied by esquires and the
magistracy, and may also suggest that the homogeneity of the
upper classes within the county community transcended their
economic diversity.

In calculating the averages in table 1 and in producing the
figures below, the arbitrary decision was made to exclude houses
with less than five hearths, though owned by men designated
esquire, since these are almost certainly secondary property.
Nevertheless the inclusion of what are almost certainly some
small, secondary houses will have somewhat distorted the
picture, and produced averages in table 1 that are too low.

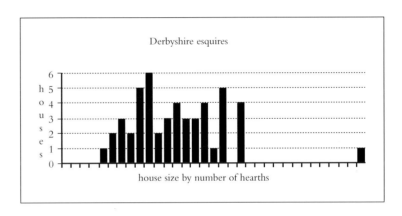

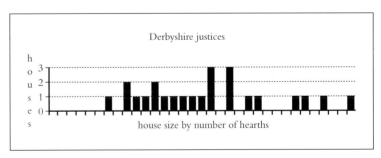

Fig. 1   Derbyshire: numbers and sizes of houses from the hearth tax
of 1662–70

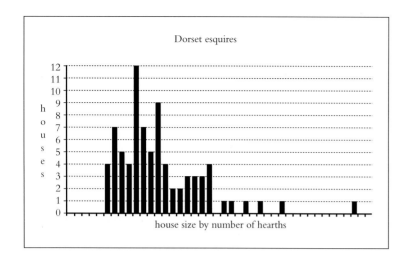

Dorset esquires

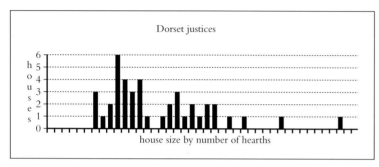

Dorset justices

Fig. 2   Dorset: numbers and sizes of houses from the hearth tax of 1664

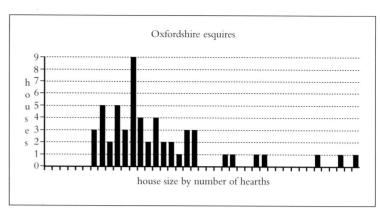

Oxfordshire esquires

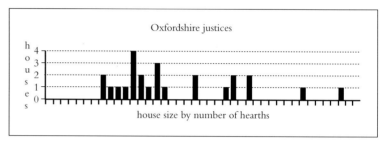

Oxfordshire justices

Fig. 4   Oxfordshire: numbers and sizes of houses from the hearth tax of 1665

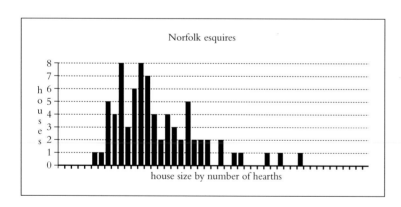

Norfolk esquires

Norfolk justices

Fig. 3   Norfolk: numbers and sizes of houses from the hearth tax of 1664

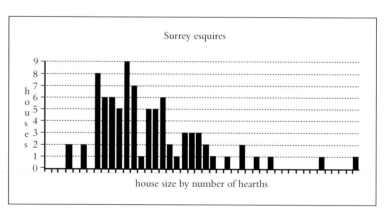

Surrey esquires

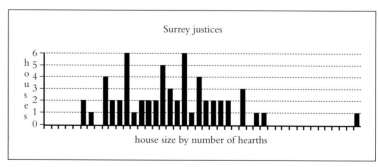

Surrey justices

Fig. 5   Surrey: numbers and sizes of houses from the hearth tax of 1664

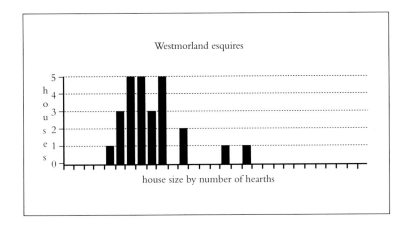

Westmorland esquires

house size by number of hearths

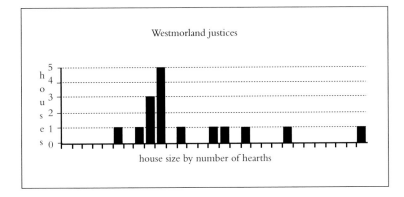

Westmorland justices

house size by number of hearths

Fig. 6   Westmorland: numbers and sizes of houses from the hearth tax of 1662–74

While the caveats set out in the first paragraph must be borne in mind in considering individual houses, the following list of a few of the houses illustrated in this book, with the number of their hearths declared in the tax returns and (where available) the principal occupant, may make it easier to visualise what houses of a certain size were actually like:

Plate	House	Hearths	Occupant
166	Gaythorne Hall, Cumbria	7	
24	Chantemarle, Dorset	13	
241–2	Hall Court, Herefordshire	14	? Elizabeth Webley
63–5	Shaw, Berkshire	16	Sir Thomas Dolman
297–8	Ufton Court, Berkshire	16	Mrs Perkins, widow
231–2	Morley Old Hall, Norfolk	17	William Sidley
330–31	Wood Dalling, Norfolk	17	Edward Bulwer
170–71	Anderson, Dorset	17	John Tregonwell
206–7	Tissington, Derbyshire	18	William Fitzherbert
151	Pendell House, Surrey	18	Richard Glyde
15	Barlborough Hall, Derbyshire	21	Francis Roades
60	Kentwell Hall, Suffolk	24	Sir Thomas Darcy
194–5	West Woodhay, Berkshire	25	Mrs Rudyard
120	Lulworth Castle, Dorset	40	Humphrey Weld
174–5	Quidenham Hall, Norfolk	40	Sir John Holland
81–3	Hengrave Hall, Suffolk	51	Sir Edward Gage
198–200	Coleshill, Berkshire	56	Sir George Pratt
153	Blickling Hall, Norfolk	58	Sir John Hobart

The range of house sizes indicated in these tables and graphs can be compared with contemporary calculations by Gregory King, who (probably in the 1690s) calculated from the hearth tax and from other information figures both for the average number of people in upper-class households and the number, nationally, of houses of a certain size (tables 2–3).

Table 2   Numbers of houses and sizes of households, c. 1690, from Gregory King[1]

Houses	Hearths	Number in household
5000	8	6.5
3000	9	7.5
2000	10	9.5
3000	11–20	14
2000	over 20	30

1   *Dorset Hearth Tax Assessments, 1662–64*, ed. C. A. F. Meekings, Dorset Archaeology and Natural History Society, xxxv, 1951.

Table 3 Numbers in five ranks of society, household size and income, from Gregory King[2]

Rank or title	Number of families	Number in household	Income per family
Lords	160	40	£3200
Baronets	800	16	£800
Knights	600	13	£650
Esquires	3000	10	£450
Gentlemen	12,000	8	£280

2 Laslett 1983, 1st edn 1971, 3–7.

Too much precision must not be attached to these figures, and comparisons with calculations for earlier dates must be treated with some reserve. But they are sufficient to confirm that the majority of houses with more than around twenty-two hearths belonged to men of the rank of knight or above (table 1, p. 6), as well as to show the overlap in size between the houses of the richer esquires and those of men of higher rank. The fact that King's figures for household numbers given in tables 2–3 do not wholly agree (table 2 indicating 7000 houses with households of more than 9.5 people, table 3 only 4560 with more than 10) is due at least in part to the fact that a few of those lower gentry who would have been described as 'gent' or 'mr' (particularly merchants or innkeepers) had houses and households substantially larger than the average for their class. In addition, many higher gentry families owned more than one house but probably did not maintain full households in a secondary seat. Allowing for such factors as these, the figures correspond closely enough to give a rough idea of the size and number of upper-class houses and households at the end of the seventeenth century.

Bibliography

General

Anon. 1868
'The English Courtier and the Country-gentleman: of Cyvile and Uncyvile Life' (first published 1579), in Hazlitt 1868, 1–93

Ashton 1978
Robert Ashton, *The English Civil War: Conservatism and Revolution 1603–1649*, London, 1978

Aubrey 1947
John Aubrey, *Aubrey's Brief Lives* (written before 1693), ed. Oliver Lawson Dick, London, 1947

Aylmer 1961
G. E. Aylmer, *The King's Servants: The Civil Service of Charles I, 1625–1642*, London, 1961

Aylmer 1973
G. E. Aylmer, *The State's Servants: The Civil Service of the English Republic, 1649–60*, London, 1973

Baker-Smith 1989
Dominic Baker-Smith, 'The Cultural and Social Setting', in *The Cambridge Guide to the Arts in Britain*, ed. Boris Ford, Cambridge, 1989, 23–45

Barker 1948
Ernest Barker, 'The Education of the English Gentleman in the 16th Century', *Traditions of Civility*, Oxford, 1948, 124–58

Batho 1967
Gordon Batho, 'Landlords in England', in Finberg 1967, 256–305

Bean 1968
J. M. H. Bean, *The Decline of English Feudalism, 1215–1540*, Manchester, 1968

Beckett 1986
J. V. Beckett, *The Aristocracy in England, 1660–1914*, Oxford, 1986

Blomefield 1805
Francis Blomefield, *An Essay towards a Topographical History of the County of Norfolk* (written before 1752), 2nd edn, London, 1805, 11 vols

Boorde 1870
Andrew Boorde, *Dyetary of Health* (written 1554), ed. F. J. Furnivall, Early English Text Society, extra ser. 10, 1870

Bramston 1845
The Autobiography of Sir John Bramston (written 1683–99), ed. Lord Braybrooke, Camden Society, XXXII, 1845

Brereton 1868
N. B[rereton], 'The Court and the Country' (first published 1618), in Hazlitt 1868, 171–212

Burton 1660
Robert Burton, *Anatomy of Melancholy* (first published 1621), 7th edn, London, 1660

Carew 1602
Thomas Carew, *Survey of Cornwall*, London, 1602

Carpenter 1986
Christine Carpenter, 'The Fifteenth-century English Gentry and their Estates', in Jones 1986, 36–50

Carpenter 1992
Christine Carpenter, *Lordship and Polity: A Study of Warwickshire Landed Society 1401–1499*, Cambridge, 1992

Caspari 1954
Fritz Caspari, *Humanism and the Social Order in Tudor England*, Chicago, 1954

Castiglione 1928
Baldassare Castiglione, *Il libro del cortigiano* (1531), trans. Thomas Hoby as *The Book of the Courtyer* (first published 1561), ed. W. H. D. Rouse, London, 1928

Charlton 1965
Kenneth Charlton, *Education in Renaissance England*, London and Toronto, 1965

Chartier 1989
Roger Chartier, ed., *History of Private Life III: Passions of the Renaissance*, Cambridge, Mass., and London, 1989

Chaudhuri 1989
Sukanta Chaudhuri, *Renaissance Pastoral and its English Development*, Oxford, 1989

Chauncy 1700
Henry Chauncy, *The Historical Antiquities of Hertfordshire*, London, 1700

Cholmley 1870
Memoirs of Sir Hugh Cholmley (written *c.* 1655), New Malton, 1870

Clay 1985
Christopher Clay, 'Landlords and Estate Management in England', in Thirsk 1985, 119–251

Collier 1989
Stephen L. Collier, *From Divine Cosmos to Sovereign State*, New York and Oxford, 1989

Cooper 1967
J. P. Cooper, 'Social Distribution of Land and Men, 1436–1700', *Economic History Review*, 2nd ser., xx/3, 1967, 419–40

Cooper 1976
J. P. Cooper, 'Patterns of Inheritance and Settlement by Great Landowners from the Fifteenth to the Eighteenth Centuries', in *Family & Inheritance: Rural Society in Western Europe 1200–1800*, ed. Jack Goody, Joan Thirsk and J. P. Thompson, Cambridge, 1976

Cornwall 1988
J. C. K. Cornwall, *Wealth and Society in Early Sixteenth Century England*, London, 1988

Coss 1995
P. R. Coss, 'The Formation of the English Gentry', *Past and Present*, CXLVII, 1995, 38–63

Cressy 1976
David Cressy, 'Describing the Social Order of Elizabethan and Stuart England', *Literature and History*, III, March 1976, 28–44

Currie and Lewis 1994
C. R. J. Currie and C. P. Lewis, eds, *English County Histories: A Guide*, Stroud, 1994

Dowling 1986
Marion Dowling, 'The New Learning in the Schools', *Humanism in the Age of Henry VIII*, London, 1986, 112–39

Dugdale 1730
William Dugdale, *The Antiquities of Warwickshire* (first published 1656), ed. William Thomas, London, 1730, 2 vols

Elias 1978
Norbert Elias, *The Civilising Process, I: The History of Manners*, Oxford, 1978

Elton 1994
G. R. Elton, 'Humanism in England', *Studies in Tudor and Stuart Politics and Government*, IV, Cambridge, 1994, 209–30

Elyot 1880
Thomas Elyot, *The Boke named The Governour devised by Sir Thomas Elyot* (written 1531), ed. H. H. S. Croft, London, 1880, 2 vols

Evelyn 1955
John Evelyn, *Diary* (*c.* 1660–1706), ed. E. S. de Beer, Oxford, 1955, 6 vols

Everitt 1966
A. M. Everitt, 'Social Mobility in England', *Past and Present*, XXXIII, 1966, 56–73

Everitt 1969
A. M. Everitt, *Change in the Provinces: The Seventeenth Century*, Leicester University Department of English Local History, occasional papers, 1969

Fiennes 1947
Celia Fiennes, *The Journeys of Celia Fiennes* (written *c.* 1690–1700), ed. Christopher Morris, London, 1947

Finberg 1967
H. P. R. Finberg, ed., *The Agrarian History of England and Wales, IV: 1500–1640*, Cambridge, 1967

Fletcher 1986
Anthony Fletcher, *Reform in the Provinces: The Government of Stuart England*, New Haven and London, 1986

Friedman 1970
D. M. Friedman, *Marvel's Pastoral Art*, London, 1970

Fuller 1662
Thomas Fuller, *The History of the Worthies of England*, London, 1662

Fumerton 1991
Patricia Fumerton, *Cultural Aesthetics: Renaissance Literature and the Practice of Social Ornament*, Chicago and London, 1991

Gent 1981
Lucy Gent, *Picture and Poetry, 1560–1620: Relations between Literature and the Visual Arts in the English Renaissance*, Leamington Spa, 1981

Gent 1995
Lucy Gent, *Albion's Classicism: The Visual Arts in Britain*, London and New Haven, 1995

Gent and Llewellyn 1990
Lucy Gent and Nigel Llewelyn, eds, *Renaissance Bodies: The Human Figure in English Culture c. 1540–1660*, London, 1990

Gerard 1900
Thomas Gerard, *The Particular Description of Somerset drawn up by Thomas Gerard of Trent* (written *c.* 1630), ed. E. H. Bates, Somerset Record Society, xv, 1900

Given Wilson 1987
Chris Given Wilson, *The English Nobility in the Late Middle Ages*, London, 1987

Gleason 1969
J. H. Gleason, *The Justices of the Peace in England, 1558–1640*, Oxford, 1969

Guy 1988
John Guy, *Tudor England*, Oxford, 1988

Habakkuk 1940
H. J. Habakkuk, 'English Landownership 1680–1740', *Economic History Review*, X, 1940, 2–17

Habakkuk 1994
John Habakkuk, *Marriage, Debt and the Estates System, English Landownership 1650–1840*, Oxford, 1994

Habington 1895
Thomas Habington, *Survey of Worcestershire* (written 1634–7), ed. J. Amphlett, Worcestershire Historical Society, I, 1895

Hammond 1904
Lieutenant Hammond, *Relation of a Short Survey of 26 Counties . . . by a Captain, a Lieutenant, and an Ancient* (written *c.* 1632), ed. A. G. Wickham Legg, London, 1904

Harrison 1877
William Harrison, *Harrison's Description of England in the Year 1577*, ed. F. J. Furnivall, London, 1877, 2 vols

Hart 1994
Vaughan Hart, *Art and Magic in the Court of the Stuarts*, London, 1994

Harte 1976
N. B. Harte, 'State Control of Dress and Social Change in Pre-Industrial England', in *Trade, Government and Economy in Pre-Industrial England, Essays presented to F. J. Fisher*, ed. D. C. Coleman and A. H. John, London, 1976, 132–65

Hay 1988
Denys Hay, 'Renaissance Education and the Governors', *Renaissance Essays*, London, 1988, 389–96

Hazlitt 1868
W. C. H[azlitt], *Inedited Tracts*, London, 1868

Heal 1984
Felicity Heal, 'The Idea of Hospitality in Early Modern England', *Past and Present*, CII, 1984, 66–93

Heal 1990
Felicity Heal, *Hospitality in Early Modern England*, Oxford, 1990

Heal and Holmes 1994
Felicity Heal and Clive Holmes, *The Gentry in England and Wales, 1500–1700*, London, 1994

Hexter 1962
J. H. Hexter, 'The Education of the Aristocracy in the Renaissance', *Reappraisals in History*, London, 1962, 45–70

Hoby 1902
Thomas Hoby, *The Travels and Life of Sir Thomas Hoby* (written 1547–64), ed. E. Powell, Royal Historical Society, Camden Society 3rd ser., IV, 1902

Hodgson 1820–58
John Hodgson, *History of Northumberland*, Newcastle upon Tyne, 1820–58, 5 parts

Howarth 1985
D. J. Howarth, *The Earl of Arundel and his Circle*, New Haven and London, 1985

Howell 1892
James Howell, *Epistolae Ho-Elianae: Familiar Letters* (first published 1645–55), ed. Joseph Jacobs, London, 1892

Hutchins 1861
John Hutchins, *History of Dorset* (first published 1774), 3rd edn, London, 1861

James 1978
Mervyn James, 'English Politics and the Concept of Honour', *Past and Present*, suppl. 3, 1978

Jones 1986
M. E. Jones, ed., *The Gentry and Lesser Nobility in Medieval Europe*, Gloucester, 1986

Kelso 1924
Ruth Kelso, *The Doctrine of the English Gentleman in the Sixteenth Century*, Chicago, 1924

King 1656
Daniel King, *The Vale Royall of England* (text by William Webb, c. 1622), London, 1656

Kipling 1977
Gordon Kipling, *The Triumphs of Honour: Burgundian Origins of the Elizabethan Renaissance*, The Hague, 1977

Kristeller 1979
P. O. Kristeller, *Renaissance Thought and its Sources*, New York, 1979

Lander 1977
J. R. Lander, *Conflict and Stability in Fifteenth Century England* (first published 1969), 3rd edn, London, 1977

Larkin 1983
Stuart Royal Proclamations II: Royal Proclamations of Charles I, Oxford, 1983

Larkin and Hughes 1973
Stuart Royal Proclamations I: Royal Proclamations of James I, Oxford, 1973

Laslett 1983
Peter Laslett, *The World we have Lost Further Explored* (first published as *The World we have Lost*, London, 1971), London, 1983

Leland 1904
John Leland, *The Itinerary of John Leland in or about the years 1535–1543*, ed. Lucy Toulmin Smith, London, 1904, 5 vols

MacFarlane 1973
Alan MacFarlane, *The Nobility of Later Medieval England*, London, 1973

MacFarlane 1978
Alan MacFarlane, *The Origins of English Individualism*, Oxford, 1978

Major 1964
John M. Major, *Sir Thomas Elyot and Renaissance Humanism*, Lincoln, Nebraska, 1964

Manning 1992
Brian Manning, *1649: The Crisis of the English Revolution*, London, 1992, esp. pp. 49–71

Martin 1986
John E. Martin, *Feudalism to Capitalism: Peasant and Landlord in English Agrarian Development*, Basingstoke and London, 1986

Mathew 1948
David Mathew, *The Social Structure in Caroline England*, Oxford, 1948

Mendyk 1989
Stan A. E. Mendyk, *Speculum Britanniae: Regional Study, Antiquarianism and Science in Britain to 1700*, Toronto, Buffalo and London, 1989

Mercer 1962
Eric Mercer, *English Art 1553–1625*, Oxford, 1962

Mertes 1988
Kate Mertes, *The English Noble Household, 1250–1600: Good Governance and Politic Rule*, Oxford, 1988

Miller 1986
Helen Miller, *Henry VIII and the English Nobility*, Oxford, 1986

Mingay 1976
G. E. Mingay, *The Gentry, the Rise and Fall of a Ruling Class*, London, 1976

Morgan 1986
D. A. L. Morgan, 'The Individual Style of the English Gentleman', in *Gentry and Lesser Nobility in Late Medieval Europe*, ed. Michael Jones, Gloucester, 1986, 37–58

Morrill 1993
J. S. Morrill, *The Nature of the English Revolution*, London, 1993

Ogden and Ogden 1955
H. V. Ogden and M. S. Ogden, *English Taste in Landscape in the 17th Century*, Ann Arbor, 1955

Peacham 1962
Henry Peacham, *The Compleat Gentleman* (first published 1622), ed. Virgil B. Heltzel, Ithaca, NY, 1962

Peck 1991
Linda Levy Peck, ed., *The Mental World of the Jacobean Court*, Cambridge, 1991

Postan 1983
M. M. Postan, 'Feudalism and its Decline', in *Social Relations and Ideas: Essays in Honour of R. H. Hilton*, ed. T. H. Aston *et al.*, Cambridge, 1983

Prest 1986
Wilfred R. Prest, *The Rise of the Barristers*, Oxford, 1986

Reresby 1991
John Reresby, *Memoirs of Sir John Reresby* (written *c.* 1680), 2nd edn, ed. Andrew Browning, London, 1991

Sharpe 1992
Kevin Sharpe, *The Personal Rule of Charles I*, New Haven and London, 1992

Simon 1965
Joan Simon, *Education and Society in Tudor England*, Cambridge, 1965

Slingsby 1836
Henry Slingsby, *The Diary of Sir Henry Slingsby of Scriven* (written 1638–48), ed. Daniel Parsons, London, 1836

Smuts 1987
R. M. Smuts, *Court Culture and the Origins of a Royalist Tradition in Early Stuart England*, Philadelphia, 1987

Smuts 1991
R. M. Smuts, 'Cultural Diversity and Change at the Court of James I', in Peck 1991, 99–112

Smyth 1883
John Smyth, *Lives of the Berkeleys* (written 1618), ed. Sir John Maclean, Gloucester, 1883, 2 vols

Spring 1993
Eileen Spring, *Law, Land and Family: Aristocratic Inheritance in England 1300–1800*, Chapel Hill and London, 1993

Starkey 1992
David Starkey, 'England', in *The Renaissance in National Context*, ed. Roy Porter and Mikulus Teich, Cambridge, 1992, 146–63

Stone 1965a
Lawrence Stone, *Crisis of the Aristocracy, 1558–1641*, Oxford, 1965

Stone 1965b
Lawrence Stone, ed., *Social Change and Revolution in England, 1540–1640*, London, 1965

Stone 1966
Lawrence Stone, 'Social Mobility in England', *Past and Present*, XXXIII, 1966, 16–55

Stone 1972
Lawrence Stone, *The Causes of the English Revolution, 1529–1642*, London and Henley, 1972

Stone and Stone 1984
Lawrence Stone and Jeanne C. Fawltier Stone, *An Open Elite? England 1540–1880*, Oxford, 1984

Stow 1908
John Stow, *Survey of London* (first published 1603), ed. C. L. Kingsford, Oxford, 1908, 2 vols

Strong 1973
Roy Strong, *Splendour at Court: Renaissance Spectacle and Illusion*, London, 1973

Strong 1986
Roy Strong, *Henry, Prince of Wales and England's Lost Renaissance*, London, 1986

Stubbes 1879
Phillip Stubbes, *Phillip Stubbes' Anatomy of Abuses in England* (written 1583), ed. F. J. Furnivall, New Shakespere Society, I, 1877–9

Sutton 1981
Denys Sutton, 'Early Patrons and Collectors', *Apollo*, CXIV, 1981, 282–97

Thirsk 1967
Joan Thirsk, 'The Farming Regions of England', in Finberg 1967, 1–112

Thirsk 1969
Joan Thirsk, 'Younger Sons in the Seventeenth Century', *History*, LIV, 359–77

Thirsk 1985
'Agrarian Change', in *The Agrarian History of England*, ed. Thirsk, V: *1640–1750*, pt II, Cambridge, 1985

Thompson 1924
Elbert Thompson, *Literary Bypaths of the Renaissance*, New Haven, 1924

Thompson 1983
John A. F. Thompson, *The Transformation of Medieval England, 1370–1529*, London and New York, 1983

Turner 1979
James Turner, *The Politics of Landscape: Rural Scenery and Society in English Poetry, 1630–1660*, Oxford, 1979

Whinney 1964
Margaret Whinney, *Sculpture in England 1530–1830*, Harmondsworth, 1964

Whinney and Millar 1957
Margaret Whinney and Oliver Millar, *English Art 1625–1714*, Oxford, 1957

Williams 1973
Raymond Williams, *The Country and the City*, St Albans, 1973

Williams 1995
Penry Williams, *The Later Tudors: England 1547–1603*, Oxford, 1995

Woolley 1981
William Woolley, *William Woolley's History of Derbyshire* (written *c.* 1715), ed. C. Glover and P. Riden, Derbyshire Record Society, VI, 1981

Wrightson 1982
Keith Wrightson, *English Society 1580–1680*, London, 1982

Wrightson 1991
Keith Wrightson, 'Estates, Degrees and Sorts', in *Language, History and Class*, ed. P. J. Corfield, Oxford, 1991, 30–52

Wrigley and Schofield 1981
E. A. Wrigley and R. S. Schofield, *The Population History of England 1541–1871: A Reconstruction*, London, 1981

Zagorin 1969
Perez Zagorin, *The Court and the Country*, London, 1969

Architectural

Ackerman 1990
J. S. Ackerman, *The Villa*, London, 1990

Airs 1975
Malcolm Airs, *The Making of the English Country House, 1500–1640*, London, 1975

Airs 1978
Malcolm Airs, 'The Designing of Five East Anglian Houses', *Architectural History*, XXI, 1978, 58–67

Airs 1994
Malcolm Airs, ed., *The Tudor and Jacobean Great House*, Oxford, 1994

Airs 1995a
Malcolm Airs, *The Tudor and Jacobean Great House: A Building History*, Stroud, 1995

Airs 1995b
Malcolm Airs, ed., *The Seventeenth Century Great House*, Oxford, 1995

Alberti 1988
Leon Battista Alberti, *De re aedificatoria* (written 1452), ed. and trans. Joseph Rykwert, Neil Loach and Robert Tavernor as *On the Art of Building in Ten Books*, Cambridge, Mass., and London, 1988

Ambler 1913
Louis Ambler, *The Old Halls and Manor Houses of Yorkshire*, London, [1913]

Anderson 1995
Kristy Anderson, 'Learning to Read Architecture in the English Renaissance', in Gent 1995, 239–86

Babelon 1989
J.-P. Babelon, *Chateaux de France au siècle de la Renaissance*, Paris, 1989

Bacon 1858
Francis Bacon, 'On Building' (first published 1625), *The Works of Francis Bacon*, ed. James Spedding, VI, London, 1858, 482–7

Barley 1986
Maurice Barley, *Houses and History*, London, 1986

Barley 1990
Maurice Barley, *The Buildings of the Countryside*, London, 1990

Bold 1989
John Bold, *John Webb: Architectural Theory and Practice in the Seventeenth Century*, Oxford, 1989

Bold and Chaney 1993
John Bold and Edward Chaney, eds, *English Architecture Public and Private: Essays for Kerry Downes*, London and Rio Grande, 1993

Bold and Reeves 1988
John Bold with John Reeves, *Wilton House and English Palladianism*, London, 1988

Brett-James 1935
N. G. Brett-James, *The Growth of Stuart London*, London, 1935

Cherry 1988
Bridget Cherry, 'The Devon Country House in the Late 17th and 18th Century', *Proceedings of the Devonshire Archaeological Society*, XLVI, 1988, 108–35

Colvin 1995
Howard Colvin, *A Biographical Dictionary of British Architects 1600–1840* (first published 1954), 3rd edn, New Haven and London, 1995

Colvin and Harris 1970
Howard Colvin and John Harris, eds, *The Country Seat: Studies in the History of the British Country House*, London, 1970

Connor 1977
T. Connor, 'The Making of *Vitruvius Britannicus*', *Architectural History*, XX, 1977, 14–30

Connor 1987
T. Connor, 'The Earliest English Books of Architecture', in Georgian Group 1987, 61–8

Cornforth and Hill 1966
John Cornforth and Oliver Hill, *English Houses: Caroline 1625–1685*, London, 1966

Craven and Stanley 1982–4
Maxwell Craven and M. Stanley, *The Derbyshire Country House*, Derby, 1982–4, 2 vols

Evelyn 1723a
John Evelyn, *A Parallel of Architecture both Ancient and Moderne by Roland Freart Sr. de Chambray* (first published 1664), London, 1723

Evelyn 1723b
John Evelyn, *Some Account of Architects and Architecture* (first published 1697), London, 1723

Figueiredo and Treuherz 1988
P. de Figueiredo and J. Treuherz, *Cheshire Country Houses*, Chichester, 1988

Friedman 1989
Alice T. Friedman, *House and Household in Elizabethan England: Wollaton Hall and the Willoughby Family*, Chicago and London, 1989

Gage 1822
John Gage, *History and Antiquities of Hengrave in Suffolk*, London, 1822

Garner and Stratton 1913
Thomas Garner and Arthur Stratton, *The Domestic Architecture of England during the Tudor Period*, London, 1913

Georgian Group 1987
Georgian Group, *Inigo Jones and the Spread of Classicism*, London, 1987

Gerbier 1662
Balthazar Gerbier, *Principles of Building*, London, 1662

Gerbier 1663
Balthazar Gerbier, *Counsel and Advice to All Builders*, London, 1663

Girouard 1959
Mark Girouard, 'The Development of Longleat House between 1546 and 1572', *Archaeological Journal*, CXVI, 1959, 200–222

Girouard 1962
Mark Girouard, ed., *The Smythson Collection of the Royal Institute of British Architects*, Architectural History, V, 1962

Girouard 1978
Mark Girouard, *Life in the English Country House*, New Haven and London, 1978

Girouard 1983
Mark Girouard, *Robert Smythson and the Elizabethan Country House*, New Haven and London, 1983

Girouard 1992
Mark Girouard, *Town and Country*, New Haven and London, 1992

Gotch 1894
J. A. Gotch, *The Architecture of the Renaissance in England*, London, 1894

Gotch 1902
J. A. Gotch, *Early Renaissance Architecture in England*, London, 1902

Grenville 1997
Jane Grenville, *Medieval Housing*, Leicester, 1997

Guillaume 1988
Jean Guillaume, ed., *Les traités d'architecture de la Renaissance: Actes d'un Colloque tenu a Tours . . . 1981*, Paris, 1988

Gunther 1928
R. T. Gunther, *The Architecture of Sir Roger Pratt*, Oxford, 1928

Harris 1979
John Harris, *The Artist and the Country House*, London, 1979

Harris and Higgott 1989
John Harris and Gordon Higgott, *Inigo Jones: Complete Architectural Drawings*, New York, 1989

Harris, Orgel and Strong 1973
John Harris, Stephen Orgel and Roy Strong, *The King's Arcadia: Inigo Jones and the Stuart Court*, London, 1973

Harris and Tait 1979
John Harris and A. Tait, *Catalogue of the Drawings of Inigo Jones, John Webb and Isaac de Caus at Worcester College, Oxford*, Oxford, 1979

HKW
The History of the King's Works, ed. H. Colvin, 5 vols, London, 1963–82 [I and II: *The Middle Ages*, 1963; III: *1485–1660*, pt 1, 1975; IV: *1485–1660*, pt 2, 1982; V: *1660–1782*, 1976]

Howard 1987
Maurice Howard, *The Early Tudor Country House: Architecture and Politics, 1490–1550*, London, 1987

Jenkins 1961
Frank Jenkins, *Architect and Patron*, London, 1961

Johnson 1994
A. W. Johnson, *Ben Jonson: Poetry and Architecture*, Oxford, 1994

Jope 1961
E. M. Jope, 'Cornish Houses, 1400–1700', *Studies in Building History*, ed. Jope, London, 1961, 192–222

Kingsley 1989–92
Nicholas Kingsley, *Country Houses of Gloucestershire*, Gloucester 1989, Chichester 1992, 2 vols

Knowles and Pitt 1972
C. C. Knowles and G. Pitt, *History of Building Regulations in London 1189–1972*, London, 1972

Kruft 1994
Hanno-Walter Kruft, *A History of Architectural Theory from Vitruvius to the Present*, London and Princeton, 1994

Kuyper 1980
W. Kuyper, *Dutch Classicist Architecture: A Survey of Dutch Architecture, Gardening and Anglo-Dutch Architectural Relations, 1625–1700*, Delft, 1980

Lees-Milne 1951
James Lees-Milne, *Tudor Renaissance*, London, 1951

Lees-Milne 1953
James Lees-Milne, *The Age of Inigo Jones*, London, 1953

Lubbock 1995
Jules Lubbock, *The Tyranny of Taste: The Politics of Architecture and Design in Britain 1550–1960*, New Haven and London, 1995

Miller 1994
Henry A. Miller, 'Models in Renaissance Architecture', in H. A. Miller and V. M. Lamugnani, *The Renaissance from Brunelleschi to Michelangelo: The Representation of Architecture*, Milan, 1994, 19–74

Mowl and Earnshaw 1995
Timothy Mowl and Brian Earnshaw, *Architecture without Kings: The Rise of Puritan Classicism under Cromwell*, Manchester, 1995

North 1981
Roger North, *On Building: Roger North's Writings on Architecture* (written c. 1690), ed. Howard Colvin and John Newman, Oxford, 1981

Onians 1988
John Onians, *Bearers of Meaning: The Classical Orders in Antiquity, the Middle Ages and the Renaissance*, Princeton, NJ, 1988

Oswald 1933
Arthur Oswald, *Country Houses of Kent*, London, 1933

Oswald 1959
Arthur Oswald, *Country Houses of Dorset* (first published 1935), 2nd edn, London, 1959

Pantin 1957
W. A. Pantin, 'Medieval Priests' Houses in South-west England', *Medieval Archaeology*, I, 1957, 118–46

Platt 1994
Colin Platt, *The Great Rebuildings of Tudor and Stuart England*, London, 1994

Pugin 1840
A. Pugin, *Examples of Gothic Architecture*, London, 1840

Pugsley 1992
Steven Pugsley, 'Land Society and the Emergence of the Country House in Tudor and Early Stuart Devon', in *Tudor and Stuart Devon*, ed. T. Gray, M. Rowe and A. Erskine, Exeter, 1992, 96–118

Raine 1852
James Raine, *A Brief Historical Account of the Episcopal Castle or Palace of Auckland*, Durham, 1852

RCHM Cambridgeshire
Inventory of the Historical Monuments of Cambridgeshire, London, 1969–72, 2 vols

RCHM Dorset
Inventory . . . of Dorset, 1952–75, 5 vols

RCHM Essex
Inventory . . . of Essex, 1916–23, 4 vols

RCHM Herefordshire
Inventory . . . of Herefordshire, 1931–4, 4 vols

RCHM Hertfordshire 1910
Inventory . . . of Hertfordshire, 1910

RCHM Hertfordshire 1992
J. T. Smith, *English Houses 1200–1800: The Hertfordshire Evidence*, 1992

RCHM Lancashire
Sarah Pearson, *Rural Houses of the Lancashire Pennines, 1560–1760*, 1985

RCHM Middlesex
Inventory . . . of Middlesex, 1937

RCHM Northamptonshire
John Heward and Robert Taylor, *Country Houses of Northamptonshire*, Swindon, 1996

RCHM Westmorland
Inventory . . . of Westmorland, 1936

RCHM West London
Inventory . . . of . . . [West] London, 1925

RCHM West Yorkshire
Colum Giles, *Rural Houses of West Yorkshire 1400–1700*, 1984

Reid 1980
Peter Reid, *Burke's and Savills Guide to Country Houses II: Herefordshire, Shropshire, Warwickshire, Worcestershire*, London, 1980

Robinson 1991
John Martin Robinson, *A Guide to the Country Houses of the North West*, London, 1991

Schofield 1994
John Schofield, *Medieval London Houses*, New Haven and London, 1994

Serlio 1982
Sebastiano Serlio, *L'architettura* (written 1537–51); trans. Robert Peake as *The Five Books of Architecture*, London, 1611, repr. New York, 1982

Serlio 1996
Sebastiano Serlio, *L'architettura*, Book VI (unpublished); ed. Myra Nan Rosenfeld as *Sebastiano Serlio: On Domestic Architecture*, Cambridge, Mass., and London, 1978, repr. New York, 1996

Shute 1563
John Shute, *The First and Chief Groundes of Architecture*, London 1563

Smith 1975
Peter Smith, *Houses of the Welsh Countryside*, London, 1975

Smith 1992
Christine Smith, *Architecture in the Culture of Early Humanism*, New York and Oxford, 1992

Strong 1979
Roy Strong, *The Renaissance Garden in England*, London, 1979

Summerson 1958
John Summerson, 'Three Elizabethan Architects', *Bulletin of the John Rylands Library*, XL, 1957–8, 202–28

Summerson 1966
John Summerson, ed., *The Book of Architecture of John Thorpe*, Walpole Society, XL, 1966

Summerson 1993
John Summerson, *Architecture in Britain, 1530–1830* (first published 1953), 9th edn, New Haven and London, 1993

Tait 1987
A. A. Tait, 'Post-Modernism in the 1650's', in Georgian Group 1987, 23–35

Taylor 1892
M. W. Taylor, *The Old Manorial Halls of Westmorland and Cumberland*, Kendal, 1892

Thompson 1987
M. W. Thompson, *The Decline of the Castle*, Cambridge, 1987

Thompson 1993
David Thompson, *Renaissance Architecture: Critics, Patrons, Luxury*, Manchester, 1993

Thornton 1978
Peter Thornton, *Seventeenth Century Interior Decoration in England, France and Holland*, New Haven and London, 1978

Thurley 1993
Simon Thurley, *The Royal Palaces of Tudor England*, New Haven and London, 1993

Tinniswood 1989
Adrian Tinniswood, *A History of Country House Visiting*, Oxford, 1989

Turner and Parker 1859
Hudson Turner and J. H. Parker, *Some Account of Domestic Architecture in England from Richard II to Henry VIII*, Oxford, 1859

Tyack 1994
Geoffrey Tyack, *Warwickshire Country Houses*, Chichester, 1994

Wells-Cole 1997
Anthony Wells-Cole, *Art and Decoration in Elizabethan and Jacobean England: The Influence of Continental Prints 1558–1625*, New Haven and London, 1997

Wittkower 1988
Rudolf Wittkower, *Architectural Principles in the Age of Humanism* (first published 1952), 4th edn, London and New York, 1988

Wood 1965
Margaret Wood, *The English Medieval House*, London, 1965

Vitruvius 1960
Vitruvius, *De architectura*, ed. and trans. M. H. Myers as *The Ten Books of Architecture*, 1914, repr. New York 1960

Wotton 1624
Henry Wotton, *Elements of Architecture*, London, 1624

Index of Persons

Index of Places

This index includes both extant buildings and ones that have been demolished. Houses, in England, which stand complete or of which some significant part exists, are identified by Ordnance Survey grid references. London boroughs are given as LB. Pre-1974 counties are given in square brackets. Plate numbers are italicised.

Acorn Bank, Cumbria [Westmorland] [NY617282] 234, 236, *277*

Acton Court, Avon [Gloucestershire] [ST677843] 83, 112, 294, 319, *67, 334*

Albourne Place, West Sussex [Sussex] [TQ254165] 178

Albury, Surrey 324–5, 327, *335*

Aldermaston Court, Berkshire 47, 106, 181, 184, 316, *191, 192*

Amboise, Indre-et-Loire, France 311

Amesbury Abbey, Wiltshire 242

Ampney Crucis, Gloucestershire, church 319

Ampthill Lodge, Bedfordshire 35, 110

Anderson Manor, Dorset [SY881977] 166, 168, 198, 199, 308

Annesley Hall, Nottinghamshire [SK504524] 282

Apethorpe, Northamptonshire [TL023953] 265

Appleton House, Nun Appleton, North Yorkshire [Yorkshire West Riding] 327

Appuldurcombe, Isle of Wight 321

Arlescote Manor, Warwickshire [SP389487] 218

Ashbourne, Derbyshire, church 17

Ashbury, Oxfordshire [Berkshire], Manor Farm [SU262853] *208*

Ashby de la Zouche Castle, Leicestershire [SK631165] 65

Ashby St Ledgers, Northamptonshire 302

Ashley Park, Walton on Thames, Surrey 131, 136–7, 155–7, *135*

Ashton Manor House, Somerset 55

Aspeden, Hertfordshire 51, *34*

Astley Hall, Lancashire [SD574184] 321

Aston Bury, Hertfordshire [TL276218] 166, 313

Aston Hall, West Midlands [Warwickshire] [SP078899] 41, 155, 287, 316, *237*

Athelhampton Hall, Dorset [SY770942] 198, 264, 276, 308

Audley End, Saffron Walden, Essex [TL525382] 47, 98, 106, 109

Aynho Park, Northamptonshire [SP513331] 194

Azay le Rideau, Indre-et-Loire, France 311

Bagshot, Surrey, Royal Lodge 116

Bailleul, Seine Maritime, France 337 n.102

Bakewell, Derbyshire, Holme Hall [SK218694] 196

Barlborough Hall, Derbyshire [SK477783] 26, 41–2, 100, 107, 146, 196, 289, *15*

Barlborough Old Hall, Derbyshire [SK477773] 211, *231, 232*

Barlborough, Derbyshire, Park Hall [SK463788] 198

Barnham Broome Hall, Norfolk [TG080081] 207

Barnham Court, West Sussex [Sussex] [SU956034] 176, *184*

Barningham Hall, Norfolk [TG147354] 168

Barrington Court, Somerset [ST397183] 75, 78–9, *58, 59*

Barton on the Heath, Warwickshire, Manor House [SP257326] 106

Bassingthorpe Hall, Lincolnshire [SK967285] 265

Bay Hall, Pembury, Kent 178

Baynards, Surrey [TQ086368] 79, 256

Bayworth, Berkshire 307

Beaupre Hall, Norfolk 206

Beckford Hall, Hereford and Worcester [Worcestershire] [SO975355] 210

Beckington Castle, Somerset [ST802516] 144

Beckley Park, Oxfordshire [SP578120] 112, 115, 118, 311, *102, 103*

Belton House, Lincolnshire [SK928394] 242

Benthall Hall, Shropshire [SJ658025] 316

Bentley Hall, Hungry Bentley, Derbyshire [SK177381] 196

Beoley, Worcestershire, church 17

Berkeley, Gloucestershire 256, 266

Betchworth Castle, Surrey 142

Bidston Hall, Merseyside [Cheshire] [SJ286902] 118, 135, 158, 160, 183, *114, 115, 160*

Bingham's Melcombe, Dorset [ST772022] 23, 198, 264, 308, *11*

Bisham Abbey, Berkshire [SU847850] 23, 28, 91, 259–60, *16, 300, 301, 323*

Bishop Auckland, Durham, Auckland Castle [NZ214302] 226, 232, 234, 236, 291, 321, *273*

Bishopsbourne, Kent 301

Bishops Cleeve Manor, Hereford and Worcester [Worcestershire] [SO958960] 285

Bletchingdon Hall, Oxfordshire 204, 316

Blickling Hall, Norfolk [TG179287] 44, 155, 159, 164, *152*

Blois, Loir et Cher, France 311

Bolsover Castle, Derbyshire [SK471703] 124, 190

Bonivet, Vienne, France 311

Bourne, Lincolnshire, Red Hall [TF095196] 143, 146–7, 160, *146, 147*

Bourne Park, Kent [TR182531] 242

Bourton House, Bourton on the Hill, Gloucestershire [SP177324] 156–7, *155*

Bowringsleigh House, Devonshire [SX718445] 308

Boynton, North Yorkshire [Yorkshire North Riding] [TA139578] 341 n.6

Bradford on Avon, Wiltshire, The Hall [ST829608] 15, 143, 204, 214, 317, 319, *4*

Bradley Manor, Newton Abbot, Devonshire [SX848708] 198

Braithwaite Hall, East Witton, North Yorkshire [Yorkshire North Riding] [SE117858] 222, *259, 260*

Bramshill, Hampshire [SU758596] 155

Branthwaite Hall, Dean, Cumbria [Cumberland] [NY066253] 234, 235

Bridge Place, Kent [TR175543] 178, 266

Broadlands, Hampshire [SU355203] 106, 291

Broome Park, Kent [TR218482] 51, 178, 227, *189*

Broughton Castle, Oxfordshire [SP419382] 65, 311, 317

Browsholme Hall, Lancashire [SD684453] 292

Brympton d'Evercy, Somerset [ST521154] 258, 259, 284, 306, *299*

Buckden Palace, Cambridgeshire [Huntingdonshire] [TL193678] 65

Buckhurst, Sussex 254

Burghley House, Cambridgeshire [Northamptonshire] [TF049061] 109, 111, 240, 308, 311, 313, 317, *328*

Burton Agnes, Humberside [Yorkshire North Riding] [TA103633] 103, 107, 162, 207

Burton on Trent, projected house for Lord Paget, Staffordshire 42

Cadhay, Devonshire [ST079962] 320

Calke Abbey, Derbyshire [SK367227] 100

Callowden Lodge, Warwickshire 33

Callowden, Warwickshire 266

Cambridge, Trinity College Hall 40

Camden House, Gloucestershire 131

Cannington, Somerset, Blackmore Farm [ST245387] 70–72, 74, 261, 296, 306, 310, *50, 51*

Cannington, Somerset, Gurney Street Manor [ST263394] 70–72, 74, 261, 309, *52, 53, 54*

Canons Ashby, Northamptonshire [SP576508] 65, 289, *44, 318*

Canterbury, Kent, monastic hall 310

Subject Index

Photograph Credits

All illustrations are Crown copyright, National Monuments Record, with the exception of the following:

Warden & Fellows of All Souls College, Oxford 316, 317
Courtesy of the Society of Antiquaries of London 24, 34, 112, 177, 192, 335
Michael Baker 291
By permission of the Marquess of Bath, Longleat, Warminster 17
British Architectural Library, RIBA, London 23, 107, 276, 322, 331
By permission of the British Library 5, 195
Courtesy of the Trustees of the British Museum 71, 150
Christ's Hospital, Horsham, Museum and Archive 148
N. Cooper frontispiece, ill. p. 52, ill. p. 54, 3, 9, 27, 33, 37–8, 40–42, 53, 58, 80, 92–3, 99, 107, 120, 124, 133, 140, 142, 145, 147, 152, 166, 167, 176, 183, 188–9, 204–5, 219, 228, 231, 239–41, 243, 248, 254, 259, 263, 265, 277–80, 283, 287, 299, 303, 307, 336

Country Life Picture library 10, 14, 16, 18, 56, 62, 91, 102–3, 186, 196, 198, 200, 210–11, 291, 296, 310, 323–4, 332
Devonshire collection, Chatsworth; by permission of the Duke of Devonshire and the Chatsworth Settlement 179
Duchas, The Heritage Service, Dublin 154
Hertfordshire Archives & Local Studies 190
County Archivist, Lancashire Record Office, Preston 321
Courtesy The Landmark Trust 54
James Mackinnon 126
Manchester Central Library, Local Studies Unit 226
Marianne Majerus 246
National Maritime Musum, London 104
National Trust photograph library/John Hammond 105, 124
National Trust photograph library/Christopher Hurst 2

Private Collection 1
Royal Commission on the Ancient and Historical Monuments of Wales; Crown Copyright 156
Courtesy of the Marquess of Salisbury, Hatfield House 22, 117
William Salt Library, Stafford endpapers
Courtesy of the Trustees of Sir John Soane's Museum, London; photographs copyright the Conway Library, Courtauld Institute of Art 70, 118, 122, 127–9, 131–2, 138–9, 149, 164
Suffolk Record Office, Ipswich 302
East Sussex Record Office, Courtesy of Lord Hampden 135
Col. L.T. Tomes 32
Courtesy of the Trustees of the Victoria & Albert Museum, London 106
Courtesy of the Provost and Fellows of Worcester College, Oxford 178
West Yorkshire Archive Service, Leeds 29, 319